Nineteenth Century
Inland Centers
and Ports

Publisher's note: This book is one of a four-book series comprising Vol. 1 of the AAG Project.

The four books are:
1. Cities of the Nation's Historic Metropolitan Core
2. Nineteenth Century Ports
3. Nineteenth Century Inland Centers and Ports
4. Twentieth Century Cities

Association of American Geographers

Comparative Metropolitan Analysis Project

Vol. 1   Contemporary Metropolitan America: Twenty Geographical Vignettes. Cambridge: Ballinger Publishing Company, 1976.

Vol. 2.   Urban Policymaking and Metropolitan Dynamics: A Comparative Geographical Analysis. Cambridge: Ballinger Publishing Company, 1976.

Vol. 3.   A Comparative Atlas of America's Great Cities: Twenty Metropolitan Regions. Minneapolis: University of Minnesota Press, 1976.

Vignettes of the following metropolitan regions are also published by Ballinger Publishing Company as separate monographs:

- Boston
- New York-New Jersey
- Philadelphia
- Hartford-Central Connecticut
- Baltimore
- New Orleans
- Atlanta
- Chicago
- St. Paul-Minneapolis
- Seattle
- Miami
- Los Angeles
- Detroit

Research Director:
John S. Adams, University of Minnesota

Associate Director and Atlas Editor:
Ronald Abler, Pennsylvania State University

Chief Cartographer:
Ki–Suk Lee, University of Minnesota

Steering Committee and Editorial Board:
Brian J.L. Berry, Chairman, Harvard University
John R. Borchert, University of Minnesota
Frank E. Horton, Southern Illinois University
J. Warren Nystrom, Association of American Geographers
James E. Vance, Jr., University of California, Berkeley
David Ward, University of Wisconsin

Supported by a grant from the National Science Foundation.

CONTEMPORARY METROPOLITAN AMERICA

3

Nineteenth Century Inland Centers and Ports

Association of American Geographers
Comparative Metropolitan Analysis Project

John S. Adams, Editor
University of Minnesota

Ballinger Publishing Company • Cambridge, Massachusetts
A Subsidiary of J.B. Lippincott Company

International Standard Book Number: 0-88410-425-7 (set)

Library of Congress Catalog Card Number: 76-56167

Printed in the United States of America

Library of Congress Cataloging in Publication Data
Main entry under title:

Contemporary metropolitan America.

Includes bibliographies and index.
CONTENTS: pt. 1. Cities of the Nation's historic metropolitan core.—pt. 2. Nineteenth century ports.—pt. 3. Nineteenth century inland centers and ports.—pt. 4. Twentieth century cities.
1. Cities and towns—United States. I. Adams, John S., 1938-   II. Association of American Geographers. Comparative Metropolitan Analysis Project.
HT123.C635   301.36'3'0973   76-56167
ISBN 0-88410-425-7 (set)
      0-88410-467-2 (pt. 1)
      0-88410-464-8 (pt. 2)
      0-88410-465-6 (pt. 3)
      0-88410-466-4 (pt. 4)

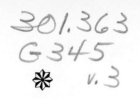
Contents

Chapter Six
The Twin Cities of St. Paul and Minneapolis
Ronald Abler, The Pennsylvania State University, *John S. Adams, John R.*
Borchert, University of Minnesota

List of Figures

CHAPTER FOUR–CHICAGO

CHAPTER FIVE-DETROIT

List of Tables

✳ *Chapter One*

Metropolitan Pittsburgh: Old Trends and New Directions

Introduction

One of the more spectacular approaches to a large American city by car is the one into Pittsburgh from the southwest through the Fort Pitt tunnels and across the Fort Pitt bridge, directly into the heart of the central business district (Figure 1). Until the exit from the tunnels, Pittsburgh is hidden from view by hills. Upon exiting there is an unobstructed view of features that set Pittsburgh apart from other metropolitan areas—the compact central business district, called the Golden Triangle; the junction of the Monongahela and Allegheny rivers to form the Ohio River; an iron and steel plant and other heavy manufacturing installations along the rivers; numerous bridges; the new sports stadium across the Allegheny River from the Golden Triangle; and residential communities on the hillslopes. Not discernible, however, are large areas of deteriorating, low income housing lying adjacent to the central business district that are as much a part of Pittsburgh as the more visible examples of industrial and commercial activity.

Pittsburgh provides a fascinating laboratory for the study of urban patterns and problems because the physical setting and historic development have combined to create a unique economic and social character. Most of the emphasis in this study will be on the changes occurring since 1950, as largely revealed by the U.S. Census.

The Pittsburgh SMSA, with 2.4 million people in 1970, was the only major metropolitan area in America that failed to increase in population during the previous decade. Between 1960 and 1970 there was a loss of less than 0.5 percent, or 4,000 people, but this loss came after a long period of slow growth following World War I. A half century before, the Pittsburgh SMSA had already attained close to 60 percent of its 1970 population, and from that date on population growth increased at a steadily decreasing rate, registering only an 8 percent increase between 1950 and 1970, which was the smallest increase among the SMSAs over one million in population size in 1970. During this same twenty year period, the New York and Newark metropolitan areas gained over 20 percent in population; St. Louis, Chicago, Philadelphia, Detroit, Cleveland, and Milwaukee all increased over 30 percent; and several SMSAs in the South and West, such as Houston, Miami, and San Diego, more than doubled in size. As a direct consequence of these growth trends, the Pittsburgh SMSA has experienced a relative decline in population size. From a ranking of sixth among SMSAs in 1950, Pittsburgh dropped to ninth in 1970.

Population loss has been even more pronounced in the central city, which declined by 23.1 percent between 1950 and 1970. The only central city of an SMSA over one million in size to have experienced a higher percentage loss during this period was St. Louis, which declined by over 27 percent.

The lack of population growth is not necessarily bad for a city, particularly when most contemporary large cities are struggling with traffic congestion, poverty, and shortages of

Figure 1. Pittsburgh central business district, the Golden Triangle. The Monongahela River on the right, the Allegheny River on the left, join to form the Ohio River. Photo by Norman W. Schumm.

adequate housing. However, population losses in Pittsburgh probably reflect reactions to unsatisfactory living and working environments that stem in part from the industrial base and associated high pollution levels. Since the 1920s Pittsburgh has been experiencing consistent net outmigration, leading to a declining and aging population. Pittsburgh's specialization in heavy industry—iron and steel, metal fabricating, and machinery—was a real asset during the latter part of the nineteenth century and the beginning of the twentieth century when manufacturing was one of the nation's fastest-growing industries. Now that both the national and local economies are more service oriented and the focus of the iron and steel industry has shifted

away from the Pittsburgh region, the concentration in heavy industry has become something of a drag for the Pittsburgh economy. While great strides have been made in the direction of industrial diversification, with over 2,300 different manufacturing plants based in the Pittsburgh area, the industrial mix is still dominated by heavy industry.

In the Pittsburgh area, large population losses have not been limited to the central city. Many communities, particularly those with heavy industrial bases located along major rivers and railroad lines, have also suffered severe population losses since 1950. This metropolitanwide pattern of population decline in both central city and suburbs is one of the most significant features of the Pittsburgh urban and regional system.

The effects of economic change on social and demographic structure have resulted in distinctive environmental and demographic patterns. This has been revealed in a comparison by Flax of indicators describing social and economic conditions plus attitudes toward political and social involvement in the eighteen largest SMSAs. Only in educational attainment does the Pittsburgh SMSA score about average for the eighteen metropolitan areas in the study. For all other indicators, Pittsburgh is either significantly above or below average. Pittsburgh compares favorably with the other metropolitan areas in its social and attitudinal dimensions, ranking second in expressions of community concern as shown through contributions to the United Fund, fourth on citizen participation in the presidential election in 1968, and fifth in racial equality as measured by the ratio of white and black unemployment rates. On the other hand, Pittsburgh compares unfavorably in indicators that represent good working and living conditions, ranking very low on poverty, per capita income, unemployment, air quality, and housing conditions.

Needless to say, Pittsburgh is an exceptional city. Pittsburgh is the third most important location of major corporate headquarters after New York and Chicago. Underlying southwestern Pennsylvania is one of the richest coal regions in the world. Making use of the coal, the Pittsburgh region produces nearly one-fifth of the nation's steel output. But there has been virtually no significant industrial growth in the metropolitan region since World War I. As a result of the so-called "Pittsburgh Renaissance" in the late 1940s and early fifties, Pittsburgh has an unusually vibrant and active central business district, but inadequate and substandard housing covers close to half the city. Employment levels are unstable, revealed perhaps most dramatically by the fact that in 1961 the black unemployment rate of the Pittsburgh SMSA was over 11 percent. Yet, according to FBI statistics, Pittsburgh has a relatively low crime rate compared to other large urban centers such as Detroit, New York, Chicago, and Los Angeles.

Place, people, problems, and prospects, in that order, provide the thematic framework for this study of Pittsburgh. The major objective is to unravel those patterns and processes that give this urban region a distinctive flavor, sifting out issues that seemed particularly salient in a brief but perceptive glimpse into a complex urban and regional setting.

A Place of Regional and Physical Complexity

Pittsburgh is the core of a relatively compact urban system within Allegheny, Beaver, Washington, and Westmoreland counties—the Pittsburgh SMSA. The SMSA does not include the entire region of influence. The Daily Urban System, defined by counties that send at least 5 percent of their labor force to work in the central county of Allegheny, consists of the four SMSA counties plus Butler, Armstrong, and Fayette; and at least some daily commuting to the central county occurs from within an area that covers southwestern Pennsylvania and adjacent parts of Ohio, West Virginia, and western Maryland. However, the SMSA does provide an adequate geographical framework for an introduction to Pittsburgh because the rough terrain of the region, the dense land use patterns, and an underdeveloped transportation network sharply curtail interaction between the central city and outlying areas.

Pittsburgh is part of both the industrial heartland of the United States and the largest economically depressed region in the country, Appalachia. In patterns of terrain, land use, and economic activity, the Pittsburgh metropolitan area reflects characteristics of both regions. Major corporate headquarters, iron and steel plants, and well-to-do suburban communities are juxtaposed with strip mines and old mining and mill towns, many of which are declining in population and suffering from urban blight.

Lying within fossil-fuel-rich, soil-poor Appalachia, Pittsburgh is strongly east-west oriented. Pittsburgh has been a major gateway connecting the populous eastern seaboard to the Midwest, placing this city in an advantageous position with respect to resources, the national market, and regional leadership (Figure 2). However, the irregular terrain, numerous rivers, and underdeveloped transportation system have restricted Pittsburgh's region of direct influence to southwestern Pennsylvania plus nearby parts of West Virginia and Ohio along the Ohio River. Even in this region, adjoining the SMSAs of Wheeling and Steubenville-Weirton in the northern panhandle of West Virginia and adjacent Ohio and the Johnstown area to the east have developed independently of Pittsburgh. Perhaps only when the Pittsburgh Pirates or Steelers make a run for a divisional title, or for Christmas shopping, major arts performances, or other specialized needs does Pittsburgh's regional influence become more in line with its population size and economic strength.

Lack of good direct links between Pittsburgh and places within Appalachia has prevented Pittsburgh from becoming an important refuge for people of this depressed region. Instead, Appalachian outmigrants have tended to bypass Pittsburgh when moving northward for metropolitan centers such as Chicago, Cleveland, and Detroit. The drying up of opportunities for unskilled workers in Pittsburgh has reduced the inflow, but the barriers to movement imposed by the terrain and transportation have certainly been critical factors.

Adjacent SMSAs are afflicted with similar economic and environmental problems. An

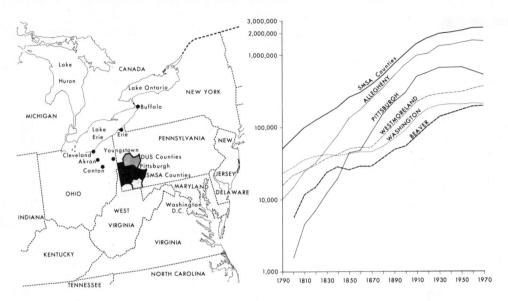

Figure 2. Population change in the Pittsburgh area

additional four counties (Butler and Armstrong to the north and Greene and Fayette to the south) are in the orbit of Pittsburgh's economic and cultural pull. Three of these four counties have declining populations. This illustrates how important it is to gain a sense of Pittsburgh's natural environment, because so much of this city's economic and social character is intertwined with the physical setting.

THE PHYSICAL SETTING

This major metropolitan complex is part of an extensive dissected plateau that has a prominently hilly terrain with frequent steep gradients (Figure 3). In the Laurel Highlands at the eastern margin of the SMSA, elevations of nearly 3,000 feet are found. Cutting through this rugged terrain are numerous drainage lines that feed into the incised Monogahela and Allegheny rivers that join to form the Ohio River. River pool level at the forks of the Ohio, where Pittsburgh was first settled, is measured at 710 feet above sea level, and the local relief is of an order of 500 feet. Downstream to the northwest, elevations decline and the hills become less steep.

The numerous hills and narrow valleys present a challenge to urban development. Large tracts of flat land suitable for industry and

settlement are limited. A great deal of land leveling and sculpturing has had to be undertaken. The transportation system has had to adapt itself to the surroundings by winding along the valleys, climbing over and sometimes through the hills, and bridging the rivers. Though the numerous residential developments that cling to the hillslopes have no fear of flooded basements, there is the danger of land slides and subsidence. The East Street valley, shown in Figure 4 looking south toward the Golden Triangle, illustrates how transportation and housing have adapted to the terrain. This winding road is the major approach to downtown Pittsburgh from the north. Plans call for an interstate limited access highway which would eliminate most of the buildings at road level and make access to the dwellings on the slopes difficult. Strong local opposition to the conversion of the road to an expressway has delayed construction for many years, even though most of the properties along the road have been acquired by the state and many buildings have been torn down.

Needless to say, site acquisition and movement of people and commodities have never been simple in the Pittsburgh area. There has been a long history of fierce competition between residential, industrial, and transportation users for the stretches of flat land that are found in the valleys.

Slope Map

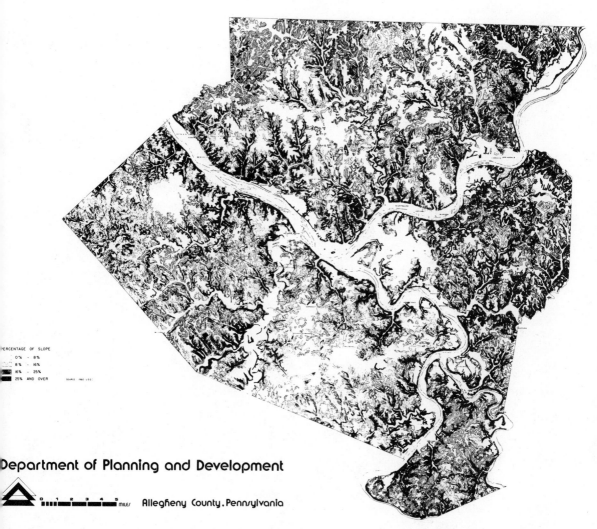

Figure 3. Slope map. Used with permission of Allegheny County Department of Planning and Development, Pittsburgh.

Nearly a seventh of the region's area is taken up by hills over twenty-five degrees in slope, and this otherwise unusable land provides a pleasing forest cover. Besides providing visual stimulation, these green breathing spaces often serve as parks and recreational areas. Though the numerous hills in the city of Pittsburgh form serious barriers to transportation, the many steep wooded slopes provide a most welcome contrast to the gray tones of the built-up area and significantly enhance the attractiveness of the city.

Massive continental ice sheets of ages past touched on the northwestern corner of the metropolitan area. The volume of meltwater that resulted had a profound effect on major rivers and their valleys. Floors of the valleys became covered with a thick mantle of gravelly alluvium that is a primary source of ground water. Terraces formed above river levels. Aban-

Figure 4. East Street valley, 1967. Photo courtesy of Urban Redevelopment Authority, Pittsburgh.

doned channels, after streams returned to their old courses, are prominent surface features. The great Allegheny, Monongahela, and Ohio rivers were keys to the historical development of the region. Besides providing unlimited water supply, their confluence served as an early natural corridor for westward movements of people and materials.

One liability of extensive and full drainage throughout the area has been a long history of flooding in confined valleys, with two devastating floods in recent times. In 1936 the St. Patrick's Day floodwaters swirled twenty-one feet above flood stage, extensively damaging property in the valleys but taking few human lives. Although precipitation was exceptionally heavy in June 1972, the flood control system developed by the Army Corps of Engineers for the upper Ohio drainage basin kept the muddy waters to 10.8 feet above flood stage.

The humid continental climate provides a five to six month frost-free period typical of midwestern and mid-Atlantic states. The summers are long and warm and the winters cold. Precipitation averages around thirty-seven inches and is spread rather evenly throughout the year. Conditions at the eastern margin are modified by the higher elevations. An important dimension of this particularly moist climate zone is the relatively high percentage of cloudy days. In the Pittsburgh area, less than one-fifth of the days in a year are cloud free. The overcast condition is sometimes blamed solely on pollution, for which Pittsburgh has been popularly recognized—an erroneous and unfortunate conclusion since this city has been trying to overcome the negative impression created by the excessive emissions of coal-burning home furnaces and heavy industrial plants prior to World War II. However, there is no question that Pittsburgh still has a serious pollution problem, although significant improvements have been made in recent years. Heavy industry still represents an important sector in the regional economy, the automobile has become a major polluter, and the terrain and climate are complicating factors.

Major river valleys, where most industrial activity is located, act as traps for airborne pollutants that would otherwise be flushed away from a prairie metropolis. Moreover, prevailing west-to-east winds cause a smog and particle fallout to the east of the polluting sources, making hilltop areas of southwestern and northwestern sections of the metropolis relatively free of air pollution (Figure 5). The fact that these are also the locations of some of the highest income neighborhoods in the metropolitan area is not coincidental.

POPULATION DISTRIBUTION AND LAND USE

Rough terrain and major rivers have produced a dispersed pattern of settlements and a winding, irregular transportation system centered on Pittsburgh (Figure 6). Adaptation of residential, commercial, and industrial developments to the physiography and natural resources of the Pittsburgh urban region has given rise to a distinctive urban morphology that consists of industrial concentrations along river valleys, discontinuous suburban developments, and dense, though broken, patterns of residential and commercial land use in the central city. In these respects, Pittsburgh is a modern metropolis with urban morphology and land use patterns resembling the late nineteenth century city.

The early history of the area, marked by strong dependence on major rivers and railroad lines, has left a visible imprint on geographical arrangement of urban components. Today, there are more people and more continuous built-up areas, but the blueprint for spatial patterns of growth was well established before the turn of the century by numerous mining and industrial centers established along major routeways to take advantage of the region's resources.

Over half of the land area in the four SMSA counties is either vacant or unusable, largely because of the irregular terrain. Only a tenth of the total land area is used for urban development. The remainder consists of farm land, bodies of water, and forested areas. Forest cover is particularly extensive in the eastern part of Westmoreland County, where extensive wooded areas have been declared state forest and game reserves. Allegheny, the most urban of the four counties, has close to 30 percent of its area built upon, with rural farm land insignificant. Agricultural land covers more area in larger and more peripheral Washington and Westmoreland counties, but the economic contribution of agriculture to the regional economy is slight.

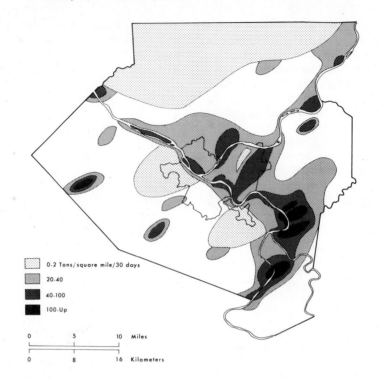

0-2 Tons/square mile/30 days

20-40

40-100

100-Up

0   5   10   Miles

0   8   16   Kilometers

Figure 5. Dust fallout in Allegheny County, circa 1967. Used with permission of Allegheny County Department of Planning and Development, Pittsburgh.

Even though population is unevenly distributed throughout the SMSA, there is a high degree of regularity in the overall pattern, because the central city of Pittsburgh and transportation corridors have served as controlling forces (Figure 7). In 1970 Allegheny County accounted for 67 percent of the population of the SMSA, reflecting the gravitational force exerted by the central city. Here population densities reach their peak and fall away rapidly with distance from this urban core except for linear extensions of urbanized area conforming to the three rivers and major railroad lines (Figure 8). Pittsburgh's density was 9,420 people per square mile, compared to 2,420 for the urbanized area excluding the central city and a low 222 people per square mile for the remainder of the SMSA.

Since the 1950s, suburbanization has more than offset the tendency for people and activities to concentrate as close as possible to the central city. Pittsburgh now accounts for a little over 20 percent of the population of the SMSA, making this city one of the smallest central cities among major metropolitan areas.

Rough terrain and rivers have cut up the ur-

ban region into quite discrete components, creating an attractive small town atmosphere in many parts. In the central city, where housing densities are high and buildings large, numerous parks, cemeteries, and wooded hillsides soften the harshness and crowding of a big city. Sprawled out strings of older, dense communities occupy major river valleys, while smaller prongs of settlement extend into the tributaries. Newer, more spacious, suburban housing developments stretch over hilltops and outer fringes of the urbanized area, away from industrial centers. These patterns reflect the tendency for living and working places to concentrate initially around the central city and outlying industrial centers and then to decentralize in conjunction with pedestrian, streetcar, and automobile mobility. These stages are similar to patterns of urban growth experienced by other major urban centers in the Midwest and Northeast.

Housing in the central city and multinucleated settlements consists of an unusually diverse mixture of building materials and architectural styles that seem to be more a manifestation of the terrain and the time

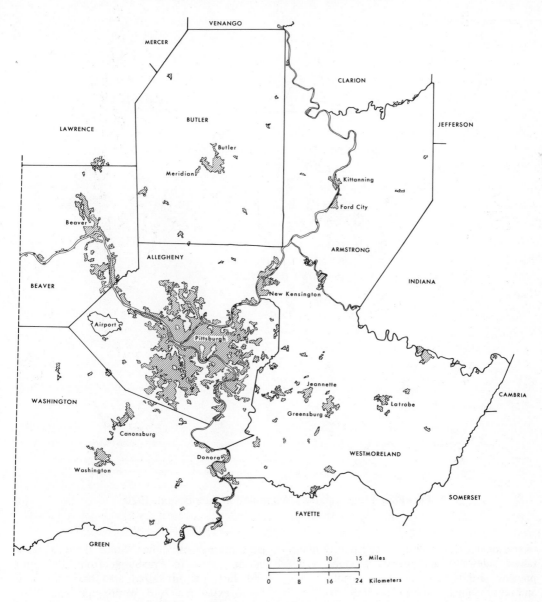

Figure 6. Pittsburgh urban and regional system.

period built than anything else. Absent from Pittsburgh are large developments of ethnic type housing. Only in churches and civic and social clubs can cultural influences be detected. The hillside house with its publicly maintained "stairstreet" is probably the only type of dwelling distinctive of Pittsburgh (Figure 9). Another unique feature may be the extensive use of locally produced stained-glass windows in large dwellings built between 1880 and 1920.

Much of the housing in the Pittsburgh metropolitan area is old. Even in the urban periphery, relatively new high cost residential developments share space with dense, motley housing units of mining and mill towns. The advanced age of housing has taken its toll, but housing problems in Pittsburgh are often more related to environmental considerations since much of the old housing is still structurally sound. High housing densities, poor access to jobs and shopping centers, lack of adequate

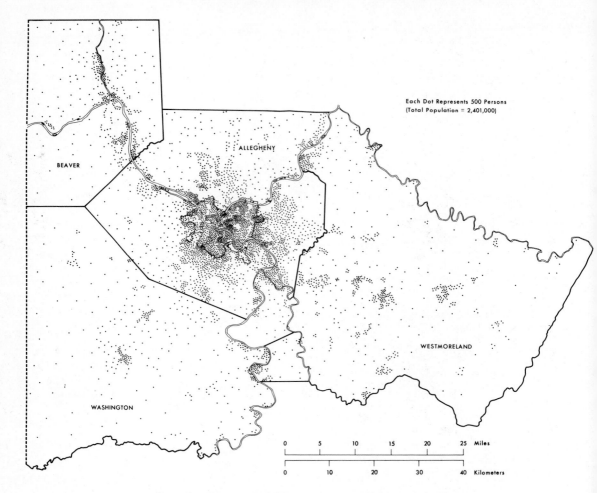

Figure 7. Pittsburgh SMSA, population distribution, 1970.

recreational space, pollution, and poorly maintained sidewalks and streets produce a depressing atmosphere in many central city
and suburban neighborhoods (Figure 10).

Transportation systems in the Pittsburgh
area are also affected by the rolling physiography and intense competition for limited
sites suitable for large scale land development. The highway system is an imbalanced,
radial network that feeds into downtown
Pittsburgh. Adequate beltways around the
central city do not exist. A parkway, extending east-west, offers the only major divided,
limited access route through Pittsburgh. This
artery feeds directly into the central business
district, adding congestion to a downtown
already constricted by major rivers. A traveler
risks heavy traffic through the city and traffic

jams during rush hours. Since there is much
better access to Pittsburgh from the south
and east, the urbanized area has tended to
favor expansion into Washington and Westmoreland counties. The daily commuting rates
from these two counties to Allegheny County
are almost twice as high as from other counties
within the daily urban system.

Most of the main railroad lines conform to
the easier gradients of the river valleys. Major
railroad lines do extend away from the rivers,
but these have been constructed at the great
cost of tunneling abutting hills and bridging
rivers and deep valleys. This regional railroad
network moves the bulk of the raw materials
and commodities into and out of the region,
in contrast to the period before the middle
of the nineteenth century when the navigable

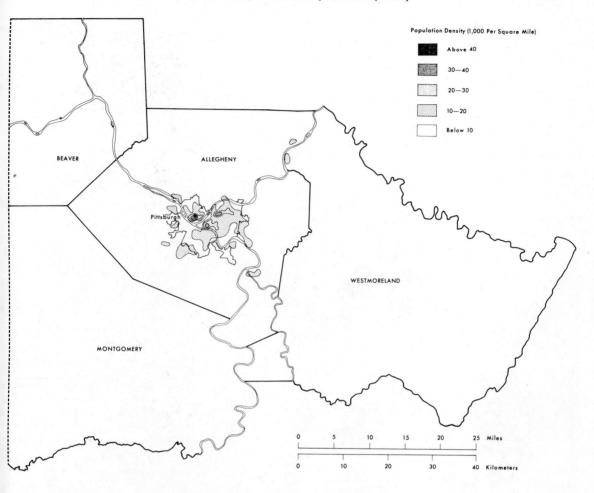

Figure 8. Population densities, 1970.

rivers handled most of the traffic and gave the original impetus to economic development. Inland water transportation was revived in the twentieth century, when a modernization program provided the entire Ohio and Monongahela rivers and the lower seventy-two miles of the Allegheny River with a nine foot draft by 1929. Fewer, but larger and more efficient, locks and dams are replacing the old ones, substantially increasing the navigational capabilities of the system. Nevertheless, the combined competition of the railroad and trucks precludes a return of the region's waterways in their earlier prominence in moving goods and supplies. At present, the movement of coal accounts for two-thirds of the river traffic.

Until relatively recently, local access to the major rivers was blocked by industry, ware-

houses, and dumps. Heavy pollution and foul odors made the river offensive for recreational use. Marinas and small boat harbors now dot the waterways; new waterfront parks are being developed, with Point State Park, at the apex of Pittsburgh's central business district, as the best example.

The Pittsburgh metropolitan area has a political structure to match its terrain. There are 310 townships, boroughs, and cities in the SMSA, and close to half have populations under 2,500. Early patterns of settlement led to the founding of numerous mining and mill centers. These later became the nuclei for the separate urban developments that today are part of the metropolitan area. Many minor civil divisions in Allegheny County were also formed from the dispersal of population away from the central

Figure 9. Hillside houses with a stairstreet. Photo courtesy of Urban Redevelopment Authority, Pittsburgh.

city of Pittsburgh and subsequent incorporation of these suburban settlements.

Until the turn of the century, annexation and consolidation of nearby areas was a normal part of Pittsburgh's growth. Many consolidations involved large communities, as when Allegheny City, with a population of 130,000 in 1900, consolidated with Pittsburgh in 1906 (Figure 11). Such political expansions of the central city came to a halt with the attainment of political power by suburban areas. Until the 1920s the state legislature controlled annexation and consolidation decisions. When this power was given back to local communities by an amendment to the state constitution, they could successfully block attempts by the central city to absorb contiguous communities. The establishment of many countywide authorities for the provision of water, sewage, power, and public transportation encouraged political separatism from the central city. Suburban communities were able to acquire metropolitanwide services and yet remain free from high taxes and social problems of the central city. Moreover, some suburbs were hindered from ready access to the city and would have gained little from joining it. Consequently, the city of Pittsburgh has remained at approximately its present size of fifty-five square miles since the 1930s, except for annexion of a largely

Figure 10. A Street scene in a deteriorating neighborhood. Photo by James K. Hoeveler.

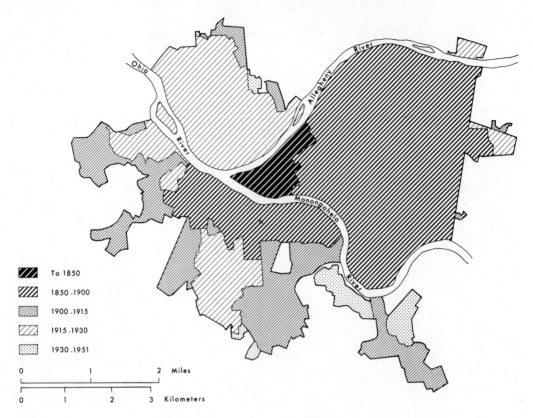

Figure 11.   Map of political annexation.

uninhabited area. The Pittsburgh metropolitan area suffers not only from the social and monetary costs of political fragmentation derived from duplication of services and lack of coordination between local government agencies, but also from the failure of the tax base of many communities to expand in proportion to need. Both the central city and numerous minor civil divisions in suburban areas, particularly the industrial communities, have experienced loss of an adequate financial base through heavy population declines. To exacerbate matters, the small size of most of these independent communities makes them much less capable of providing needed local services and rehabilitation programs to serve their populations. The proliferation of municipalities of various sizes and financial viability has led to inequities in services and competition and suspicion among local governments, not to mention failure in developing metropolitan-wide strategies to combat social and economic

problems that extend beyond municipal boundaries.

For example, Allegheny County is a conglomeration of 129 separate municipalities, with the city of Pittsburgh being by far the largest. With the central city declining in population for several decades and shrinking away from metropolitan leadership, the county government has assumed a larger role. A decade and a half ago the city operated on a budget higher than that of the county, but now the budget of the former is considerably less. With the exception of garbage collection, police, and fire protection, the central city provides only those social services that are paid for or subsidized by some larger governmental unit.

Since 1960 the county has added thirteen new departments, bureaus, or agencies. Some are subsidized by state and federal government, and all require county funding. Included are the bureaus of drug rehabilitation, waste management systems, consumer protection, public information; the fire fighting academy; the police training academy; public defender's office; county planning and development; the minor judiciary; adult services; child welfare service; the mental health–mental retardation program; the Model Cities agency; and the Office of Economic Opportunity. The Allegheny County Sanitary Authority, Greater Pittsburgh International Airport, county hospital, department of recreation and conservation all have expanded in operation. In 1965 the county created the Allegheny County Community College system. Two year colleges and preprofessional programs are now available at three permanent campuses, with an enrollment of 17,000 students.

The Port Authority was established by the county in 1964 to provide for regional mass transportation. Since that time, questions relating to management and improvement of the county-run mass transit system have been constant sources of friction between the county and central city governments. Pittsburgh has no direct voice in mass transit policymaking decisions, but is the one municipality most affected by them since most public transit commuting occurs between the suburbs and central city. The infighting reached a peak over a proposal introduced by the Port Authority, soon after it was established, called the Early Action Program. It was designed to improve existing bus and streetcar lines and introduce Skybus, an innovative, rubber-wheeled vehicle, to operate on an elevated ramp that carried with it the astronomical price tag and controversy of a new and untested scheme. Concerned that the eventual cost of Skybus would far outweigh commuter benefits, Pittsburgh's mayor and the leadership of several communities along the proposed Skybus route have used various stalling tactics to block progress on the Early Action Program. Thus the hopeful, promised program of an innovative public transport system was tied into knots by political inaction.

The large conglomeration of heterogeneous places, with many separated from Pittsburgh by inconvenient access, have contributed to feelings of independence between central city and suburban communities. Fear of metropolitanism, distrust of the central city, and a normal resistance to change combined to defeat a county home rule charter in 1974.

While physical features, population distribution, land use, and political structure are important attributes of the Pittsburgh urban region, it is a changing economic environment, perhaps more than anything else, that has been responsible for Pittsburgh's sense of place. Thus, before proceeding with the discussion of economic patterns and the people that inhabit this region, let us turn first to the story of Pittsburgh's economic growth.

A CHANGING ECONOMIC ENVIRONMENT

Pittsburgh gained its early prominence as a gateway to the West through a combination of geographical and economic advantages. The confluence of the Monongahela and Allegheny rivers, forming the Ohio, was a strategic location during the settlement and taming of this region. The British seized Fort Duquesne from the French in 1758 and founded Pittsburgh on the same site. Ever since George Washington's first reconnaissance of the area in 1763, settlers had been aware that this location offered a command position over the major waterways of the Ohio country. In the early years Pittsburgh served chiefly as an outpost for pioneers moving westward, since the narrow valleys and dissected uplands prevented the region from achieving much importance as an agricultural center.

During the early period of settlement, additional communities developed adjacent to major waterways or at important crossroads. This was a region of rich resources with excellent river transportation to facilitate exploitation. But no other place could match the natural advantages inherent in the location of Pittsburgh. Initial local influence was soon transformed into regional, then national, importance. Boatbuilding and metal industries sprang into prominence, and Pittsburgh's manufacturing career had begun. In 1790 Pittsburgh was a hardy hamlet of 376 persons; by 1810 it had attained a population of nearly 5,000, far exceeding the size of other communities in the region.

Expansion of Pittsburgh's industrial base was associated with the establishment of settlements close to the fringe of the growing town. Local enterprise, trade, and convenience to services and opportunities of Pittsburgh gave initial support to these smaller places. Many of these peripheral communities sooner or later were absorbed by the city, resulting in a mixture of land use and in winding, seemingly chaotic streets aligned to meandering rivers and interrupted by steep hills and dead ends that still puzzle local residents and are anathema to strangers.

Pittsburgh gained local importance prior to the Civil War, but it was not until after this conflict that this city became regionally, and then nationally, important. Exigencies of the Civil War greatly increased the demand for manufactured items. At approximately the same time, coke replaced charcoal as the fuel source in iron manufacturing, bringing about an abrupt shift in the distribution of iron-making facilities from forest locations, the bases for charcoal supply, to the river sites that formed collecting points for coking coal. This gave unrivaled advantage to the Pittsburgh region which was underlain by rich, flat seams of bituminous coal, some reaching eight feet in thickness. Iron-making technology at this time favored locations near coal deposits since much more coal than iron ore was required in iron-making. Coal mining activity became the catalyst for rapid industrial expansion, and Pittsburgh experienced "boom town" growth. Before 1914, Pittsburgh's population had reached over a half million, with 40 percent of the work force engaged in manufacturing. All the integrated iron and steel plants that exist today in the area had been established.

Pittsburgh of the mid-1920s stood as a heavy industry giant. Two-thirds of the manufacturing wage earners worked in metal and metalworking industries. The region produced nearly one-third of the nation's output of finished and rolled steel. It ranked fourth in the U.S. in capital surplus profits of banking institutions. The world's largest tube and pipe mill, structural steel plant, rail mill, wire manufacturing plant, bridge and construction fabricating plants were here. Pittsburgh led in the manufacture of electrical machinery, steel railroad cars, fire brick, glass, tin plate, vanadium, and white lead. It possessed the world's largest aluminum finishing works, airbrake manufacturing plant, glass manufacturing plant, and cork manufacturing plant. Two-fifths of the nation's coal supply came from within a hundred miles of Pittsburgh, with rail haul tonnage amounting to 30 percent of the total national rail tonnage. Pittsburgh's rivers were equally active.

Rapid growth in manufacturing and coal industries created high demand for cheap, unskilled labor. Immigrants from Europe and later blacks from the South filled many of the job opportunities. Prior to World War I, nearly one-quarter of the population of this region consisted of European immigrants, and 70 percent of the foreign-born work force was employed in manufacturing.

Reliance on heavy industry tended to magnify effects of short term changes in the regional and national economy. When the business cycle turned down in the past, the Pittsburgh area felt the unemployment blow much harder than the United States as a whole. Spiraling manufacturing and population growth were halted abruptly by the great economic depression of the 1930s, with the strongest adverse impact being felt by the capital goods industries. On the other hand, in times of high demand for durable goods—such as during the world wars and the Korean conflict—the economic picture was bright. By 1950 factories were providing nearly 43 percent of all district jobs, but for the next decade and a half Pittsburgh's manufacturing base shrank without corresponding gains in tertiary industries. Herein lies an economic shortcoming in the Pittsburgh region that still has not been satisfactorily resolved (Figure 12).

Geographic Patterns of Economic Acitivites

Economic activities in the Pittsburgh metropolitan area are geographically concentrated and functionally specialized. Allegheny County accounted for two-thirds of total employment in the SMSA in 1970 and outlined the center of commercial and industrial activities in the urban system, while Pittsburgh with its Golden Triangle served as the location for major businesses and corporate headquarters. Though Pittsburgh's share of metropolitan employment declined by about 14,000 workers between 1950 and 1970, primarily through movement of population and industry to the urban periphery, the central city maintained its position as the major focus of business and commercial activity.

Concentration in space is matched by industrial specialization in heavy manufacturing, although the degree of specialization in the production of iron and steel is not as high as might be expected, given the frequent reference to Pittsburgh as the "steel city." There is no question that manufacturing is an important

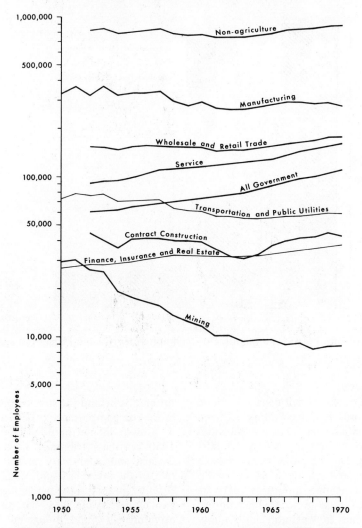

Figure 12. Pittsburgh area employment structure, 1950–1970.

segment of Pittsburgh's economic structure, and in 1970 this declining sector still accounted for almost one-third of the employed work force (Figure 13). The extent of economic specialization does not become clear until manufacturing itself is broken down into its components. Over four-fifths of those employed in secondary industries were involved in the production of durable goods and 50 percent in the iron and steel industry alone. Moreover, employment in the iron and steel industry maintained its relative importance in manufacturing between 1950 and 1970, even though manufacturing employment as a whole declined by nearly 31,000 workers—or 10 percent—during this period.

Between 1950 and 1970 employment in the Pittsburgh SMSA displayed a mixed pattern of gains and losses. Allegheny, Beaver, and West-moreland counties experienced increases in employed work force, while the trend in Washington County held steady. The combined effects of these trends showed a 7.7 percent increase in employed work force for the SMSA, which was almost equivalent to its percentage population increase. Over half of the gain came after 1960, in spite of the slight loss in population incurred during this time.

Wide variations in employment changes among minor civil divisions seem related more to fluctuations in manufacturing employment, particularly heavy manufacturing, than to any

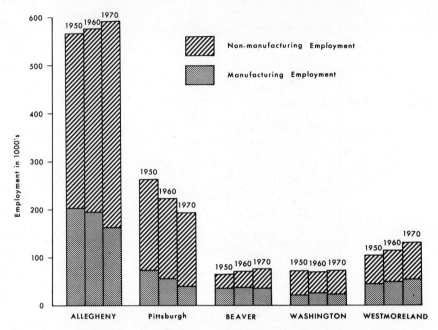

Figure 13. Manufacturing and nonmanufacturing employment in the Pittsburgh area, 1950, 1960, and 1970.

other single factor. Minor civil divisions, found along major transportation corridors, suffered major losses in employment. Large proportions of their work force were engaged in the older heavy industries. On the other hand, growth areas tended to serve as locations for newer assembly and fabricating industries, or were suburban to Pittsburgh or to regional centers such as Greensburg in Westmoreland County and Washington in Washington County.

The city of Pittsburgh also lost considerably in manufacturing employment during this twenty year period. By 1970 this segment of its work force was reduced by nearly half. Pittsburgh's eclipse as a manufacturing center began after World War II when industries began to move to the urban periphery. Changing production techniques increased the need for space. Increased use of trucks lessened the need for industrial concentration along railroad lines. Rising land costs, along with higher taxation and congestion, made the relatively open suburban areas far more attractive. The largest single employer in the city is still Jones and Laughlin Steel Company, a legacy of this city's industrial past. The University of Pittsburgh's full time employees place this educational insti-

tution just behind the steel company, indicative of the rising importance of services.

Growth in metropolitan employment since 1950 can be attributed to expansion of the tertiary and quaternary sectors and contraction of the secondary and primary sectors, the latter by an amazing 68 percentage points. Rapid growth in services is a sign of a diversifying economy on a solid, though imbalanced, manufacturing base. Diversification in manufacturing is occurring as well, and the importance of the primary metals industry is waning. Greater demands are being made for skilled labor, and new growth is occurring in fabricating industries. This last development bodes well for the future quality of living environment, since this type of industry tends to be less polluting and more compatible with other types of land use than heavy manufacturing.

Degrees of intensity and industrial mix of manufacturing in the Pittsburgh region vary with distance from the regional core and the major rivers, the heaviest concentrations being found along the latter (Figure 14). Heavy manufacturing along the Monongahela is the most intense, followed by activity along the Ohio and then the Allegheny. Manufacturing

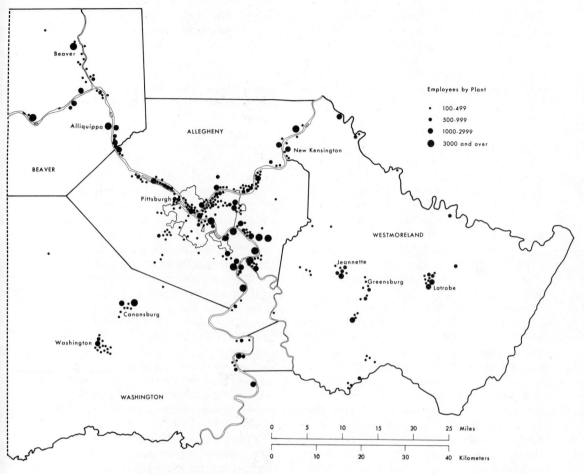

Figure 14. Manufacturing plants of 100 employees or more, 1970. Data Source: *Industrial Directory of the Commonwealth of Pennsylvania.* Harrisburg, 1972.

away from the rivers tends to be located in communities along major railroad lines, giving the spatial pattern of these industries a more clustered appearance.

The old heart of Pittsburgh's industrialized district is found along both sides of the Monongahela, extending from the Golden Triangle southward to Clairton. The alternate spacing of industrial plants, with their large furnaces, rolling mills, stock piles of ore, coal, and scrap steel, in the inside bends of the meandering river valley creates an intensity of metal prodution rarely exceeded anywhere else. The elongated iron and steel facilities combined with converging barge, train, and truck traffic make the narrow, winding Monongahela River valley one of the most congested and polluted

areas in the Pittsburgh region. The recent switch to basic oxygen furnaces in steel production, plus environmental controls on smoke emissions and waste disposal, have improved the situation significantly in recent years, but there is still much to be done to upgrade living and working conditions. Physical improvements represent only partial solutions. The nature of industrial activity in general, plus the failure of many industries to modernize older and less efficient facilities, has led to decreasing employment opportunities. This gave rise to social and demographic scars that will not be eradicated for years. Some of the most distressed communities in the Pittsburgh region are located here.

Manufacturing along the Ohio and Allegheny rivers resembles that along the Monongahela, although the manufacturing land use is not as intense nor as specialized in iron and steel. Along the Ohio, manufacturing facilities tend to be spaced at wider intervals than in the two other valleys. The Allegheny River valley is the least industrialized of the three and has a greater diversity in industry.

The distribution of industrial concentrations in the Pittsburgh metropolitan area has remained relatively stable since the 1950s. Three reasons can be cited for this: (1) the rough terrain and absence of beltways around the Pittsburgh area that have discouraged large scale dispersal away from the few large sites suitable for industrial development; (2) the large land use requirements and high capital costs in physical plants that have made them relatively immobile; and (3), perhaps most importantly, the lack of significant new growth in manufacturing.

While the interplay of various physical and economic factors has contributed to inertia in manufacturing location trends, important changes have transpired in recent years that have led to some redistribution and diversification. These changes have included significant decreases in both manufacturing firms and employment in the Pittsburgh region as a whole and especially in the central city, and an increasing proclivity for manufacturers to avoid already congested and polluted transportation corridors and to select major highways and industrial parks for new industrial developments, expansions in plant capacity, and relocation. Also, there has been substantial growth in research and development facilities attached to major corporate headquarters based in Pittsburgh. The influx of these sophisticated and innovative types of industry represents an important trend, not because of their effect on employment in general since they require small numbers of highly skilled technicians, but for their favorable contribution to Pittsburgh's image and intellectual climate. This city has suffered unduly from heavy industry and mill worker stereotypes. Smoke, strikes, and stagnation have been assumed to be accurate descriptors of Pittsburgh, when in fact the situation here is probably no worse than in other major industrial centers.

Rebuilding the Downtown

One of the most important chapters in Pittsburgh's economic history occurred within the two decades after the Second World War. The central business district, known as the Golden Triangle, was then revitalized, and continues to remain an exceptionally strong regional focal point. Restricted by the Allegheny and Monongahela rivers, this compact 370 acre wedge occupies the original corporate limits of the city of 1816.

The rebuilding of the downtown area was the main objective of what has been called the Pittsburgh Renaissance. The city, though prosperous through the Second World War, was choked with smoke, floods were frequent, rivers carried raw sewage, and the region lacked convenient automobile access to the downtown. The need for preserving and protecting the stability of the commercial business center of the region became imperative. Since the end of the 1930s no new construction had taken place in the grimy downtown, and an estimated two-fifths of the district's buildings were blighted or vacant (Figure 15). The Republican corporate elite associated with R.K. Mellon's financial power and the local Democratic leadership decided to work together to revitalize the central business district, which they hoped would serve as a starting point for the economic resurgence of the metropolitan area as a whole.

The Allegheny Conference on Community Development was the principal instrument for formulating the basic plans and obtaining the cooperation of government and business. In the early phase, four basic projects were considered essential—a park at the apex of the business district where the two rivers meet; smoke control; flood control; and a limited access highway. Contributing agencies in the development program included an Urban Renewal Authority, a Public Auditorium Authority, a broad communitywide waste disposal system, and a Stadium Aurthority. The Southwestern Regional Planning Commission, which shares staff and facilities with the Pittsburgh Regional Planning Association, became the major planning agency for the Pittsburgh region.

By 1949, thirty-six acres for Point Park were acquired by the state. A quarter of a century later an attractive park had become a reality, though a good part of it is occupied by a landscaped highway interchange. Comprehensive smoke control legislation of the 1940s became countrywide by 1960, substan-

Figure 15. Pittsburgh's central business district in the late 1940s. Photo courtesy of Greater Pittsburgh Chamber of Commerce.

tially reducing soot pollution, although odorous smog and black dust are still too prevalent. Much of the success came automatically when natural gas and petroleum began to replace coal for power and heating. Pollution controls applied to commercial and industrial facilities were also helpful. Army Corps of Engineers projects in the watershed of the Allegheny and Monongahela rivers substantially reduced the threat of devastating floods.

The limited access Penn-Lincoln Parkway, linking downtown with the Pennsylvania Turnpike to the east and the major airport to the west, was a costly engineering project, as the highway had to bridge streams, tunnel through hills, and cling to the hillsides. Fortunately, because of the irregular terrain along the route, only a small number of families had to be displaced. While Pittsburgh's business core has not been overwhelmed by dehumanizing freeways, the lack of adequate, rapid access routes to the Golden Triangle continues to be a pressing problem. During rush hours the city center becomes nearly inaccessible and highly polluted from traffic jams. Parking lots and parking garages occupy large portions of highly valued commercial core land, though the two underground parking facilities show good surface use as parks, malls, or buildings. Poor public transport services compound the problem of access to the business district. Suburban railroad services are largely a thing of the past. The streetcar system has been reduced to only a segment of its former extensive network. Bus services suffer from traffic congestion and narrow streets. A Public Parking Authority, the first agency of its kind in the country, was created to build public garages to handle the ever increasing stream of vehicles in the Golden Triangle.

Between 1950 and the mid-1960s more than a quarter of the triangle was rebuilt, beginning with the twenty-three acre landscaped Gateway Center office complex that Equitable Life Assurance Society financed (Figure 16). In 1972, thirty-one buildings were twenty stories or more. Some were built prior to World War I, such as the twenty-one story H.C. Frick building, which was intended to show the financial might of one of the great industrial leaders of the city. Of more recent vintage is the massive sixty-four story U.S. Steel building. New structures have enabled the city to maintain its position as the third leading corporate headquarters of the country, according to Fortune Magazine's listing of the 500 leading American corporations. Gulf Oil, U.S. Steel, Westinghouse Electric, Rockwell International, Alcoa, National Steel, H.J. Heinz, and PPG Industries, with sales over a billion dollars, are headquartered here. Over 100,000 people are employed in the central business district, with

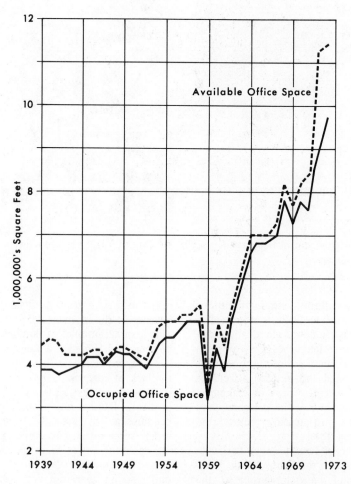

Figure 16. Change in CBD office occupancy. Source: Building Owners and Managers Association of Pittsburgh.

about two-thirds employed by office establishments. This number has remained stabilized for several years.

During the day, the Golden Triangle is a busy place of business, government, education, and retailing. The three large department stores are located here, sports events take place in an arena and stadium which adjoin the business district, and a performing arts hall has an active calendar. After dark, first run theatres, restaurants, and night clubs show signs of flourishing. Though suburban shopping malls now compete with the central business district for retail sales, serious suburban business office competition has been limited to two quite secondary centers—Greentree and Monroeville.

The Pittsburgh Renaissance was a significant achievement. Over a twenty year period, a congested and ugly commercial industrial center was transformed into a vibrant and viable one, primarily through efforts of private investors. Even though Pittsburgh's population declined by 25 percent after reaching its peak in 1950, the vitality of the central core has increased. Nevertheless, the renaissance has fallen short of its original goals. Redevelopment was largely confined to the Golden Triangle point where new, modern structures now stand in stark contrast to surrounding slums. Much of the Golden Triangle itself is visually unexciting. Parks and new buildings were built in piecemeal fashion, without an integrated plan, and have little architectural harmony with each other or their surroundings. A much more serious criticism has been raised that public welfare was too often given secondary consideration to corporate welfare, as evidenced by the thousands of low income families in the Lower Hill District adjacent to the downtown, that were displaced by the Civic Arena and apartments for middle and high income families.

The path taken by Pittsburgh's economic history and responsive inmigration shows that there are two important dimensions to this city—Pittsburgh as a steel and manufacturing center; and Pittsburgh as a place of ethnic diversity. These two interrelated facets are captured well in the locally popular legend of Joe Magarac, a massive Hungarian or Slovak steel worker about whom a song and many tales have been written. Magarac was supposed to be strong, brave, skillful, and kind—idealized traits for the dangerous and difficult task of spending a lifetime working with molten steel. He is the Paul Bunyan of the steel mills, as revealed by excerpts from a song written by Jacob Evanson entitled, "Joe Magarac, That's the Man":

> He was sired in the mountain by red iron ore
> Joe Magarac, that's the man!
> He was sired in the mountains by red iron ore
> Raised in a furnace—soothed by its roar.
> Steel-heart Magarac, that's the man!
>
> His shoulders are as big as the steel-mill door,
> Hands like buckets, feet half the floor.
>
> Joe never sleeps, but he's got to eat,
> Hot steel soup, cold ingots for meat.

The legend has it that Joe Magarac was never seen until disaster was about to strike. Then he would appear to perform feats of miraculous strength and bravery, such as holding together with his bare hands a split fifty ton ladle of molten steel while endangered workers scampered to safety.

That is the legend of Joe Magarac. His occupation is symbolic of Pittsburgh's industrial structure. There remains the questions of the kind of person Magarac represented, and it is to a discussion of the people of Pittsburgh that we now turn.

A People of Many Faces

Migration has had a profound impact on the social composition of the Pittsburgh metropolitan area—perhaps more than any other single component of population change. Fluctuations in the economy of the Pittsburgh region have been triggering agents for population movements into and out of the region that have left their indelible marks. Inmigration of Europeans, particularly from Southern and Eastern Europe prior to World War I, and of blacks has endowed Pittsburgh with a rich ethnic background that is one of its most important cultural features. Net outmigration since the 1920s has decreased the labor supply and contributed to an aging population, with associated housing and health care needs for the elderly that represent one of the most pressing problems of the Pittsburgh region.

Rapid expansion in the industrial and mining sectors during the late nineteenth and early twentieth centuries were primarily responsible for the inflows. Europeans came into the area in response to the demand for cheap unskilled labor in the steel mills, other heavy industrial plants, and the coal mines. Both the central city of Pittsburgh and outlying industrial and mining centers were destinations for these immigrants. In 1930 over half of the population of Allegheny County was of foreign stock. Forty years later, about 24 percent of the population of the SMSA and 26 percent of Pittsburgh was still of foreign stock, with the most important groups being those of Italian and Polish descent (Figure 17).

The central city of Pittsburgh accounted for only one-quarter of those of foreign stock, reflecting the dispersal pattern of settlement throughout the SMSA, although many of the immigrant families who settled initially in the central city presumably joined the flow to the suburbs.

Blacks from the South were recruited during the industrial boom of World War I, when the immigration from Europe was severed. With the passage of quota restrictions on immigration during the 1920s, blacks from the South continued their trek northwards. The largest steel firms in 1918 employed 7,000 blacks, which was more than three times the figure of a few years before. Blacks were also first introduced into the coal mining industry in large numbers as strikebreakers in the 1920s. In 1930, 50 percent of the blacks in Allegheny County were within the twenty to forty-four age group, clearly reflecting the recency of inmigration and the need for labor in the mills and mines. By 1970, this same age cohort only accounted for 28 percent of the black population.

Patterns of black movement into the urban region resembled in form the destination patterns of European immigrants before them, except the movement was more highly directed toward the steel mill communities. On arriving in the Pittsburgh metropolitan area, blacks tended to settle in residentially segregated neighborhoods in the central city and in industrial centers along transportation corridors, particularly the iron and steel complexes along the Monongahela and Ohio rivers. However, far

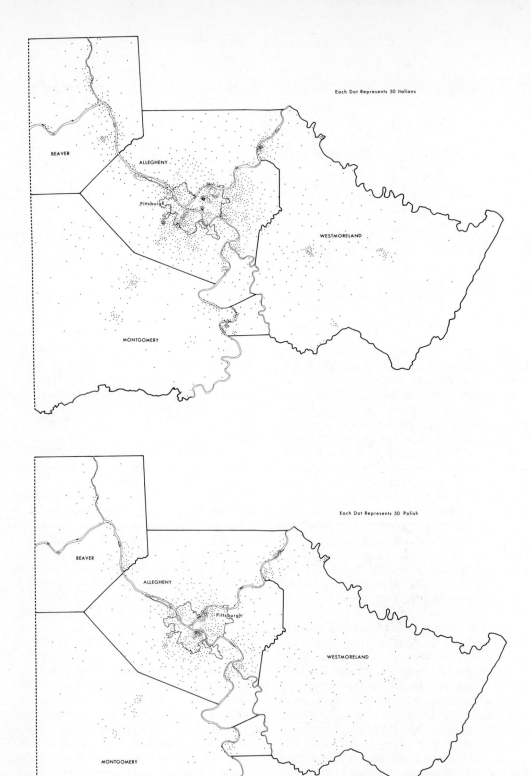

Figure 17. Italians and Poles in Pittsburgh.

greater proportions moved into areas of low cost housing in the central city that had been vacated by recent European immigrants who had begun to move to the less congested and polluted urban periphery. Thus, blacks became the most concentrated major ethnic group in the SMSA, with 61.8 percent found in Pittsburgh alone. This percentage in the central city is high compared to other major ethnic groups in the Pittsburgh region, but it is very low with respect to major metropolitan areas in the Midwest and Northeast. The location of nearly 40 percent of the black population in suburban areas is related primarily to the dispersal pattern of industrial centers and associated residential areas found along transportation corridors in all counties of the SMSA. Many sizable black concentrations in these centers date back to the early 1900s. Suburbanization of a small number of blacks since the 1960s has also added to the number found outside the central city.

Pittsburgh has never been a part of major black movement from the South, although blacks were actively recruited by industrialists during and immediately after World War I. In recent years, most black inmigrants have come from other northern cities. Lack of direct rail connections between major southern cities and Pittsburgh may be one reason. Another may have to do with the fact that Pittsburgh's rapid economic development lagged behind that of New York, Philadelphia, Detroit, and Chicago. By the time Pittsburgh began actively to seek out black labor, migration streams had already been well established between the South and the other urban centers.

In 1970 blacks represented only about 7 percent of the population of the Pittsburgh SMSA. In the central city, where they numbered a little over 105,000, they constituted about 20 percent of the total. Even this is a relatively small percentage for a central city of a SMSA with over 2.4 million in population. The complex physical and political structure of the Pittsburgh SMSA has caused black neighborhoods to be highly fragmented. At least seven separate black ghettos can be identified within Pittsburgh and adjacent area, and many other important concentrations are scattered throughout the urban region (Figure 18).

In the central city, the Hill District, East Liberty, Homewood-Brushton, and Manchester are the most important black neighborhoods, accounting for over two-thirds of the total. The Hill District, adjacent to the Golden Triangle, is the largest, having been one of the first areas in the city to receive large numbers of blacks. This neighborhood was formerly inhabited by Russian Jews who settled next to the commercial center of Pittsburgh during the late nineteenth and early twentieth centuries to take advantage of immediate access to employment opportunities. The rising affluence of these early occupants during World War I and the 1920s made it possible for them to move away from a neighborhood that was becoming increasingly congested and polluted. Reduction in demand for housing and the incompatability of business and residential land uses lowered housing values. The subsequent conversion of many formerly large single family residences into multifamily units and the location there of early public housing projects transformed the Hill District into the largest low cost housing development in the city. Blacks settled there because they could not afford the higher housing and transportation costs associated with suburban living, or were discouraged from securing a home in the suburbs because of social pressure and real estate discriminatory practices.

During the last two decades, Pittsburgh's black population has increased slowly, growing mainly by natural increase and not by inmigration, in contrast to the rapid gain in blacks through inmovement which has been the common pattern among major metropolitan areas in the North. Between 1960 and 1970 blacks experienced a gain of only 4.2 percent in the central city. The remainder of Allegheny County and the rest of the metropolitan area displayed almost no change in black percentage.

Close to half of Pittsburgh's population is either of foreign stock or black. The extent of ethnic diversity is reflected by ethnic churches and cultural events, such as the very popular annual Pittsburgh Folk Festival, but only marginally by neighborhood patterns (Figure 19). Neighborhoods with a strong ethnic flavor are more the exception than the rule, except for distinct black and white communities. Residential mobility through the years has led to a mixture of most white ethnic groups. Only a few areas, such as Squirrel Hill (with its large Jewish population), Spring Hill (with a strong German element), Mt.

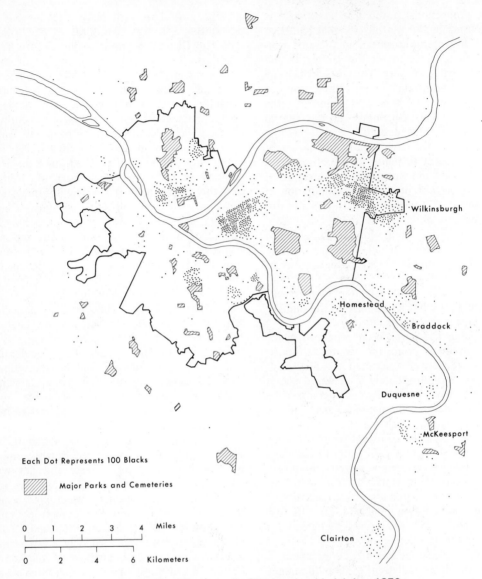

Figure 18. Blacks in the Pittsburgh and vicinity, 1970.

Washington (with its many Italians), and Polish Hill remain as stable ethnic enclaves. The Pittsburgh Planning Department does identify over sixty neighborhoods, but most are the result of income difference and rough terrain, which often hinders access between contiguous areas, or a planning convenience since they conform to census tract boundaries. The bringing together of many diverse groups may have fostered an element of tolerance for those of different backgrounds, leading to the common

expression by local residents that Pittsburgh is a city of friendly people.

Of course, a spirit of goodwill is not shared by all. Discrimination is a major problem in Pittsburgh, just as it is in other major metropolitan areas. Problems of poverty, health

Figure 19. Ethnic congregations. Used with permission of Nationality Rooms Program, University of Pittsburgh.

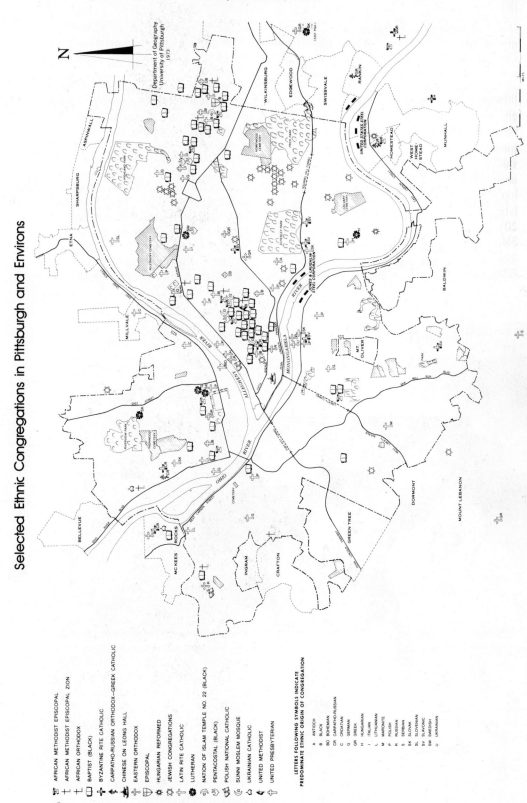

Selected Ethnic Congregations in Pittsburgh and Environs

AFRICAN METHODIST EPISCOPAL
AFRICAN METHODIST EPISCOPAL ZION
AFRICAN ORTHODOX
BAPTIST (BLACK)
BYZANTINE RITE CATHOLIC
CARPATHO-RUSSIAN ORTHODOX—GREEK CATHOLIC
CHINESE ON LEONG HALL
EASTERN ORTHODOX
EPISCOPAL
HUNGARIAN REFORMED
JEWISH CONGREGATIONS
LATIN RITE CATHOLIC
LUTHERAN
NATION OF ISLAM TEMPLE NO 22 (BLACK)
PENTACOSTAL (BLACK)
POLISH NATIONAL CATHOLIC
SUNNI MOSLEM MOSQUE
UKRAINIAN CATHOLIC
UNITED METHODIST
UNITED PRESBYTERIAN

LETTERS FOLLOWING SYMBOLS INDICATE
PREDOMINATE ETHNIC ORIGIN OF CONGREGATION

A   ANTIOCH
B   BLACK
BO   BOHEMIAN
CR   CARPATHO-RUSSIAN
C   CROATIAN
G   GERMAN
GR   GREEK
H   HUNGARIAN
I   ITALIAN
L   LITHUANIAN
M   MARONITE
P   POLISH
R   RUSSIAN
S   SERBIAN
SK   SLOVAK
SL   SLOVENIAN
SV   SLAVONIC
SW   SWEDISH
U   UKRAINIAN

care, and substandard housing face blacks and the elderly alike. Blacks suffer additionally from racial discrimination. Four-fifths of all poor families are white, but more than half of all black families are poor.

Migration has been a positive force, providing needed labor for industrial growth and giving the region its rich mixture of different peoples, each adding to the cultural flavor of numerous neighborhoods. On the negative side, redistribution of population in the region as well as net outmigration from the SMSA have resulted in widespread patterns of population loss among minor civil divisions (Figure 20). As mentioned in the introduction, the SMSA lost population between 1960 and 1970, and although the amount was negligible, it symbolizes the extent of the problem. This net

outmigration has resulted in the loss of many of the potentially most productive members of the work force and has produced a general aging of the population.

Numerous communities in suburban areas—especially those with significant proportions of their work force engaged in heavy industry—have suffered greatly from net outmigration, many losing up to one-third of their population since 1950. Some mill towns within greater Pittsburgh along the Monongahela River, such as Braddock and Rankin, have been particularly hard hit. They have suffered from both structural shifts in the regional economy and competition for jobs and services from the metropolitan area.

Minor civil divisions that experienced gains in population from 1950 to 1970 were either

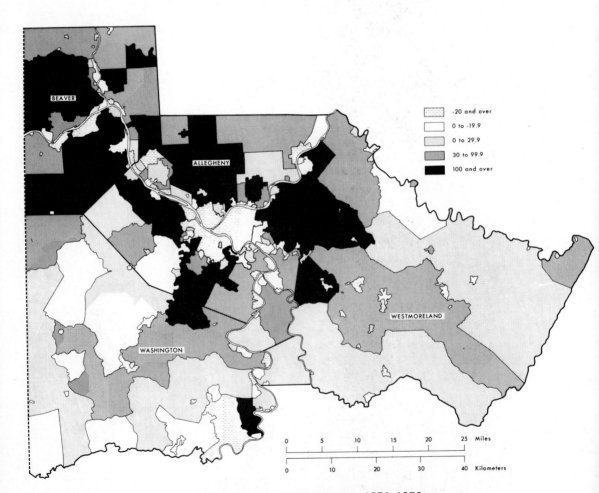

Figure 20. Population change, 1950–1970.

suburban to Pittsburgh or to industrial communities and removed from railroad corridors. The only major exceptions are mining and farming areas in the western portions of Washington County that have low population densities, few large settlements, and are not part of the urbanized area.

Significant population losses throughout the metropolitan region since 1950 are dramatic examples of migration effects, but of far greater long range consequence have been changes in age and sex structure brought on by fifty years of persistent net outmigration. In 1950 the largest age cohorts in both the SMSA and city of Pittsburgh were in the twenty to thirty-nine age group. After a span of only twenty years, gaps appear in the young adult ages where bulges were before, the outcome of natural aging of the population and departure from the region of many within this age group (Figure 21).

Pittsburgh is becoming a place of old and young people. In 1970, 43.1 percent of the population of the SMSA was under eighteen or over sixty-five years of age. Median ages for the SMSA and the central city were 32.2 and 33.7, respectively. These values compare dramatically with the national figure of 27.7, a difference of about five years. Were it not for the age and family size characteristics of blacks, the differences would have been even more exaggerated, particularly in the central city where the blacks make up a little over 20 percent of the population. The median age for this group in the SMSA in 1970 was twenty-six, slightly younger than in 1950, in contrast to the aging trend experienced by the whites. Yet, even then the black population median age was over three years above the national median age for blacks.

The deficit of females in the fifteen to forty-four age group, and the disproportionate numbers of the elderly, have resulted in low birth rates and high mortality rates for the metropolitan area in general, with the higher mortality rates in the central city and industrial communities along transportation corridors. In 1973 Allegheny County, as well as the central city, registered more deaths than births, giving this country the distinction of being one of the few metropolitan counties in the U.S. to have experienced natural decrease. Since minor civil divisions that have experienced heavy population losses since 1950 are found throughout the metropolitan area, the generalization that central city residents tend to be older than those in suburban areas does not readily apply in the Pittsburgh case. Although there are many middle and upper income white collar suburbs with young populations, industrial communities located in suburban areas have relatively old populations, some with a median age of over forty years.

As a consequence of these trends, health care and housing for the elderly have become critical problems in the Pittsburgh SMSA. The

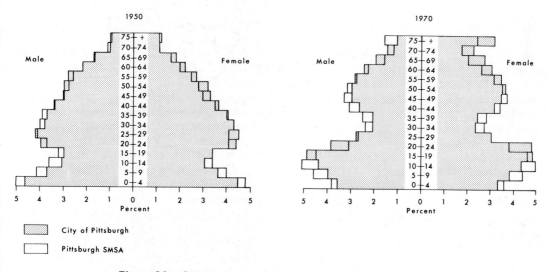

Figure 21. Age structure of the population, 1950 and 1970.

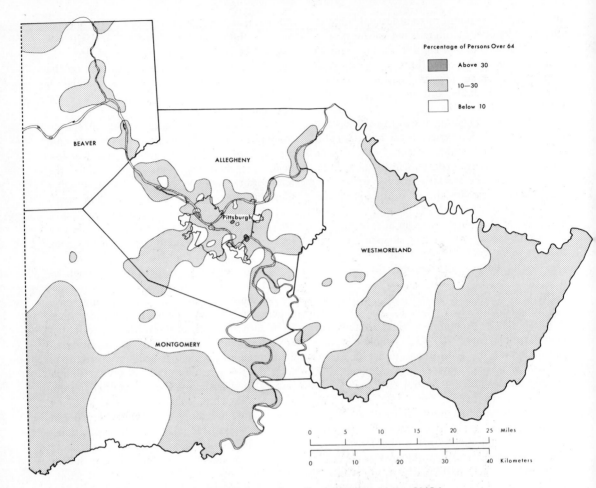

Figure 22. Persons sixty-five and older in the SMSA.

dispersed nature of the elderly throughout the urban region and dense concentrations in specific locations have complicated the task of meeting the needs of this particular group (Figure 22). For many industrial communities in which the median age is over forty years, the situation has reached crisis proportions. Old, poor people with no families and completely dependent on public assistance for sustenance, tragically blending in with the urban blight that surrounds them, have become a common sight.

DISTRIBUTION AND DELIVERY OF HEALTH CARE

Nearly thirty years have passed since the tragedy in Donora, an industrial community about thirty miles south of Pittsburgh on the Monongahela. Excessive levels of air pollution over a three day period caused substantial increases in serious illnesses, particularly among the elderly, resulting in twenty deaths. The industrial and demographic characteristics that led to this well-known incident are still contributing to medical problems. An aging population, large numbers of low income families, and high levels of air pollution are difficult challenges for a health care system more suited to serving younger families in the middle and upper income categories.

Hospitals and physicians tend to be distributed in accordance with population within the SMSA (Figure 23). The major concentration of general and specialized hospitals is found in the city of Pittsburgh, primarily in the Oakland area. Here there are twenty-nine separate health

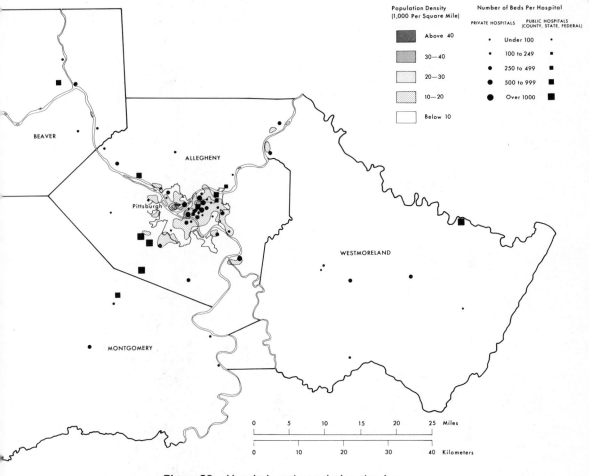

Figure 23. Hospitals and population density.

services, including five major hospitals; various clinics for X-rays, methadone treatment, abortion consultation; and a number of offices for the dispensing of family planning and health care information. Suburban hospitals cater to general health care needs. Patients requiring specialized health care services are transferred to the central core.

This hierarchically arranged health care system tends to work well for those who can afford it. But the elderly and low income families have difficulties gaining entry to the health care system, and getting proper care once they are admitted. While the central city is well equipped with wide-ranging medical facilities, hospitals and physicians are scarce in industrial communities along major river valleys and in older mining towns, making the question of health care for the elderly particularly difficult. Even

though a little over 10 percent of the SMSA population is over sixty-five years of age, they make up close to half of all poor households. Nearly two-thirds of the elderly are poor. This age group is distributed throughout the metropolitan area, but major concentrations are found in low income neighborhoods in the central city and along major river valleys, where geriatric health care facilities are inadequate.

If net outmigration continues at about the same pace as it has in recent years and the population continues to fail to replace itself, a short term labor shortage may develop that will reduce the ability of the economy to expand rapidly in labor-intensive industries. Other opportunity areas to be affected will be those in education, recreation, health care, and other services catering to children and young people.

Problems in a Declining Region

Population and housing problems of the Pittsburgh region derive from the patterns and processes highlighted in the previous sections. The long history of settlement, changing economic structure, an aging population, and racial discrimination have created urban and social distress in many parts of the urban region. Of course, out of these same processes have come countervailing forces of ethnic diversity, relatively low crime rates, an expanding service sector, and ample green spaces that have tended to offset the negative forces and lend themselves to a relatively high degree of social stability. But for the poor, the aged, and victims of discrimination, positive factors fall short of canceling out frustrations, insecurity, and anger. Pittsburgh is an urban region beset with population and housing problems.

Following a general introduction into the geographical distribution of depressed areas, brief capsules about selected problems are presented, beginning first with demographic changes and housing. These two interrelated issues are perhaps two of the more difficult problems that confront the Pittsburgh metropolitan area. Mass transit, recreation, and air and water pollution are three additional problems that pose special challenges.

In most major metropolitan areas in the Midwest and Northeast, population and housing attributes vary systematically with increasing distance from the downtown. Patterns of metropolitan expansion have included construction of new housing in attractive surroundings for middle and high income families in the suburbs. Central cities tend to be plagued by poverty, substandard housing, unemployment, and a host of other problems, while in suburban areas family incomes tend to be higher, housing of higher value, and the quality of life generally better. This horizontal polarization of low income and affluent families, of substandard and standard housing, and other paired indexes reflecting discrepancies in living conditions between central cities and suburbs also applies to the Pittsburgh area (Figure 24). For example, in 1969 the median family income of $8,800 for the central city was decidedly lower than the $10,132 suburban median family income. Also, the median age for central city residents was 33.5 compared to 31.6 for those in outlying areas, and nearly 14 percent of the central city population was over sixty-five years of age, while outside the city the figure was a little less than 10 percent. As for housing, the mean value of owner-occupied housing units in the central city was $14,735 in 1970, while it was $18,105 in the suburbs. Similarly, differences in unemployment, occupational structure, and crime that favor the suburbs can also be cited. But, the generalization that central cities have more severe population and housing problems than suburban areas tends to break down when the Pittsburgh SMSA is disaggregated into minor civil divisions.

A unique vertical dimension in population and housing problem areas in the Pittsburgh SMSA derives from the early industrializa-

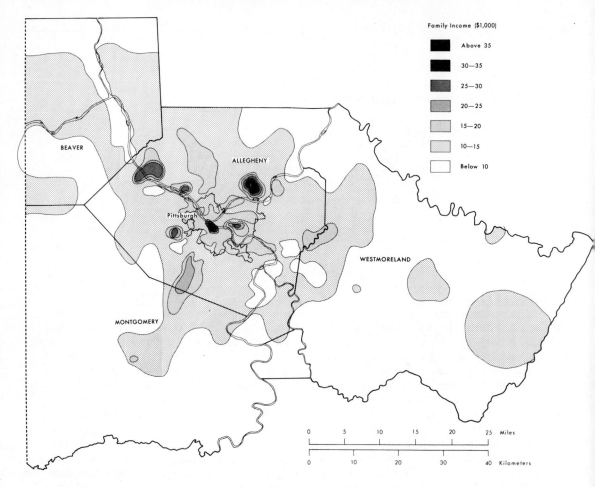

Figure 24. Median family income, 1969.

tion of major river valleys. Communities on the valley floors can be distinguished from those on surrounding hilltops. Industrial centers along the major river valleys formed the nuclei for settlements that were subsequently transformed from rapidly growing, viable communities to economically depressed areas as jobs were lost through modernization or closures of industrial plants and the movement of people away from the persistent lack of jobs, congestion, and pollution. Thus, industrial communities on the narrow valley bottoms and adjoining areas generally suffer from problems of poverty, inadequate health care for the elderly, unemployment, and deteriorating housing. Settlements on the bluffs overlooking the valleys are much better off in these respects. Partly because of the above conditions the family income deficit, or the amount of money re-

quired to bring all family incomes up to the poverty level, is twice as high in the suburbs as it is in the central city (Figure 25).

INDUSTRIAL COMMUNITIES

Perhaps no other single feature is more representative of the history and geography of the Pittsburgh metropolitan area than these industrial communities situated along major river and transportation corridors (Figure 26). Many were established during the latter part of the eighteenth century as trade and mercantile centers, but not until after the Civil War did economic and transportation developments give them a competitive advantage over settlements located away from the rivers. The railroad generally followed major river valleys, representing paths of least resistance through the rough ter-

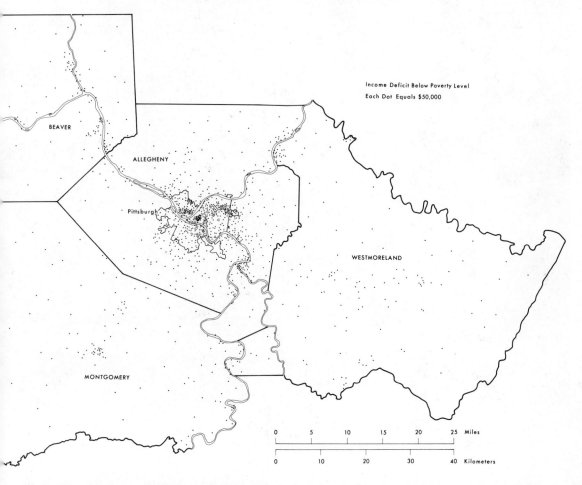

Figure 25. Poverty in the Pittsburgh area. Each dot represents $50,000 needed to bring households at that location up to the poverty line in 1969.

rain. Ready access to railroad and river transportation plus plentiful water supply for use as a coolant and for waste disposal made these riverine communities valuable sites for heavy industry.

Concentration of iron and steel production and ancillary manufacturing firms in these communities gave rise to a process of circular and cumulative economic and population growth that continued unabated until after World War I. Since that time many of these highly specialized industrial communities have declined in population. Only those with diversified economic bases and located some distance from Pittsburgh have managed to avoid significant population losses.

In 1970 in the Pittsburgh SMSA, sixty-six minor civil divisions and urbanized townships with over 2,500 in population size had at least 18.5 percent of their work force engaged in blue collar occupations. Compared to other minor civil divisions, excluding Pittsburgh, these industrial communities tended to be smaller in population size, older in population and housing, ethnically more diverse, more in need of urban renewal, higher in mortality rates, and to have other correlates of declining, depressed areas.

Two types of industrial communities can be identified on the bases of time of development and function—older industrial communities located along major rivers and railroad lines; and more recently established communities removed from major transportation corridors that serve as residential areas for industrial centers. In either case, the percentage of blue

Figure 26. An iron and steel plant and adjacent housing along the Monongahela River, Pittsburgh. Photo courtesy of Greater Pittsburgh Chamber of Commerce.

collar workers is relatively high. These communities differ markedly in economic, population, and housing patterns from other suburban areas in the metropolitan region.

The older industrial communities are classic examples of mill towns. In general, most residents owe their livelihood to one or two industrial plants, and shutdowns or even cutbacks in production send reverberations of unemployment, decreased patronage of local stores, and other job-related ramifications through the entire community. Patterns of land use and economic activity strongly reflect economic origins and intense competition over the years for use of limited, river-terraced areas. Flat stretches of land along the transportation corridors are largely occupied by industrial facilities, residential areas being relegated to the hillslopes. High land use densities, narrow streets, and incompatible land uses prevail, typified by the location of residential areas alongside industrial establishments. Noise, pollution, traffic congestion, and other negative externalities for residential areas amount to poor living and working conditions. Central business districts, usually near the factory and railroad district, display the size and diversity of shops and businesses of formerly prosperous times. Now the numerous deteriorating and boarded-up buildings are painful reminders of social and economic decay.

The distribution of problem areas in both the central city and suburbs emphasizes the need for metropolitanwide coordination in housing and population programs.

DEMOGRAPHIC PROCESSES IN THE CENTRAL CITY

Changes in demographic composition of Pittsburgh have been brought on by massive outmovements of whites (mostly to the suburbs), natural decrease for the older whites that remained, and higher replacement level capacities of younger black families.

The suburban trek by whites in Pittsburgh actually began in the mid-1850s, as the wealthy moved to Allegheny City across the Allegheny River from downtown and to Bellevue further to the northwest, on the Ohio. The escape from pollution and congestion in the central city to more pleasant surroundings in the urban periphery was just as important then as it is today. Before the 1860s, when most travel was by foot, railroad, or private horse-drawn carriage, outlying estates were for summer residences only. The advent of the streetcar in the late nineteenth century lowered the money-time costs of commuting, permitting the growth of predominantly middle class suburbs outside the central city, such as Wilkinsburg to the east, Aspinwall to the north, and Mt. Oliver, Ingram, and Crafton to the south. Increasing use of the automobile after 1920 and expansion of the road network, which only measured fifty-six miles of improved roads at the beginning of the century in Allegheny County, expanded significantly the commuting radius of the central city. The completion of the Liberty Tunnels through the hills to the south in 1924 opened up still more attractive areas for Pittsburgh residents.

These transportation developments facilitated outmovements of whites to the suburbs, particularly after 1950. Most of the one-quarter loss in Pittsburgh's population over the next two decades can be attributed to this heavy outmovement. Since the movers to the suburbs tended to be younger and have higher incomes than those who remained. Pittsburgh's demographic structure and tax base were severely affected. Births of whites declined sharply and deaths increased. From 1967 to 1973 white deaths per year actually outnumbered white births, with the largest deficit coming at the end of the period when 5,509 deaths were matched against only 3,357 births. The inability of whites to replace themselves has not yet occurred in Allegheny County outside the central city, an important destination for younger white families moving out of the city or into the Pittsburgh region from outside the metropolitan area. Here white birth rates have been consistently higher than death rates, although the difference has narrowed in recent

years. From 1967 to 1973 annual white death rates held steady at about 9.5 per 1,000, but annual birth rates dropped from 14.5 to 10.6.

In contrast to the declining numbers of whites in Pittsburgh, blacks have gained in numbers, but at a rate much lower than the normal increase in blacks in major metropolitan areas in the North because natural increase and not inmigration has been primarily responsible. In 1970, the median ages for black males and females were eight and ten years younger respectively than white males and females. Moreover, there was very little difference between the median age for black females in the central city or the SMSA as a whole, whereas the median age for white females in the central city was 38.4 while for the SMSA it was 33.9. The younger age structure for blacks has meant relatively high rates of natural increase. From 1967 to 1973 black births per year were approximately 1.6 times higher than deaths, quite a contrast to the pattern for whites. Moreover, in 1973 black births amounted to over one-third of the total births in the city, and blacks constituted only one-fifth of the population. As a consequence of these opposing demographic trends and white outmovement, from 1950 to 1970 blacks increased by 26 percent while whites declined by 31 percent. During this time Pittsburgh also increased from 12 to 20 percent black. This is a small percentage increase, considering the large decline in white population, and reveals that natural increase for blacks was initially relatively low, and inmigration of this group into Pittsburgh has been negligible since 1950.

High levels of outmovement combined with natural decrease for whites have lowered population densities in the central city and opened up the housing market for low income families. At the same time, the increasing numbers of the elderly and the poor have increased the need for health, education, and welfare programs at a time when the tax base of the city has been lessened by the move to the suburbs of middle and high income families and commercial enterprises. A small number of high cost condominiums and apartments have opened in the downtown area, heralding the return to the central city of a growing, though still small, number of families in the higher income brackets. But it will take a massive infusion of young white families before this group again experiences natural increase. The percentage of the elderly in Pittsburgh, which will probably continue to rise for many years, was already 13 percent in 1970.

The diminishing number of whites in Pittsburgh, concomitant with expanding numbers of blacks in dense, low cost housing areas in the inner city, has contributed to high levels of residential segregation. In 1950, the Hill District was the only neighborhood identifiable as a black ghetto at the census tract level. By 1970, three more predominantly black neighborhoods had been formed from many tracts that were only 15 to 20 percent black in 1950.

Black concentrations in the central city suffer from a combination of poor living conditions and a central location that is no longer economically advantageous, since most of the rapidly growing employment areas are found in suburban areas, necessitating some reverse or inside-out commuting. This can be time consuming, since the mass transit system is geared more to serve commuters who live in the suburbs and work in the central city. Fortunately, the Golden Triangle has maintained its prominent position as the business-commercial center of the metropolitan area. However, jobs in the Golden Triangle have become more of the clerical, administrative, and professional variety, requiring high skills, and less of the laborer and service worker kind, forcing these occupational groups to travel relatively long distances away from the central city to find work.

High levels of residential segregation in the central city and in outlying industrial communities have been major stumbling blocks for the attainment of racially integrated schools. (Figure 27). Three predominantly black high schools (Westinghouse, in the eastern part of the city; Fifth Avenue, near the downtown; and Schenley, further to the east in Oakland) and numerous all-black elementary schools are found in the black ghettos of the central city (Figure 28). The patterns of school enrollment over time display a gradual but seemingly inexorable increase in the proportion of black pupils in central city public schools. Busing and school consolidation to counteract segregated schools have never operated on a significant scale.

Poor housing conditions and racial tensions have not been conducive to wholesome school environments. The stereotype of the inner city school generally holds in the central city. An added dimension is the lack of confinement there of racial tension as a problem in urban education. Some of the most racially troubled schools in the Pittsburgh area are found on the fringes of the city—such as in Wilkinsburg, where the black ghetto of Homewood-Brushton on the eastern edge of the city has recently expanded outward, and in outlying industrial communities such as Braddock, Rankin, and Clairton that have had large numbers of black residents for some time. In these communities, black-white percentages are more nearly equal. Many of these suburban communities also have numbers of upwardly mobile black families, who bring high expectations and, perhaps, low thresholds for frustration when their expectations go unfulfilled.

HOUSING

Characteristics, quality, and distribution of housing tell a great deal about a place. Whether an area is rapidly growing, stable, or declining in population is usually reflected in housing adjustments made in accordance with income, social status, space needs, and locations of workplace, schools, shopping centers, and recreational facilities.

The lack of significant influx of population into the Pittsburgh SMSA since at least World War I, and the long history of settlement in the region, have contributed to the accumulation of a relatively old housing stock. In 1970 close to half of the housing units in the metropolitan area were built before 1940, with major concentrations of old housing located in the central city and in industrial communities (Figure 29). In many of these places row houses built for mill workers during the early parts of the twentieth century are still very much in evidence.

The lack of population growth in the region and an insecure economic situation have produced a depressed housing market. Since 1960, new housing starts have averaged only about 10,000 per year and have been primarily limited to suburban areas some distance from the central city and transportation corridors. Federally subsidized housing units have been compensating factors. In 1970 close to one-third of all housing starts in the SMSA and over half of new rental units were federally assisted. Federally subsidized housing was even more sig-

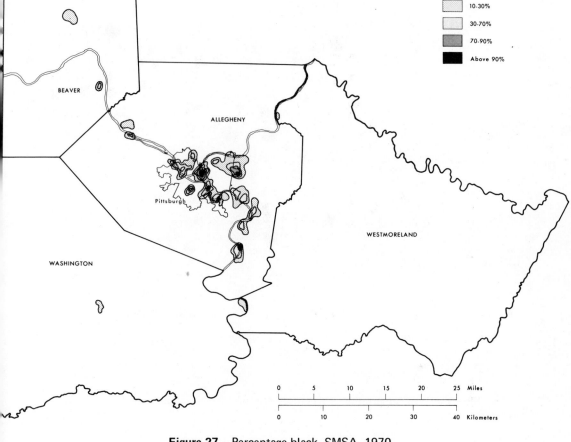

Figure 27. Percentage black, SMSA, 1970.

nificant in the central city, accounting for near-ly 60 percent of the total from 1968 to 1972. This has also made the housing market par-ticularly vulnerable to cutbacks in federal funding for housing. The moratorium on Fed-eral Housing Administration loans in 1973 contributed in part to the sharp decline in housing starts during that year. In the metro-politan area only 9,300 new houses were start-ed, the lowest level since 1969. The downward turn in housing production has also been a function of the shortage of mortgage money, rising housing costs, and the deficit of people in the thirty to forty age bracket who normally make the highest demand for single family dwellings. Half of the families and unrelated individuals in the SMSA received less than $10,000 in income in 1969, representing those of lower and lower middle income. Thus need

is great for inexpensive housing units. Since population growth of the metropolitan area has leveled off, turnover of existing housing units is becoming an increasingly important mechan-ism of housing change. This puts a premium on programs to maintain and rehabilitate the pres-ent housing supply.

The aging population has also caused an increase in multifamily dwellings, which went from only 9 percent of housing starts in 1961 to 31 percent in 1970. Condominiums account-ed for a small but growing fraction of the total housing starts. As the population of the metro-politan area grows increasingly older, multi-family dwellings in both central city and suburbs will continue to gain in importance. In the former, apartments already account for over half of the total housing units. Attractiveness of the central city as a place to live should be

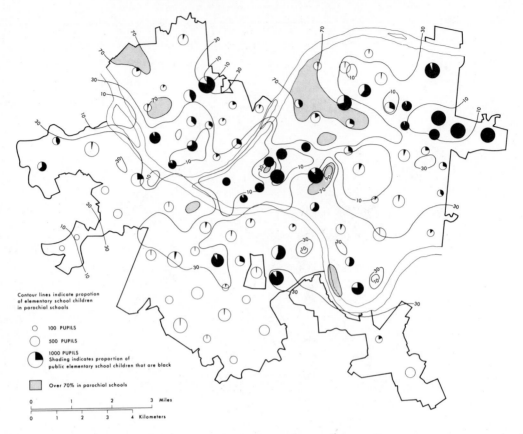

Figure 28. Blacks in Pittsburgh public elementary schools, 1969, and parochial elementary school attendance patterns, 1970.

enhanced by this trend, particularly for those who work there. The change from one apartment to another does not necessarily involve such a drastic modification in lifestyle as would be the case for the owner of a detached unit who might stand to lose some privacy, space, and emotional attachment to property ownership with the move to the central city.

The worst housing conditions in the Pittsburgh metropolitan area are found in low income neighborhoods in the central city, along major transportation corridors, and in isolated mining communities away from the region's waterways. These tend to be areas of older housing, of neighborhoods that have lost their initial locational utility to the metropolitan area, and of economic or racial transition (Figure 30). Housing values in suburban communities range from estates valued at $100,000 and up in Sewickly Heights to industrial communities along major rivers, such as Rankin and

Braddock, where poorly maintained houses sell for $10,000 to $12,000. Since nearly one-half of the poor are elderly and over one-fifth are black, these groups suffer the most in relative terms from hardships of blighted housing, and stand to gain the most from urban renewal. Unfortunately, public housing has accounted for only 5 percent of housing starts since the mid-1960s, and most of these recent units have been for the elderly.

In the city of Pittsburgh, new house construction has lagged well below the rate for the metropolitan area as a whole, which was very low by national standards. In 1970, nearly 80 percent of the housing in the city was over thirty years old. High rates of net outmovement of middle and high income families and rising proportions of low income families have obviously had an impact. Mortgage loans, already scarce in recent years because of tight monetary policies and high interest rates, may be even

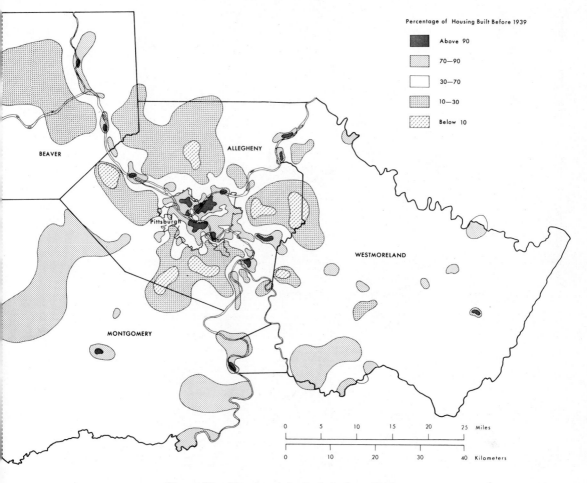

Figure 29. Housing units built before 1940.

more difficult to obtain for old housing that is structurally suspect and a seemingly poor investment for banks.

During the 1960s decade, authorized building permits for new housing units averaged approximately only 1,300 a year for a sum total of about 14,000 units. This housing unit increase fell far short of the 10,000 or so units demolished under the auspices of various urban renewal and highway construction programs and the estimated 40,000 units of the very old housing stock that deteriorated into the substandard category. As a consequence, the actual number of housing units in Pittsburgh declined from 196,000 at the beginning of the decade to around 190,000 units in 1970. Taking into account the number of standard units estimated to have been lost through deteriora-

tion, as many as 50,000 housing units, or roughly one-quarter of the total in 1960, had become substandard or were lost to the housing market entirely. In spite of this, a housing shortage never developed in the city because of two decades of substantial outmovement. Pittsburgh has more than an adequate supply of housing, and overcrowding is not a problem. The housing unit vacancy rate actually increased from 3.7 percent in 1960 to 7.7 percent in 1970, with most of this change accounted for by unrented units in low income neighborhoods.

The percent of occupied housing units with 1.01 or more persons per room, an index for overcrowding, declined from 17 percent in 1950 to 10 percent in 1960 and then to a low of 6 percent in 1970. In 1970, only two census

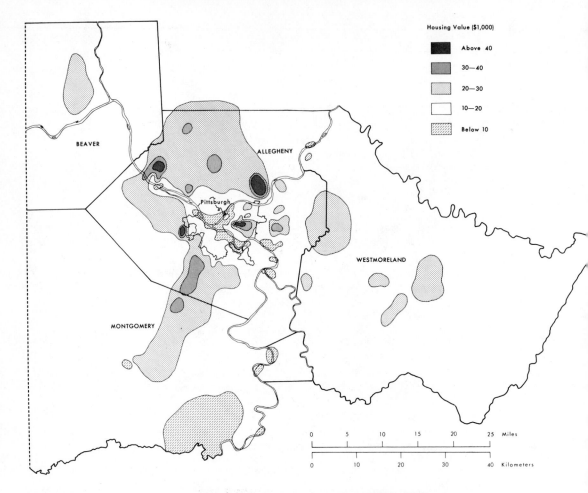

Figure 30.   Median housing value, SMSA, 1970.

tracts in the city could be considered seriously overcrowded, and both contained public housing projects.

Outmovements of whites and the gradual increase of blacks have obviously combined to reduce residential densities in Pittsburgh, opening up the number of alternative locations where low income families can reside. However, the advanced age of most of the housing does present a dilemma. While old housing does not necessarily mean inadequate housing—as evidenced by long established well-to-do neighborhoods such as Squirrel Hill, Point Breeze, and Shadywide that contain some of the oldest housing in the city—occupants of old housing must have the skills and requisite funds for structural maintenance or else age soon takes its toll. It is likely that outmigration has

removed some of the very people with the financial resources to maintain their old homes.

In large measure, Pittsburgh is a city of low and lower middle income families. The median family income in 1969 was only $8,000, and 26.8 percent of all families were either below the poverty level or in the near poor category, the latter defined as families with incomes less than 125 percent of the poverty level. This same year the median sales price for the relatively few new homes that were put up for sale was $25,400, and new rental units were renting for over $100 per month. Needless to say, the few new housing units that were put on the market were too expensive for close to half of the city's residents.

Of course, the housing problem involves more than simply fitting families and individuals into a given number of housing units. If this was all there was to it, Pittsburgh would have an excellent housing situation. Data can be misleading. Both blacks and whites have been pulled to the suburbs by what they perceive to be better living situations just as much as they have been pushed by negative features of the central city. Solutions to housing problems in Pittsburgh lie not only in rehabilitation and maintenance of housing units but, perhaps more importantly, in the improvement of streets, sidewalks, recreational facilities, or those other ingredients of adequate neighborhoods.

Given the income structure and sluggish housing market, federally subsidized housing has dominated real estate activity in the city to a much greater extent than the SMSA as a whole, particularly after 1968, when a Federal Housing Act was enacted. For the next four years, federally subsidized units averaged close to two-thirds of all housing starts. Nearly three-quarters of these housing benefits were directed toward Homewood-Brushton, East Liberty, and East Hills, all predominantly black neighborhoods. The effects of the moratorium have become evident through housing starts that are at an all-time low, and long waiting lists for public housing. In 1973 only 202 new housing units were started, while 5,000 were demolished or deteriorated into the substandard category.

It is unfortunate that the Pittsburgh Renaissance was so short-lived and limited in spatial extent. The same spirit of commitment that worked so well in the downtown never materialized when it came to the question of regenerating neighborhoods (Figure 31). Many of the mistakes usually associated with urban renewal have also been committed in Pittsburgh (Figure 32).

During the late 1950s and early 1960s, urban renewal strategies consisted of tearing down blighted areas and replacing them with commercial and civic structures or high rent apartments such as the Civic Arena and Chatham Center complex that was carved in the Lower Hill District, a formerly black neighbohood. Another characteristic of public housing developments was to concentrate poor and moderate income families in public housing and rental housing in separate projects and exclusive areas. The city of Pittsburgh was the focus of most of this publicly sponsored build-

ing activity, and approximately 70 percent of subsidized units were located there, with black neighborhoods in the eastern section of the city accounting for over half of the units. A trend toward decentralization in subsidized housing is now taking hold as attention is shifting more and more to the depressed areas along the major river valleys.

From 1940 to 1970, nineteen public housing projects were built in the central city, and the present 9,907 units provide homes for about 40,000 people. These projects are generally located on somewhat isolated, vacant hilltops, where services for low income families are virtually nonexistent. Most of these projects are three story walk ups. Although the monotonous architecture, broken windows, and litter-strewn grounds clearly identify them as public housing, the decision to avoid constructing high-rises, except for housing the elderly, has probably been a factor in avoiding some of the public housing disasters of St. Louis and New York City. Nevertheless, public housing in Pittsburgh still suffers from common complaints of mismanagement, high incidence of crime, and poor situations from the hilltop locations that make walking to and from shopping and service centers arduous.

ACTION Housing, a private, low profit agency established by the Allegheny Conference for Community Development in 1957, has been primarily responsible for the provision of subsidized housing units for families with too much income to qualify for public housing but not enough to participate in the private housing market without financial assistance. In 1959, through grants and loans from thirty business and financial institutions, an innovative $1.6 million revolving loan plan referred to as the Pittsburgh Development Fund was set up by ACTION Housing to serve as seed money to encourage involvement of private financiers and building contractors in developing low cost housing. Since its introduction, the Development Fund has generated $55.4 million worth of housing, and has been responsible for around 2,800 new and rehabilitated housing units in the metropolitan area and 65 percent of total FHA-subsidized housing starts in the central city. These accomplishments include seven major housing developments—namely, Spring Hill Gardens, East Hills Park, Sheraden Park, Liberty Park, Penn Circle Towers, Greenway Park, and Palisades.

Figure 31. The Lower Hill: a black neighborhood adjacent to the Golden Triangle with deteriorating housing and old and new public housing. Photo courtesy of Urban Redevelopment Authority,
Pittsburgh.

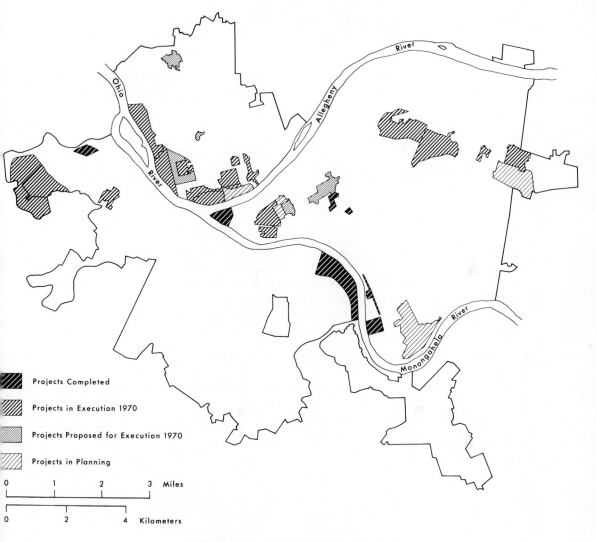

Figure 32. Urban renewal areas.

East Hill Park in the eastern section of the city provides living space for up to 800 families and is the most impressive project. Besides providing modest but decent living quarters within the reach of the average family in Pittsburgh, this low cost housing development is next to a major shopping center and has good mass transit connections with the rest of the city.

As mentioned, public and subsidized housing developments have tended to increase segregation by income and race and have accomplished little in the way of promulgating neighborhood solidarity. In an attempt to promote integration

and stronger attachment to neighborhoods for the beneficiaries of publicly supported housing, Pittsburgh City Planning and the Housing Authority have recently put into practice a "scattered site housing strategy." This entails advocating a change in federal policy to permit qualified residents in a neighborhood chosen as the site for a public housing project to be given first choice for most of the units; leasing housing units to low income families in some of the better neighborhoods; and, finally, combining public and subsidized housing on the same site. If implemented successfully, these strategies will replicate some aspects of the private housing market by providing more diversified housing and neighborhood alternatives for low income families.

MASS TRANSIT

Mass transit in Pittsburgh is a marvelous adaptation of a variety of vehicles to a physically complex region. Active use is made of buses, trolley cars, and cable cars. Buses, the most important mode, are well suited to the rough terrain, numerous narrow streets, and scattered population distribution. Pittsburgh has always lacked the high residential densities in corridors emanating out from the city to support a system of train and subways with much greater carrying capacities.

The metropolitanwide mass transit system—Port Authority Transit (PAT)—was formed in 1964 from thirty-three private bus and trolley car companies operating in the Pittsburgh area. In the decade or so leading up to the public takeover, these formerly independent companies had been caught in the vicious circle of declining riders, increasing fares, reduction in service, followed by still fewer riders, brought about by the common use of the automobile. Frequent cutbacks in service, except along the most profitable routes, and sporadic transit fare increases were unacceptable trends, since so many low income people were dependent upon mass transit for their working and shopping trips. Increasing automobile-related congestion and pollution in the Golden Triangle provided visible evidence that an integrated and expanded mass transit program was long overdue.

Formation of PAT was a necessary beginning for a metropolitanwide transit program designed both as a service and a means of reducing congestion and pollution. While mobility was facilitated for those with no other means of transportation and within walking distance of a transit route, only a small fraction of commuters have been willing to take mass transit instead of driving to work. Close to 80 percent of PAT riders are "captive" or have no other means of transportation. The controversy generated by PAT's so-called Early Action Program, the only serious attempt to date to modernize the transit system, has been one major reason for the failure of mass transit to attract auto drivers. An ineffective campaign to promote mass transit as an alternative to the automobile has been another.

Yet Pittsburgh does seem to possess the ingredients for a successful mass transit system. The Golden Triangle is the major focus of work trips into the central city, easing somewhat the logistics of getting commuters to their jobs. Residential areas are spread out, but the numerous bridge and tunnel bottlenecks take away some of the advantage of private automobiles. For example, residents in the north and south sides of Pittsburgh must cross the Allegheny or Monongahela to get downtown. Only those to the east of the city have real flexibility in route choice. Lastly, but perhaps most importantly, increasing numbers of low income and elderly central city residents ensure an expanding base upon which to operate extensive but subsidized mass transit.

The question of subsidy is critical. PAT has been unable to maintain metropolitanwide service and still make a profit. In 1973, the average fare of 40 cents was 15 cents short of the break even point, given the number of riders, amounting to a loss of $19 million. The state paid for two-thirds of this deficit, the county for the remaining third. Senior citizens now ride for free, their fares being covered by the state lottery.

Since 1972 PAT has stepped up its efforts to publicize the benefits of commuting via public transit and to improve the overall quality of the system. Seventy new buses will be added in 1975. Many old buses and trolley cars have been painted in bright mod style colors and design. Price decrease incentives have been instituted. These include weekly, monthly, and annual permits at a savings over equivalent daily fares; cheaper fares on special days during off rush hours; weekend family passes; and a "wild card" bus that alternates among the routes giving surprise free rides.

These innovations have already had detectable influences. According to a survey of the American Public Transit Association, in September 1974 PAT had 8,558,000 passengers, an 11.8 percent increase over the same month the previous year. This was the highest percentage increase among the major cities in the survey. Not included were Los Angeles, Detroit, Boston, Oakland, and San Francisco, because they do not keep cumulative records of ridership.

RECREATION

The Pittsburgh metropolitan area has been endowed with large stretches of open space, even in the densely built-up areas, because of the numerous ridges, river valleys, and steep gradients. Green spaces throughout the urban region are pleasing to the eye. In the central city, they offer a refreshing contrast to the otherwise congested mixture of streets and buildings. Large undeveloped areas and the extensive water resources would seem to provide wide-ranging possibilities for recreational activities, but this potential has never been fully realized. Generally speaking, residents of the Pittsburgh metropolitan area suffer from a shortage of total acreage of recreational land uses and the irregular geographic distribution of local and regional parks. This deficiency has come from the destruction of many areas suitable for parks and the failure to provide for adequate open space during urban expansion. According to the land use and trip behavior survey conducted by the Southwestern Pennsylvania Regional Planning Commission (SPRPC) in 1967, covering the four SMSA counties plus contiguous Butler and Armstrong counties, regional parks in the six county area covered approximately 70,000 acres. While this represented a 100 percent increase over regional park acreage in 1950, SPRPC estimates this to be 30,000 acres short of the desirable number of acres, based on the population size of the region.

Industrial development has meant the exploitation of energy and transportation resources at the expense of the natural environment. Little provision was made for open space during the establishment of industrial centers and associated communities along the major river valleys. Principal concerns were for economic productivity and not for the quality of life for the workers. Space that was not preempted by industrial complexes and transportation links became dense housing developments, leaving virtually no space for recreation except where the gradient was too steep for other uses. Industrial plants and railroad tracks that ran parallel to the rivers cut off access to the major waterways. Moreover, the dumping of sewage and industrial waste into the rivers made the question of access almost irrelevant.

Coal mining areas away from the rivers have also been destructive. Many of the region's waterways have become polluted from acid drainage into streams and rivers from underground mine flows. Strip mining has rendered land unsuitable for recreation activities, and the unsightly blight adversely affects adjacent places. State laws requiring reclamation of strip-mined land have as yet had little impact.

The geographic distribution of parks is also part of the problem. Residents of the central city and affluent suburban areas are relatively well served by local and regional parks if private transportation is available. However, low income residents of industrial communities along major valley floors suffer not only from a lack of local parks but from lack of convenient access to regional parks.

The 1967 SPRPC survey revealed that recreational trips are highly sensitive to distance, with large, well-equipped parks near major population clusters receiving the most visitors. North and South parks in Allegheny County accounted for over one-half of all trips to regional parks in the area. This strong preference for nearby parks places residents of valley communities at a disadvantage, since most major parks in the metropolitan area are located away from major rivers, beyond the rural-urban fringe where population densities are low. Consequently, low income families were underrepresented in visitations to regional parks, and about two-thirds of the park visitors were those of middle and high income who make up less than one-half of the population.

In contrast to the situation in the valley communities, residents of Pittsburgh are well situated with respect to outlying regional parks and have good access to small parks, playground areas, and swimming pools that are well spaced throughout the city. The city also has a population large enough to support a wide variety of recreational activities. The city zoo is housed in Highland Park. The Oakland-Schenley Park area and Frick Park provide various recreational possibilities, including a public golf course, tennis courts, hiking trails, Phipps Conservatory for flower shows, and the first class Carnegie Museum Art Gallery and Library complex. On the North side, there is again a diverse mix of educational and recreational facilities in Riverview Park and parks around Allegheny Center, consisting of an aviary, planetarium, and the Old Post Office Museum which specializes in the early history of the area. Theaters, nightclubs, restaurants, and sports arenas in the Golden Triangle provide a diversity of high quality social events. Varied activities and continual comings and goings of pedestrian and automobile traffic have had a lot to do with keeping the downtown relatively safe.

The Point State Park at the tip of the Triangle, and proposals to improve a small area called Market Square which is becoming a nightclub and discotheque center for the city, are indicative of the continuing commitment on the part of civic leaders to preserve and upgrade the cultural and recreational role of the Golden Triangle.

AIR AND WATER POLLUTION

Air pollution in Pittsburgh has long attracted attention. Even in the early nineteenth century concerned citizens were advocating smoke abatement. Anthony Trollope, an English novelist, wrote, "Pittsburgh is without exception the blackest place which I ever saw." The *Report of the Economic Survey of Pittsburgh* in 1912 stated, "The first fundamental need in Pittsburgh is the eradication of smoke." Even today, the name "Smoky City" is still associated with the Pittsburgh area. Yet the begrimed citizen of the past associated the smoke of the mills with prosperity. The ominous sign for him was when smoke stacks were without their plumes, for this meant people were out of work. In reality, much of the smoke in the cooler seasons came from the tens of thousands of residential furnaces burning bituminous coal.

Soon after the Second World War, air quality in Pittsburgh underwent dramatic improvement. Trains switched from steam to diesel fuel, individual homes converted from coal furnaces to cleaner burning natural gas, and industries began applying new technology for reducing smoke. A relatively tough smoke control law became applicable to all of Allegheny County, and in the next seven years there was at least a 90 percent improvement. In 1946 there were 298 hours of "heavy smoke" in Pittsburgh; by 1953 this had been reduced to sixteen.

Though the worst aspects of "dirty" air pollution have been brought under control, air quality is still a serious problem. The valley corridors of the region tend to function as natural traps for foul air, smoke, and soot. Brisk winds can clean the sinuous valleys of smoke and the pungent smell of sulfur, but much of the time the wind does not blow strongly enough to dissipate all the toxic gases and atmospheric dirt. A dangerous condition results during inversions, when warmer air overrides cooler air and traps it in the valleys, resulting in the rapid build-up of smog.

Particulate matter and sulfur dioxide are monitored at seven different locations in Allegheny County and provide an index of air quality. Either on a composite county index or for a given locality, the levels of particulate matter and sulfur dioxide are at present significantly in violation of existing federal standards. The federal Clean Air Act mandated that the county had to meet its twenty-four hour and annual air quality standards by July, 1975, which the county failed to do. Automobile pollution is not a top priority concern, though in some areas—such as the Golden Triangle—these emissions can reach dangerously high levels.

In recent years industry, iron and steel mills, and electric power plants have spent considerable sums of money on pollution control, because of increasing pressure from the county Variance Board, the state Department of Environmental Resources, and concerned citizen groups. In 1967, air pollution was unquestionably high, but Pittsburgh had less suspended particulate matter than New York, Buffalo, Philadelphia, and Chicago.

In general, water quality in the Pittsburgh region is also unsatisfactory. The extensive drainage system of southwestern Pennsylvania provides an abundant water supply for consumption and sewage disposal for numerous municipalities in the Pittsburgh metropolitan area. Industry, particularly electric power plants and iron and steel mills, accounts for the bulk of water usage. Most of the water is returned to the streams after being used for cooling and waste disposal. As a consequence, the streams are polluted by industrial waste, sewage, and thermal pollution. Acidity of the streams from coal mining is an additional problem.

Communities along the major rivers and tributaries have either developed their own treatment plants for both water and sewage or have joined together to form authorities.

Municipalities away from the rivers are either linked to a river-based system or obtain water from wells or reservoirs. Sewage disposal is handled in much the same way. Minor civil divisions are either connected to a treatment plant that disposes into one of the rivers, or use on-lot septic tanks in the absence of public sewage facilities.

Problems arise in these service systems from the lack of cooperation among many contiguous municipalities and the advanced age of many of the systems, requiring frequent repairs of ruptured or clogged pipes.

The water and sewage systems of Pittsburgh and surrounding areas in Allegheny County mirror those of the metropolitan area as a whole. Water supply is no problem. The major city filtration plant serves twenty-four out of the thirty-two wards, while remaining wards are provided for by local water authorities based outside the city. Since population is expected to remain stabilized at about its present level in the foreseeable future, no plans are in the offing to expand the purification and sewage treatment systems. However, the Pittsburgh water supply system is an old one, requiring frequent maintenance and replacements. Many of the water pipes in some of the older neighborhoods have become nearly clogged by the build-up of materials, causing periodic water shortages.

The Allegheny County Sanitary Authority (ALCOSAN), formed in 1959, provides a single sewage treatment plant for Pittsburgh and seventy-two other municipalities. Since the urbanized area is beginning to expand into areas not served at present by this public sewage service, localized problems of sewage disposal may increase on the urban fringe in the near future. This is already happening in Plum Borough, on the eastern edge of Allegheny County, which has excellent access to the central city ensuring continued population growth. This borough is one of the largest areas to the east of the city without a public sewage system.

Age is also a problem for Pittsburgh's sewage system. The average age of city sewer pipes is sixty-two years, and many segments date back 125 years. The combination of advanced age and the inability of many sewer lines to handle runoff during periods of heavy rain have created nine major sewage problem areas in the central city. The largest problem sections are

found in the eastern section of the city and in the south side, along Saw Mill Run Boulevard where sewers often back up, spilling untreated sewage into streets and streams.

Acidity of the streams is one of the more serious water quality problems for the metropolitan area, even though coal mining in the region has declined for over half a century. Mine acid drainage increases each time a mine shaft is opened or abandoned, or the surface is stripped to get at the coal. The exposure of sulfur-bearing minerals to air and water forms sulfuric acid. When the acidity of a stream increases so that the pH level falls below six (a "pH value" of less than seven indicates acidic properties), fish life is endangered and the water becomes increasingly corrosive and unpalatable. During the low periods of summer and fall, acidity of streams becomes more concentrated.

A mine-sealing program, initiated by the state in 1937, and more recent stringent strip mining laws have had little impact on the control of mine acid discharges. New deep or surface mines must have a plan of drainage approved by the Sanitary Water Board, but the penalties for noncompliance have been inadequate.

PROSPECTS IN A REGION OF POPULATION SIZE STABILITY

What lies ahead? It is difficult to say in this age of unpredictability, but one thing is certain: the patterns, processes, and problems reviewed in this study are certain to have an influence on future events, at least in the short run. Of these, stabilization of the population size of the metropolitan area, diversification of the economic base, and preservation of the Golden Triangle as the business and cultural center will figure prominently in the course of future developments.

Stabilization of the population size of the Pittsburgh metropolitan area at about its present level, with net outmigration and low rates of natural increase, is of major consequence. Spatial expansion of the urbanized area, already slow, should become even more gradual, particularly since the rising cost of energy is placing greater value on propinquity. This, plus inconvenient access to outlying areas, makes coalescence of the Pittsburgh urban complex with the Cleveland-Youngstown, Ohio, area very doubtful anytime in the near future. Changes in land use patterns will come about more from redistribution of people and economic activities within the region, rather than inmovement from the outside. The city of Pittsburgh and major transportation corridors will continue to exert gravitational-like forces on these patterns.

While population size of the metropolitan area is expected to hold steady, net outmigration and low rates of natural increase will continue to bring about a general aging of the population, particularly in the central city and in outlying industrial communities. The central city will continue to lose population to the suburbs, but not at the rate of the last two decades. Outmovement of whites, low replacement levels for whites that remain, and higher rates of natural increase for blacks will result in the continued slow rise of the relative importance of blacks. However, change in racial composition of Pittsburgh is also slowing down. Blacks are beginning to move out of the central city in significant numbers.

The lack of population growth in the metropolitan area is symptomatic of underlying economic conditions. To a large extent, the future of Pittsburgh rests in the economic front. Specialization in heavy industry in the past contributed to pollution, population losses, and urban decay, although Jane Jacobs' reference to Pittsburgh as a "ruined city" has never been appropriate, not even before the "Pittsburgh Renaissance." In deference to those who feel that Pittsburgh suffers from a bad reputation, she wisely pointed out that "[a]rtificial symptoms of prosperity or a 'good image' do not revitalize a city, but only explicit economic growth processes for which there are no substitutes." There are reasons to be optimistic here. This time, however, economic growth will be generated more ·by business, commerce, and light industry. The heavy industrial phase of economic productivity is over. Pittsburgh may lose Jones and Laughlin Steel Works, its only integrated iron and steel plant. Industrial parks away from river and railroad lines have become the site for new industrial establishments. Major corporations with headquarters here have promoted the expansion of research and development facilities. Research and teaching programs associated with the major universities (University of Pittsburgh,

Carnegie-Mellon, and Duquesne) have bolstered the intellectual climate of the central city.

The dominant position of the Golden Triangle is symbolic of diversification of the urban economy. Large scale displacement of business activity away from the city center will probably not occur in Pittsburgh. Greentree and Monroeville are growing rapidly, but they will remain as secondary centers. The office occupancy rate of the Golden Triangle is close to 90 percent. New buildings are under construction, with the thirty-four story Equibank building the most prominent new structure. A convention hall, twin movie, shopping mall, and restaurant complex are soon to be built in the area.

The preservation of the Golden Triangle as the business, cultural, and sports center of the metropolitan area is a real positive factor for the future. Yet the image of Joe Magarac will not be erased. Pittsburgh has its roots in industrial and mining communities in outlying areas. Production of iron and steel, heavy machinery, and coal will continue to make significant, though diminishing, contributions to the regional economy. Moreover, widespread urban blight and poverty in these communities, as well as in residential areas surrounding the Golden Triangle, are grim reminders that many inhabitants of this region have never benefited from renewal in the downtown.

The overall quality of life must be improved so that it is shared by all. From sheer numbers alone, Pittsburgh has the mandate to become a leader in the formulation and implementation of housing, income maintenance, and health care programs for the elderly and low income families. The attainment of a relatively constant population size may be a real planning advantage. Since the question of expansion is not so important, emphasis can be placed on the maintenance and upgrading of existing services and facilities. Public and low cost housing must be expanded. The mass transit system must be improved not only to ensure a means of mobility for those with no other transportation, but to help sustain the Golden Triangle by reducing automobile congestion and pollution. More progress in pollution control is also needed, a charge that will become increasingly difficult to meet if air and water quality standards are lowered to promote the use of coal as a primary energy source. In addition, cleaning up and making more accessible the major waterways, the development of river front parks, and improvements in the distribution and quality of recreational facilities need to be assigned high priorities.

Political fragmentation of the metropolitan area will function as a major stumbling block for the successful implementation of programs to combat metropolitanwide problems. Unfortunately, income and racial distinctions between the central city and suburban communities, plus unworkable consolidation laws, make the prospects for eventual metropolitanwide government almost out of the question. Although the hope is dim for unification of political subdivisions, efforts should at least be made to combine the numerous public and private agencies with overlapping responsibilities in planning and delivery of social and health care services. To name a few, there are Southwestern Pennsylvania Regional Planning Commission, Allegheny County Planning, City Planning, Allegheny Conference for Commu-

nity Development, Chamber of Commerce, Penn's Southwest, Pittsburgh Convention and Visitor's Bureau, Three Rivers Industrial and Development Association (TRIAD), ACTION Housing, Golden Triangle Association, Urban Redevelopment Authority, and Regional Industrial Development Corporation. Special districts that cross over political boundaries have been used relatively successfully to provide mass transit, water and sewage service, and pollution control. The application of this strategy to the many agencies involved in urban planning and development will not be a panacea, but it may lead to more efficient and economical services.

In conclusion, the future of the Pittsburgh metropolitan area is closely tied to what happens to social and living conditions in the central city and outlying areas now suffering from poverty and urban blight. The Renaissance of the 1950s needs to be revitalized, this time to promote social, not corporate, welfare.

Bibliography

Allegheny County Planning Commission. *Development Sketch-Plan*. Pittsburgh, 1970.

Baldwin, Leland. *Pittsburgh: The Story of a City*. Pittsburgh: University of Pittsburgh Press, 1938.

Flax, Michael J. *A Study of Comparative Urban Indicators: Conditions in 18 Large Metropolitan Areas*. Washington, D.C.: Urban Institute, 1972.

Jacobs, Jane. *The Economy of Cities*. New York: Random House, 1969.

Klein, Philip. *A Social Study of Pittsburgh*. New York: Columbia University Press, 1938.

Lorant, Stefan. *Pittsburgh: The Story of an American City*. Garden City, N.Y.: Doubleday, 1964.

Lowe, Jeanne R. *Cities in a Race With Time*. New York: Random House, 1967.

Lubove, Roy. *Twentieth Century Pittsburgh*. New York: John Wiley & Sons, 1969.

Southwestern Pennsylvania Regional Planning Commission. *Physical and Man-Made Features of the Region*. Pittsburgh, 1965.

———. *Issues in a Region of Contrasts*. Pittsburgh, 1968.

———. *Historical Analysis of the Region*. Pittsburgh, 1967.

Pittsburgh Regional Planning Association. *Economic Study of the Pittsburgh Region*. Vol. V1–V4. Pittsburgh: University of Pittsburgh Press, 1963.

Swetnam, George. *Pittsylvania Country*. New York: Dell, Sloan and Pearce, Inc., 1951.

Wagner, Walter, et. al. *Geology of the Pittsburgh Area*. Harrisburg: Pennsylvania Geological Survey, 1970.

Holdsworth, J.T., *Report of the Economic Survey of Pittsburgh*, n.d., no publisher. Letter of Transmittal, 1912.

Pennsylvania Industrial Directory, Commonwealth of Pennsylvania, Harrisburg, Pa. (published every three years).

 *Chapter Two*

The St. Louis Daily
Urban System

Frontispiece The face of St. Louis. After Gateway Arch was completed in 1965, the entire St. Louis riverfront-downtown took on a new appearance. Busch Memorial Stadium (left center) opened in 1966 and new office buildings, apartment complexes, hotels, and parking ramps added to the area's changing complexion. Photograph courtesy of Convention and Tourist Board of Greater St. Louis.

Introduction

The St. Louis Daily Urban System consists primarily of the St. Louis SMSA. Included in the SMSA are eight counties and the city of St. Louis, which is also legally an independent county as defined by the city charter (Figure 1). According to the 1970 United States Census, the population of the St. Louis SMSA was 2,410,784 and it ranked as the tenth largest SMSA in the United States. The main population concentrations are St. Louis City

Figure 1. The Daily Urban System, the SMSA, and the city of St. Louis.

and St. Louis County. The primary emphasis in this study will be on these two areas, as they are the two most important entities within the SMSA. Several additional Illinois and Missouri counties lying outside the SMSA are also included in the St. Louis Daily Urban System. These counties are included in the commutershed for St. Louis industries and contain consumers who utilize and support the wholesaling activities, retail establishments, and recreational and cultural opportunities offered by the SMSA.

The topics addressed include history and historical geography of the St. Louis region; population and economy; the physical setting (ecology and the environment, land use and transportation); housing and urban renewal; current regional topics and problems (intergovernmental relations, public health, education, public safety, political behavior, and the St. Louis central business district); and future trends for the area. The main discussion with respect to each of these topics will reflect on the present situation. However, attention must also be directed toward the evolution of these patterns and the prospects for the future.

The discussion of each topic notes the similarities that exist between the St. Louis metropolitan area and other metropolitan areas. However, the area is also unique, and an attempt has been made to highlight this uniqueness.

In a discussion of this type there is a great deal of overlap from one topic to another, and hopefully these overlaps have been synthesized to give the reader both a clear and composite view of the St. Louis area.

History and Historical Geography of the St. Louis Region

St. Louis was founded as a fur-trading post by Pierre Laclede, a French Canadian fur trader, in the mideighteenth century. Laclede chose this site at the confluence of the Missouri and Mississippi rivers because of its nodal situation in the vast inland waterways of the United States. The location was also chosen because of its advantageous access to the fur-trapping areas of the interior portion of the continent, by way of the rivers that drained the area. In 1763, as part of the Treaty of Paris, France transferred the land from the Appalachians to the Mississippi River to Great Britain. The French settlers living in southern Illinois moved across the river. This influx of settlers caused the trading post to expand into what became known as Laclede's Village. Laclede gave it the official name St. Louis in honor of King Louis IX of France. In 1803 the Louisiana Purchase was consummated and St. Louis was included in the area which France sold to the United States.

The "Town of St. Louis," which had a population of nearly 1,200, was incorporated by the Territorial Court of Common Pleas in 1809. Expansion at this time occurred close to the Mississippi River and primarily in a north-south direction (Figure 2). By the early 1820s the population of St. Louis was over 5,000.

Missouri achieved statehood in 1821, and on December 9, 1822, the state legislature passed an act to incorporate St. Louis as a city with a mayor-council form of government. From 1822, the time of incorporation, to 1876, when the citizens voted the final limits of the city's boundaries, St. Louis grew rapidly. However, despite the phenomenal growth of this era, several ominous events occurred that have continued to affect St. Louis even to the present.

The decade from 1830-1840 saw the population of the city increase from 6,694 to 16,649. Events occurring during the decade included the laying of the cornerstone for St. Louis University, which opened in 1829 and was the first institution of higher learning west of the Mississippi. The westward expansion of the nation and the beginning of steamboat traffic were also of importance to the city.

From 1840 to 1850 St. Louis continued to grow rapidly both in area and population. The population increased from 16,649 to 160,733 and land development had occurred approximately six miles westward from the river. Immigration, particularly of Germans, accounted for a large proportion of the population increase. The growth in area formed a star-shaped pattern and occurred along the public transit lines (horse-drawn omnibus) and rail lines.

The most significant period in the history of St. Louis was from 1850-1870. This was the period of the economic rivalry between Chicago and St. Louis, when Chicago emerged as the great city of the Midwest and St. Louis retreated to a poor secondary position. The classic account of this rivalry is Wyatt Belcher's, *The Economic Rivalry Between Chicago and St. Louis 1850-1880*. The decade of 1850-1860 was the "golden age" of steamboating, and St. Louis occupied the premier location. St. Louis served as

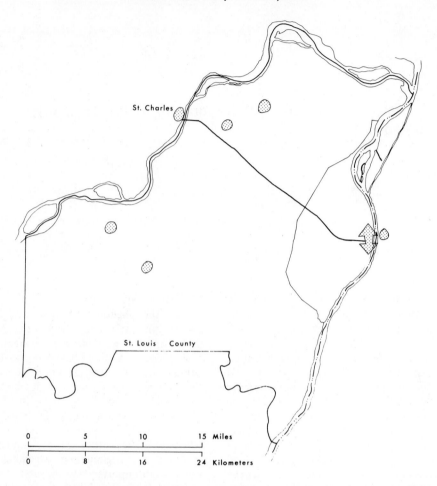

Figure 2. Expansion of St. Louis along the Mississippi River around 1800. Source: Bruce Heckman, "Maps of the Spatial Expansion of the St. Louis Metropolitan Area, 1800–Future," unpublished (Clayton, Mo.: St. Louis County Planning Commission, 1973).

a break in bulk point between the larger steamboats that could navigate the lower Mississippi and the smaller steamboats needed to navigate the upper Mississippi. As a consequence, St. Louis felt her natural locational advantage would automatically dictate her being the major center of the Midwest. However, while St. Louis enjoyed the splendor of her position, Chicago energetically and effectively emerged as the rail center of the Midwest. Belcher outlines a number of reasons why Chicago proceeded to overwhelmingly surpass St. Louis during this era. The business leadership of St. Louis was very conservative and failed to adjust to the revolutionary effect of the railroads, while Chicago's leaders were more astute. Another significant factor was that St. Louis

aligned herself with New Orleans to compete with Chicago and the East for the business of the West. This alignment proved to be a case of extremely bad judgment, as St. Louis had no grain elevators while Chicago had many, water transportation was unreliable and almost no navigation was possible five months per year, and New Orleans became more and more aligned with the South and cotton. However, it was the Civil War which made Chicago's economic victory over St. Louis both quick and sure. Missouri became a slave state as part of the Missouri Compromise, and a great difference of opinion existed among the business leaders of St. Louis as a result of this decision. Two other factors associated with the Civil War severely hampered the economy of St.

Louis. Navigation was suspended on the lower Mississippi for much of the war and this isolated St. Louis from the port of New Orleans. Also, tolls were extracted on all commerce out of St. Louis, placing her in a very disadvantaged position with respect to Chicago. By 1860 Chicago had become the rail center of the Midwest, and rail lines extending westward (e.g., the Hannibal and St. Joseph Railroad) all connected with Chicago, thus depriving St. Louis of much of her economic hinterland.

By 1870 St. Louis had become the nation's fourth largest city, with a population of 310,000 and an area of 17.98 square miles (Figure 3). However, Chicago had already surpassed St. Louis in population.

Particularly significant in the 1870s was the Missouri Constitution of 1875, which when ratified in the 1880s made St. Louis the first home rule city in the nation. Following this action, the residents of St. Louis in 1876 voted the final extensions of the city's boundaries, which separated the city from St. Louis County and fixed the present physical limits of the city. This act by the voters of the city was hailed as a very progressive act, but proved in the long run to be unwise, since it froze the city's growth possibilities and has created a number of problems that will be discussed in other sections.

By 1880 Chicago's population reached 503,185 while St. Louis had only reached 350,518, and Chicago's economic superiority had become apparent.

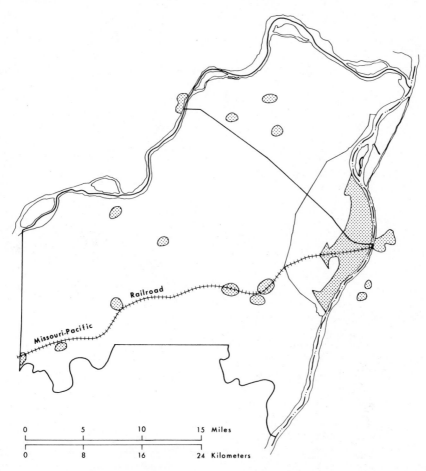

Figure 3. By 1870, a railroad along Meramec valley begins to pull urban development outward from the St. Louis core as post-Civil War western expansion strengthens the original settlement patterns. Source: Bruce Heckman, "Maps of the Spatial Expansion of the St. Louis Metropolitan Area, 1800–Future," unpublished (Clayton, Mo.: St. Louis County Planning Commission, 1973).

The remainder of the nineteenth century saw growth in St. Louis City occurring primarily in a west-northwest direction. This pattern evolved as the result of the omnibus routes and horsecar lines, and became even more pronounced with the construction of cable car lines and electric trolleys. Also, for the first time growth extended outward from St. Louis City into St. Louis County. This thrust was in a southwestward direction following the Missouri-Pacific Railroad (Figure 4). The east side across the river in Illinois also was beginning to develop. Even at this early date the effect of the Mississippi River as a permeable barrier can be seen, as

the St. Louis metropolitan area, both then and now, exhibits the truncated circle effect common to other metropolitan areas that are located with their initial core on the bank of a major river (e.g., Detroit and Windsor). By the turn of the century all the evidence indicating the development of a large American city was present. The central business district was rapidly expanding. Supporting activities, such as wholesaling, began to ring the business district. Manufacturing had expanded in narrow strips along rail lines, forming industrial corridors that are still present today. The wealthiest residents were beginning to settle in large homes around the newly established

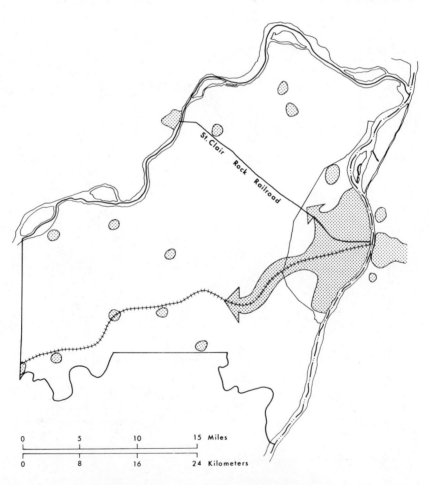

Figure 4. By 1900, the railroad continues its pull on development outward from St. Louis. Expansion northwest follows the St. Charles River Road. Source: Bruce Heckman, "Maps of the Spatial Expansion of the St. Louis Metropolitan Area, 1800–Future," unpublished (Clayton, Mo.: St. Louis County Planning Commission, 1973).

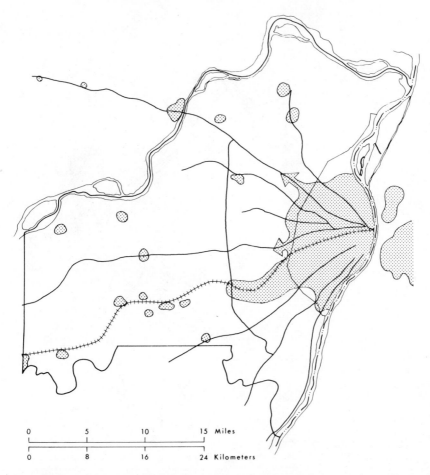

Figure 5. By 1920, small communities form at the end of trolley loops on the western edge of the city of St. Louis. Source: Bruce Heckman, "Maps of the Spatial Expansion of the St. Louis Metropolitan Area, 1800–Future," unpublished (Clayton, Mo.: St. Louis County Planning Commission, 1973).

parks located on the city's periphery, and the poor were concentrated in multifamily dwellings near the industrial area.

One of the highlights in the history of St. Louis occurred in 1904, when the St. Louis World's Fair (Louisiana Purchase Exposition) was held in Forest Park, in the city's west end. Over twenty million visitors were attracted to St. Louis, and many of the features of the fair remain integral parts of the park today. The fair provided the impetus for residential development near the park both in St. Louis and beyond the city limits in what are now the suburbs of Clayton and University City. The concentration of hotels and apartments in the area also received their initial boost at this time.

It was in the decade from 1910–1920 that the first signs of visible urban blight occurred in St. Louis. The old industrial riverfront deteriorated, and multifamily dwellings both north and south of downtown were deteriorating.

By 1920 many small communities were beginning to come into existence on the western edge of the central city (Figure 5). These communities formed at the end of the trolley lines, at the turn around points (loops), and the residents utilized this form of mass transportation for commuting purposes.

St. Louis City by 1940 was fully developed except for small portions in the extreme north and south. The impetus for this growth was the steady and substantial expansion of St. Louis'

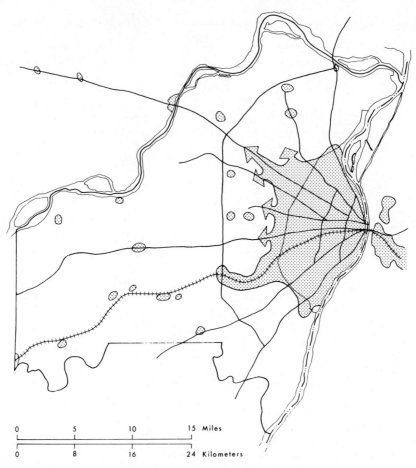

0   5   10   15 Miles

0   8   16   24 Kilometers

Figure 6. The northwestern extension of the built-up area becomes even more pronounced by 1930. A major north-south road helps in filling of areas between radial development corridors. Source: Bruce Heckman, "Maps of the Spatial Expansion of the St. Louis Metropolitan Area, 1800–Future," unpublished (Clayton, Mo.: St. Louis County Planning Commission, 1973).

diversified industry until the Great Depression of the 1930s. The city had become the world's greatest producer of beer, shoes, and several lesser products. Expansion in St. Louis County in the 1920s and 1930s continued to be westward, with the primary thrust in a northwest direction and to a lesser degree to the southwest (Figures 6 and 7).

The post–World War II growth patterns are shown in Figures 8, 9, and 10. Patterns of the 1950s, 1960s, and 1970s are the result of the same general factors common to all large metropolitan areas. Among the contributing factors were: (1) the more widespread use of the automobile; (2) postwar housing programs of the federal government; (3) the postwar federal highway construction program; (4) the decentralization of employment opportunities; and (5) the construction of a major metropolitan airport. The result has been one of America's most exclusively automobile-oriented cities.

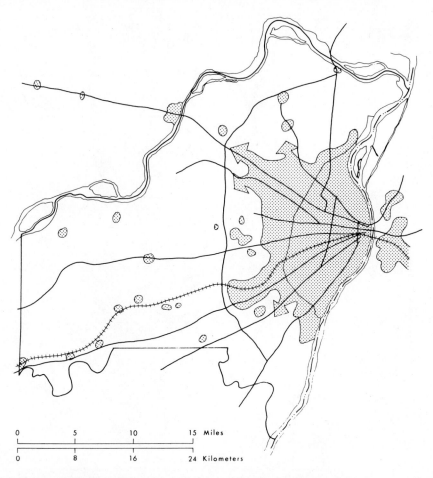

Figure 7. The southwestern area widens as automobile movement supplements rail lines by 1940. West central area continues to fill in. Source: Bruce Heckman, "Maps of the Spatial Expansion of the St. Louis Metropolitan Area, 1800–Future," unpublished (Clayton, Mo.: St. Louis County Planning Commission, 1973).

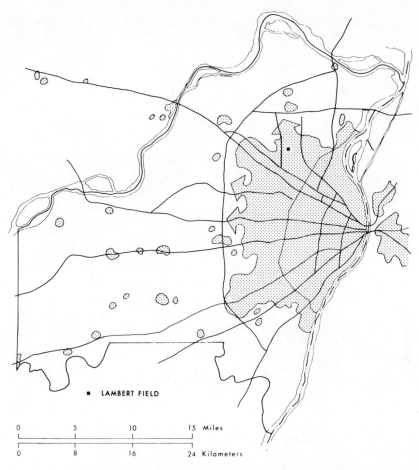

Figure 8. Through 1950, postwar housing and highway programs spur general expansion. The pull of the airport stimulates a growth pattern to the north. Source: Bruce Heckman, "Maps of the Spatial Expansion of the St. Louis Metropolitan Area, 1800–Future," unpublished (Clayton, Mo.: St. Louis County Planning Commission, 1973).

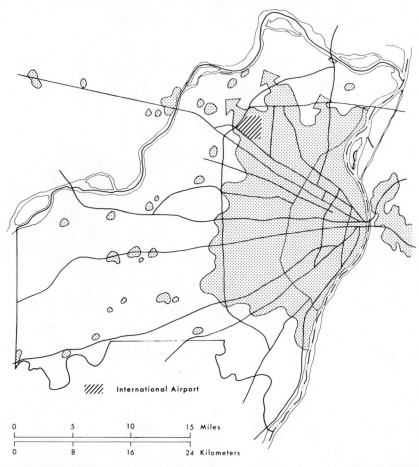

International Airport

0   5   10   15 Miles

0   8   16   24 Kilometers

Figure 9. By 1960, industries near the airport continue to pull development into their neighborhood. Decentralization of other employment centers spurs suburban growth. Location of downtown St. Louis becomes increasingly peripheral to built-up urban area. Source: Bruce Heckman, "Maps of the Spatial Expansion of the St. Louis Metropolitan Area, 1800–Future," unpublished (Clayton, Mo.: St. Louis County Planning Commission, 1973).

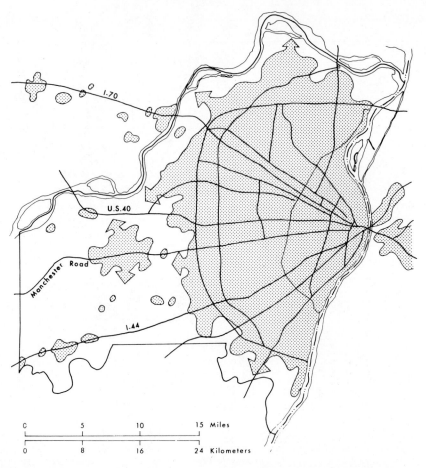

Figure 10. By 1970, new and upgraded radial and circumferential highways permit compact extension of the built-up urban area. Source: Bruce Heckman, "Maps of the Spatial Expansion of the St. Louis Metropolitan Area, 1800–Future," unpublished (Clayton, Mo.: St. Louis County Planning Commission, 1973).

Population and Economy, Past to Present

St. Louis and East St. Louis, the two major cities in the region, have suffered large population losses and a change in the composition of their populations since 1950. The population of St. Louis has declined from 857,000 in 1950 to 622,000 in 1970. Prior to 1950, when St. Louis City reached its peak population total, the city had experienced a continual and rapid growth since its inception. Before 1940 St. Louis City had always had more than 50 percent of the entire population in the metropolitan area. However, in 1950 St. Louis had only 48 percent of the area's population, and by 1970 this figure had been reduced to 26 percent. The reasons for this decline are numerous and were mentioned previously (the widespread use of the automobile, federal housing policies, etc.). Compounding the problem of population decline in St. Louis and East St. Louis has been the changing composition of their populations. For example, from 1950–1970 St. Louis' white population declined by 48 percent while the black population increased by 60 percent. What has resulted is a central city population consisting more and more of blacks and elderly whites, while the middle and upper income whites have fled the city. This has meant an increased demand for more and more city services—police protection, welfare, recreation, schools, etc.—while the city's ability to pay for these services has diminished drastically. This population decline and shift in composition has been a common postwar experience of America's major cities, but no other large American city approached the

proportion of St. Louis' population loss in the 1960s.

The situation in East St. Louis (the major city on the east side) has been similar. The population of East St. Louis declined from 82,000 in 1950 to 69,000 in 1970. The composition of the population has also shifted, and by 1970, 69.1 percent of the population of East St. Louis was black. The conditions discussed with respect to St. Louis City also apply to East St. Louis.

While the population of the major cities in the region has been decreasing dramatically, the population in the surrounding counties has risen sharply. St. Louis County has experienced a population increase from 406,000 (23 percent of the area's total) in 1950 to 952,000 (40 percent of the area's total) in 1970. However, population shifts have also occurred in St. Louis County, and composition has changed in some areas. The older major central suburban centers that ring St. Louis City have for the most part suffered a population decline or have stagnated. These suburbs have also experienced an influx of blacks from the central city. On the other hand, certain areas in north, west, and south St. Louis County have experienced sharp increases in population. Included are unincorporated St. Louis County, and suburbs such as Florissant (3,737 in 1950 to 65,912 in 1970), Ballwin (incorporated in 1956 and a 1970 population of 5,031), and Bridgeton (202 in 1950 to 19,992 in 1970). St. Clair County, which is the major Illinois county included in the study area, has seen its population increase from 205,995 in 1950 to 285,176 in 1970, while the major city in the county (East St. Louis) suffered a substantial decrease in population.

The remainder of the counties in the metropolitan area have remained basically the same in terms of their share of the metropolitan population. Two exceptions should be noted. St. Charles County and Jefferson County have entered periods of rapid growth, and their proportional share of the area's population has increased rapidly. Jefferson County, which today contains about 5 percent of the area's population, has been projected to contain 10 percent of the region's population by 1990.

Another important facet of the population shifts in the St. Louis metropolitan area is the population shifts of the black population since 1940. Black migration patterns on the east side of the Mississippi River are not readily apparent, with the majority of the black population remaining concentrated in specific large cities (East St. Louis, Madison, and Alton). Consequently, these will not be dealt with, as they are not well documented. On the other hand, black migration patterns are apparent in both St. Louis City and St. Louis County.

In 1940 the black population in the city of St. Louis was 108,765, or approximately 12.5 percent of the total population. At this time blacks were highly concentrated on the outer fringes of the central business district. The primary ghetto—Mill Creek—extended westward from the downtown area to the St. Louis University campus (Figure 11). No distinct pattern of black settlement existed in St. Louis County at this time, but one major concentration of blacks did exist in Kinloch, a nearly all-black town, which dates back to the Civil War.

By 1950 no large scale movement of blacks had occurred, but rather the existing black areas had undergone substantial increases in density. This was a period of heavy inmigration of blacks into the city, which in turn created pressure in the existing ghetto, setting the stage for rapid ghetto expansion. Also, by 1950 no set migratory pattern for the blacks into St. Louis County had been established.

From 1950–1960 the black corridor extending outward from downtown St. Louis in a northwesterly direction reached the city limits. This expansion of the ghetto was the result of population pressures caused by inmigration into the existing black community. It moved in the direction of available low cost housing served by accessible arteries of transportation. Black migration into St. Louis County was still occurring at a very slow rate, with only a few isolated pockets discernible at this time.

The decade of the 1960s saw a rapid increase in the black population in St. Louis. This brought about both an increase in density in the existing ghetto and a massive spread in the areal extent of it. By 1970 nearly all of St. Louis north of a line drawn straight west from the downtown area could be characterized as nearly all black. The exceptions were the industrial area along the river north of the downtown area, which has virtually no population; the Mill Creek area (formerly the city's worst slum) directly west of the downtown area, which was the location of one of the nation's largest urban renewal projects in the 1960s; and extreme north St. Louis, which has had a large influx of blacks since 1970. In addition to the black population encompassing north St. Louis almost entirely, there has been some black migration into south St. Louis. However, this movement has been minimal and not likely to increase rapidly in the near future as there exist two physical barriers—Highway 40 and Interstate 244—separating north and south St. Louis. In addition, neighborhood associations are numerous in south St. Louis, and their role in stopping blight and encouraging neighborhood stability has prevented vacancies that possibly would be occupied by blacks from occurring. Perhaps the most noteworthy occurrence with respect to the black population in the 1960s was the extension of the black corridor into St. Louis County. Suburbs west and north of the city— such as University, Winston, Hillsdale, and Pine Lawn—have seen a substantial increase in their black populations. Blacks have also dispersed into many other areas of St. Louis County, but not in such numbers as to form a spatial pattern.

On the basis of the spatial shifts described, certain generalizations can be made. The northwestern migration corridor, which by 1970 extended from the edge of downtown St. Louis to the boundary of the city and beyond into St. Louis County, developed in an area where low cost housing existed (below the median

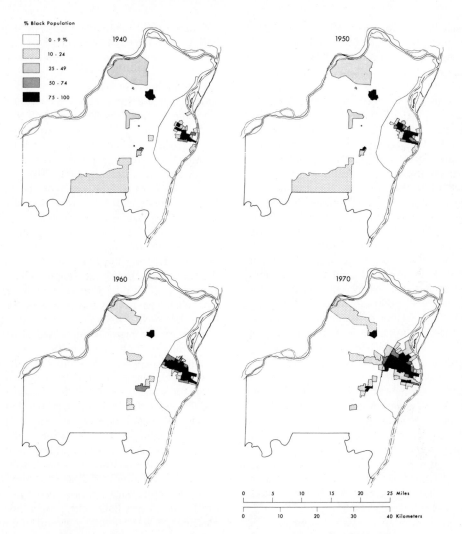

Figure 11. Expansion of black neighborhoods in the St. Louis area, 1940–1970.

for the city of St. Louis). This was also a corridor in which a vast number of rental dwellings were available. It has only been recently that the black population has moved into areas with a high proportion of owner-occupied dwellings.

Projecting future black migration is a difficult task, as there exists a unique set of circumstances. First, the present corridor of black migration has now extended itself northwest to a point where it has encountered Interstate 70, several parks, golf courses, and cemeteries that interrupt the present extension of the black population. For the black population to continue to move northwestward would require a movement across this area, which runs

counter to accepted notions of ghetto expansion. The second uncertainty is the degree to which economic gains will be made by the black community in the future. If blacks rise to income levels enjoyed by other groups, the possibility exists that the black population will disperse throughout St. Louis County. However, we can more logically expect perhaps that the Rock Hill, Brentwood, and Maplewood southwest of St. Louis will receive an influx of black residents, as a sizable concentration of blacks already exists in that area.

The economy of the St. Louis area since World War II has been one of the slowest growing of any metropolitan area in the nation. From 1958–1968 one industry—aircraft and parts—accounted for over 40 percent of the total growth in manufacturing jobs in the St. Louis region, and one firm—McDonnell-Douglas—accounted for the bulk of this growth. Highlighting the problem is the fact that one product—the F-4 fighter in the 1960s and, more recently, the F-15 fighter—accounted for most of the employment. The automobile industry is the second largest employer. General Motors, Ford, and Chrysler all have automobile assembly plants in the area.

Since 1970, the situation has become bleaker. For example, the total number of jobs in the St. Louis metropolitan area declined by about 61,200 between 1970 and 1973. This downward trend in jobs occurred despite the growth of employment in the nation as a whole. If the St. Louis area had gained at the national rate in the last three years, employment would have risen by 110,000 jobs instead of dropping 61,200. The decline in employment affected both manufacturing and nonmanufacturing jobs. The biggest decline, however, has been in manufacturing. The only exceptions to the general decline were lumber and furniture manufacturing, mining, retail trade, and state and local government.

Despite the generally bleak statistics that describe the economy of the St. Louis region, disparities exist within the region. The city of St. Louis has declined in almost all economic activities, while the bulk of the region has remained relatively constant, and St. Louis County has exhibited sharp gains.

As regional retail sales rose from $2.4 billion in 1958 to $3.7 billion in 1967, the St. Louis City share dropped from 48 to 32 percent, while the St. Louis County share rose from 27 to 40 percent. The other counties have remained steady, although slight increases in retail sales and establishments have occurred in St. Charles and Jefferson counties, and slight decreases have occurred in the major Illinois counties (St. Clair and Madison). Future trends in retailing are difficult to predict. However, certain observations seem to be plausible on the basis of population shifts and other factors. St. Louis City can be expected to continue its economic decline. At present a large proportion of the retail sales in downtown St. Louis are to Metro-East residents, as there is no major regional shopping center on the east side of the river. However, one of the largest regional shopping centers in the metropolitan area—

Fairview Heights shopping center, to be located within easy access of Belleville, East St. Louis, and Collinsville on the east side—will soon be competing with downtown St. Louis for this major market. Retailing in St. Clair County should increase substantially as a result, while Madison County can be expected to decline slightly because of this new shopping center. St. Charles and Jefferson counties should continue to grow in retailing because of an anticipated population growth. The growth in retail sales in St. Louis County can be expected to slow down in the future as its population begins to stabilize.

Data available indicated the same trends with respect to industry as were evident in retailing. Historically, St. Louis City has been the dominant industrial center of the area. However, St. Louis County has mounted a stiff challenge to the supremacy of St. Louis City. In 1967–1968, St. Louis County got twenty of the region's thirty-two new plants, St. Louis City only four. Of the 170 industrial expansions between 1966 and 1969, St. Louis County accounted for ninety, St. Louis City only forty-eight. In 1970 St. Louis County had 29 percent of all industrial parkland acreage in the region and 76 percent of the Missouri portion of the total (Figure 12). This leads to the conclusion that, at least in the near future, St. Louis County should solidify its position as the new industrial center of the area. However, it can be assumed that, unless St. Louis County takes the proper preventive measures, it will eventually give in to industrial and residential blight and follow the cycle of the city of St. Louis. Sound zoning, provision for proper land use mixture, and building code enforcement can prevent St. Louis County from deteriorating as St. Louis has.

Perhaps the most crucial question facing the St. Louis metropolitan area is, Why does the economy of St. Louis lag behind the nation as a whole, and what can be done about it? A great deal of the problem is obviously historical and can be traced back to the economic rivalry with Chicago discussed above. Those who have studied the question more recently have laid the blame on local bankers. It has been alleged that the local banking community might have done a great deal more to encourage and promote local economic growth. Perhaps this is partially true, but if conditions for investment in the region were good, it

○ INDUSTRIAL PARK

■ INDUSTRIAL ZONED LAND

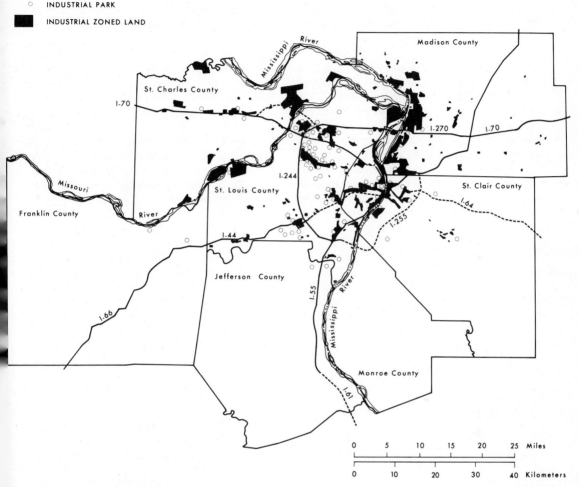

Figure 12. Industrial zoned land and industrial parks in the St. Louis area, 1970. Source: East-West Gateway Coordinating Council.

seems that outside banking interests from other cities would have been quick to finance projects in the St. Louis area. It has also been alleged that the narrow interests and parochial rivalries of local civic, business, and political leaders have had an adverse effect on the local economy. This factor has no doubt had an adverse effect on the area. City-suburban conflict prevails in all major metropolitan areas. However, the separation of city and county, and the resulting strength of the St. Louis County government, has hindered economic growth in the area. Rather than working together, city and county have often assailed the plans of one another rather than presenting a united front (for example, the controversy over the location of a new metropolitan air-

port to be discussed below). It also appears plausible that older cities such as St. Louis have experienced their period of rapid growth. The newer boom cities of the South and West, such as Memphis, have severely cut into the trade area of St. Louis.

The problem facing St. Louis and the entire metropolitan area is how to achieve economic growth. In older cities with hinterlands that are rather slow-growing, such as those of St. Louis, it seems that promoting existing industry is the best hope for sustaining economic growth. However, St. Louis does have one advantage not possessed by other cities. Its location near the confluence of the Missouri and Mississippi rivers is an ideal location for taking advantage of the barge traffic on the Mississippi, and, thus, for industries that can utilize barge transportation. A series of articles by Gerald Meyer in the *St. Louis Post-Dispatch* discussed St. Louis' role as a port in detail. St. Louis has always handled more barge tonnage than any other inland port on the Mississippi. However, in recent years growth in barge tonnage in St. Louis has leveled off, while other ports have been growing rapidly. St. Louis is the one port of any size on the Mississippi at which no work has been completed or planned. Memphis, on the other hand, has spent $42 million on its port facilities, and has seen the tonnage handled jump 90 percent in the last eleven years and 30 percent in the past three years. In addition Memphis has attracted many industries seeking waterfront locations. Even Vicksburg has spent $4,664,500, and has seen its tonnage increase 133 percent in the last eleven years and 90 percent in the last three years. While these and other cities have expanded their port facilities substantially, St. Louis has sat idly by. If St. Louis would create a St. Louis Port Authority, and expand its port facilities, it would seem that this could lead to substantial economic growth for the entire metropolitan area, but particularly for the central city, which desperately needs revitalization.

The Physical Setting

One of the most pressing problems in metropolitan areas today is air and noise pollution, and St. Louis is no exception. However, according to a recent report by the Environmental Protection Agency, St. Louis was among a number of urban areas where there was an improvement in air quality in the last decade. St. Louis has shown a long term downward trend in airborne particulates, smoke, dust, and sulfur oxide pollution.

The highest concentration of pollutants is in the four most urbanized areas—St. Louis City, St. Louis County, St. Clair County, and Madison County (Table 1). Pollution has not only decreased in the previous decade, but in more areas pollutants showed a downward trend from 1970 to 1971. There are wide disparities within each general area noted in Table 1. For example, the highest concentration of most types of pollutants was found at a sampling station in Granite City, located in Madison County, Illinois. Granite City is the home of many large industrial plants, such as Granite City Steel. Wide disparities also exist in other areas. In St. Louis County the heaviest concentrations of pollution occur in the inner suburbs, while the outermost portions of the county compare quite favorably with the rural counties of the region.

It is expected that levels of air pollutants will continue to decline in the more urbanized portions of the area, while the more rural counties will see their levels rise as urbanization extends itself more fully into what are now basically rural areas.

One type of pollution that has been virtually ignored in most American cities, St. Louis not excepted, is noise pollution. St. Louis is in the process of drafting a noise pollution ordinance. Areas in which the city's air pollution office feels a beginning could be made in attacking noise pollution include construction standards for soundproofing and road standards to eliminate as much road noise as possible.

A second problem of environmental concern in the St. Louis metropolitan area is the status of the area's water and sewage treatment plants. Of the ninety separate water facilities in the area, sixty-three will need expansion by 1985. Meanwhile seventy-four of the region's eighty-two municipal sewage treatment facilities need to be upgraded, expanded, or both by 1985. Many of the small sewage plants in the area have been alleged to be dumping huge quantities of improperly treated sewage into rivers and streams, resulting in a threat to the personal health of many of the area's residents. The Citizens for Clean County Water have alleged that this is the case in the outermost two-thirds of St. Louis County, which is served by a complex network of sewage-handling operations. The proposed solution to this problem, at least in St. Louis County, is to expand the highly successful Metropolitan Sewer District (MSD) to include all of St. Louis County.

Another aspect of the environment affected by urban-industrial complexes is the weather. The St. Louis area was the site of the field proj-

Table 1. Air Pollution in the St. Louis Area

| | Ranges at Reporting Stations, July–December 1971 | | |
	Dustfall (tons per square mile per month)	Suspended Particulates (micrograms per cubic meter of air)	Sulfation (micrograms of SO_3 per 100 square centimeters per day)
Jefferson County	5–18	*	0.15–0.35
St. Charles County	11–13	59–93	0.12–0.42
St. Louis County	11–31	53–126	0.29–2.07
St. Louis City	9–48	64–152	0.36–1.55
Madison County	16–32	78–179	0.02–0.02
Monroe County	15**	72**	*
St. Clair County	15–35	84–124	0.02**
Franklin County	*	*	*

*No data
**Only one sample

Source: Missouri Air Conservation Commission, *Missouri Air Quality* (Jefferson City, Mo., 1971); State of Illinois Environmental Protection Agency, *Illinois Air Sampling Network Report,* 1971 (Springfield, Ill., 1972).

ect called METROMEX (Metropolitan Meteorological Experiment) conducted by scientists—working independently, but cooperatively—from the Argonne National Laboratory, University of Chicago, Illinois State Water Survey, and the University of Wyoming. The scientists studied urban-related alterations in precipitation processes and quantitative changes in surface precipitation. Although the study was incomplete, historical data on St. Louis revealed summer increases in the immediate downwind area of rainfall (10–17 percent); moderate rain days (11–23 percent); heavy rainstorms (80 percent); thunderstorms (21 percent); and hailstorms (30 percent). Figure 13 illustrates the pronounced spatial variation in thunder days, number of storms with rainfall more than or equal to one inch, and the percent of total summer rainfall in storms producing one inch or more during 1971–1972. In all cases, the greatest frequencies are in the Edwardsville area, which is "downstorm" from St. Louis. On the basis of these findings, there appears to be no doubt but that the weather in the region is affected by the St. Louis urban-industrial complex.

Several factors have been attributed to an increased demand for recreational facilities in the St. Louis area and in the nation as a whole. Among these are a general population increase, increase in income, and increases in mobility and leisure time.

A recent study by the East-West Gateway Coordinating Council analyzed the metropolitan and regional parks of the area using a standard of twenty acres per 1,000 population for regional parks and five acres per 1,000 population for metropolitan parks. It was found that the existing acreage was 13.8 acres per 1,000 population for metropolitan and regional park facilities in the St. Louis area. The entire region was found to have a shortage of regional and metropolitan park facilities. St. Charles, Jefferson, Franklin, and the Metro-East counties were found especially lacking. St. Louis City basically has adequate park facilities, and they are pointed to as a major factor in why St. Louis did not experience any race riots in the 1960s when most other major cities did. St. Louis County also has a rather extensive county park system. Figure 14 shows the existing and proposed park facilities in the entire metropolitan area. It can be seen that St. Charles County and the Metro-East counties are the areas expected to lag in the development of park facilities.

Almost all of the proposed development in Franklin and Jefferson counties, and much of the proposed development in St. Louis County, hinges upon the building of the Meramec Park Dam and the recreational facilities that would result. The resulting lakes and recreation sites would have tremendous economic and social value for the entire region. Flood control is

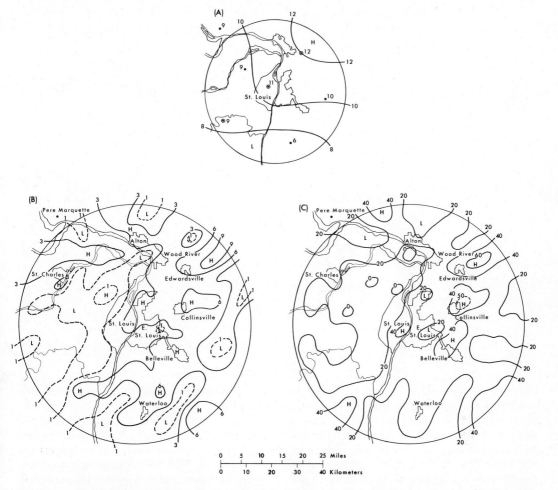

Figure 13. Weather modification in the St. Louis area. (A) Thunder day patterns, 1971–72. (B) Number of storms with rainfall of an inch or more, recorded at 225 rain gauges, June-August, 1971–72. (C) Percentage of total summer rainfall coming from storms yielding an inch or more, 1971–72. Source: Stanley A. Chagnon, Jr., and Floyd A. Huff, "Enhancement of Severe Weather by the St. Louis Urban-Industrial Complex," Mimeo (Urbana: Illinois State Water Survey, 1973).

also needed in the area. This is very apparent in light of the devastating flooding of the Meramec River in the spring of 1973. In addition the lakes would also help meet the area's growing problems of water supply. The recreational development that would occur would have a tremendous economic impact on the area, as would the building of the $87,500,000 project itself. The project has however been opposed by the Sierra Club and other environmental groups. These groups have up to the present time succeeded in delaying the project. However, it appears that the project ultimately will be built, as the combined bene-

fits to the region outweigh the environmental concerns associated with the project.

One other aspect of recreation in the area is worth mentioning. The St. Louis area is the home of Six Flags Over Mid-America. This elaborate amusement park, located in southwestern St. Louis County, provides a high class amusement park for the residents of the area, but has also drawn tourists to the area and provided needed summer jobs for many high school and college students.

Land use and transportation are also important aspects of the metropolitan area's physical setting. Significant increases are

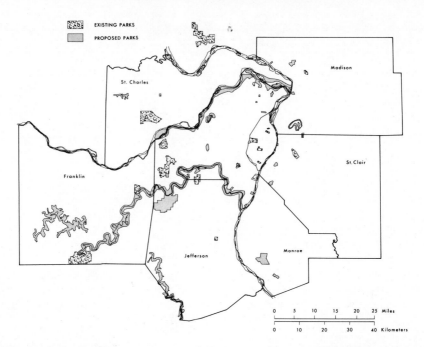

Figure 14. Existing and proposed parkland in the St. Louis area, 1970. Source: East-West Gateway Coordinating Council.

expected in the amount of land devoted to residential and recreational land use (Table 2). Slower growth is expected to occur in the amount of land devoted to commercial, industrial, and public and semipublic use. To increase the amount of land used by the above-mentioned activities, the amount of underdeveloped and extractive land necessarily will diminish. If these projections are borne out, urbanization will obviously be spreading into the more rural counties of the area.

Transportation in the St. Louis metropolitan area can be most effectively discussed in two parts. First, internal modes of transportation are discussed, with an emphasis on the current Bi-State Development Agency crises. Second, St. Louis' national transportation linkages are discussed, with an emphasis on the controversy

Table 2.   Land Use in the St. Louis Area, 1966 and 1990

Land Use	1966		1990	
	Acres (1,000)	*Percent*	*Acres (1,000)*	*Percent*
Residential	175	16	260	24
Commercial	15	1	24	2
Industrial	36	3	51	5
Public and Semipublic	38	4	54	5
Recreational	29	3	110	10
Extractive	538	49	537	40
Undeveloped	272	25	167	15
Total	1,103	100	1,103	100

Source: East-West Gateway Coordinating Council; Illinois Department of Transportation; Missouri State Highway Commission, *St. Louis Area Transportation Study: Streets, Highways and Transit* (St. Louis, Mo., 1973).

regarding whether a new international airport should be built in the region, or the present facility (Lambert International) expanded.

Internal mobility in the St. Louis metropolitan area is highly dependent on the automobile and is becoming even more so. In the twelve months ending August 31, 1972, the Bi-State Transit System—St. Louis' only significant form of public transportation—carried an estimated 53.4 million passengers. This compares to 114.9 million passengers carried in 1957 by the old Public Service Company, and 78.9 million passengers carried on Bi-State buses in 1967.

The Bi-State Transit System, operated by the Bi-State Development Agency, was formed in 1963 by consolidating fifteen private bus companies. It serves about 1.9 million persons in the metropolitan area and provides some form of service into all of the metropolitan area except Clinton County, Illinois, and Franklin County, Missouri. About 80 percent of the service is provided in Missouri and 20 percent in Illinois. The declining use of mass transportation due to higher fares, crime, and other impediments, coupled with the fact that Bi-State was the last major metropolitan transit system to remain unsubsidized, pushed the Bi-State Transit System to the brink of financial collapse in the spring of 1973. This would have left the St. Louis metropolitan area without any form of mass transportation.

If Bi-State had been allowed to fold, it would have had dire consequences for the metropolitan area, as 150,000 daily riders would have either been forced to use automobiles, or to drop out of the work force and onto the welfare rolls. The lack of mass transit would also have meant a loss of rides for the young, elderly, and physically handicapped. Downtown St. Louis, which serves those who utilize mass transit, would have suffered a further economic setback. It would also have been a blow to any proposed rapid transit system for the future, which would depend on buses to operate feeder routes.

Emergency subsidies were provided by the Missouri and Illinois state legislatures, St. Louis City, St. Louis County, and several other municipalities in the area. These subsidies provided the necessary additional funds to keep Bi-State in operation until June 30, 1973. In the meantime, the disaster of a major metropolitan area being without any form of mass transportation was averted. In early June 1973, the Missouri legislature approved enabling legislation allowing St. Louis City and St. Louis County to levy a 0.5 percent sales tax earmarked for mass transit subsidy. During the week of June 24-30, 1973, both the St. Louis County Council and the St. Louis Board of Aldermen approved the 0.5 percent sales tax. It became effective on July 1, 1973. It is estimated that this tax will provide Bi-State with a $19 million subsidy per year. With the additional funds available Bi-State has advanced a plan whereby fares will be reduced to 25 cents. The plan will cut the fare for senior citizens to 15 cents during nonpeak hours, and transfers will be free. Bi-State has also proposed a 12.5 percent increase in bus mileage, including service to areas not now served, and the establishment of a minibus route. In addition, several new buses will be provided.

As the fuel crisis becomes more serious and gasoline shortages and price hikes occur, more people may turn to mass transit. If middle class commuters begin to use mass transit in the St. Louis area, then bus service will probably be improved substantially and the possibility of a more elaborate mass transit system may become a reality in St. Louis.

The final form of internal mobility is the bicycle. The use of bicycles by those who commute short distances has been gaining favor in St. Louis, as in other cities. As a result, the city has instituted a "safe lane" for cyclists extending from Forest Park, on the city's west end, to the downtown area.

In terms of national transportation, St. Louis is well situated. The metropolitan area is served by five interstate highways—I-44, I-55, I-70, I-244, and I-270—Amtrak, and Lambert International Airport. The controversy over whether a new international airport is needed, or whether Lambert should be expanded to meet the future air travel needs of the region, has shared the limelight with the Bi-State crisis as two of the most important issues in the region.

Almost 5.6 million passengers used Lambert Field in 1971. This represented a decline of 100,000 from 1970, and decline of 340,000 from 1969. Despite the current decline in air travel, it is generally, but not universally, agreed that Lambert as it presently stands is inadequate for the future air travel needs of the area. Sites have been proposed for a new airport in St. Louis and St. Charles counties, Missouri, and in Monroe County, Illinois. The Missouri sites have for the most part been eliminated from consideration because plans for financing were never seriously studied. Originally, the Monroe County site near Waterloo and Columbia, Illinois, was favored, as Illinois Governor Ogilvie and St. Louis Mayor Cervantes together pushed for the building of a new airport at that site. It was also expected that officials in Washington, D.C., would support the Illinois site because Illinois had a Republican governor and a Republican senator, while Missouri had a Democrat governor and two Democrat senators. In addition, Missouri's governmental officials were not actively pushing a Missouri site. As a result of the November 1972 elections, Illinois acquired a Democrat governor, and Missouri a Republican governor. Consequently, Washington adopted a hands off position and said that the decision should be made locally. Also, Mayor Cervantes was defeated in his reelection bid by a fellow Democrat, John Poelker, who favored expansion of Lambert International Field.

The economic implications of the decision whether to expand Lambert or build a new facility are a very important consideration. To expand Lambert obviously would benefit St. Louis County, while to build a new facility in Illinois would hurt the economy of St. Louis County and provide a tremendous boost for Metro-East. The effect of either decision on the city of St. Louis is the subject of much conjecture and controversy.

Housing and Urban Renewal

When one speaks of St. Louis, the topic of conversation immediately turns to the Pruitt-Igoe public housing projects, the Black Jack zoning controversy, the Gateway Arch, or Busch Stadium. The first two deal with housing, while the latter two are the result of the massive urban renewal projects undertaken in St. Louis.

A wide range of housing exists in the St. Louis metropolitan area. The continuum ranges from Pruitt-Igoe (average monthly rent $40 per unit according to the St. Louis Housing Authority) to Ladue (median home value over $50,000).

One of the most rapidly increasing types of housing in the area is the multifamily dwelling unit found in apartment complexes. A recent study prepared by the St. Louis County Department of Planning discussed the impact of these units locally, and it has implications for national planning. The fact that multifamily units annually make up over 40 percent of the nation's housing starts shows the importance of this type of housing nationally. In 1970 St. Louis County contained 54,608 multifamily dwelling units, which accounted for approximately 19 percent of the county's total housing units. From 1960–1970 over 40 percent of the new dwelling units built in St. Louis County were multifamily, and in 1969 and 1970 48 percent were multifamily. Several factors have contributed to this growth in the number of multifamily units, both locally and nationally. Included are rising land and construction costs and higher mortgage rates, all

of which have led young couples to give up or delay homeownership in favor of apartment life. This cost factor is even more significant when comparing St. Louis County to neighboring Jefferson and St. Charles counties. Houses on the average are about $3,000 higher in St. Louis County than for similar units in the other two counties.

Despite the increase in the number of apartment complexes, they are still viewed unfavorably and objected to when proposed for certain areas. Apartments are alleged to increase the tax burden on single family homeowners, to overcrowd schools, to overburden all forms of municipal services, and to bring undesirable elements into the area. To dispel these notions, the planning commission, as part of their study, conducted a cost-revenue analysis and other related studies. It was found that apartment complexes, because of their densities, more than paid their way in taxes. Real estate tax on the complexes, personal property tax, and payment of sales tax, combined with their "multiplier effect" on business activities, yield a high return for the municipalities or areas in which they are located. The second criticism, that apartment complexes overburden the schools, was also dismissed. The number of children in apartment complexes is far below the number found in an equal number of single family dwelling units. Apartment dwellers for the most part tend to be single, or newly married couples with either no children or children of preschool age, or couples who have grown children. Apartments were also found not to overburden other types of municipal services. Swimming pools, recreation facilities, and internal roads are usually provided by the complex. The final major criticism, that apartments bring an undesirable element into the area, was also refuted in St. Louis County. The new apartment complexes existing in suburban America usually have a young highly educated group of residents, whose social-economic status is often above that of other residents of the area.

Another form of housing, and one often embroiled in controversy, is public housing. Data availability limits the consideration of public housing, and those who occupy it, to St. Louis City. However, there is also public housing in East St. Louis, Granite City, and Alton on the east side.

There were 7,902 units of public housing constructed in St. Louis from 1942 to 1968, of which 4,734 were occupied in 1973 by over 16,000 persons (Table 3). The occupancy rates range from nearly 100 percent in the Blumeyer

project to only 8.5 percent in the Pruitt project (23.5 percent for Pruitt-Igoe combined). Table 4 shows certain characteristics selected to show the depressing situation characterizing St. Louis's public housing occupants. The combination of a high number of persons per household, a low ratio of males to females, a low median age, a high percent of families with female head of household, a low median income, a low percent of "employable" persons employed, and a high percentage of families in which no one is employed provide a spawning ground for crime, vice, and drug use. In almost all categories Pruitt and Igoe exhibit the worst situation, culminating in what must be a feeling of hopelessness for the residents (Table 4). Life and its social consequences for Pruitt and Igoe is described by Lee Rainwater in *Behind Ghetto Walls, Black Families in a Federal Slum,* based on a series of lengthy interviews with residents of the two projects.

The major question of both national and

Table 3. Conventional Public Housing, St. Louis Housing Authority

Project	Date Completed	Number of Buildings		Original Number of Dwelling Units	Occupied Units, June 14, 1973
Carr Square Village	1942	53	2&3 story	658	636
Clinton Peabody Terrace	1942	53	2&3 story	657	619
John J. Cochran Garden Apartments	1953	4	12 story	703	482
Captain Wendell Oliver Pruitt Homes	1955	20	11 story	1,653	142
William L. Igoe Apartments	1956	13	11 story	1,085	503
George L. Vaughn Apartments	1957	4	9 story	647	404
George L. Vaughn Buildings for Elderly	1963	1	9 story	112	107
Jos. M. Darst Apartments	1956	4	9 story	645	393
Anthony M. Webbe Apartments for Elderly	1961	2	9 story	580	297
		1	12 story		
		1	8 story		
Arthur A. Blumeyer Apartments for Elderly	1968	2	14 story	1,162	1,151
		42	2 story		
		2	15 story		
Total				7,902	4,734

Source: Ethan Z. Kaplan, *The Residents of St. Louis Public Housing: A Socio-Economic and Demographic Report* (St. Louis: Health and Welfare Council of Metropolitan St. Louis, December 1972), page 3.

Table 4. Selected Characteristics of Public Housing Residents in St. Louis

	Persons per House-hold	Male-Female Ratio (x 100)	Median Age	Families With Female Head (Percent)	Median Years in Public Housing	Median Family Income	"Em-ploy-able" Persons Em-ployed (Percent)	House-holds With No Em-ployed Persons (Percent)
Total St. Louis City	2.8	84						
Total Public Housing	3.4	68	18.0	69	5	$2,470	46	62
Carr Square	3.0	67	28.2	67	10	2,408	50	63
Peabody	3.5	70	17.8	67	6	2,234	48	55
Cochran	4.3	73	14.0	72	4	2,777	42	60
Pruitt	4.7	64	16.5	79	10	2,386	31	69
Igoe	4.3	69	16.4	77	9	2,345	32	73
Vaughn	3.7	71	16.4	75	6	2,019	40	66
Darst/Webbe	3.9	71	15.0	75	5	2,297	35	66
Webbe (only)	3.3	66	16.1	76	6	1,872	76	77
Blumeyer	2.3	61	32.3	60	4	2,619	62	57

Source: Ethan Z. Kaplan, *The Residents of St. Louis Public Housing: A SocioEconomic and Demographic Report* (St. Louis: Health and Welfare Council of Metropolitan St. Louis, December 1972), p. 3.

local interest is, How did Pruitt and Igoe decline to their present situation. Pruitt and Igoe today consist of thirty eleven story buildings. Three addresses had been demolished by 1975, with most of the remainder scheduled for demolition. None of the original 2,738 units is occupied. Before demolition, the unoccupied buildings stood empty with jagged glass in the windows, as though they had been fire-bombed. The sight was truly one of America's ugliest. Aside from its sheer size and inappropriate design, the forces that contributed to the decline of Pruitt-Igoe included low income, high densities, and unstable families—all of which were far worse than in other public housing projects in St. Louis. Ineffective project management also contributed to the decline. Prior to the rent strike of 1968-1969, space rentals were set irrespective of income. Simultaneously, money reserves were depleted and the inadequate maintenance stopped altogether. Also noteworthy is the fact that Pruitt and Igoe were built for the working poor, but became a massive concentration of welfare recipients. It is the author's contention that the only solution to Pruitt-Igoe is complete demolition. Thirty-three eleven story buildings simply created too dense a population of underprivileged residents. What more fertile ground for crime and drugs could exist than

this extremely high density of impoverished residents?

Another important facet of housing in St. Louis has been urban renewal. Urban renewal has both eliminated and provided housing in the city, although it must be recognized that urban renewal is not a housing program. Eight major projects were begun between 1939 and 1970. Three more have been proposed.

St. Louis' first urban renewal project focused on the redevelopment of the riverfront area composed of decrepit warehouses and shanties. The impetus for the project occurred in 1955 when President Eisenhower designated the original settlement site of the village of St. Louis as a national historic site, and the project became known as the Jefferson National Expansion Memorial. However, the project was underway prior to this designation. Site clearance had begun in 1939, but the federal share of the funds (three to one basis) was delayed by World War II. In 1947 an architectural competition was held for the redevelopment of the riverfront area. Over 170 entries were received, and the $50,000 prize was awarded to Eero Saarinen for his design featuring a 630 foot catenary arch of stainless steel (Figure 15). The arch is the tallest monument in the United States; it com-

Figure 15. The 630 foot stainless steel Gateway Arch is a tribute to the early pioneers and westward expansion.

memorates the Louisiana Purchase and symbolizes St. Louis as the Gateway to the West. Riding to the top of the arch and viewing the St. Louis metropolitan area and its surroundings has become a nationwide tourist attraction. Landscaping continues in the area today making it one of the nation's longest and emptiest redevelopment projects. The area was cleared and the arch built in what appears today as a wind-swept wasteland. It is a prime example of an area that was massively leveled, but not, at least yet, treated to compensating renewal.

Plaza Square, a dilapidated slum area only a few blocks from city hall and Union Station in downtown St. Louis, was the first Title I Urban Renewal Project in St. Louis, and several sig-

nificant events occurred prior to and during redevelopment of the area. In 1954 St. Louis redevelopment received a boost when the state of Missouri enacted the Missouri Urban Redevelopment Corporation Law, which, though limiting profits to 8 percent per year on project costs, provides developers with twenty-five years of partial tax relief. Also, in 1951 the Land Clearance for Redevelopment Authority, which is the city's key agency for urban renewal, was created. The function of the authority is to buy and clear blighted areas using federal loans, and then sell the property to private interests who agree to redevelop the area in accordance with a prescribed plan. Sixteen acres were redeveloped in Plaza Square, resulting in construction of 1,090 middle and upper income apartments in six multistory buildings, as well as the rehabilitation of two churches, and the construction of a small park, some shopping facilities, and an office building.

St. Louis' largest urban renewal project, Mill Creek Valley, located directly west of downtown and extending to St. Louis University in midtown, was undertaken in 1954. Involved were one hundred blocks of the worst blighted, rat-infested slums in the city. A preliminary survey taken in 1954 showed that 99 percent of the structures in the area needed major repairs. Eighty percent of the structures were without private bath and toilet and 67 percent lacked running water; the crime rate was four times the city average. At the time the project was started, the annual property tax revenue was $365,000 in the area; and the city was spending seven times that amount to provide police, fire, health, and welfare services for the area. When completed, 83.5 acres were used for middle income housing, 132 acres for industrial sites, twenty-six acres for commercial expansion, 208 acres for highways and rights of way, and twenty-two acres were given to St. Louis University for expansion. The developed area includes the nationally known Leclede Town, one of the nation's most successfully integrated lower middle class housing developments. One serious consequence of the Mill Creek project was that even though blight was eliminated in this area, 1,772 very low income black families were displaced and moved into other areas of the city.

The Kosciusko project, which began in 1957, was unique and significant in that land was made available to local industry for expansion of existing facilities. When completed, 134.4 acres were provided for industrial use, 24.4 acres for commercial use, and 62.4 acres for public right of way. This was an example of wise planning, as the area was located immediately south of downtown in an area where industrial and commercial facilities needed room for expansion, and one of the reasons blight had occurred in the area was because of the mixture of land uses. There was also a relocation problem associated with this project as 664 families were displaced and they settled primarily in areas which were already blighted.

The Grandel project was undertaken by a group of local black businessmen. Grandel, located two miles northwest of the central business district, was designed to serve as a shopping center for the nearby low rent housing project (Blumeyer) residents. The project consisted of only 6.7 acres and was completed in 1970.

The Civic Center redevelopment project, first proposed in 1958, cost over $109 million and was a non-federally-assisted project. The area redeveloped comprises a portion of downtown St. Louis. Included in the redevelopment area are Busch Stadium, Stouffer's River Front Inn, the Spanish Pavilion from the New York World's Fair, Keiner Memorial Fountain and Mall, Pet Milk's seventeen story world headquarters, the Equitable Building, a high-rise office complex, and parking garages for 7,400 cars. This is truly one of the nation's most impressive non-federally-assisted redevelopment projects. The area serves as the southern anchor for downtown St. Louis, with the newly approved convention center to serve as the anchor on the north. However, the wisdom of approving and assisting this project must be questioned. This area contained a number of fine nineteenth century commercial buildings that, if they had been left and restored rather than destroyed, would have made St. Louis more graphically a true memorial to the national expansion.

The West End Urban Renewal project begun in 1965 differs from those discussed previously in that the project was intended to be a rehabilitation and conservation program with the majority of structures to be retained and rehabilitated. The fact that this project deals with rehabilitation and conservation is very important as this area contains many of St. Louis' fine nineteenth and early twentieth century homes, and the rehabilitation of these homes rather than their destruction will help keep alive the memories of this early heritage of St. Louis' private streets and the urbane life associated with them. The area involved is located in the central west end of the city and consists of seventy-five blocks containing 2,600 structures on a 693 acre tract. Currently only about 600 structures of the 2,015 structures programmed for rehabilitation have actually been rehabilitated.

The DeSoto-Carr Urban Renewal Project commenced in 1970. The area, which was declared blighted back in 1959, is located on the near north side of the city's central business district. The area has been planned primarily as a clearance and redevelopment area with limited rehabilitation of some existing commercial and industrial structures. The city's new convention center soon will be constructed in this area, and this undoubtedly will provide the catalyst for new hotels, restaurants, and related businesses in the area. The convention center on the near north side together with Busch Stadium on the near south side are to serve as the anchors for a revitalized downtown St. Louis.

In addition to the urban renewal projects discussed, St. Louis currently has three unfunded renewal applications—LaSalle Park, Mill Creek North, and the West End Amendatory.

Urban decay (blight) is also a problem of major concern in the St. Louis metropolitan area, and it is perhaps the number one visible problem in St. Louis City. Detailed studies have recently been completed by Charles Leven of the Washington University Institute for Urban and Regional Studies and the St. Louis County Planning Commission describing the state of decay in the St. Louis metropolitan area.

According to Leven et al., the reasons for the severity of urban decay in East St. Louis include the intensity of the population shift from the cities to the suburbs and the drastic change in the composition of the remaining population, discussed previously. A second major factor causing blight in St. Louis and East St. Louis is that the two cities not only have lost population, but the population loss has been accompanied by corresponding losses in all types of employment—for example, the decline in the meat packing industry in East St. Louis and the shoe industry in St. Louis. Not only has St. Louis declined in manufacturing jobs, but wholesaling and retailing have also declined in the central city. Another factor affecting the spread of blight was the condition of the housing at the time the population shifts began to occur. The housing by the end of World War II needed repairs due to the money shortage of the 1930s and the materials shortages during World War II. This was compounded by the fact that the housing no longer suited the aspirations and the lifestyle of the postwar affluent. Also aggravating the situation were urban renewal projects that displaced thousands of the poorest blacks,

who then occupied the housing already showing signs of blight, hastening the process. In addition, "redlining"—where mortgages for buying or property improvements are impossible to obtain in certain areas of the city and insurance is also impossible to obtain at normal rates—became a prevalent practice in St. Louis. By the 1960s almost all of north St. Louis was "redlined." St. Louis' position also changed with respect to the national circulation system. The loss of the economic contest to Chicago, mentioned previously, is still felt today. Chicago continues to grow rapidly while St. Louis struggles to grow at all.

With these and other conditions prevalent in the city, blight spread rapidly in the 1950s and 1960s. Figure 16 shows the extent to which blight is prevalent today in St. Louis, and the areas that are susceptible to the encroachment of blight. This pattern exists despite the demolition of 34,596 dwelling units in the city between 1950 and 1970. The number of vacancies in the city has also risen from 4,426 to nearly 23,000, despite the large number of demolitions.

St. Louis County, the main suburban area to which city residents escape from problems such as blight, has its own blighted areas. A recent St. Louis County Planning Commission report pinpointed areas as substandard (to a greater or lesser degree) which contain over 300,000 people (34 percent of the county population). Most of the blight and deterioration is occurring in the older county municipalities, with unincorporated areas affected to a lesser degree. Forty-five of the county's municipalities are suffering from some kind of deterioration. The St. Louis County report placed communities in four classifications of deterioration. In comparison to blight in the inner city, only category one, including communities and areas of the county deficient in all functional areas, compares to conditions in the city. The four county municipalities in this category are the black communities of Kinloch and Wellston, and the white communities of Valley Park and Times Beach. Wellston is adjacent to north St. Louis, and is an extension of the black corridor. Kinloch is a black community in north St. Louis County, and dates back to the Civil War. Valley Park is in southwest St. Louis County, and Times Beach is a rural type community in extreme southwest St. Louis County. All four communities show large amounts of deteriorating housing, low family income, high infant mortality, high venereal disease rates, and low assessed valuation. The other three categories include communities deficient in key functional areas, cities with areas of deterioration, and municipalities deficient in code enforcement. To stem the tide of blight the county has recommended razing several vacant and dilapidated buildings. The other major program that would help fight blight would be enactment of a countywide minimum housing code. This has previously been proposed, but has been defeated by the voters in a countywide referendum.

Inadequate housing is not only a problem of St. Louis and St. Louis County; and, though concentrated in the four most urbanized counties, the problem is not restricted to them. A regional housing plan utilizing at least four major approaches in combination has been proposed by the American Institute of Planners (St. Louis section) to alleviate the problem in the St. Louis metropolitan area. The four major approaches are:

(1) Market assistance whereby information and counseling is provided to prospective low and moderate income families that lack adequate housing, (2) Regulatory and fiscal incentives whereby local codes, ordinances and services are oriented to help preserve and rejuvenate older neighborhoods, (3) Housing construction assistance whereby local government and nonprofit organizations encourage federally assisted housing, in some cases on a fair share basis throughout the metropolitan area, and (4) Housing allowance whereby the poor are provided direct income supplements with which to secure housing in the conventional market.

The final aspect of housing in the metropolitan area discussed here is the Black Jack zoning controversy, which has gained nationwide attention. Black Jack is a relatively affluent north St. Louis County suburb, which was incorporated in the late 1960s so that it could adopt its own zoning ordinance rather than be controlled by that of St. Louis County. The incorporation occurred as the result of an overwhelming majority vote by the citizens

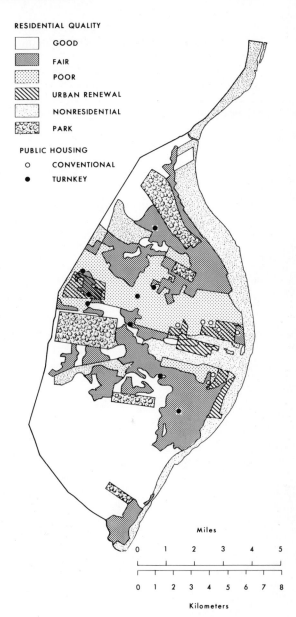

RESIDENTIAL QUALITY

☐ GOOD

▓ FAIR

▒ POOR

▨ URBAN RENEWAL

░ NONRESIDENTIAL

▨ PARK

PUBLIC HOUSING

○ CONVENTIONAL

● TURNKEY

Miles
0 1 2 3 4 5

0 1 2 3 4 5 6 7 8
Kilometers

Figure 16. The residential quality of St. Louis, based on housing quality, safety, schools, and other considerations when choosing a place to live. Source: St. Louis City Plan Commission.

of the area. The county zoning ordinance allowed the construction of multiple dwellings in many areas of Black Jack, and a low income apartment complex was proposed for one of these areas. The federal government has argued that Black Jack used its zoning powers illegally for the explicit purpose of discriminating against blacks. The city of Black Jack, on the other hand, has argued that low income housing is inconsistent with the upper middle class values of the area, and that racial discrimination was not a motive, as several blacks already lived in the city at the time of the rezoning. The case has still not been resolved in the federal courts, but the decision rendered may possibly have very significant national ramifications regarding how a city may use its zoning powers. It is entirely possible that zoning itself may be weakened by the court decision.

Current Regional Topics and Problems

Intergovernmental relations are a topic of daily concern as the St. Louis Daily Urban System consists of parts of two states, nine counties, and approximately 200 municipalities. In addition, several single purpose districts exist —school districts, fire protection districts, water and sewer districts, etc.—that overlap the municipalities.

Political fragmentation has resulted in similar types of problems in most metropolitan areas today. However, two facets of the fragmented governmental structure in the St. Louis metropolitan area warrant specific mention. The first is that St. Louis City is itself an independent county, and is not a part of St. Louis County. This has led to many problems, as the entire financial burden for services in the central city must be borne exclusively by the city without any funds from St. Louis County. Perhaps this problem is best illustrated by comparing the St. Louis situation with that of another major metropolitan area. In Chicago, the primary hospital for the poor is Cook County Hospital. It serves almost exclusively the indigent of the central city, and is financed by all the residents of Cook County including those who live outside the city of Chicago. In St. Louis the two city hospitals serve the indigent of the central city, but receive their operating funds exclusively from the central city. Certain measures (for example, a 1 percent city income tax paid by everyone who works in the city regardless of the place of residence) have been enacted by the city to help alleviate this govern-

mental arrangement. The second feature of the governmental structure in the St. Louis area that warrants specific mention is the strength of the St. Louis County government. Over 332,000 people live in unincorporated areas of suburban St. Louis County. This population is greater than those of many major cities (e.g., Des Moines, Honolulu, and Tulsa), and has given rise to perhaps the strongest county government in the United States. The county supervisor, elected directly by the voters of St. Louis County, is considered equal to the mayor of St. Louis as a political power.

The fragmentation that exists can best be illustrated by considering St. Louis County. St. Louis County has a population of 951,971, of which 95.8 percent reside in urbanized areas. Within the boundary of St. Louis County there are ninety-four incorporated cities, towns, and villages ranging in size from the village of Champ with a population of nineteen to Florissant with a population of 65,908. The number of municipalities in St. Louis County is the second greatest in the United States; only Cook County, Illinois, has more. There are also about seventy other separate taxing bodies, including fire protection districts, school districts, and sewer districts. There are even three street lighting districts and a sidewalk district. In addition there are about seventy-one nontaxing political areas, such as legislative districts. The composite picture is a total of approximately 236 political subdivisions in St. Louis County, or one for every two square miles.

The true magnitude of the problem can best be illustrated by considering police protection in St. Louis County. The St. Louis County Police Department provides protection for all unincorporated areas of the county and to certain municipalities that contract with the county. At present there are seventy police departments in the county. The inadequacy of the police protection in many areas is illustrated by the fact that forty-three departments have no regularly assigned detectives. Some municipalities receive their police protection during certain hours (usually daylight) from a municipal police force, and then receive their evening protection from the St. Louis County police force. The result is highly fragmented, and oftentimes inadequate, police protection for many of the residents in St. Louis County. However, the Major Case Squad, created in 1965 to handle cases that create much public interest, represents an important example of consolidation. The squads pool the investigative talents of several detectives from St. Louis City and six of the surrounding counties in Missouri and Illinois. With a county government as large and strong as that of St. Louis County, a single countywide police force would seem to provide more adequate and equitable police protection for the citizens of St. Louis County.

To alleviate governmental fragmentation in the greater St. Louis area three proposals for city-county consolidation have been advanced. Attempts at consolidation, which required a majority vote in both the city and county for passage, were defeated by the voters in 1926 and 1959. In addition, a state constitutional amendment, which would have allowed a federation between city and county, was defeated by the voters in 1930. The 1926 proposal received a majority vote in the county, but was defeated by city voters, while the 1959 proposal was rejected by county and city voters alike. The change in vote illustrates the changing conditions characterizing our cities as the twentieth century has progressed.

Political integration has been achieved in St. Louis in some areas. Among the successful attempts at obtaining cooperative agreements are the Metropolitan Sewer Districts (MSD), Bi-State Development Agency, the Zoo-Museum District, the Junior College District, and East-West Gateway Coordinating Council. The MSD, created in 1954, provides sewer service at a lower cost than could be offered by the individual municipalities to St. Louis City and a large portion of St. Louis County.

The Bi-State Development Agency was established in 1949 and began operating the area's buses in 1963. Although presently the subject of much controversy, it represents a fairly successful attempt at the integration of a specific service. Bi-State is responsible for mass transportation (bus) in the region and provides services in St. Louis City, parts of St. Louis County, and Madison County and St. Clair County, Illinois. The specific operations and problems will be discussed in a later section.

Another example of cooperation is the Zoo-Museum District, encompassing St. Louis City and St. Louis County. Prior to its creation in 1971 (majority vote by the citizens of both St. Louis City and St. Louis County) the zoo and art museum were located in the city, financed by the city, and utilized equally, if not primarily, by the citizens of the county. The creation of the special taxing district has distributed the payment equally among those who use the facilities.

The Junior College District, created in 1962, is another example of a special taxing district to provide a specific service to the residents of St. Louis City and St. Louis County. The district operates three junior colleges, two of which are located in the county (Florissant Valley and Meramec Community colleges) and one in the city (Forest Park Community College). These junior colleges provide very low cost education to several thousand students each year.

The final example of a major cooperative agreement in the area is the St. Louis area council of governments known as the East-West Gateway Coordinating Council. It was created in 1965 and all municipalities in the St. Louis SMSA are eligible for membership. Several important suburban areas have neglected to join, as they feel the council is merely a forum for the views of the mayor of St. Louis and the supervisor of St. Louis County. The primary function of the council is planning and making recommendations for the entire region. Enforcement of these plans depends upon the voluntary compliance of the areas in question, as the only power that the council has is the A-95 review power over certain federal funds available to municipalities.

Many other specific cooperative agreements have been entered into by mutual agreement. The majority of these involve a contractual arrangement between St. Louis County and a single county municipality.

The Alliance for Regional Community Health, Inc., feels that when discussing public health in the St. Louis metropolitan area two basic problems appear at the forefront. The first is the relationship between availability and accessibility of health care services, as the areas with the greatest concentration of physicians also have some of the poorest health indicators. The second concerns the problem of health care in the rural areas of the metropolitan area, which is related to a scarcity of health resources such as hospitals and physicians.

The St. Louis metropolitan area has forty-six hospitals. Only nine of these are located outside of St. Louis City, St. Louis County, and St. Clair County (Figure 17). Six of the nine hospitals located outside the three previously mentioned areas are in Madison County. This leaves only three hospitals in St. Charles, Jefferson, Franklin, and Monroe

counties. In addition, 2,500 out of the 3,000 physicians in the area are located in St. Louis and St. Louis County. That the entire area depends heavily on St. Louis City and St. Louis County for hospital care is apparent. Hospitals in the remainder of the counties primarily serve their own residents, with St. Clair County also serving several residents of Madison County. This dependence on the big counties shows the need for expanded health services in the rural counties. Figure 17 suggests the distances people in rural areas have to travel when they require hospitalization. On the other hand, over 70 percent of the patients in the area receive their care in St. Louis City and St. Louis County. These health services, which serve the needs of the region, are inaccessible to many who need these services the most in the inner city.

Providing health services to the poor of the central city appears to be the number one health problem in the area. Health problems are most acute for the poor, and they are unable to pay the high cost of health services. They may live in the shadows of the area's best hospitals, but are unable to afford the care available at their doorstep. Figure 18, showing the general health of residents in the city of St. Louis, corresponds closely to the geo-

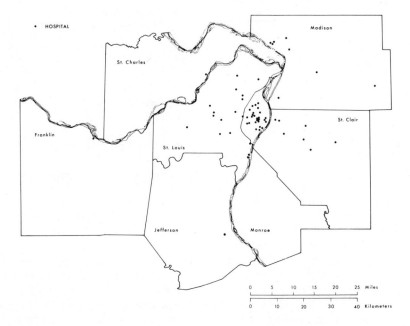

Figure 17. Hospitals in the St. Louis area, 1970. Source: East-West Gateway Coordinating Council.

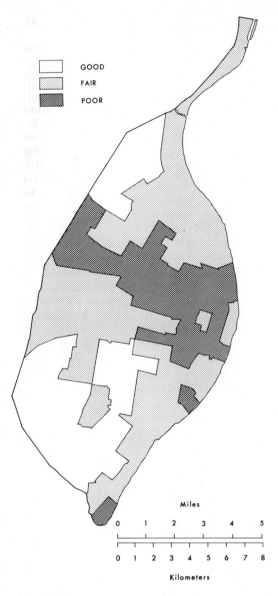

GOOD

FAIR

POOR

Miles

| 0 | 1 | 2 | 3 | 4 | 5 |

Kilometers

| 0 | 1 | 2 | 3 | 4 | 5 | 6 | 7 | 8 |

Figure 18. Average levels of general health of city residents.

graphical pattern of residential quality. Areas of poor general health are also the areas of poor residential quality. The poorer the area in terms of health strata, the more active tuberculosis cases, the more sanitation complaints, the higher the number of reported rat bites, the higher the number of illegitimate births, the higher the infant mortality rate, the lower the percentage of children in kindergarten immunized for diphtheria, pertussin, and typhoid, the lower the percentage of children in kinder-

garten immunized for polio, the higher the number of children with elevated lead levels, and the higher the number of syphilis cases. The area of poor health strata can also be seen to correspond closely to the location of the black population in St. Louis. This relationship can be attributed to the disadvantaged economic situation in which many St. Louis blacks find themselves.

The St. Louis metropolitan area is the home of thirty-six institutions of higher learning. The four major universities are the University of Missouri–St. Louis, Southern Illinois University–Edwardsville, Washington University, and St. Louis University. Of the thirty-six colleges and universities in the area, ten are in St. Louis City, sixteen in St. Louis County. One small college worth noting specifically is Marillac College, which closed at the end of the 1972-1973 academic year. Marillac was the only four year college in the United States operated solely to educate nuns. Its closing exemplifies the plight of private schools attempting to stay open despite rising costs and declining enrollments.

An important aspect of higher education in St. Louis is an innovative cooperative doctoral degree program announced early in 1973 between Southern Illinois University–Edwardsville, St. Louis University, and Washington University. Under terms of the agreement the three universities will exchange students, faculties, and academic resources on a contractual basis to provide doctoral degree programs to students from the three universities. The program involves private and public institutions and crosses state lines. If this program succeeds, it will provide a model to be followed in higher education by other universities located in close proximity to one another. To share rather than duplicate resources and programs seems particularly significant in these times of financial troubles for our nation's universities.

As in most major metropolitan areas, the major problem in elementary and secondary education in the St. Louis area is to provide an equal educational opportunity for all. This poses a serious problem, as resources are obviously not evenly distributed throughout the metropolitan area (Table 5). The assessed valuation per pupil ranges from $50,690 in Clayton to only $3,733 in Kinloch, and the amount spent per pupil per year ranges from $1,816

Table 5. St. Louis City and St. Louis County School Districts, 1971–1972 School Year
(Selected Characteristics)

District	*Average Daily Attendance*	*Amount Spent per Pupil*	*Assessed Valuation per Pupil*
Affton	4,034	$1,018	$18,467
Bayless	2,072	774	12,070
Berkeley	4,438	1,030	23,636
Brentwood	1,553	1,242	27,302
Clayton	2,190	1,816	50,690
Ferguson	16,936	841	10,151
Hancock	2,076	847	11,679
Hazelwood	22,336	813	12,412
Jennings	2,807	1,107	22,109
Kinloch	1,084	1,016	3,733
Kirkwood	7,971	1,021	16,484
Ladue	5,290	1,479	31,537
Lindberg	10,847	855	14,685
Maplewood-Richmond Heights	2,712	1,054	19,984
Mehlville	10,589	857	12,894
Normandy	8,037	965	13,351
Parkway	19,233	878	13,790
Pattonville	10,839	934	16,656
Ritenour	11,882	862	12,058
Riverview Gardens	8,654	858	11,807
Rockwood	8,164	894	14,081
University City	6,668	1,208	18,144
Valley Park	888	927	13,313
Webster Groves	6,898	1,052	15,146
Wellston	1,914	1,053	12,526
St. Louis City*	95,625	757	16,712

*Data for St. Louis is for 1970–1971 school year. At that time thirteen St. Louis County School Districts had a lower per pupil expenditure. It can be assumed that the figure for St. Louis City has also risen proportionately.

Source: Department of Education, St. Louis County, Clayton, Mo.

in Clayton to $774 in the Bayless School District. Clayton is the location of the county government center, several high-rise office buildings, and many shopping facilities, restaurants, and expensive homes. Kinloch, on the other hand, is one of the four communities classified as severely blighted by St. Louis County. However, it should be noted that Kinloch, despite its pathetically low valuation per pupil, ranks in the upper half of the St. Louis County school districts in the amount spent per pupil. This reflects the result of impressive efforts to achieve equalization by use of state and federal funds. The data for St. Louis City is from 1970-1971, and that for the county from 1971-1972. In 1970-1971 St. Louis City was ninth highest in assessed valuation per pupil, and thirteenth in amount

spent per pupil. However, St. Louis, because of its size, receives the bulk of the publicity, yet its educational resources were better than average in comparison to the St. Louis County districts, and certainly much better than the local resources available in Kinloch. Many proposals advanced in other areas, such as the creation of a metropolitan school district (actually just St. Louis City and St. Louis County), or a change in the method of financing education (i.e., elimination of the total dependency on property tax), have also been proposed in St. Louis. Any attempt to create a metropolitan school district (i.e., to combine the St. Louis City and various county school districts) would meet stiff opposition, in that it would eliminate local control over the schools, which is contrary to the desires of many people. On the other hand, an equalization of resources available for education must somehow be achieved. This does not mean that every school district need have the same amount to spend per pupil, but rather that no district fall below an adequately established minimum. People who are willing to pay higher taxes for better education should be allowed to do so, but all districts should be brought up to an acceptable minimum. The decline in the number of students—e.g., St. Louis County schools saw their total enrollment decrease for the first time in twenty years in 1972-1973—should help alleviate the financial crises of our schools, as more money will be available to educate fewer students.

Another educational topic of interest in St. Louis, as in many cities, is the continuing decline in the number of students attending Catholic elementary and high schools. Enrollment has declined by nearly 50 percent in the Catholic elementary schools from 1960 to present, and by nearly 30 percent in the Catholic high schools. The enrollment decline has resulted in the closing of twenty-four Catholic elementary schools and five Catholic high schools in the city. The most substantial drop has occurred in north St. Louis. A number of factors have played a role in the enrollment decline and subsequent school closings. Included is the change in racial composition that occurred in north St. Louis during the 1960s. Once the school age population in an area is essentially black, the parochial school enrollments have become black as well. The fraction of the total enrollment attending parochial schools usually drops abruptly, and the school hangs on for a few years, then closes. In racially changing areas, parochial schools are often chosen by minority families as a preferred alternative to the public schools, but the number of Catholic families with school age children has declined, and the ability and willingness of the remaining residents to pay for private education has lessened, while the price has increased. Partially compensating for this decline in elementary parochial school enrollment in the central city is the relatively high proportion of elementary school students who attend parochial schools in parts of south and north St. Louis County, where the majority of the white residents who left the central city settled (Figure 19). West St. Louis County has

a very low proportion of its elementary students in parochial schools, and this can be attributed partially to the fact that it is the new growth area and is inhabited by newcomers to the metropolitan area. The same general pattern exists for high school students in both the city and SMSA, except that the percentage attending parochial schools is lower nearly everywhere. This can be attributed to the higher tuition rates charged for high school students and less interest in parochial school education by high school age youth. One additional area of high parochial school enrollment, not mentioned previously, is Belleville in Metro-East. Belleville's heritage is that of an old German community that has long had a large number of Catholics and many children attending parochial schools.

As in America's other metropolitan centers, the highest crime rate in the St. Louis metropolitan area is found in the central city. In the St. Louis area the basic causes of crime—low income, high unemployment, the lack of job opportunities, low levels of education, one parent families, and the physical deterioration of buildings—are found to the greatest extent in St. Louis and East St. Louis.

The magnitude of the crime problem in the city of St. Louis can best be illustrated by comparing the number of crimes in St. Louis with the number of crimes in St. Louis County. In 1972 St. Louis (population 622,236) recorded 266 homicides, 546 rapes, 5,296 robberies, and 3,329 assaults. St. Louis County with its far greater population (951,971) recorded only forty-one homicides, 145 rapes, 779 robberies, and 644 assaults in 1972. The city dweller is ten times as likely to be the victim of a crime against person as is the county dweller. However, the trend is slowly reversing. According to the FBI, crime in St. Louis City decreased by 4.1 percent during 1972, while crime in St. Louis County increased by 6.4 percent, which is more than triple the national suburban crime increase of 2 percent. The St. Louis Law Enforcement Officials Association blames the increase in crime in the county on the influx of federal high impact anticrime funds into the city, which has caused the criminals to shift their operations to the more fertile area of St. Louis County.

Within both St. Louis City and the county crime rates are not uniform. A "crime cor-

Figure 19. Parochial school attendance patterns in St. Louis, 1970.

ridor" extends from the central business district through the north side and then northwest into the first tier suburban communities such as Wellston and University City. This area of high crime in St. Louis City corresponds closely to the area of low income and black population concentration in the city. It is within the black community that many of the perpetrators of crime are found, but it is also in the black community that the victims of crime are found. On the other hand, in St. Louis County the amount of crime in areas is almost directly proportional to population. The outlying areas with high crime rates are the locations of major highway intersections where a large number of commercial establishments are located. Throughout the remainder of the area, crime seems to be proportional to population, with the most rural areas, Monroe and Franklin counties, experiencing the least crimes.

The lack of adequate police protection is of greatest concern in the unincorporated areas of St. Louis County. The St. Louis County Police Department, which serves unincorporated St. Louis County, is woefully undermanned. The department has only 444 officers, who must serve 347 square miles (69.5 percent of the county area) with a population of 320,000. The remainder of the county, 152 square miles with 630,000 residents, is served by 1,240 officers. One unified county police force would better serve the needs of all the residents of St. Louis County. However, to achieve this goal the residents of the county's municipalities would have to be convinced that their police protection would improve rather than suffer. Currently St. Louis City spends 53 percent of the region's local government outlay for criminal justice services, including police, courts, prosecution, defense for indigents, and corrections. St. Louis County spends 45 percent of the regional total. For the most part county-by-county outlays correspond to population. St. Louis, as would be expected, is an obvious exception.

In many respects the political behavior of the St. Louis metropolitan area resembles other metropolitan areas. Since 1948 St. Louis City has voted solidly Democratic for mayor, president, U.S. senator, U.S. representatives, and governor. St. Louis County, on the other hand, has turned in majorities for Republican candidates at all levels. However, effective gerrymandering has now diminished the chance of St. Louis County electing a Republican to Congress. St. Louis County voters have been split into districts controlled by St. Louis City voters and rural Democratic counties. There is no doubt but that the Republican majority in St. Louis County has been denied their right of representation. St. Charles County has become more Republican as it has become suburban. Franklin and Jefferson counties are solidly Democratic in statewide elections, but Franklin County supported Richard Nixon for president in both 1968 and 1972—reflecting the voting behavior in much of rural Missouri, which is characterized by a long-standing Democratic tendency, but a recent rejection of national Democratic candidates perceived as being too liberal.

The Illinois counties in the metropolitan area are in traditionally Republican "downstate." Clinton and Monroe typify this traditional Republican stronghold. St. Clair County is the exception to downstate Illinois and is strongly Democratic. Madison County, with its urban-rural mix, cannot be described as leaning strongly toward either party.

Currently, the most significant aspect of political behavior in the area is the effect it may have on where a new metropolitan airport, if built, will be located. The changes that occurred in the last election, when Illinois elected a Democrat to succeed a Republican as governor and Missouri elected a Republican to succeed a Democrat as governor, could well influence the location of a new airport.

Although many aspects of the city of St. Louis itself have been discussed elsewhere, it seems appropriate to devote special attention to the status of downtown St. Louis. When Americans think of a city other than their own if they happen to live in a major metropolitan area, they think of the tall buildings and activities associated with the downtown area, rather than the housing, shopping, and other features of suburbia.

From the completion of the downtown urban renewal projects in the mid-1960s until the fall of 1972 the central business district of St. Louis stagnated. During this period a general climate of discouragement existed, and the city of St. Louis indeed looked like a dying central city. Population was declining at the fastest rate of any major city in the nation, the number of vacant buildings per capita was the highest in the nation, and downtown St. Louis stagnated, while Clayton, the seat of the strong St. Louis County government, built high-rise office buildings at an unbelievable rate. Clayton became a second central business district for the metropolitan area, making the St. Louis area unique in that a suburban center had risen to challenge the position of the central city as the economic center of the metropolitan area. However, since October of 1972 many events have occurred that have created a new climate of optimism with respect to downtown St. Louis, and that indicate that the downtown area is ready to assert its position as the economic, cultural, and entertainment center for the metropolitan area.

The first significant event, and probably the catalyst for the events that have followed, was the announcement by the Mercantile Trust Company of a plan to redevelop six blocks in the north end of downtown St. Louis over a ten year period at a cost of $150 million. The first buildings to be constructed were to be a thirty-five story bank tower costing $25 million, and a $1.5–$2 million multilevel parking garage. Other buildings to be constructed as part of the project include a $36 million 800 room luxury hotel; and a twenty-four story office building, a twenty-six story office building, and a fifty-one story skyscraper, which will be St. Louis' tallest building. A significant feature of the project is that 43 percent of the six block area will be open space preserved for trees, shrubs, flowers, fountains, and sculptures.

Closely following the announcement of the Mercantile Center was the approval, by the voters of the city on November 7, 1972, of the construction of a new convention center to be financed by $25 million worth of revenue bonds. The center was to be completed by January 1976, replacing outdated Kiel Auditorium. The three story building will contain 200,000 square feet of exhibit space, thirty meeting rooms, and an additional 8,500 temporary seats. Constructed adjacent to the facility will be a $60 million convention plaza consisting of two hotels, a shopping mall, office buildings, and parking garages. The new convention center should prove extremely valuable to the city's economy.

A third major redevelopment project was recently announced for the north side of the downtown area. Boatmen's National Bank planned to construct a $20 million twenty-two story office tower, a $3 million 150 unit housing complex, and 640 underground parking spaces. A significant feature of the design was the proposed use of a new type of aluminum having a satin finish and sheathed in a bronze mirror material to catch the reflections of the Gateway Arch and the old courthouse.

A fourth major redevelopment proposal was announced by the St. Louis City Planning Commission. This is the creation of a "New Town In Town." Financing has not yet been obtained for the proposed project, but if it is this project could be the most significant of all in terms of revitalizing the city. The proposed area is a 1,250 acre tract in midtown St. Louis, and would anchor the downtown area on the west. There are presently 16,000 persons and 5,750 dwelling units in the area. Since 1960 the area has lost one-third of its population and 40 percent of its dwelling units. It is proposed that 14,250 new housing units would be built in the area, and that the redevelopment area would have a population of 40,000 at the completion of the twenty year project. The new housing units would be 20 percent high income, 35 percent middle income, 30 percent moderate income, and 15 percent low income. The housing in the area would feature high-rise apartments on the tops of hills, terraced low-rise apartments and townhouses on slopes, and single family homes built around a lake in the lowland areas. A peoplemover transportation system utilizing small, computer-controlled transit cars would be installed along Grand Boulevard to facilitate travel between the various institutions, shopping and entertainment areas, and housing in the area. Industry in the "New Town" would reflect the area's site as a transportation center in the St. Louis region, and in the nation as a whole. The area has many strengths that will be of help in insuring success if the project is undertaken. Included are the Lafayette Square Restoration Area, St. Louis University (main and medical campuses), Powell Symphony Hall, Bethesda and Incarnate Word hospitals, eight elementary schools, and the Work-Study High School.

Two other proposals are worth noting. First is the proposed construction of a 330 room luxury hotel tower adjacent to the Spanish Pavilion. The so-called "jewel" of the 1964-1965 New York Word's Fair, which was purchased by St. Louis and moved here, is now vacant. Another proposal for the use of the Spanish Pavilion has been to open an aqua-center in it. The hotel proposal appears the soundest. It has also been proposed that a new hockey arena be built near Busch Memorial Stadium. This would replace the old arena, which has limited use due to the lack of air conditioning. This would obviously help the downtown area.

Downtown St. Louis is also attempting to reassert itself as the center of nightlife in the area. A new entertainment center—the New Gaslight Square—is being developed in the downtown area by private nightclubs.

If all the proposals noted become a reality, downtown St. Louis will be on the verge of reasserting itself as the center of the metropolitan area. The plans imply a functional change for the downtown area. The downtown area grew as a center of retailing, wholesaling, and finance. The revamped downtown will be based on a strengthened financial and office sector and an expansion of entertainment facilities. If the downtown area again begins to thrive, it can also be expected that proportional increases in retail trade will follow.

The Future of the St. Louis Metropolitan Area

Speculating on the future of any metropolitan area is a risky undertaking. However, certain observations can be offered based on conditions in the area.

The economy is the backbone of any metropolitan area, and, as described previously, the economy of the St. Louis metropolitan area is basically stagnant and precariously based on a few key industries—primarily McDonnell-Douglas and automobile assembly. St. Louis is not located in the boom areas of the South and West. Consequently, the most logical course of action for the area to follow is to concentrate on keeping what industry it has, and encouraging these industries to expand in this area rather than elsewhere, if and when they contemplate expansion.

The direction of future growth in the metropolitan area will be determined by the two basic transportation issues facing the region. First, will Lambert International Airport be expanded or will a new facility be constructed at the Columbia-Waterloo site? This decision will determine whether the present west-north-western expansions of the metropolitan area will continue, with massive growth occurring in St. Charles County and extreme west St. Louis County, or whether the new growth area will be in Metro-East near the new airport, if it is constructed. The second transportation issue is whether the St. Louis region will build a new mass transit system. If fuel shortages develop, limiting the number of cars in the area, perhaps St. Louis will finally act

positively on a mass transit system. This would promote growth along the transit corridors.

Another highly important concern for the future of the area is increased intergovernmental cooperation in the area. Particularly acute is increased cooperation between St. Louis City and St. Louis County, as these two areas contain nearly 75 percent of the area's population. However, it is highly important that all the counties and municipalities in the area cooperate in solving problems dealing with crime, education, pollution, and transportation. All problems are areawide. Certain problems obviously can be solved best at the local level, but this should not be used to promote parochial interests at the expense of cooperation to solve mutual problems. Great value can be obtained from the East-West Gateway Coordinating Council, as it provides a forum in which the views of governmental units, large and small, are heard. Hopefully, many of those municipalities that do not currently belong will join, so that they too can provide an input of their views and learn from the experiences of others.

The number one problem of the future in the metropolitan area will remain for some time the revitalizing of St. Louis City. The population decline and change in its composition; the decline in retailing and in industry; and the crime rate, blight, vacant buildings, etc., do not paint a bright future for the city. However, the outlook presently is more optimistic than it has been for some time. If the construction proposed for downtown begins on schedule, the proposed projects such as the "New Town In Town" become a reality, and solutions are found to the area's economic woes the city may again begin to prosper. The future of the metropolitan area is much like that of other established metropolitan areas. Problems abound, but if solutions can be found to the problems, St. Louis can once again signify America's greatness, as she did in the era of national expansion when she enjoyed her greatest splendor.

Bibliography

Alliance for Regional Community Health, Inc. *The Final Report of the Health Facilities Planning Committee,* St. Louis, October 1971.

American Institute of Planners (St. Louis Metropolitan Section). *St. Louis Housing: A Regional Problem.* St. Louis, December 1972.

Belcher, Wyatt Winton. *The Economic Rivalry Between St. Louis and Chicago 1850–1880.* New York: Columbia University Press, 1947.

Bracco, James, and Grzesik, Steven. "Studies in Black Migration: St. Louis City–St. Louis County, 1940–1970." Manuscript, Department of Geography, St. Louis University, 1973.

Bradley, Robert A., and Thran, Sally. "Measuring St. Louis Residential Quality." *St. Louis Post-Dispatch,* April 3, 1972.

Chagnon, Stanley A., and Floyd A. Huff. "Enhancement of Severe Weather by the St. Louis Urban-Industrial Complex," Mimeographed. (Urbana: Illinois State Water Survey, 1973).

East-West Gateway Coordinating Council. *Comprehensive Planning Status Report for the St. Louis Region, 1970–1971 Edition.* St. Louis, April 1971.

Heckman, Bruce. "Maps of the Spatial Expansion of the St. Louis Metropolitan Area, 1800–Future." Clayton, Mo.: St. Louis County Planning Commission, 1973.

"Job Total Here Drops 61,200 in Last 3 Years." *St. Louis Post-Dispatch,* January 1973.

Kaplan, Ethan Z. *The Residents of St. Louis Public Housing: A Socio-Economic and Demographic Report.* St. Louis: Health and Welfare Council of Metropolitan St. Louis, December 1972.

Leven, Charles L., et al. *Urban Decay in St. Louis.* St. Louis: The Institute for Urban and Regional Studies, Washington University, March 1972.

Meyer, Gerald. [Series of articles on St. Louis as a Port.] *St. Louis Post-Dispatch,* May 1973.

Missouri Air Conservation Commission. *Missouri Air Quality.* Jefferson City, 1971.

Missouri Law Enforcement Assistance Council, Region 5. *Criminal Justice System Description: 1973.* St. Louis, October 1972.

Rainwater, Lee. *Behind Ghetto Walls: Black Families in a Federal Slum.* Chicago: Aldine Publishing Company, 1970.

State of Illinois Environmental Protection Agency. *Illinois Air Sampling Network Report: 1971.* Springfield, Ill., November 1972.

St. Louis County Planning Commission. *Apartments in St. Louis County.* Clayton, Mo., 1972.

——. *Evaluation: Municipalities and Unincorporated Communities: Report I.* Clayton, Mo., 1973.

U.S. Bureau of the Census. *U.S. Census of Population: 1970, Number of Inhabitants.* Final Report PC (1) - A1. Washington, D.C.: U.S. Government Printing Office, 1971. Pp. 116–19.

——. *U.S. Census of Population and Housing: 1970. Census Tracts.* Final Report PHC (1) - 181. Washington, D.C.: U.S. Government Printing Office, 1972.

Voorhees, Alan M. and Associates, Inc. *History of Urban Renewal: St. Louis Mo.* Highlights of Findings. St. Louis, March 1970.

 *Chapter Three*

The Northeastern Ohio
Urban Complex

Frontispiece. Downtown Cleveland, looking northward. (Photo courtesy of Greater Cleveland Growth Association).

Acknowledgements

In this study we have utilized the findings of much research previously published by individuals and agencies concerned with the urban development of Northeastern Ohio and, in the course of the current project, have utilized special studies prepared for the project by many students and faculty of Kent State University, and especially of that university's Department of Geography and its Center for Urban Regionalism. The present publication represents a summary of such studies, as well as a synthesis, by the principal authors, of the regional concepts that have emerged in the course of the project.

Especially appreciated are the efforts of the following members of the Kent State University student body, faculty, and staff for their contributions to the project. Thomas Corsi, in addition to contributing major portions of the sections on population and ethnicity, served as principal editorial assistant throughout the project. Betty Gombert, provided indispensable secretarial services as well as patience and persistence which greatly expedited the completion of the manuscript. Dr. William Ross contributed much of the material on environmental quality, as did Dr. Richard Raymond on employment trends.

Students contributed much background material, in the form of theses and term papers, including some of the latter which were prepared in connection with a series of graduate seminars on Northeastern Ohio. Thomas Brumbach contributed research and papers on railroads, interurbans, and rapid transit; Marsden Burger on railroad history; Thomas Corsi on population, race, and ethnic groups and their spatial distributions in the Cleveland area, and Laura Brown on the Akron area; Norman Dietrich and Al Sulin on location and relocation of industry; Wayne Dust and Kenneth Lederman on intermetropolitan coalescence along the highways; James Kastelic on problems of the Lake Erie shoreline; and Andrew Schoolmaster on history of parks and recreation and on open space preservation. Collaborating on the section on environmental quality under the direction of Dr. Ross were members of his seminar—Randal Beeson, Donald Fred, Gary Gezann, Mark McElvray, Andy Schoolmaster, and Martin Williams.

Many public agencies furnished information and materials. Among them are: Tri-County Regional Planning Commission, Northeast Ohio Areawide Coordinating Agency (NOACA), Regional Planning Commission of Cuyahoga County, Cleveland and Akron city planning commissions, Stark County Regional Planning Commission, State of Ohio Departments of Natural Resources and of Transportation, Ohio Turnpike Commission, and many others.

Finally, those who participated in the project at Kent State University appreciate the enthusiastic encouragement and cooperation of the headquarters staffs of the Association of American Geographers Comparative Metropolitan Analysis Project in Minneapolis and Iowa City.

Introduction: General Characterization*

Northeastern Ohio is a region with a multi-nucleated urban structure that is coalescing along its principal transportation corridors. In common with many of the other older industrialized regions, Northeastern Ohio has, in recent years, witnessed a declining rate of economic and population growth relative to the nation as a whole. This, together with the physical, functional, and locational obsolescence of many of the industrial plants located in the region, has been accompanied by substantial decentralization and deconcentration of industry within and from the region. This dispersion has encouraged cross-commuting and the spreading out of residential and commercial land use, while the traditional central areas have suffered decline. Many centrally located tracts now have high vacancy rates both of land and of remaining buildings, urban renewal has met with indifferent success, and there are some indications that a number of the massive central city redevelopment projects are out of scale with the contemporary and prospective demand. The planning activities of the region are fragmented. As in most urbanized regions, there is a multiplicity of municipalities and special function agencies, while regional planning agencies generally lack success.

*Since the manuscript was prepared several of the railroads have changed their status. Major portions of the Penn Central and the Erie Lackawana are now included within ConRail (Consolidated Railroad Corporation). The B&O and the C&O are now included in the Chessie System. The former Cleveland and Shaker Heights transit systems are part of the Regional Transit Authority.

DEFINITION OF THE NORTHEASTERN OHIO URBANIZED REGION

Late in April 1973 the governor of Ohio announced the boundaries of proposed planning regions within the state, in accordance with federal requirements for planning assistance and financial aid for a wide variety of programs. This definition of Northeastern Ohio is used in this repoit. The nine county region includes Cuyahoga, Lake, Geauga, and Medina (the Cleveland Standard Metropolitan Statistical Area); Summit and Portage counties (the Akron SMSA); Stark County (the Canton SMSA); Lorain County (the Lorain-Elyria SMSA); and Wayne County (Figure 1), which is not included in any Standard Metropolitan Statistical Area.

Cleveland and Akron are clearly the most important urban concentrations within the region. The two cities are often in conflict. This has been especially evident in recent years with respect to regional planning, and the conflict has escalated in the light of the federal requirements for regional planning and for review agencies.

Stark County has had a separate regional planning agency for a number of years. Active county planning agencies have existed for some time in Cuyahoga and Lorain counties, among others, while Summit, Medina, and Portage counties have been served by a single agency, the Tri-County Planning Commission, with headquarters in Akron.

In accordance with federal requirements,

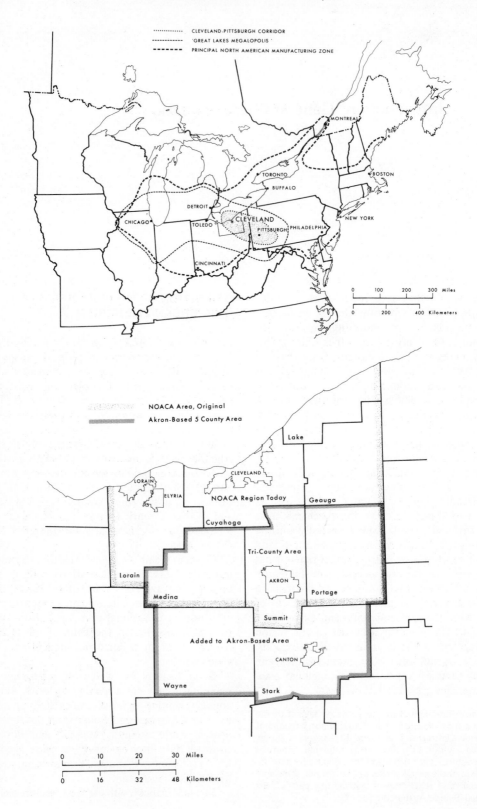

the Northeastern Ohio Areawide Coordinating Agency (NOACA) was organized in 1968. This agency has been the official regional planning and review agency for seven counties— Cuyahoga, Lake, Lorain, Geauga, Medina, Summit, and Portage. The federal government has maintained that the tricounty area—Summit, Medina, and Portage counties, with Akron as the major center—should not have an official review agency as such but that the Tri-County Planning Commission should clear proposals through NOACA.

In April 1973, the state of Ohio announced its decision to reorganize the regional planning and review functions within the nine county area by setting up two agencies: one, based in Cleveland, to include the four northern counties (Cuyahoga, Lake, Geauga, and Lorain); and the other, based in Akron, to include five counties (Summit, Medina, and Portage, previously included in the Tri-County Planning Commission area, together with Stark County, which has had its own county-regional planning agency, and Wayne County, which previously had none. In addition, the state proposed the creation of an administrative district to include all of the nine counties.

HISTORICAL DEVELOPMENT TO THE EARLY TWENTIETH CENTURY

In less than 200 years Northeastern Ohio developed from a virtually unexplored wilderness to one of the major urban and industrial concentrations of North America. In the late nineteenth century it was one of the leading growth areas of the United States, with manufacturing constituting the major part of its economic base. Subsequently, the area reached economic maturity, with slower growth of population and employment. In common with other older mature industrialized regions, it has recently contributed a smaller proportion of the nation's population and economic expansion.

The present landscape of the region has many elements which condition the present land use, population, and economic patterns as a result of historical development. The rectangular grid pattern of land subdivision, the

Figure 1. (a) Northeastern Ohio in the core areas of North America. (b) Planning regions of Northeastern Ohio.

grid of roads one mile apart in the rural areas, the rectangularity of the street pattern in most of the cities, and the governmental pattern of generally rectangular rural townships and of counties resulted from the federal land survey principles and their application in the Northwest Territories Ordinance of 1787, followed by the survey, under the Connecticut Company, by Moses Cleaveland in the closing years of the eighteenth century. The area constitutes part of the Western Reserve of Connecticut, which, in turn, represents the territory which Connecticut claimed west of the Appalachians after all the other original coastal states gave up their territorial aspirations west of the mountains. The southern boundary of the Western Reserve corresponds approximately to the southern boundary of our study area, while the western boundary is 125 miles west of the Pennsylvania-Ohio boundary. Within the Western Reserve are many other evidences of the early ties with southern New England: the architecture of many of the older buildings and their newer imitators constitute a distinctive "western reserve" modification of the New England style; the central parks in many of the communities including the famous Public Square of Cleveland are reminiscent of the "commons" and "greens" of southern New England towns; and the remaining covered bridges are similar to those of New England.

Significant urbanization of the area began with the canal era. New York State completed the Erie Canal, joining the Great Lakes with the Atlantic Seaboard, in 1825. Immediately, the state of Ohio began the construction of several canals to bring the benefits of low cost all-water transportation to the area of the state between Lake Erie and the Ohio River. Canals greatly reduced the cost and ease of travel and of transportation of the produce of the state to the eastern markets. One of these canals, the Ohio and Erie, was to traverse the state from Cleveland to Portsmouth. It was opened as far as the subcontinental drainage divide, thirty miles up the Cuyahoga valley from Cleveland, in 1827, and it was in that year that Akron was founded. Cleveland's growth then was accelerated, and it soon outdistanced other localities on Lake Erie as the region's major port and city. Subsequently, branch canals were opened, and for a while Cleveland and Akron had a direct waterway connection with Pittsburgh.

During the last half of the nineteenth century northeastern Ohio became an industrialized region, based upon a dense network of railroads, Great Lakes transportation, and the convergence of iron ore, coal, and limestone, which formed the resource base of the burgeoning iron and steel industry; oil and natural gas, which stimulated America's first large petroleum and petrochemical industries; salt and other minerals within the region; and good glacial soils, which furnished the base for a thriving, but later relatively declining, mixed farming and dairy industry. The combination of location astride both east-west and north-south transportation routes, on the one hand, and the proximity of and access to natural resources on the other, were complemented by aggressive local entrepreneurs; among them were John D. Rockefeller, Marcus Hanna, B.F. Goodrich, and others who laid the foundations for many of the region's industries that today are of national and international importance.

Population and Economic Base

POPULATION GROWTH

Between 1890 and 1960, except for the 1930–1940 Depression period, the growth rate in the nine county Northeastern Ohio region exceeded the growth rate of the country as a whole, the East North Central states (Ohio, Indiana, Illinois, Michigan, and Wisconsin), and Ohio (Figure 2). Between 1960 and 1970, however, the population of the nine county region expanded less rapidly than the total population of the United States and of the East North Central states. The nine county region is a mature industrial area that grew most rapidly in the early years of the twentieth century and now is growing more slowly than other regions of the country.

The growth patterns of the SMSAs furnish convincing documentation that the region has reached maturity (Figure 3). From 1920 through 1970, the region's SMSAs, with few exceptions, have been growing at a slower pace than those of the nation as a whole. In the three decades since 1940, only the population growth rate for the Lorain-Elyria SMSA has surpassed the average growth rate for all SMSAs in the nation. The region's SMSAs would have been much further behind national trends had it not been for the rapid growth of suburban areas around central cores. Throughout the post–World War II era, suburban areas of Cleveland and Akron have expanded at faster rates than the average of suburban areas in the nation.

In 1900, the city of Cleveland represented 80.0 percent of the combined populations of Akron, Canton, Cleveland, Elyria, and Lorain. In 1970, these five cities reported a total population of 1,267,993. Cleveland's 1970 population of 750,903 equaled 59.2 percent of the total—a twenty percentage point decline between 1900 and 1970. This last figure, perhaps, underestimates the decline of the city of Cleveland. If the population of Cleveland is compared with the combined population of the region's four SMSAs (3,372,486), a more striking result is apparent. Cleveland's population equals only 22.0 percent of the total population of the four SMSAs. This summarizes the trend of the past thirty-five to forty years: the central cities and especially the region's central node (Cleveland) have declined rapidly. The central cities of Lorain and Elyria were the only central cities to experience population gains between 1960 and 1970.

ECONOMIC BASE

Northeastern Ohio is fundamentally a region of heavy basic manufacturing. A high proportion of its most important industries is mutually interrelated, and forms an integrated series of stages from the processing of basic raw materials from both within and without the region to the final assembly into durable goods. On the other hand, service industries, such as finance and government, are underrepresented in comparison with the rest of the nation. Since the region is dominantly urban, agriculture, of course, plays a very minor role. The

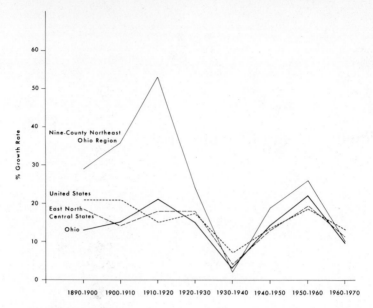

Figure 2. Northeastern Ohio population growth compared with larger areas, 1890-1970.

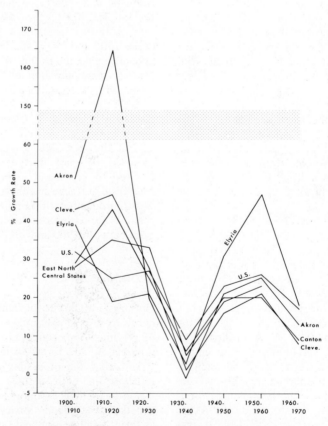

Figure 3. Relative rates of population growth of SMSAs: northeastern Ohio, north central states, and United States, 1900-1970.

region is largely dependent upon the rest of the nation and the world for its foods and fibers.

Northeastern Ohio, therefore, is primarily a region containing a blue collar population of industrial workers. Many of the regional attributes spring from this fact: the strong emphasis upon vocational training in its educational systems as contrasted with the middle class white collar emphasis in many other regions; the expenditures, both by individuals and governments, upon physical goods rather than services; and the relative reluctance to adopt forward-looking planning for the future.

A pertinent measure of this set of characteristics is the relatively low level of its educational institutions. Ohio ranks fiftieth among the 50 states in support of public "higher" education, in spite of the fact that it is sixth in per capita income. Paradoxically, two large urban state universities in the region—Cleveland State and Akron U—have grown phenomenally in recent years.

Among the manufacturing industries, three are outstanding. Iron and steel leads in employment (18.9 percent of the total durable manufacturing employment), and is a significant localizing factor in the next two ranking manufacturing categories—motor vehicles and equipment (15.3 percent of the total durable manufacturing employment), and electrical machinery (10.4 percent of the total durable manufacturing employment). Northeastern Ohio also ranks very high in the manufacture of a wide variety of other durable metal goods and machinery, ranging from heavy earthmoving equipment to household appliances.

The iron and steel industry is heavily localized in the lower Cuyahoga valley, principally in Cleveland and its immediately contiguous industrial suburbs, and in Lorain, Canton, and Massillon. The automobile industry is scattered throughout the region—in large plants in Cleveland, Brook Park, Lordstown, Lorain, Twinsburg, and elsewhere, and in hundreds of smaller plants throughout Northeastern Ohio. The state ranks second to Michigan in the production of motor vehicles and parts, and its participation in that industry represents an easterly extension of the core automobile belt of southern Michigan. The automobile industry constitutes the largest single market, in turn, for many of the industries heavily represented in Northeastern Ohio. These include primary iron and steel, machinery, metal fabricating, and, of course, the rubber industry, the world center of which

remains in Akron, despite declines in employment and production, both relatively and absolutely, compared with other regions.

The industrial "mix" in Northeastern Ohio does not portend well for the future. In the first place, service occupations and industries are very underrepresented in comparison with other regions and with the nation as a whole. With increasing concern for the quality of life, education, entertainment, travel-related, and other industries and occupations will increase more rapidly than will goods production, and particularly production of durable goods, in which Northeastern Ohio predominates. In the second place, Northeastern Ohio generally does not have its proportional share of the "growth" industries—the sophisticated electronics, aerospace, or similar industries that require highly educated personnel and that carry on extensive research and development activities. Those parts of the nation that can offer greater amenities, including climate, have witnessed greater growth of those types of industries than has Northeastern Ohio. Nevertheless, in recent years, several of the region's industries have established or increased research and development activities, with a significant number of research laboratories and other facilities, especially in the suburban areas from Cleveland to Akron, as well as in the fringe areas around some of the other cities.

There is little doubt, however, that the large scale industries that have constituted the principal impetus for urbanization in Northeastern Ohio for the past century will continue to be dominant in the region. They are, however, faced with some serious challenges. One is the fact that, in some instances, the optimal-sized plant for achieving maximum economies of scale may be smaller now than in the past, as the result of technological change. At the same time, there is a tendency in such industries to establish plants closer to the markets, so that the traditional centers of the industries may face relative, if not absolute, decline. Automobile assembly plants are now scattered. The tire industry is gradually deconcentrating toward the automobile assembly plants for marketing of original equipment and to the more rapidly growing populous areas for distribution of replacements. The metalworking industries are also following their industrial customers, who, in turn, tend to move with the general population movements.

Other conditions combine with those men-

tioned above to challenge the dominant industries of Northeastern Ohio. Plant sites for the
heavy primary metal industries are scarce: they
generally require large tracts of land on water
bodies. The lower Cuyahoga valley is filled with
industries, and many of their facilities are old
and increasingly noncompetitive. Modernization of the plants is difficult, for many facilities would have to be shut down for long
periods while replacement on the same site
took place, and meanwhile production would
be lost to competitors. This problem is reflected and accentuated by the establishment and
expansion of huge steel works in other regions.
The petroleum and petrochemical industries
face a similar problem. In addition, the recent
emphasis upon environmental quality involves
very substantial expenditures by industry in
order to reduce, and hopefully to eliminate, air
and water pollution. It is usually more economic and practicable to design new plants to
incorporate provisions for environmental quality control than to refit older plants. Thus,
there is an added incentive to phase out the
older marginal and submarginal plants in favor
of new ones, usually at new locations.

Finally, many of the industries of Northeastern Ohio are inefficient, high cost industries,
not only because of plant and product obsolescence, but also because of high relative
costs of labor.

Many of the semiskilled and skilled members
of the labor force are highly unionized, and, in
spite of a high level of skill and long experience,
their high wage rates in some instances create a
regional comparative disadvantage. Many of the
labor practices in Northeastern Ohio industry
reflect technological and other conditions of
the past. In numerous instances, these practices
produce higher costs for industry than they
would incur in other regions. While it is often
true that substantial differentials among regions with respect to labor costs and efficiency
are, in the long run, reduced or eliminated, the
short run effects may include outmigration or
unfavorable rates of growth among regions as,
for example, in the movement of the textile
industry from New England to the South a
generation ago, and in the virtual termination
of the meatpacking industry in Chicago a
decade ago. Some of the important industries
in Northeastern Ohio face similar threats now.

Finally, the recent and current emphasis

upon the employment of previously disadvantaged minority groups, particularly blacks
and Spanish-Americans, as evidenced by equal
opportunity and "affirmative action" programs,
is causing a shift in industrial location, to the
general disadvantage of Northeastern Ohio,
and especially to the central cities and inner
suburban industrial communities of the region.
Industrialists are extremely unwilling to discuss
this, for obvious reasons. Consequently, typical
questionnaire and interview surveys never
openly reveal the relationships between minorities and industrial location trends, but
there is without doubt a close relationship.
Since Northeastern Ohio is predominantly a
region in which blue collar occupations, often
involving relatively low levels of skills, predominate, the region has long attracted immigrants,
not only among blacks and Spanish-Americans,
but also among Appalachian whites, who have
also been occupationally and educationally disadvantaged. Since the disadvantaged tend to be
somewhat higher in proportion to the total
population in Northeastern Ohio than in some
other regions, this factor may contribute toward
the slower rate of industrial growth here than
elsewhere.

At the intrametropolitan scale, since the disadvantaged tend to concentrate in the older
areas of the cities rather than toward the newer
peripheral areas, some industrialists tend to locate their plants as far as practicable from the
concentrations of the disadvantaged and minority populations. This further accentuates
the economic, cultural, and social differences
between inner city areas on the one hand and
the peripheral and suburban areas on the other.
Public transportation in many of the urbanized
areas of Northeastern Ohio is insufficient to
compensate for the increased spatial separation
between the concentrations of minority population that constitute prospective labor pools,
on the one hand, and the outlying and suburban locations of new and extensive industry,
on the other. Thus, these considerations combine with other less subtle ones to contribute
to the deconcentration of industry from inner
city areas and the more rapid rate of industrial
growth outside the central cities.

In summary, Northeastern Ohio is a mature
region whose population and industrial growth
has in recent years been at a somewhat slower
rate than that of the nation as a whole. Al-

though its basic heavy industries will probably dominate in the region's economic base for many years to come, the indications are that service industries and occupations, as elsewhere, will grow faster than manufacturing of durable goods, which are no longer the "growth" industries. The recent awareness of the magnitude of the fuel shortage underscores the seriousness of Northeastern Ohio's heavy dependence upon automobiles, trucks, and highways, both as sources of employment and as the overwhelmingly dominant mode of intraregional transportation. The region's industrial complex is especially vulnerable, since a high proportion of its basic industries depend for their markets upon manufacture of motor vehicles. On the other hand, Northeastern Ohio must compete with many other regions for most nondurable goods production and for service employment. In this competition, its location in the middle of the continent's principal urban-industrial belt can be an advantage if its people and industries are sufficiently innovative.

The Physical Setting of the Cleveland and Akron Urbanized Areas

TERRAIN AND URBAN PATTERN OF CLEVELAND AND CUYAHOGA COUNTY

The terrain within Cleveland and Cuyahoga County has been important to a much greater degree than in many other cities in the pattern of physical development and the arrangement of land uses and functions. The principal features that have been instrumental in the shaping of the city's pattern, in addition to the Lake Erie shoreline, are (1) the Cuyahoga valley, which bisects the city and divides it into eastern and western segments; (2) the Appalachian Plateau and its borders, including the bluffs paralleling Lake Erie; and (3) the other streams flowing in deep valleys to Lake Erie (Chagrin River, Euclid Creek, Doan Brook, and Rocky River (Figure 4). The deeply incised valleys of the Rocky River west of the city and the Chagrin River to the east are both crossed by high level bridges that link the city with some of its outer suburban areas.

The Cuyahoga Valley

The Cuyahoga valley itself is a major barrier within the city. In addition to many low level bridges, some of which are movable to permit passage of lake vessels in the lower six miles of the river, there are a few high level bridges, some approaching a mile in length, that join the two portions of the city and, south of the city, the southwesterly and southeasterly suburban areas. In northern Summit County, the valley is crossed by two pairs of high level via-ducts that carry Interstate 271 and the Ohio Turnpike. Closer to Cleveland, another pair of long, high viaducts is currently under construction to carry an additional east-west interstate freeway. The lower portion of the Cuyahoga River meanders across a low, flat delta, known locally as "The Flats," which is the site of many of Cleveland's heavy industries, including its primary steel plants, chemical and paint manufacturing plants, and oil refineries and tank farms. The lower six miles of the river are maintained as a federal navigation project, with a twenty-three foot channel for lake vessels. The largest lake vessels are excluded and handled at lakefront bulk terminals. The original mouth of the river was nearly a mile west of the present river entrance, which is artificial. The original lower channel is filled in lakeward, and separates a peninsula, incorrectly but popularly known as Whiskey Island, from the mainland.

Moses Cleaveland platted Cleveland's central business district, which focuses upon the public square, on the upland spur between Lake Erie and the lower Cuyahoga. The CBD is confined by bluffs to the northeast and southwest to a triangular area. Immediately across the Flats, on the westerly upland and centering upon West 25th Street, is the original business district of what, until 1854, was a separate municipality, Ohio City. The area is now linked to downtown Cleveland by high level bridges across the Flats.

Some of the principal tributaries of the Cuyahoga to the east and west are partially in

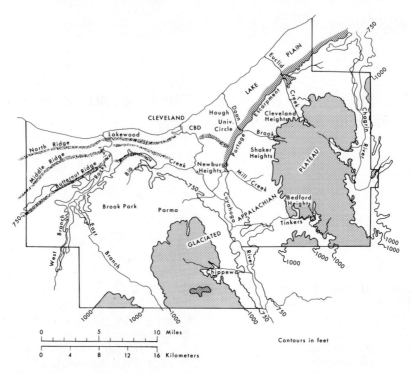

Figure 4. Major physiographic features of Cleveland and Cuyahoga County.

public park reservation. Others have been utilized as routes for railroad lines and highways. Big Creek, the northernmost major westerly tributary, partly in park land, is the locus of a branch of the B&O Railroad and, more importantly, the route of Interstate 71, Cleveland's principal highway to Hopkins Airport, the westerly portion of the Ohio Turnpike, Columbus, and other southwesterly cities. Mill Creek, which extends through the lowland into the southeasterly suburbs, is an industrial locus, and mainline railroads occupy a portion of its valley. Tinkers Creek, the dominant tributary flowing into the Cuyahoga from the east, has a deeply entrenched valley, which is in part reserved for a portion of the Cleveland Metropolitan Park District. Chippewa and Brandywine Creek valleys, west and east of the Cuyahoga, respectively, are still wooded and may constitute part of the proposed national park, which would include the Cuyahoga valley between Akron and the southern limit of the present Cleveland suburban industrial development.

All of these streams have deep valleys, V-shaped in their upper courses and flat-bottomed near Lake Erie, where the meanders of the streams have cut steep-sided slopes exposing the horizontal sedimentary rocks of the Allegheny Plateau. Of the three major rivers in metropolitan Cleveland that flow generally northward into Lake Erie, only the lower Cuyahoga has a valley sufficiently wide and flat to permit extensive industrial development. Here access by lake shipping has facilitated primary manufacturing, but at the same time has, until recent restrictions were instituted, encouraged industry to use the river as a disposal facility for its liquid and solid wastes. In addition, the Flats area, in spite of the largely artificial channel, is not accessible to the largest lake and ocean vessels because of restricted depths and, more especially, because of the sharp meanders. One meander, close to downtown Cleveland, is called "Collision Bend."

The Appalachian Plateau and its Borders

The upland, with horizontal rocks laid down in an ancient ocean some 400 million years ago and subsequently uplifted, constitutes a portion of the vast Allegheny Plateau. The surface is gently to moderately rolling and consists in part of glacial deposits, which were scoured out from what became the Great Lakes basin by the continental glaciers, the last of which receded from the area a few thousand years ago. The southern limit of glaciation, marked by terminal moraine, is near Canton in the southern portion of the nine county area.

The northward-facing edge of the Appalachian Plateau is another dominant physical feature that has conditioned the pattern of occupance and development of the urban area. It is a steep bluff, as much as 250 feet in height, that separates the plateau from the Lake Erie coastal plain, and it is generally parallel to the lakeshore. East of the Cuyahoga valley, the differences in the character of development and occupance between the upland, on the one hand, and the lake plain, on the other, are very conspicuous. The low to lower middle income, high density residential areas of the lake plain communities of Glenville and Collinwood in Cleveland, and the contiguous suburb of East Cleveland, in recent years largely occupied by the immigrant black population, contrast sharply with the adjacent middle to upper class residential areas of the upland communities of Cleveland Heights, University Heights, Shaker Heights, and South Euclid. Only very recently have the inmigrant groups to any extent entered the upland suburban communities east of Cleveland proper. The northward-facing bluff itself is marked, in part, by open land uses—a major park and a cemetery, which separate Cleveland Heights from East Cleveland. The bluff itself is sometimes known as the Portage Escarpment, and locally as Murray Hill. Between the lakeshore and the escarpment, the mainline routes of the former New York Central (now Penn Central) and Nickel Plate (now Norfolk & Western) railroads between Chicago and Buffalo are the axes of a lineal development of industry. Lakeward of this industrial axis are middle to upper middle suburban areas, notably Euclid, whose residences, including recent high-rise apartment structures, command views over the lakeshore bluff.

West of the Cuyahoga, the bluff, which separates the lake plain from the plateau upland, is much less conspicuous. A short distance west of the river mouth and Whiskey Island, the bluff separates Edgewater Park, one of the few areas of public recreational access to the lake, from the Ohio City upland development. Through Lakewood, Rocky River, Bay Village, and other western suburbs, there are three terraces separated from one another by slopes facing northwest. Though generally parallel to the lakeshore, they diverge in a westerly direction. These slopes—old beach ridges—were formed in successive stages of the postglacial recession when drainage of the predecessor of Lake Erie, blocked by the retreating ice sheet in the St. Lawrence valley, was temporarily arrested for periods of a few hundred years each. This allowed beaches and sand dunes to form. These beach ridges, from south to north, are known as Butternut Ridge, Middle Ridge, and North Ridge. They separate the succession of steplike terraces, each of which in turn was formed as the bottom of the retreating postglacial lake. Being well drained and free from flooding each spring, they were used by the early settlers as loci for roads to the west and southwest. Today, a major road follows each of the ridges: Lorain Road (State Route 10) on the southernmost, Butternut Ridge; Center Ridge Road (U.S. 20) on Middle Ridge; and Detroit Road (Ohio 254) on North Ridge. Each of these roads forms the axis of a ribbon of commercial and other development to the west of Cleveland.

Chagrin River, Euclid Creek, Doan Brook, and Rocky River

West of Cleveland, the deep valley of Rocky River, about 150 feet below the upland and bordered by steep bluffs, is largely a county forest reservation. Similarly, the Chagrin River, east of Cleveland, is partially in public open space.

In addition to the three major northward-flowing rivers in the metropolitan area of Cleveland, there are two other streams that enter Lake Erie within the area—Euclid Creek and Doan Brook. Euclid Creek, the easterly of the two, has had little impact upon urban development, but Doan Brook, with its associated pattern of land uses, today is a major feature of the urban pattern, not only of the city of Cleveland, but also of the adjacent suburb of Shaker Heights. Within these two municipalities Doan Brook is the axis of continuous open space, largely in parks.

The Doan Brook park development is not

fortuitous. It resulted from the donations of five men—William J. Gordon, John D. Rockefeller, Jephtha H. Wade, and the Van Sweringen Brothers. The first three made their fortunes in Cleveland in the late nineteenth century and established country estates along the brook. When the spreading city, extending along the axes of the major streets, such as Euclid Avenue, reached and surrounded their properties, they each donated their estates to the city for park purposes. The present parks, named for their donors, form a continuous strip from Gordon Park, bordering the mouth of the brook at the Lake Erie shore, through Rockefeller Park, separating the communities of Hough to the west and Glenville to the east, to the municipal border of Cleveland, beyond which the chain of parks continues into Shaker Heights.

Wade Park is an especially noteworthy focus within Cleveland. It is the core of an area known as University Circle, which is the principal concentration of Cleveland's cultural institutions, four miles from downtown. Here are Case Western Reserve University, the Art Museum, the Cleveland Institute of Art, Natural History Museum, Historical Society Museum, several major religious institutions, and Severance Hall, home of the famed Cleveland Orchestra. Cleveland is almost unique among large cities in that the major cultural institutions are located not downtown and not scattered, but concentrated in one area. Only the Cleveland Public Library remains downtown. Wade Park, in spite of deteriorated residential surroundings in Hough and Glenwood, is a magnificent setting for these institutions. Some years ago, in an attempt to arrest and reverse the decline of the surrounding areas, the institutions formed the University Circle Foundation and proposed a comprehensive plan for redevelopment of the nearby areas. Although some of the institutions expanded into new structures, the University Circle plan aborted for financial reasons. Today, Wade Park stands as the principal buttress against the further encroachment of deterioration.

Two small streams in parallel courses make up the headwaters of Doan Brook. Both streams have been dammed to form artificial lakes—the Shaker Lakes—which, together with the connecting stream courses, are maintained as parks within the city of Shaker Heights.

Shaker Heights, a middle to upper income residential suburb, contains some of the largest and highest cost residential properties within the metropolitan area. It originated as a large scale real estate development by O.P. and M.J. Van Sweringen after 1906. Urbanization in the city of Shaker Heights proceeded rapidly until the occurrence of the Great Depression in 1929 and resumed after World War II. The development of eastern Shaker Heights is still continuing in the 1970s. The lakes form major attractions within the community, and there are rigid controls of density and architecture throughout the portion of Shaker Heights adjacent to the lakes.

Some of Cleveland's more affluent families have moved east of Shaker Heights, to the Chagrin valley, where large estates in Gates Mills and Hunting Valley border the public park reservations.

In general, Cleveland is a metropolitan area with an attractive variety of relief and with alternative choices of natural environment. The situation will perpetuate as long as appropriate programs for scenic conservation are realized.

Local Climates

Of some importance to the residential pattern of metropolitan Cleveland are the local climates within the area. Summers tend to be hot; winters are moderately cold, but generally with heavy cloud cover. Two local climatic conditions are of some significance: the effects of proximity to Lake Erie are related to both. The lake tends somewhat to moderate the extremes of winter cold and summer heat for several miles inland, especially in the easterly portion of the metropolitan area, where the shoreline is nearly at right angles to the direction of the prevailing northwesterly winds. On the other hand, the orientation of the shoreline with respect to the winds causes the formation of a prominent "snow belt" in the easterly suburbs. The snow belt is a short distance inland from the lake and is beyond the escarpment that parallels the shore. Picking up moisture from passage over the Great Lakes, the winds become saturated. When the winds hit the shore and then rise over the escarpment, they tend to cause heavier precipitation in the easterly suburbs. The resulting snow belt represents the western end of an extensive belt, which extends for several hundred miles in a narrow band paralleling the northeasterly trending shore of Lake Erie and the south shore of Lake Ontario, from Cleveland to upstate New York. Frequently, during winter storms, heavy snowfall in some of Cleveland's eastern suburbs causes some inconvenience and disruption of transportation, when areas to the west and south may be free of snow.

THE AKRON AREA SETTING

The word "Akron" is from the Greek *akros,* which means "high," and Akron is the central city of Summit County. These names indicate the essential physical characteristic of the Akron urban area: it is located astride the drainage divide between the streams flowing northward into Lake Erie, which drains northeastward through the St. Lawrence to the Atlantic Ocean, and those flowing southward to the Ohio River and, thence, down the Mississippi River to the Gulf of Mexico. The Akron area is on the subcontinental divide (Figure 5). Most of the city of Akron and its nearby easterly suburban area is within the drainage basin of the Cuyahoga River. The western and southern suburban areas drain into the Tuscarawas. Akron's location on the drainage divide has had a major bearing upon its history and is reflected in its present pattern of land uses and activities.

The Cuyahoga River, with headwaters in Geauga County to the northeast of the Akron area, flows southwesterly and makes a U-shaped turn in the northern part of Akron. From this point, it flows northward through a deep and scenic valley and enters Lake Erie just west of downtown Cleveland. Its largest tributary, the Little Cuyahoga, flows generally west and northwest to join the Cuyahoga in northern Akron. Both rivers flow through gorges, where they have eroded steep-sided bluffs in the horizontal sedimentary rock formations, at several points. Some stretches of these gorges constitute the axes of major units in the Akron Metropolitan Park District, which has been instrumental in preserving much of the scenic value of the streams and their valleys. On the other hand, the gorges have presented problems in the internal development of the cities and towns. They have necessitated, in some instances, the construction of long, high level bridges and viaducts to connect the upland spurs.

The Cuyahoga valley was the original transportation corridor between Akron and Cleveland. The Ohio and Erie Canal, which connected Akron and Cleveland in 1827, was the original impetus for the founding of Akron. The canal is still visible for most of its course. In downtown Akron, it passes under some of the buildings, and the masonry walls of the original canal locks are still in place in certain segments of the route. A branch canal follows the course of the upper Cuyahoga to just above Kent, where it strikes overland, across the drainage divide at Ravenna, to a connection eastward with the upper tributaries of the Mahoning and Ohio rivers.

The Cuyahoga River itself, relatively unpolluted in its upper course as far as Akron, is in part a series of pools, behind multiple purpose dams. One of these, just northeast of Kent, forms Lake Rockwell, a major unit in Akron's water supply system. Another, at Cuyahoga Falls, is the site of a small hydroelectric power plant.

Downtown Akron occupies a low point in the drainage divide, a col that was utilized by the canal in climbing, by a series of locks, to the summit of the divide in the southwestern portion of the city, where Summit Lake supplied much of the water for the canal, which flowed from there in both directions. South of the city, the Portage Lakes, a chain of "kettle" lakes formed mainly by glaciation but partly augmented by artificial reservoirs, also supplied water to the canal. Today those lakes constitute nodes of attractive residential development along their shores, with water-based recreation and a small state park fronting on one of the lakes. From Akron, a valley trending southwestward constitutes a transportation corridor to and beyond the industrial satellite suburb of Barberton, which is characterized by a number of chemical and fabricating plants. The corridor, originally the route of the canal, is followed between Akron and Barberton by the three railroads serving Akron—The Erie Lackawanna, Chessie System (B&O), and the Penn Central.

The valley in central Akron, trending northeast-southwest, together with the transportation access, is closely articulated with the local street pattern, which is rectangular, oriented to the axis of the valley. Main Street parallels the

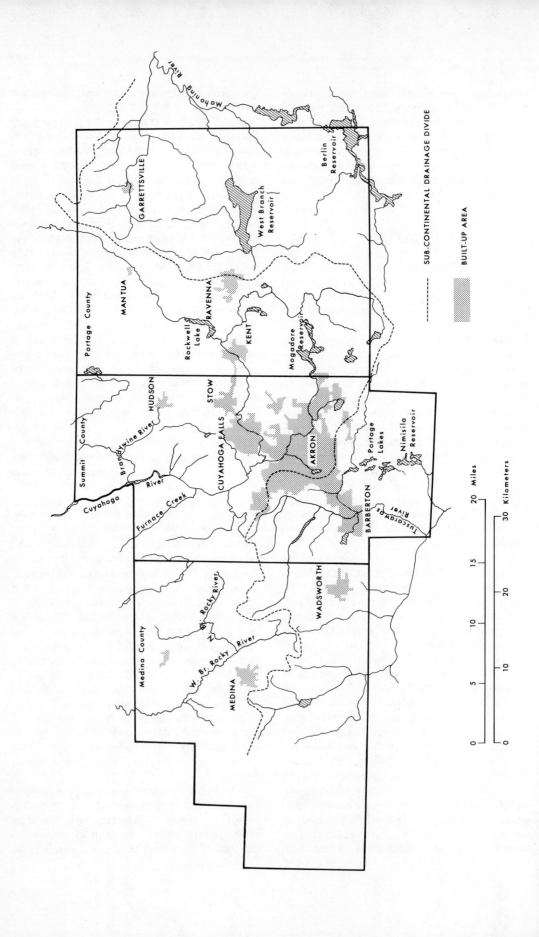

SUB-CONTINENTAL DRAINAGE DIVIDE

BUILT-UP AREA

canal route a few hundred yards to the east and represents an important deviation from the general pattern of the streets of the city and region, which are oriented to the rectangular land survey.

In general, then, the Akron urbanized region can be characterized physically as a moderately rolling upland surface, bisected by a sub-continental drainage divide and interrupted by relatively deep, steep-sided stream valleys. It contains numerous lakes, some artificial and some natural, the latter as the result of glaciation.

Figure 5. Major physiographic features of Akron metropolitan area.

The Changing Ethnic and Racial Pattern of Cleveland and Akron

Both Cleveland and Akron are characterized by a high degree of ethnic and racial segregation, and by rapid changes in the occupancy of many of their neighborhoods and communities. The conflicts between the expanding black population and the adjacent areas with concentrations of white ethnic populations exploded in 1966 and 1968 in violence. In Cleveland the balance of political power between the white ethnics and the black population has dominated the political scene during the past decade. Cleveland was one of the first two major American cities, and by far the largest of the two, to elect a black mayor, but at the end of his second two year term he was replaced by a white ethnic. In Cleveland, there is a conspicuous dichotomy between the East Side of the city, with an expanding area of predominantly black population, which now extends into some of the contiguous inner suburban area, and the West Side, which is predominantly white ethnic. In Akron a similar segregation exists, differing from that of Cleveland mainly in scale.

POPULATION SHIFTS IN THE CITY OF CLEVELAND AND ITS SUBURBS

The increasing industrial and commercial activity in the late nineteenth and early twentieth centuries brought to the city many thousands of immigrants in search of employment. By 1900, three-quarters of the city's population was either foreign born or had foreign-born or mixed parents. Throughout the early twentieth century, immigrants coming to Cleveland were primarily from areas now included in five nations—Poland, Hungary, Germany, Czechoslovakia, and Italy. The immigrants were separated from the older residents of the area, many of whom had New England origins, by language, by customs, and often by religion, and they were shut off from political power. As a result, they often settled in ethnic enclaves in and around downtown that were and are contiguous to the industrial activity of the Cuyahoga valley (Figure 6). Eventually the immigrants gained some political power, but their ethnic loyalties and in many instances their enclaves remained.

The next major immigration into the Cleveland area was that of blacks from the Deep South and Appalachia during the 1940s. The black residents of the city have since expanded rapidly. By 1970 over 38.0 percent of Cleveland's total population was black, almost all of its east of the Cuyahoga valley. The original concentrations of blacks were in the central neighborhoods (Figure 7a). From here, the black population expanded to the northeast through the Hough and Glenville areas (Figures 7b and 7c) and, during the 1960s, into the suburban East Cleveland area (Figure 7d). The black population also expanded from the central neighborhoods to the southeast through the Kinsman, Woodland Hills, Mt. Pleasant, Corlett, and Lee-Miles areas and, during the 1960s, into the contiguous suburban communities of Cleveland Heights and Shaker Heights (Figures 8 and 9). Black immigrants into the city from the

Figure 6. Communities in Cleveland (including Lakewood, East Cleveland, and Bratenahl). Source: Michael Papp, *Ethnic Communities of Cleveland*, (Cleveland State University, 1971).

southern states came to the neighborhoods close to the city's center, while blacks who have been residents of the city for a longer time tend to migrate to the predominantly black areas in the northeast and southeast corners of the city or to the contiguous suburbs. The path of expansion of the black population from the central area has largely followed the path of expansion of the city's Jewish population.

The first Jewish concentration was that of the early immigrants, primarily from Germany and Hungary, between 1839 and the 1880s, in the central neighborhoods. These early Jewish settlers were overwhelmed in the early years of the twentieth century by the flood of immigrants from Eastern Europe, who located in the Central neighborhood; by World War I the Jewish population of Cleveland was estimated to be 60,000. From this origin, the center of the Jewish population in the city shifted, in succession, to the Glenville, Kinsman, Mt. Pleasant, and Lee-Miles areas. Today, the Jewish population, although partly dispersed, is heavily concentrated in the suburbs of Cleveland Heights, Shaker Heights, Mayfield Heights, and Beachwood. Black migration has generally occupied the homes vacated by Jewish residents

who were headed for suburban communities. Even today, the black population of the area is expanding into the suburbs of Cleveland Heights and Shaker Heights.

The major cluster of black residents on Cleveland's West Side occurs in one census tract in the Puritas-Bellaire neighborhood. This concentration, however, has not expanded for decades. It originally consisted of railroad employees who worked or reported for work in the nearby railroad yard. In addition, there are some blacks in the Near West Side who are mainly occupants of two public housing projects.

The ethnic enclaves of the city since World War II have largely constituted barriers to the expansion of the black community. Particularly strong barriers existed in the Collinwood, Norwood, Broadway, Woodland Hills, and University neighborhoods—all with ethnics representing more than 30 percent of the total population (with the exception of the University neighborhood in which ethnics make up 23.0 percent). Yet, within the past decade, the barriers to the black population—especially in the Woodland Hills, South Collinwood, and Norwood neighborhoods—have loosened. This

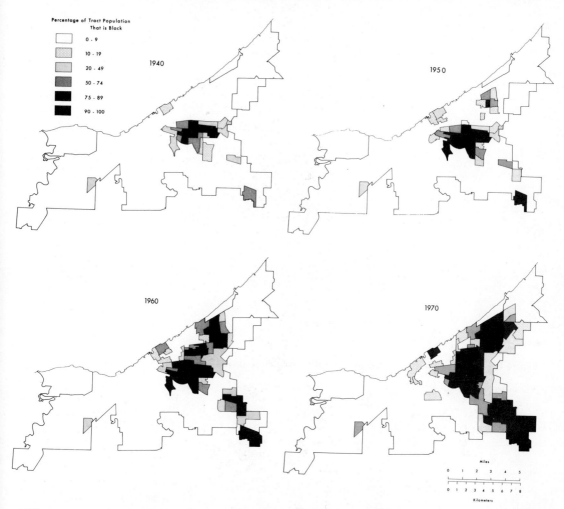

Figure 7. (a, b, c, d) Black population as a percentage of tract population: Cleveland, Lakewood, Bratenahl, and East Cleveland. Source: U.S. Bureau of the Census.

is a result of the breakup of certain ethnic neighborhoods with the migration of the younger generation to the surrounding suburbs. The movement of blacks into these formerly ethnic strongholds constitutes an expansion of the city's predominately black areas and not an integration of blacks and white ethnics.

The city has experienced a much smaller influx of Spanish-speaking and Appalachian white populations. These people have located primarily in the Near West Side, Tremont, and Goodrich neighborhoods. Many Appalachians, but not Spanish-speaking people, have located in the North Broadway area. Throughout the city, the neighborhoods of blacks and Spanish-Americans are distinct and physically separate.

THE PREDOMINATELY BLACK COMMUNITIES OF CLEVELAND

The Cuyahoga River represents more than a physical boundary between the West and East sides of Cleveland. With a few exceptions, it is the boundary between the predominately white communities and the predominately black areas. However, at present, the latter do not constitute a homogeneous grouping. As the black community has expanded during the past three decades, blacks who could afford to have begun to occupy areas away from the original nodes of black immigration. The Cleveland City Planning Commission, in a study of 2,000 individuals who had moved between 1965 and

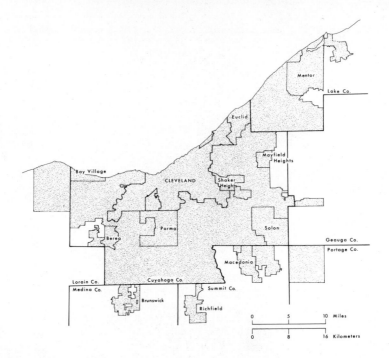

Figure 8. Cleveland urbanized area and suburban communities.

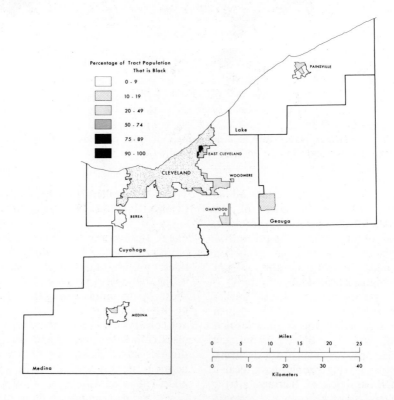

Figure 9. Black population as a percentage of tract population, Cleveland suburban area, 1970.

1970, established the following results. Approximately 90 percent of those who had moved into the Mt. Pleasant, Corlett, and Woodland Hills communities between 1965 and 1970 came from the central or downtown areas. Approximately 45 percent of those who had moved into the Lee-Miles community during the same time period came from Mt. Pleasant, Corlett, and Woodland Hills. Approximately 64 percent of those who had moved into Glenville during the same time period came from the Hough and Central areas. As mentioned, blacks have moved, as well, into the contiguous suburbs of East Cleveland, Cleveland Heights, and Shaker Heights.

The newer areas of black migration within the city limits—especially Corlett, Mt. Pleasant, and Lee-Miles, and to a lesser degree Glenville—are significantly different from the older black areas (Central, Central West, Central East, Kinsman, and Hough) in a number of respects. For instance, larger percentages of black families in the newer communities are homeowners. An average of 88.65 percent of the families in the Lee-Miles census tract own their homes while in the census tracts of the Central West area an average of only 3.17 percent own their homes. The older predominately black areas have high vacancy rates, as census tracts in such areas average a vacancy rate of over 10 percent. In the Hough area alone, the vacancy rate is 16 percent. In the newer black neighborhoods the rates are substantially lower. Not only are the vacancy rates higher in the older areas, but more of the units are substandard. Census tracts in the older community areas average at least 7 percent of all housing units with incomplete plumbing facilities. In the majority of newer predominately black areas, this is a problem in less than 1 percent of all housing units. The only significant new construction since World War II throughout the entire predominately black area occurred in the Lee-Miles community, where 15 percent of all houses were built since 1960. In the Central West community, 9 percent of the housing units were built since 1960, mainly in urban renewal projects, including multiple unit public housing. On the other hand, the construction in the Lee-Miles area was single family detached units. In short, as black residents have moved outward from the city's center, a vacuum has developed with many vacant and substandard units.

The black residents of Glenville, Lee-Miles,

Corlett, and Mt. Pleasant have higher employment rate and higher status occupations than the residents of the older black-occupied areas. Unemployment among males sixteen years of age and older in the newer predominately black areas averaged about 5 percent at the time of the 1970 census, while unemployment among males in the older black communities averaged over 11 percent. The situation for female employment was similar. A higher percentage of the workers in the newer black areas are professionals or managers than are the workers of the older black areas. More of the workers in the older black communities are employed as laborers or service workers. Financially, families in the newer black areas are better off than families in the older black areas. Census tracts in the older neighborhoods average more than 16 percent of all families with income less than 50 percent of the poverty level. The corresponding figure for the new black areas is 5 percent. Furthermore, census tracts in the new neighborhoods average more than 40 percent of all families with income more than three times the poverty level. The corresponding figure for older neighborhoods is 20 percent.

CLEVELAND'S WHITE
ETHNIC AREAS

Like the black communities of the East Side, the white communities of the West Side are not homogeneous. The Near West Side, Tremont, Clark-Fulton, Jefferson, and Denison areas were nearly completely built up before World War II. The new construction on the city's West Side has concentrated in the Riverside, Puritas-Bellaire, South Brooklyn, and Edgewater neighborhoods. As on the East Side, there is a tendency on the West Side for residents to move from neighborhoods close to the city's center to more distant areas. In addition, there is little movement within the city from the East Side to the West Side or vice versa. The Cleveland City Planning Commission reports that 30 percent of those who had moved into the West Side or Jefferson communities between 1965 and 1970 came from the Near West Side or Tremont areas. Over 42 percent of those who had moved into the Clark-Fulton and Denison areas between 1965 and 1970 came from the Near West Side or Tremont areas. Approximately 50 percent of those who had moved into the Puritas-Bellaire or Riverside communities between 1965 and 1970 came from the Near West Side, Tremont, Clark-Fulton, Denison, West Side, or Jefferson communities.

The obvious movement of individuals away from the close-in neighborhoods (primarily the Near West Side and Tremont areas) can be explained in terms of the social and economic differences between those communities and the outlying communities. The close-in neighborhoods average only 25 percent of the families who own their home, while the outlying communities have over 50 percent homeowners. In fact, the census tracts in the Puritas-Bellaire and Riverside community area average in excess of 75 percent homeownership. The vacancy rate in the Tremont and Near West Side areas is not as great as on the East Side. Nevertheless, it is more substantial than the vacancy rate in the outlying portions on the West Side. The same situation applies to the percentage of dwelling units in the Tremont and Near West Side areas without complete plumbing facilities. Approximately 6 percent of the housing units in Tremont and the Near West Side fall into these categories, while an average of only 1 percent of the housing units in the outlying areas are deficient. In short, the Tremont and Near West Side areas have substantial vacancies and substandard housing.

Many residents who had sufficient finances have fled the area. Indeed, since World War II there has been a large influx of Spanish-speaking population. In both areas, the Spanish-Americans comprise more than 10 percent of the population. They are generally more mobile, have higher unemployment rates, and are poorer than the outlying residents on the West Side. For example, unemployment among males sixteen and over in the Tremont and Near West Side areas averaged over 7 percent at the time of the 1970 census, while the corresponding figure for the outlying communities was between 2 and 3 percent. Census tracts in the Near West Side and Tremont areas also average more than 6 percent of all families with incomes less than 50 percent of the poverty level. Census tracts in the outlying areas averaged 2 percent.

The outlying neighborhoods on the West Side have large concentrations—in all cases more than 25 percent of the total population—of foreign-born whites or native whites of foreign or mixed parentage. The major ethnic

groups of the Clark-Fulton, Denison, and South Brooklyn areas are Czechoslovakians, Italians, Germans, and Polish (Figure 10). The major ethnic groups of the West Side, Jefferson, Puritas-Bellaire, and Riverside community areas are German, Hungarian, Czechoslovakian, Italian, and Irish in origin.

In sum, the Tremont and Near West Side areas are substantially below the outlying areas of the West Side with regard to a number of social and economic characteristics. However, the conditions in both the Tremont and Near West Side areas are appreciably better than those in the Central community areas of the East Side. In Riverside, Puritas-Bellaire, and Edgewater there are concentrations of the city's highest-priced housing. For example, along the shores of Lake Erie in the Edgewater area, as well as in the contiguous suburb of Lakewood, there is a series of impressive high-rise apartment buildings, many residents of which hold important positions in the city's major business organizations.

As mentioned earlier, many white ethnic communities on the East Side of Cleveland have dissipated, leaving a vacuum into which the blacks expand. Nevertheless, there are still some very tightly knit white ethnic strongholds on the city's East Side. The North Broadway and South Broadway areas are among them. There has been little expansion of the black population of the Kinsman and Corlett areas into the Broadway communities. Over 32 percent of the population of both Broadway communities is of foreign stock. There the major ethnic groups are Polish, Czechoslovakian, and Italian. The two communities are very old, over 90 percent of the housing units having been built before 1939. Yet few of the dwellings are either substandard or vacant. The areas are occupied mainly by blue collar workers with middle incomes.

Two additional ethnic strongholds on the city's East Side, the Collinwood and University communities, have become focal points for incidences of racial tension during the past decade as the ethnic groups felt that the expanding black community threatened their neighborhoods. The Collinwood and University areas—particularly an area within the University community called Murray Hill—have large concentrations of persons of Italian origin. Both the University and Collinwood areas are older residential areas with many blue collar workers,

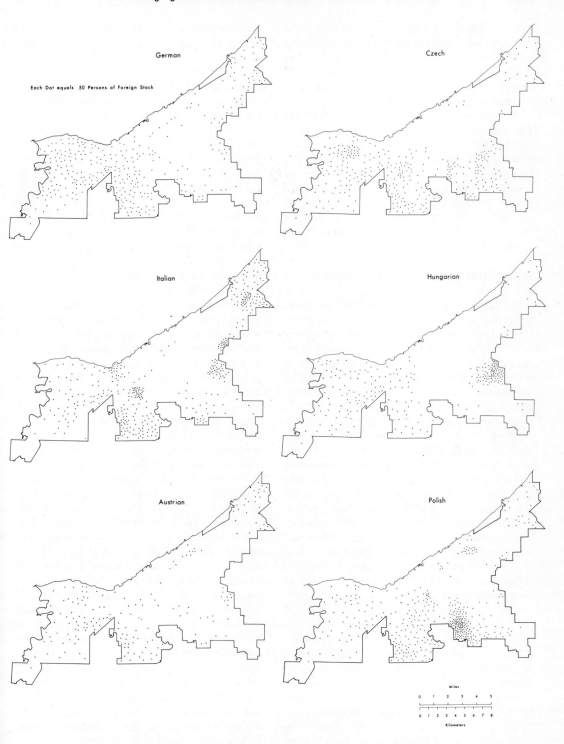

Figure 10. Ethnic concentrations in Cleveland. One dot equals fifty persons.

many of whom are employed in the steel mills and auto factories. The University area includes Case Western Reserve University and other institutions. The university has expanded into the ethnic neighborhoods, and this constitutes a source of friction.

In summary, although there has been a considerable erosion of the ethnic concentrations on the city's East Side, followed by the expansion of the black community, strong ethnic communities do remain. Many ethnic individuals have achieved financial security and moved to suburban areas. Other ethnics, with inadequate incomes or with strong feelings toward community identity, have remained in the city.

SUBURBAN AREAS OF CLEVELAND

Extending outward in every landward direction from the city of Cleveland are numerous suburbs. Many have high income and high status families and some of these contain large numbers of white ethnics. The suburban black population constitutes a majority of the total population in East Cleveland, and a smaller, but not inconsequential, percentage of the total population in Cleveland Heights, Shaker Heights, Warrensville Township, Garfield Heights, Maple Heights, Bedford, and Woodmere (Figure 9). These suburban communities form a wedge extending northeast, east, and southeast from the predominantly black-populated areas which they adjoin in the eastern portions of the city of Cleveland. The movement of blacks into East Cleveland was accompanied by an exodus of whites from that suburb, such that by the early 1970s little integration existed in East Cleveland. There have been some efforts to maintain "neighborhood balance" in Cleveland Heights and Shaker Heights in order to reduce white residents' fears of "declining property values." The efforts have initially been mildly successful, although insufficient time has passed to test their long term effectiveness.

Many suburban communities constitute strongholds for white ethnic groups. In many suburbs over 30 percent of the total 1970 population was of foreign stock. Two leading ethnic groups in many suburbs south of Cleveland originated in areas that are now parts of Czechoslovakia and Poland. A leading ethnic group in many west side and east side suburbs

is of German origin. The leading foreign origins of the population in the suburban areas, as a whole, in order of magnitude, are Italian, Polish, Czechoslovakian, German, Russian, Hungarian, British, Austrian, and Irish.

As in most American metropolitan areas, the present suburbs were largely developed within the post–World War II period. In 1939 the following suburbs had over half their present housing already constructed—East Cleveland, parts of Shaker Heights, Chagrin Falls, parts of Berea, and Kirtland Hills. In contrast, over three-fourths of the present housing units in the city of Cleveland antedated 1939. Since the end of World War II, the bulk of the area's new housing construction has occurred in the suburban areas. By contrast, in Cleveland only 6 percent of the existing housing units have been built since 1960.

In addition, the suburban areas tend to have higher percentages of families owning their homes. In Cleveland, only 43 percent of the housing units were owner-occupied, whereas in Cuyahoga County outside Cleveland 68.6 percent were owner-occupied. Furthermore, the vacancy rates are lower in the suburban areas than in Cleveland—2.4 percent as contrasted with 6 percent in Cleveland.

Family incomes in most suburbs are substantially higher than in Cleveland. In no suburban area was the mean 1970 income lower than $10,000. A noteworthy wedge of very high income prestigious suburbs—including Shaker Heights, Warrensville, Beachwood, Pepper Pike, Gates Mills, Hunting Valley, and Chagrin Falls—extends east from the eastern city limit of Cleveland to and beyond the Chagrin valley. In each of these suburbs the mean 1970 family income exceeded $20,000. In fact, mean family income in Hunting Valley reached $49,509. The occupations of the suburban workers tend to cluster in the higher status managerial and professional areas. In the following suburbs more than 50 percent of the employed persons are engaged in managerial or professional occupations—Shaker Heights, University Heights, Pepper Pike, Chagrin Falls, and Moreland Hills. In Cleveland, approximately 12 percent of the workers are engaged in such occupations.

Thus, the suburban area of Cuyahoga County resembles that surrounding many other American cities in that the incomes, occupational status, and age and quality of housing tend to be considerably higher or better than in the central city. Another resemblance is in the existence of a conspicuously prestigious extremely high status wedge of suburbs, in this instance extending in an easterly direction. As in many other metropolitan areas, some of the inner suburbs have recently experienced rapid population change as the predominantly black-occupied area has extended beyond the central city municipal boundary.

THE POLITICAL DYNAMICS OF CLEVELAND

During and since the 1960s, Cleveland has experienced the political awakening of the black community. Initially powerless and unorganized, the black population became united on certain objectives and achieved some notable results.

In the early 1960s, the leaders of the black community engaged in various protests (sit-ins, boycotts, etc.) to stimulate the School Board to promote integration. When, in January 1964, the black protests centered upon the Murray Hill School in "Little Italy," fighting broke out as various whites attacked blacks who were driving through the neighborhood. The black protests against segregation were unsuccessful. Furthermore, shortly after the incident, the Cleveland School Board pledged to "upgrade the quality of neighborhood schools" instead of promoting integration. Such pledges seemed temporarily to placate the black leaders, who increasingly were becoming more interested in "black power" and less in integration.

In the November 1965 election for mayor of the city, Carl B. Stokes, a black, ran as an Independent against Ralph S. Locher, the white incumbent Democratic mayor. Although Stokes lost the election by a slim margin, his participation in the election gave hope to the black residents that a black mayor of Cleveland was a realistic possibility.

Cleveland's first serious racial riot occurred in the summer of 1966 in the Hough community. For a week during July, large sections of Hough were destroyed. Looting, vandalism, and sniper fire were prevalent throughout. Over 2,000 National Guard troops were called in to quell the disturbance. Four black people were killed and there was extensive property damage.

The incident served further to polarize the black and white communities in the city.

During the summer of 1967, a number of major cities across the country had violent racial disturbances, yet Cleveland experienced no serious disorders. Perhaps the hopes of black residents were encouraged by the second effort of Carl B. Stokes who, in 1967, defeated Ralph S. Locher in the Democratic mayoral primary election as a result of a very high turnout of voters in the predominately black wards and only a moderate turnout in the predominately white wards. Stokes then narrowly defeated the Republican candidate, Seth B. Taft, a member of the nationally known Taft family, thus becoming the first black mayor of a major American city. In the 1967 election, Stokes received over 90 percent of the votes in the primarily black wards and approximately 20 percent of the votes in the predominantly white wards (Figure 11).

Stokes began his administration with great hope. Many white businessmen believed that the presence of a black mayor would be a guarantee against further racial disturbances. Such hopes were further buoyed when no riots occurred in the city in the aftermath of Martin Luther King's assassination in the spring of 1968. Stokes, having heard the news of the death of the national leader, walked the streets of the city's ghetto and encouraged the people not to engage in violence. Indeed, Stokes was given credit for averting violence in the city during that evening.

In May 1968 he initiated a major program—"Cleveland—Now!"—to raise over $11 million to rehabilitate the ghetto area and to provide employment to ghetto youths. By July, the campaign had raised over $4 million and had secured additional revenue from federal matching funds.

However, on July 23, 1968, Stokes suffered a major setback in his efforts to ease racial tensions. In Glenville, a group of black nationalists and Cleveland policemen engaged in a shootout that ended in the death of three policemen and four blacks. The particular shooting incident also set off a full scale riot in the Glenville area, especially along Superior Avenue, a major thoroughfare. As in the Hough riot, extensive property destruction and looting took place in the Glenville incident.

The Glenville riot was the turning point in the career of Mayor Stokes. From then on, dis-

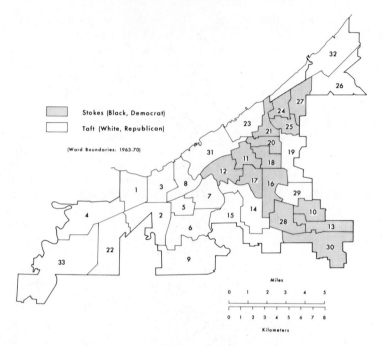

Figure 11. Mayoralty election results, 1967, by wards, Cleveland.

satisfaction with his administration increased and distrust among the whites intensified. Support for the "Cleveland—Now!" program evaporated as it was revealed that the black nationalists who had engaged in the shootout had received funds from the program. Yet, despite the dissatisfaction, in November 1969 Stokes narrowly defeated Ralph J. Perk, a Republican white ethnic, in the election for mayor. As in 1967, Stokes won by receiving over 90 percent of the vote in predominantly black wards, and approximately 20 percent of the vote in primarily white wards. Perk did extremely well in wards with a high percentage of ethnic population.

Stokes spent much of his second term in political infighting with the leaders of the City Council. The division of the city into thirty-three wards produces ineffective government. The interests of each councilman are too parochial, and stand in the way of promoting unified solutions to citywide problems. One particularly bitter controversy involved a proposal by Stokes to build public housing in vacant lots in the Lee-Miles area. The black residents of this area made it clear that they did not want public housing there. The argument they advanced centered upon lack of sewer and

water facilities, inadequate schools, and poor police protection. Yet, in spite of these public arguments, there was the unstated motive that the residents had moved to the Lee-Miles area to get away from the Hough-Central ghetto and did not want the ghetto extended into their middle class neighborhood. The public housing project has not been constructed in the Lee-Miles area. Public housing projects for the city's West Side were also blocked by residents in those areas. Indeed, throughout his second term, Stokes was in constant battle with the City Council over his programs.

In announcing that he would not seek re-election, Stokes attempted to line up support in the black community for James Carney, a wealthy white real estate developer, in the 1971 Democratic primary election against City Council President Anthony Garofoli, a strong ethnic candidate and leader of the anti-Stokes forces in the City Council. Carney defeated Garofoli by a wide margin as a result of his vote-getting ability in the predominantly black wards. For the general election, however, Stokes threw his support to Arnold Pinkney, the black School Board president and an independent candidate. In the general election, Carney's opponents were Perk and Pinkney.

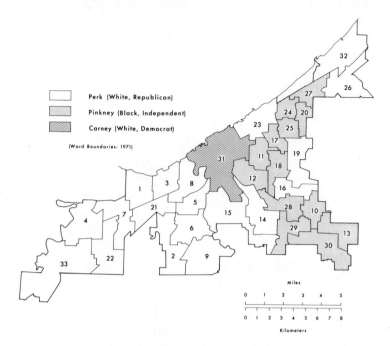

Figure 12. Mayoralty election results, 1971, by wards, Cleveland.

Perk, as in 1969, ran extremely well in areas of high white ethnicity. This time, however, Perk won election as Mayor by plurality with 38.1 percent of the votes (Figure 12).

The major goal during Perk's first term as mayor was to reverse the previous administration's financial policies, which he had claimed were bankrupting the city. Perk was able to achieve a balanced budget largely through federal financial assistance. Late in his first term, Perk initiated a Model Cities program for the Hough area. Cleveland was the last city in the nation to start such a program. However, actual benefits to the Hough residents have been minimal, since the program early in 1974 was still tied up in charges of irregularities, which have involved the Model Cities director and various aides in the Perk administration. Incidents of alleged payment for nonwork and overpayment have been uncovered by investigators.

Yet the Model Cities' difficulty did not prevent Perk's reelection in 1973. In the nonpartisan primary election (first utilized by the city in 1973), Perk and Carney were the two top vote-getters, although Perk had substantially more votes than Carney (Figure 13). In the aftermath of the primary, Carney suddenly withdrew and his place on the ballot was taken by Mercedes Cotner, a white former

City Council member and compromise candidate of the Democratic organization. Perk easily defeated Cotner in the general election.

In preparing its strategy for the 1973 mayoralty election, the black community faced two divergent opinions. Louis V. Stokes, congressional representative from the area and leader of a black-controlled political organization independent of the Cuyahoga County Democratic organization, felt that the black community should support a black candidate for mayor. However, other black leaders believed that the black community should support a white candidate in exchange for certain concessions from the Democratic party. Thus, the blacks who favored cooperation with the Democratic organization instead of competition won a temporary victory.

Although the percentage of the city population that is black has increased rapidly since the 1940s, the rate of increase will be leveling off because many blacks are now moving out of the city and into suburban areas. The entire West Side of Cleveland, however, remains almost entirely white and shows no signs of change in this respect. Thus, black leaders of the city recognize that they will need the support of significant numbers of white political leaders and voters to achieve effective action.

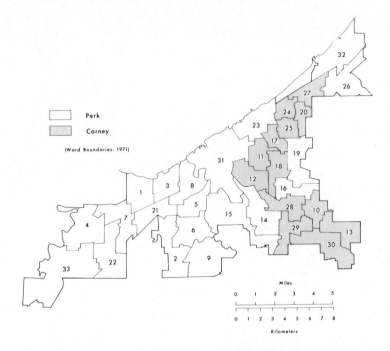

Figure 13. Mayoralty primary election results, 1973, by wards, Cleveland.

ETHNIC POPULATION PATTERNS IN AKRON

Although the role of ethnic population in the political and economic life of Akron is probably less conspicuous than in Cleveland, there are noteworthy ethnic concentrations in the city, in addition to a substantial black population. Also, a significant proportion of the population consists of migrants and their descendants from rural Appalachia, particularly from West Virginia and eastern Kentucky, attracted by the employment opportunities in local industry during the periods of the two world wars.

The most significant growth occurred during the 1910-1920 decade, when Summit County increased its population by 164.3 percent and the city of Akron by 201.8 percent. Much of that increase consisted of immigrants from abroad, who either settled directly in Akron or moved there from intermediate residence in other parts of the United States, and of immigrants from Appalachia. There were relatively few blacks; as late as 1940 they constituted only 5 percent of the total population, or 12,000 people. By 1970, however, there were 48,000 blacks in Akron, constituting 17.5 percent of the city's population. In the rest of Summit County, the blacks constituted 1.5 percent of the total population. As in most cities, the preponderant proportion of the black population lives within a short distance of the central business district, and is highly clustered. The principal areas of black concentration in Akron are within a mile or two of the downtown area, particularly in the community areas of South Akron and East Akron, the latter oriented especially along Wooster Avenue, a major southwesterly trending street which was the main axis of racial disturbances, especially during the summer of 1968 (Figures 14 and 15).

Akron's white ethnic population consists mainly of five principal groups of European origin. The largest single group is the Italian population, followed by German, Hungarian, Czechoslovakian, and Russian.

The population of Italian origin predominates in the entire northeastern quadrant of Akron (Figure 16). This area, consisting largely of modest single family homes, has been occupied by Italian population since its original settlement. Members of that group who have moved up the socioeconomic scale have tended to relocate near the edge of the city directly south of the downtown area, especially in the community of Firestone Park.

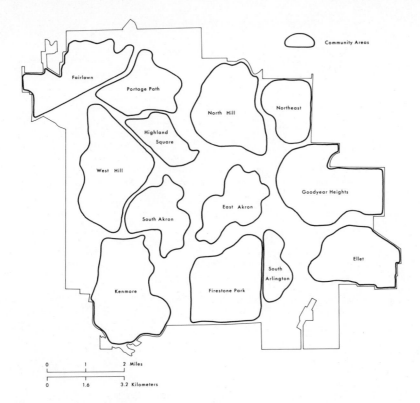

Figure 14. Community areas of Akron.

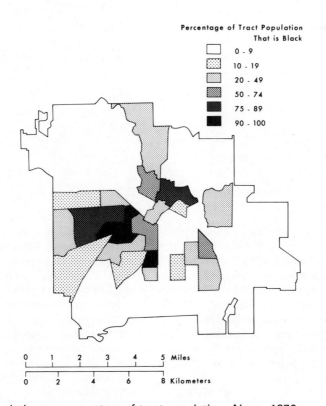

Percentage of Tract Population
That is Black

- 0 - 9
- 10 - 19
- 20 - 49
- 50 - 74
- 75 - 89
- 90 - 100

Figure 15. Black population as a percentage of tract population. Akron, 1970.

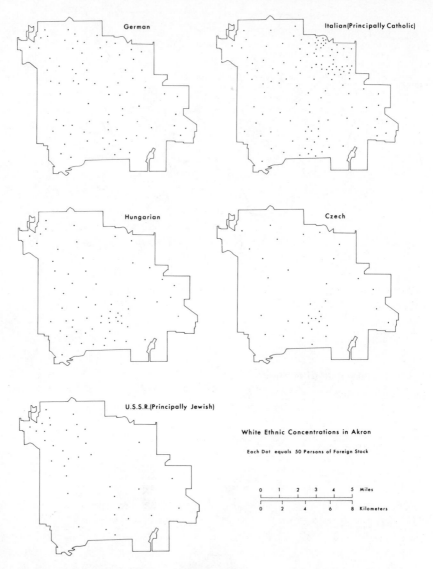

Figure 16. White ethnic concentrations in Akron, 1970.

The northwestern portion of Akron—including both the Fairlawn community within the city and the contiguous suburb of Fairlawn, both of which are upper income areas of large homes—contains a high proportion of persons of Russian and other east European origins. These people are predominantly Jewish, and the northwestern quadrant contains a number of prominent Jewish institutions, as well as one of the metropolitan area's two largest regional shopping centers.

A visual comparison of the maps of Akron's black population and its principal ethnic groups (Figures 15 and 16) shows a high degree of segregation. The ethnic areas have tended to resist integration firmly, particularly in the southwestern and eastern portions of the city. Only the central western portion has witnessed any significant degree of integration, and there the population composition has been gradually changing for many years. To the northwest, the high cost housing and lack of available middle income housing has served to inhibit racial or ethnic change.

The area to the south and west of downtown Akron has been declining for many years and has witnessed a succession of ethnic groups; it is now the principal locus of the city's black population. The Akron Metropolitan Housing Authority has developed many projects in that area and has achieved some degree of integration. An extensive area immediately southwest of the central business district, known as Opportunity Park, is the site of the largest urban renewal activity in the city; here federally assisted housing for both lower and middle income is, by law, integrated.

Intraregional Employment and Dynamics

In recent years Northeastern Ohio has retained its character as an area of predominantly heavy durable goods manufacturing, although the character of such activity has changed. It is still a region of primary metals manufacturing, in spite of relative declines in that category, but the market for metal production has been augmented by rapid, almost spectacular, expansion in industries that utilize the metals, and particularly in automobile manufacturing and in other industries that are suppliers to the automobile plants. In addition, the chemical industry has substantially increased, based upon naturally occurring resources within the region, such as salt, and other chemicals supplied from elsewhere by the region's excellent transportation.

The locational trends of manufacturing plants are producing significant changes in population, land use, and employment locations. The larger central cities have experienced a noteworthy decline in manufacturing establishments, employment, and population, while the suburban areas, and the rural areas between the metropolitan centers, are growing.

These trends underline the urgent need for closer cooperation among the many government and planning units within the nine county region. With a rapid increase in jobs outside the central cities; with outmigration of middle class persons and families to the suburban areas and beyond; with continued rapid increases in low income, unemployed, and minority group members; and with decreased central city job opportunities, the imbalance constitutes a major challenge to government, transportation, land use, and other interests to coordinate their facilities, operations, and plans.

EMPLOYMENT TRENDS, 1960 TO 1970

Total employment in the Northeast Ohio region increased 22.3 percent between 1960 and 1970, slightly less than the increase registered for the nation as a whole (24.6 percent) but appreciably above that for the six state region (18.8 percent). Large gains in both absolute and relative terms were registered in all but two of the service categories. The two exceptions were personal services and entertainment and recreational services. Employment in durable goods manufacturing increased slowly and there was an actual decline in employment in the nondurable goods sector.

When the performance of the Northeastern Ohio economy is compared to that of the six state region, a number of differences emerge. Employment in Northeastern Ohio grew more rapidly than employment in the six state region in a number of other categories—construction, communications, wholesale and retail trade, and business and repair services. The performance of manufacturing employment was poorer in Northeastern Ohio, with the durable sector growing less rapidly and the nondurable sector declining more rapidly than was the case in the six state region.

Since national employment grew much more rapidly than employment in the six state region, it is not surprising to find that the Northeastern Ohio growth performance appears in a less favorable light when compared to the nation as a whole. Only in agriculture and communications did employment in Northeastern Ohio grow more rapidly (or decline more slowly) than employment in the entire U.S. The performance in a number of categories—construction, wholesale and retail trade combined, and business and repair services—appears essentially the same. In all remaining categories national growth was significantly more rapid than growth in Northeastern Ohio. In terms of absolute numbers, the disadvantage of Northeastern Ohio seems particularly marked in manufacturing and perhaps in some service areas—e.g., professional and personal services. It thus appears that both the six state region and Northeastern Ohio share certain characteristics which have recently put them at a disadvantage relative to the rest of the nation. Within the six state region, however, Northeastern Ohio seems to occupy a relatively favorable position.

The figures pertaining to the detailed subcategories illustrate interesting changes in the industrial composition of Northeastern Ohio and the six state region.

Primary iron and steel employment fell by 22.1 percent in Northeastern Ohio while remaining virtually unchanged in the six state region as a whole. The six state region excluding Northeastern Ohio showed an increase of 7.8 percent in primary iron and steel employment.

Two additional important categories performed about the same in both areas. Employment in electrical machinery rose by about 15.0 percent; and machinery, except electrical, employment went up by 21.0 percent to 22.0 percent.

Northeastern Ohio's relative losses in primary iron and steel were partially offset by stronger growth performances in fabricated metals (+38.1 percent to +12.6 percent for the six states) and motor vehicles and motor vehicle equipment (+24.6 percent to +16.1 percent for the six states). Although these figures graphically illustrate a rapid change in the industrial composition within Northeastern Ohio, the 1970 employment profile still shows a very heavy concentration in primary iron and steel.

In the nondurable sector a few industries were responsible for very large declines in em-

ployment. The combined total of jobs lost in Northeastern Ohio was over 15,000 for the following industries—meat products, dairy products, bakery products, newspapers, and rubber products. Large losses in employment were also registered in the six state region in meat products, dairy products, and bakery products. The six state region showed small gains in newspapers and rubber products. The six state region excluding Northeastern Ohio showed a gain of 6.8 percent in rubber products employment. This pattern is similar to that exhibited by primary iron and steel, although the movement of employment from Northeastern Ohio to the rest of the six state region is less pronounced in the case of rubber products. Nevertheless, if this movement persists it could be quite serious, since rubber products account for 33.4 percent of Northeastern Ohio employment in nondurable manufacturing. One category, plastic products, accounted for large gains in employment in both Northeastern Ohio (4,497 jobs or 151.3 percent) and the six state region (109.3 percent).

Nearly 80 percent of the large increase in employment in professional services was accounted for by two categories. In Northeastern Ohio employment in educational services increased by 48,756, representing a gain of 90.8 percent, and employment in medical services rose by 31,067, or 60.3 percent. Similar increases were registered in the six state region.

Cleveland is the dominant employer in the region, accounting for 54.4 percent of the area's total. There seems to be some tendency for Cleveland to be a net provider of services to the rest of the region. Cleveland accounts for significantly more than its share of employment in communications, wholesale trade, finance, insurance and real estate, business and repair services, and professional services other than medical and educational. There are, however, two quantitatively important service categories in which Cleveland accounts for slightly less than its share of total regional employment. These categories are retail trade and educational services, which together account for 40.0 percent of total service employment in the region. Thus, the tendency for Cleveland to export services to the rest of the region is not pervasive.

In the manufacturing sector, primary iron and steel dominates the economies of Lorain-Elyria (43.8 percent of total SMSA manufacturing employment), Youngstown-Warren (35.0

percent), and Canton (23.0 percent). This industry is very small in Akron and accounts for only 7.9 percent of Cleveland's manufacturing employment. Motor vehicle employment is important in Lorain-Elyria (27.2 percent of manufacturing employment), Youngstown-Warren (17.2 percent), and Cleveland (12.1 percent). Machinery accounts for 29.4 percent of Canton's manufacturing employment and 27.8 percent of Cleveland's. The rubber industry, dominant in Akron, accounts for 37.8 percent of manufacturing employment, followed by machinery (15.3 percent), and fabricated metals (14.3 percent).

In general, industrial diversification appears greatest in Cleveland and smallest in Lorain-Elyria. Youngstown-Warren and Akron are also heavily dependent upon single industries.

The 1960 to 1970 changes in employment in primary iron and steel and motor vehicles for the region's SMSAs illustrate marked intraregional location changes in these industries. Primary iron and steel employment fell quite rapidly in Youngstown-Warren and Cleveland, more moderately in Canton, and significantly less in Lorain-Elyria. The difference was due primarily to a rapid increase in blast furnace and rolling mill employment in Lorain-Elyria. Motor vehicle employment fell in Cleveland and increased moderately in Lorain-Elyria and very spectacularly in Youngstown-Warren (+794.2 percent). The latter is accounted for by the expansion of the General Motors plants at Lordstown.

Overall employment in the region increased by 22.3 percent; Cleveland's increased by 20.0 percent. In Akron, the decline in rubber products employment was more than offset by increases in fabricated metals and machinery. The poor performance of Youngstown-Warren was largely due to decline in primary metals.

NORTHEASTERN OHIO AS A CORPORATE HEADQUARTERS LOCATION

The three largest cities of the nine county Northeastern Ohio region—Cleveland, Akron, and Canton—have, in the past decade, maintained their relative position nationally with respect to the number of headquarters of large industrial companies that are located within them. In nearly every instance, the companies that maintain corporate headquarters in North-

eastern Ohio also operate their principal plants, or at least one or more of their larger plants, within the region. A study of the locations of the headquarters of the 500 largest American industrial organizations, as listed in *Fortune* magazine, was undertaken for 1961 and 1971. In both years, the New York region had three times as many headquarters as its next nearest rival—Chicago. Pittsburgh ranked third in 1961; Los Angeles third in 1971. There is thus a very clear advantage for headquarters locations in very large urban concentrations, where "external economies" are maximized. The attractions of large urban concentrations are thus cumulative.

Cleveland, as expected, dominates Northeastern Ohio with respect to corporate headquarters. It headquarters sixteen major industrial firms, ranging from steel (Republic Steel), chemicals (Diamond Shamrock), and industrial tools and equipment (Midland-Ross), to office equipment (Addressograph-Multigraph), electronic components (TRW), paints (Sherwin-Williams), and mining and lake shipping (Hanna Mining). Akron and Canton, on the other hand, are more specialized. Major companies headquartered in Akron are all rubber companies of national and worldwide importance; four of the five largest in America are headquartered in Akron, and one of them recently completed a large headquarters office building contiguous to its main plant. One of them also controls an aerospace industry with substantial, though declining, employment in Akron: Goodyear, famous for the lighter than air craft of the 1920s and 1930s, is an important producer of parts for present-day airplanes and spacecraft. Canton is the home of Timken Roller Bearing, which is an important market for the nearby steel mills, and the Hoover Company, which is famous for household appliances.

A shift of managerial activity toward dynamic regions away from the "core region" of the continent seems to have taken place between 1961 and 1971, although New York and Chicago, the two largest centers, have maintained their dominance. Although Cleveland has maintained its relative position as a corporate headquarters location, the other two largest centers between New York and Chicago, equidistant from Cleveland—Pittsburgh to the southeast and Detroit to the northwest—have not fared as well. Cleveland moved from ninth among the metropolitan areas of the United States in 1961 with respect to the number of industrial corporate headquarters, with fifteen, to fifth in 1971, with sixteen.

MOVEMENTS OF INDUSTRY WITHIN NORTHEASTERN OHIO

Because of the predominance of manufacturing activity in the nine county Northeastern Ohio region, which is the subject of this study, and because of the multiplier effect that manufacturing exerts upon other employment, such as professional and other services, the relative changes in the location of manufacturing establishments and employment among the cities and other portions of the region are highly significant.

In general, the principal cities of the region have, in recent years, experienced substantial declines in industrial employment and population, while areas peripheral to the central cities have experienced growth in employment and population.

Cleveland and Cuyahoga County

Since the earliest days of settlement in Northeastern Ohio, Cleveland has had the largest concentration of industrial establishments and employment within the region. In Cuyahoga County, which includes Cleveland and has half the population of the nine county region, industrial plants began to locate in suburban areas in the early part of the twentieth century. By 1929, 208 plants located within the county but outside of Cleveland, representing less than 8 percent of the industrial establishments of the county. By 1971, the proportion of industrial establishments in suburban Cuyahoga County had reached 35 percent. Furthermore, there has been an absolute decline in the number of manufacturing establishments within the city of Cleveland since 1954.

Within Cleveland and Cuyahoga County, industry is largely located within three general areas. The largest single area, and the most intensively developed, is the "Flats," or the lower Cuyahoga valley, which bisects Cleveland into eastern and western components. This area has the advantage of providing water transportation of raw materials—although with serious restrictions on the sizes of vessels—but the disadvantages of having very inadequate areas for operations or expansion. A second, and widespread, type of industrial location in Cleveland

and Cuyahoga County is along the numerous railroad lines. Typically, these lines form the axes of long, attenuated industrial developments on either or both sides of the rights of way. Third, industries have, largely since World War II, located in industrial parks or elsewhere, mostly in suburban areas, that are accessible to freeways for heavy trucking, but may be with or without direct railroad access. Some suburbs, predominantly or exclusively residential, have restricted or prevented industrial development. Among them are Shaker Heights, Pepper Pike, and Fairview Park. Other suburbs, mostly older ones, attracted substantial industry early in the twentieth century when Cleveland's industrial land became scarce. Some of these suburbs, such as Brooklyn and Newburg Heights, are primarily industrial in character and contain homes of workers in nearby plants. Others, such as Euclid and Lakewood, contain, in addition to a variety of industries, homes of middle and upper middle class families who may or may not be employed in the nearby establishments.

A study of industrial relocation between 1960 and 1972 revealed that there were at least 403 establishments that relocated within the city of Cleveland, or from Cleveland to the Cuyahoga County suburbs. The study did not identify industries that may have moved in the reverse direction, but it is known that they were very few. Nor did the study consider industries that may have terminated their operations within the area without relocation, or with relocation between sites outside of Cuyahoga County.

The study revealed that the moves were generally proportionally distributed among the different classifications of manufacturing industries, with the machine and fabricated metals industries accounting for most of the establishments that relocated. Because of the extremely large size of the plants and the great capital investments, the primary metals industries had few relocations. Of all the moves, over three-fourths were establishments with under fifty employees. Two types of establishments—namely, apparel, and printing and publishing—had very few moves. The central business district has been a natural location for both types of establishments. The apparel establishments depend upon female employees who require mass transportation—available in sufficient quantity only into and out of the central city. The printing and publishing establishments depend upon a location near central city offices—the primary outlet for their services.

Three types of relocations by manufacturers may be identified. The first type, characterized by textile and apparel, printing and publishing, and miscellaneous products establishments, as expected, involved short distance moves principally within the central business district of Cleveland or its immediately contiguous fringe area. The second type of move, represented by such industries as furniture, transportation equipment, and technical instruments, is very diverse and generally the result of the need for increased spaces. These tended generally, but not exclusively, to be peripheral movements. The third type of move is diverse, falling into no particular pattern. It includes centrifugal, centripetal, and crosstown moves.

The relocation of industry within Cleveland and Cuyahoga County was by no means uniform in every direction. On the contrary, there has been a strong directional bias. Establishments which relocated within Cleveland moved primarily to the southwest and the northeast. This is, in part, a reflection of the alignment of the lakeshore and the railroads, which generally trend in those directions within the city. On the other hand, industries that moved from the city to the suburbs tended to favor the southeastern suburbs where the available land subtends a wider arc, and the southwest, where most of the industrial parks were developed and where the Cleveland-Hopkins International Airport constituted an attractive force. Between 1960 and 1972, the average distance between old and new locations was 2.2 miles. The new locations averaged over two miles farther from the city center than the old sites.

Why did the industries relocate? A stratified random sample of the industrialists who were questioned ranked the reasons in the following order—need for more space, lack of parking and loading space, lack of land for expansion, obsolete facilities, opportunity for more efficient facilities, vandalism and the high crime rate in the inner city, technological changes, personal preference, transportation problems, displacement by highway construction or urban renewal, expiration of lease, expensive land costs, high municipal taxation, and poor municipal services. None of these reasons, nor their relative rankings, are surprising. In general, they conform to findings of studies made in other cities. It is clear that, in Cleveland as in most other cities, centrifugal forces predominate in industrial location. Industries outgrow their central locations and seek room for expansion.

The decentralizing trends that were evident in Cleveland and Cuyahoga County with respect to relocation of industrial establishments and employment were revealed by the statistics regarding total and net changes in industrial employment, both within the Cleveland SMSA and in Northeastern Ohio as a whole. In Cuyahoga County, the influx of major manufacturers of transportation equipment in the area surrounding Cleveland led to an increase of over 24,000 jobs in the county since 1950. A notable increase in foundries outside Cleveland, but within the county, replaced the loss of foundries within the city.

Decline of Central City Industries

Throughout Northeastern Ohio, certain industrial groups tended to abandon central city sites while others seemed to cling to such sites. The industries that abandoned central sites included metal fabricating, grey iron foundries, textiles, and technical instruments. These types of industries are characterized by comparatively large size, large ground area per employee, nuisance features (odors, noise, high fire hazard, etc.), specialized buildings, serious problems of waste disposal, and large quantities of bulk inputs, including fuel and water. On the other hand, the industry groups that tended to retain central locations were women's apparel, men's clothing, small job printing, metal assembling and service plants, and metropolitan newspapers. Their principal characteristics are unspecialized buildings; employment of specialized, highly skilled workers; high employment density in proportion to site areas; comparatively small scale; ability to utilize older and partially obsolescent buildings; close contact with the local market; seasonality and fluctuating labor force; and, in some instances, significance of style or timeliness.

The manufacturing establishments which moved into Northeastern Ohio followed the same location pattern as to central sites, with one important exception. New metal assembling and service plants moved into sites outside the central cities.

The increase in the motor vehicle industry

is by far the most significant trend in manufacturing, and in employment, in Northeastern Ohio during the past two decades. In 1950 there were only two such plants employing 3,000 or more, but by 1972 there were several very large additional ones. They not only contributed to the net growth of employment in the region, but also served as replacements for declining central city industries. Many of the new plants located in small communities or rural areas such as Twinsburg and Hudson, drawing upon the labor force from as far away as Cleveland, Akron, and beyond. The huge Lordstown complex, just east of the easterly boundary of the nine county area, has also had a very great influence upon employment and commuting patterns within the area since it competes for labor with the industries throughout the region. This and other plants manufacturing motor vehicles and equipment are sufficiently large as to constitute probable nucleii for extensive surrounding urbanization and are major contributors to intermetropolitan coalescence.

Meanwhile, the dominance of the motor vehicle manufacturing industry is substantially reducing the diversity of the region's industrial base: in 1968, 12.5 percent of manufacturing employees in Northeastern Ohio were engaged in manufacture of transportation equipment, whereas the percentage was only 8.5 in 1949. In addition, of course, this industry is a major localizing force, attracting to the region many industries that are suppliers to the vehicle manufacturers. Between 1949 and 1968, in addition to nearly 100,000 additional jobs in the motor vehicle manufacturing plants, fabricated metal products increased by over 32,000 jobs; and it is quite possible that the steel and rubber industries would have fared much worse than they did were it not for the increasing

market for their output within and near the region created by the motor vehicle manufacturers.

Industry in the Akron Metropolitan Area

In the Akron SMSA, the rubber industry declined by 10,796 employees, in spite of an increase of forty-three establishments. Because of the relation of plastics to the rubber industry —they both involve polymer chemistry—and because plastics are included statistically in the rubber industry, the increase in establishments is largely accounted for by plastics manufacturing, which, in turn, is in part composed of "spin-off" establishments using former rubber workers. A decline in population of the city of Akron between 1960 and 1970 was largely related to decline of the rubber industry within the city. While the city was experiencing a decline in employment and population, the SMSA increased its population as new and expanding industries located in the suburban and rural areas, in some instances stimulating nearby residential development.

The Canton SMSA experienced the same trends, with an increase in industry, especially in transportation equipment, electrical machinery, printing, and food products. At the same time, the city of Canton experienced a decline in population and employment, with a sharp decrease in jobs in the primary metals manufacturing industry.

The Lorain-Elyria SMSA and the city of Lorain continued to increase in population through 1970. While the primary metals industry in that metropolitan area lost 11,014 jobs, it was replaced by new and expanded plants in transportation equipment and chemicals. The former is accounted for by a large Ford plant, and by the American Shipbuilding Plant at Lorain, the largest shipyard on the Great Lakes.

Intermetropolitan Coalescence and Internal Transportation

Northeastern Ohio is a significant node or focus for the network of transportation of the entire North American continent, and it also has access by major routes to the other continents. Few regions anywhere have as many facilities connecting them with the rest of the world—by railroad, waterway, highway, pipeline, and air—nor are many as favorably located with respect to other major nodal regions. Northeastern Ohio is, on the one hand, within the western flank of the North Atlantic trade route connecting the core region of North America with its counterpart in western Europe. This trade route generates by far the world's densest intercontinental traffic by sea and air. The position of the region relative to that route has been substantially reinforced by the enlargement of the St. Lawrence Seaway in 1959; by the construction of the network of interstate express highways, both within the region and connecting it with ports on the Atlantic, Gulf, and Pacific coasts; by the development of intermodal transportation techniques including containers, railroad piggyback, and unit trains; and by the growth of jet air transportation, including air cargo movements. With relation to all of these, Northeastern Ohio is favored by excellent internal facilities and good external connections.

THE MAJOR CORRIDORS

The region developed most of its present larger cities, and many of its smaller ones, during the period in the nineteenth century and early twentieth century, when public carrier transportation dominated. The waterways, especially the Great Lakes, and in particular the railroads carried virtually all except very short distance passenger and goods transportation. These carrier routes commonly paralleled one another and formed transportation corridors or routes that crossed the region in several directions. They reinforced the "nested hierarchy" pattern of interregional relationships. On the one hand, the core region of the northeastern quarter of the United States and nearby Canada, which extended from the western Great Lakes to the Atlantic seaboard and also extended across the Atlantic to western Europe, was, and is, developed along the east-west transportation corridors. Lake Erie, which extends along the main east-west line of movement, and the railroads, and later the highways, immediately contiguous to and paralleling the lakeshore and passing through Cleveland, constitute the northernmost east-west corridor. The middle east-west corridor is served by the main lines of the Erie-Lackawanna and Chessie (B&O) railroads, passing through Youngstown, Ravenna, Kent, and Akron, and, more recently, by the Ohio Turnpike just north of the railroads. The southerly east-west corridor was originally developed along the former line of the Pennsylvania Railroad (now Penn Central), and later along the Lincoln Highway (US 30), including Alliance, Canton, and Massillon. Thus, we can recognize three parallel corridors, served by rail and highway, along which chains of cities developed like beads on a string (Figure 17).

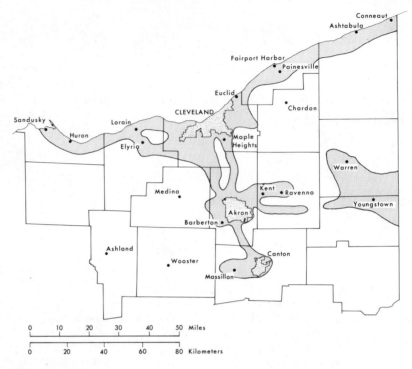

Figure 17. Major intermetropolitan corridors of Northeastern Ohio.

Intersecting these east-west alignments are the northwest-southeast and the north-south ones. One important corridor has developed along the railroads, which connect the Lake Erie ports of the region with interior points—notably Youngstown, Pittsburgh, and other cities along the Ohio River—as well as the coal fields of Appalachia in southeastern Ohio, western Pennsylvania, and nearby West Virginia. These rail lines carry coal northward and iron ore southward, as well as a variety of other goods, and, formerly, passengers. Each of the lake ports—Conneaut, Ashtabula, Fairport Harbor, Cleveland, and Lorain—has one or more railroad lines carrying bulk northbound coal, southbound ore, and general freight. Later, the railroads were paralleled by highways radiating from the lake port cities, especially from Cleveland. These highways are of two types. In addition to the rectangular grid of section line roads, there are the standard intercity highways that form a network of state and national routes and, more recently, the limited access expressways. Among the latter are the Ohio Turnpike, bisecting the region along approximately the commutershed divide between

Akron on the south and Cleveland on the north; Interstate Route 77, the main highway link along the Cleveland-Akron-Canton north-south corridor; and Interstate 71, the principal northeast-southwest route joining Cleveland with Columbus, Cincinnati, and other major southwesterly cities.

The original corridor, which opened up settlement in the region by making it possible to utilize the all-water route to and from the East, was the lower Cuyahoga valley between Cleveland and Akron, followed by the Ohio and Erie Canal. Today, the Cuyahoga valley is no longer an important long distance, or even intraregional route. It contains only minor roads and a local railroad branch.

On the parallel uplands, the preexpressway highways form main axes of interurban coalescence between Cleveland and Akron. These are Highway 8 to the east of the valley and Highway 21 to the west. They form a dual corridor, on the upland. Several highways connect Youngstown, just to the east of the region, with Cleveland and Akron, respectively.

The transportation corridors connecting Cleveland, Akron, and Youngstown form a triangle, with a double base to the west (Cleveland-Akron), along the edges of which ridges of urbanization are rapidly filling in. These ridges will eventually join these three cities with each other to form a hollow triangle. Similarly, coalescence of urbanized areas is taking place along the principal highways that link Akron with Canton—first along the conventional highway joining the two cities (State Route 8), and more recently along the route of the limited access expressway (Interstate 77). Since the construction of the latter, several major developments adjacent to interchanges along the route have begun to serve as nodes or growth centers for urbanization in their vicinities. These include the Belden Mall Shopping Center, the Stark County campus of Kent State University, and the previously established Akron-Canton Airport, which is Northeastern Ohio's second most important air carrier facility.

Cleveland-Youngstown

The edge of the triangle between the southeastern suburbs of Cleveland and the Youngstown area, for which U.S. 422 serves as the principal axis, is substantially less urbanized than the other two sides of the triangle. The continuity of urban development is interrupted by the extensive Ravenna Arsenal in eastern Portage County and by the West Branch Reservoir just to the south of it. The Ohio Turnpike, completed in 1956, has few interchanges between the northeastern portion of the Akron urbanized area (Gate 13: Streetsboro) and the Warren-Youngstown complex. Consequently, it has not influenced urbanization to any great extent.

On the other hand, urbanization is virtually continuous between Cleveland and Akron and between Akron and Youngstown, along the major prefreeway highway routes. In order to ascertain the extent of interurban and intermetropolitan coalescence, studies were made of the land use and land value patterns along the respective highway routes.

Cleveland-Akron

Between the inner southerly suburbs of Cleveland and the northern parts of Akron, State Route 8, the principal highway route (the last gap in parallel Interstate 77 was closed in mid-1973), and U.S. 21, east and west of the Cuyahoga valley, were investigated (Figure 18).

Within a fifteen mile stretch between the southern end of the Cleveland urban area and the northern boundary of Cuyahoga Falls there is a three mile stretch of moderate to low residential density and relatively large vacant parcels. This "break" shows definite signs of filling in with such urban land uses as industrial developments and residential construction in the near future.

It was found that land values decrease away from the northern and southern ends of the corridor, and gradually reach a low point between the two principal cities. This supports the previous conclusion that there is a minor break in urbanization approximately halfway between the ends of the corridor because land values are lowest there. Also, land values reach secondary peaks along the route, at major intersections, and decrease at a decreasing rate away from each of the intersections or nodes along the route. These findings indicate that urbanization is not continuous along Route 8, but, rather, varies according to location with respect to the nearest node. The combined pattern of the two relationships—distance from the ends of the corridor and distance from the nearest intermediate node—produces a series of peaks and troughs, lower near the middle and higher near the ends of the corridor.

Land uses along U.S. 21 west of the Cuyahoga valley indicate continuous urbanization, though varying in form, along the entire sixteen mile stretch between the outer limits of the Cleveland and of the Akron urbanized areas. Richfield Township, in the middle of the study area, has recently become heavily developed with truck terminals due to the presence of the three limited access highways nearby. The truck terminals have apparently offset the tendency for this area to have the least urbanization and the lowest land values. The location midway between Cleveland and Akron, on the other hand, was very favorable for the trucking industry, not only for access to the freeways for the long hauls, but also for convenience to both Cleveland and Akron.

In contrast to the pattern on the parallel highway east of the Cuyahoga valley, the pattern of land values along U.S. 21 west of the valley shows an insignificant relationship between distance from the ends of the corridor and the level of land values. Land values showed a general pattern of decline with increased distance from intermediate nodes.

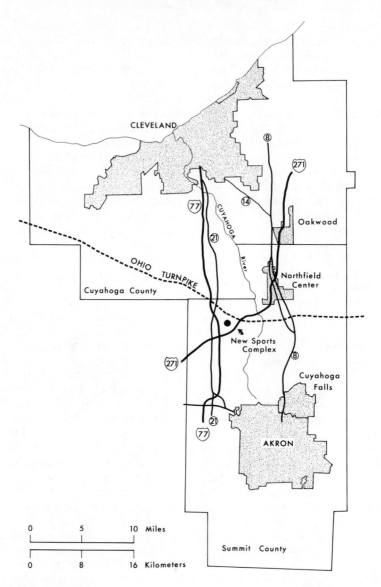

Figure 18. Cleveland-Akron corridor.

Thus, of the two highway corridors between Cleveland and Akron, Route 8, east of the Cuyahoga valley, is less continuously urbanized and has more variation in urban land uses in relation to distance from the nodes. West of the valley, along U.S. 21, urbanization is continuous, but this occurrence has been relatively recent, especially midway between the two major cities.

Several prospective developments, announced early in 1973, indicate an intensification of the continuous urbanization between Cleveland and Akron. A very large shopping center, exceeding in size any so far built in northern Ohio, if not in the nation, is to be constructed southeast of Cleveland, and a major sports complex, in part to replace the present facilities in Cleveland, is under development just west of the Cuyahoga valley in Richfield Township, adjacent to the intersection of the Ohio Turnpike, U.S. 21, and Interstates 77 and 271. These and the associated facilities, such as related retail and service establishments, including motels, are expected to be growth centers for surrounding urban residential and other developments. This will fill in the urbanization between Cleveland and Akron. With these developments, the Cleveland-Akron corridor will be quite analogous in general character to those between Dallas and Fort Worth, Texas, and between Seattle and Tacoma, Washington, all three of which are approximately the same length.

Akron-Youngstown

Between the urbanized area of Akron on the west and Youngstown on the east, State Route 18 has long been the major connection. Recently, it has been paralleled very closely by Interstate 76 (formerly I-80S, renumbered in 1973) immediately to the north.

In order to determine the extent of urban development and intermetropolitan coalescence between Akron and Youngstown, a study of land uses and land values was made along Highway 18, and the changes between 1960, 1966, and 1972 were investigated. The period before and after the construction of Interstate 76, a limited access freeway, was studied. The highest land values were located at settlements along the highway and at the eastern end, at the former interchange, now closed, with the Ohio Turnpike. Lower land values coincided with small clusters of residential development. Decline of value with increasing distance from either end of the highway stretch was relatively unimportant in comparison with the nodes of high value.

Some changes over time became apparent. Most striking is the fact that the highest land values have become much higher than the surrounding land values. This is the result of the advantages of freeway accessibility at various intermediate points where roads connected the two parallel highways and of the convenient location near the low order commercial establishments at the several intermediate hamlets that are located near freeway interchanges. Proximity to the cities at both ends had a strong influence on land values. Whereas in 1960 the only significant internodal areas of relatively high value land seemed to be near two intermediate hamlets, in 1972 the entire corridor had at least incipient development. This indicated a linkage of the urban frontiers of the two cities and was the first significant indication of intermetropolitan coalescence.

Land value profiles of transverses to Highway 18 tended to be simpler. In most cases, they tended to show a definite decrease in land value with increasing distance from the corridor itself. That relationship became stronger with time, as the corridor developed at a faster rate than did the hinterland. In some instances, however, "leapfrog" exurban development, off the corridor itself and some distance from the freeway interchanges, weakened the dominance of the corridor by creating additional nodes of high land value. Such development, nevertheless, supported interurban coalescence. Certain relationships are evident: (1) consistent dominance of the nodal "beads on a string" pattern over the pattern of declining land values with distance from the corridor ends, although distance from the end of the corridor was also significant; (2) a fairly consistent drop in correlation of land values with distance from both the ends and the intermediate nodes with increasing recency, particularly since 1966, as a result of filling in between nodes and an elevation of the land value levels in the midsection of the corridor due to the outward spread of urbanization; and (3) a sharp drop in land values near the peak intersections followed by more gentle decreases. Since 1966, there has been a notable blurring of the effects, seen between 1960 and 1966, of the nodal pattern due to the improved access provided by the opening of parallel freeway Interstate 76, which makes the entire corridor easily accessible to commuters to and from both the Youngstown and Akron urbanized areas. Thus, the urban frontier between the two cities, separated by a fairly small gap before 1972, has disappeared due to opening of I-76.

The several major cities of Northeastern Ohio, therefore, are connected by more or less clearly identifiable corridors along which urban expansion has produced interurban coalescence, very pronounced between Cleveland and Akron, rapidly developing between Akron and Canton, less pronounced between Akron and Youngstown, and incipient between Youngstown and Cleveland. Each of the major nodes, furthermore, consists of two or more subsidiary nodes, identifiable as separate municipalities, originally developed around the respective central business districts. Thus, Akron is continuous with Cuyahoga Falls, Silver Lake, Stow, Kent, and Ravenna to the northeast, and Barberton to the southwest. Canton has North Canton, and, to the west, Massillon.

Youngstown, Niles, and Warren form a continuous southeast-northwest high density urban corridor along the Mahoning River. Cleveland has a complex-multinodal structure, with many satellite and suburban communities. Finally, there is strong evidence of a continuous urban corridor along the shore of Lake Erie, including Painesville–Fairport Harbor, Euclid, Cleveland, Lakewood, Rocky River, Bay Village, Avon Lake, and Lorain, among other nodes, and extending east and west, with few substantial breaks, along the entire lakeshore from Buffalo to Toledo.

Commuting Patterns: The Journey to Work

Virtually all of the nine county area can be traversed in any direction in less than one hour even with the lowered speed limits imposed in late 1973 and early 1974. Thus, there is a tendency for multidirectional commuting, principally along the highways, both old and new, that constitute the axes of the several corridors. There is, to a very significant degree, a communality of labor market and housing market areas, with substantial overlap, throughout the region. In spite of the identification of the commutershed boundaries between cities, identified, as described above, by low points in the land value profile and low density of development, there is considerable through traffic, not only across the region to and from outside points, but also between the cities and counties within the region. These movements take place along the highway axes of the several corridors. Few regions are as completely dependent upon automobile transportation as Northeastern Ohio.

The dominance of Cleveland and Akron is clearly shown in Figure 19. This shows the number of journeys to work that originate or terminate in each of the two cities. The destinations or origins of those journeys are in the seven county NOACA area. Although the Ohio Turnpike, midway between the two cities, is generally considered to mark the approximate boundary between the commutersheds of the two cities, it will be noted that there is considerable overlap, with a substantial number of work trips to Cleveland originating in Medina, Summit, and Portage counties. Also, a lesser number of trips to Akron originate in Cleveland and Cuyahoga county. The greater gravitational

pull of Cleveland, as compared with Akron, is evident, as is the significant number of trips in both directions between the two cities. Indeed, the dominance of the two cities within their respective counties is depicted. In spite of deconcentration of commercial and industrial employment, the central cities still dominate; of all the work trips from Portage to Summit County, half go to the city of Akron, and of the Lake to Cuyahoga County trips, 54 percent end in the city of Cleveland.

Figures 19 and 20 show the county-to-county work trips within the seven county area, both between contiguous and adjacent counties and across intermediate counties. Again the dominance of Cleveland and Akron is shown, with Cleveland clearly exerting the greater pull. However, the overlap of commuter areas of the several major nodes within the region is also shown. A significant number of trips not only extend for distances of fifty miles or more but also pass through or bypass the two principal cities. For example, trips between Ashtabula and Lorain-Elyria bypass Cleveland, and trips between Cleveland and Canton bypass Akron.

The commuting across county lines between home and work is also depicted in Figure 21a, which shows the percentage of workers resident in each of the nine counties who worked in the county of residence. It will be noted that the percentage varied from less than half in the case of three peripheral and predominantly rural counties—Medina, Lake, and Geauga—to over 80 percent in two predominantly urban counties—Cuyahoga, containing Cleveland and many industrial suburbs; and Stark, containing Canton. Summit and Lorain counties occupied an intermediate position with between 71 and 80 percent of the workers employed in the counties of residence. Although Lorain County contains a number of large industrial employers, its proximity to the Cleveland industrial complex gives it the dual status of an employing area as well as a dormitory area for Cleveland and inner suburbs. Summit County, on the other hand, is dominated by Akron with its contiguous suburbs, notably Barberton and Cuyahoga Falls, but the extreme northern part of the county is clearly within the Cleveland commuting orbit.

The net result of these intercounty daily

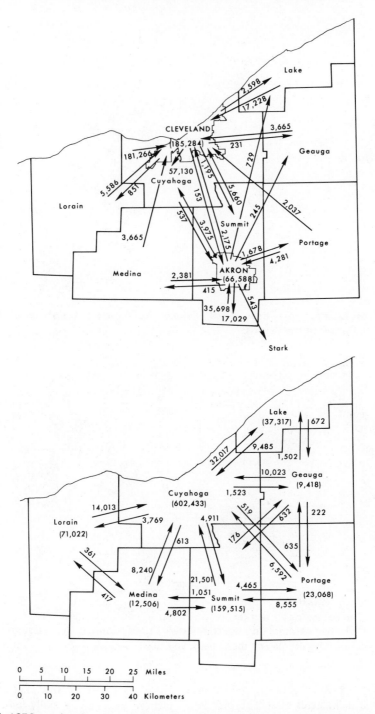

Figure 19. (a) 1970 work trips to and from Cleveland and Akron. (b) 1970 work trips—internal and adjacent counties. Source: Northeastern Ohio Areawide Coordinating Agency and U.S. Bureau of the Census.

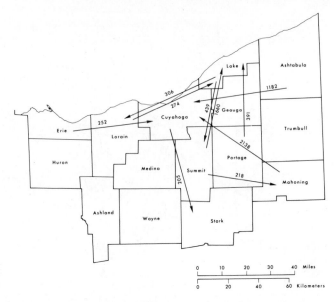

Figure 20. Cross-County work trips, 1970. Source: Northeastern Ohio Areawide Coordinating Agency and U.S. Bureau of the Census.

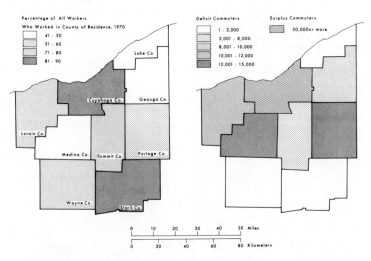

Figure 21. (a) Percentage of all workers who worked in county of residence, 1970. (b) Deficit or surplus in total number of cross-County commuters, 1970. Source: Northeastern Ohio Areawide Coordinating Agency, U.S. Bureau of the Census, and Stark County Regional Planning Commission.

movements to and from work is shown in Figure 21b, which indicates the net surplus or deficit of commuters—in other words, the extent to which each of the counties has more or fewer workers resident in the county than persons who work in the county. Only Cuyahoga County has more inbound than outbound daily commuters. While the county is a rather crude areal unit for this kind of statistical depiction, the maps generally indicate that Cleveland and its closer industrial suburbs continue to exert the heaviest attraction for employment, while many other portions of the nine county region have a dominant dormitory function. Were the time available in this study to utilize available statistics on smaller areal units, such as townships and individual municipalities, it could be demonstrated that, within several of the counties containing large centers of industrial employment such as Summit and Stark counties, the cities, Akron and Canton, would dominate over the closer suburbs in generating intracounty movements between home and work.

It is clear from most of the available evidence that the Northeastern Ohio nine county region has a pattern of urbanization that is internally cohesive and that has overlapping employment and housing market areas with substantial cross-commuting. Furthermore, although urban-oriented residential development has taken place in many parts of the region not immediately contiguous to urbanized areas or to major highways, the earliest and most prominent urban developments between the larger nodes or centers exist along and close to the principal intercity highway routes of the pre-freeway era and in proximity to access and egress points along the newer freeways.

PUBLIC PASSENGER TRANSPORTATION WITHIN THE REGION

As in most urban regions of the United States, public mass transportation within the region has suffered a precipitous decline in recent decades. The automobile is the overwhelmingly dominant mode in all parts of the region, except for a few areas in the inner portions of Cleveland where the remnants of a once extensive street railway and bus network are now supplemented by four rapid transit routes which radiate from the Terminal Tower, facing the Public Square, the core of the city.

Except for these rapid transit lines, which are suffering a continuing decline in numbers of riders, there is no passenger train service within Northeastern Ohio for internal movements.

A few intercity buses serve the principal nodes within the region, but their role in commuting is insignificant. Many communities, including some fairly large ones, have neither internal nor external public passenger transportation services and are entirely dependent upon automobile transportation.

In common with many other cities throughout the nation, those cities of Northeastern Ohio that have any public transportation at all have witnessed conversion of their transit operation from that of private franchised car-

riers to public operations, which, in turn, cannot meet rapidly increasing costs by increasing fares proportionately and, consequently, can be maintained only by public subsidy. In any event, the daily ridership in every instance is only a small portion of the volume of a few years ago. Akron and its neighboring suburbs of Cuyahoga Falls and Barberton in 1972 voted to subsidize its metropolitan bus system and, with federal subsidy aid, has restored a moderately adequate service along major high density routes.

In Cleveland and its suburbs within Cuyahoga County, public takeover of formerly privately operated local transportation services came much earlier. In 1942, the city of Cleveland took over an extensive local street railway system, and by 1954 the streetcars were gone, to be replaced, where traffic demanded, by buses. A short time later, the Cleveland Transit System (CTS) opened a rapid transit line. At present, the Cleveland SMSA is the smallest metropolitan complex to be served by rail rapid transit. But the CTS line was not the first rapid transit line in the Cleveland area.

Oris P. and Mantis J. Van Sweringen, brothers who were in the real estate business in Cleveland, in 1906 purchased a tract of 1,366 acres, formerly occupied by an agricultural colony of a religious sect, the Shakers, and proceeded to plat it along what was, for that time, a modern suburb, known today as the city of Shaker Heights. They planned the development to attract primarily upper income executives who worked in downtown Cleveland. Their development, located along two branches of upper Doan Brook, southeast of Cleveland, developed rapidly after it was platted in 1911, but it lacked adequate transportation to the center of Cleveland. To remedy the situation, they planned a rapid transit line. Two branches were constructed within their development. The branches converge at Shaker Square, just within the easterly city boundary of Cleveland. To obtain a right of way into downtown Cleveland, the brothers, having been refused permission to use Cleveland streets or the Nickel Plate (New York, Chicago and St. Louis) Railway, purchased the railway outright. In 1918, the Shaker Rapid began service and, with its completion by the Van Sweringens in 1930, operated—as it still does—into the Cleveland Union Terminal, facing the Public Square, which the Van Sweringens completed just before their bankruptcy in the Great Depression. The Shaker Rapid was subsequently taken over by the city of Shaker Heights. The present "Shaker Rapid" consists of track jointly operated with the CTS Rapid in the Cyahoga Valley, track parallel to the Nickel Plate road (now Norfolk & Western), a stretch of private grade-separated right of way to Shaker Square, and then two branches in the median strips of parallel boulevards through Shaker Heights, to terminals, which, although originally regarded as temporary, contain extensive nearby parking facilities. These terminals enable the transit line to draw from an extensive suburban area beyond its easterly extremities. Around one terminal, at Van Aken Square, an intensive complex of shopping facilities and office buildings has developed.

The Cleveland Rapid Transit, which opened in 1955, originally stretched from the present Windermere terminal in East Cleveland through the downtown terminal complex. From the terminal, the transit system proceeded in a southwesterly direction to a temporary terminal. In 1968, the system was extended to the Cleveland-Hopkins Airport, in the southwesterly portion of the city. Virtually the entire line is constructed on grade-separated right of way parallel to what was a main line of the New York Central Railroad (presently Penn Central), thereby minimizing costs and problems of land acquisition. Unlike the Shaker Rapid, which is operated by streetcar type rolling stock, the CTS Rapid is operated with heavy duty rapid transit type cars, in up to six car trains during the rush hours.

Unfortunately, the two rapid transit systems were built to different technical standards. Both are publicly operated, but their physical integration has not been accomplished, except for a short stretch leading into the Union Terminal, which they share. Both systems also share a common problem of declining patronage. In the case of CTS, the middle class and more affluent residential areas are not directly served, although there is some integration with the extensive CTS bus system. In the case of the Shaker Rapid, the suburb of Shaker Heights, which owns the line, is primarily dependent upon the automobile, although much reverse commuting, such as by domestic servants and workers in the Van Aken Square district, helps to improve the load factors on the line.

The CTS Rapid Transit reached its peak traffic in 1960, with over eighteen million passengers, but then had a precipitous decline to under thirteen million passengers in 1972. The Shaker Rapid, concurrently, had a steady decline in riders, from six and a half million in 1955 to below four million in 1972. With the current interest in minimizing use of private automobile transportation in urban areas, not only to reduce congestion and pollution but also to save fuel, and with increased recognition of the need to provide public transportation for the aged, infirm, young, and low income people, there is a desire to improve and extend the rapid transit lines. On the other hand, to connect the areas of maximum traffic generation between home and work, major extensions would be required, and the existence of express and other highway routes capable of handling buses makes such extension very doubtful.

The extensive CTS bus network, operating on city streets, serves Cleveland and nearby suburbs. In addition, several suburbs (Euclid, for example) have municipal bus operations, internally, that connect with the CTS system. Some suburbs, such as North Olmsted, have bus systems that provide service directly to downtown Cleveland. Bus patronage and service, however, has been declining even more rapidly than rapid transit patronage and service. Although statistics on the number of bus riders on the CTS system are not available, the number of vehicle miles of service on that system declined from 36.6 million in 1957 to 19.2 million in 1972, a 47.5 percent decline.

Selected Regional Problems of Northeastern Ohio

The nine county area of Northeastern Ohio is characterized by a variety of problems, many of which are mutually interrelated and the solutions to which involve the resolution of politically sensitive public issues. In addition to the usual problems arising out of the conflicts between ethnic and socioeconomic groups within the urbanized areas, and the central city-suburban dichotomy, Northeastern Ohio, because of its multinucleated nature, has a number of special problems; some of these are long-standing and are especially difficult to solve because of lack of public interest, or lack of adequate organizations and agencies to deal with them, or both.

THE STRUCTURE OF REGIONAL PLANNING

There are serious conflicts among the various definitions of the region for planning purposes, and the problem of drawing appropriate regional boundaries is politically sensitive. Under the Demonstration Cities and Metropolitan Planning Act of 1966, the federal government required the creation and operation of regional planning agencies, the majority of whose members were to be elected public officials. The certification by such agencies that any public programs or projects within a broad series of defined categories were in conformance with a comprehensive metropolitan plan was required in order to obtain federal assistance for the projects and programs. Each such agency was to be certi-

fied by the federal government's Department of Housing and Urban Development. These agencies, in each state, were to be set up by the state. Whereas in most metropolitan areas there was little difficulty in identifying the boundaries of such planning units, in Northeastern Ohio the problem was—and is—complicated not only by the city-suburban dualism, intensified by the ethnicity and racial segregation within the city of Cleveland, but also by the strongly divergent views and localisms prevailing in both the Cleveland and Akron regions with respect to the relations between the two overlapping centers. On the other hand, three active regional planning agencies on the periphery of the Cleveland-Akron complex, previously set up, functioned well in the new context. There are Mahoning and Trumbull counties (Youngstown-Warren SMSA), Stark County (Canton SMSA), and Lorain County (Lorain-Elyria SMSA). The first two received the needed federal certification; the latter operated through the Northeast Ohio Areawide Coordinating Agency (NOACA), an agency that has been the subject of much political fighting and uncertainty since its creation in 1968. The Tri-County Regional Planning Agency, covering Summit, Portage, and Medina counties, operated semiindependently, but NOACA is the certified metropolitan planning agency through which Tri-County secured federal approvals. In mid-1973 this situation was fluid, with the state recommending a consolidation of the Tri-County and Stark County regional planning agencies, and the addition of

Wayne County, heretofore without a planning agency, to serve the Akron complex, and a four county agency (Cuyahoga, Lake, Geauga, and Lorain) to succeed NOACA. On the other hand, as part of a plan to divide the state into administrative districts for decentralization of many state governmental and administrative functions, a nine county administrative district was proposed. As a first step in implementing the proposals for the Akron-centered region, a five county Council of Governments was in process of organization in mid-1973. It was hoped that such a council would constitute the nucleus of the future regional planning agency.

Much of the difficulty with NOACA sprang from the ethnic and racial friction, reflected in spatial segregation, between Cleveland and its suburban and outlying areas. Cleveland at one time withdrew from NOACA, and with the withdrawal NOACA temporarily lost its federal certification. The certification was restored when a change in administration in the city of Cleveland resulted in the city rejoining the planning agency. Many suburbanites have viewed with apprehension the dominance of Cleveland, with its large black and lower income populations, and the consequent concentration of problems in the inner city. On the other hand, many people in Cleveland were fearful of the dilution of the political strength of the blacks and ethnics in Cleveland by inclusion of the large white and middle to upper income populations of the suburban areas. Cleveland, as a city, has its boundaries relatively close to the downtown area, and the "overspill" into the inner suburbs of minorities and low income people has reduced the middle income population and areas within Cleveland to a much smaller percentage of the total metropolitan population than is common in most other metropolitan regions.

Many individuals in the Akron region resented the dominance of both Cleveland and its suburbs in NOACA and favored separation with a regional agency based upon Akron. It is an important regional issue whether the communalities between Cleveland and Akron are, or should be, more significant than the separate identities of the two overlapping metropolitan complexes.

Within the nine county urban region of Northeastern Ohio, we here identify several more specific problems for separate brief consideration.

STRENGTHENING OF THE ECONOMIC BASE

We have seen that the economic base of Northeastern Ohio had had a slower rate of growth in recent decades than that of many other regions of the United States. In spite of a relative decline in some of its traditional capital and durable goods manufacturing industries, the region is at the same time falling behind most of the rest of the nation in the service occupations. Service employment is relatively underrepresented; financial, professional, and personal services appear to be at a somewhat lower level than in many other regions. There are frequent complaints of a "brain drain," an outmigration of qualified high level personnel. The amenities of the region, in spite of many famous Cleveland institutions, are not among the region's attractions, nor is the climate. On the other hand, the more important growth of industry has been in the durable consumer goods lines, particularly motor vehicles, and in the industries in which the vehicle manufacturers constitute major markets. The growth potential for many of these industries is limited for the following reasons—a slowing up in demand for vehicles, due to slower population growth; saturation of the market for second cars; an emphasis upon smaller cars resulting from the environmentalist movement; and a greater demand on the part of services for disposable consumer income.

ECONOMIC DEVELOPMENT ACTIVITIES

The fragmentation of the region into a number of metropolitan areas has, to some extent, hindered economic development activities. The Greater Cleveland Growth Association, in spite of its somewhat anachronistic name, has been an asset to the region, but its areal extent of concern is rather limited. Similarly, the economic development efforts on the part of the state of Ohio, centered in its Department of Economic Development, have tended to emphasize the northeastern part of the state somewhat less than would be the case if Ohio did not have other large metropolitan areas elsewhere, such as Toledo, Columbus, Dayton, and Cincinnati, that divide the state's economic development efforts.

The location of existing transportation facilities, on the other hand, in the urban region of Northeastern Ohio continues to favor the region in industrial location. The region has one of the densest nodes of railroad lines in the nation. Its position astride the east-west trunk lines, together with the lines connecting the Lake Erie cities with the southern hinterland, provide excellent freight services. The regional railroads have not been slow to adopt new technology, including unitized intermodal transportation such as containers, piggyback, and unit trains. In 1973, progress by the railroads had, however, been substantially impeded by the bankruptcy of two of the largest systems serving the region. Northeastern Ohio has a very real and substantial interest in the successful outcome of efforts to reorganize and revitalize the northeastern railroad network.

MASS TRANSPORTATION

The concentration of interregional and arterial highways in Northeastern Ohio, similarly, is an important asset in the prospective enhancement of the economic base of the region. The highways provide unexcelled access in all directions, in spite of localized congestion in the central areas of Cleveland and some of the other nearby cities. On the other hand, the presence of the highways has acted to the detriment of intercity public passenger transportation, which, except for a few bus lines connecting the larger cities, is virtually nonexistent. There have been many proposals for maintaining, under some form of public operation, the few remaining urban local transit systems in the face of continuing declines in ridership. The basic problems are insufficient population density to generate enough mass transit riding, and the diffuse pattern of origins and destinations of trips due to urban decentralization. In Cleveland, extension of the CTS system to include the rest of Cuyahoga County, and perhaps beyond, has frequently been proposed. Without substantial infusion of federal financial assistance, it is impossible to see how the system could become economically viable. As we have seen, both of the rapid transit systems in the Cleveland area—CTS and Shaker Rapid—have suffered continuing losses of traffic in recent years, and the spiraling fare levels create a very discouraging prospect for the future. The Akron metropolitan bus system, on the other hand, was revived in 1972, when Akron, Cuya-

hoga Falls, and Barberton voted overwhelmingly to subsidize its operation from tax revenues. This is based upon the assumption that, although fares could not possibly justify the operation, the larger public benefits make continued availability of public transit essential. Perhaps the current interest in the reduction of atmospheric and environmental pollution, combined with the prospect of fuel shortages and increased federal aid, will at least arrest the decline and perhaps revive public mass passenger transportation in the urban areas of Northeastern Ohio.

PORT DEVELOPMENT

The dependence of many of Northeastern Ohio's basic manufacturing industries on water transportation continues to be very significant. The primary metals industries, especially iron and steel, receive ores from the upper lakes, eastern Canada, and abroad, and limestone from other areas of the Great Lakes; the chemical industry is a heavy user of lake transportation; Appalachian coal is marketed in the upper lakes and in nearby Canada. More recently, the enlargement of the St. Lawrence Seaway has been followed by the development of substantial direct overseas general cargo traffic, in which the ports of Northeastern Ohio—Conneaut, Ashtabula, and Cleveland—compete with westerly Great Lakes ports but, more significantly, with salt water ports, easily reached by rail and the interstate highway systems.

In bulk traffic, Conneaut, Ashtabula, and Lorain are characterized by continuing heavy receipts of iron ore, which are moved inland by rail to the Pittsburgh, Youngstown, and other steel-producing districts (Figure 22). Coal is moved in the opposite direction, to upper lake and nearby Canadian destinations. To handle the many millions of tons of such bulk traffic, highly specialized wharfside machinery constitutes a distinctive waterfront landscape. In recent years, in spite of access to wider territories because of the enlarged seaway, which enables eastern Canadian ores to compete with Lake Superior ores in Northeastern Ohio, the ore traffic has not been increasing. At the same time, the coal movements have leveled off for a number of reasons—the substitution of alternative fuels for domestic space heating, industrial and railroad use, and use in utility

Figure 22. Northeastern Ohio railroads, 1970.

plants; the development of unit trains and train-load rates, which are competitive with the rail-water routings of coal; and the concern for the environmental effects of the use of coal fuel.

In Cleveland, the bulk movements are handled largely at a complex terminal on Whiskey Island, west of the Cuyahoga River, where the largest lake and ocean vessels, able to travel the seaway and the connecting channels between the lakes, can be handled; and up the meandering Cuyahoga River, where access is handicapped by limited depth, sharp turns, and numerous bridges. A proposal has been made to transfer bulk movements to and from the upriver plants to a conveyor belt at a lake-front terminal. This would avoid using the river. Meanwhile, several vessels intended for upriver access are under construction.

Within the Great Lakes, internal package freight and passenger movements, which terminated with World War II, have been replaced at the major Great Lakes ports by direct over-seas general cargo movements, handled largely by scheduled cargo liner services moving through the St. Lawrence Seaway. Manufactures move in both directions through the seaway. In Northeastern Ohio, both Cleveland and Ashtabula have a variety of services to and from every continent. These services, however, are subject to great year-to-year fluctuations, depending upon economic, political, and military conditions in various parts of the world and upon the political climate in the United States. Recently, steel imports were prominent among the general cargo movements; this has recently declined. The development of container ships for general cargo movements on the major ocean routes, the expansion of interstate highways, the growth of railroad piggyback and container traffic, and the increasing prospect for unit trains have greatly reduced the potentials for increasing general cargo traffic through the Great Lakes ports. The ports of Northeastern Ohio cannot, as can the lake ports farther west, compensate for this by further development of export grain traffic. One Great Lakes shipping line has instituted a feeder containership movement, transferring at Montreal. The development of barge-carrying ships may have some applicability to the Great Lakes. Nevertheless, the prospects for continued substantial general cargo movement at a level envisioned by the more optimistic promoters of the seaway a couple of decades ago scarcely seem realistic in the light of subsequent developments.

The general cargo facilities at the port of Cleveland are in the hands of a county port authority, which, in 1972, announced long range plans for considerable extension of the port. The prospects of early implementation of the plans seem dim. Most of the expansion is proposed off downtown Cleveland, where prospects are good, in many people's minds, for location of a major regional airport serving Northeastern Ohio.

REGIONAL AIRPORT

In addition to many general aviation airports which serve the region, Northeastern Ohio has one major and several lesser airports serving scheduled airlines. The largest is Cleveland-Hopkins International Airport, in the southwest corner of the city. It is a "large hub," normally ranking fifteenth or sixteenth in the nation in traffic volume. Because of its location, between a built-up area and the gorge of the Rocky River, it is incapable of being greatly expanded in area. In 1973, a feasibility study was authorized for a major regional airport in Northeastern Ohio. The interests in Cleveland tend to favor, if a new airport is to be built, a site in Lake Erie offshore from the central business district. Many problems are involved: determination of prospective traffic volumes for both passengers and cargo; costs of acquisition and construction at several alternative sites; ecological and environmental effects including noise, air, and water pollution; landward access; and regulation of nearby land uses. The present Cleveland airport may be adequate for many years, particularly with the emphasis upon larger planes, fewer flights in proportion to traffic, and prospective development of STOL and VTOL (steep takeoff or landing and vertical takeoff or landing) aircraft for short flights, and the possible development of new methods of ultra-high-speed land trans-

portation. Meanwhile, other airports in the region, notably Akron-Canton and Youngstown-Warren-Sharon airports, can serve, along with several of the general aviation facilities, as "reliever" airports. These facilities put off, or possibly eliminate, the ultimate necessity for another major regional facility. In any event, if a new airport were to be built, it would occupy a substantial area of many square miles, would cost upward of $1 billion, and would take at least a decade to plan and build. If it were to be built, however, it would undoubtedly form the locus of a very intensive nearby industrial and commercial development employing some 50,000 people. If the airport were to be built at an offshore site opposite central Cleveland, it would materially facilitate a reversal of the downward trend in activity in the downtown area and, in part, counteract the tendency for regional activities to decentralize. The incompatible effects upon the lake, noise pollution, and traffic generation would require considerable study before a decision could be made.

LAKE ERIE SHORELINE

Northeastern Ohio, and especially Cleveland, have not taken maximum advantage of the Lake Erie shoreline as a unique resource. In comparison with other Great Lakes urbanized areas—especially Chicago, Milwaukee, and Toronto—the shoreline land uses are not developed in accordance with comprehensive planning principles, and public access to the lakeshore is deficient.

There are several characteristics of the lakeshore which have, in the past, accentuated problems of shoreline development. In the first place, the lake, throughout most of Northeastern Ohio, is bordered by steep bluffs, formed from the horizontal sedimentary rocks and the glacial overburden by erosion. The shoreline is leeward of the prevailing winds, which sweep across the lake from the northwest, especially during the stormy winter season, and the waves undercut the bluffs, with the full fetch of the wide lake behind them. The southwest-northeast alignment of the shore throughout most of Northeastern Ohio places the shoreline at almost right angles to the winds and waves. Although the erosion problem is acute throughout most of the extent of shoreline, it is especially critical in the northeastern suburbs of Cleveland and farther eastward. Recession of the bluffs has been accompanied by loss of extensive land, and many homes have been undermined and have fallen into the lake. Because of the fragmentation of riparian ownership and the lack of comprehensive shoreline planning, the small scale efforts to reduce shore erosion by means of groins and breakwaters has been ineffective. Except for the federal breakwater that protects the harbor on both sides of the Cuyahoga River entrance and extends for nearly five miles eastward paralleling the shore, there is no large scale erosion control project.

A second condition adversely affecting development of the Lake Erie shore in Northeastern Ohio is water pollution. Lake Erie, in recent years, has received nationwide publicity as a "dying" lake, due largely to industrial pollution. The lake is far from "dead" in spite of pollution, which is partly of local origin within the region and partly the result of heretofore largely uncontrolled industrial, municipal, and other effluents discharged into the lake from outside the region, notably from the urban areas bordering the Detroit River and the Maumee (Toledo), and from Canada, immediately across the lake. At present, commercial and sport fishing is adversely affected, and the few public beaches, such as in Edgewater and Gordon parks in Cleveland and Headlands State Park near Fairport Harbor, are frequently closed to swimming.

The recent concern for pollution control, both in the United States and in Canada, and the many regulations recently initiated may eventually reduce the problem, but the lake has a long way to go before pristine conditions are restored. Meanwhile, careful treatment of the water supply of Cleveland and other lakeshore communities, which take their public supplies from the lake, is required.

In spite of the adverse conditions of the lakeshore and the lake itself, including frequent treacherous storms, recreational boating is highly developed on Lake Erie. However, the several marinas are insufficient to meet the demand.

In proximity to downtown Cleveland, the wide area of the Flats merges with the lake plain, and the bluffs are absent from the lakeshore. Here, partly on artificial fill, is the major portion of Cleveland's port; the Burke Lakefront Airport, a general aviation facility which occupies over a mile of shoreline; and

other facilities, with recreation on the immediate shoreline almost totally absent, in sharp contrast with downtown shoreline development of park areas in several other major Great Lakes cities. In the summer of 1973, plans were announced for the development of a multimillion dollar recreational area in the Flats.

East and west of downtown Cleveland, most of the shoreline is in private riparian ownership; except at street ends, the public does not have any direct access. Small lakefront parks in Euclid, Lakewood, and elsewhere are separated from the shore by bluffs. The long term cyclical fluctuations in lake level create wide beaches in certain years. Nevertheless, these beaches are not very accessible. During high water stages, the beaches disappear and backward erosion of the bluffs is a serious problem.

In short, the failure to view the regional shoreline as a major resource and the lack of comprehensive planning and development are reflected in a fragmented ownership pattern, with a high percentage of the shore fronted by private developments and with inadequate public access. The fragmentation of the adjacent land areas into many local governmental units further complicates the problem of planning for and implementing comprehensive attacks upon the shoreline problems—pollution, erosion, inadequate public access, inadequate provision for recreational boating, a disorderly and largely unplanned utilization of Cleveland's downtown lakefront, and a general public lack of awareness of the possibilities for utilization of the lakeshore as a major regional resource. The prospect of a large offshore regional airport is tending to obscure the larger issues involved in regarding the shoreline as a totality.

OPEN SPACE PRESERVATION

Although Lake Erie with its uninterrupted vistas toward the northern horizon is the largest open space available to the people of Northeastern Ohio, there is a continuing and acute need to preserve open space in the landward portions of the region in the face of peripheral expansion of urbanization and of the intermetropolitan coalescence or "urban sprawl." There is, additionally, the need to provide open space in the inner city areas, where population density is at a maximum and, because of low incomes, mobility—the ability to reach extensive recreational areas—is at a minimum. Open space in Northeastern Ohio is becoming a prime commodity as demand for urban uses of land increases due to population increases and deconcentration from older areas of the central cities.

Much of the public open space in Cuyahoga County is held by the Cleveland Metropolitan Park District (Figure 23). That agency, established in 1917, controls 14,400 acres in thirty municipalities within Cuyahoga County and Hinckley Township in Medina County. The system is being expanded at an average rate of 200 acres per year. Many of the properties are along stream valleys. A major portion of the units within the system are interconnected to form a semicircular belt of "reservations" and parkways nearly encircling the city—hence the popular designation of the "emerald necklace." Among the stream courses within the system are Rocky River, Big Creek, Euclid Creek, and portions of the Chagrin River. In most instances, the streams and their tributaries occupy deep, steep-sided gorges, and the district has been a major force in preserving the scenic amenities of the metropolitan area. Financing

has been mainly by a series of ten year tax levies for capital expenditures, supplemented by other bond issues. Current plans call for the acquisition of an additional 8,400 acres by 1980.

Summit County established a similar park district in 1925. A number of the scenic areas in the vicinity of Akron, such as portions of the Cuyahoga Valley, are within the control of the Metropolitan Park Board of Summit County. Both the Cuyahoga and Summit County park districts were guided in their early stages by Frederick Law Olmsted, Jr., and his colleagues in what was probably the most noted firm of landscape architects in America. The Summit County system consists of ten major sites totaling 5,500 acres. Other counties subsequently established metropolitan park systems—Lake County in 1958, currently with seven parks covering 1,600 acres; and Lorain County in 1957 with ten sites and 10,000 acres. Stark County established a park district in 1967. In addition, there are state parks and other regional park and open space facilities in the various counties. Two noteworthy state parks are Nelson-Kennedy Ledges, near Garrettsville in Portage County, a 167 acre tract

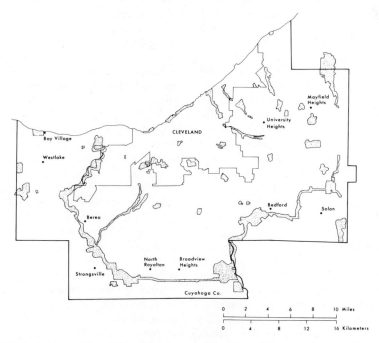

Figure 23. Principal areas of public open space, Cuyahoga County. Source: Regional Planning Commission, Cuyahoga County.

containing a geologically interesting and scenic rock outcrop conglomerate; and Punderson State Park, in Geauga County, containing a lake and facilities such as a lodge and cabins within its 728 acres. In addition, open space is preserved in Northeastern Ohio by designating areas as wildlife preserves. In addition to these public open spaces, much of the remaining open space is in private hands, and there is a considerable development of commercial recreation facilities.

The Ohio Department of Natural Resources provided a statewide plan for outdoor recreation in 1971, with an inventory and analysis for each county in Ohio. While it does not provide specific steps for land acquisition, it sets the stage for further efforts in preservation and development of open space. If the proposed federal open space planning requirements are instituted, open space planning in Ohio would have a head start.

The region is particularly favored by location of many scenic features and natural woodlands close to accessible population. While these areas offer opportunities for preservation as natural areas in many instances, and for development of active recreation in other instances, their preservation constitutes a challenge to the region. Furthermore, a problem that the region shares with most other urbanizing areas is how to preserve an open character between major urban concentrations. This gives a form and structure to the urbanized areas, mitigates the effects of urban sprawl, and provides for recreational demands. Many institutions, such as camps, campuses, and county clubs, require not only extensive areas of open space for their own operations, but also an essentially nonurban environment with contiguous open space. The preservation of such open type land uses, as well as agriculture, in the face of the prospects for continued urban expansion, is a major problem for planners in Northeastern Ohio.

One possible solution, among others, is the development of clusters of higher density outside the present established limits of urbanization. Such clusters can be single function—apartment developments, shopping centers, etc.—or multifunctional.

At a smaller scale, cluster planning of residential and other developments utilizes higher densities in limited areas in order to provide more open space. It is becoming increasingly popular as more and more developers realize its advantages. Much of the present zoning, based upon the prevalence of individual uses of relatively small conventional lots, is obsolete. Planned unit development (PUD) zoning, which is being adopted by an increasing number of jurisdictions, is more suited to the larger scale, extensive developments that are characteristic of the urbanization process in recent years.

Another area of special concern, where steps taken in the near future may insure subsequent preservation of amenities, is the Cuyahoga Valley, particularly between the northern limits of Akron and the southerly suburbs of Cleveland, a stretch of over twenty miles of superb scenery and natural beauty. Portions of this area were recently designated for purchase as a state park. In 1973, the U.S. Congress had before it a bill to create a national park in this area, to include not only the valley bottom, but also the slopes and sufficient adjacent upland area to protect against incompatible encroachments upon the scenic character of the valley. Since many prospective developments in, and particularly in proximity to, the valley are imminent, action upon this bill is particularly timely. The proposed park would be of sufficient size so that the river and adjacent areas could provide not only for preservation of most of the scenic quality, but also for limited areas of active recreation, accessible to many people, within the heart of the multimetropolitan complex of Northeast Ohio.

Many other areas of Northeastern Ohio offer opportunities, because of terrain and water bodies, for either conservation as open space or for carefully controlled recreational development. Many of the natural lakes of the region form the foci for private residential developments, either where there is little or no public access—as, for example, at the Twin Lakes north of Kent—or where some public access is provided—as in the Portage Lakes area south of Akron. A number of multiple purpose reservoirs have been developed, primarily for flood control or water supply and incidentally for recreation. The Mogadore Reservoir is a recreation facility of some importance, and the recently created West Branch Reservoir is the site of a state park. On the other hand, Lake Rockwell, behind a Cuyahoga River dam north of Kent, furnishes a major part of Akron's public water supply, but, in spite of great scenic beauty, the public is denied access.

ENVIRONMENTAL QUALITY

Like many other urban regions of the United States, Northeastern Ohio experiences considerable environmental disruption. These adverse conditions include the familiar gamut of air, water, noise, and aesthetic problems, and they are especially acute in the lower Cuyahoga basin, although many other portions of the region have also been adversely affected by the lack of concern, until very recently, for the quality of the environment. Northeastern Ohio has been unable to generate effective improvement mechanisms. Efforts have generally been frustrated by the prevailing provincialism of the population, political bickering, the fragmentation of the region into numerous units of local and special function governments, agency duplication, and an emphasis upon home rule. Only very recently has federal intervention been manifest to any extent, and the current emphasis upon environmental quality is evidence that, in the long run, in spite of numerous obstacles, the physical quality of the air and water of Northeastern Ohio may be improved.

Problems of air and water pollution are generally beyond the ability of local governments to handle. A number of planning agencies—including the Three Watersheds District (Cuyahoga, Rocky and Chagrin river basins)—were formed to deal with specific problems such as water management and problems that transcend individual local jurisdictions including counties. Agencies such as the Northeastern Ohio Areawide Coordinating Agency (NOACA) and the Tri-County Planning Commission are very vulnerable to local pressures since, until very recently, participation by local governments has been strictly voluntary. How the recent federal requirements for overall regional planning will ultimately prove their effectiveness remains to be seen.

Air Quality

There are at least twenty air pollution control agencies, districts, or regions attempting to monitor, regulate, and control air quality within the urbanized region of Northeastern Ohio. Many of these agencies conflict with and duplicate the work of others. Power to enforce regulations is complicated. However, consistent with the home rule provisions of the Ohio constitution, many cities have delegated this responsibility, and a concerted effort has been made to avoid a centralized enforcement agency. The result is that the overall level of air quality has deteriorated. The recent requirements for air quality standards and for mandatory consideration of environmental impact in connection with federal aid projects and programs offer some hope for improvement in the not too distant future. Meanwhile, the air pollution, particularly on the lee sides of the major cities, close to the principal concentrations are located constitutes a major challenge. How the changes in federal, state, and industrial pollution but heavy traffic concentrations are located constitute important challenges. How the changes in federal, state, and local air pollution control regulations resulting from the fuel shortages of late 1973 and early 1974 will affect air quality in the region remains to be determined as the result of experience.

Water Pollution

Water pollution, like air pollution, is a compelling and urgent problem in Northeastern Ohio. The Cuyahoga River, in its lower course, has achieved nationwide recognition as one of the most polluted major streams in the nation. Lake Erie has international notoriety as a dying lake. Whether these dubious distinctions are completely justified or not, both the river and lake undoubtedly require much cleaning up. Not only are industrial wastes disposed into the waters, but many of the suburban and unincorporated residential areas continue to discharge their wastes into the surface waters. With recent, more stringent regulations, there are prospects of improvement, but the specific planning for sewage treatment and water pollution abatement generates numerous interregional conflicts the resolution of which may be extremely difficult.

Much of the pollution in Lake Erie is beyond the control of the Northeastern Ohio region. It is true that the Cuyahoga, Rocky and Chagrin rivers, as well as minor streams with their pollution, discharge into the lake. However, much of the pollution of Lake Erie originates outside the region, especially along the Detroit River. Since the lake forms part of the international boundary with Canada, the control of pollution in the lake is, in part, an international problem. Several international agencies are dealing with the problem.

Meanwhile, the few beaches that are available for public access, as well as the privately held shoreline, are adversely affected by the quality of the lake water. Cleveland's public beaches, in spite of attempts to mitigate the pollution by chlorination in the semienclosed beach areas, are frequently closed to bathers and swimmers. Sport and commercial fishing are adversely affected by the pollution. Similarly, many of the inland lakes and streams are polluted. Although some local governments have joined forces for combined attacks on water pollution, there is as yet no comprehensive plan for water management in the drainage basins of Northeastern Ohio.

Solid Waste Disposal

Disposal of solid wastes in the nine county region also constitutes a major problem. Not only city garbage, but also solid by-products from sewage treatment plants must be disposed. In Northeastern Ohio plans have been developed to ship solid or semisolid wastes to areas within and outside the producing region by means of trucks, railroads, and pipelines. Some studies propose shipment of semisolid waste sludge by pipeline to storage basins and aerated lagoons in northern Wayne County and eastern Stark County. Liquid effluents would also be shipped out of the region to storage basins and treatment plants in western Ohio. The waste sludge would then be used in landfills and for strip mine reclamation in southeastern Ohio.

Electric Power Generation

Environmental quality in Northeastern Ohio would be much more of an acute problem than now is the case if the area did not, in effect, export environmental disruption out of the region, especially in the case of the electric power industry. Northeastern Ohio is somewhat unique in that a very large proportion of the power consumed in the region comes from generating plants outside the area. Although there are a few thermal plants along the Lake Erie shoreline (two in eastern Cleveland, one each in Avon Lake and Painesville) and some small hydroelectric plants, as at Cuyahoga Falls, most of the power is produced along the Ohio River and east and west of the region along Lake Erie and

is transmitted to the region by a grid. The Ohio River plants, in particular, utilize coal mined in southern Ohio and West Virginia and discharge thermal wastes into the Ohio River. The several companies (Ohio Edison and its subsidiary Pennsylvania Power, the Cleveland Electric Illuminating Company, the Ohio Power Company, and the Duquesne Light and Power Company) are linked in CAPCO (Central Area Power Coordinating Group), which is a generating and distribution consortium designated to take advantage of the system reliability and capital investment benefits of large scale power production and distribution. CAPCO in turn is tied to consortiums in other states through the East Central Area Reliability group (ECAR) and other groups. CAPCO anticipates that these ties will provide steady power supplies and prevent massive breakdowns such as the November 1965 eastern blackout. While regional ties are important for short term problems, solutions to the long term energy problem require that each company and consortium construct its share of power plants to feed the system. Studies indicate that current building programs of CAPCO and companies forming the consortium will be able to meet demand through 1980 and, given that projects are on line when scheduled, the power system is reliable. Thus, it does not appear that industrial growth will have to be curtailed in Northeastern Ohio through 1980. Existing plans of CAPCO call for nuclear energy to supply a considerable portion of the demand after 1980. Many of these plants, particularly the proposed Perry plants on Lake Erie, are located within the region and have already been objected to by the environmentalists. As more and more power plants are built within the region, close to urban areas, there may well be long court battles to ensure strict compliance with environmental standards or to stop construction, or both. Given the long lead time required for planning and construction of nuclear plants, any serious delays could impede the reliability of the CAPCO system beyond 1980, particularly because of the combination of environmental constraints and the oil shortage.

Proximity of the Northeastern Ohio region to vast deposits of coal in the nearby portions of the Appalachian plateau may prove, in the near future, to be a decided attraction for industry and for further urban development, since, unlike other regions that are largely dependent upon petroleum fuels or limited hydropower resources, the supply of coal seems adequate for the long run future. The siting of generating plants, the control of their effluents, and the location of transmission lines, however, constitute important battlegrounds between those desiring further economic expansion in the region, on the one hand, and the environmentalists, on the other.

OUTLYING COMMERCIAL CENTERS

Since the early 1950s, Northeastern Ohio has witnessed a spectacular shift in its commercial retailing and service functions, and, to a lesser but nevertheless important extent, its office administrative functions. At the same time, the old central business districts, which long constituted the cores of the region's cities, have almost universally suffered not only a relative, but an absolute, decline. The multinucleated character of the region's urban pattern has been reinforced by the development of numerous planned, large scale shopping centers, office parks, and combination facilities, which not only compose foci of surrounding and nearby residential growth, but also comprise, in themselves, important centers of employment and of traffic generation. In some instances, the volume of retail sales in any one of several large shopping centers rivals, or even exceeds, that of the central business districts of the major cities of the region. The location of such new centers has been, together with the highway system that makes them accessible, a major factor in intermetropolitan coalescence. Many of the new large "regional" shopping centers are located beyond the limits of the heretofore urbanized areas, and some of them depend upon substantially more than the trade of a single city.

As in most North American urban regions, the older pattern of retailing and service establishments consisted of those in the central business districts, outlying nucleations most commonly associated with crossings, transfer points, or terminals of mass transportation routes, and ribbons of intermittent commercial developments along the major arterial streets. All of these earlier elements of the commercial pattern survive, though many of them with difficulty, while ribbons continue to develop along some of the major highways, as indicated

earlier, where limited access does not restrict their development.

A recent study of regional shopping centers in Cuyahoga and western Lake counties by the Real Property Inventory of Cleveland found that slightly over half of all retail stores and service establishments within the area were in planned regional shopping areas. By type of establishment, the percentage ranged from 31.2 for wholesale establishments to 89.0 percent for apparel stores and 82.0 percent for general merchandise stores. These figures are especially amazing in light of the fact that comprehensively planned shopping centers were virtually unknown a generation ago.

The first planned shopping center in the nine county region, and one of the first anywhere, was the Shaker Square Center, developed in 1928 by the Van Sweringen brothers at the west end of their Shaker Heights suburban area, just within the city limits of Cleveland, where the two branches of their transit line converge. Although that center is not modern, in that it is intersected by streets; does not have a covered mall; and has limited parking, it remains today as one of the prestige retail concentrations of the region. Small by contemporary standards, it contains fifty-three establishments with just over 100,000 square feet of selling area and parking for 1,000 cars. A larger, but less comprehensively planned, shopping and office building center developed at the outer terminal of one of the Shaker Rapid lines between 1947 and 1956, but by the latter year the boom in comprehensively planned regional shopping centers was well under way.

A large proportion of the major regional planned shopping centers were built in the region between the mid-1950s and the late 1960s, although several of the very largest are of more recent development, including Midway Mall between Lorain and Elyria, opened in 1966; Richmond Mall, opened in the same year; Chapel Hill Mall in Akron; and Belden Village in Canton (Figure 24). The earlier regional centers consisted of one or more rows of shops, with two, three, or four department stores, an open mall, and a surrounding sea of parking. The major regional centers built in recent years typically have covered malls, with year round controlled climate. Some of the older centers, such as Westgate just beyond the westerly city limit of Cleveland, subsequently had their malls roofed. The typical large re-

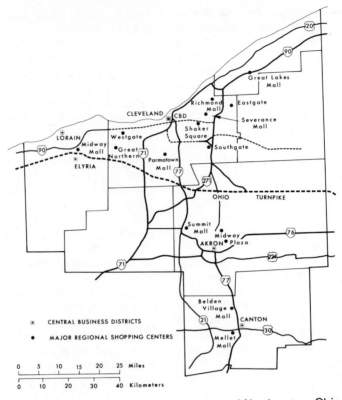

Figure 24. Major regional shopping centers, urbanized areas of Northeastern Ohio.

gional shopping center has upward of 400,000 square feet of selling space; from under fifty to over one hundred individual retail and service establishments, including at least two major department stores or branches; and parking for from 1,000 to nearly 10,000 cars. A few of the centers are multilevel, with stairways, ramps, and escalators facilitating access to the various levels. Nearly all are located within easy access of at least one freeway, and many are near two or more major highway routes. Early in 1973, plans were announced for the development of the region's, and possibly the nation's, largest regional shopping center, to be located in an easterly suburb of Cleveland and to contain at least 1.8 million square feet of shopping area.

These regional shopping centers draw from very extensive areas, in many instances from as far as thirty miles. The region's medium-sized and larger cities compete, not only with one another, but also with the central business districts of more than a single city. Unless the ad-

jacent areas plan for shopping centers and for the consequences of their location, monotonous urban sprawl results. Among the problems in the immediate vicinities of the shopping centers are intensive generation of traffic, especially if major highway access is inadequate; decline of the older shopping areas in the vicinity; and, sometimes, general unsightliness, including the growth of "parasitic" nearby establishments, which may not be subject to the rigid controls of those within the centers proper. Transition zoning may consitute a problem.

One of the problems associated with planned shopping centers is that many municipalities and townships need to attract more development than the market may justify, with a view toward maximizing tax revenues from the real property taxes paid by the development, from the sales taxes generated by the establishments, and from wage taxes paid to the local governments by the employees. The result, in too many instances, is an oversupply of land zoned for commercial uses and the encouragement of uneconomic expansion of retail, service, and industrial facilities.

DECLINE OF CENTRAL BUSINESS DISTRICTS

The cores of the principal cities of the nine county region have been affected in many ways by the spread of the region's population and activities and the coalescence of the urban settlement of the region. The very nature of the "downtowns" has been rapidly changing. In some respects, they may be regarded as responses to nineteenth century transportation technology and are, at least partly, anachronistic. While in most cities of the region the downtown area may still be the site of major activity, their relative, and in many instances absolute, importance has continued to decline.

Regional and community shopping centers, industrial and office parks, highway-oriented hotels, and new clusters around large airports all have contributed to the reduction of the importance of many downtown functions and the elimination of others. On the other hand, in the larger cities, the office function has increased in relative importance within the central business district, in spite of the establishment of many office functions in other parts of the respective metropolitan areas. Entertainment, retail shopping, and other functions generally associated with central business districts are having great difficulty, where they survive at all. Most downtowns die at night. In a few instances, as in Cleveland and Akron, high-rise apartment developments, and institutional nodes such as central city-oriented universities and colleges, constitute essentially newly established, central area functions.

Downtown Cleveland, although continuing as the most important single node in Northeastern Ohio, has been hard hit by the numerous trends above noted. With the peripheral growth of retailing, several major department stores have closed, but downtown Cleveland still remains as the locus of numerous specialty establishments and the largest units of many regional and national chain operations within the region also remain. On the other hand, several very large retail establishments have closed in recent years and have not been replaced in downtown Cleveland. The shortage of hotels of sufficient size and quality to attract major conventions has undoubtedly hurt the center, in spite of relatively good facilities for exhibitions and the presence on the downtown lakefront of a large municipal stadium. As in most cities, wholesaling and light manufacturing in and near the central business district, formerly occupying numerous multistory loft buildings, have largely evacuated the central area. The classic "core frame" or "zone of wholesaling and light manufacturing" has largely been vacated, occupied by marginal businesses that cannot afford high rents and rely upon occupance of "filtered down" buildings, or devoted to extensive areas of limited access highway interchanges and parking facilities.

Downtown Cleveland occupies a relatively confined area and is limited on all sides by pronounced physical barriers—on the north and northeast by the lakefront, although much landfill has been placed for public functions, including the Burke Lakefront Airport, the general cargo portion of the port, the municipal stadium, and public parking; on the west and southwest by steep bluffs bordering the flats of the Cuyahoga valley, here occupied by remaining loft buildings and heavy industry; and on the east by the Innerbelt Freeway. The Public Square, dominated by the tall Terminal Tower, remains as the major focus of the city. The railroad terminal no longer functions for intercity travel, and part of the main concourse is used for tennis courts. Under the building, however, the rapid transit lines converge, while nearby buildings of the vast Van Sweringen development of the 1920s continue in their original functions—a department store, a hotel, two office buildings, and the main post office. Surrounding the Public Square are office buildings, some relatively new, while almost immediately contiguous to the northeast is the Mall, the locus of a cluster of public buildings including city hall, the county courthouse, the public library, and the exhibition hall.

Euclid Avenue, extending eastward from the Public Square, is the main retail axis of Cleveland and contains the largest concentration of shopping facilities in the region, although the facilities are substantially reduced from several years ago. The concentration of offices and retail establishments at the western end, near the Public Square, is in much healthier condition than is the eastern end of the CBD. This is in large part due to the concentration of Cleveland's rapid transit lines at the west end. There is no other rapid transit station within the downtown area, and internal distribution of people within the area is by bus, including local shuttle buses. There are recurrent plans for a subway, with several stations in the area, to connect with the existing CTS rapid transit, but no tangible progress has been made in recent years. Meanwhile, ridership on public transit, both rapid and bus, has been declining, and the availability of downtown parking, in spite of the changing character of the area, continues as a problem. Since the office function is more important now, relative to retailing, all-day parking demand has increased in proportion to short term demand.

Several major projects and proposals have been and are being considered or are being developed to revitalize the downtown area of Cleveland. Perhaps the most spectacular is the prospective airport in Lake Erie, for which feasibility studies are now under way. A new hotel and a multifunctional apartment-office-shopping complex are under construction on the edge of the present retail district. Finally, the recent development of a high density campus for Cleveland State University, at the east edge of downtown Cleveland, bordering the Innerbelt Freeway, may have some effect in revitalizing the deteriorated eastern side of the CBD.

Akron's central business district, similarly, has been declining for a number of years. Main Street, paralleling and east of the old canal, is the principal axis. Two large department stores face each other across the street, and the core is sharply defined, with serious atrophy around the edges. A large hotel structure, near the center of downtown Akron, has stood vacant for several years, although plans were recently announced to convert the building into a moderate income apartment building. As in Cleveland, a major inner city university on the fringe of the downtown area is regarded by local interests as a revitalizing force: the University of Akron, with a newly expanded, high density campus, is immediately east of downtown Akron, separated from it by several railroad lines, which occupy a narrow valley between downtown and the campus. Between the university and downtown, a newly completed Center for the Performing Arts is regarded by many Akronites as a spur toward new

vitality downtown. Earlier attempts to revitalize downtown Akron have not been completely successful. Cascade Plaza, a multipurpose development near the northern end of downtown Akron, consists of a large skyscraper office building, a smaller office structure, a hotel, and a parking garage, the latter underneath a landscaped plaza that gives visual unity to the project. However, Cascade Plaza, because of its magnitude, is out of scale with the rest of downtown Akron, and has accelerated the vacancies of other structures in the central area. On the other hand, it has stimulated a few additional developments nearby, which are to a limited extent slowing up the decline of the northern portion of the central business district. These include a public library and a federal office building. Immediately west of the core of Akron is a stretch of a few hundred yards of elaborate expressway, unconnected at either end and virtually useless.

In spite of these several new developments and others, downtown Cleveland and downtown Akron are both considerably less significant, both relatively and absolutely, than formerly, and there is serious doubt that either will ever again achieve the dominance that it once had. Similarly, the downtown areas of other Northeastern Ohio cities—Canton, Youngstown, Warren, Alliance, Massillon, Lorain, Elyria, and Cuyahoga Falls among them—not only have lost much of their former importance, but also have deteriorated—especially on their fringes, where vacant land is common. Express highways, parking lots, and vacant buildings are symptomatic of the shifting patterns of activity within the region.

CITY-SUBURBAN DICHOTOMY AND METROPOLITAN COORDINATION

As we have seen, Northeastern Ohio is a multinucleated urban region—a "conurbation"—with many regional problems that transcend the individual city areas and call for coordinated solutions on the part of local governments, special function governments, counties, the state, and the federal government. In some instances, the conflicts between regional identity on the one hand and local identity on the other have not been resolved sufficiently to permit the necessary public actions toward solution of regional problems. At a more local scale, some of the most compelling problems have not been approached with sufficient objectivity because of the conflicting interests of the various racial and ethnic groups, which, as we have seen in Cleveland, vitally affect the democratic process and tend to dominate election results. These circumstances are by no means unique to Northeastern Ohio; they are present to a greater or lesser degree in most urban areas of the United States. In spite of all attempts in the past decade or two to reduce the impact and extent of racial segregation, the dichotomy of interest between white and black, and between various white ethnic groups, still dominates many of the local and regional issues in Northeastern Ohio. Especially conspicuous are the conflicts between the eastern and western halves of the city of Cleveland, and between the central city on the one hand and the suburban areas on the other. The spatial patterns within the city and the metropolitan area of Cleveland relative to the various population groups spring not only from socioeconomic differences, but also from racial and ethnic differences. The upwardly mobile persons and families seek to secure what they consider a better way of life by moving into better housing, by using what they believe to be better schools, and by migrating to the suburbs to achieve status. Thus, the urban frontiers advanced and finally coalesced in the form of urbanized corridors that connect the principal cities of the region.

Although local rather than regional issues tend to dominate in public concern, there were indications in early 1974 of increasing interest on the part of many people in metropolitan and intermetropolitan problems. The formation decades ago of the metropolitan park districts in the Cleveland and Akron areas, and the more recent realization that problems of water management, air pollution control, energy, employment, and commuting transcend local administrative boundaries, offer hope that appropriate organizations and programs will lead toward at least mitigation, and hopefully solution, of some of these problems. The state of Ohio, under federal pressure, has planned to supersede the two major regional planning agencies with new agencies, the boundaries of which would presumably be more realistic, and to create a new administrative district for the nine counties with which this study is concerned. Mass transportation, which is very

much underdeveloped, is beginning to be approached on a regional basis; a regional transportation authority was created in Akron and adjacent suburbs in 1972; there is an active movement to create one in Portage County in 1974, and there are prospects for creation of a metropolitan transit authority with power to extend the Cleveland Transit System. Finally, Mayor Perk of Cleveland, late in 1973, proposed the creation of a metropolitan government to include Cleveland and the suburban areas of Cuyahoga County.

Racial, ethnic, and socioeconomic differences and apparent conflicts of interest once again were brought to the fore in connection with the proposal for metropolitan government for the Cleveland region. Some of the black leaders have accused the mayor of Cleveland of using the prospect for metropolitan government as a device for diluting the political influence of Cleveland's black population: particularly significant is the fact that the black population is moving to some of the suburbs in increasing numbers. Contributing to the movement is the rising affluence among some of the black families, antidiscrimination laws such as open housing requirements and school busing, increasing population pressures and continuing decline in the quality of many areas of the inner city, and the relatively more rapid increase of employment opportunities in suburban areas. In 1970, blacks constituted 38.3 percent of the population of the city of Cleveland, whereas they were only 19.1 percent of Cuyahoga County's population and 16.1 percent of the population of the four county Cleveland Standard Metropolitan Statistical Area.

In summary, the nine counties, including four metropolitan areas with overlapping commuting areas and much community of interest, but also numerous differences and conflicts, do not differ in many respects from many other older urbanized industrial regions. The principal differences are in the multinucleated nature of the region, the several major nodes and arterial internodal alignments of which form a conurbation or network, somewhat resembling the better known and larger eastern Megalopolis, but unique in that the intermetropolitan coalescence is taking place along several transportation corridors rather than a single one.

Bibliography

Akron Metropolitan Area Transportation Study. *Existing Land Use and Development.* Akron, 1967.

——. *Land Use and Development Forecast,* 1968.

Cleveland City Planning Commission. *Cleveland Today . . . Tomorrow: The General Plan of Cleveland.* Cleveland, 1952.

——. *Downtown Cleveland, 1975.* Cleveland, 1959.

——. *Lakefront Study Summary.* Cleveland, 1962.

——. *Summary of the Two Percent Household Survey.* Cleveland, June 1972.

Cleveland/Seven County Transportation/ Land Use Study. *A Framework for Action: The Comprehensive Report of the Cleveland/ Seven County Transportation/Land Use Study.* Cleveland, 1969.

Duncan, O.D., et al. "Cleveland." *In Metropolis and Region,* by O.D. Duncan et al. Baltimore: The Johns Hopkins Press, 1960.

Hatcher, Harlan. *The Western Reserve, The Story of New Connecticut in Ohio.* Rev. ed. Cleveland: The World Publishing Company, 1966.

Krumholz, Norman. "Cleveland's Fight for a Fair Share of the Region." *Planning, the ASPO Magazine,* November 1972, pp. 275–78.

Leigh, Warren W. *Rubber Industry, With Particular Reference to the Tri-County Region of Ohio.* Akron: Tri-County Regional Planning Commission, 1965.

Papp, Michael. *Ethnic Communities of Cleveland.* Cleveland: Cleveland State University, 1971.

Raup, Hallock F., and Smith, Clyde. *Ohio Geography, Selected Readings.* Dubuque, Iowa: Kendall/Hunt Publishing Company, 1973.

Regional Planning Commission, Cuyahoga County. *Land Development, Housing Cuyahoga County.* Cleveland, 1972.

——. *Land for Growth: A Study of its Availability in 32 Outlying Communities in Cuyahoga County.* Cleveland, 1964.

——. *Open Space in Cuyahoga County.* Cleveland, 1961.

Stark County Area Transportation Study. *Stark County Comprehensive Transportation Plan.* Canton, 1970.

Stark County Regional Planning Commission. *Physical Geography, A Planning Dimension.* Canton, 1960.

Tri-County Regional Planning Commission. *The Development of the Region.* Akron, 1962.

——. *Industrial Development.* Akron, 1965.

U.S. Army Corps of Engineers, Buffalo District. *Flood Plain Information, Cuyahoga River, Cuyahoga and Summit Counties, Ohio.* 1969.

Wolf, Laurence G. "The Metropolitan Tidal Wave in Ohio, 1900–2000." *Economic Geography* 45, 2 (April 1969): 133–54.

Work Projects Administration, Writers' Program. *The Ohio Guide.* New York: Oxford Unviersity Press, 1940.

Chapter Four

Chicago:
Transformations of
an Urban System

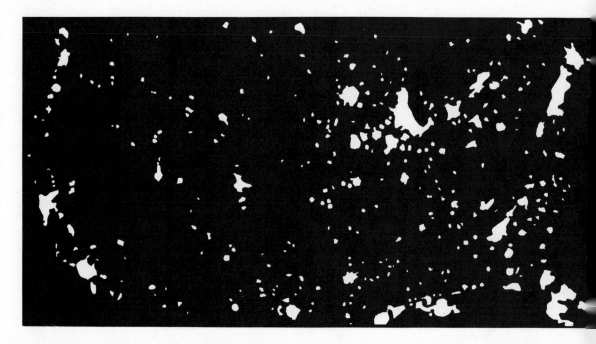

Frontispiece. A composite U.S. Air Force satellite image of America by night reveals the urbanization pattern.

Preface

On a clear night, the satellite passing over the United States picks out the pattern of urbanization by the configuration of lights (Frontispiece). On the northeast coast, Megalopolis stretches from Boston to Washington, but almost as extensive is the belt of lights around the southern end of Lake Michigan that extends in fingerlike tentacles across northern Illinois. The heart of this region is Chicago, numerically and psychologically the nation's Second City. The purpose of this study is to provide some insights into processes that make continual change the essence of the region, and in particular to probe the nature of change in the 1960s and the changes in the nature of change that will produce further transformations in the decades to come.

The study is a team effort. A variety of scholars and students examined different facets of life in the metropolis and contributed insights in the form of working papers. Selections from these papers were assembled into a working draft by the editor and the draft was then circulated to each member of the team for comments, criticisms, and suggestions that in turn helped the editor refashion the first draft into a document that, it is hoped, captures some of the essential spirit of a dynamic and challenging urban region.

With severe size limitations, the group had to eschew comprehensiveness, hoping instead to provide insights into the ways in which contemporary urbanization processes are unfolding in the heart of midcontinent America. The difficulties of writing by committee were recognized—too often a committee has in mind an Arabian stallion, but its joint picture turns out to be an aging and clearly disreputable hippopotamus—and so the editor takes full responsibility for the selections made from team members' contributions, and the often outrageous liberties he took with the materials he selected. For the good will and forbearance of his friends and colleagues he is grateful. In return, it is his hope that the result expresses the challenge of a region that continually elicits men's strongest emotions, a region in which, in Carl Sandburg's words, "tomorrow shall have its own say-so" as "new laughing men come and put up a new city" ("The Windy City").

A Process Not a Place

put the city up; tear the city down
put it up again; let us find a city.
—Carl Sandburg
"The Windy City"

It is a truism that the initial patterns of any system, like the first tracks through a virgin forest, shape its future. Traditions become established, routines are set, vested interests develop, an aura of legitimacy comes to surround existing ways and becomes in time conventional wisdom. In short, "structure" is an outgrowth of the past and becomes a shaping tool of the future.

Nowhere is this truism more relevant for understanding the geography of a city than in Chicago. Yet it does not, as in New Orleans, arise from special people rooted for a long time in a special place. Chicago is less a place than it is a process. American cities have always been dynamic; Chicago has been one of the most dynamic of all—as Carl Sandburg said, "a tall bold slugger set vivid against the little soft cities" ("Chicago Poems"). Old landmarks, whatever their merits, have been continuously discarded and replaced by new ones, and one group of residents by another, in the continuation of that special metabolism that propelled Chicago from a swampy Potawatomi wild onion patch to the world's fourth largest metropolis in less than a century. "Structure", then, is not in Chicago the constraining geometry of a static form; it is the incessant beat of underlying rhythms.

Tempora mutantur, et nos mutamor in illis. Yet in the brief span of Chicago's thrust to global importance a variety of observant visitors has borne witness to the emergence of themes that even today define the pathways of change. *She-kag-ong,* the wild onion place, was a focus for Indian trails and was recognized as a strategic location in 1673 by Père Marquette and Louis Jolliet, soon becoming the key portage route in the chain of waters carrying men and goods from the Mississippi valley along the St. Lawrence to French Canada.

The first permanent settlement, a trading post, was established in the 1770s at the mouth of the Chicago River by Jean Baptiste Point du Sable, a dark-skinned pioneer born of a Quebec father and a Negro mother. Fort Dearborn was built on the site in 1803 to secure land ceded by the Indians after their defeat at Fallen Timbers by "Mad Anthony" Wayne. Its garrison massacred in 1812, the fort was reestablished in 1816 to control the portage route, ceded by the Sacs and Foxes, running southwest from Chicago to Ottawa, Illinois.

A variety of settlers drifted to a site that seemingly afforded but little promise. As a visitor observed in 1823:

> The appearance of the country near Chicago offers but few features upon which the eye of the traveler can dwell with pleasure. There is too much uniformity in the scenery. ... The village ... consists of but few huts, inhabited by a miserable race of men, scarce-

ly equal to the Indians from whom they are descended ... its name, derived from the Potawatomi language, signifies either a skunk, or wild onion; and each of these significations has been occasionally given for it.
—William H. Keating
Narrative of an Expedition to the Source of St. Peter's River, 1823

It was the strategic location, not any quality of the site, that provided the impetus for growth. Chicago was platted in 1829, grid system style, at the northern end of a canal planned by the Illinois legislature to replace the portage linking Lake Michigan to the Mississippi. The raw frontier town began to take shape. Two visitors in 1833 both spoke of the diversity of its inhabitants and its continual uproar, traits that have persisted since:

The inhabitants are a singular collection of beings. All nations and kindred and people and tongues. Black and white and red and grey, and they live in all manner of ways.... I was surprised to observe the masculine appearance of the women.
—Colbee C. Benton
A Visitor to Chicago in Indian Days: Journey to the Far-Off West

I have been in many odd assemblages of my species, but in few, if any, of any equally singular character as with that in the midst of which we spent a week in Chicago. This little mushroom town is ... crowded to excess.... You will find horse-dealers and horse-stealers,—rogues of every description, white, black, brown, and red—half-breeds, quarter-breeds, and men of no breed at all .... in an uproar from morning to night.... The interior of the village was one of chaos of mud, rubbish and confusion.
—Charles Joseph Latrob
The Rambler in North America

Work on the canal began in 1836, and although it was not to be put into use for a decade, a speculative boom set in, the first of many that resulted in a pulsating tempo of growth that Homer Hoyt later called the "Chicago building cycle." By 1846 another visitor to Chicago could write:

Any one who had seen this place, as I had done five years ago ... would find some difficulty in recognizing it now when its population is more than fifteen thousand.

It has long rows of warehouses and shops, its bustling streets; its huge steamers, and crowds of lake-craft, lying at the wharves; its villas embowered with trees; and its suburbs, consisting of the cottages of German and Irish laborers, stretching northward along the lake, and westward into the prairies, and widening every day. The slovenly and raw appearance of a new settlement begins in many parts to disappear. The Germans have already a garden in a little grove for their holidays, as in their towns in the old country, and the Roman Catholics have just finished a college for the education of those who are to proselyte the West.
—William Cullen Bryant
Letters of a Traveller

Rapid construction of new housing was made possible because of another trait that Chicago established early to facilitate its rapid growth and change—architectural innovation. In 1832 it was what came to be known nationwide as "Chicago construction"—the balloon frame developed by Augustine Taylor and George Washington Snow. "If it had not been for the knowledge of the balloon frame," a *New York Tribune* article said in 1855, "Chicago and San Francisco could not have arisen as they did, from little villages to great cities in a single year." Later in the century, too, Chicago was to influence the nature of American urban development through its architectural innovations, for her architects simultaneously pioneered the garden suburb, the planned satellite city, and the steel-frame skyscraper, exercising a style-setting role in both the outward expansion and the upward thrust of the American metropolis. In return, these architects were acclaimed as the "Chicago School," the first of many such schools that resulted from Chicago's accumulating intellectual leadership in a variety of technical, artistic, and professional fields.

Even as the canal was first coming into use in 1847 visitors sensed the town's growth prospects:

Chicago is destined, some day hence, and no very far-off day neither, to be one of the largest cities in the Union; and the wisdom of its projectors, in carrying out its wide streets, is every where apparent.
—J.H. Buckingham
Illinois as Lincoln Knew It

Yet the pace of change astounded even the most aggressive civic boosters. One visitor who returned after a decade's absence observed in 1857 that:

Chicago ... [was] ... a vast mud puddle ... during my first year.... Twelve years have passed, and what a change in its appearance as well as in its population, which is now 120,000! The ... streets have been raised by several feet and paved with planks or stone.... It is now a city in which private and public buildings compare favorably in size and style with the most splendid structures in the capitals of Europe.... Chicago has under gone a complete transformation ... having extensive parks, magnificent buildings and attractive villas surrounded by beautiful flower parterres, orchards, and terraces, it now really deserves the name it has adopted, the Garden City. It is now displaying, perhaps in a greater degree than any other city in the Union, one of the most indisputable proofs of the industrial advance and virile power which ... has lifted ... the great, robust nation.... The canal became the first powerful force leading to the present greatness.... However, the web of railroads which Chicago has spun around itself during the last ten years is the thing that more than anything else has contributed to its wealth and progress ... one of the most important business centers in the Union ... [and] ... it has already become the center for great iron-manufacturing mills.... This city will become the central metropolis of the great North American continent.

—Gustaf Unonius
A Pioneer in Northwest America,
1841-1858

By 1850 Chicago had become the focus of the lines of transportation and communication that linked east with west, a role that it has maintained to the present with each successive innovation in the means of moving goods, people, messages, and ideas. In 1850, one railroad entered the city; by 1856 it was the focus of ten trunk lines that fanned out, fixing the fingerlike form of the metropolis before they radiated throughout the fertile Middle West. Dockside and railside, Chicago's industries burgeoned. Lumber from the northern lakes moved through the port onto the rails, and thence to the prairies; Chicago's preeminence in the nation's furniture trade dates from this time. In return, midwestern grain moved from the plains. The Board of Trade organized the buying and selling and became the base point anchoring the spatial pattern of midwestern grain prices. A speculative and innovative spirit came to characterize the city's commercial life, so much so that an English novelist visiting Chicago in 1862 could write:

Chicago is in many respects the most remarkable city among all the remarkable cities of the Union. Its growth has been the fastest and its success the most assured.... Chicago may be called the metropolis of American corn.... Men in these regions do not mind failures, and, when they have failed, instantly begin again. They make their plans on a large scale.

—Anthony Trollope
North America

As with grain, so with cattle and hogs. The Union Stockyards were organized beyond the city's southern limits in 1865, replacing a dozen closer installations, and were surrounded with a ring of packing houses that were said to use everything, even the squeal. The Armours, Libbys, and Swifts were joined as Chicago's ruling oligarchs by the McCormicks, who supplied the Midwest's agricultural implements, and the scions of the steel mills, who supplied the rails. State Street, "that great street," emerged as the retail core as a consequence of the initiative of hotelier Potter Palmer and retailers Marshall Field and Levi Leiter. Almost overnight, the rebuilding they sparked created a new commercial core, an early example of the several transformations of the city led by its commercial leaders—admittedly in their own self-interest, but increasing also with a public-spirited rhetoric of civic improvement.

They also produced a distinctive social geography by their choices. Field and Philip Armour built elegant homes which drew the city's elite around them, creating exclusive residential areas along the avenues south of the city center—Wabash and Michigan, Indiana and Prairie, Calumet and South Park. Elsewhere, European immigrants flocking to work in the city's factories crowded into mean wooden cottages on small lots, without paved streets or sewers, segregating themselves into tightly knit ethnic neighborhoods. Swedes and Norwegians, Germans and Irish all had their separate districts; the Irish stronghold was Bridgeport, which remains even now—with the residence of Mayor Richard J. Daley—the symbolic center of the Irish machine.

Meanwhile, the horse-drawn omnibus already had set in motion a movement of the middle class that its successors—cable cars, electric lines, commuter railroads, elevated and subway trains, and the automobile—simply extended, the shift away from the business center to fashionable neighborhoods along the lakeshore and at the edge of the city. Commuters' suburbs grew like beads along the commuting lines leaving Chicago. Hyde Park and Kenwood, Austin and Norwood Park, Ravenswood and Rogers Park (all subsequently annexed) grew, as did Blue Island and Riverside, Oak Park and Park Ridge, Evanston, Winnetka, Highland Park, and Lake Forest beyond what came to be the city's end-of-the-century legal limits (Figure 1). Spaciousness and environmental amenities were the qualities emphasized in advertising. These qualities were epitomized by Frederick Law Olmsted's planned garden suburb, Riverside, conceived as an alternative to the gridiron town. Laid out in 1869, Riverside's roadways were "formed to curved lines to make a gracious and harmonious whole," "an elegant drive, a handsome park, and a delightful suburban city," thus setting the style for what later became "conventional" American suburbia—a suburbia subsequently to be provided by Chicago's suburban Oak Park architect Frank Lloyd Wright with its equally conventional ranch-style home, a derivative of his "prairie houses" such as Hyde Park's Robie House (1909).

Meanwhile, the trait captured by Harold Mayer when he called Chicago the "City of Decisions" surfaced once again. The central city remained a quagmire. Drainage and sewage disposal were critical problems. The public water supply was polluted and inadequate. Public open space was unavailable. The civic leadership, a powerful oligarchy of downtown businessmen and major industrialists—a pattern repeated many times since—had the city council act on their behalf, making major decisions boldly and decisively to reshape the downtown area. In 1855–1856 the council declared that the grade of the city's downtown be elevated out of the mud. In the next few years, buildings were raised bodily and new drainage and streets constructed many feet higher than before. A water system was constructed by 1867, with in-

take cribs two miles out at the bottom of Lake Michigan, and by 1870 a new park and boulevard system ringed the city. Visitor after visitor commented upon one Chicago trait above all —its dynamism—as in 1871:

> All is astir here. There is no such thing as stagnation or rest. . . . You catch the contagion of activity and enterprise . . . —circulating, whirling—
>
> —Sara Clark Lippincott
> *New Life in New Lands*

In 1871 Chicago burned down. One-third of the population was made homeless. Both fine residential neighborhoods and the jerry-built ethnic enclaves were destroyed, along with the commercial and industrial core, in the four square miles that were gutted. Rebuilding began immediately. The following year an observer commented:

> I was much struck by the prominent evidences of the devastation caused by the great fire in October last year, and also by the strenuous and very wonderful efforts which have been made to repair its ravages. New and handsome buildings are being rapidly erected . . . now the city is rising from its ashes . . . more wonderful than ever. . . . (It) has a population estimated to number over 300,000.
>
> —John Watson
> *Souvenir of a Town in the United States of America and Canada*

Only five years later another said:

> The city was built by giants and for giants. It has its own unique characteristics . . . everything is symmetrically laid out . . . everywhere are innovations. . . . On the sidewalks there is tremendous movement. Crowds of people, both white and colored, hurry in all directions . . . a new gigantic city was being erected . . . scaffolding after scaffolding. . . . What strikes one most . . . is . . . vitality and also the most incredible energy of the inhabitants.
>
> —Henry Sienkiewicz
> *Portrait of America*

Figure 1. Municipalities within the Chicago SMSA, and the officially designated "community areas" within the city of Chicago.

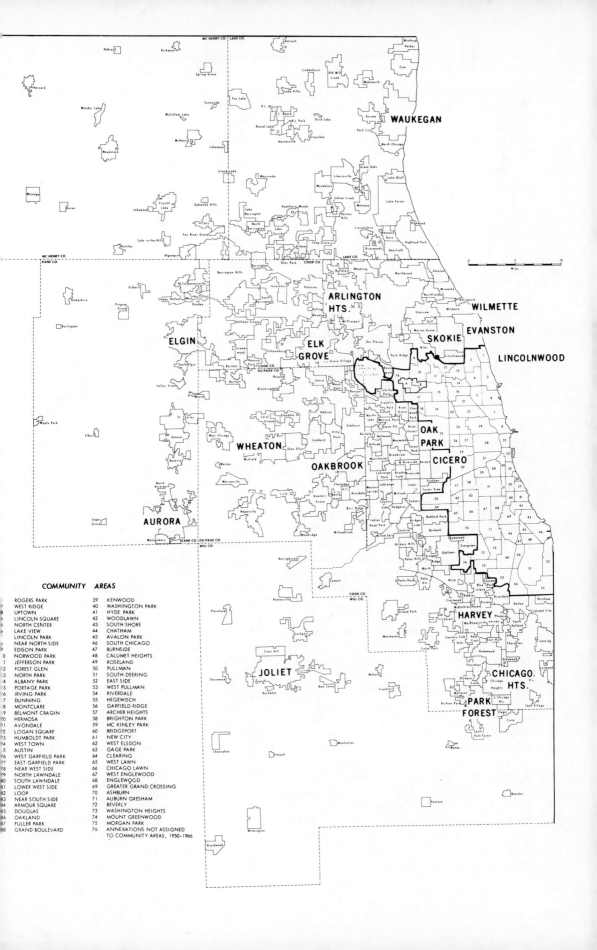

MC HENRY CO. LAKE CO.

WAUKEGAN

MC HENRY CO.
KANE CO.

COOK CO.
LAKE CO.

ARLINGTON
HTS.

WILMETTE

ELGIN

ELK
GROVE

SKOKIE

EVANSTON

LINCOLNWOOD

OAK
PARK

CICERO

WHEATON

OAKBROOK

AURORA

KANE CO. DU PAGE CO.
WILL CO.

HARVEY

COOK CO.
WILL CO.

JOLIET

CHICAGO
HTS.

PARK
FOREST

COMMUNITY AREAS

1	ROGERS PARK	39	KENWOOD
2	WEST RIDGE	40	WASHINGTON PARK
3	UPTOWN	41	HYDE PARK
4	LINCOLN SQUARE	42	WOODLAWN
5	NORTH CENTER	43	SOUTH SHORE
6	LAKE VIEW	44	CHATHAM
7	LINCOLN PARK	45	AVALON PARK
8	NEAR NORTH SIDE	46	SOUTH CHICAGO
9	EDISON PARK	47	BURNSIDE
10	NORWOOD PARK	48	CALUMET HEIGHTS
11	JEFFERSON PARK	49	ROSELAND
12	FOREST GLEN	50	PULLMAN
13	NORTH PARK	51	SOUTH DEERING
14	ALBANY PARK	52	EAST SIDE
15	PORTAGE PARK	53	WEST PULLMAN
16	IRVING PARK	54	RIVERDALE
17	DUNNING	55	HEGEWISCH
18	MONTCLARE	56	GARFIELD RIDGE
19	BELMONT CRAGIN	57	ARCHER HEIGHTS
20	HERMOSA	58	BRIGHTON PARK
21	AVONDALE	59	MC KINLEY PARK
22	LOGAN SQUARE	60	BRIDGEPORT
23	HUMBOLDT PARK	61	NEW CITY
24	WEST TOWN	62	WEST ELSDON
25	AUSTIN	63	GAGE PARK
26	WEST GARFIELD PARK	64	CLEARING
27	EAST GARFIELD PARK	65	WEST LAWN
28	NEAR WEST SIDE	66	CHICAGO LAWN
29	NORTH LAWNDALE	67	WEST ENGLEWOOD
30	SOUTH LAWNDALE	68	ENGLEWOOD
31	LOWER WEST SIDE	69	GREATER GRAND CROSSING
32	LOOP	70	ASHBURN
33	NEAR SOUTH SIDE	71	AUBURN GRESHAM
34	ARMOUR SQUARE	72	BEVERLY
35	DOUGLAS	73	WASHINGTON HEIGHTS
36	OAKLAND	74	MOUNT GREENWOOD
37	FULLER PARK	75	MORGAN PARK
38	GRAND BOULEVARD	76	ANNEXATIONS NOT ASSIGNED TO COMMUNITY AREAS, 1950-1966

Joining these inhabitants were distinctive new immigrant groups:

> The chief Polish center is Chicago.... The small area occupied by them in the city —a sector sneeringly referred to by the Germans as *Polakei* ... is along Milwaukee Avenue.... The Poles of Chicago are united through Polish societies whose aims are to assist new arrivals, to protect their members from foreign influences, and to preserve their national spirit.
>
> —Henry Sienkiewicz
> Ibid.

As well as the Poles, Czechs, and Italians, and both European and Russian Jews, a variety of other nationality and ethnic groups poured in and created their own enclaves. The enclaving, in turn, produced strong identification with named local subcommunities, some seventy-five in all, that even today remain part of the social identity of the city. The named communities are widely perceived by residents and outsiders alike to have a particular social character and they thus influence individuals' locational choices and serve to pattern the social geography of the city.

The fire enabled the old inner city to be refashioned. The business center was rebuilt with taller buildings at higher densities, old frame residential areas were replaced by block after block of apartments, and workers were forbidden by municipal ordinance to live in frame structures within the "brick area" downtown, to avoid further fires. The changes were more than merely incremental. Limitations placed on building heights by masonry technology led to the invention of the steel-frame skyscraper by William Le Baron Jenney, to the early masterpieces of the "Chicago School" architects Dankmar Adler and Louis Sullivan, and to the vertical growth of the city, supported by other innovations—the caisson foundation that could support tall buildings in the mud, and the Otis elevator. Bold decisions led to the linking of radiating mass transportation routes in a downtown elevated "Loop" of rails encircling the business center. They also produced a new Sanitary District that, moving more earth than was involved in building the Panama Canal, reversed the flow of the Chicago River from Lake Michigan to the Mississippi system in 1900 to carry away Chicago's effluents and protect its public water supply and beaches. The "Loop" elevated line opened in 1897, encircling a mas-

sive central business district including the State Street shopping core; the Board of Trade and the adjacent La Salle Street financial center; hotels that serviced a growing convention business; the city government, Art Institute, Civic Opera, and the city's medical and dental complex; the leading social and political clubs; and the wholesale and produce markets. The scale of the concentration was unprecedented. Chicago had become the epitome of the core-oriented nineteenth century industrial metropolis.

Along the streetcar lines which followed both the gridiron streets and the radial routes inherited from the Indian trails, there developed ribbons of small businesses (with flats above). In the neighborhoods behind, three to six floor walk up apartment buildings replaced many of the areas once occupied by one story frame houses. At major streetcar intersections, more important outlying business centers developed. And in 1884, Potter Palmer moved from Michigan Avenue south of the Loop to Lake Shore Drive north of it. Just as in the 1860s his actions created State Street, this move created the Gold Coast. Following his leadership, Chicago's leading families moved from the South Side avenues to the Near North Side. Their former mansions were quickly subdivided and underwent rapid social transformation, all the more so because just west of the avenues other newcomers, southern Negroes, were forming a dense cluster around Sixteenth and State—the Black Belt. Many of the Negroes had been brought north as strikebreakers, and they encountered both racial prejudice and job-related enmity by Chicago's blue collar ethnics. They turned inward and created Black Chicago, a city within the city.

As the civic leadership moved, so did the affluent. Meanwhile, the middle classes continued to flock into new suburbs constructed along the radiating mass transit lines, to be replaced in older suburbs that had by then been absorbed into the continuous urban development by upwardly mobile working class ethnics who, Americanized in Chicago's melting pot, left the crowded innermost city neighborhoods to those least able to take advantage of the city's opportunities, and to new poverty stricken immigrants pouring in from Eastern Europe. Urban sociologists of another "Chicago School," Robert E. Park and Ernest W. Burgess, called this a process of "invasion and succession."

And it was in the slums of the West Side that another pioneer, Jane Addams, opened her Hull House and took the first giant step in the creation of a new profession, social work.

The crowding of the central city also meant that new locational opportunities had to be created for industry. This was accomplished by the building of a succession of circumferential railroads, culminating in the Chicago Outer Belt Line (Elgin, Joliet, and Eastern Railroad) that formed an outer arc thirty-five miles from the Loop, and by another invention, the organized industrial district. Where the Outer Belt Line crossed the railroads radiating from Chicago, a crescent of industrial satellite cities grew up—Waukegan, Elgin, Aurora, Joliet, and Chicago Heights. Each was heavily populated by the new immigrants, and this has colored their social and political life since. Chicago Heights was created as a planned factory town, with industry segregated from housing, and so, later, was Gary. Another such venture was George Pullman's innovative company town, a showpiece planned workingmen's community that was built between 1880 and 1884 and named for him and his company.

The first organized industrial district in the United States was the Central Manufacturing District, built on the innermost belt railroad north of the Union Stock Yards, along the Chicago River, in 1890. It was followed quickly by the Clearing Industrial District on the Southwest Side and soon each of the outlying industrial satellites, as well as new industrial suburbs such as Cicero, developed their organized industrial districts. Heavy industry moved to Calumet Harbor to the south, and to Indiana Harbor, constructed by the federal government across the state line in northern Indiana. Each new industrial concentration also carried with it its workingmen's enclave populated by the new Eastern European immigrants, its middle class residential area, and a small black ghetto, laying down a social fabric that has persisted to the present, setting the tone and style of contentious conflict-laden local political life.

While this was taking place, the world flocked to Chicago in 1893 to see the World's Columbian Exposition and its White City, which extolled the City Beautiful. Their judgements varied. Rudyard Kipling (cited by B.L. Pierce) grumped that "[h]aving seen it, I urgently desire never to see it again. It is inhabited by savages." Others saw the social

polarization and the governmental problems that afflict Chicago even today:

> Chicago, queen and guttersnipe of cities, cynosure and cesspool of the world! ... The most beautiful and the most squalid, girdled with a two fold zone of parks and slums ... the great port.... The great mart ... widely and generously planned with streets of twenty miles, where it is not safe to walk at night ... the chosen seat of public spirit and municipal boodle, of cutthroat commerce and munificent patronage of art; the most American of American cities, and yet the most mongrel; the second American city of the globe, the fifth German city, the third Swedish, the second Polish. ... Where in all the world can words be found for this miracle of paradox and incongruity ... a land of giants—a land where the very houses are instinct with almost ferocious energy and force.... [I]f Chicago is the lodestone that attracts the enterprise and commercial talent of two hemispheres, it is also the sink into which to drain their dregs. The hundred and twenty thousand Irish are not a wholesome element in municipal life. On the bleak west side there are streets of illiterate, turbulent Poles and Czechs.... Out of this rude and undigested mass how could good government come?
> —George W. Steevens
> *The Land of the Dollar*

> The government of Chicago ... seems to reach the lowest depths of municipal efficiency
> —Sidney Webb
> *Beatrice Webb's American Diary, 1898*

Yet others were not so pessimistic, seeing hope in the city's energy and capacity to act:

> Chicago is awake, and intelligently awake, to her destinies. ... Discontent is the condition of progress, and Chicago is not in the slightest danger of relapsing into a condition of inert self-complacency.
> —William Archer
> *America To-Day: Observations and Reflections*

This capacity had been seen before, and was already being expressed in the grand design for the Sanitary District of Chicago, an autonomous body covering 185 square miles in 1889 (currently 860 square miles), with elected officials and independent taxing authority. But this was not enough. In 1906 the Merchants' Club commissioned Daniel H. Burnham to prepare his *Plan of Chicago*. Burnham knew that small measures are the work of little minds, for he said, "[m]ake no little plans. They have no magic to stir men's blood and probably themselves will not be realized. Make big plans; aim high in hope and work, remembering a noble logical diagram once recorded will never die but long after we are gone will be a living thing, asserting with growing intensity."

True to his own admonitions, Burnham planned a monumental City Beautiful. The 1909 Chicago Plan was adopted by the city in 1910, becoming the guideline for city policies until World War II. These policies ultimately produced a monumental civic center, a lakefront preserved in a belt of continuous parks and beaches, a greenbelt of forest preserves encircling the built-up area in Cook County, streets and landscaped boulevards that would hurry movement and ease circulation, and an east-west highway stretching from the city center to the prairie beyond.

These plans were realized during a quarter century of unprecedented boom in which the skyline of the Loop rose while at the same time the "Magnificent Mile" of North Michigan Avenue was built in the back of the Gold Coast. The metropolitan population grew rapidly, and as densities increased, building styles changed as an apartment boom transformed the inner city. And a new device, the automobile, freed suburban development from the commuter rails, just as new employment centers were created in additional outlying organized industrial districts (Figure 2).

There followed a stagnant quarter century of the Great Depression and World War II, during which blight increased in the older inner city and both racial and socioreligious conflicts became more profound as a growing population competed for a limited housing supply. It was during this later period that some have said Chicago developed a neurotic "Second City" mentality because she never quite topped New York to become the first city of America.

Yet out of the Depression came new forces such as the Federal Housing Administration's loans for suburban housing, and slum clearance and public housing programs in the central city. Just before World War II, the city completed a land use survey and developed a master plan for residential land use in Chicago to replace the Burnham Plan. New subways and superhighways were contemplated and extensive residential redevelopment was proposed. These plans had to await the end of postwar controls, however. What they subsequently affected was a metropolis described in 1945 as:

the metropolis of the West. To describe this great city, now the fourth largest in the world, defies one's powers.... Here is a city of nearly four million souls, with another two million in satellite communities round it; composed of almost all Caucasian nationalities, Negroes, and Orientals, and dependent on agriculture, mining, oil, electricity, the seaborne traffic of the Great Lakes or the canals and rivers, and the most intricate texture of railroads and highways on earth.... Huge city of swamp and prairie, one community of many communities, *communitas communitatum;* it is both a Pittsburgh and a Detroit; a financial and commercial granary, slaughter-house, and inland seaport; a repository of great wealth and great poverty; a center of learning; metropolis of ... the heart of America ... [and] ... a national metropolis too, because of its position.... It is a part of all American life. To find a blasé Chicagoan would be a relief, so keen, so hungry and thirsty for new experiences, so curious, so divinely discontented and unsatisfied are Chicagoans of all income brackets and national origins. That is why Chicago holds the quintessence of the Midwest. In Chicago all the extremes and extremism of the region reach a grand climax. Within a minute or two's walk of the splendid stores and hotels and offices in the Loop you pass the flophouses of West Madison ... ; the terrible slums and Negro district near the Stockyards; ... the hangouts of the bums.... It is natural, in the region of greatest mobility in America, that the Germans' *bummeln* should have thus passed into the general slang....

Who are the Chicagoans? ... They come from almost every race and people.... Germans form solid districts all over.... Poles with their pseudobaroque Catholic Churches ... make whole areas look like Cracow or Lodz. Czechs and Slovaks keep their homes and little gardens more neatly and reproduce Brunn or Pilsen.... Italians of all kinds, too, ... keep their feast days and market days as if in the old country and live in solid blocks of the city.... Here is a potent source of variety and difference as well as vigor and restlessness....The variety of suburbs is bewildering.... The home of the middle-class.... They have commu-

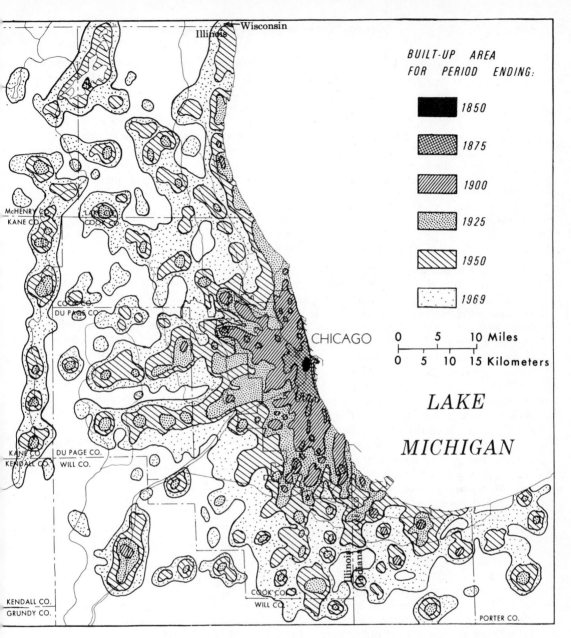

Figure 2. Chicago's growth rings, 1850–1970.

nity sense and community achievement to their credit ... the sense of community is and always was, strong in this region. But, in making these communities, the community sense has been taken away from the city center. The problems of Chicago ... are left at or near the center: The "inner ring" of solid and densely settled residential areas where the manual workers live; the area of slums, dilapidation, or overcrowding.... The tempo of life in Chicago has to be experienced to be believed ... this gives to the sur-

face of things in Chicago an impression of perpetual motion, like the surface of the sea ... in Chicago things happen, and people seem to think, and even more, in waves.

–Graham Hutton
Midwest at Noon

Relying on the continuing advantages of its strategic location, impelled by a speculative spirit that remained the driving force behind continuing innovation, led by a responsible if self-interested civic leadership willing to think boldly about the city's future, dynamic, changing, yet also:

> not a single town; more than any other American city (Chicago) is an agglomeration of towns of huge dimensions, grouped round the business center; the various districts are much more watertight than those of New York; the emigrants have not fused into a single whole. Many of them speak their native tongue, have their own papers, and develop a kind of chauvinism that leads to brawls and quarrels.
> —Simone de Beauvoir
> *America Day by Day*

Black Chicago, denied equality of opportunity, had turned inward to create a city within the city. Tightly knit inner city ethnic communities maintained old social bonds and developed new ones, and in their competitive struggle for existence gave their residential enclaves the Darwinian semblance of "natural areas." Around them, the affluent and the middle class had withdrawn to their pastoral retreats in suburbia or to the exclusiveness of their high-rise towers strung northward from the city center along the Lake Michigan shore.

Chicago, in the very pace of its growth and change, had developed by the end of World War II into the archetypal industrial metropolis. As it developed it both followed and led, quickly responding to national trends, but also experimenting, innovating, and becoming a style setter. No city could claim so many schools. The Chicago School of Architecture had in the 1880s provided the ideas and technologies that enabled American cities to grow both up and out; after World War II new members led by Mies van der Rohe developed new high-rise styles and building technologies that helped reshape downtown office cores. The Chicago School of Urban Sociology had provided both an overview and minute dissection of the social process that accompanied the drive to industrial dominance; after World War II a new generation of Chicago social scientists provided new interpretations of the changing social structure. The Chicago School of Economics was and is associated with laissez faire principles of growth. The Chicago School of Psychological Functionalists and Philosophical Pragmatists included such renowned scholars as John Dewey, George H. Mead, E.S. Ames, and James Rowland Angell. Adler and Sullivan, Burnham and Root, Wright and van der Rohe, Burgess and Park, Faris and Dunham,

Shaw and McKay, St. Clair Drake and Cayton, Addams and Merriam, Wirth, Hoyt, and a myriad of other scholars and students had made Chicago the most imitated and best researched city in the world. Its concentric zones of development, reflecting each upswing of the Chicago real estate cycle, radiating development axes, reflecting both the location of transportation lines and the relative prestige of different suburban sectors, its tightly knit community areas, processes of invasion and succession, neighborhood territoriality, and many other traits had been codified as empirical generalization, raised to the status of universal theory, and become the conventional wisdom of students of urbanization throughout the world. Often invalidly, many of the world's cities have been studied in ways that have been moulded by these Chicago theories.

Yet one penalty of lagged emulation for the imitators is that the innovative continue to innovate, and this has certainly been true of postwar Chicago. The metropolis has experienced and indeed led in many of the trends that have transformed metropolitan America in the last two decades. This fact emerges if one inspects the list of Chicago "firsts" for which its civic boosters, perhaps betraying their Second City psychosis, continually search.

In 1904, the superlatives had been those of the midwestern industrial metropolis:

> Chicago has pushed ahead more rapidly than any other city in the history of mankind.
> She is the greatest of railway centers.
> Chicago is the greatest cattle market in the world.
> Chicago is the largest grain market.
> Chicago is the biggest market for agricultural machinery.
> Chicago does the largest mail-order business.
> The largest trading in ready-made clothing.
> She has the finest wholesale dry-goods establishment in the world.
> She is the largest hardware market in the world.
> Chicago is the biggest furniture market.
> —William E. Curtis
> *Chicago Record-Herald*
> November 18, 1904

The civic boosters could see no obstacle to the continuing progress of the city:

> She is moving upward and onward,
> With victory on her lips,

And a dauntless eye and a strenuous cry,
To a world that she outstrips.
                                    —Horace Spencer Fiske
                                    The March of Chicago, 1903

In 1974, the Chicago Association of Commerce and Industry, the biggest continuing civic booster for "Chicagoland"—the six county Chicago SMSA plus Lake and Porter counties of Indiana—could still see nothing but "progress." Asking the question "Why should firms invest in Chicago?" they compiled an impressive list of "firsts" that was instrumental in moving the city's bond rating to an unusual top flight level among the nation's major metropolitan areas.

First, reiterating the most basic theme in Chicago's history, they focused on the region's role as the nation's principal transportation hub. "More tons of freight" they noted "move out of Chicago by rail and highway than any other area in the country." "The region has the nation's greatest trucking and wholesaling complex." "Chicago leads in wholesale sales." "Manufacturing shipments are greater than those of any other region." "Chicago dominates in many retail sales categories." And in modern transportation, Chicago has remained the fore, for O'Hare Airport is the nation's busiest.

Chicagoland's growth was found to have been unmatched in the late 1960s, and the Association of Commerce and Industry labeled Chicago the nation's "Construction City," as indicated by the following statistics:

Millions of Dollars of New Construction 1966-1971

1	Chicago	7,809
2	Los Angeles	7,732
3	New York	7,280
4	Detroit	4,752

Millions of Dollars of Plant and Equipment Expenditures 1964-1969

1	Chicago	3,826
2	Detroit	3,291
3	New York	2,992
4	Los Angeles	2,899

Millions of Dollars and Numbers of New Housing Units Constructed 1965-1971

1	Chicago	5,211	335,707
2	Los Angeles	4,783	291,891
3	New York	4,606	306,164
4	Detroit	3,177	196,724

The growth was shown to have two expressions. First, even though Chicago could not top New York's concentration of head-quarters or of the administrative functions of major corporations, Chicago was growing rapidly in these respects while New York was losing:

Fortune "Top 500" Headquarters

		1956	1972	Gain or Loss
1	New York	145	112	-33
2	Chicago	50	55	+ 5
3	Los Angeles	16	21	+ 5
4	Pittsburgh	23	15	- 8

Increase in Branch Office or Administrative and Auxiliary Employment

		1962	1970	Percent Increase
1	New York	117,948	240,735	204
2	Chicago	55,558	139,897	252
3	Detroit	57,942	106,103	183
4	Pittsburgh	31,924	60,558	189

This control-function impact was most evident in the city center, where Chicago is now adding office space more rapidly than any other metropolis and has joined New York in the league of major skyscrapers with the new and distinctive products of her architects, who pioneered once again—this time in methods of constructing large buildings with less steel such as Sears Tower, the world's largest, and the distinctive multifunctional John Hancock Center:

Private and Public Office Space in Central City

		Completed 1965-1972	Total 1972
1	New York	79,590	243,688
2	Chicago	21,146	68,271
3	Washington	32,866	55,300
4	Los Angeles	26,415	53,174

		Added 1973-1974	Total 1974
1	New York	15,077	258,765
2	Chicago	17,417	85,688
3	Washington	6,350	61,650
4	Los Angeles	4,760	57,934

Yet more profound in its consequences than the upward thrust of the city center has been the massive outward movement of employment and population, as Chicago's suburbanization has proceeded at a greater pace than in any other metropolitan region:

Growth of Suburban Population, 1960-1970

1	Chicago	941,000
2	Washington	856,000
3	New York	747,000
4	Los Angeles	700,000

Civilian Employment Change,
1960-1970

		Suburban	Central City	Total
1	Chicago	548,000	–211,000	337,000
2	New York	353,000	–339,000	141,000
3	Detroit	326,000	–156,000	170,000
4	Washington	323,000	9,000	332,000

In this list of "Chicago firsts" one can sense the massive transformation that has reshaped the fabric of the metropolis and it is to the elements of this reshaping that we now turn. We begin with the nature of suburbanization, for it has been in the suburbs that new modes of life have been fashioned. Next we deal with the consequences of suburbanization for the central city: polarization between Black Chicago and the residual white ethnic community, and the successive attempts by the city's business and political leadership to reshape and revitalize the city core. Finally we look at the metabolism of the metropolis and the ways in which change occurs. Of particular interest is the interaction between the grand designs of the city's leaders and the accumulative small changes in the everyday behavior of Chicagoans, for in such interactions lie the emergent form of metropolitan America.

The Suburban Frontier

The suburb and the quest for status are shaping the American personality of the future as the frontier once shaped the American personality of the past.

—Charles Abrams

In 1970 the Chicago "Daily Urban System" extended over four states, including several metropolitan areas (Figure 3), having changed significantly during the 1960s. An outward thrust along the Northwest Tollway had brought Rockford into Chicago's daily orbit, commuting intensities had increased both southward along extensions of the Calumet Expressway and eastward across northern Indiana, while, simultaneously, as decentralization proceeded apace, many suburbs found that smaller percentages of their residents now worked in Chicago while increasing proportions of the central city's residents now commuted to the suburbs (Figure 4). Close to a million new highly mobile middle class white residents now lived in a broad outer ring of child-rearing suburbs, encircling a low mobility ring of pre-depression suburbs whose aging residents were being joined by central city blue collar ethnics fleeing racial change in a high mobility ring within the central city, the belt of ghetto expansion housing black middle class child-rearing families who, at last, were escaping the decaying low mobility neighborhoods of the traditional inner city ghettos located behind the elegant high-rise apartment and condominium developments of Chicago's lakeshore (Figure 5). An intricate chain of events had unfolded.

The massive growth of suburbia had both permitted and was made possible by rapid decentralization of economic activities from the central city and it resulted in declining relative dependence of the suburbs on central city jobs and increases in reverse commuting flows from the central city to the suburbs. The rapid growth of the suburban housing stock both facilitated and was impelled by accelerated suburbanization of white families from the central city and produced an accelerated filtering of the housing stock from one income level to another, improvement of housing conditions for most central city residents, rapid ghetto expansion, abandonment of the oldest of the central city's housing in the heart of the traditional ghetto communities, and decreasing central city densities. Central city decay, in turn, resulted in massive public intervention into low income housing markets and urban renewal, and dramatic private initiatives to regenerate the city core.

CHANGES IN TRANSPORTATION

At the heart of all of these changes were changes in the metropolitan transportation system, thus repeating Chicago's most basic relationship. Since its founding near the mouth of the Chicago River, transportation has been a primary factor in Chicago's growth and development. Early settlement was strongly affected by water transportation, with improvements such as the Illinois and Michigan Canal stimulating rapid

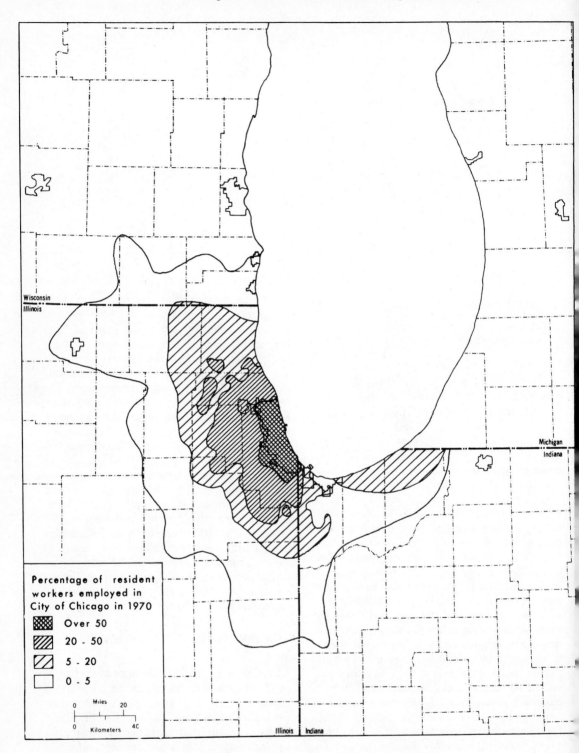

Figure 3. Chicago daily urban system in 1970, as measured by percentage of workers residing in each census tract commuting to the city of Chicago.

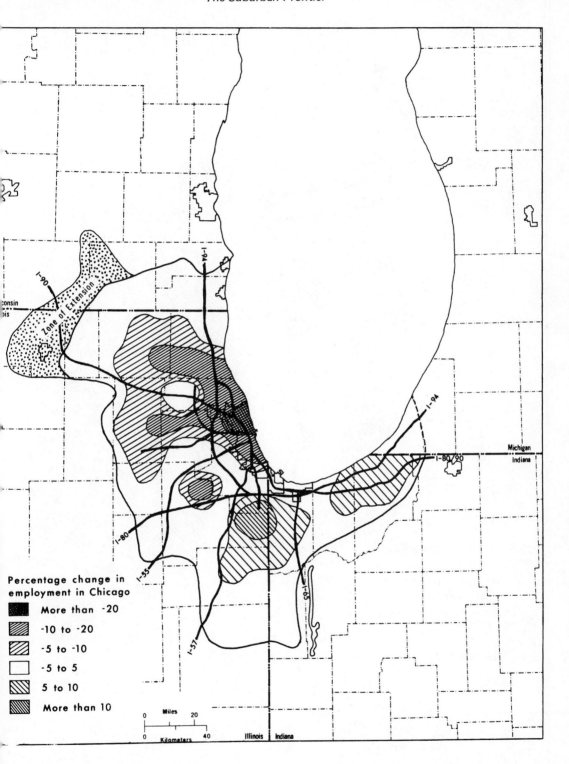

Figure 4. Changes in commuting intensities and the commuting area 1960–1970, shown against the pattern of expressways within the Chicago Daily Urban System.

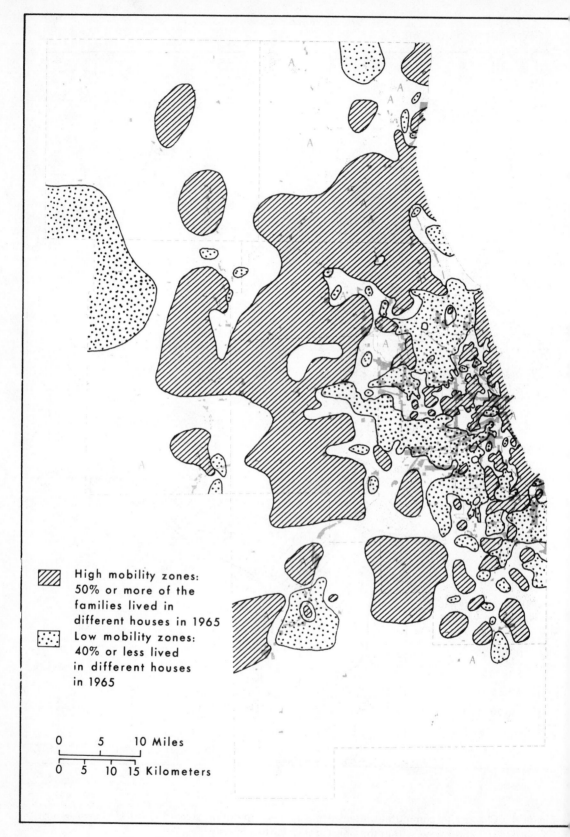

Figure 5. Bands of high and low population mobility, 1965–1970.

growth. Settlement spread further as ribbons of population along the railroads and mass transit routes (compare Figure 2 with Figure 6). And, more recently, the area has undergone widespread decentralization with the coming of the automobile. Because of the importance of changes in transportation we will deal with them in some detail before we return to the principal theme of this section, the role of the suburbs as the leading edge of metropolitan growth.

The Expanding Freeway Network

The most far-reaching changes have been associated with increasing use of the motor vehicle and the spreading freeway network. Automobile ownership has increased much more rapidly than population. Reflecting higher socioeconomic levels, less dependence on mass transportation, and different life styles, the suburbs have almost twice the number of cars per household as the central city's ratio of 0.81. Paralleling the rise in automobile ownership has been the growth of the expressway and tollway network, which started in 1956 when the network in the Chicago-Gary area totaled only 53 miles. By the end of 1972 it had expanded almost tenfold to total 506 miles (Figure 7). Most of the increase was financed by the federal government as part of the National System of Interstate and Defense Highways, approved by Congress in 1956.

In 1956 there were only disconnected segments of the future network. With the exception of Lake Shore Drive, which was of pre–World War II construction, the other segments had been completed in the 1950s. After 1956, construction started on additional expressways which had become part of the master plan for the area in the 1940s. The basic plan consisted of a number of expressways radiating from the CBD: the Kennedy Expressway was built to the northwest, the Eisenhower Expressway, including its Lake Street Extension, extended west to realize the last component of the Burnham Plan; the Stevenson Expressway and I-55 were extended southwest; and the Dan Ryan Expressway and I-57 reached south. Thus, by the end of the 1960s Chicago had four new expressways leading out of the CBD in addition to the north and south segments of Lake Shore Drive. All but Lake Shore Drive joined directly with other expressways

or tollways passing through the metropolitan area. Complementing the expressways, three tollway systems were completed. The 157 mile Indiana Toll Road reached the Illinois border in 1958, the western segment of a tollway network that was to reach the East Coast. The seven and three quarter mile Chicago Skyway was built hurriedly to handle the expected dumping of Indiana Toll Road traffic into the already congested southeastern corner of Chicago. It was intended to carry traffic to a junction with the Dan Ryan Expressway, affording access to the metropolitan area freeway system.

The third and largest of the tollway systems was developed by the Illinois State Toll Highway Commission. It consists of three segments: the Northwest Tollway running seventy-seven miles from the Kennedy Expressway to the Wisconsin border; the East-West Tollway running twenty-seven miles from the Eisenhower Expressway to beyond Aurora; and the seventy-eight mile Tri-State Tollway which bypasses Chicago and links northwest Indiana with southeast Wisconsin.

The Indiana and Illinois tollways have exceeded load expectations and have been successful financially. The Illinois tollway system, despite demands for lower tolls, has, instead, elected to expand and is currently extending the East-West Tollway to Rock Falls, Illinois. The Chicago Skyway, in contrast, has been a financial disaster, with sinking fund installments and interest to bond holders in default. The Chicago Skyway traffic projections were grossly overestimated. It also was hurt by the construction of alternate freeway routes. Vehicles and revenues are slightly less than half of initial projections. Increased tolls have not significantly relieved the financial situation.

With other service-feeder segments now built, the expressway and tollway system possesses both radial routes which converge at the CBD and both inner and outer circumferential routes that tie the radials together. An inner distribution loop encircles the CBD, while the outer belt circumferential (the Tri-State Tollway) runs from Indiana to Wisconsin. A planned middle circumferential, the Crosstown Expressway running along the western city limits, is mired in controversy and construction is unlikely to be started. As urban development continues to spread, more distant expressways are contemplated including one running south-

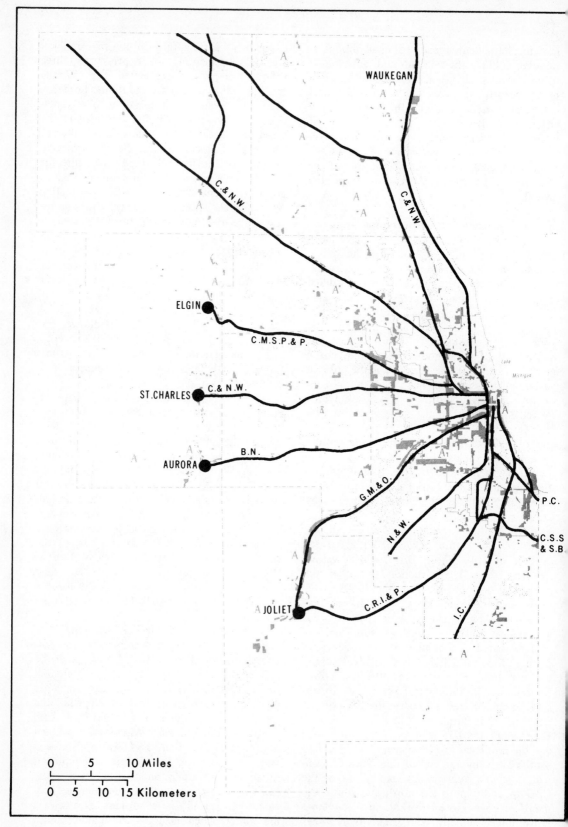

WAUKEGAN

C.&N.W.

C.&N.W.

ELGIN

C.M.S.P.&P.

ST.CHARLES C.&N.W.

B.N.

AURORA

G.M.&O.

P.C.

N.&W.

C.S.S
& S.B

JOLIET

C.R.I.&P.

I.C.

Lake
Michigan

```
0     5     10 Miles
0   5   10   15 Kilometers
```

Figure 6. Chicago's commuter railroad network.

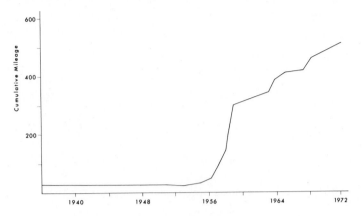

Figure 7. Expressway mileage in the Chicago area, 1936-1972.

ward from Lake County through DuPage County into Will County and another even farther west running through the rapidly growing Fox River valley.

The expressways opened vast tracts of land on the periphery of the urbanized area to suburban development. Initially the movement outward followed the basic high accessibility population corridors. Soon population began to diffuse, however, filling the vacant gaps. This outward migration brought about a decline in Chicago's commercial and industrial dominance. Rings of large, modern suburban shopping centers, almost always freeway-oriented, drained business from the central city. Industry increased rapidly in the suburban areas, often seeking expressway proximity rather than a more traditional railroad location. More jobs are now found in the surrounding metropolitan area than in Chicago, whereas in 1950, 78 percent of the employment was in Chicago. Some of the industry was new but much had relocated from Chicago causing a net loss of jobs there. Some 211,000 jobs and 220 factories were lost in the last decade alone. People living in the suburbs increasingly found there were interesting opportunities for employment besides those in Chicago, increasing the proportion of trips between origins and destinations other than the CBD.

Minority groups living in the inner city, on the other hand, were especially hard hit as many jobs moved to the suburbs and commuting to them was difficult because mass transportation could not adequately serve the dispersed industrial locations in the suburbs.

The result was overwhelming reliance on the automobile (by those who could afford one) and a growing amount of reverse commuting—people leaving the city in the morning for work and returning to Chicago in the evening. Between 1960 and 1970, for example, the number of Chicagoans who reverse commuted to jobs in the suburbs increased from 88,900 to 206,500—or 132 percent. In Elk Grove Village, adjacent to O'Hare Airport, for example, about 75 percent of the 25,000 people employed there reside in Chicago, resulting in traffic jams in both directions during the morning and evening rush hours.

The expressway system had some other incidental results in the city. Traffic was reduced on many paralleling arterial streets, and the overall accident rate per mile driven in the area declined. Land values near the expressways rose, compensating for the loss of tax revenue because of property demolition along the rights of way. Yet despite the construction of some thirty inbound expressway lanes, the number of vehicles entering the CBD daily has not changed appreciably, although there was an increase when the expressways first opened, necessitating construction of additional Loop parking facilities that now occupy an estimated one sixth of the surface area (Figure 8).

Problems of Mass Transit

While the overwhelming number of people now travel by automobile (over eleven million passenger trips daily), almost two million passenger trips daily are still by mass trans-

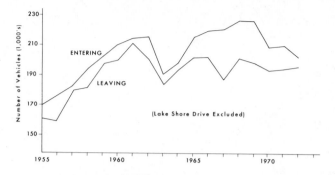

Figure 8. Changes in numbers of vehicles entering the CBD, 1955-1973.

portation. But mass transit use has been declining because of automobile competition. A declining number of passengers, coupled with other factors such as the inflationary cost squeeze, has resulted in a decline in service and equipment. All major modes of mass transit have been affected adversely.

The Chicago Transit Authority, by far the largest mass transit agency, serving Chicago and a number of the suburbs with integrated bus, elevated, and subway service, experienced a total traffic decline of 38 percent from 1955 to 1971. The decline was much greater for the bus lines—44 percent—and that largely after 1966 (Figure 9). The rapid transit has benefited not only from its speed and convenience but also from its reliability, virtually unaffected by automobile congestion and weather, and with downtown stations linked by underground walkways.

In recent years the elevated subway system has benefited from major extensions. Emulating the pioneer median strip rapid transit service established in the Eisenhower Expressway in 1958, a similar median service was opened in 1969 in the Dan Ryan Expressway, connected with the Lake Street elevated line to provide through service from the western suburbs, through the Loop, to Chicago's South Side. The following year an extension of CTA's west-northwest route was opened along the Kennedy Expressway. Bus routes in the areas of the new facilities were realigned to serve as feeders into the new stations to provide improved service to the CBD (Figure 10). A measure of the success of the new service is the fact that the 95th Street terminal on the Dan Ryan rapid transit now handles 20,000 entering passengers a day.

Yet despite these improvements, including the acquisition of new air-conditioned buses and rapid transit cars, the decline of passengers has continued without interruption since the end of World War II. Ridership is off some 65 percent since 1947 when CTA began operation as a successor to much older private companies. In the same period the automobiles registered in the city have nearly doubled to over a million—or from one car per 6.4 persons to one car per 3.5 persons.

With falling ridership, rising labor costs (consuming 82.5 percent of gross revenues of this labor-oriented industry), a large bonded indebtedness, and much needed equipment replacement, the CTA has been experiencing deficits since 1964 and has been suffering a hand to mouth existence, with one financial crisis after another. Only sporadic, last minute government aid has kept the CTA from more service curtailments, more fare increases, and possible financial disaster. By 1973 the state government had begun to recognize that an unsubsidized CTA was no longer capable of financial existence and that the CTA needed aid on a regular basis, as is the case with virtually every large transit system in the country.

The commuter railroads created Chicago's fingerlike population corridors (Figure 11). After experiencing a steady post–World War II decline in ridership, the commuter railroads as a whole showed a 7.5 percent increase during the 1960–1970 decade. They were the only form of mass transit in the area to show an increase.

Much of this increase is due to the decentralization of population into suburban areas and to the relatively good service to the CBD

Figure 9. Passenger volumes carried by Chicago's public transportation systems, 1960-1971.

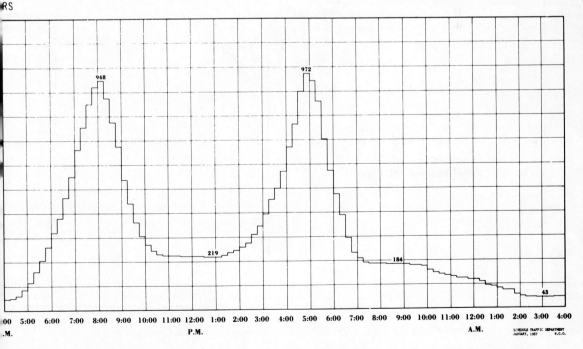

Figure 10. Scheduling of the CTA's rapid transit cars by fifteen minute periods on Friday, December 30, 1966. (Courtesy Chicago Transit Authority)

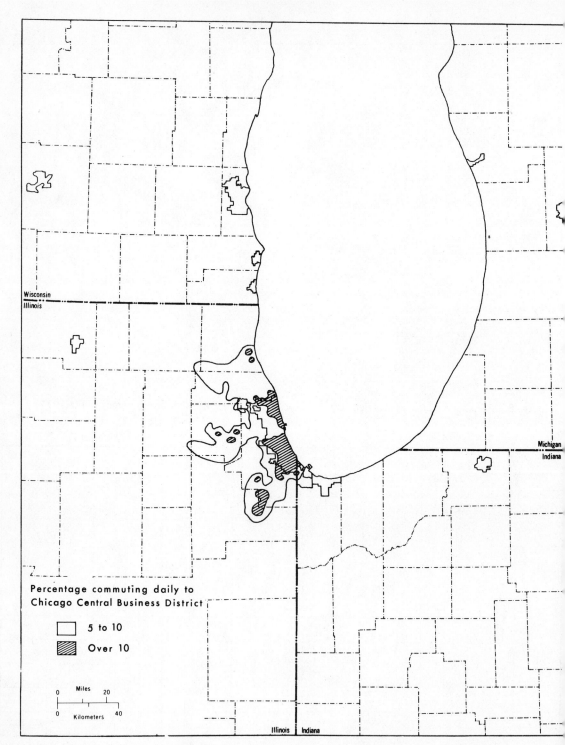

Figure 11. Percentage of the labor force commuting to the Chicago CBD in 1970.

rendered by a number of the railroads. Unlike the CTA which provides relatively comprehensive service in Chicago, the railroads are geared to carrying people from suburbs to the CBD. The increase in passengers, however, is not necessarily translated into economic success; actually the commuter railroads as a whole are experiencing increasing economic difficulties which threaten the continuance of their service.

The railroads have suffered from similar problems that plague the CTA—inflation, rising labor costs, auto competition and new expressways, maximum use of equipment only during the two workday peak periods, etc. They have tried to meet these problems in a number of ways. The most drastic was outright abandonment, as in the case of three electric interurban routes—the Chicago, Aurora, and Elgin Railroad in 1959 due to opening of the competing Eisenhower Expressway; the Shore Line route of the Chicago North Shore and Milwaukee Railroad in 1955; and its Skokie valley route in 1963, also due largely to increased expressway competition.

Other methods used by the railroads to combat their financial difficulties were to curtail service, raise fares, cut costs wherever possible, and abandon close-in stations to concentrate on longer hauls. The only railroad making a profit on its commuter service, the Chicago and North Western Railway, attacked the problem in a different manner. Besides instituting the above measures, it improved its services with better equipment and service, instituted numerous innovations, and vigorously promoted its three suburban routes, totaling 175 miles. It also benefited from the abandonment of the two competing interurban railroads. But after reaching a profit peak on commuter service in 1968, the profit has declined steadily since.

The changing percentage of passengers carried by the various carriers in the last twenty-five years is the consequence of differences in the growth of the areas served, the establishment of the expressway network, the elimination of certain competing railroads, and the quality of service. Among the lines, the Chicago North Western, the Burlington Northern, and the Milwaukee Road each have about doubled their share of the market. They serve the fast-growing suburbs to the north, northwest, and west. The Illinois Central Gulf and the Rock Island, by comparison, have experienced substantial percentage declines due to the slower growth of their south suburban hinterlands and, more importantly, to the change in population composition of much of their hinterland within South Chicago from white to black. Many of their South Side stations in the city have declined sharply in patronage or been eliminated entirely because the journey to work patterns of the blacks are not nearly as CBD-oriented as were those of the whites who were displaced. The opening of the Dan Ryan median rapid transit also has had an adverse impact on both railways. The Illinois Central Gulf estimates that since 1969 when the CTA Dan Ryan service opened, its patronage between 75th Street and 111th Street has declined about 65 percent.

The suburban bus lines are by far the smallest of the three major components of mass transit in the area. They are also the ones that have declined the most precipitously in ridership in recent years: suburban bus lines (serving the suburbs around Chicago) by 36.3 percent and satellite bus lines (serving municipalities in the outer area of the region) by 71.3 percent.

The twelve suburban and six satellite bus lines are the most marginal of all public transit operations. They range in size from West Towns Bus Company with 138 buses to Lindberg Transportation Company with one. They operate older equipment in areas of low density where most families have at least one automobile. Frequency of service except during rush hours is limited. In some instances the buses are feeders to rapid transit or commuter railroads, while a few lines carry passengers directly to the Loop. They often provide the only reasonable service for people who do not have automobiles.

The focal point of employment, shopping, and transportation of the Chicago SMSA through the years has been the Chicago CBD. Transportation service to the CBD generally has been good. Fortunately, valuable and regular comparative data are available on the mode of travel people have utilized to reach the CBD from an annual passenger Cordon Count that has been compiled since 1926, and is shown in Table1. As these data show, the number of people entering the CBD has been quite stable. Even going back to 1926 the decline has only

Table 1. Daily Number of Passengers Entering CBD[a]

Year	Buses and Streetcars	Subway and Elevated	Railroad	Private Auto	Taxicabs and Out-of-Town Buses	Total
1926	294,998	256,286	118,857	166,367	44,878	880,859
1950	177,369	199,351	138,741	288,659	76,125	800,233
1960	124,235	258,757	115,318	285,283	80,020	864,733
1972	96,495	236,784	110,723	270,487	85,846	805,224

[a]The CBD as defined in the passenger Cordon Count is bounded by Roosevelt Road, Lake Michigan, and the river. The count was taken from 7:00 A.M. to 7:00 P.M. in May 1975.

been about 8 percent. Indeed, with the rapid growth in recent decades of the area north of the Chicago River, and to a lesser extent to the west of the river, it is possible that broader definition of the CBD for all the years would have yielded a much smaller total decline—if any at all. The mode of transportation has also changed surprisingly little since 1950 except for a sharp decline in the number coming into the CBD via CTA. For the entire SMSA surveys show that only 3 percent of all auto passengers make a daily trip to Chicago's central area, thirty-nine percent of bus passengers, and 81 percent respectively of rapid transit and commuter railroad passengers.

Changes in External Passenger Flows

Since 1960 the automobile, aided by the new interstate highway system, has continued to dominate intercity passenger travel to and from the Chicago area. Air travel has increased substantially, but travel has held fairly steady, and rail travel has declined sharply. Nationally in 1967, according to the U.S. Bureau of the Census, the auto accounted for 86.2 percent of intercity trips, planes 8 percent, buses 2.6 percent, trains 1.4 percent, and other 2.4 percent.

Following the national trend, intercity rail passenger service out of Chicago fell drastically during the 1960s with one train schedule after another being abandoned. In 1971 the creation of the federally supported Amtrak system stabilized, at least temporarily, rail service to and from Chicago. In 1973 Chicago, as previously, had the greatest number of scheduled trains in the nation, some twenty-three daily, including high speed, French-built Turbo Train service on the Chicago-St. Louis route. Additionally, the Rock Island operates one train a

day to Peoria and one to Rock Island, Illinois, and there is service to Dubuque.

The rapid erosion in intercity passenger service facilitated consolidation of all Amtrak intercity passenger service into Union Station downtown; the two daily Rock Island trains still use the La Salle Street Station. One result has been continued deterioration of areas surrounding the old stations, especially those little used. The Grand Central Station has already been torn down. But much land has been released for potential redevelopment, as will be seen in the following section.

Bus transportation out of Chicago has been improved by the spreading interstate highway network. The main results have been the shortening of running times and the instituting of more express service between Chicago and other large cities. This often resulted in the curtailing of some of the service to smaller communities, especially those not near the expressways. Besides the downtown Trailways and Greyhound stations and a few small suburban stations, Greyhound developed three new convenient substations at CTA rapid transit terminals—the 95th Street Dan Ryan, the Skokie Swift, and the Jefferson Park Kennedy terminals.

The decade of the 1960s witnessed a rapid growth in Chicago air passenger traffic, with about 95 percent using O'Hare International Airport, the world's busiest airport. O'Hare averages 1,700 arrivals and departures daily or better than a plane a minute on a twenty-four hour basis. It is served by thirty-one scheduled carriers including seventeen with direct international services. Of the total passenger volume, approximately 50 percent were travelers who landed at O'Hare to take a connecting flight.

Increasing traffic at O'Hare brought problems of both air and land access congestion, while the smaller Midway Airport which it replaced with the advent of jet aircraft soon resembled a ghost scene as did its once bustling ancillary commercial area. Concomitant with the rapid growth of air traffic were rapid commercial and industrial developments. Dozens of hotels and motels were built in the area to accommodate the air travelers and the growing number of meetings and conventions held in the vicinity of the airport. In this, O'Hare was following in the well-established transportation-related paths of Chicago's role as an ideal meeting place and distribution center. Chicago's first convention—the 1847 River and Harbor's Convention—debated the topic of inland navigation. Until the 1950s, because water and rail transportation focused on center city terminals, there was a downtown concentration of service functions for transient populations. Two gatherings in particular left visible symbols of their magnitude upon the internal structure of the city; the 1893 Columbian Exposition hosted 27,500,000 visitors, a figure matched by the 1933-1934 Century of Progress Exposition and its 28 million guests and 1,527 official conventions. A network of downtown-oriented facilities capable of flexibility and sufficient size developed to meet both these heroic and lesser-sized gatherings. In return, Chicago has benefited enormously. During 1972, eight million conventioneers and tourists spent over $850 million while attending more than 1,000 conventions. Using a conservative ratio of five to one injected dollars, this activity amounted to more than $4 billion cycled through the economy of Chicago, providing 100,000 jobs and numerous business opportunities. Beyond raw numbers and dollars, this influx of differing peoples and activities contributes to the atmosphere of vitality and cosmopolitanism found only in the world's great cities. Residents of Chicago share in and benefit from this industry in terms of jobs, income, entertainment, parades, trade shows, and cultural and athletic events.

The concentration of air traffic at O'Hare, and the accessibility created by the tollways and expressways, has meant that the 19,000 hotel rooms of the downtown concentration—complemented by McCormick Place and adjacent exposition halls, the only facilities capable of housing the largest trade shows—have now been joined by a newer terminal-convention complex of more than 7,000 hotel and motel rooms adjacent to O'Hare. There, transients are served and myriad business meetings and smaller conventions are held.

The Changing Freight Network

Chicago also remains a major focal point for national freight movement and for local traffic interchange. An estimated eighty-six tons of goods per capita are handled by the area's transportation network compared to fifty-four tons per capita nationally.

Exact freight data are difficult to obtain. A study based on an analysis of available secondary data conducted by the Chicago Area Transportation Study estimated that approximately 588 million tons of goods are handled annually in the six county Chicago SMSA and Lake and Porter counties, Indiana. The estimated division by mode in 1965 is: rail, 54.25 percent; truck, 22.45 percent; water, 12.24 percent; pipeline, 11.05 percent; and air, 0.07 percent (of 588,445,000 tons total).

Evidence indicates that the absolute tonnage of all modes has been increasing steadily in recent years. Air cargo has been increasing the most rapidly, but still represents less than 1 percent of total freight.

The huge freight operations of the area are handled by a vast complex of facilities:

RAIL	17	line haul railroads
	4	belt line railroads
	8	industrial switching railroads
TRUCK	843	for-hire carriers
	360	moving van lines
AIR	23	scheduled carriers of air cargo
WATER	42	scheduled overseas carriers
	14	barge lines
	64	commercial waterway terminals
PIPE	21	carriers of petroleum and petroleum products and 7 refineries
	3	carriers of natural gas
	4	utility companies
OTHER SERVICES	138	warehouses
	56	freight forwarders

Waterway Traffic. Waterway traffic has grown rapidly, spurred by the opening of the St. Lawrence Seaway in 1959, the widening of the Calumet Sag Channel, and the development of new port facilities, especially at Lake Calumet. Annual traffic in 1970 totaled 80,708,486 tons for the entire area. Bulk cargo for the steel mills comprises most of the tonnage; about a third of the tonnage consists of barge traffic on the inland waterways. The port of Chicago handles about a third of total Great Lakes overseas trade. It is visited annually by over 600 foreign vessels representing forty-two steamship lines. In the 1950s, before the opening of the St. Lawrence Seaway, only about one-third as many much smaller foreign ships called at the port of Chicago annually.

There has been a shift among the Chicago waterway facilities in recent years in the amount of freight handled. Downtown Navy Pier has declined in tonnage and may be phased out because of limited facilities, congestion near the CBD, and desirability of the location for other uses. Only sixty-two foreign ships called at Navy Pier in 1972. The Calumet River and Lake Calumet waterways have been deepened to the standard twenty-seven foot depth, have had obstructive bridges removed, and have had their facilities improved. However, they still lack good container facilities, and early traffic growth has been halted by labor problems and dockside theft. A completely new industrial-public facility port at Burns Harbor in the center of the Indiana sand dunes is too recent a construction to have affected the port of Chicago as yet. Traffic, however, has been somewhat affected by the declining use of river and channel frontage by industries that utilize waterfront facilities.

Rail Freight. The railroads' share of intercity freight has declined substantially. Carloadings in the Chicago area declined from 1,206,225 in 1959 to 1,064,937 in 1968. Some of this reflects larger boxcars, elimination of less than carload (LCL) traffic, and the use of bypass routes, but one consequence has been underutilization of some of the maze of railroad facilities. A CATS survey showed that 38 percent of facilities studied were underutilized. This is especially true of the often outmoded facilities on the fringe of the CBD, notably to the south, but the situation

has, in turn, opened vast tracts of land for grandiose residential developments now planned. These facilities originally served the industrial and commercial concerns that were concentrated in the CBD area. Railroads also had direct connections with the then much-used local waterway facilities. Many of these facilities, some also previously important in handling the passenger trains of the past, have been moved farther out to more modern, spacious, and less congested facilities such as those at Markham, Proviso, Bensenville, and the new yards at Burns Harbor. The trend is for the development of huge classification yards far beyond the urbanized perimeter; the Burlington Northern, for example, is planning a major facility west of Aurora.

Consolidation of facilities is now proving to be cost saving, speeding the time it takes for freight cars to move through the Chicago rail network and making available for development large and valuable parcels of unneeded railroad land (fifty-two square miles are occupied by rail rights of way and yards in the Chicago area).

Since the mid-1950s, Chicago railroads have instituted many other important technological changes that have helped them competitively. Besides better equipment and increased automation, the railroads have developed the unit train, the piggyback trailer on flatcar (TOFC), the container on flatcar (COFC), and auto rack service.

In 1970 seven single commodity, low cost, through route unit trains direct from source to consignee were operating in the area. They included coal trains to public utilities, coking coal and iron ore trains to Indiana steel mills, and an experimental thirty-five car train transporting liquid sludge from the Chicago Sanitary District to downstate Illinois.

TOFC and COFC services allow the railroads to give door-to-door intermodal service, to handle former LCL as well as high value business, and to service the increasing number of industries in suburban locations where there are no direct rail connections. In the last twenty years some twenty-one TOFC-COFC yards have been put into operation, almost wholly in the southern and western parts of the area; thirteen of these facilities are located in the city of Chicago and average over thirty acres in size. In many cases the railroads have converted obsolete, underused, inner city yards into TOFC-COFC facilities to provide loading and unloading sites central to established industrial and commercial areas and highways. This type of specialized service has been increasing at an annual rate of about 15 percent in the Chicago area, though it only accounts for perhaps about 5 percent of the carloadings.

The use of roll on–roll off auto rack cars has allowed the railroad industry to increase its share of new car shipments from only 8 percent in 1959 to over 50 percent at present. Chicago has seven auto rack depots located mainly in the southern and western parts of the Chicago Switching District. They serve mainly as regional receipt-distribution centers.

Despite these recent improvements, much remains to be done to improve railroad efficiency in the Chicago area. Past unplanned growth has produced both overcapacity and duplicate facilities. Within the Chicago Switching District, there are still 131 freight yards, more than fifty places where railroads cross other railroads, eighty-five separate rail routes parallel to other rail routes, and over 5,700 miles of trackage. The system of belt railroads has helped somewhat, as have mergers and the recently installed joint electronic scanning system; however, there is much consolidation and realignment still to be achieved.

Trucking. For the Chicago area the trucking industry is important both as an intrametropolitan distributor of goods and for its longer range intercity operations. It is also important for its role in freight forwarding and as the ultimate distributor of sizable quantities of the goods handled by the other major transportation modes—rail, water, air, and pipeline.

Freight handled has grown steadily and the industry has exhibited a greater locational flexibility than have the other modes of transportation. Terminal facilities have been moving outward, away from congested inner city areas, reflecting the rapid merger of trucking firms and the opening of expressways. The merger of trucking companies has led to fewer but larger trucking terminals. The new Gateway Transportation Company trucking terminal in Chicago Ridge is the world's largest, having 285 loading bays. But the number of for-hire trucking carriers is still large, with some 843 listed for the eight county area. Often, mergers result in a special kind of filtering: the movement of smaller or local carriers to terminals vacated by the larger firms that often have moved to newer and larger facilities farther out from the inner city.

There has been a strong concentration of new terminals along the Stevenson Expressway in the area east of the Tri-State Tollway and also along some stretches of major West Side arterial streets such as Pulaski and Cicero avenues. The need for interline exchange of goods has fostered locational concentrations, although the growth of numerous national carriers may cause the importance of this to decline. Clusters of truck terminals have been established in some of the southwest suburbs—Bedford Park, Chicago Ridge, Oak Lawn, Summit, and Alsip. However, 69 percent of the truck terminals are still located in Chicago, mainly on the South and Southwest sides. Freight forwarders have located near O'Hare. City plans calls for more truck terminals in the Lake Calumet area. Only 12 percent of the region's terminals are currently located in the seven counties outside of Cook County; the largest concentrations outside of Cook County are in the Gary-Hammond area in Indiana and in Fox River valley in Illinois.

A very recent trend for some of the larger intercity carriers has been to ring the area with terminals in satellite cities to handle the traffic of those areas. Satellite terminals have been established by a number of companies in Waukegan, Elgin, Aurora, Joliet, and Chicago Heights. Both building and operating costs are lower and there is less congestion than in Chicago. Indications are that Chicago has lost some interchange business as a result.

Pipelines. Pipelines, whose limited visibility often masks their crucial importance, also are one of the area's fastest growing freight transport modes, handling in 1965 over 11 percent of the freight tonnage of the area. Connected with the network of twenty-four pipelines that carry petroleum, natural gas, and refined products are seven underground gas storage facilities and seven oil refineries—four of which (including the two largest) are located in the Whiting-East Chicago area of Indiana, with the other three along the inland waterway network. Chicago is a major inland hub for the petroleum and natural gas industry.

The area's facilities have been further increased by the twenty-six inch Chicap petrole-

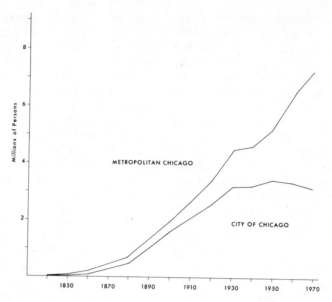

Figure 12. Population growth of the city of Chicago and the Chicago metropolitan area, 1830–1970.

um pipeline which became operational in 1969, by the opening of the new Union Oil refinery near Lemont in 1971, and the opening of the Mobile Oil refinery near Joliet in 1973. In addition there were sizable expansions by a number of other refineries in the area. In recent years refinery capacity growth has averaged about 8 percent annually and the increase in natural gas use has been about the same.

THE CHANGING HOUSING STOCK

Facilitated by changes in transportation, the city of Chicago's population declined 5.2 percent from 3,550,000 in 1960 to 3,369,000 in 1970 while the SMSA's population increased 12.2 percent from 6,220,000 to 6,977,000 because of a net increase in the suburban population of 958,000 (Figure 12). Between 1960 and 1970, 481,553 new housing units were built in the metropolis—four times as many apartments as single family homes in the central city and three times as many housing units in the suburbs as in the central city. With a 24 percent increase in the metropolitan housing stock but only a 12.2 percent increase in the population, a major transformation of the region's residential fabric occurred, and there was a withdrawal of 218,968 of the least-desirable housing units from the stock.

In the period 1960–1970, 257,590 of the new units were occupied by white home-

owners and 146,029 by white renters, another 13,934 by black homeowners and 27,153 by black renters, and 27,934 of the units were vacant in 1970. Because the number of households in the metropolitan area increased in the decade by only 285,729—143,174 white homeowners and 25,797 white renters, 45,065 black homeowners and 49,573 black renters, a ratio of 1.7 new housing units to each new family—a massive chain of successive housing moves was initiated as families living in older neighborhoods moved to homes vacated by the new suburban homeowners and renters, and so on down the chain of housing values. The resulting effects rippled progressively inward from the suburbs to the core of the city. For example, of the 54 percent of Chicago's suburbanites who reported in 1970 that they had lived in a different residence in 1965, one-half had come from other suburbs in the metropolitan area and one-quarter had come from Chicago. The remaining quarter were immigrants from outside the metropolitan area, generally moving into communities "approved" by real estate companies and banks, and advertised in *Chicagoland's Community Guide* (Figure 13).

Figure 13. Residential areas "recommended" to intercity executive transferees in *Chicagoland's Community Guide* by the Chicago Association of Commerce and Industry.

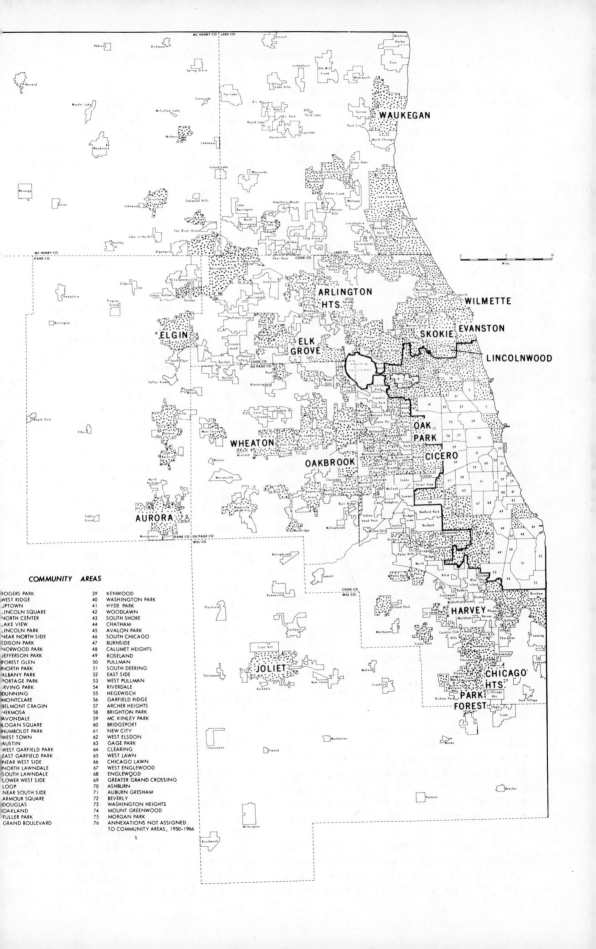

COMMUNITY AREAS

1	ROGERS PARK	39	KENWOOD
2	WEST RIDGE	40	WASHINGTON PARK
3	UPTOWN	41	HYDE PARK
4	LINCOLN SQUARE	42	WOODLAWN
5	NORTH CENTER	43	SOUTH SHORE
6	LAKE VIEW	44	CHATHAM
7	LINCOLN PARK	45	AVALON PARK
8	NEAR NORTH SIDE	46	SOUTH CHICAGO
9	EDISON PARK	47	BURNSIDE
10	NORWOOD PARK	48	CALUMET HEIGHTS
11	JEFFERSON PARK	49	ROSELAND
12	FOREST GLEN	50	PULLMAN
13	NORTH PARK	51	SOUTH DEERING
14	ALBANY PARK	52	EAST SIDE
15	PORTAGE PARK	53	WEST PULLMAN
16	IRVING PARK	54	RIVERDALE
17	DUNNING	55	HEGEWISCH
18	MONTCLARE	56	GARFIELD RIDGE
19	BELMONT CRAGIN	57	ARCHER HEIGHTS
20	HERMOSA	58	BRIGHTON PARK
21	AVONDALE	59	MC KINLEY PARK
22	LOGAN SQUARE	60	BRIDGEPORT
23	HUMBOLDT PARK	61	NEW CITY
24	WEST TOWN	62	WEST ELSDON
25	AUSTIN	63	GAGE PARK
26	WEST GARFIELD PARK	64	CLEARING
27	EAST GARFIELD PARK	65	WEST LAWN
28	NEAR WEST SIDE	66	CHICAGO LAWN
29	NORTH LAWNDALE	67	WEST ENGLEWOOD
30	SOUTH LAWNDALE	68	ENGLEWOOD
31	LOWER WEST SIDE	69	GREATER GRAND CROSSING
32	LOOP	70	ASHBURN
33	NEAR SOUTH SIDE	71	AUBURN GRESHAM
34	ARMOUR SQUARE	72	BEVERLY
35	DOUGLAS	73	WASHINGTON HEIGHTS
36	OAKLAND	74	MOUNT GREENWOOD
37	FULLER PARK	75	MORGAN PARK
38	GRAND BOULEVARD	76	ANNEXATIONS NOT ASSIGNED TO COMMUNITY AREAS, 1950-1966

A consequence was that many Chicago families were enabled to improve their housing condition dramatically during the decade, while downward pressure was exerted on the prices of older housing units. New home prices inflated at 9.9 percent annually 1965–1971, while older single family homes in Chicago inflated in price at an annual rate of 4.5 percent. In addition, discriminatory pricing of identical units—blacks paying more than whites—was eliminated. Not only was there a dramatic improvement in the housing condition of Chicago's central city minorities, as over 128,000 units were transferred from white to black occupancy, but 63,000 of the worst units in the city could be demolished at the time that tens of thousands of additional undesirable units were being abandoned. The Chicago region thus provides a classic example of filtering mechanisms at work, because housing surpluses rather than housing deficits characterized Chicago's housing market.

In spite of these changes, however, segregation between black and white remained profound. Polarization by race increased between the central city and the suburbs, and within the crescent of late nineteenth century industrial satellites. In the decade, 352,057 new housing units were constructed, but in the entire six county suburban area, only 4,188 out of 223,845 new single family dwellings were sold to blacks, and only 3,712 out of 11,290 new apartments were rented to blacks. In addition, some 3,208 blacks purchased homes previously owned by whites and 2,153 blacks moved into apartments previously rented by whites. In contrast to the net increase of 287,000 white families in suburbia, only 13,261 new black families were able to obtain residences outside the central city, most in or contiguous to the "minighettos" of the region's industrial satellites. In 1970, less than 500 black families lived in white suburban neighborhoods.

Contrast this picture with that of the central city. There was a net decline of 41,500 white homeowners and 76,900 white renters in the central city in the decade. Net increases in the central city's black population consisted of 37,669 new homeowners (more than doubling black homeownership in the decade) and 43,708 new renters.

The complex dynamics of white-to-black filtering in the central city were as follows: some 128,829 units were transferred from white to black occupancy, allowing net increases over new construction of 28,008 in black homeownership and 20,267 in black rental of better quality flats and apartments than previously had been occupied. In addition, 63,000 black families were able to move into better quality housing from dilapidated and other units that were demolished in the decade within the area of the 1960 ghetto, and finally, there was a net increase by 1970 of 17,554 vacant units in the black residential area of 1970, precursors to abandonment.

These facts do not support those who argue that there is a housing shortage in metropolitan Chicago; there is not for those able to pay. To the extent that people have been able to participate in Chicago's private housing market, the normal market mechanism of filtering has delivered increasing supplies of improved quality housing and has both permitted and impelled the demolition of the worst housing in the worst neighborhoods. To the extent that unmet needs have not been met, it is for those subgroups beset by incapacity and/or financial inability to participate in the private market on an equal footing, i.e.:

1. Those *financially afflicted,* including the elderly poor, the welfare poor, and the sick and infirm poor, unable to participate in normal housing market channels on any basis, and thus left the dregs unwanted by any market participant.
2. Those *institutionally afflicted,* dominantly minority group members who have been unable, due to the web of discrimination that still afflicts the housing market, to gain access to suburban residences close to the metropolitan area's new and expanding job centers.

In the first case, the problem is one of financial access; in the second, one of geographic access, to which we now turn.

SUBURBANIZATION OF JOBS AND THE CHANGING JOURNEY TO WORK

Accompanying these housing shifts, Chicago lost 211,000 jobs and the suburbs gained 548,000 jobs in the 1960s. In these ten years, Chicago's jobs declined at more than twice the rate of its population loss (–12 percent versus –5 percent) and suburban jobs grew twice as fast as suburban population (71 percent versus 35 percent). Northwest Cook County gained by far the most jobs and people in the decade, adding 149,400 jobs and 222,800 people (222,620 whites but only 180 blacks) to the areas surrounding O'Hare Airport. In relative terms, there was a gain of 262 percent in jobs, and 135 percent in white population. DuPage County registered the second largest relative gains in jobs (131 percent) and people (59 percent)—82,300 jobs; 177,000 white and 970 black residents.

This massive suburbanization of jobs has meant that fewer suburbanites now work in Chicago and that more Chicagoans now work in the suburbs. Chicago, with 52 percent of the metropolitan jobs and 48 percent of the labor force, still has 11 percent more jobs than labor force—but the city's jobs do not match the skills of its labor force, nor do the suburbs' jobs match their labor force. Thus, there are more than twice as many reverse commuters from Chicago as in 1960: 18 percent of Chicago's labor force now works in the suburbs, compared to 7 percent ten years ago. There is another difference too. In 1960, Chicago's suburban commuters lived in the ring of white collar neighborhoods closest to the suburbs (Figure 14). By 1970, there were pockets of reverse commuters throughout the central city (Figure 15), with Chicago's blue collar labor force making up the largest gainers among the reverse commuters. In 1970, 18 percent of Chicago's laborers worked in the suburbs, compared to 7 percent in 1960; 21 percent of its craftsmen worked in the suburbs, compared to 10 percent in 1960; and 22 percent of its factory workers worked in the suburbs, compared to 8 percent in 1960.

Correspondingly, suburban residents now rely less on Chicago workplaces and more on local industry. For example, only 36 percent of Park Forest's labor force now work in Chicago compared with 56 percent in 1960, with the bulk of the remaining labor force working in South Cook County. The proportion of DuPage County's labor force working in Chicago fell from 37 to 23 percent, with 49 percent now working in the county compared with 42 percent in 1960.

Chicago continues to dominate both the lower- and higher-paying jobs, while progressively greater proportions of upper income groups live in suburbia (Figure 16). Because the new homes

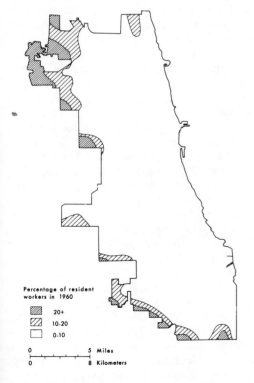

Percentage of resident workers in 1960

- 20+
- 10-20
- 0-10

0   5 Miles
0   8 Kilometers

Figure 14. Percentage of the labor force resident in Chicago's census tracts commuting to work in areas of Cook County outside the city in 1960.

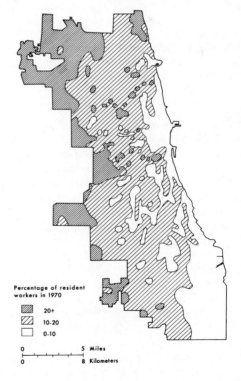

Percentage of resident workers in 1970

- 20+
- 10-20
- 0-10

0   5 Miles
0   8 Kilometers

Figure 15. Patterns of "reverse commuting" by city residents to suburban Cook County in 1970.

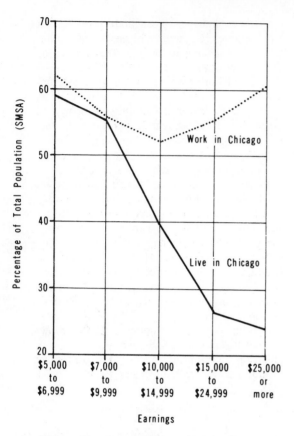

Figure 16. Differential place of residence and place of work of heads of household, classified by income in 1970.

and workplaces are more dispersed and are less accessible by public transportation, the average work trip is longer—thirteen versus seven miles one way—and automobile commuters have increased by one-third. A majority of Chicago residents now drive to work (53 percent in 1970, up from 45 percent in 1960), while the overwhelming majority of suburbanites now commute by car (80 percent at present, up from 69 percent in 1960 in the case of DuPage residents).

The proportion of automobile commuters is generally higher for workers working in the suburbs than for the residents living in them. Work trips to the city center can still be made by railroad; work trips to growing suburban job centers cannot. Nonetheless, as noted earlier, there has been a corresponding decline in commuting by public transportation. The proportion of commuters going by bus fell from 19

to 14 percent (from 30 to 20 percent for Chicago residents) and that of railroad and subway commuters from 12 to 9 percent (from 13 to 10 percent for Chicago residents). Thus, the suburbanization of jobs has aggravated the congestion of expressways and surface roads while contributing to the underutilization of the financially hard-pressed CTA and suburban bus and railroad companies.

Blacks and Spanish-speaking workers have been doubly penalized by the shift of jobs from Chicago to the suburbs. A disproportionate number of these workers are in the blue collar occupations, where the jobs are suburbanizing, and are in the moderate income brackets which means that they are priced out of new suburban housing. But they are excluded from suburban housing on racial as well as economic grounds. As we have already seen, the black worker, no matter what his income or his profession, is not free to move to most suburbs. For example, only 15 percent of Chicago area black households earning over $50,000 live in the suburbs.

There is abundant evidence of the adverse effect that distance has on the ability of blacks and other minorities to find more employment in the suburbs. If work trip origins and destinations among the major suburban areas for black and Spanish-speaking workers are examined, it is found that Chicago sends 14 percent of its black labor force and 20 percent of its Spanish labor force to suburbs, but depends on other areas for only 2.5 percent of its black work force and 8 percent of its Spanish work force. In contrast, for all workers, Chicago depends on the suburbs for 28 percent of its work force. In the outlying counties, too, the proportion of black and Spanish people working in the same county is much higher than for white workers.

The greater resistance to distance in the commuting patterns of black and Spanish workers is due partly to their lower rates of car-ownership and to their lower earnings. Only half of the Chicago area's black households and two-thirds of the Spanish households own cars, compared to four-fifths of white households. Black and Spanish workers earn on the average only two-thirds as much as white workers. The more people earn, the more time and money they are willing to spend commuting.

It is sometimes said that the main reason why only 10 percent of Chicago area blacks live in the suburbs is that most blacks cannot afford the cost of suburban housing. It is also sometimes contended that the main reason why only one-fifth of Chicago black workers work in the suburbs is that most blacks are not qualified to fill the jobs available in the suburbs.

There are relatively easy ways to test these two hypotheses. If one matches the housing expenditures of black households with the type and cost of housing in the suburbs, it will be found that in a colorblind housing market about two-thirds of the Chicago area blacks could afford to move from their present communities to white communities in Chicago and the suburbs.

There are similar measurable differences between the white and black labor force that permit the redistribution of the Chicago area black labor force, given a hypothetical colorblind job market. Characteristics of occupation, industry, and earnings are the major measures of differences between the qualifications (in the marketplace at least) of white and black workers. Although blacks have significantly increased their representation in white collar jobs since 1960 (from 6 to 10 percent), their occupational distribution continues to be heavily concentrated in unskilled and semi-skilled manual occupations. Although they make up 14.5 percent of the labor force today, blacks count only 5 percent of all managers, 6 percent of all salespeople, and 8 percent of all professional workers.

Still, black workers have made major inroads in most industries, particularly since 1960. Their most striking advances in the last ten years have been in machinery (up from 4 to 10 percent of the jobs), public utilities (6 to 15 percent), retail trade (6 to 12 percent); and finance and insurance (4 to 9 percent). However they continue to be substantially under-represented in the latter industry, as well as in construction (9 percent), wholesale trade (9 percent), and printing (9.5 percent), even though these industries are concentrated in the central area of Chicago. Similarly, blacks make up but 8 percent of retail salesworkers, in yet another highly centralized industry which involves no unusual technical skills or apprentice training.

On the other hand, blacks continue to dominate the occupations of service workers (26 percent), laborers (25 percent), and household workers (55 percent), and the industries of primary metals (25 percent), government (29 percent), and personal and household services (31 percent).

The greatest differences in black participation rates are found in the earnings categories. The proportion of black workers declines drastically as earnings go up—down from 21 percent for workers earning between $3,000 and $7,000, to 16 percent in the $7,000 to $10,000 bracket, to 7 percent in the $10,000 to $15,000 range, and to 2 percent for those earning over $15,000.

How would black employment in the suburbs increase if black workers were able to obtain work in a colorblind job market? In an exercise similar to the redistribution of black households in a colorblind housing market, black workers have been reallocated among the twenty largest suburban areas based on black participation rates in occupational, industrial, and earnings categories. It is assumed that these three characteristics are appropriate measures of job qualification and remuneration and that matching black participation rates for each category of these characteristics to the employment base of the twenty suburban areas reasonably removes the barrier of distance currently separating black housing from the suburban jobs for which they potentially qualify.

This method of reallocating black workers is illustrated in Table 2 using the example of the employment base of Arlington Heights. Participation rates of the Chicago area black labor force by occupational, industrial, and earnings categories are given in column 1. These rates are used as multipliers of the 1970 population of workers working in Arlington Heights (column 2) in the calculation (in column 3) of the potential black workers who would occupy these jobs if there were a colorblind housing market. The results are 1,903 potential black workers redistributed by the occupational profile; 2,065 workers by the industrial profile; and 1,902 by the earnings profile, for a composite average of 1,957 black workers—13.4 percent of the existing population of 14,600. This contrasts with the existing 169 black workers who make up only 1.1 percent of the work force.

Similar calculations were made for Chicago and the nineteen other suburban areas and the results are presented in Table 3. The last two

Table 2.   Calculation of Potential Black Employment in a Hypothetical Colorblind Housing Market

	SMSA Percent Black Workers	Arlington Heights	
		All Workers 1970	Potential Black Workers Col. 1 X Col. 2
All Workers	14.5	14,600	
Occupations			
Professional	8.3	2,603	216
Manager	4.7	1,228	58
Sales	6.1	1,326	81
Clerical	13.7	3,672	504
Craftsmen	10.3	1,927	194
Operatives	22.1	1,256	278
Laborers	25.1	696	175
Service	25.8	1,522	393
Total Potential			1,903
Industries			
Construction	9.1	1,029	94
Manufacturing	13.8	2,284	315
Transportation, Communication, and Public Utilities	15.4	1,494	230
Wholesale and Retail Trade	11.5	3,311	381
Finance, Insurance and Real Estate	8.8	942	83
Business and Repair Services	12.3	322	40
Personal Services	30.5	616	188
Professional and Real Estate Services	16.1	3,456	556
Public Administration	28.8	481	139
All Other Industries	14.5	269	39
Total Potential			2,065
Earnings			
$1, to $999	14.1	1,391	196
$1,000 to $2,999	11.7	2,656	311
$3,000 to $4,999	21.0	1,786	375
$5,000 to $6,999	21.3	1,987	423
$7,000 to $9,999	16.2	2,461	399
$10,000 to $14,999	6.7	2,470	165
$15,000 to $24,999	2.7	1,060	29
$25,000 or More	1.7	242	4
Total Potential			1,902

columns juxtapose the actual percentage black employment and the calculated composite percentage (columns 2 and 6). Whereas the actual black employment percentage ranges from less than one to more than twenty, no urban area would have fewer than 10 percent or more than 15 percent black workers, and eighteen of the twenty areas would have work forces of between 12 and 14 percent black workers in the hypothetical situation. Black workers in the city of Chicago would decrease from 305,107 to 221,907 and 170,300 blacks

would work in the suburbs, compared with the 82,000 now working there. The proportion of Chicago area blacks working in the suburbs would shoot up from the present 21 to 44 percent!

INDUSTRIAL PARKS AND THE CHANGING LOCATION OF INDUSTRY

The other component of changing journey to work patterns is the relocation of industry. In

Table 3. Actual and Potential Black Employment in Municipalities of 50,000 or More and Counties in the Chicago SMSA, 1970

	Actual 1970		Potential Black Workers Redistributed According to				Percentage Black	
	All Workers	Black Workers	Earnings	Occupation	Industry	Composite	Actual	Composite
Cook County	2,320,914	366,673	326,240	322,811	331,882	326,978	15.8	14.1
Arlington Heights	14,600	169	1,902	1,903	2,065	2,065	1.1	13.4
Berwyn	10,272	66	1,363	1,389	1,337	1,363	0.6	13.2
Chicago	1,506,549	305,107	224,786	210,354	230,580	221,907	20.3	14.7
Cicero	45,844	5,044	6,035	7,255	5,763	6,351	11.0	13.9
Des Plaines	33,038	1,018	4,057	4,459	3,965	4,160	3.1	12.6
Evanston	36,047	5,205	4,790	4,781	4,790	4,787	14.4	13.3
Oak Lawn	12,386	385	1,605	1,739	1,623	1,656	3.1	13.4
Oak Park	17,305	1,009	2,137	2,265	2,274	2,225	5.8	12.9
Skokie	41,737	2,927	5,284	5,583	5,038	5,302	7.0	12.7
Rest of Cook County	603,136	50,787	74,373	83,083	74,743	77,400	8.4	12.8
DuPage County	145,303	2,592	17,585	8,880	15,985	17,762	2.0	12.2
Elmhurst	14,472	302	1,853	1,811	1,848	1,837	2.1	12.7
Rest of DuPage County	130,831	2,592	15,732	17,069	14,137	15,925	2.0	12.2
Kane County	98,694	3,355	12,341	13,598	11,608	12,516	3.4	12.7
Aurora	31,136	1,137	3,692	3,959	3,526	3,726	3.7	12.0
Elgin	21,298	612	2,885	3,135	2,707	2,909	2.9	13.7
Rest of Kane County	46,260	1,606	5,764	6,504	5,375	5,881	3.5	12.7
Lake County	143,463	8,656	17,827	15,487	13,379	15,564	6.0	10.9
Waukegan	26,774	1,707	3,054	3,555	3,262	3,290	6.4	12.3
Rest of Lake County	116,689	6,949	14,773	11,932	10,117	12,274	6.0	10.5
McHenry County	33,671	217	4,120	4,601	4,092	4,271	0.6	12.7
Will County	79,685	5,376	9,282	10,841	9,885	10,002	6.8	12.6
Joliet	35,790	2,783	4,429	4,876	4,541	4,615	7.8	12.9
Rest of Will County	43,895	2,593	4,853	5,965	5,344	5,387	5.9	12.3
SMSA	2,821,393	387,171	387,171	387,171	387,171	392,209	13.7	13.7

this relocation, organized industrial districts have played a leading role, changing the scale of locational decisionmaking from the firm to the complete industrial park. A pulsating growth intimately related to and reflecting the pace of the regional economy has produced a progressive expansion in the number and variety of industrial parks since the Union Stock Yards were created in 1865. By 1974, the fourteenth annual survey of metropolitan parks listed a total of 356 parks occupying 51,362 acres within an eight county area of northeastern Illinois and northwestern Indiana, representing an increase of 298 parks and 41,756 acres between 1960 and 1974.

Today's industrial park is an outgrowth of the earlier organized industrial district, developed to provide a complete location package to a manufacturer. In establishing an industrial district, the developer eliminated the need for an individual manufacturer to carry out the functions of land purchase, zoning conformance, site development, or plant construction. The district provides access to proper transportation modes; utilities, including water and sewerage; proper streets and docks; and maintenance and security.

The forerunner of Chicago's industrial districts was the Union Stock Yards, established in 1865 by railroad and meatpacking interests. At that time the city had a population of 200,000, and milling and meatpacking were the primary industrial employers. The stockyard operation proved very successful and the yards remained on the same site for 106 years. Finally, in 1971, the Union Stock Yards closed and the operation, now much reduced in size, relocated close to Joliet. However, the original site still exists, being transformed into a modern industrial park in the heart of the city.

At the turn of the century, the concept of the organized industrial district became a reality when the Central Manufacturing District opened in Chicago on a tract immediately north of the stockyards, offering the array of services of the contemporary park. Central was soon joined by the Clearing Industrial District, whose first package deal as an industrial district was made in 1909. Central's development proceeded at a faster pace than Clearing's because of its more favored location near the center of Chicago and the need at that time to rely on horse-drawn drayage. As a result Central developed a more intensive type of land use

based on the multistoryed factory building. Clearing was located farther from the city and developed at a later stage, when the truck had started to replace the horse for intracity distribution. The change made possible the development of single story buildings on less expensive land, establishing a trend that continues to the present.

The original districts had to rely exclusively on the railroads for intercity carriage and were tied to rail locations. The rail network implanted on the region that linear fingerlike pattern of industrial land use that still prevails. After 1953, as the expressway networks evolved, the truck assumed new importance, however, and was reflected in locational decisions that accelerated the process of metropolitan decentralization.

Figure 17 shows the spatial pattern of the 356 industrial parks now in the metropolitan area. These parks accounted for much of the 16.7 million square feet of new plants built between 1960 and 1970. In terms of both value and number, northern Cook County's growth has been the most significant, located as it is at the innermost end of the region's principal growth direction. The primary catalyst has been O'Hare Airport at the intersection of the Tri-State and Northwest tollways. DuPage County has maintained a steady rate of expansion, characterized by standards of extreme high quality. The Oak Brook cluster is almost as important as that of O'Hare. Further afield, both Lake and Kane counties have expanded rapidly, also combining prestigious industrial parks, high status residential developments emphasizing quality environments, and distinctively modern office complexes and shopping centers. Lake County lies along the northern axis of metropolitan expansion that follows Interstate 94, while Kane expects to participate in new growth largely via the development of new towns that are already planned along the extension of the East-West Tollway currently under construction.

Despite the absence of attractive prestige parks similar to those located to the north and west, southern Cook County also has recorded a 400 percent growth rate in parks over the decade. These are "bread and butter" industrial parks linked to the heavy industry of the region. In general, land values of parks in southern Cook are lower than elsewhere in the county, but numerically the parks have grown

Figure 17. Location of Chicago planned industrial districts in 1972.

Industrial District (1972)

0   5   10 Miles

0   5   10 15 Kilometers

steadily as important changes in the transport network have closed major gaps in the expressway system. These include the opening of Interstates 80 and 57.

Finally, Lake and Porter counties in Indiana accounted for only sixteen parks of 3,530 acres in 1974, understandable because of the concentration of long-established large scale heavy industries located there. Steel plants, oil refineries, cement manufacturing, chemical plants, and primary food-processing firms dominate employment in this sector, and there are none of the environmental amenities that encourage industrial parks.

The spatial pattern has the following elements: prewar parks are strung along the railroads, whereas modern parks are aligned along the expressway system; major clusters are found around O'Hare Airport and in the Oakbrook area of eastern DuPage County; and another tight grouping of high quality parks is located immediately north of Chicago in the communities of Lincolnwood, Skokie, Morton Grove, and Niles, developed around decisions to operate from close-in locations, but in a political, economic, and social climate different from that of the central city. The unique character of the area is epitomized by one of its newest parks, Tam-O'Shanter Industrial Fairways. Built on nine holes of the former championship golf course, the asking price for sites is $2.29 per square foot or $100,000 per acre.

This pattern of industrial parks is carried over into the sites chosen by relocating or new industries in the Chicago region, and in the directions of industrial decentralization from the central city (Figure 18). Moreover, prestige parks located in the prestige communities also have become a focus for major office developments, as Figure 19 reveals. In all, there were twenty-five million square feet of new office development in Chicago's central business district between 1960 and 1972, and fourteen million square feet were built elsewhere in the SMSA—over nine million in the suburbs and less than five million elsewhere in the city of Chicago.

The broad differences in attractiveness of different parts of suburbia to prestige parks, office developments, and the like are reflected in the range of land values of industrial park sites throughout the region. The highest values —$2.29 to $2.50 per square foot—are in the

northern Cook sector which includes the O'Hare complex. Likewise, parks in eastern DuPage have asking prices as high as $3.00 per square foot in the vicinity of Oak Brook. Within the city, the Southwest Side—with a number of well-located parks—commands an asking price of $1.36 to $2.29 per square foot. Southern Cook has the lowest range inside the commercial zone—$0.46 to $1.50 per square foot—and has commensurately low status industrial and residential development.

THE CHANGING SCALE OF RESIDENTIAL AND RETAIL SUBURBANIZATION

The prestige-related pattern of decentralization carries over into many other facets of metropolitan life. Figure 20 shows the broad differences in socioeconomic status of Chicagoland's suburbs in 1970 based upon the median family incomes of their residents. The greatest growth has been outward within the region's more prestigious residential sector (Figure 21).

This is not to say that suburban growth has been absent in other sectors; it has not. Lower status suburbs have burgeoned, as have mobile home parks adjacent to them. Apartment complexes have sprung up around O'Hare and there are many condominium developments and new retirement villages in the western and northwestern suburbs. Apartment construction has been particularly rapid since 1965 alongside railroads and expressways in the lower-income parts of suburbia. On the other hand, some areas are not changing at all, except that their residents are aging. There is a growing awareness of the resulting suburban differences, as suggested by an article that appeared in the *Chicago Daily News* in January 1974. The story began:

> When Stanley Lieberman was transferred to Chicago from New Jersey, he bought his house by telephone. It was simple: He liked his old house, so he picked an almost identical one in Buffalo Grove built by the same company.
> Mary Edgren moved to a new apartment-with-a-balcony in Schaumburg after 13 years on Chicago's North Side because now she's just a 10-minute drive from her job.
> Joseph Klbacka moved to a three-flat in Brookfield about five miles west of Gage

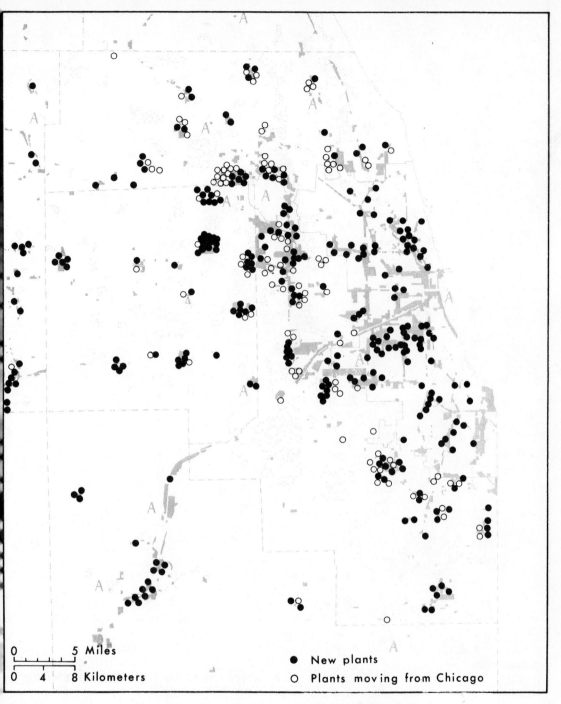

Figure 18. Plant locations and relocations, 1966–1970.

Park, where he and his new bride grew up. "It's our own life, but familiar enough to feel like home," he says.

That's how Chicago's suburbs grow: Some have taken a big leap, pulling in new jobholders from around the country. And some are slowly and steadily transplanting bits of ethnic Chicago.

Some are so dynamic, changing so fast, it's impossible to predict what they will be like in five years. Some aren't changing at all, except that the citizens are growing older. Their future, too, is certain.

"I think most of our members are on pensions and Social Security," said Rev. John Stankevicius, pastor of St. Anthony Roman

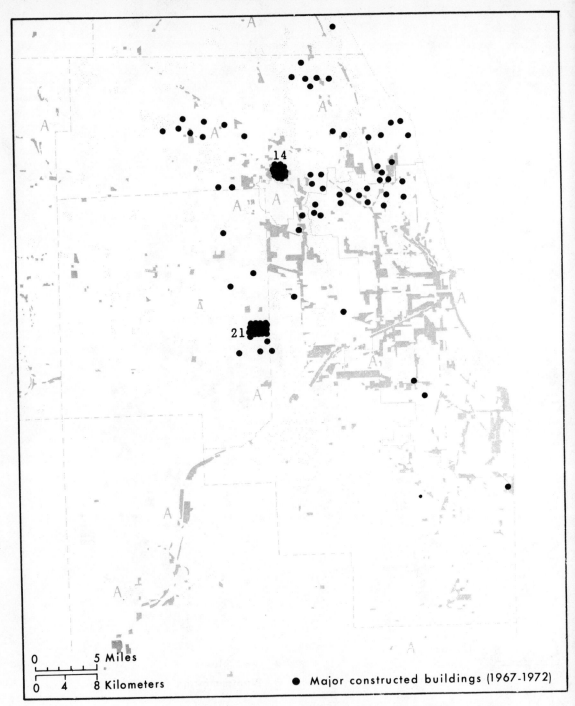

Figure 19. Major new office buildings constructed outside the Loop, 1967–1972.

Catholic Church in the northern part of Cicero, just south of Roosevelt Rd. "The three parishes in this area have only about 160 children among them."

The grown children of his parishioners, he added, move west—to La Grange Park, Brookfield, Westchester.

The net result of changes of these kinds is that an increasingly fine-grained set of community distinctions has emerged, a mosaic of community types, each catering to a particular group with a particular lifestyle by offering housing types, physical design, and a package of environmental amenities that convey a

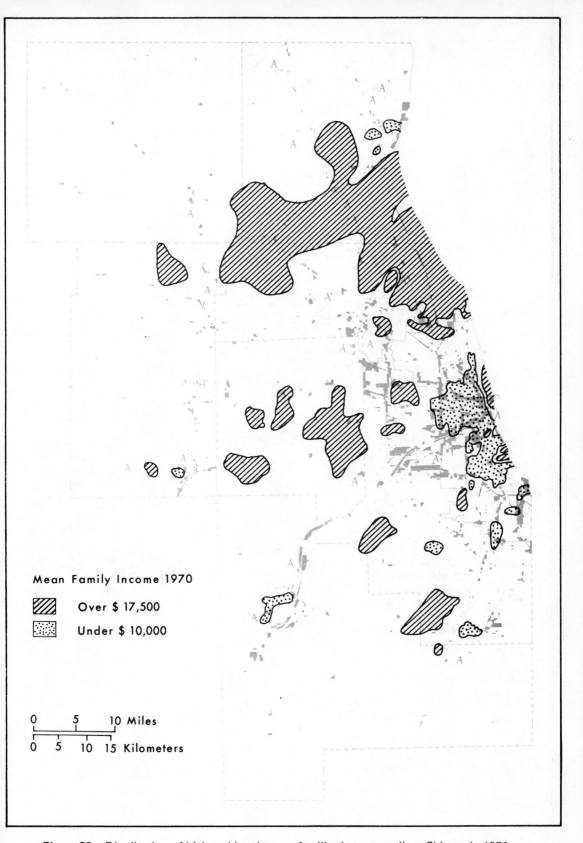

Figure 20. Distribution of high and low income families in metropolitan Chicago in 1970.

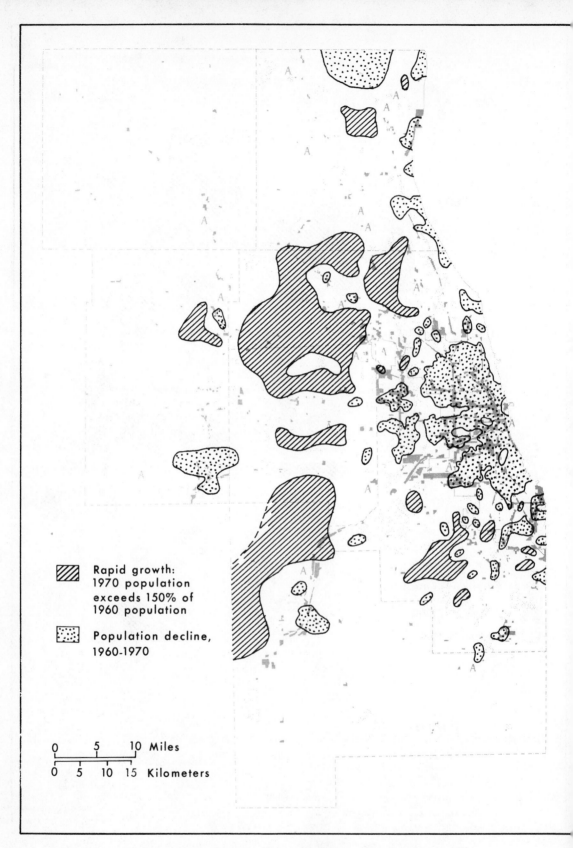

Figure 21. Population change in the Chicago SMSA, 1960-1970.

particular image. The image is all-important to groups whose lifestyle differences are related to occupational attainment and status perceptions on the one hand and to stage in life cycle on the other, and who are further differentiated by ethnic background, race, religious affiliations, and political attitudes, for it is the type of housing unit, the package of amenities, and the community's overall image that determine whether or not a new resident will choose to move into a community or an existing resident will be satisfied and will elect to stay.

Life cycle and status differences among suburbs have, of course, been remarked many times before. What perhaps is notable about Chicago's suburbanization is the persistence of ethnic and socioreligious ties. The high mobility outerzone mapped in Figure 5 is middle class, child-rearing, and WASP. The lower mobility zone within it, and the outlying crescent of industrial satellites, is blue collar Catholic. For example, the fastest-growing group in Oak Park in the last decade has been families of Irish descent from the West Side of Chicago. They replaced families of Swedish, German, and English descent who went west to Elmhurst and Lombard and Glen Ellyn and Wheaton, and were themselves replaced by blacks. In the years between 1960 and 1970, Oak Park lost about a fourth of its families of German and Swedish extraction.

Chicago's ethnic concentrations have not scattered around the area as people have left the city. Rather, there has been outward movement within well-marked corridors to form new ethnic concentrations in the older inner ring suburbs. As a result, forty suburbs now have a higher percentage of first and second generation Americans than Chicago, which had about 19 percent in the 1970 census, compared with 30 percent in 1960. Families of Czechoslovakian descent from Chicago's Southwest Side and from Cicero and Berwyn moved to La Grange Park, Brookfield, Downers Grove. First and second generation Polish families poured out of Logan Square and Humboldt Park in the city to Chicago's far Northwest Side and on to Park Ridge, Des Plaines, Mt. Prospect, and Arlington Heights. Jewish families from Rogers Park moved to Evanston, Skokie, Niles, Morton Grove, Wilmette, Winnetka, and Highland Park. Jewish families from Skokie and Highland Park moved into new towns farther northwest like Buffalo Grove.

As a result of these residential changes in the suburbs, each community is becoming increasingly homogeneous in socioeconomic status, age structure, religion, and ethnic affiliation, while differences among communities are becoming more sharply drawn. Rather than homogenized Americans produced by some mythical melting pot, there is an increasingly pluralistic set of subgroups within a fractionated society that has built for itself a complex suburban mosaic.

The differences are not immutable. Just as individual mobility and choices produce and maintain the character of a given area, many can change it too. In addition, developers have found that new lifestyles can be invented by constructing significantly different communities with distinctively different "images." As a result, these major developers have taken the initiative in determining suburban growth directions, replacing the traditional instrument of suburban growth, the small scale builder constructing a few single family homes each year. The unit of development has switched to that of the entire planned community and new towns are now being built in Will County to the south, along the Fox River valley corridor to the west, and in Lake County to the north. The Fox River valley developments were sparked by the construction of the National Accelerator Laboratory (the world's largest nuclear particle accelerator) in the area just east of Batavia in DuPage County. The Will County development—Park Forest South—is planned to grow to 100,000 people by 1990 and is being developed by a consortium headed by the Manilow interests who were originally involved in the construction of the nation's first post–World War II new town—Park Forest, just to the north. Park Forest South's industry park is growing. Part of its image is that it has built alternative types of housing to the conventional suburb. Located amidst woods and lakes, it is the home of a new state university, Governor's State. Similarly, the major development announced for the Fox valley corridor is a new town east of Aurora to be built by Urban Investment and Development Company, created by Philip Klutznik, another of the Park Forest partners, who was also responsible for building Oak Brook and the Old Orchard and River Oaks shopping centers. The first phase of the Aurora development will cost $1 billion and involves 3,800 acres with a 1.2 million square feet enclosed mall, 14,000 residential units in a wide range of homes and apartments; a transportation center consolidating rail, bus, and cab services; industry and office parks; and an educational services park consolidating public educational facilities. New Century Town in Lake County is also an Urban Investment venture and centers on a large recreational area with twin lakes, as well as having two "research and development parks."

Alongside these new towns, other distinctive outlying development types have emerged: Leisure World is now building the first of its outlying retirement villages, offering a "safe," well-serviced pastoral retreat to the more affluent elderly; and "swingles" apartment and condominium complexes are multiplying, particularly in the ring of communities surrounding O'Hare Airport. In both cases these represent alternatives to apartment life in the city somewhere in the Gold Coast, Near North Side, or along the northern lakeshore.

As residential differentiation has increased in these ways, so has the differentiation of service provision. Table 4 shows how retail sales and medical practitioners suburbanized

in the period 1950–1970. As this happened, differentials in, for example, physicians available to the rich and the poor became profound (Table 5). Many of the suburbanizing physicians are now clustering in new medical-dental complexes offering a broad array of specialist services. Likewise, there is continuing pressure for inner city hospitals to close after they have established suburban branches.

Similar changes have taken place in retailing. Just as the scale of residential decentralization has changed as image-making developmental leadership has moved into the hands of a small number of major corporations, so the pattern of retail suburbanization also has been set by a few developers who have constructed fifteen major regional shopping centers and over 100 smaller plaza-type centers. Regional shopping centers first appeared in the Chicago area in the early 1950s. Only four regional centers were built and operating until 1960. They were open malls with plenty of parking and, most important, each center was more than twenty-five miles from any of the other three and at least thirteen miles from the Loop. These centers did not really compete with each other as planned centers do today. Expressways were just starting to span the area and shop-

Table 4.   Some Measures of Suburban Growth in the Chicago SMSA

	Percentage in Central City			Percentage in Suburbs			Change in City's Percentage 1950–1970
	1950	*1960*	*1970*	*1950*	*1960*	*1970*	
Private Practice							
Physicians' Office	80	66	53	20	34	47	−27
Population	70	58	48	30	42	52	−22
White	68	51	39	32	49	61	−29
Black	90	91	90	10	9	10	0
Retail Sales	73	60	50	27	40	50	−23
Hospital Beds	70	68	63	30	32	37	−7

Table 5.   Physician-Population Ratios in the Ten Most Affluent and Ten Poorest Communities in the Chicago SMSA, 1950–1970

	1950	*1960*	*1970*
Ten Most Affluent Communities	1.78/1,000	1.36/1,000	2.10/1,000
Ten Poorest Communities	0.99/1,000	0.46/1,000	0.26/1,000
Difference Between Most Affluent and Poorest Communities	0.79/1,000	0.90/1,000	1.84/1,000

pers' preferences for a center usually depended on how close it was. Competition came from the central business districts of the industrial satellites and inner suburbs, but most of these quickly succumbed, despite repeated attempts at downtown resuscitation. As a result, the innovative regional shopping center rapidly became a success, catering to high mobility suburbanites with a wide variety of goods and an increasing array of services.

Gaps between centers were filled during the 1960s. By 1969 eleven regional shopping centers were doing business in the Chicago area. Their combined total retail sales came to an estimated $775 million out of a total of $1,908 million in all suburban plaza-type centers,

which compares with $906 million in Chicago's central business district in the same year.

Today there are fifteen major regional centers in the area including recently opened Woodfield Mall, Lakehurst, New Century Town, and Lincoln Mall (Figure 22). As these new centers have been added, competition has increased as downtown Chicago's department and other stores have sought to saturate the suburban market. The seven department store giants—Marshall Field; Carson, Pirie, Scott; Goldblatt's; Wieboldt's; Sears Roebuck; Montgomery Ward; and J.C. Penney—together have built over forty branches in the fifteen regional centers. Forty-five apparel chains have almost 200 stores in the same centers. As a result of

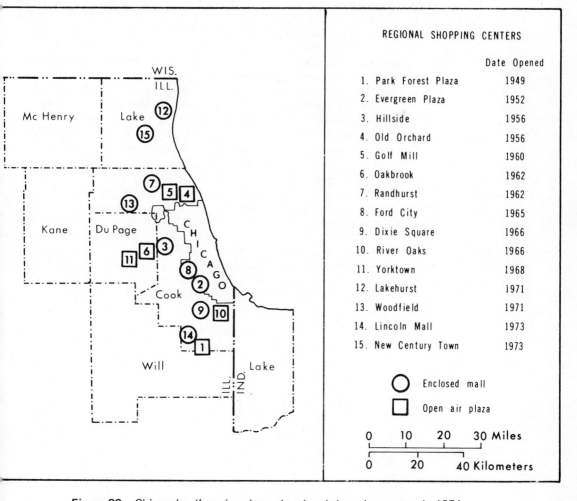

Figure 22. Chicagoland's major planned regional shopping centers in 1974.

competition, the pattern of retailing throughout suburbia has oriented itself to these new nodes.

To attempt to reduce competition, there is now a tendency to create centers that are structurally and aesthetically distinctive. Their daily operation includes offering free services, entertainment, and activities for the shoppers. The retail development is thus tending to become a "recreational shopping park." Recreational shopping is a key term for describing the atmosphere of the new regional centers, involving the attempt to divert the customer's attention from the tiresome aspects of shopping to pure fun, new things, exciting surroundings, and entertainment. All of Chicago's regional centers have become involved in the concept of recreational shopping. The type of facilities, of course, limit what kind of recreational opportunities the centers can supply. Two basic facility designs exist—the open air mall that offers the traditional shop-to-shop environs with traffic moving outdoors, and the enclosed mall where shoppers step from the parking lot into complexes and do not return outdoors until they leave. Woodfield Mall, the world's biggest, developed jointly by the Taubman Company and Sears Roebuck (Homart Development Company) along with Marshall Field and J.C. Penney, shows the recreational shopping potentialities of the enclosed mall. It sits on a 191 acre site with two million square feet of shopping on three levels. Walkways are interconnected by carpeted ramps, escalators, and elevators. More than 100 contemporary skylights, some more than twenty feet across, provide natural light to three story sculptures, live vegetation, and secluded reading nooks. Other features, in addition to its landscaped, two level parking area for 10,000 cars, include

a Greek amphitheatre capable of seating 600 persons for special events; recessed, semiprivate living room areas for conversation and relaxation; movies; ice skating; and an attractive exterior landscaping design to eliminate a sense of overwhelming size in the retail complex of 215 stores of all kinds. Woodfield epitomizes the principles its developer, A. Alfred Taubman espouses: "If you must go out and spend your money, you might as well enjoy it."

Together with recreational shopping, the other solution of shopping center developers to increasing problems of competition and the difficulties of establishing a unique image is to develop a "package" of housing and a prestigious office park along with the retail center, thus linking back to the drive to new town development. The concept is that of a self-contained community which includes a regional shopping center as its hub with residential units (both single family and multiple) surrounding the center. Industrial and commercial space is also planned as an integral part of the community. New Century Town has been planned as such a development by Urban Investment and Development Corporation and Homart, the Sears development subsidiary, as are the new towns being built in the Fox valley. In such ventures, the planned regional shopping center has thus turned old retail relationships around. Rather than following the spread of the market, the role of the new planned center is to exercise an imagebuilding style-setting role that sets the tone for subsequent residential growth. It has thus become another example of the saliency of large scale entrepreneurial decisionmaking in determining the pattern of urban growth, deliberately creating the distinctive point of focus about which other elements making up the fabric of spatial organization may crystallize.

Polarization of the Central City

When a few Negro families do come into a white neighborhood, some more white families move away. Other Negroes hasten to take their places. . . . This constant movement of Negroes into white neighborhoods makes the bulk of white residents feel that their neighborhood is doomed to be predominantly Negro, and they move out. . . .

—Gunnar Myrdal
An American Dilemma

The social history of Chicago during the 1960s was that of the departure of white middle class Protestants to suburbia, leaving behind a deepening cleavage between an outer ethnic ring and inner city minorities (Figure 23). The economic history was that of decentralization of jobs and business, except those highest order financial, administrative, and control occupations that supported the massive private redevelopment of the Loop and the extension of a lakeside ribbon of high-rise apartments and condominiums northward from the Gold Coast (Figure 24). The political history was that of an entrenched Democratic machine fighting for its survival, by using a variety of federal programs to ensure that major hospital and university complexes would remain in the city, to create a climate conducive to private redevelopment, and to reward supporters and punish opponents.

That changes in society, economy, and polity were intertwined, with the most sensitive issue being that of race, is nowhere more clearly illustrated than in the history of public housing in Chicago.

In the early years of the nation's public housing program, the Chicago Housing Authority (CHA) sought to build public housing throughout Chicago. The City Council, in the belief that most prospective public housing tenants were black, proposed, however, to restrict such housing to ghetto areas. Since each alderman had a veto over site selection in his ward, CHA went along with the City Council.

As a result, CHA administered regular (family), elderly, and Section 23 (leasing) public housing to keep blacks out of white areas. Regular public housing was located in ghetto neighborhoods and the elderly and leasing programs were located in what were, at the time, all-white neighborhoods (Figure 25). In four public housing projects located in white neighborhoods, quotas kept the number of black tenants at a minimal level. In projects for the elderly, tenant assignment policies ensured that white elderly occupied most of the housing in white neighborhoods. Only in racially changing areas were "integrated" projects to be found and these projects ultimately became all black as the surrounding neighborhoods changed. Leased housing was treated in the same fashion. Tenant selection was delegated to landlords by CHA, giving them the right to refuse tenants because of "undesirability." Landlords were allowed to select tenants who were not on CHA's almost all-black waiting list. In sum, the white elderly were placed in public housing in white areas, while blacks were located in ghetto projects.

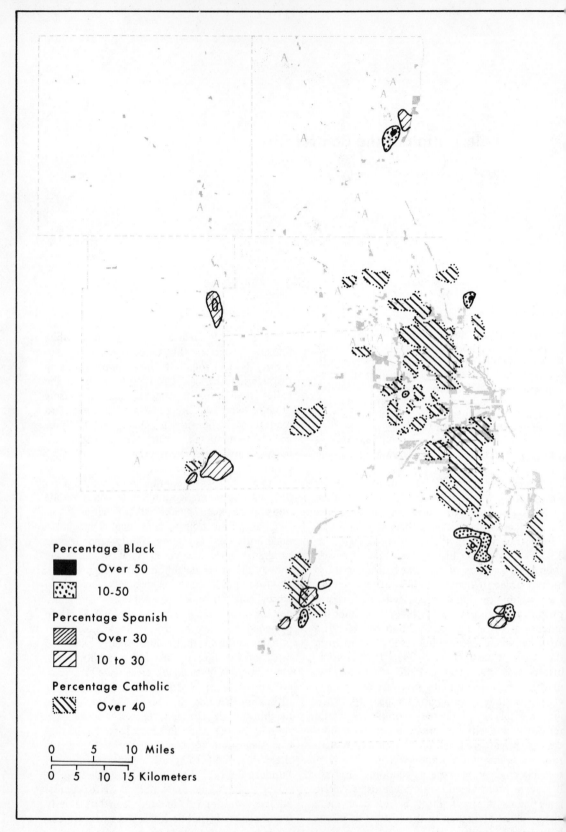

Figure 23. (A) Catholic, black, and Spanish population concentrations in suburbia.

Figure 23, continued. (B) Black, Spanish, and Catholic neighborhoods in the city of Chicago and the inner suburbs.

Throughout the 1960s federal civil rights laws and regulations produced no changes. While HUD was aware that CHA was violating HUD regulations covering racial discrimination, it opted to serve rather than regulate the local constituency. Finally, however, in August 1966, fair housing interests filed suit in U.S. District Court accusing CHA of discrimination against blacks (Gautreaux v. CHA). Judge Richard B. Austin, in February 1969, found CHA

Figure 24. The northward extension of a ribbon of high-rise development is one of the more striking features of recent growth along Chicago's lakeshore.

guilty as charged and issued an order designed to promote integration by construction of public housing in all-white areas. Before any new public housing could be constructed in the ghetto or areas likely to undergo racial change, several hundred new units had to be constructed in all-white areas. But CHA refused to abide by the court's directive and HUD refused to enforce compliance. All public housing construction in Chicago ceased during the 1969–1974 period.

It was only under continuing pressure from Judge Austin that CHA finally announced plans in 1973 for a program of scattered site public

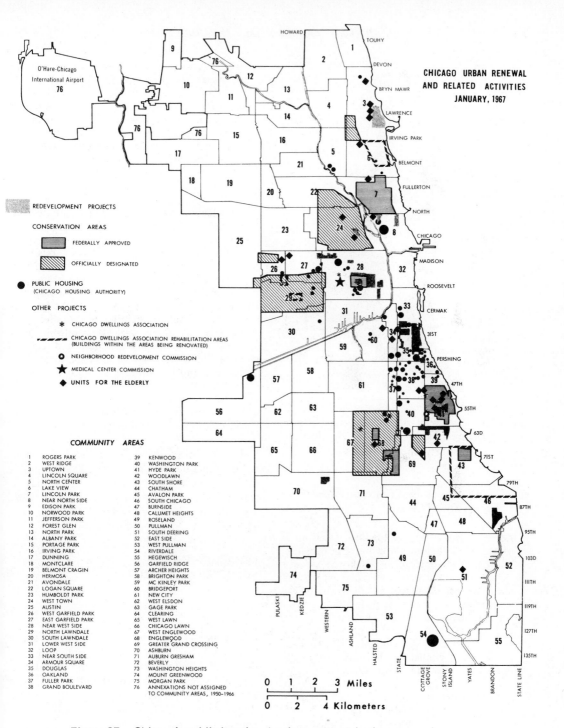

Figure 25. Chicago's public housing developments and urban renewal areas.

housing in the white Northwest and Southwest sides of the city (Figure 26). Residents of the white neighborhoods were aghast. The attitudes that lay behind the ward politicians' earlier vetoes of public housing surfaced in an attempt by a consortium of nineteen Northwest Side and Southwest Side white community organizations to use the National Environmental Policy Act of 1969 to prevent CHA from acting in accordance with Judge Austin's ruling. The ar-

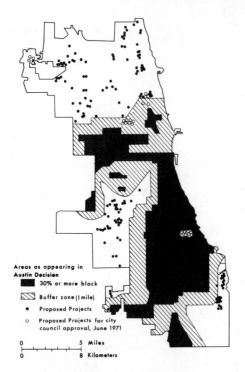

Figure 26. Scattered site public housing: proposed developments following the Austin decision, and actual City Council approvals.

gument of the Nucleus of Chicago Homeowners Association (No CHA) was

> As a statistical whole, low-income families of the kind that reside in housing provided by the Chicago Housing Authority possess certain social class characteristics which will and have been inimical and harmful to the legitimate interests of the plaintiffs.
>
> Regardless of the cause, be it family conditioning, genetics, or environmental conditions beyond their control, members of low-income families of the kind that reside in housing provided by the Chicago Housing Authority possess, as a statistical whole, the following characteristics:
>
> (a) As compared to the social class characteristics of the plaintiffs, such low-income family members possess a higher propensity toward criminal behavior and acts of physical violence than do the social classes of the plaintiffs.
>
> (b) As compared to the social class characteristics of the plaintiffs, such low-income family members possess a disregard for physical and aesthetic maintenance of real and personal property which is in direct con-

trast to the high level of care with which the plaintiffs' social classes treat their property.

> (c) As compared to the social class characteristics of the plaintiffs, such low-income family members possess a lower commitment to hard work for future-oriented goals with little or no immediate reward than do the social classes of the plaintiffs.

> . . . . .

> By placing low-rent housing populated by persons with the social characteristics of low-income families described above in residential areas populated by persons with social class characteristics of the plaintiffs, defendant CHA will increase the hazards of criminal acts, physical violence and aesthetic and economic decline in the neighborhoods in the immediate vicinity of the sites. The increase in these hazards resulting from CHA's siting actions will have a direct adverse impact upon the physical safety of those plaintiffs residing in close proximity to the sites, as well as a direct adverse effect upon the aesthetic and economic quality of their lives (Plaintiff's brief, *No CHA* v. *Chicago Housing Authority*, 1973)

U.S. District Court Judge Julius J. Hoffman ruled against the No CHA suit on November 26, 1973, saying that "[i]t must be noted that although human beings may be polluters, they are not themselves pollution." However, the attitudes that produced the suit remain.

INVASION AND SUCCESSION REVISITED

In the early twentieth century, research in plant ecology at the University of Chicago stimulated sociologist Robert E. Park to view social change in the city in terms of ecological processes of competition between population groups for natural areas of the city, leading to processes of invasion and succession and the dominance by one group over another. His colleague, Ernest W. Burgess, mapped the spatial consequences. Outward migration of upwardly mobile groups and their replacement in a growing city by new migrants created a concentric city structure—a commercial core fringed by industry, workingmen's homes, middle class housing, and commuter housing. These five concentric zones were further divided into smaller natural areas on the basis of

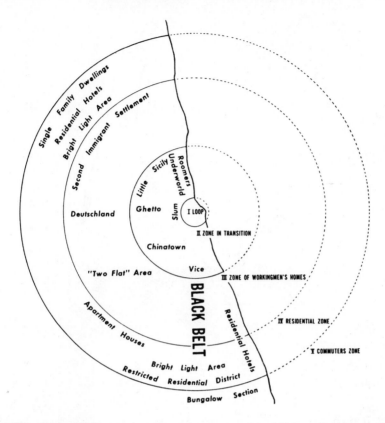

Figure 27. Ernest W. Burgess's concentric zone model of Chicago's urban ecology.

race, ethnicity, or type of residence (Figure 27).

At the time of the original delineation of Chicago's natural areas, blacks made up but 4 percent of the city's population, and the Black Belt seemed an insignificant competitor for *Lebensraum* against such redoubtable kingdoms as Deutschland, the Ghetto, Little Sicily, Polonia, and Bohemia. But in the fifty years since, Deutschland and Little Sicily have given way to blacks, the Ghetto changed from Jewish to black, Polonia retrenched to a Polish corridor on the Northwest Side and retreated behind a Curzon line on the Southwest Side, and Bohemia became a Sudetenland on the southern frontier of the black West Side annexations.

Burgess later divided the city into seventy-five "community areas," partly on the basis of local self-identification, partly on the basis of socioeconomic and ethnic homogeneity, and partly on the basis of his own wishful thinking about what the community structure of the city "ought" to be. So many people referred to Burgess' areas by the names he gave them that most of them became indelibly marked on the perceptual map of the city in the decades that followed, decades that made a shambles of his original concentric zones. The changes have been so profound, and so much related to race, that it is perhaps easier to understand the social dynamics of the central city during the 1960s in terms of five zones of racial change. These are shown in Figure 28, which juxtaposes the zones with Burgess' seventy-five community areas:

1. The 1960 Ghetto—communities that were over 50 percent black in 1960.
2. The 1970 Ghetto Extension—communities that became over 50 percent black between 1960 and 1970.
3. The Ghettoizing Zone—communities that were between 10 and 50 percent black in 1970.

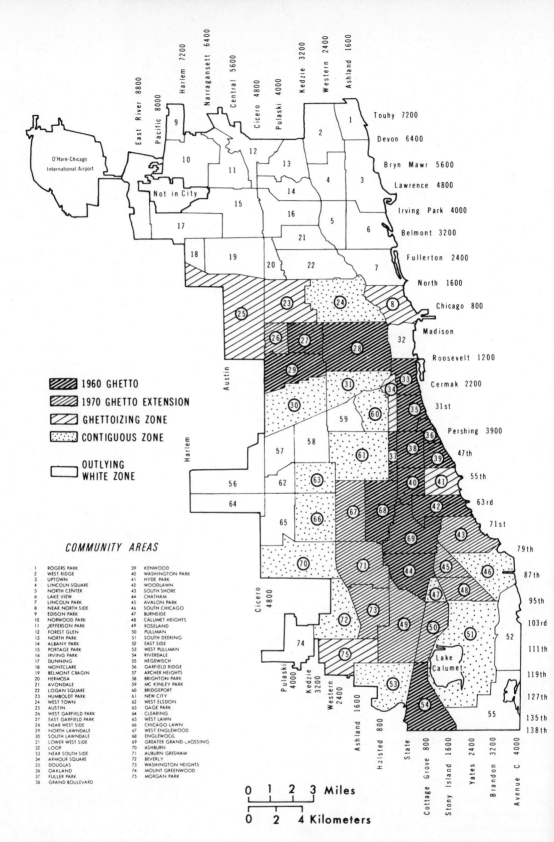

Figure 28. Chicago's seventy-five officially designated community areas, with the city's five racial zones of the 1960s.

4. The Contiguous Zone—communities under 10 percent black in 1970 contiguous to black communities; some Spanish and some white.
5. The Outlying White Zone—the remaining communities, refuges for the inner city ethnics.

Chicago experienced a net loss of 5 percent in population during the decade, but the figure is deceptive, for the black population increased by 288,000, whereas the white population declined by over 470,000. Yet in spite of this, the 1960 ghetto lost 18 percent of its people, the 1970 ghetto extension gained 11 percent as child-rearing black families replaced older whites, and the three outlying zones lost about 4 percent of their population (Figure 21). The 1960 ghetto saw its proportion of children drop by one-sixth while that of the ghetto extension increased by one-third, the contiguous zone increased by 5 percent with the influx of new Spanish-speaking Chicagoans, and the outlying white zone lost 11 percent of its child population, with inevitable consequences for public elementary school enrollments (Figure 29).

Chicago's slight net loss of 6,000 housing units was the result of 125,800 units built since 1960, less 131,900 units lost through demolition. Private housing construction amounted to 106,800 units, about 9 percent of the city's housing stock in 1970. The lowest rate of new private construction was in the contiguous zone, amounting to only 5 percent of the 1970 stock, while the highest rate occurred in the white outer zone, where it neared 11 percent of the 1970 stock. Only 19,000 public housing units were built in the period 1960-1967— either in the 1960 ghetto, where they made up close to 6 percent of the housing stock in 1970, or in the ghetto extension.

Declining aggregate demand enabled 131,900 housing units—11 percent of the 1960 housing stock—to be demolished in the city in the decade, more than half of these in the black neighborhoods of the 1960 ghetto and the biracial zone. Almost a fourth of the 1960 ghetto's housing and a tenth of the biracial zone's housing were demolished, either by urban renewal or as a result of abandonment. The 1970 ghetto extension had by far the lowest demolition rate of any zone—under 3 percent —reflecting the greater demand for housing in this zone.

Figure 30 shows the spatial pattern of abandoned housing units demolished between 1965 and 1971. Concentrations in the 1960 ghetto and in North Side poverty areas paralleling the Gold Coast and extending north to Uptown are evident. In part, the high rates of abandonment in these areas were a result of declining demands due to depopulation as filtering took place, as was noted earlier. However, lagging aggregate demand as the old ghetto areas have become virtually exclusively concentrations of the welfare poor has had other more profound effects.

Price decreases for rental property have been so severe that disinvestment and deterioration through decreased maintenance also appear to have resulted, producing an accelerating and more contagious form of abandonment. Concentrations of welfare families, usually in neighborhoods where the abandonment process has reached significant levels, display the most profound pathologies—high unemployment rates, particularly among young males, and high levels of female-headed households with children, frequent school problems, drug addiction, crime, and vandalism. The concentration of such problems among a significant proportion of the population of any given neighborhood has become the identifying mark of "collapsed neighborhoods" from which the working poor—black as well as white families, with children—have fled or in which they will refuse to seek living quarters voluntarily. These concomitantly have been areas in which public services have deteriorated or vanished, whether as a precursor or as a consequence of the foregoing developments.

Increasing the pressures on rental and older housing have been newer federal housing programs, as well—the concentration of federally funded Section 221(d)(3) and 236 units in the very areas where surpluses exist (Figure 31); and the construction of Section 235 single family units largely in the southward ghetto extension zone, where they enabled persons who might otherwise have been forced to stay in the 1960 ghetto to move away (Figure 32).

The vacancy rate is another measure of the results of the housing changes and was highest in the 1960 ghetto and ghettoizing zone (over 6 percent) and lowest in the 1970 ghetto extension (under 1 percent). The city's overall vacancy rate climbed by one-fourth during the decade—from 3.7 to 4.6 percent, despite the demolitions and abandonments.

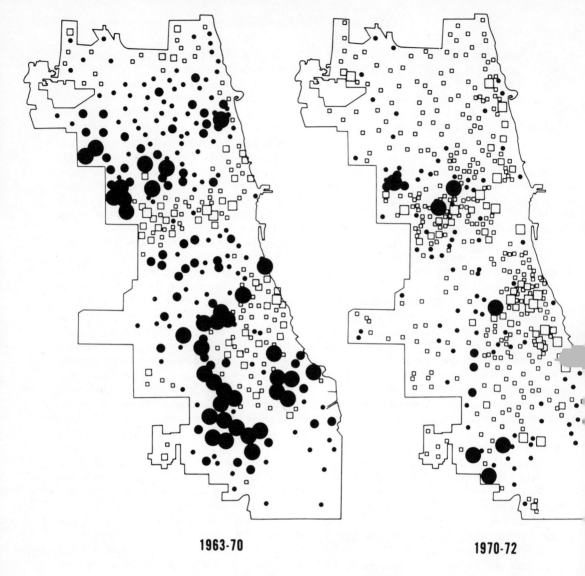

1963-70 1963-70

1970-72

Percentage Change in Public Elementary School Enrollments

Percentage Increase		Percentage Decrease	
● More than 50		☐ More than 50	
● 25-50		▫ 25-50	
• 0-25		▫ 0-25	

Figure 29. Changes in public elementary school enrollments, 1963–1972, showing the effects of ghetto expansion.

Population per housing unit went down for the city—from 3.1 to 2.9 and for all zones except the 1970 ghetto extension where it went up from 3.0 to 3.1 as younger black families with children moved in. The proportion of single family housing also declined—from 27 to 24 percent in the city—with the construction of new rental units along the northern lakeshore. The sharpest contrast among zones in 1970 was between the 1960 ghetto and the 1970 ghetto extension, with respective single family housing proportions of 12 and 38 per-

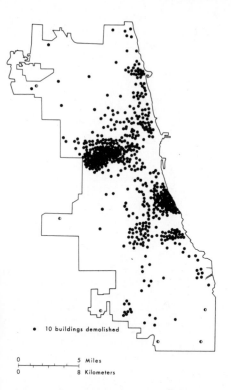

0 • 10 buildings demolished

0   5 Miles
0   8 Kilometers

Figure 30. Court-ordered demolitions by the city of Chicago and by private owners between 1965 and 1971. Source: Austin Sullivan, Building Department, City of Chicago.

cent; black expansion has been into good quality middle class areas and, as a result, black home ownership jumped by 38,000—more than 100 percent.

The concentration of new construction on rental housing has also affected housing values. The somewhat newer rental housing stock yielded a median monthly rent of $108, up 8 percent since 1960 in constant 1970 dollars. The single family housing stock aged by almost ten years and suffered a decline in median home value of $2,200, or 9 percent, from $23,400 in 1960 to $21,200 in 1970. Rent gains were lowest in the 1960 ghetto and the 1970 ghetto extension. Greatest rental gains occurred in the contiguous and white zones.

The Rolling Tide of
Residential Resegregation

What these changes reflect is a rolling tide of residential resegregation as blacks have moved away from traditional ghetto areas either to replace whites moving to the suburbs or to displace whites who, for a period, have fought aggressively against ghetto expansion. Yet this process of racial transition has not always been the rule in Chicago, nor has the now prevalent fearful white attitude toward black neighbors. There was a time before World War I when the few blacks in the city found housing on the basis of what they could afford and seemed to get along well with their white neighbors. Many of the city's first blacks were concentrated in what Burgess called the Black Belt, but in the early 1900s it was more properly the Poor Belt, occupied by immigrant whites as well. There were not enough blacks to constitute any sort of threat to the whites, rich or poor.

This pre-1915 pattern of black settlement and white reaction to it has been described as a "filtering-in" process. When neighborhoods did change, it was most often because they were run down and the whites wanted better housing. As they moved out, blacks could move in. But then came a great migration of blacks from the South during World War I. That changed the whole race relations equation by starting a steady wave of black immigration that has continued until the late 1960s, although slowed by depressions and speeded by wars. Industrialists helped to bring about the great migration, needing cheap labor to man the factories and strikebreakers to combat the newly assertive white labor unions. Until the United States entered World War I, the increased black population continued to be accommodated in close-in hand-me-down white neighborhoods as the prosperous former occupants moved farther out. But in 1917, war controls produced a housing shortage and the whites became reluctant to relinquish their homes. Property owners' associations were formed with the specific purpose of maintaining all-white neighborhoods. The resulting increase in racial tension, fired by union anger, was one of the prime causes of the infamous Chicago race riot of 1919.

The postwar years were prosperous ones, but the blacks came into Chicago faster than they could be absorbed into the few neighborhoods that were ripe for transfer from the white to the black housing market. Blacks shared in the prosperity and had money to spend on better housing. That meant that economics alone would not be enough to keep all the blacks in the Black Belt.

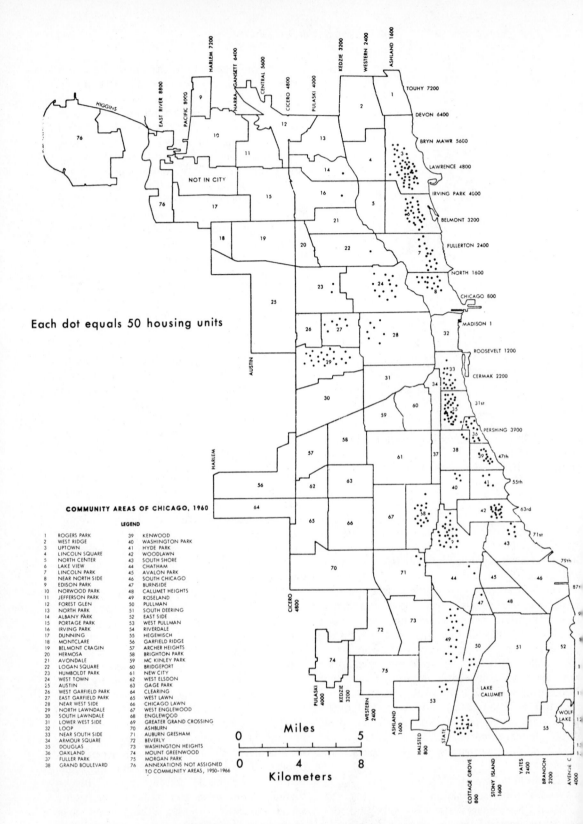

Each dot equals 50 housing units

COMMUNITY AREAS OF CHICAGO, 1960

LEGEND

1	ROGERS PARK	39	KENWOOD
2	WEST RIDGE	40	WASHINGTON PARK
3	UPTOWN	41	HYDE PARK
4	LINCOLN SQUARE	42	WOODLAWN
5	NORTH CENTER	43	SOUTH SHORE
6	LAKE VIEW	44	CHATHAM
7	LINCOLN PARK	45	AVALON PARK
8	NEAR NORTH SIDE	46	SOUTH CHICAGO
9	EDISON PARK	47	BURNSIDE
10	NORWOOD PARK	48	CALUMET HEIGHTS
11	JEFFERSON PARK	49	ROSELAND
12	FOREST GLEN	50	PULLMAN
13	NORTH PARK	51	SOUTH DEERING
14	ALBANY PARK	52	EAST SIDE
15	PORTAGE PARK	53	WEST PULLMAN
16	IRVING PARK	54	RIVERDALE
17	DUNNING	55	HEGEWISCH
18	MONTCLARE	56	GARFIELD RIDGE
19	BELMONT CRAGIN	57	ARCHER HEIGHTS
20	HERMOSA	58	BRIGHTON PARK
21	AVONDALE	59	MC KINLEY PARK
22	LOGAN SQUARE	60	BRIDGEPORT
23	HUMBOLDT PARK	61	NEW CITY
24	WEST TOWN	62	WEST ELSDON
25	AUSTIN	63	GAGE PARK
26	WEST GARFIELD PARK	64	CLEARING
27	EAST GARFIELD PARK	65	WEST LAWN
28	NEAR WEST SIDE	66	CHICAGO LAWN
29	NORTH LAWNDALE	67	WEST ENGLEWOOD
30	SOUTH LAWNDALE	68	ENGLEWOOD
31	LOWER WEST SIDE	69	GREATER GRAND CROSSING
32	LOOP	70	ASHBURN
33	NEAR SOUTH SIDE	71	AUBURN GRESHAM
34	ARMOUR SQUARE	72	BEVERLY
35	DOUGLAS	73	WASHINGTON HEIGHTS
36	OAKLAND	74	MOUNT GREENWOOD
37	FULLER PARK	75	MORGAN PARK
38	GRAND BOULEVARD	76	ANNEXATIONS NOT ASSIGNED TO COMMUNITY AREAS, 1950-1966

Figure 31. Federally subsidized multifamily housing projects built in the city of Chicago as of August 1972 under Sections 221(d)(3) and 236 of the federal housing legislation.

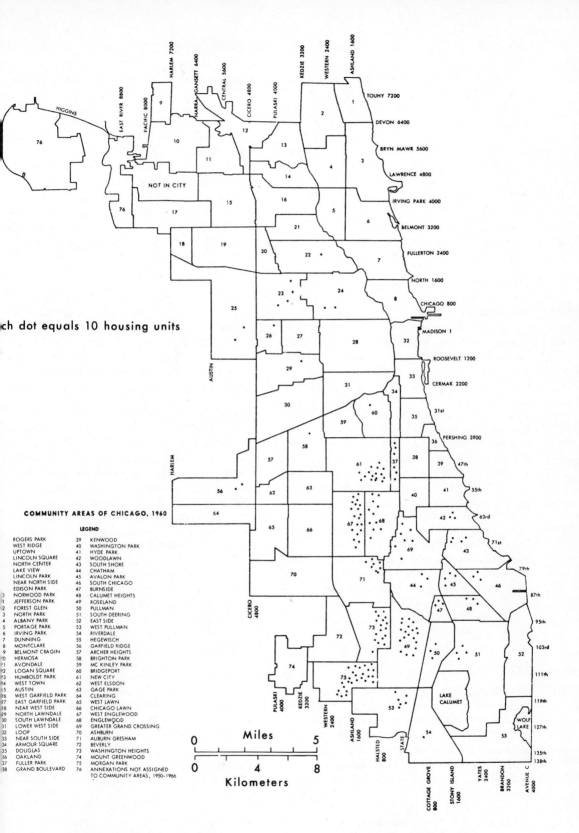

Figure 32. Section 235 single family housing built in Chicago as of August 1972.

One way in which whites tried to maintain neighborhood "stability" was through outright violence. There was a rash of bombings in the years around 1920, aimed not only at blacks moving into white neighborhoods, but also at the black or white real estate brokers responsible.

But there were subtler ways that worked better in the long run. One was an article in the code of ethics of the National Association of Real Estate Boards which warned brokers never to "be instrumental in introducing into a neighborhood ... members of any race or nationality whose presence will clearly be detrimental to property values in that neighborhood." Blacks were perceived to be such a group.

Another way, promoted by both property interests and by white residents themselves, was the restrictive covenant. That was a clause written into property deeds to bar the selling or renting of property to a member of any named minority. By 1930, according to one estimate, property owners' associations and neighborhood improvement associations had succeeded in getting 75 percent of the housing in the city covered by such covenants.

Before the covenants took wide effect in the late 1920s, blacks had expanded the Black Belt as far east as Cottage Grove Avenue and as far south as 63rd Street. But then the Depression slowed migration from the South, and the combination of covenants and joblessness brought expansion of the Black Belt almost to a halt for more than a decade. Crowding worsened after 1940 when thousands more blacks came North to work in war plants. With no additional housing available, population density in black neighborhoods rose to 90,000 people per square mile—more than four times the figure for nearby white neighborhoods.

In the years following World War II, the dam burst. The days of price and rent controls were over, and thousands of veterans returned to get educations and start families. Federal highway programs opened new suburban areas to settlement, and loan guarantees from the Federal Housing Administration and Veterans Administration made it possible for whites to move into them—not blacks, though, because federal officials feared they would lower property values and jeopardize the government's big investment in all those three bedroom ranches, and they expressed such fears in the FHA Appraisers' Handbook.

The housing blacks obtained was in city neighborhoods abandoned by whites. After the United States Supreme Court decision in 1948 that restrictive covenants were not enforceable in court, racial transition gradually accelerated throughout the 1950s. By 1960, the ghetto had spread west and south to meet the earlier pockets of black settlement in Englewood and Roseland, and a new pocket had been created by a public housing project at 44th Street and Cicero Avenue. By the 1970s, the black residential areas had swept west and south to the city limits.

Thus, a broad overview of sixty years of racial transition indicates that the rate of black population growth and government economic policies have been the major factors influencing the *rate* of transition, for they combine to create surpluses or shortages in housing—under conditions of surplus black areas expand, while when shortages arise the white community stands fast. Determinants of the *directions* of black expansion have been the quality of housing, the resources of blacks, public transportation routes, and the existence of barriers of nonresidential land use. Black expansion took place in the city's western and southern middle-class sectors. And under conditions of expansion, *resegregation* has been an inevitable result. Whites complain of panic-peddling and block-busting and believe that entry of blacks into their neighborhoods will destroy property values. They complain of rising crime rates. Further, the perceived quality of the public schools is one of the main reasons that make people with children decide to move into a particular neighborhood and a perceived loss of quality in the schools is one of the main reasons that make them decide to move out. In Chicago, the quality of education is demonstrably the worst in the inner city schools attended by most poor black children.

It is small wonder, then, that black parents, too, want to escape the ghetto to a neighborhood—usually white—with a better school. The tragedy is that these education-hungry black families often create a problem in their new neighborhood schools—overcrowding—which is a powerful reason for the whites in the neighborhood to start thinking that the quality of education has gone down. The pat-

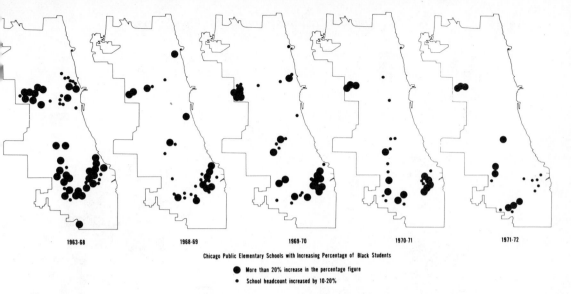

Figure 33. Racial change in Chicago's public elementary schools, 1963–1972.

tern of increasing public elementary school enrollments unerringly traces out the wave of ghetto expansion (Figure 33), while the elevated levels of property turnover in changing neighborhoods reveal that ghetto expansion in the 1960s involved more than whites moving out and blacks moving in as part of a "normal" process of residential mobility—i.e. there has been accelerated white flight to suburbia (Figure 34).

Many of the complaints of the white population thus seem valid: public elementary school enrollments skyrocket in the ghettoizing neighborhoods and a variety of measures of educational inputs and outputs and their relationships show that performance is significantly lower under ghetto conditions. The percentage of children ready for first grade is lower in the ghetto (Figure 35); traditionally the Chicago Board of Education assigned the most inexperienced teachers to the ghetto schools (Figure 36); and results of standardized tests reveal the poorer performance of ghetto children (Figure 37). A number of explanations have been put forth to explain these gaps—biased tests, segregation, social discrimination, the inexperienced teachers, the home environment, family size, inadequate nutrition and health care, heredity, and the confounding of race with social class and recency of migration to the city. Whatever the explanations given, however, the differences are real, and they contribute to the white flight. The continuing white exodus is revealed clearly enough in the racial headcounts in the public

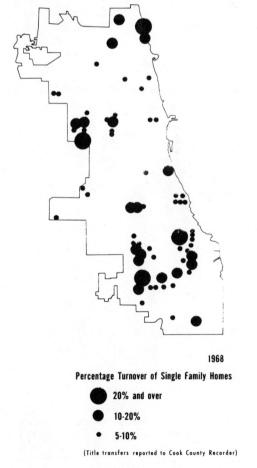

1968

Percentage Turnover of Single Family Homes

● 20% and over

● 10-20%

• 5-10%

(Title transfers reported to Cook County Recorder)

Figure 34. Turnover rates in the sale of single family homes in Chicago in 1968.

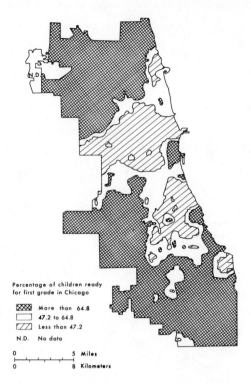

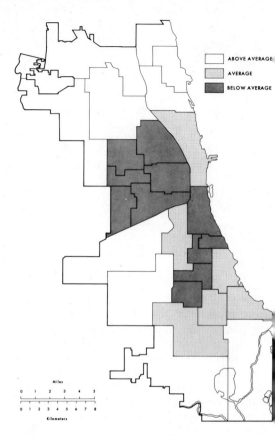

Figure 35. Percentage of children ready for first grade in Chicago in 1971.

Figure 37. District performance of Chicago public school pupils on standardized tests during the 1970–1971 school year.

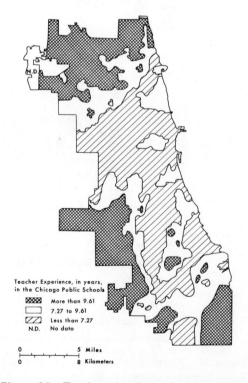

Figure 36. Teacher experience, in years, in the Chicago public schools in 1971.

elementary schools (Figure 38) and the public high schools (Figure 39).

Shifts in Chicago's Older Ethnic Communities

The expansion of Black Chicago and the departure of the white middle class from the central city to new suburbs has left a belt of traditional ethnic communities in between (Figure 23). Within the central city, these communities have been under increasing pressure, and have been relocating, as indicated by steadily falling Catholic elementary and high school enrollments (Figures 40 and 41). The far Northwest and Southwest sides of the city and, beyond the central city, older pre–World War I suburbs, have become refuges for the Catholics. To cite three examples, Chicago's Polish population declined by 26 percent as the traditional Near Northwest communities of Humboldt Park and Logan Square came

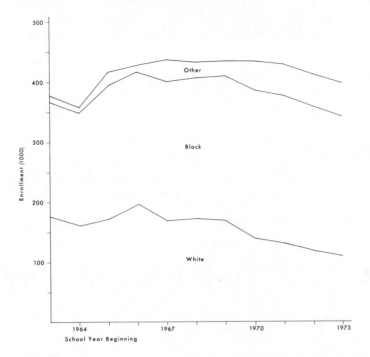

Figure 38. Changing Chicago public elementary school enrollments by race, 1963–1973.

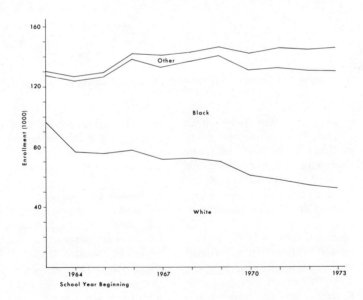

Figure 39. Changing Chicago public high school enrollments by race, 1963–1973.

under pressure from new Spanish-speaking immigrants. A 28 percent decline in the Italian population came about as the Near West Side communities came under pressure from both blacks and Spanish-speakers. The Chicago Irish declined by 33 percent, leaving both Austin and the Southwest Side. Meanwhile,

some forty close-in northern and western suburbs emerged with a greater foreign stock population than Chicago (18.6 percent), for example, Lincolnwood (40.0 percent) and Berwyn (33.8 percent).

Meanwhile, the city's Czech and other central European populations withdrew to Cicero

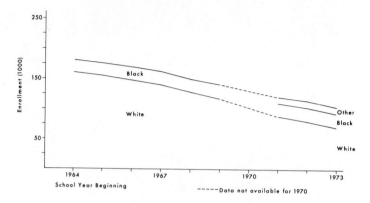

Figure 40. Changing Chicago Catholic elementary school enrollments by race, 1964-1973.

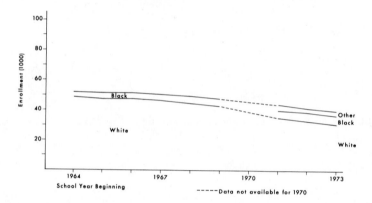

Figure 41. Changing Chicago Catholic high school enrollments by race, 1966-1973.

and, as Italians displaced them there, to La Grange Park, Jews left South Shore and South Chicago to concentrate in the north lakeshore apartment developments, in the northernmost city communities of Rogers Park, West Ridge, and North Park, and over the northern city limits in Lincolnwood and Skokie (See Figure 42).

Part of the numerical decline of the ethnics is a statistical artifact. Without new immigrants many families are now passing beyond the "second generation" through which they are traced in the decennial census, and the census therefore reports them as declining. But this does not mean that ethnic identity vanishes in the grandchildren and great-grandchildren; indeed, traditional family ties remain in many blue collar ethnic communities. Ethnic integrity remains strong among groups relocating both to the city's Northwest and Southwest sides and to the older inner suburban ring. Through-

out the region, evidence of ethnicity remains strong in the life of neighborhoods, in their shops and restaurants, their associations and newspapers.

Spanish Chicago

Meanwhile, a new force has arisen in Chicago's racial and ethnic mosaic. The growing ethnic communities are the Spanish-speakers—the Mexicans, Puerto Ricans, and more recently the Cubans. The number of Latins in Chicago doubled between 1960 and 1970, making them a minority group second only to the blacks. In the 1970 census almost a quarter of a million Chicagoans answered some Spanish indicator question affirmatively, and several distinctively different Spanish communities developed (Fig-

Figure 42. Changes in six ethnic communities in Chicago, 1960-1970.

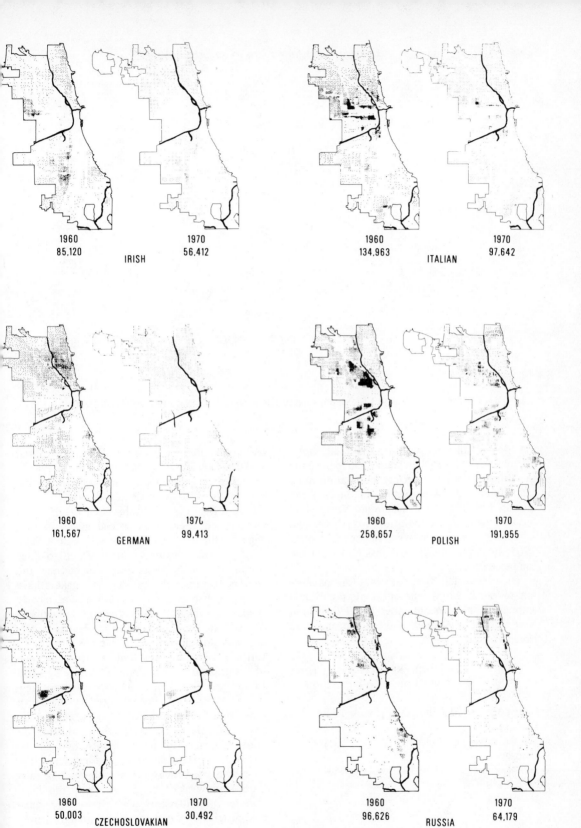

1960	1970	1960	1970
85,120	56,412	134,963	97,642

IRISH   ITALIAN

1960	1970	1960	1970
161,567	99,413	258,657	191,955

GERMAN   POLISH

1960	1970	1960	1970
50,003	30,492	96,626	64,179

CZECHOSLOVAKIAN   RUSSIA

Each dot equals 60 persons

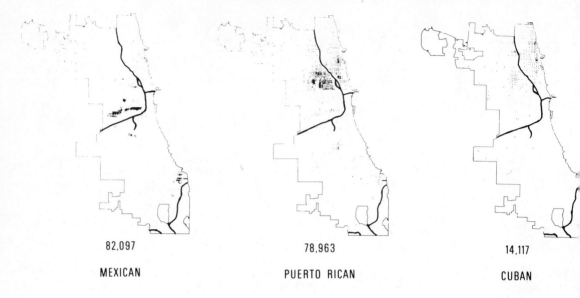

82,097   78,963   14,117

MEXICAN   PUERTO RICAN   CUBAN

Each dot equals 60 persons

Figure 43.   Chicago's Mexican, Puerto Rican, and Cuban communities in 1970.

ure 43). While most other national group populations decreased by about 35 percent in the decade, the Puerto Rican population more than doubled (144 percent) and the Mexican increased by 84 percent. We do not have a good measure of Cuban population growth because they were counted as West Indians as late as 1960; however, their 1970 residential pattern can be charted.

The growth has been such that Chicago now ranks fourth in Spanish-speaking population among major American cities in 1970, behind New York, Los Angeles, and San Antonio, and ahead of Miami:

	Spanish-speaking Population	Percent of Total Population
New York	1,278,630	16.2
Los Angeles	481,668	17.1
San Antonio	335,950	51.4
Chicago	247,343	7.3
Miami	151,914	45.4
U.S. Total	9,589,216	4.7

It was the industrial boom created by World War I that first brought large numbers of Mexicans to Chicago. Many came from the south-

western United States where they had worked several generations on farms and in vineyards, in railroad construction and mining. Some arrived directly from Mexico during the same period. The United States Census of 1920 enumerated them as a special group in Chicago for the first time and counted 1,265. They lived in three locations which related to their economic roles: these locations became the centers from which the Spanish-speakers have more recently expanded. One group, mostly single men, lived in railroad camps and worked on railroad construction and maintenance. Occupying old railroad cars converted into dormitories or older housing built adjacent to some of the original railroad yards, they often walked to the yard and rode to work sites on crew trains. A second group, attracted by the heavy industry of the steel mill area, settled in the old residential sections of West Pullman and South Chicago on the far South Side of the city. The third area of early Mexican settlement was the Hull House neighborhood a mile south and west of the Loop. From this location they could easily reach the central business district or the many nearby manufacturing establishments.

Since the 1920s Mexicans have remained a rapidly growing immigrant group. For a time during the Depression of the 1930s, the city lost many Mexicans because limited job skills and discriminatory hiring practices caused them to suffer an extremely high unemployment rate. They returned to Mexico rather than compete with white Americans who were now willing to work at jobs they had considered fit only for Negroes and "foreigners." However their numbers grew from 1,200 in 1920 to 7,000 in 1940, 9,000 in 1950, 44,686 in 1960, and 82,057 in 1970 (with many illegal immigrants assertedly uncounted). By 1960 Chicago ranked as the city with the largest Mexican settlement outside the southwest, surpassed only by Los Angeles, San Antonio, and El Paso.

The Mexican population grew by 84 percent in Chicago and 92 percent in the SMSA during the decade. The mainstream of Mexican expansion is now the former Bohemian corridor vacated by the Czechs. Thus Mexican population grew 164 percent in Pilsen and fifteenfold in South Lawndale. Further south, Mexicans displaced Poles in Back of the Yards and South Chicago.

Puerto Ricans mostly came to Chicago after World War II after living for a time on the East Coast. In the 1960s direct air service to Chicago from the islands plus continued migration from New York City more than doubled the Puerto Rican population (from 32,371 in 1960 to 78,963 in 1970). Puerto Ricans in Chicago now almost equal Mexicans. Displaced from the Near North Side and the Near West Side by urban renewal and by private middle class redevelopment and from East Garfield Park by blacks, Puerto Ricans filled the void left by native whites in Lincoln Park and Lake View and by Poles and Italians in Humboldt Park and Logan Square.

There were very few Cubans in Chicago before the establishment of the Castro government in 1959, so few that the U.S. Census included them in a general category of "West Indies" in the 1960 census. An effort was made in the early sixties to disperse the overwhelming number of refugees who had flooded into the Miami area. The 1970 census counted 19,000 Cubans in the Chicago metropolitan area and 14,000 in the city.

The first refugees to flee Cuba were the professional and white collar people who felt that their lives would be adversely affected by the new government which had taken over the

island. They came with limited financial resources and often were unable to use their special training because of language problems. Many had to go through a retraining period or meanwhile had to accept lesser positions. Physicians became lab technicians and medical researchers; lawyers joined real estate and insurance firms.

Those who did factory work often became supervisors, especially over other Spanish-speaking employees, because of their background. Many moved up, improved their economic position, and moved out of the central city to nearby suburbs after only a short time in the city. Their professional background and short term accomplishments gives many Cubans a feeling of superiority over other Latins to the point where they have little desire to associate or identify with them.

This is reflected in their residential pattern. Two-thirds of the city's present-day 14,000 Cubans live dispersed in five North Side communities, particularly Uptown, Logan Square, and Lake View.

Putting the numbers together, it emerges that three-quarters of the Spanish-speakers are clustered into ten of the city's community areas, and expansion is to the northwest, from Humboldt Park in particular, as indicated by the changing pattern of Spanish school enrollments in Chicago's public elementary schools (Figure 44). Meanwhile, small Spanish concentrations also have developed in the outlying ring of industrial satellites; there, too, Spanish neighborhoods are found adjacent to the black ghettos:

	Number	Percent
Blue Island	1,745	7.6
Aurora	5,412	7.3
Waukegan	4,460	7.2
Chicago Heights	2,884	7.0
Romeoville	778	6.1
Summit	695	6.0
West Chicago	562	5.5
Elgin	2,933	5.2
Melrose Park	1,186	5.2
Joliet	3,195	4.1

In all of these areas, the increase in size and density of the Spanish-speaking population has been of high visibility. The Mexicans especially have tried to preserve their rich cultural heritage. Their civic associations

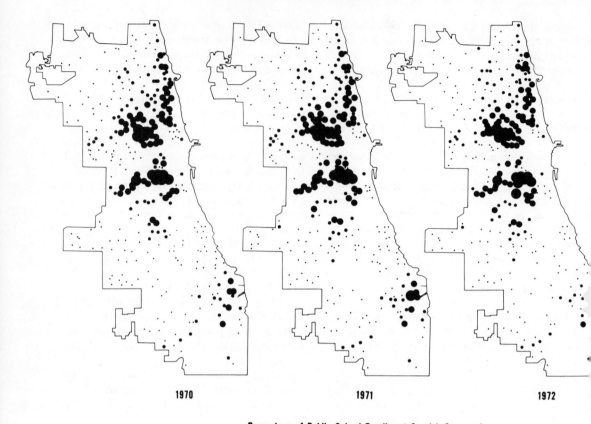

1970   1971   1972

Percentage of Public School Enrollment Spanish Surnamed

●   **More than 80%**

•   **25-80%**

•   **5-24%**

·   **Less than 5%**

Figure 44. Percentages of Chicago's public school enrollments with Spanish surnames, 1970–1972.

sponsor parades, dances, and rodeos. They have developed small business districts in which the establishments are owned and operated by Mexicans to satisfy Mexican tastes. The commercial area in the Far South has strengthened during the past decade in response to the growing consolidation of Mexicans there. In the Central West, New City or Back of the Yards, the area to the south of the canal, has also grown to service the incoming population there. The area north of the canal-Eighteenth Street—may be in jeopardy, however, as it now borders on the black community. Its continued existence may depend more upon the future movement of blacks into the area than on anything the Mexicans may do.

There is less visible evidence of the Puerto Rican presence. Their business ventures tend to satisfy the more general needs of their community. They own such things as grocery stores, dry cleaners, barber shops, driving schools, etc. Sometimes the only ethnic feature about these activities is the Spanish language. However, special Puerto Rican parades and observances are on the increase. They have joined the many national groups which sponsor a yearly parade through the community and down State Street in celebration of their ethnic background.

The one characteristic associated with all these groups, the Spanish language, has made itself evident throughout the city. Movies, books, periodicals, and advertising in Spanish are found in abundance throughout the Latin settlements. Schools have special instruction in Spanish, and English is taught as a second language to Latin children. Various agencies sponsor English language and other adult education programs. Also, many of the Catholic churches in the area conduct mass and hear confession in Spanish. By 1970 there were also several television and radio programs broadcast in Spanish and several public service programs dealing with problems peculiar to the Spanish-speaking population. There was also the request for several Spanish-speaking public defenders and that laws be made available in Spanish so that Latin Americans would be less apt to accidentally break the law or risk misrepresentation in court. Most of these acknowledgements of the importance of the growing Spanish-speaking population have taken place during the past decade.

THE GEOGRAPHY OF WEALTH AND POVERTY

Not only is there a polarity in the city between blue collar ethnics, the blacks, and the Spanish, there is also a profound polarity in the juxtaposition of wealth and poverty.

Poverty is an affliction of the minority group member in the ghetto. There were signs of improvement between 1960 and 1970, largely due to declining unemployment rates and increasing reliance of the unemployed upon public aid. The number of families in the city beneath the poverty line declined from 12.5 percent (109,000) in 1960 to 10.6 percent (88,000) in 1970, with a corresponding thinning of the spatial pattern of poverty. The improvements benefited white Chicago far more than the black neighborhoods, however; poverty concentrations remained disproportionately black or Spanish-speaking. Figure 45 shows that poverty is most profound in the heart of the city's ghetto, largely by virtue of the concentration of single parent minority families in high-rise public housing developments surrounded by abandoned neighborhoods. Fifty-one thousand of the city's 88,000 poverty families in 1970 were black and many of the 37,000 poor "whites" reported in the census were in fact members of the Spanish community.

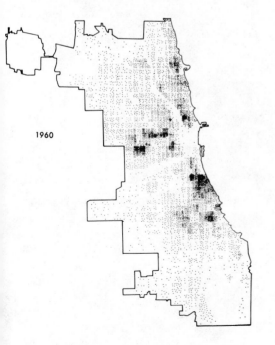

1960

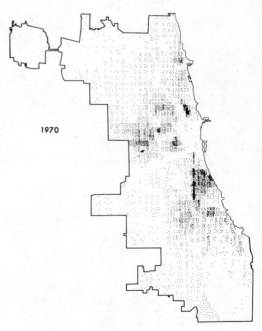

1970

1 dot equals 20 family units

Figure 45. Chicago's poverty population, 1960 and 1970.

Juxtaposed with these poverty areas are the city's most affluent residential areas (see Figure 20)—the high-rise apartment strip extending northward along the lakeshore from the Gold Coast to the city limits (Figure 24); the outlying ethnic refuges in the northwestern and southwestern fringes of the city where new single family housing was still being constructed in the 1950s and 1960s; and the South Side lakefront urban renewal areas of Lake Meadows–Prairie Shores and Hyde Park–Kenwood.

Lake Meadows is an apartment community that was privately redeveloped by the New York Life Insurance Company in what had been one of the worst slum areas of the city (Figure 46). With an adjoining apartment complex developed later at Prairie Shores, it provides relatively inexpensive integrated living close to the Loop, the Michael Reese hospital complex, and the Illinois Institute of Technology.

Further south, in Hyde Park-Kenwood, a massive federally funded urban renewal project preserved the community for future generations of University of Chicago faculty and students and families liking the lifestyle that a university provides. Deteriorated housing was torn down and new townhouses and apartments constructed; what were perceived to be the incipient sources of blight were eliminated. Old shopping streets were knocked down and replaced by modern shopping centers. As a result, private capital has poured into the area to build high-rise apartments along the lake, and the university, after a period of uncertainty, experienced a dramatic renaissance. Hyde Park is one of the few communities in which racial integration works in its own way: as one observer is alleged to have said, "In Hyde Park black and white stand shoulder to shoulder against the poor."

That comment serves to highlight the polarization of rich and poor. Just south of the

Figure 46. Aerial view of the Lake Meadows–Prairie Shores urban redevelopments.

University of Chicago is Woodlawn, probably Chicago's best known ghetto community. It is the home of TWO (The Woodlawn Organization), the city's most effective black community organization, established by Saul Alinsky. It is also the headquarters of the notorius Black P Stone Nation, and backyard and community laboratory to the university.

Largely because of the presence of these organizations, Woodlawn became the recipient of about $35 million of federal, university, and foundation support for experimental programs in housing, education, employment, youth, law enforcement, health, and welfare. Some of the best brains in the nation ghostwrote the plans and helped the community sponsors implement programs. Probably no other neighborhood in the nation had as much money and brainpower lavished upon it in the 1960s. In addition, Woodlawn has the best locational advantages of Chicago's ghetto communities, flanked by two large and beautiful parks to the east and west, by two affluent communities to the north and south, and connected to downtown by two expressways and two rapid transit systems.

Out of these inputs, with university aid and state financing to step around the opposition of Mayor Daley's democratic machine to the incipient independent black political organization represented by TWO, the community organization has moved ahead with its own redevelopment plans. One TWO-planned and managed housing development, Woodlawn Gardens, is now in place and operating, together with its own shopping center, and a second development is nearing completion.

Yet while this was being accomplished, Woodlawn still lost 34 percent of its people and 24 percent of its housing.

In the week of July 5, 1971, the *Chicago Daily News* published a series of five articles describing the "4-year epidemic" of fires in Woodlawn and identifying 165 abandoned buildings, many gutted by fire, and 195 sites where buildings had recently been razed. The reporters found fear and suspicion among firemen and the remaining residents that the fires had been set, that there was a "conspiracy" to complete the demolition of the community and rebuild for the benefit of real estate speculators. The fires, of which there were 1,600 in 1970 alone, follow the same pattern. Owners are sued by the city for building code viola-

tions, largely brought on by tenant abuse, vandalism, and deferred maintenance. The landlord cannot afford to correct the violations, and abandons the building. Tenants are ordered to move, after which the fires begin.

Lack of a private market and an income base lie at the root of the problems. Woodlawn's housing is simply no longer economically viable to the private real estate operator. Thus, much of Woodlawn stands in stark contrast to its Hyde Park neighbor today. Hyde Park, with a major institution providing continuing support for the local housing market, was able to use federal support to regenerate itself. Woodlawn, without such strong institutional backing, was not.

THE LOOP AND THE NORTHERN LAKESHORE: SELECTIVE GROWTH

Standing in stark contrast to the devastation of much of the old ghetto areas is the transformation that has taken place in the Loop; along North Michigan Avenue's Golden Mile; in the Gold Coast; and northward in a strip of communities extending from the entertainment and "swingles" districts of the Near North Side, through the neighborhoods being upgraded by upper income private renewal (Lincoln Park, Old Town, and New Town), and continuing in a lakeside strip of condominiums with an affluent, more elderly, and heavily Jewish population.

It was the declining fortunes of the Loop and particularly of the State Street shopping core during the 1950s that sparked a series of actions by the downtown business community that, with the active support and participation of the city government, helped realize the growth potentials afforded by the growth of the service industries and the continuing concentration of headquarters and administrative functions in the downtown areas of America's biggest cities.

State Street was being buffeted in a variety of ways—by construction of more than one hundred planned shopping centers and close to 150 discount stores in the city and suburbs; by the changing population, income, and buying habits of the population remaining in the city; and by decentralization of both employment and population. As one of the city's leading appraisers, Walter Kuehnle, has shown, daily shoppers in the CBD declined precipitously from the end of World War II until the mid-1960s (Figure 47), as did the total numbers of persons downtown during the business day (Figure 48), with the inevitable consequence of declining retail sales (Figure 49), felt more profoundly during the 1950s and early 1960s by the downtown specialty shops (Figure 50) than by the main line department stores (Figure 51), although rising costs did force upon them a real profit squeeze before taxes; net profits of the five main State Street department stores stood in 1962 at a low of only 30 percent of the 1948 level (Figure 52). Growth of retail selling space in outlying plaza-type shopping centers had particularly profound effects (Figure 53). A crisis of major proportions was at hand.

But in 1958 a coalition of new young "organization men" who had moved to the fore in Chicago's businesses and public utilities formed what has proven to be a durable coalition with first term Mayor Daley and the city's traditional civic leadership. This coalition, operating by quiet consensus, produced thirty-two million square feet of new office space in the central area over the next sixteen years, turned the Near North Side into Chicago's wealthiest neighborhood, and set in motion the privately financed redevelopment of a succession of neighborhoods to the north—Lincoln Park, Old Town, and New Town—as well as supporting urban renewal as a means of locating a new university (Chicago Circle campus of the University of Illinois) on the Loop's western fringes, preserving the integrity of major hospital complexes on each side of the Loop, and enabling The University of Chicago to flourish in Hyde Park-Kenwood. The whole was capped by a new civic center fronted by a massive Picasso sculpture and a federal complex constructed in the "Chicago Bauhaus" style of Mies van der Rohe.

The basic decisions related to the headquarters locations of private businesses—insurance companies such as Prudential and John Hancock; major corporations like Standard Oil; and trading giants like Sears Roebuck and Montgomery Ward all agreed to rebuild in the city center. An office boom of unprecedented proportions began in the late 1960s

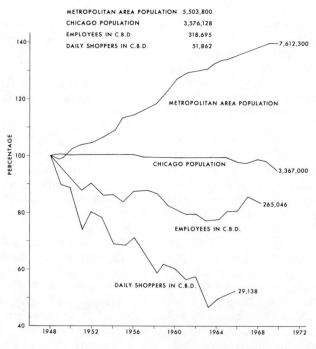

Figure 47. Change in employees and daily shoppers in the Chicago CBD, compared with change in the population of the city and the Chicago metropolitan area.

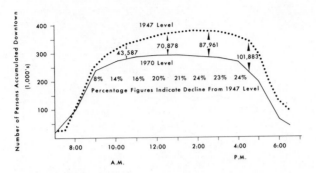

Figure 48. Numbers of persons downtown during the business day, 1947 and 1970. Source: City of Chicago, Bureau of Street Traffic.

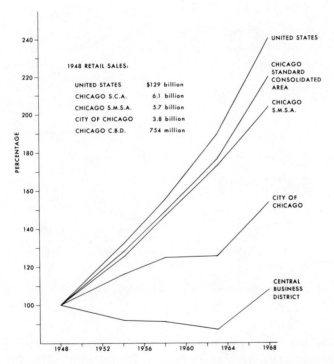

Figure 49. Retail sales in the CBD, city of Chicago, Chicago metropolitan area, and the United States, 1948-1967.

(Figure 54), capped by the world's largest skyscrapers (Figure 55). The city's skyline was transformed, and the boost to employment was felt not only in State Street fortunes, but also resulted in the emergence of North Michigan's "Magnificent Mile" as the metropolitan area's most exclusive shopping complex. This complex is soon to be cemented by the completion of Water Tower Plaza, a $100 million complex with a sixty-three story hotel-apartment tower atop an eleven story shopping-office center adjacent to the John Hancock Center (which pioneered the self-contained multilevel parking, office, apartment, service, and shopping complex that now characterizes the city's new highrise giants). Six hundred thousand square feet of shops are being built on six levels around

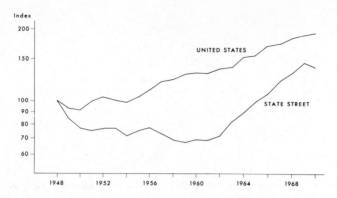

Figure 50. Retail sales index for women's wear, State Street and U.S., 1948-1970.

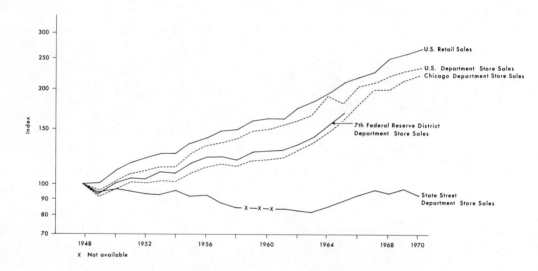

Figure 51. Department store retail sales indexes, 1948-1970.

a central atrium in the Water Tower Plaza, and Chicago's leading retailer, Marshall Field and Co., will be the main tenant.

The increases in office employment contributed in turn to housing demand in the central area and Near North Side. The central area of the Near North Side, the west bank of the Chicago River, and the Loop proper gained more than 25,000 jobs between 1962 and 1968. One result was an opportunity that Chicago's developers quickly realized—to construct new apartment complexes for the young unmarrieds and newlyweds close to the Near North night spots. Further north, more elegant buildings were built fronting the lake for the more elderly affluent.

The "Chicago 21" Plan

By the early 1970s the old coalition had grown complacent and listless. Its 1958 plan for $3 billion in new construction had been completed, but at the same time other signs of malaise had begun to appear in the Loop. Theaters and restaurants, plentiful in 1958, were closing. Downtown Chicago had become the commercial center for the black community. Many of the successes were suddenly beginning to look like liabilities to Chicago's white business elite and to Mayor Daley's party organization in a city rapidly moving toward a black majority. By building up the city center as a prestige office location, Chicago corporations had brought in 25,000 new white collar jobs,

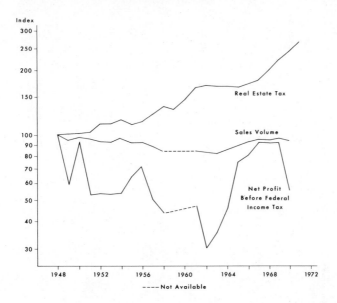

Figure 52. State Street department stores' sales and net profits (index), 1948–1972.

created a $490 million annual convention trade, established a $1.9 billion real estate investment, and put 33 percent of the city's tax base on 4 percent of its land. The cost had been considerable, however. Between 1968 and 1972, demolition and rising real estate assessments forced out of the central area 13 percent of the small retailers, 15 percent of the entertainment spots, and 8 percent of the restaurants.

The response has been a new superplan—the "Chicago 21" plan—produced by the Central Area Committee, a regrouping of the 1958 coalition and the city government. What is proposed is a $15 billion, thirty year program to convert the city's central core into "a vision of the Central Community of the 21st Century."

At the core of the proposal is a thriving financial and office center built around the Sears Tower, the First National Bank and Standard Oil buildings, and the Civic Center. Running along Wabash and State streets will be a refurbished shopping district converted to plazas, malls, and street fairs, and anchored on North State Street by a cultural-entertainment complex. Making all those developments possible will be the infusion of an outer bank of permanent Loop residents squeezed on rail yards along the Chicago River (Figure 56) and a simultaneous rebirth of the innermost ethnic neighborhoods.

Figure 53. Growth in total retail selling space of plaza type shopping centers in the Chicago metropolitan area, 1950–1974.

Other highlights of the plan include:

1. Construction of a South Loop New Town by 1985 on 650 acres of unused railroad property south of the Loop for upwards of 120,000 persons.
2. Limited expansion of the Central Business District to the south edge of the Loop and across the river to the north and east.
3. Creation of a recreational and open space belt along the riverfront in the form of

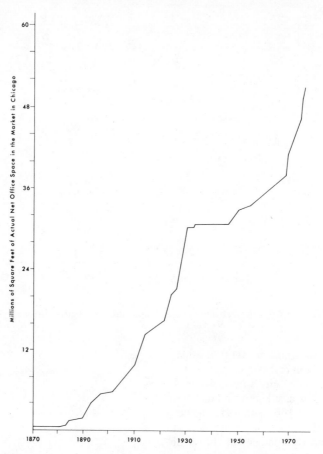

Figure 54. Millions of square feet of actual net office space on the market in Chicago, 1870–1970.

esplanades, parks, and open spaces and expansion and enhancement of the lakefront.

4. Continued development of the Illinois Center—eighty-three acres of land northeast of the central business district of which fifty-three will be devoted to parks and plazas, built on railroad air rights.

5. Replacement of the Loop and Ravenswood elevated lines with a subway and relocation of the Jackson Park line.

6. Establishment of a distributor subway to the north, west, and south edges of the CBD connecting John Hancock Center, Chicago Circle Campus, and McCormick Place.

7. Establishment of a ring of parking lots at outlying areas for commuters who use public transportation.

8. Improvement of conditions in public housing, with Cabrini-Green serving as a test

case in converting apartments to owner-occupied units.

The plan was the result of a "shirtsleeves relationship" developed over a two year series of monthly closed meetings between top city planners and the second echelon of "hot shot" young executives of Chicago's twenty-one major corporations. The meetings were held ostensibly to review the developing Chicago 21 report. But their broader purpose was to fix a certain common perception of the Loop's—and Chicago's—problems on the city and industry.

City officials came away with a basic understanding that the Loop firms wanted their office investments protected with a whole new community of middle and upper income live-in residents supporting their prestige center. In general, the city agreed to this. There was

Figure 55. The Loop skyline in 1973. To the left is Sears Tower, the world's largest building, and to the right are the Standard Oil and John Hancock buildings.

dickering as to specifics. But the discussion did produce a silent consensus, essentially a strategy for development that emerges with the following elements.

Social. Here the watchwords are "balanced use"—that is, rebuilding the Loop's residential and cultural prestige so it is on a par with the office and convention accommodations. Planners foresee a gradual, simultaneous growth of apartments and scattered cultural-entertainment spots, each making the other more attractive and both drawing customers from the pool of Loop office workers.

This means, in effect, that the Loop will increasingly become a community predominantly of the rich and well-off that lives along the river, works in the financial center, shops along State Street or Michigan Avenue, and dines in between.

But it also means a massive economic thrust to improve schools, transportation, recreation, safety, and the general "livability" of the Loop, since the typical Loop worker is a family man who picks his home by these criteria.

Racial Strategy. All the Chicago 21 retail and housing proposals therefore point toward a gradual "whitening" of the Loop. As long as blacks do not constitute a large share of the middle and upper income brackets, prestige housing on the river will be predominantly white. Thus, those stores marked as underutilized and ripe for more prestigious development

Figure 56. Comparison of the south Loop skyline today, and as contemplated by the Chicago 21 Plan.

are curiously the same ones that have survived by catering to the new Loop blacks.

But in the city, where the population and hence political power will shift to a black and Latino majority by 1985, even the Chicago 21 planners recognized that it would be self-defeating to invest $15 billion in the Loop and then shut out minorities. Therefore, the final layer in preparing the Loop for an infusion of white collar residents is preparing the white collar classes for a greater proportion of blacks through more minority recruitment and hiring in major firms and greater private financial support of minority owned businesses.

The timetable remains looseknit. After all, $15 billion is to be spent over thirty years. Moreover, enormous logistical problems remain. The South Loop rail yards, for example, although prized, are now owned by some fifty partnerships, including the Penn Central Railroad now tied up in backruptcy court. True to the admonitions of Daniel Burnham, though, Chicago 21 is no little plan.

Mid-Chicago Economic Development

Meanwhile, active planning by a business-city coalition under the direction of the Mayor's Committee for Cultural and Economic Development also has led to a variety of initiatives to attract employment back to other parts of the central city. Principally, these efforts have focused on two portions of Chicago designated as economic redevelopment areas and lying at the core of the old South Side and West Side ghettos: the Stockyards Redevelopment Area in 1967 and the Midwest Impact Area (incorporating portions of Lawndale, East and West Garfield Park, and Humboldt Park) in 1970. These were recommended initially in the Mid-Chicago Economic Development Study, conducted by the Center for Urban Studies, University of Chicago, between 1964 and 1966. Planning and programming efforts focused on the stimulation of new industrial development and on industrial conservation.

Results are now appearing. Within the square mile which contained the old packing town-stockyards complex there have been developed the Morgan Industrial District, a planned industrial park by the Central Manufacturing District, the Hammond-Columbia complex, and the Ashland Industrial District.

Similarly, within the Midwest Impact Area, several large scale economic development ventures have been started. These include an eighty acre industrial park being developed by the North Lawndale Economic Development Corporation on the site of the old International Harvester Tractor Works. The same developer is creating a twenty acre shopping center. In the north end of the Midwest Impact Area, Northwestern Mutual Life Assurance Company and Northwestern Industries have co-ventured the development of a major industrial park—the Northwestern Center for Industry.

In these projects alone, more than 7,500 new jobs already have been created following about $120 million of private investments, and they have the potential to create directly an additional 40,000 jobs.

Private Redevelopment of Chicago's North Side

While federally financed urban renewal programs were transforming large tracts of South Chicago, and city-backed corporate-financed developments were renovating the Loop, a third consortium was at work. More loosely knit and operating on a smaller scale, private landowners, real estate firms, and land development corporations were quietly rejuvenating selected portions of Chicago's North Side. The process, as in the previous two, resulted from a basic need, in this instance housing.

Not all whites joined the exodus to the suburbs during the period 1960–1970. Those unwilling or unable to leave sought alternative locations. The choice of residential location was influenced by the individuals' stage in life cycle. Families with school age children sought areas containing newer single family dwellings and all-white schools. The only Chicago communities which could supply these requirements were those at the periphery of the city, contiguous to suburban communities. Older, childless couples, on the other hand, moved to the more conveniently located residential units of the Gold Coast if affluent, the lakeshore communities to the north of the Gold Coast if less so, and to Chicago's Madison Street skid row if poverty stricken. Developers followed the more affluent, building a wall of high-rise apartments and condominiums northward along the lake.

However, there remained a sizable minority group, the young singles or newly married. The suburbs, with their family structuring, were not appealing. Suburban apartment complexes designed for "swingles," with their subliminal promises of social and sexual freedoms, had not yet come into existence. Instead, this group was drawn toward the Loop with its increase in white collar jobs and the excitement of its entertainment districts. Residential choices were limited. The south shore communities of Hyde Park, Woodlawn, and South Shore were in the throes of urban renewal and/or racial change. The conveniently located Gold Coast was prohibitively expensive and was preempted by the more elderly. The remaining choices were the north shore communities of Near North, Lincoln Park, Lakeview, Uptown, and Rogers Park. Yet these communities experienced a net population loss during the period 1960–1970 of 3.2 percent. But a closer examination of the census tracts within these communities located immediately adjacent to Lake Michigan indicates a net population gain of 19.3 percent, with a net gain of the white population of 13.5 percent. It is this narrow strip that has attracted private development in order to meet the demand for the specialized housing needs of the young, white middle class.

Emergence of Old Town. First observed in the late 1950s, the processes associated with private urban development have steadily progressed northward from origins in the northern edge of the Near North Side and the southern boundary of the Lincoln Park community. The area was ideal. It was directly west of the Gold Coast and contained a multimix of three and four story brownstones. Rents averaged from $40–80 a month versus the Gold Coast's, which exceeded $150. Young residents converged upon the area. However, the new population lacked retail facilities. Wells Street between 1200 N.–1900 N. provided the solution. Commercial rents were low, large warehouse-type structures dotted the street and were ideally suited for conversion into interior malls containing many small boutiques. Old Town was born.

Psychedelic, novelty, and clothing shops lined Wells Street. New shops opened weekly, and competition reduced individual shops' sales. The youth market could not sustain the level and number of existing stores, selling what was basically and same type of merchandise, however. Attempts to control the merchant

mix, a characteristic of every new planned shopping center, were absent.

Attempts to lure the affluent Gold Coast residents failed because of the lack of appropriate merchandise. The area was perceived to have a high crime rate, and the elderly eschewed contacts with both the swingles and the increasing numbers of blacks who appeared on the street. Therefore, by the mid-1960s, Old Town sought to enlarge its market attraction by diverting some of the tourist-conventioneer traffic from the traditional Rush-Oak Street entertainment center. B-bars and strip joints appeared, closely followed by the House of Horrors, Ripley's Believe-It-Or-Not Museum, and the Royal Wax Museum. Area residents now viewed Old Town as a grossly overcommercialized tourist strip. Expansion or migration to an immediately adjoining area was impossible. Hemmed in on the east by the luxurious Gold Coast which had further encroached westward to Clark with the building of the high-rise and townhouse units of the Carl Sandburg Village, invaded by the black Near West ghettos, and blocked by the commercial district to the south, the disenchanted youthful founders of Old Town could only look north.

The adjoining community of Lincoln Park appeared to be the logical site. However, several factors combined to exclude this community area. Accessibility was poor—especially via rapid transit to the Loop. Hostility on the part of residents toward an expansion of "hippie" Old Town provided difficulties. But most significant was the fact that the area was undergoing a process of land reclassification by the Department of Urban Renewal and realtors were assembling large tracts of land for developments of high-rise and townhouse residential units.

From Old Town to New Town. The southeastern part of Lake View, the next community area to the north, was destined to become the new "hot" area. The community boasted easy access to the Loop and the lakefront and good transportation. Southeast Lake View contained a multiethnic mix of families, senior citizens, and young people. It had a long and well-established homosexual community around Clark, Belmont, and Diversey. The local business strips, although dormant, offered a variety of commercial spaces that could be rented for less than $4 per square foot.

However, the zone east of Broadway lacked an adequate supply of housing to meet the increasing demand. But in Chicago, where demand means development, the problem was quickly solved. Housing units increased from 16,707 in 1960 to 24,012 in 1970—a 44 percent increase. The majority of the increase was a result of one of Chicago's most infamous and controversial structures—the four plus one unit.

In the late 1960s these structures sprang up, replacing the older three to six family unit apartment building that had been there before with shoddily built, cramped, thin-walled, forty to one hundred unit structures. Designed to avoid the costly fire resistant construction required by law of five story apartment buildings, the wood and concrete four plus ones were built with four floors of apartments on the top of open parking spaces half below ground level. Rents ranged from $150 for a studio to $195 for one bedroom apartments and were quickly filled. During the period 1960-1970 they experienced a diverse rent increase of 31 percent, from $139 to $182, while the average size of the units declined from 3.4 to 3.2 rooms—net result, higher rents for smaller units.

The residential structure of the zone immediately to the west also was affected but in a somewhat different manner. The basic dwellings were two and three story multiunit dwellings with an intermingling of single family dwellings. Many of the dwellings had been converted to rooming houses and offered sleeping rooms and small, furnished, low rent units. Demolition of existing structures and their replacements by larger units with a greater number of apartments was prevented by zoning ordinances. Thus this area was characterized by deconversions (reduction of the number of units in a dwelling with a corresponding increase in the size of the remaining unit), renovation, and restoration of the many Victorian buildings. As a result the number of residential units decreased from 14,319 to 11,695, or 22 percent in the decade. During this period the average size of the residential units increased from 3.1 to 3.4 rooms and rents increased over 56 percent. This zone now supplies the demand for larger units, but at a corresponding increase in rental rates.

The residential structure of the community was not the only segment affected by private development. Paralleling the demand for housing was an awareness of an opportunity to provide goods and services for these new residents. The growing commercial potential of the area attracted opportunistic businessmen to the Broadway commercial ribbon. "New Town" was to emerge after a complete restructuring of the existing commercial facilities had taken place.

With the increased demand for commercial space, rents spiraled upward. The effects can be seen in the transformations within the business sector which have occurred during the past five years. In 1969 the neighborhood's needs were satisfied by 139 retail and service units lining Broadway between Diversey and Belmont. The service sector accounted for 39 percent of all business operations. Five years later this figure had been reduced to 18.4 percent. Especially hard hit were services such as auto repair and moving and storage firms which required large amounts of low rent space. Smaller marginal operations—shoe repairs and independent laundries and cleaners—were unable to absorb rising rents. Professional services were also adversely affected. Another sector of the business community, food and related goods, registered a sharp decline from an initial 12 percent to 4.9 percent. Most distressing to the local community was the elimination of 50 percent of the area's supermarkets, from twelve in 1969 to six in 1974. This posed a problem for the elderly, who were forced to travel greater distances for basic food items.

Yet spectacular gains were registered in the general merchandise (+153 percent), wearing apparel (+76.5 percent), and dining and entertainment categories (+82.8 percent). These goods and services are directed at the groups with the largest amounts of disposable income—the young singles or newly married couples without children. Herein lies the social impact of the redevelopment of the retail structure of New Town. Rapidly, it came to serve a smaller segment of the local community. This fact has not escaped the local merchants. In an effort to enlarge what was initially a local market to include all of Chicago, its northern suburbs, and tourists, a $12.5 million shopping plaza is under construction inside the Old Century Theater at Clark and Diversey. The center is scheduled to contain over 110,000 square feet of rental space, over sixty shops, and a parking garage for 550 cars.

What is the impact of this project upon the area's business community? The core of New Town's business strip is now gravitating toward the new plaza, with rents now being based upon proximity to the expectant traffic-generating shopping plaza. Shops are realigning themselves, with those unable to support high rents delegated to the least desirable and peripheral locations.

The nearby area of gay bars and restaurants are seeking new low profile locations as they have done in the past. The rows of antique shops, artist studios, and craft workshops are under pressure to migrate even further northward. This puts them into competition for space with the existing Spanish and Oriental shopping districts in Uptown. Only a few types of businesses can survive in an area now containing some of the highest commercial rents in Chicago.

It should further be noted that this rent structure has also influenced the nature of the business operations. Initially the area was comprised predominantly of independent merchants, both those long established in the neighborhood and the newer younger entrepreneurs. However, as initial investment and operating costs increased, the number of independent shopkeepers has declined. Franchise and chain store operations are now appearing. Even then, there are indications that development has been excessive. Shops are beginning to open and close with disturbing frequency, while vacancy rates are gradually increasing. The community's major concern now is that they will evolve into a bawdy strip of B-bars, strip joints, and game parlors, the fate which befell Old Town.

Ecology of the Lakeshore Communities. In the competition for space, the degree to which each group is affected varies according to their need, ability to pay, and the nature and location of available space. As a result Lake View, as well as the majority of Chicago's north shore communities, has developed a very particular socioeconomic pattern. While Lake View remains a multiethnic mixture of peoples, four distinct layers can be detected running in north-south ribbons from Lake Michigan. Each strip is separated by little more than a single street, yet is divided by attitudes, values, and expectations.

The easternmost layer has been the most stable and affluent. It has always been the domain of the well-to-do, from turn of the century summer homes and mansions to the present canyon of high-rise apartments. The inhabitants are characterized by high levels of education, professional attainment, and income. With a population mainly over forty years of age (70 percent), and a large Jewish percentage, the zone's religious, cultural, and business activities are directed to Lake Shore Drive, North Michigan Avenue, and the Loop. This strip has been least affected by the private development of New Town because it has little interaction with the remaining community to the west. The area has been developed to maximum intensity usage under current zoning regulations.

This is not the case with the narrow ribbon immediately to the west. This was once Lake View's depressed zone, containing a large population of Appalachian whites, Spanish speaking groups, the elderly, and families with school age children. As private investment began to transform the area into the swinging "in" spot, rapid changes occurred. The ethnic minorities shifted westward. The poor, often synonymous with the elderly, gravitated toward the cheaper boarding houses and resident hotels on the periphery of New Town. Families were unable to obtain larger residential units, most of which had been converted into studios and one bedroom units.

Local community institutions reflected the changing composition of the population. During the period 1960-1970, the number of elementary school age children fell by 16.1 percent. The decline has continued, with the nearest elementary school experiencing a 34 percent drop in enrollment from 1971-1973. The area's churches and temples experienced similar declines in membership. This second ribbon of Lake View is now mainly populated by young (18-35), single or newly married, highly educated, white middle class residents.

These are transient residents who have little use or concern for the older established institutions of the community; they are served by their own "glitter gulch" called Broadway. This zone has become an extension of the Gold Coast with the only major differentiating characteristics being age and income.

The third ribbon, relatively speaking, is Lake View's poverty belt. The most noticeable inhabitants are the Spanish-speaking groups (principally Puerto Ricans, but including many Cubans and other South Americans). Also numbered among Lake View's poor are the Southern Appalachian whites and the elderly remains of previous ethnic groups that economic progress has left behind.

The Latino community is particularly susceptible to changes in the structure of residential rents. The Spanish-speaking population is young, the median age being 20.3 years. The Latinos are mobile; 72 percent have moved since 1965. Family size is greater (4.4 in 1970). This in part explains the fact that 24 percent of the Latin families are living in overcrowded quarters. In 1970, 82 percent of the Spanish-speaking households were renters paying less than $149 a month gross rent. Thus, when a Latin family was faced with a rent increase, it had the choice of moving or seeking smaller quarters in the same area at the same rent. The latter was often not possible as there was a great likelihood that present quarters were already overcrowded. Migration thus was rapid from the New Town area, especially to the large Latino communities of Logan Square and Humboldt Park. The continued popularity of the old Victorian graystones may pressure more movement from the area.

The last layer of Lake View has been little affected by the New Town development. It is basically an area of one and two story buildings which are largely owner-occupied. The area contains a large middle-aged and elderly German-American population as well as several other European ethnic groups. However, one can begin to see a trickle of younger families moving into the neighborhood as rent scales of the more eastern sectors rise.

Thus, all areas of Lake View have experienced the effects of the private development of New Town. In general, these effects have increased commercial and residential rents, which effectively reduced the diversity of business and residential types. Because it is market-oriented to a small segment of the population, it has resulted in a socioeconomic stratification of the community that repeats the larger polarities of the city as a whole. Those who can afford the most preempt the most desirable locations whereas the poor, elderly, and minority groups are relegated what is left over. As with Chicago 21, the costs and benefits are differentially distributed.

The Metabolism of the Metropolis

Great whirls have little whirls,
    that feed on their velocity;
and little whirls have lesser whirls,
    and so on to viscosity.
                —Lewis F. Richardson

The processes of change described in the pre-ceding sections unfold in a particular way, reflecting an intricate interweaving of the metabolic rhythms of the growing metropolis with longer term upturns and downswings of the Chicago building cycle and with the un-expected occurrence of a variety of outside shocks. The result is pulsating, reverberating growth and change, beginning in the ways in which new growth is accommodated and end-ing in the ways in which the costs and bene-fits filter to the disadvantaged.

The daily ebbs and flows of commuters, shoppers, and school children are the most familiar of the rhythms, five days a week, in metabolic cycles essential to the maintenance of the region and its parts. In turn, weekly and monthly cycles are superimposed on seasonal fluctuations which vary around longer term trends. Many aspects of seasonality may be charted. Winter peaks in demands—for exam-ple, of natural gas—are balanced around an up-ward trend that reveals the continuing growth of the metropolis (Figure 57). Summer, on the other hand, is marriage and vacation season (Figures 58 and 59). The unemployment rate peaks in the summer as school leavers enter the labor force (Figure 60). Summer is home-building season (Figures 61 and 62). Lagging

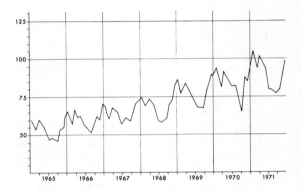

Figure 57. Natural gas delivered by pipeline to metropolitan Chicago, 1965-1971.

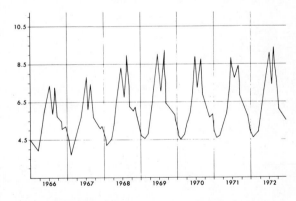

Figure 58. Marriage licenses issued, eight coun-ty metropolitan Chicago area, 1966-1972.

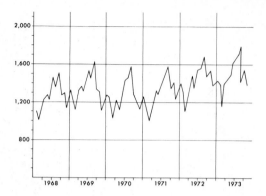

Figure 59. Number of scheduled air passenger arrivals, O'Hare and Midway airports, 1968–1973.

occurrence ... the sequence of events ju:
described may in the future be of intere
only to historians delving in the habits an
customs of "early machine age culture i
the United States," and the knowledge c
the mode of behavior of forces in the rea
estate cycle will have no value in forecas
ing the trend of future events.

Hoyt may have been correct. Chicago
growth now closely resembles that of th
nation (Table 6), as does the growth of eac
of the nation's largest metropolitan areas. Th
is a product of diversification of major metro
politan economies and the closeness of metro
politan connectivity. Indeed, the *set* of U.
metropolitan areas now functions as a uni
increasingly, the Chicago region is but on
thread in the fabric of a nationwide intermetro
politan network. Chicago's rhythms, then, ar
today those of the nation as a whole.

And yet there are changes taking place tha
will continue to alter the face of the metropo
lis. Intermetropolitan migration flows are in
creasing while flows of migrants to Chicag
from rural areas are declining and more Ch
cagoans are seeking residence in nonmetropo
litan areas elsewhere (Table 7). The flood c
black migrants into Chicago's West and Sout
Side ghettos from the Mississippi Delta tha
was such an important element in ghetto ex
pansion in the 1950s (Figure 67) fell to a trickl
in 1965–1970 (Figure 68), while emigratio
of Chicagoans westward and southward in
creased substantially (Figure 69 and 70).

Reflecting these trends, few new student
are coming to the city's high schools fror

behind the moving season, the residential vacancy rate peaks in the fall (Figure 63).

There can be sags and accelerations (Figures 64 through 66), seasonality superimposed on longer term cycles, and minor fluctuations around long term trends. There was also, in Chicago's first hundred years, the Chicago real estate cycle identified by Homer Hoyt as consisting, in sequence, of "the cycles of population growth, of the rent levels and operating costs of existing buildings, of new construction, of land values and of subdivision activity." Hoyt, however, concluded his study by saying:

The real estate cycle itself may be a phenomenon that is confined chiefly to young or rapidly growing cities ... if rapid rises or declines in land values become of rare

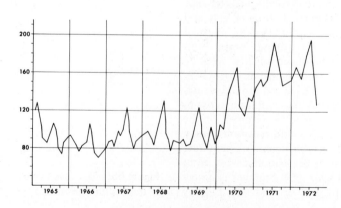

Figure 60. Number of unemployed, metropolitan Chicago, 1965–1972.

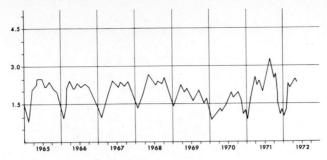

Figure 61. Building permits for single family homes, metropolitan Chicago, 1965–1972.

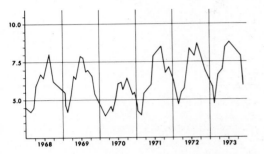

Figure 62. Real estate transfers recorded, Cook County, 1968–1972.

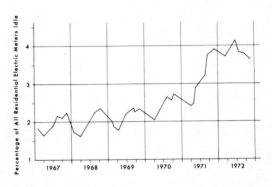

Figure 63. Residential vacancy rate, metropolitan Chicago, 1967–1972.

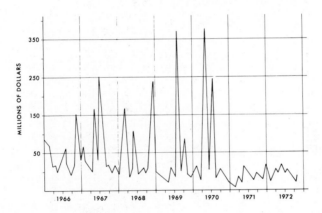

Figure 64. Industrial development investments, metropolitan Chicago, 1966–1972.

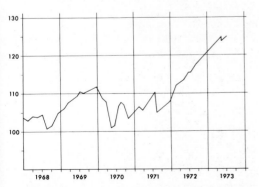

Figure 65. Index of industrial production, metropolitan Chicago, 1968–1973. Source: Illinois Bell Telephone Company.

Figure 66. Index of vacant industrial buildings, city of Chicago, 1968–1973.

Table 6. Selected Economic Indicators, Metropolitan Chicago Versus U.S.

	Metropolitan Chicago					Percent Change		U.S.					Percent Change	
	1970	1971	1972	1973^F	1974^F	72–73	73–74	1970	1971	1972	1973^F	1974^F	72–73	73–74
Personal income (billion $)	34.4	36.5	39.6	43.6	46.8	10.0	7.5	808.3	863.5	939.2	1,033	1,108	10.0	7.3
Per capita income ($)	4,548	4,774	5,132	5,600	5,965	9.1	6.7	3,943	4,164	4,492	4,900	5,218	9.0	6.3
Industrial production (1967 = 100)	106.2	107.0	115.8	124.6	128.0	7.6	2.7	106.6	106.8	115.1	125.7	128.5	9.2	2.2
Unemployment Rate (%)	3.9	4.5	4.2	3.6	3.7	–	–	4.9	5.9	5.6	4.8	5.2	–	–
Labor Force (million)	3.57	3.54	3.54	3.55	3.57	0.2	0.5	82.7	84.1	86.5	88.8	90.5	2.7	1.9
Employment (million)	3.43	3.38	3.39	3.43	3.45	1.3	0.5	78.6	79.1	81.7	84.5	85.8	3.4	1.5
*Consumer Price Index (1967 = 100)	116.3	120.8	124.3	131.5	138.9	5.8	5.6	116.3	121.3	125.3	132.9	140.8	6.1	5.9

*Data also includes Lake and Porter counties of Indiana.

F–Forecast

Source: Release by the Chicago Association of Commerce and Industry.

Table 7.   Interregional Migration: Chicago SEA 1955–1960 and 1965–1970

	1955–1960		1965–1970	
Migration To Chicago SEA	444,825		464,794	
From metropolitan areas	237,296	53.3	283,436	60.9
From nonmetropolitan areas	207,529	46.7	181,358	39.1
Migration From Chicago SEA	518,290		664,074	
To metropolitan areas	340,694	65.7	404,985	60.9
To nonmetropolitan areas	177,596	34.3	259,089	39.1

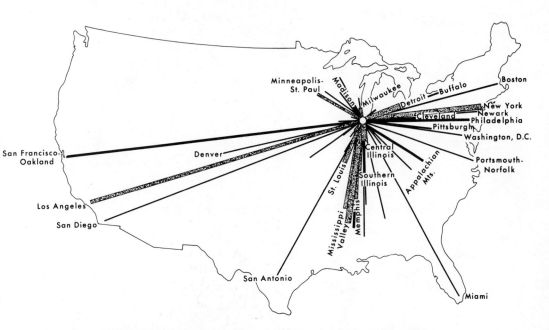

Figure 67.   Number of migrants to Chicago SEA, 1955–1960.

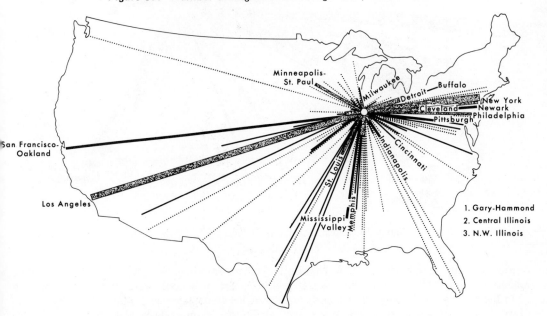

Figure 68.   Number of migrants to Chicago SEA, 1965–1970.

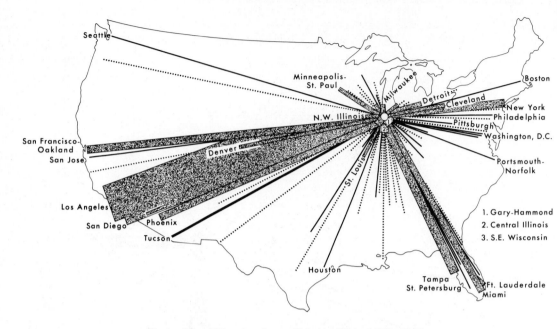

Figure 69. Migration from Chicago SEA, 1955–1960.

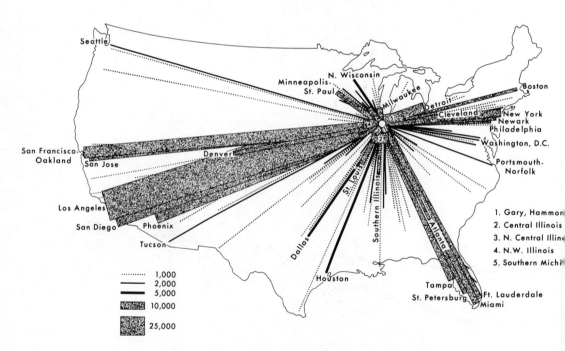

Figure 70. Migration from Chicago SEA, 1965–1970.

outside the city—a sure sign of the changing migration flows (Table 8), while students from the white schools continue to suburbanize (Table 9). As immigration has slackened, population has thinned, and birth rates have fallen, enrollments in most of the city's public elementary schools have started to dip. And while white families continue to move to the suburbs, as more leave there are fewer left to leave, and so the contribution of white emigra-

The Metabolism of the Metropolis   275

Table 8. Total Number of High School Intransfers and Percent of Group Student Enrollment Transferring from Different Origins, October 1971–March 1972

| Group Characteristics | | | Intransfers | | | | | | | | | | | | | | |
Group*	Number of Schools in Group	Total Group Enrollment	From Other Chicago Public Schools		From Vocational and Evening Schools		From Special Needs Schools		From Nonpublic Chicago Schools		From Other Illinois Schools		From Schools Out of State		From Schools Out of U.S.A.		Total	
			Number	Percent	Number	Percent	Number	Percent	Number	Percent	Number	Percent	Number	Percent	Number	Percent	Number	Percent
A	10	23,197	98	0.4	8	—	15	0.1	7	—	1	—	0	—	2	—	131	0.6
B	5	11,606	139	1.2	25	0.2	23	0.2	4	—	1	—	2	—	3	—	197	1.7
C	4	11,197	149	1.3	116	1.0	33	0.3	1	—	0	—	0	—	0	—	299	2.7
D	3	7,513	105	1.4	27	0.4	12	0.2	4	—	1	—	6	0.1	0	—	155	2.1
E	3	9,153	28	0.3	22	0.2	9	0.1	3	—	0	—	0	—	0	—	62	0.7
F	11	25,387	423	1.7	103	0.4	67	0.3	6	—	1	—	8	—	0	—	608	2.4
G	4	12,039	197	1.6	28	0.2	29	0.2	1	—	1	—	10	0.1	0	—	266	2.2
Total	40	100,092	1,139	1.1	329	0.3	188	0.2	26	—	5	—	26	—	5	—	1,718	1.7

*A—North Side white schools
B—North Side mixed schools
C—West Side black schools
D—West-Southwest mixed schools
E—Southwest Side white schools
F—South Side black schools
G—South Side mixed schools

Table 9. Total Number of High School Outtransfers and Percent of Group Student Enrollment Transferring to Different Destinations, November 17, 1971–March 31, 1972

Group Characteristics			To Other Chicago Public Schools		To Vocational and Evening Schools		To Special Needs Schools		To Nonpublic Chicago Schools		To Other Illinois Schools		To Schools Out of State		To Schools Out of U.S.A.		Dropout		Total	
Group*	Number of Schools in Group	Total Group Enrollment	Number	Percent	Number	Percent	Number	Percent	Number	Percent	Number	Percent	Number	Percent	Number	Percent	Number	Percent	Number	Percent
A	10	23,197	95	0.4	278	1.2	63	0.3	46	0.2	126	0.6	119	0.5	16	0.1	330	1.4	1073	4.7
B	5	11,606	159	1.4	271	2.3	47	0.4	40	0.3	46	0.4	83	0.7	121	1.0	552	4.8	1356	11.7
C	4	11,197	202	1.8	414	3.7	76	0.7	40	0.4	75	0.7	122	1.1	7	0.1	545	4.9	1481	13.3
D	3	7,513	108	1.4	207	2.8	44	0.6	23	0.3	41	0.6	74	1.0	27	0.4	201	2.7	725	9.7
E	3	9,153	19	0.2	59	0.6	9	0.1	5	0.1	43	0.5	20	0.2	1	0.1	108	1.2	264	2.9
F	11	25,387	443	1.8	397	1.6	127	0.5	97	0.4	92	0.4	226	0.9	1		957	3.8	2340	9.3
G	4	12,039	113	0.9	191	1.6	29	0.2	48	0.4	118	1.0	78	0.7	5		263	2.2	845	7.0
Total	40	100,092	1,139	1.1	1817	1.8	395	0.4	299	0.3	415	0.4	722	0.7	178	0.2	2,956	3.0	8,084	8.1

*A–North Side white schools
B–North Side mixed schools
C–West Side black schools
D–West-Southwest mixed schools
E–Southwest Side white schools
F–South Side black schools
G–South Side mixed schools

Table 10. 1972 Industrial Development

Movements of Facilities	Number	$ Value
Newly formed firms in city of Chicago	1	$ 600,000
Newly formed firms in suburban area	12	2,275,000
New firms moving into city from outside metropolitan area	2	1,010,000
New firms moving into suburban area from outside metropolitan area	36	25,446,000
Firms relocating from city to suburb	40	16,265,000
Firms relocating from suburb to city	4	1,550,000
Firms relocating within city	29	12,470,000
Firms relocating within same suburb	33	14,267,000
Firms relocating from one suburb to another	17	8,504,000
City-based firms establishing a branch inside city limits	15	5,441,000
City-based firms establishing branches in suburbs	15	4,277,000
Suburban firms establishing branches in city	3	2,113,000
Suburban firms establishing branches in same suburb	17	7,650,000
Suburban firms establishing branches in different suburbs	16	15,320,000
Total	240	$117,188,000

Source: Industrial Development Division, Chicago Association of Commerce and Industry.

tion to suburban growth is declining. In short, Chicago is rapidly trending to two societies. One—the suburbs, the Loop, and the northern lakeshore—is part of the nationwide inter-metropolitan system of interaction, growth and change. The other—the inner city minority—is cut off, abandoned, localized, benefiting only to the extent that filtering takes place. Reflecting this polarity and contributing to it are the region's industrial dynamics (Table 10). "Chicago 21" can be seen in light of these trends as the attempt to support and revitalize the Loop by enclosing it within a high-rise, high income womb, walled off from minority Chicago beyond.

Yet success of Chicago 21 will depend upon the willingness of whites to move back into significantly different central city developments that reuse land abandoned through railroad consolidation and relocation, industrial exodus, and residential abandonment, something that may become increasingly attractive to the more affluent suburbanite if the energy crisis continues unchecked and if the combination of legislative and legal developments following the Housing Act of 1968 leads to further suburbanization of middle class blacks. Minority concentrations are building rapidly in Park Forest, Oak Park, and Evanston, the liberal suburbs with the most forthright fair housing programs; and in Park Forest South, the new town with federal bond guarantees. Yet in these suburbs the phenomenon of white flight is repeating itself and the question that emerges is whether this flight will result in further white expansion deeper into exurbia, or in a move back into the central city, producing thereby a reversal of trends and the further transformation of the metropolis led by Chicago 21. It may be that we are on the verge of yet another change in the nature of change —but one in which a rhythm repeats itself, for, chasing the leading edge of growth, Chicago's suburbanizing minorities will find that the will-o'-the-wisp is as elusive as ever.

Bibliography

Abbott, Edith. *The Tenements of Chicago, 1908-1935.* Chicago: University of Chicago Press, 1936.

Abrahamson, Julia. *A Neighborhood Finds Itself.* New York: Harper & Brothers, 1959.

Addams, Jane. *Twenty Years at Hull House.* New York: Macmillan, 1910.

Ade, George. *Chicago Stories.* Chicago: Henry Regnery Company, 1963.

Ahmed, G. Munir. *Manufacturing Structure and Patterns of Waukegan–North Chicago.* Research Paper no. 46. Chicago: University of Chicago Department of Geography, 1957.

Algren, Nelson. *Man With the Golden Arm.* Garden City, N.Y.: Doubleday, 1949.

Andreas, Alfred T. *History of Chicago.* 3 vols. Chicago: A.T. Andreas, 1884-86.

Andrews, Robert H. *A Corner of Chicago.* Chicago: Little, Brown, and Company, 1963.

Andrews, Wayne. *Battle for Chicago.* New York: Harcourt, Brace and Company, 1946.

Appleton, John B. *The Iron and Steel Industry of the Calumet District.* University of Illinois Studies in the Social Sciences, vol. 13, no. 2. Urbana; University of Illinois, 1925.

Archer, William. *America To-Day: Observations and Reflections.* New York: W. Heinemann, 1899.

Asbury, Herbert. *Gem of the Prairie.* Garden City, N.Y.: Garden City Publishing Co., Inc., 1942.

Atwood, Wallace W., and James Goldthwait. *Physical Geography of the Evanston-Waukegan Region.* Urbana: Illinois State Geological Survey, Bulletin no. 7, 1908.

Back, Ira J. *Chicago on Foot—An Architectural Walking Tour.* Chicago: Follett Publishing Company, 1969.

Banfield, Edward C. *Political Influence.* Glencoe: Free Press, 1961.

Bellow, Saul. *Adventures of Augie March.* New York: Viking Press, 1953.

Benton, Colbee C. *A Visitor to Chicago in Indian Days: Journey to the Far-Off West.* Edited by Paul M. Angle and James R. Getz. Chicago: Caxton Club, 1957.

Berry, Brian J.L. *Commercial Structure and Commercial Blight.* Research Paper no. 85. Chicago: University of Chicago Department of Geography, 1963.

Bishop, Glenn A., and Paul T. Gilbert. *Chicago's Accomplishments and Leaders.* Chicago: Bishop Publishing Company, 1932.

Breese, Gerald W. *The Daytime Population of the Central Business District of Chicago.* Chicago: University of Chicago Press, 1949.

Bretz, J. Harlen. *Geology of the Chicago Region.* Urbana: Illinois State Geological Survey, Bulletin no. 65, pt. I. Geology of the Chicago Region, 1939; pt. II, The Pleistocene, 1955.

Bryant, William Cullen. *Letters of a Traveller.* New York: G.P. Putnam, 1850.

Buckingham, J.H. *Illinois as Lincoln Knew It.* Edited by Harry E. Pratt. Springfield, Ill.: Illinois State Historical Society, 1938.

Buder, Stanley. *Pullman: An Experiment In Industrial Order and Community Planning 1880–1930.* New York: Oxford University Press, 1967.

Burnham, Daniel H., and Edward H. Bennett. *Plan of Chicago*. Chicago: The Commercial Club, 1909.

Burnham, Daniel H., Jr., and Robert Kingery, *Planning the Region of Chicago*. Chicago: Chicago Regional Planning Association, 1956.

Campbell, Edna Fay; Fanny R. Smith; and Clarence F. Jones. *Our City–Chicago*. New York: Charles Scribner's Sons, 1930.

Casey, Robert J. *Chicago Medium Rare*. Indianapolis: Bobbs-Merrill, 1952.

Casson, Herbert N. *Cyrus Hall McCormick*. Chicago: McClurg & Company, Chicago, 1909.

Chicago Area Transportation Study. *Final Report*. 3 vols. Chicago, 1959, 1960, and 1962.

Chicago Guide, eds. *The Chicago Guidebook*. Chicago: Henry Regnery Company, 1972.

Chicago Land Use Survey. Vol. I: *Residential Chicago*. Vol. II: *Land Use in Chicago*. Chicago: Chicago Plan Commission, 1942, 1943.

Chicago Plan Commission. *Forty-Four Cities in the City of Chicago*. Chicago, 1942.

——. *Master Plan of Residential Land Use of Chicago*. Chicago, 1943.

City of Chicago Department of Development and Planning. *The Comprehensive Plan of Chicago*. Chicago, 1966.

Condit, Carl W. *The Chicago School of Architecture: A History of Commercial and Public Building in the Chicago Area, 1875–1925*. Chicago: University of Chicago Press, 1964.

Cook, Frederick F. *Bygone Days in Chicago*. Chicago: A.C. McClurg & Co., 1910.

Cowles, Henry C. *The Plant Societies of Chicago and Vicinity*. Chicago: Geographic Society of Chicago. Bulletin no. 2, 1901.

Cox, Henry J., and John H. Armington. *The Weather and Climate of Chicago*. Chicago: Geographic Society of Chicago. Bulletin no. 4, 1914.

Cramer, Robert E. *Manufacturing Structure of the Cicero District, Metropolitan Chicago*. Research Paper no. 27. Chicago: University of Chicago Department of Geography, 1952.

Cressey, George B. *The Indiana Sand Dunes and Shore Lines of the Lake Michigan Basin*. Chicago: Geographic Society of Chicago, Bulletin no. 8, 1928.

Cromie, Robert. *The Great Chicago Fire*. New York: McGraw-Hill, 1958.

Cutler, Irving. *The Chicago Metropolitan Area: Selected Geographic Readings*. New York: Simon and Schuster, 1970.

——. *The Chicago-Milwaukee Corridor: A Geographic Study of Intermetropolitan Coalescence*. Northwestern University Studies in Geography no. 9. Evanston: Northwestern University Department of Geography, 1965.

Davis, James L. *The Elevated System and the Growth of Northern Chicago*. Northwestern University Studies in Geography no. 10. Evanston: Northwestern University Department of Geography, 1965.

De Beauvoir, Simone. *America Day by Day*. London: Grove Press, 1952.

Dedmon, Emmett. *Fabulous Chicago*. Chicago: Random House, 1953.

De Meirleir, Marcel J. *Manufactural Occupance in the West Central Area of Chicago*. Research Paper no. 11. Chicago: University of Chicago Department of Geography, 1950.

De Vise, Pierre. *Chicago's Widening Color Gap*. Chicago: Interuniversity Social Research Committee, 1967.

Draine, Edwin H. *Import Traffic of Chicago and Its Hinterland*. Research Paper no. 81. Chicago: University of Chicago Department of Geography, 1963.

Drake, St. Clair, and Horace R. Cayton. *Black Metropolis*. 2 vols. New York: Harcourt Brace Jovanovich, 1970.

Dreiser, Theodore. *Sister Carrie*. New York: Doubleday, Page & Co., 1900.

Drury, John. *Old Chicago Houses*. Chicago: University of Chicago Press, 1941.

Duddy, Edward A. *Agriculture in the Chicago Region*. Chicago: University of Chicago Press, 1929.

Duncan, Otis Dudley, and Beverly Duncan. *The Negro Population of Chicago: A Study of Residential Succession*. Chicago: University of Chicago Press, 1957.

Farrell, James T. *Studs Lonigan*. New York: Vanguard Press, 1935.

Federal Writers Project. *The Calumet Region Historical Guide*. Gary: Garman Printing Co., 1939.

——. *Illinois, A Descriptive and Historical Guide*, 2nd ed. Chicago: A.A. McClurg & Co., 1947.

Fehrenbacher, Don E. *Chicago Giant: A Biography of "Long John" Wentworth*. Madison, Wisc.: The American History Research Center, Inc., 1957.

Fellman, Jerome D. *Truck Transportation Patterns of Chicago*. Research Paper no. 12. Chicago: University of Chicago Department of Geography, 1950.

Ferber, Edna. *So Big*. Garden City, N.Y.: Doubleday, Page & Co., 1924.

Field, Eugene. *Sharps and Flats*. New York: C. Scribner's Sons, 1900.

Frazier, E. Franklin. *The Negro Family in Chicago*. Chicago: University of Chicago Press, 1932.

Fryxell, F.M. *The Physiography of the Region of Chicago*. Chicago: University of Chicago Press, 1927.

Gale, Edwin O. *Reminiscences of Early Chicago*. Chicago: F.H. Revell Company, 1902.

Gilbert, Paul, and Charles Lee Bryson. *Chicago and Its Makers*. Chicago: Felix Mendelsohn, 1929.

Goode, J. Paul. *The Geographic Background of Chicago*. Chicago: University of Chicago Press, 1926.

Graham, Jory, *Chicago—An Extraordinary Guide*. Chicago: Rand McNally & Company, 1968.

Hansberry, Lorraine. *Raisin in the Sun*. New York: Random House, 1959.

Hansen, Harry. *The Chicago*. Rivers of America Series. New York: Farrar & Rinehart, Inc., 1942.

———. *Midwest Portraits*. New York: Harcourt, Brace & Co., 1923.

Harper, Robert A. *Recreational Occupance of the Moraine Lake Region of Northeastern Illinois and Southeastern Wisconsin*. Research Paper no. 14. Chicago: University of Chicago Department of Geography, 1950.

Harris, Frank. *Bomb*. Chicago: University of Chicago Press, 1963.

Harrison, Carter. *Stormy Years*. Indianapolis: The Bobbs-Merrill Company, 1935.

Hayes, Dorsha. *Chicago, Crossroads of American Enterprise*. New York: J. Messner, 1944.

Hecht, Ben, and Charles MacArthur. *The Front Page*. New York: Covici-Friede, 1928.

Hecht, Ben. *Gaily, Gaily*. Garden City, N.Y.: Doubleday, 1963.

Helvig, Magne. *Chicago's External Truck Movements*. Research Paper no. 90. Chicago: University of Chicago Department of Geography, 1964.

Hillman, Arthur, and Robert J. Casey.

Tomorrow's Chicago. Chicago: University of Chicago Press, 1953.

Hoyt, Homer. *One Hundred Years of Land Values in Chicago, 1830–1933*. Chicago: University of Chicago Press, 1933.

Hutton, Graham. *Midwest at Noon*. Chicago: University of Chicago Press, 1946.

Jensen, George Peter. *Historic Chicago Sites*. Chicago: Creative Enterprises, 1953.

Johnson, Charles B. *Growth of Cook County*. Vol. I. Chicago: Board of Commissioners of Cook County, Illinois, 1960.

Karlen, Harvey. *The Governments of Chicago*. Chicago: Courier Publishing Company, 1958.

Keating, William H. *Narrative of an Expedition to the Source of St. Peter's River, 1823*. Philadelphia: Carey and Lee, 1824. Cited in B.L. Pierce, *As Others See Chicago*. Chicago: University of Chicago Press, 1933.

Kenyon, James B. *The Industrialization of the Skokie Area*. Research Paper no. 33. Chicago: University of Chicago Department of Geography, 1954.

Kiang, Ying Cheng. *Chicago*. Chicago: Adams Press, 1968.

Kinzie, Juliette A. *Wau-Bun*. Chicago: Rand McNally Company, 1901.

Kirkland, Joseph. *The Story of Chicago*. 3 vols. Chicago: Dibble Publishing Company, 1892–1894.

Kitagawa, Evelyn M., and Karl E. Taeuber. eds. *Local Community Fact Book: Chicago Metropolitan Area, 1960*. Chicago: Chicago Community Inventory, University of Chicago, 1963.

Klove, Robert C. *The Park Ridge–Barrington Area: A Study of Residential Land Patterns and Problems in Suburban Chicago*. Chicago: University of Chicago Department of Geography, 1942.

Knight, Robert, and Lucius H. Zeuch. *The Location of the Chicago Portage of the Seventeenth Century*. Chicago: University of Chicago Press, 1920.

Kogan, Herman, and Lloyd Wendt. *Chicago: A Pictorial History*. New York: Bonanza Books, 1958.

Kupcinet, Irv. *Kup's Chicago*. Cleveland: World Publishing Company, 1962.

Latrobe, Charles Joseph. *The Rambler in North America*. London: R.B. Seeley and W. Burnside, 1836.

Leech, Harper, and John Carroll. *Armour and His Times.* New York: D. Appleton-Century Co., 1938.

Levin, Meyer. *The Old Bunch.* New York: Viking Press, 1937.

———. *Compulsion.* New York: Simon and Schuster, 1956.

Lewis, Lloyd, and Henry Justin Smith. *Chicago, the History of Its Reputation.* New York: Harcourt, Brace and Company, 1929.

Liebling, Abbott J. *Chicago, the Second City.* New York: Knopf, 1952.

Lippincott, Sara Clarke. *New Life in New Lands.* New York: J.B. Ford and Co., 1873.

McManis, John T. *Ella Flagg Young and a Half-Century of the Chicago Public Schools.* Chicago: A.C. McClurg & Co., 1916.

Masters, Edgar Lee. *The Tale of Chicago.* New York: G.P. Putnam's Sons, 1933.

Mayer, Harold M. *Chicago: City of Decisions.* Papers on Chicago no. 1. Chicago: Geographic Society of Chicago, 1955.

Mayer, Harold M. *The Port of Chicago and the St. Lawrence Seaway.* Research Paper no. 49. Chicago: University of Chicago Press, 1957.

———. *The Railway Pattern of Metropolitan Chicago.* Chicago: University of Chicago Department of Geography, 1943.

Mayer, Harold M., and Richard C. Wade. *Chicago: Growth of a Metropolis.* Chicago: University of Chicago Press, 1969.

Meeker, Arthur. *Chicago With Love.* New York: Knopf, 1955.

Meeker, Arthur. *Prairie Avenue.* New York: A.A. Knopf, 1949.

Merriam, Charles Edward. *Chicago: A More Intimate View of Urban Politics.* New York: The Macmillan Company, 1929.

Meyerson, Martin, and Edward C. Banfield. *Politics, Planning, and the Public Interest.* Glencoe, Ill.: The Free Press, 1955.

Midwest Open Land Association. *Preservation of Open Space Areas.* Chicago, 1966.

Miller, John J. *Open Land in Metropolitan Chicago.* Chicago: Medwest Open Land Association, 1962.

Moody, Walter D. *Wacker's Manual of the Plan of Chicago.* Chicago: H.C. Sherman & Co., 1911.

Moore, Charles. *Daniel Burnham: Architect, Planner of Cities.* 2 vols. New York: Houghton Mifflin Company, 1921.

Morley, Christopher D. *Old Loopy; A Love Letter For Chicago.* Chicago: Argus Book Shop, Inc., 1937.

Motley, Willard. *Knock On Any Door.* New York: D. Appleton-Century Co., Inc., 1947.

Myrdal, Gunnar. *An American Dilemma.* New York: Harper and Brothers, 1944.

Norris, Frank. *The Pit.* New York: Doubleday, Page & Co., 1903.

Northeastern Illinois Metropolitan Area Local Governmental Services Commission. *Governmental Problems in the Chicago Metropolitan Area.* Leverett S. Lyon, ed. Chicago: University of Chicago Press, 1957.

Northeastern Illinois Planning Commission. *The Comprehensive Plan for the Development of the Northeastern Illinois Counties Area.* Chicago, 1968.

———.*Open Space in Northeastern Illinois.* Technical Report no. 2. Chicago, 1962.

———. *A Social Geography of Metropolitan Chicago.* Chicago, 1960.

———. *Suburban Factbook.* Chicago, 1971.

———.*Olcott's Blue Book of Land Values in Chicago and Environs.* Chicago; G.C. Olcott and Co., Inc., 1909.

Olson, Ernst W. *History of the Swedes of Illinois.* 2 vols. Chicago: The Engberg-Holmberg Publishing Company, 1908.

Petrakis, Harry Mark. *A Dream of Kings.* New York: D. McKay & Co., 1966.

———. *Pericles on 31st Street.* Chicago: Quadrangle Books, 1965.

Pierce, Bessie Louis. *As Others See Chicago —Impressions of Visitors, 1673-1933.* Chicago: University of Chicago Press, 1933.

———. *A History of Chicago.* 3 vols. New York: A.A. Knopf, 1937-57.

Platt, Rutherford H. *Open Land in Urban Illinois.* De Kalb: Northern Illinois University Press, 1971.

Poole, Ernest. *Giants Gone—Men Who Made Chicago.* New York: McGraw-Hill Book Company, Inc., 1943.

Port Chicago Poets. Chicago International Manuscripts, 1966.

Port, Weimar. *Chicago the Pagan.* Chicago: Judy Publishing Company, 1953.

Putnam, James Williams. *The Illinois and Michigan Canal: A Study in Economic History.* Chicago: University of Chicago Press, 1918.

Quaife, Milo M. *Checagou: From Indian Wigwam to Modern City, 1673-1835.* Chicago: University of Chicago Press, 1933.

————. *Chicago and the Old Northwest, 1673–1835*. Chicago: University of Chicago Press, 1913.

————. *Chicago's Highways Old and New: From Indian Trails to Motor Road*. Chicago: D.F. Keller & Company, 1923.

Randall, Frank A. *History of the Development of Building Construction in Chicago*. Urbana: University of Illinois Press, 1949.

Royko, Mike. *Boss: Richard J. Daley of Chicago*. New York: E.P. Dutton, Inc., 1971.

Salisbury, Rollin D., and William C. Alden. *The Geography of Chicago and Its Environs*. Chicago: Geographic Society of Chicago, Bulletin no. 1, 1899.

Sandburg, Carl. *The Complete Poems of Carl Sandburg*. Rev. and enl. ed. New York: Harcourt, Brace Jovanovich, Inc. 1970.

Schiavo, Giovanni. *The Italians in Chicago: A Study in Americanization*. Chicago: Italian American Publishing Company, 1928.

Sentinel Publishing Company. *The Sentinel's History of Chicago Jewry, 1911-1961*. Chicago, 1961.

Shackleton, Robert. *The Book of Chicago*. Philadelphia: The Penn Publishing Company, 1920.

Shelford, Victor E. *Animal Communities in Temperate America, as Illustrated in the Chicago Region; A Study in Animal Ecology*. Chicago: Geographic Society of Chicago, Bulletin no. 5, 1913.

Siegel, Arthur, ed. *Chicago's Famous Buildings*. Chicago: University of Chicago Press, 1965.

Sienkiewicz, Henry. *Portrait of America*. Edited by Charles Morley. New York: Columbia University Press, 1959.

Sinclair, Upton. *The Jungle*. New York: Doubleday, Page & Co., 1906.

Smith, Alston J. *Chicago's Left Bank*. Chicago: Henry Regnery Company, 1953.

Smith, Henry Justin. *Chicago, a Portrait*. New York: D. Appleton-Century Company, 1931.

————. *Chicago's Great Century, 1833-1933*. Chicago: Consolidated Publishers, 1933.

Solzman, David M. *Waterway Industrial Sites, A Chicago Case Study*. Research Paper no. 107. Chicago: University of Chicago Department of Geography, 1966.

Steevens, George W. *The Land of the Dollar*. Edinburgh: Dodd, Mead and Co., 1897.

Taaffe, Edward J. *The Air Passenger Hinterland of Chicago*. Research Paper no. 24. Chicago: University of Chicago Department of Geography, 1952.

Terkel, Louis [Studs]. *Division Street: America*. New York: Pantheon Books, 1967.

Thrasher, Frederic M. *The Gang*. Chicago: University of Chicago Press, 1927.

Townsend, Andrew J. "The Germans of Chicago." Ph. D. dissertation in History, University of Chicago, 1932.

Trollope, Anthony. *North America*. Philadelphia: J.B. Lippincott and Co., 1862.

University of Chicago Center for Urban Studies. *Mid-Chicago Economic Development Study*. 3 vols. Chicago: Mayor's Committee for Economic and Cultural Development, 1966.

Unonius, Gustaf. *A Pioneer in Northwest America, 1841-1858*. Edited by N.C. William Olsson. Minneapolis: University of Minnesota Press, 1950.

Wagenknecht, Edward. *Chicago*. Norman: University of Oklahoma Press, 1964.

Watson, John. *Souvenir of a Town in the United States of America and Canada*. Glasgow: Shirley and Harkness, 1872.

Webb, Sidney. In David A. Shannon, ed., *Beatrice Webb's American Diary, 1898*. Madison: University of Wisconsin Press, 1963.

Wendt, Lloyd, and Herman Kogan. *Give the Lady What She Wants!* Chicago: Rand McNally & Company, 1952.

————. *Lords of the Levee*. Indianapolis: Bobbs-Merrill Company, 1934.

Werner, Morris R. *Julius Rosenwald*. New York: Harper & Brothers, 1939.

Willman, H.B. *Summary of the Geology of the Chicago Area*. Urbana: Illinois State Geological Survey, Circular 460, 1971.

Wirth, Louis. *The Ghetto*. Chicago: University of Chicago Press, 1928.

Zorbaugh, Harvey W. *The Gold Coast and the Slum*. Chicago: University of Chicago Press, 1929.

Chapter Five

Metropolitan Detroit: An Anatomy of Social Change

Acknowledgements

Many persons have provided assistance in the preparation of this study. The authors have been dependent upon the willing help of individuals in many agencies, upon the secretarial efforts of a few stalwarts during the days of final preparation, and most particularly upon the field work and suggestions of a large number of Wayne geography students during the development of the work. In particular, the authors acknowledge the expertise and assistance of Helen Willis in the Oakland Township study, of David Hartman in the Cass Corridor study, and of Paul Travalini in various phases of the work. Cartographers Larry Banka, Nick Rea, and Steve Abbey provided not only their skills, but also creative suggestions when needed. The Northwest Detroit study is a modified version of an article by R. Sinclair in the *Wiener Geographische Schriften, Festschrift Leopold G. Scheidl,* vol. 2 (1975).

Introduction to the Detroit System

The sprawling Detroit metropolitan complex of 4.2 million people forms the nation's fifth largest urban agglomeration. The city of Detroit, with about a million and a half inhabitants, lies at the heart of the system. Over eighty independent incorporated political units surround the city, nine of them with populations approaching or exceeding 100,000 (Figure 1). Suburban expansion has been rapid during the last three decades, such that the suburban population surpassed that of Detroit during the fifties, and by 1970, within the Standard Metropolitan Statistical Area alone, was 1.8 times that of Detroit.

Growth in the region has fanned out northward away from the Detroit River "hinge line" in an ever widening radius that consumes increasing segments of southeastern Michigan. Much of the development has been along a flat glacial lake plain, with the landscape becoming more rolling in the morainic belt to the northwest. Superimposed over the landscape are wide arteries and expressways that appear to stretch endlessly in all directions. Single family homes on tree-lined streets typify most parts of the region.

Detroit is a workingman's town, dominated by the automobile industry. Historically, the industry has been influential in shaping the region's growth, as industrial development jumped ahead of the built-up area, and then pulled the edge of urbanization toward it. Visitors and newcomers quickly learn that Detroit is the heartland of the American labor movement, with union activities that have na-

tionwide repercussions. The presence of the auto industry permeates all facets of life in Detroit, whether it be driving along the Chrysler Freeway, listening to a concert in Ford Auditorium, watching the construction of the Walter P. Reuther Library on the Wayne State University campus, or supporting Detroit's professional basketball team, appropriately called the Pistons.

A sameness, monotony, and lack of sophistication pervades much of Detroit's life, suggesting that auto industry principles have spilled over into many walks of life. At the same time, Detroit projects a sense of power, a dynamism, and an ability to get things done, as was illustrated after Pearl Harbor when the auto industry rapidly adapted to become the main armament supplier for the national war effort.

Detroit is one of the nation's leading black cities, and much of the social change of the last two decades is the result of the rapid increase in the size of the black community. This accelerated growth was initiated by the war time and postwar industrial expansion of the 1940s, which in turn led to large scale immigration from the South. The presence, power, and influence of Detroit's black population helped elect Coleman Young, the city's first black mayor. Many of the country's black literary, artistic, and musical leaders either are based in Detroit or began careers there. A large proportion of the city's commercial establishments, places of entertainment, and recreational events cater to the black culture. However, the

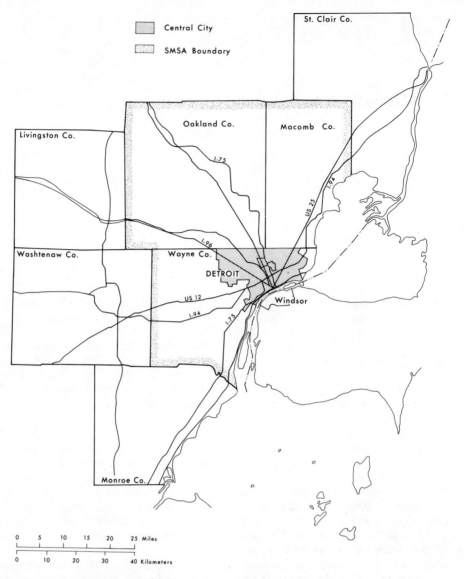

Figure 1. The Detroit Daily Urban System. All counties included send daily commuters to jobs in Detroit and Wayne County.

black presence in the central city contrasts markedly with its complete absence in most suburban communities.

Throughout its history Detroit has projected an image, a dream, a hope, and a promise to millions of unskilled workers. For many, those promises were fulfilled, the factories providing a springboard into the middle class for many of their children and grandchildren. For others the reality was disappointment, deprivation, conflict, and despair. The hopes and images are still alive today, but so are the tensions, fears, and struggles.

Detroit today projects a negative national image. Memories of the 1967 riot—the most severe and violent disturbance in recent American history—are still vivid. The city has recently achieved the dubious distinction of being the nation's homicide capital. Other alarming statistics stand out clearly—for example, fully one-quarter of the nation's abandoned HUD-owned homes are in Detroit. These images have some basis in fact. Crime and fear of crime are widespread. Protective devices, burglar alarm systems, "Beware of Dog" signs, and a swelling army of security guards have become an accepted aspect of the city's landscape. Urban decay is widespread. Many formerly prosperous commercial strips along major arteries now are characterized by vacant or boarded-up stores. Residential blight marks many neighborhoods.

The negative image, however, is misleading if applied indiscriminately. For the Detroit area also boasts attractive residential areas unsurpassed in the country. Throughout the suburban area are new and attractive shopping malls, with no apparent dearth of customers. The metropolitan area as a whole offers a wealth of outdoor recreational amenities, particularly for water-based activities. The central city itself has many quiet, tree-lined residential areas, viable ethnic communities, and highly reputed cultural and civic centers.

The Detroit area presents many faces. It is an urban region of sharp contrasts and extremes. Nevertheless, Detroit does epitomize the ills of American urban society in the mid-1970s and it might well be that our society's future depends upon how Detroit and cities like it approach, handle, and resolve what in many respects are similar problems.

This study is intended to capture the mood and the character of the metropolitan area; to complement, as well as to add to, the insights and descriptions obtained from an analysis of census data. Three themes are incorporated. The first portrays the metropolis as a mosaic of six contrasting social realms, highly interdependent but separated both by social distance and by different outlooks.

The second theme describes how the social realms of the Detroit system are engulfed by a series of external changes, including such forces as urban expansion, commercial and industrial relocation, urban renewal, expressway construction, and racial change. These forces of change and the instability they provide not only impinge upon the system, they have become an essential part of the system.

The third theme considers those forces at a more local level, recognizing that all parts of the Detroit system are not affected in the same way. This section examines, in specific areas, the chain of events set in motion by those forces and their effects both on the physical landscape and on people's lives. Three examples are chosen as representative of the important forces of change operating in different parts of the Detroit system. These are (1) an inner city community whose very survival is threatened by institutional growth, (2) a section of northwest Detroit undergoing racial change, and (3) an outlying semirural township threatened by urban sprawl.

In essence, the study is social in perspective. It analyzes the characteristics of and processes operating in basic segments of the Detroit area's social structure. It focuses upon the nature of several dominant forces of spatial change. Finally, it examines the landscape changes, and individual responses that occur as spatial change forces engulf selected parts of the system.

The Detroit System and its Regions

A SPATIAL MODEL OF THE DETROIT AREA

The Detroit system evolved as a complex mosaic of areas, each with distinctive social, economic, and physical characteristics. At first glance this mosaic appears to have little or no order or structure. What interrelationships may exist are obscured by the apparently chaotic assemblage of outlooks, lifestyles and social makeup. A spatial model is proposed to facilitate the conceptualization of the Detroit area and to provide a framework for analyzing the processes operating in the area (Figure 2).

The model divides the Detroit system into six zones. Economically, these six zones are interdependent and interacting, each performing a vital function in the total operation of the Detroit system's economy. For example, the assembly lines of the Suburban Area of Intersectoral Development are manned largely by workers from the Detroit Middle Zone. The administrative and financial offices of the Detroit Inner Zone are the work places of executives whose homes and social lives are to be found in the Suburban Area of Radial Development. Those same homes are cleaned and serviced by maids and cleaning personnel who reverse commute from Detroit's Inner and Middle Zones.

Ironically, the functional interdependence of the different zones exists alongside a condition of strict social segregation. For despite interdependent contractual relationships, residents of one zone have little social contact with those of other zones. The assembly workers who swarm to the automobile factories of the Suburban Area of Intersectoral Development return to the Detroit Middle Zone whenever the shift is over. They hardly understand, let alone participate in, the social life of their areas of employment. The women who provide maid services in the Suburban Area of Radial Development likewise return to the Detroit Inner and Middle Zones when their daily chores are performed. The executives who commute daily from this Radial Zone to the administrative offices of the Detroit Inner Zone are effectively screened from the realities of life in that zone.

The essential dichotomy between a functional and contractual interdependence of the different zones on the one hand, and a strict interzonal segregation and ignorance on the other, is an important theme of this chapter. The way in which this zonal pattern has evolved has been analyzed by Sinclair in *The Face of Detroit*. It is the concern of the present chapter to describe the zones themselves. Each zone is treated separately, starting with the Detroit Inner Zone and finishing with the Zone of Rural Change.

THE DETROIT INNER ZONE

The Inner Zone forms the hub of the Detroit system. It is a zone of contrasts, with powerful and sound business, commercial, and institutional interests juxtaposed with elements of

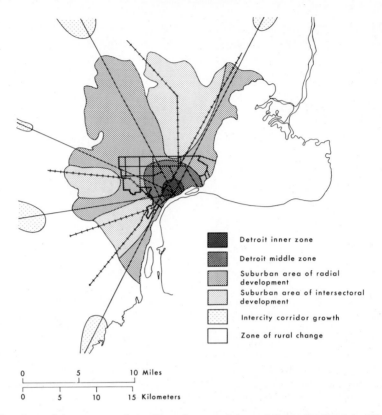

Detroit inner zone

Detroit middle zone

Suburban area of radial development

Suburban area of intersectoral development

Intercity corridor growth

Zone of rural change

Figure 2. The six activity zones of the Detroit area. Adapted from R. Sinclair, *The Face of Detroit.* (Detroit: Wayne State University-National Council for Geographic Education-U.S. Office of Education, 1970).

society that are unwanted, discarded, or simply left behind in the wake of rapid change. The overwhelming visual impressions are those of a central business district that is not what it used to be, of large and expanding public institutions, of submerged expressways that carve the area into small parcels, of decay and poverty, of vast wasteland tracts where homes once stood, and of piecemeal residential development that has sprung up in the wake of urban renewal. Feelings in the zone are highly divergent. On the one hand are the poor—suspicious, angry, frustrated, and relatively powerless as they witness their communities decay or being bulldozed out of existence. At the other extreme are those whose hope is for revitalization, in which a new commercial, business, and institutional complex will attract a middle and upper class clientele back into the city core.

Extending about three to four miles in all directions from the downtown business cen-

ter, the Inner Zone occupies a relatively small area of the Detroit metropolitan complex (Figure 2). The zone is bounded by the Detroit River to the south and Grand Boulevard on all sides. It is crisscrossed and carved up by a network of arterials and expressways, of which Woodward Avenue, running northwest from downtown, is the main arterial street.

As the original nucleus of the Detroit region, the Inner Zone has changed with every development in the area's long history, from a Great Lakes trading center centering around Fort Pontchartrain, to a commercial center serving an expanding frontier, to a thriving manufacturing area, to the business district and central core of a great American metropolis. These changes were accompanied by dramatic advances in transportation as Detroit changed from a walking city, to a horse and buggy city, to an electric railroad and horse-drawn streetcar city, to an electric streetcar city, and finally to an automobile city.

Each of those eras has left its mark upon the housing stock of the inner city. Large old mansions are found in certain sections, the legacy of the upper class of the late nineteenth century. More modest single and two family frame houses of the same general period are concentrated near the industrial areas along the railroads. Apartment hotels, scattered among single family residential areas, reflect the surge of population in the early twentieth century. At that time crowding became more common, poor quality housing was built along alleys, and single family housing was turned into multiple unit housing. By the first decade of this century, the inner city was built up, and since then housing has been noted for its succession of occupants rather than for new developments. New construction had to await the urban renewal programs of the last two decades.

The Inner Zone served as port of entry for the thousands of unskilled workers who flocked to Detroit during the first three decades of the twentieth century. As has been traditional in most American cities, these immigrants grouped together in enclaves surrounding the central business area. Virtually every one of Detroit's major ethnic groups had its original nucleus in the Inner Zone. Germans, Italians, Jews, and blacks were at some time in their settlement history concentrated in the near east side. Poles settled north of Gratiot on the east side and near the Michigan-Junction intersection on the west side. The Irish concentrated immediately west of downtown in the area known as Corktown. These ethnic colonies have long since left the inner city, expanding in a sectoral pattern into the Detroit Middle Zone and beyond. However, some residual evidence permits the reconstruction of the social history of early reception zones. In the former Germantown, for example, names and dates can still be seen on old buildings, Stroh's Brewery has remained and expanded, restaurants like Joe Muer's and Schweizer's still are culinary landmarks, and St. Joseph's Roman Catholic Church at Jay and Orleans streets is a silent sentinel of a nostalgic past.

The economic boom of World War II and the postwar period subjected the Inner Zone to pressures similar to those of the past. Southern whites and blacks, and several new minority groups, with aspirations similar to the groups which preceded them, surged to the Inner Zone to take the place of those who had migrated to other zones. These postwar immigrants remain as the most important residents of the Inner Zone.

The Inner Zone today is an area of contrast and extremes. A declining central business district, virtually cut off from surrounding areas by encircling expressways, remains the pivotal point. By day the downtown area bustles as white collar professionals from widely separated parts of the metropolitan area carry on their business activities. By early evening downtown becomes desolate as lawyers, office workers, and city employees return to outlying suburbs along arterial and expressway systems that literally dismember the Inner Zone. Retail stores in the central business district increasingly are being shunned, particularly by a middle class which resents the inconveniences of downtown shopping and now prefers outlying shopping malls. Nightlife is a shadow of its former self. Many movie theaters have closed, restaurants close earlier, and a walk along Woodward Avenue at 10:00 P.M. often can be an eerie, lonesome experience. A single bright and refreshing exception—Greektown—tends to accentuate the emptiness of the balance of the downtown area.

Four miles to the north is a second downtown, the New Center area, housing the world headquarters of General Motors Corporation, the world headquarters of Burroughs Corporation, and numerous other business and professional offices. The New Center likewise bustles with activity by day, but becomes empty by early evening.

A striking concentration of public institutions is found in the Inner Zone, particularly an expanding institutional complex that straddles Woodward Avenue and virtually links downtown with the New Center area. The Medical Center, immediately east of Woodward, is fast becoming one of the world's largest medical complexes, incorporating hospitals, nursing homes, professional plazas, and the Wayne State University Medical School. Immediately to the north is the Cultural Center with the International Institute, the Rackham Memorial Building, the Detroit Institute of Arts, and the Detroit Public Library. Adjacent to the Cultural Center are Wayne State University and the Merrill-Palmer Institute. Within this corridor are found the Detroit area's major theaters for the performing arts,

including the Ford Auditorium, the Masonic
Temple, the Fisher Theater, and Wayne State
University's Hilberry and Bonstelle theaters.
Within the Inner Zone are sports stadia including Cobo Arena, Tiger Stadium, and Olympia,
providing facilities for major league basketball,
baseball, and hockey.

The recent expansion of many of these institutions has been made possible by urban
renewal legislation. Urban renewal is also responsible for other developments. Immediately east of downtown, an extensive high- and
low-rise middle and upper income residential
development has arisen on what was Black Bottom, once the heart of the Black Ghetto. To
the west of downtown, an industrial park has
decimated and replaced the Corktown community.

This institutional landscape exists alongside another kind of landscape. It is a ravaged
landscape, characterized by blight, by empty
wastelands surrounded by white fences (the
Detroit stamp of urban renewal), by overgrown,
glass-littered playgrounds, and by residential
pockets cut off from each other by broad expressways and urban renewal "overkill." Beer
cans, trash, weeds, and broken glass comprise
much of the surface material. Stores in what
once were prosperous commercial strips are
vacant or abandoned, as are numerous industrial and office buildings. Those few stores
that remain invariably are screened by protective devices, command high prices, and
generally provide inferior goods and services.
Industry remaining in the zone faces problems of vandalism in aging structures no longer
suited to modern production methods. The
only services that appear to be thriving are
Salvation Army missions, soup kitchens, and
other social and welfare services.

The Inner Zone has both a resident population and a visitor population. The latter has no
permanent locational commitment to the zone
but comes into the zone to work, to see the
Detroit Tigers or the Red Wings, to watch a
Broadway play at the Fisher Theater, or to
partake of the "blue entertainment" readily
available in the area.

The resident population is quite different.
Essentially, the Inner Zone is the domain of
the poor and the downtrodden, those who are
"rejected," "forgotten," or "left behind" by
other elements of Detroit society. More than 25
percent of the zone's 37,000 families subsist on

incomes below the poverty level. A large proportion of the population is on welfare. Even in
1972, a relatively prosperous year, the unemployment rate for the employable population
in Detroit's Model Neighborhood, located in
the Inner Zone, was 16 percent, and almost
40 percent for eighteen to twenty-four year
old heads of households. Large numbers of people are old, single, and immobile. About half
the respondents in the Model Neighborhood
area have no access to a car. Skid row and its
accompanying institutions also are found here,
often intermingling with and imposing themselves upon adjacent residential areas.

Of the thriving ethnic groups that were present at the turn of the century, only the Poles
and the blacks remain in any great numbers,
and the continued presence of a vital Polish
community is an uncertain prospect. Several
other ethnic groups have found a niche in the
zone in more recent times. A large Mexican-
American community is located along West
Vernor and Bagley streets, and a small but
highly nucleated Maltese community resides
near Tiger Stadium. Other recent settlement has
included American Indians, Appalachian
whites, Indians, and Pakistanis.

The lifestyle of the poor in the Inner Zone is
simple, and highly circumscribed. For most it
is concerned with solving day-to-day problems.
For some it is an acute struggle for survival. In
some residential districts family life is strong,
and there is some neighborhood identity in
spite of conditions of severe poverty. For single
individuals and old persons living in apartments,
life tends to be a lonely and dull routine. For
the skid row alcoholic, life conforms to the
stereotyped pattern of day-to-day survival.
For all elements, life is highly localized. Social
activity is limited to the immediate blocks, the
corner store, the bar, and in some communities
the church. This lifestyle does not incorporate
the nearby cultural and institutional amenities
of the Inner Zone. It is not the typical Inner
City resident who frequents the Detroit Institute of Arts, who attends the symphony concerts in Ford Auditorium, who watches sports
events in Cobo Hall, and whose children are
students at Wayne State University.

Quite a different lifestyle exists in the few
middle and upper income enclaves in the Inner
Zone, such as Indian Village or the East Lafayette area. From one viewpoint life in those
enclaves is restricted and cut off from the im-

mediate environs. Yet in other ways it is free-wheeling and highly mobile. Shopping trips are made to suburban malls, friends are scattered throughout the suburbs, recreational activities might range from frequent trips to northern Michigan to less frequent journeys that are worldwide in scope.

As it has been throughout its long and dynamic history, the Inner Zone today is subjected to sweeping forces of change. Often these forces appear to oppose and contradict one another. For example, renewal has been a dominant force, as federal urban renewal projects developed some areas and private and public institutions expanded into others. At the same time, blight encompasses ever larger areas as properties decay and services deteriorate. There is some degree of relationship between those apparently contradictory forces. Many persons displaced by construction projects, unable or unwilling to move to other parts of the metropolitan area, have crowded into adjacent residential blocks causing a more rapid rate of deterioration there. An example is the migration of skid row residents and transients from their demolished Michigan Avenue area into the Woodward, Cass, and Second Avenue districts north of the central business district. Moreover, the climate of uncertainty connected with institutional expansion has lowered the incentive for property maintenance in adjacent areas.

A second apparent contradiction is the attempt, on the one hand, to bring jobs and middle and upper income residents back to the inner city while, on the other hand, businesses and jobs are departing from the area. The much discussed riverside Renaissance Center, it is hoped, will start a trend bringing businesses, people, and life back into the downtown area. As the project was being discussed and built, the headquarters of the Kresge Corporation left its Cass Park location for suburban Troy, the Michigan Automobile Association left downtown Detroit for a new location in Dearborn, and even the *Detroit News* moved many of its main operations to Sterling Heights.

A third contradiction is that developments expected to benefit the inner city and its residents are increasingly resented and opposed by those same residents. The contradiction undoubtedly stems from the history of past renewal and redevelopment which has favored commercial, industrial, institutional, and mid-dle class interests, and tended to ignore or misunderstand the plight of local residents. The result has been a climate of suspicion and resentment surrounding virtually every institutional construction project. Unfortunately that climate remains today, at a time when official attitudes toward renewal have changed greatly and developments are subject to and dependent upon local and resident control. Often the eventual result is that vast tracts of land remain idle, and new construction is stymied as local interests and development interests seek to come to terms.

Perhaps these contradictions epitomize the Inner Zone today and explain its divergent outlooks toward the future. One outlook is that of rejuvenation and revitalization, with the premise that a new commercial-institutional-residential complex will lure business back to the Inner Zone and restore its former role as the exciting hub of the metropolitan area. The other outlook is quite different. It sees the Inner Zone as the home of thousands of families and individuals who do not have the wealth, mobility, or desire to live elsewhere. For them rejuvenation is a threat, and every incoming institution becomes a potential displacement of their homes and their community life. There would seem to be no real reason why those two divergent outlooks cannot be accommodated to create a mixed and healthy environment for all who wish to live and work in the Inner Zone. Today that accommodation appears to be hindered by a legacy of suspicion and frustration derived from the past. Meanwhile much of the Inner Zone remains in a state of limbo between what was a viable and exciting past and a somewhat vague, uncertain future.

THE DETROIT MIDDLE ZONE

The Middle Zone comprises the largest part of the city of Detroit. The zone provides much of the unskilled and semiskilled factory working force upon which the automobile industry, in the suburbs as well as in the city, depends. It has become the home of Detroit's black population. The zone has been virtually transformed by recent social change. The spread of blight and neighborhood instability associated with this change is well advanced in large areas. Whether these processes continue or can be checked might well be the key to Detroit's future.

Throughout much of the zone, the initial visual impression is one of solid single family residential neighborhoods, typified by attractive tree-lined streets. Some of these neighborhoods, particularly on the east side, are inhabited by first and second generation Eastern European immigrants and have remained stable for decades. Others have become the reception zones for new immigrants from the Middle East and the Balkans. The most typical, however, are neighborhoods which only recently have become black, or which currently are undergoing racial transition. Thus, throughout much of the zone, "for sale" signs abound on front lawns, confrontations occur in the schools, and harassment of black newcomers in white areas and of the remaining whites in black areas often occurs. This social turbulence is the breeding ground for much of Detroit's physical decay and also for its reputation for violent crime.

The Middle Zone surrounds the Inner Zone in a three mile wide semicircular belt which encompasses most of the city of Detroit (Figure 2). Only the northwest and extreme northeast sections of the city are excluded. The political enclaves of Hamtramck and Highland Park are integral parts of the zone. The zone was built during Detroit's dynamic growth period between 1900 and the early 1930s. Development typically followed the pattern of the automobile industry, which first concentrated along the New York Central, Grand Trunk, and Detroit Terminal railroads that surrounded and penetrated the central parts of the city, and later jumped to the "outlying suburbs" of Highland Park, Hamtramck, and East Dearborn. Residential districts filled in the intervening areas, while the city's commercial structure was laid out on major streets, most notably along the radial arteries (Jefferson, Gratiot, Woodward, Grand River, Michigan, and Fort) that fanned out from the inner city. To a large degree the Middle Zone, along with the Inner Zone, was the Detroit system of the pre–World War II years.

Residential growth of the Middle Zone was differentiated along ethnic and class lines. Large scale immigration led to an extension of the ethnic pattern that had been established earlier in the Inner Zone (Figure 3). Thus, prior to World War II, stable residential patterns existed.

The largest ethnic settlements were Polish, one centered in Hamtramck, the other near Michigan Avenue and Junction in West Detroit. The Italian settlement had moved northeast along Gratiot Avenue. The center of Hungarian settlement was in Delray, a heavy industrial area in southwest Detroit. English, Scots, and Jews were heavily concentrated in the northwest between Woodward and Grand River avenues. The German community, though more dispersed, had moved to the northeast along Gratiot and Harper. The black community was still confined to a narrow corridor east of Woodward Avenue.

World War II and its aftermath inaugurated a transformation of the Middle Zone that in a sense has continued to the present. Two interconnected processes were involved. One was the massive immigration of blacks, whose percentage of Detroit's total population changed from 9.3 in 1940 to 44.5 in 1970. The other was the movement to the suburbs—particularly of middle or upper income white families with school children. The fact that overall suburban movement exceeded that of the black immigration has had significant consequences for the Middle Zone. First, it has meant an overall decrease in the city's population from about 1,850,000 in the 1950s to 1,511,482 in 1970. Second, it has meant that residential areas were opened up more rapidly, so that racial transition has been more rapid and more widespread than in most other cities in the country. However, the pattern of growth of the black community has not been uniform throughout the Middle Zone. In some areas, particularly on the east side, Southern and Eastern European ethnic groups, with a strong attachment to the neighborhood, the parish, the church, and the parochial school, have remained and the black community has surrounded rather than displaced them. By contrast in the northwest side, where the English, Scottish, and Jewish populations were more mobile, racial transition has been much more rapid. Most recently, as if to emphasize that residential patterns are not that simplistic, the Inner Zone has become the initial settlement area for several new immigrant groups, particularly Albanians, Yemenis, and Iraqis.

The changes of the last two decades have had a disastrous effect upon the Middle Zone's commercial structure. The prosperous radial commercial arteries and the thriving outlying

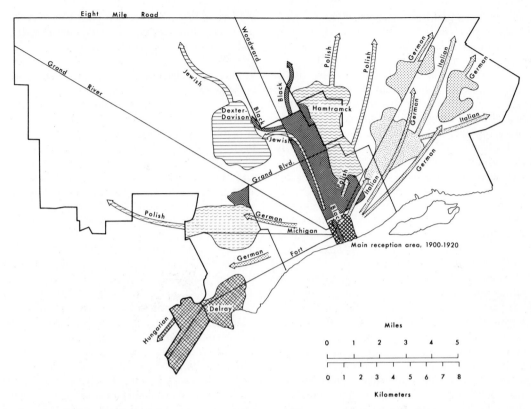

Figure 3. Detroit's ethnic communities in 1950, and major migration paths, 1900-1950.

business districts that typified Detroit's prewar and war time commercial structure have well nigh been obliterated, victims of the changing economic structure of nearby neighborhoods and the competition of suburban shopping malls. A drive along commercial arteries like Grand River and Gratiot reveals an almost uninterrupted sequence of empty stores, broken glass, boarded-up store fronts, and temporary if any occupance. Remaining businesses tend to reflect the changing socioeconomic and racial character of nearby areas. Thus, in the inner parts of the zone, stores serve a black clientele and include a high proportion of record shops, wig stores, storefront churches, barbecue restaurants, hair stylists, and party stores. Farther out businesses tend to be transitional, with large numbers of automobile showrooms, service stations, loan company offices, and real estate offices.

The industrial districts of the Middle Zone, which comprised a major part of the prewar automobile industry, have long since lost that role to the industrial corridors of the Suburban

Area of Intersectoral Development. Some districts have shells of buildings and unused facilities. Many industries that do remain occupy congested sites and structures ill-suited to modern production methods. However, several major automobile plants have remained in the Middle Zone. Dodge Main in Hamtramck, the Chrysler plant on East Jefferson, the Ford plant in Highland Park, and the Cadillac plant on Michigan Avenue are still significant units in the American automobile industry. At the same time, they employ only a part of the unskilled and semiskilled labor force of the Middle Zone. The remaining part commutes daily to the more important manufacturing employment centers in the Suburban Intersectoral Zone.

The Middle Zone houses a population that includes both middle and lower middle income blue collar and white collar workers. This population mans the assembly lines of local and suburban automobile factories, provides the civil servants for federal and local government offices, does secretarial work in downtown and local offices, performs personal services, and is engaged in social work and local teaching. Distinct differences exist between the typical black and white member of the Middle Zone. The black middle class Detroiter typically is young, married, with children and a working wife. Family income is slightly higher than the Detroit city average. His white counterpart is older, no longer has children living at home, and often is of East European descent. His family income is slightly below the average for the city. In Hamtramck, for example, 50 percent of the 1970 population was designated as foreign stock, compared to 22 percent for Detroit. Twenty-one percent of Hamtramck's population was over sixty years old, compared with 16.2 percent for the city of Detroit, and 11.9 for the metropolitan area.

These differences between the black and white populations show up in their respective life patterns. In some older white ethnic neighborhoods, life still has an old world flavor, and is slow-moving, nostalgic, and church- and community-oriented. Local markets, bakeries, ethnic food stores, bars, restaurants, and churches serve important social functions for the community and provide an important link with the past for former residents, long since moved to the suburbs, who visit the communities in which they were raised and where they still have relatives and fond memories. But there is abundant evidence that this lifestyle is on an almost inevitable decline. Even the main commercial street of Hamtramck, Joseph Campau, exhibits all the indexes of commercial blight. The extreme of decay has been reached in the Hungarian community of Delray, where deterioration is reminiscent of the worst aspects of the Detroit Inner Zone.

Life in the black community must be considered on a different scale. The Middle Zone is the source of cultural, political, and economic strength for one of the nation's leading black cities. The community has accomplished much in the last decade. Detroit's first black mayor was elected in 1973. A young generation of leaders is emerging as blacks occupy more influential positions in the city's political, economic, and cultural life. The contribution of Detroit blacks to the nation's cultural life is well known. The literature, art, theater, and music emanating from black Detroit has had a wide impact. The Motown sound remains a Detroit sound even though the company of that name has moved to the West Coast. Much of black Detroit is young, energetic, colorful, and fashionable. The church also is strong, and from its ranks have come local leaders like Reverend Nicholas Hood and Reverend Albert Cleage.

But Detroit's black community still has many long term problems. It incorporates an area that is characterized by spreading physical blight in a city plagued by deep and continuing financial difficulties. It has an unemployment rate that is higher than the metropolitan average. There is tension and mistrust between blacks and the Detroit Police Department. Discriminatory housing practices still exclude blacks from most suburbs. Increasing power at the local level means little when it can be stymied by actions at the state level. A lifestyle of increasing affluence can be frustrating if restrictions and embarrassments occur when traveling or pursuing recreational activities. To a much greater degree than their white suburban counterparts, the life patterns of middle and upper income blacks are concentrated within the limits of the Inner and Middle zones.

The Middle Zone today is subjected to forces of change which probably are more pronounced, dramatic, and visible than in any other zone. Most apparent is racial change. The zone has been a veritable case study of racial transition, with 7,000 to 9,000 housing units changing from white to black occupancy every year since 1950. The transition has been typified by contiguous "ghetto" expansion, with many of the associated symbols like rumor spreading, block-busting, panic selling, and nefarious real estate practices. Tensions have been high in areas undergoing racial change, as has been uncertainty in areas in the path of racial change. Periodically those tensions have given rise to harassment of individuals and hostilities in schools. The instability associated with the racial change process has made many attempts at neighborhood improvement quite futile, and has dashed most hopes for stable integrated communities.

Closely associated with rapid social change is an apparently relentless spread of blight. Flight of previous homeowners, postponement of upkeep investment in the face of uncertainty, deterioration during the turnover process, influx of persons with more limited means, and an overall decline in essential city services due to Detroit's declining tax base, have all played a part, as have the "spillover" effects of the deteriorating commercial structure. The continued spread of blight probably is the main overall problem in the Middle Zone, and the dominant concern of the numerous neighborhood citizen's councils that recently have formed.

One contributor to the spread of blight has come to be known as the "HUD House Fiasco." The foreclosure rate on FHA-insured mortgages in Detroit has been so great that the Department of Housing and Urban Development faces a management problem that is gargantuan in scope. Estimates from official sources of the number of HUD-owned homes in Detroit vary greatly; however, the figure probably is between fifteen and twenty thousand, or approximately 25 percent of all HUD-owned properties in the country. Most homes are either vacant or abandoned. The repair, upkeep, management, and marketing of these houses has been marked by bureaucratic inefficiency, individual corruption, and general scandal of outstanding dimensions. The physical result is that the Middle Zone is pockmarked with vacant houses, some broken down and vandalized, some falling into disrepair, some subject to rehabilitation, but all having a further blighting effect upon neighboring properties and streets.

Among the other problems of the Middle Zone is a school system that has declined in quality, that is in almost constant uncertainty concerning the adequacy of funds, and that has an increasingly bad public image. This image probably is one of the main reasons for the rapidity of suburban migration out of the zone. The school system also suffers from the rapid social upheavals that have taken place in the Middle Zone. There are some school districts where facilities are not fully utilized due to declining enrollments, many more where facilities are quite unable to handle the burgeoning influx of new pupils, some with virtually all black enrollments in racially mixed neighborhoods, and many which have become the scene for racial confrontation.

Lastly, of all the processes affecting the Middle Zone, probably the most publicized is the presence of violent crime. The Middle Zone contributes greatly to the city of Detroit's reputation as the nation's homicide capital. The high incidence of violent crime is related integrally to the tensions and frustrations created by social upheaval, but also is linked to Detroit's drug traffic and to an exceedingly high handgun ownership. Though probably not as great as the national image might imply, crime and the fear of crime have a strong influence on the life of the Middle Zone, as is visibly evident in the swelling number of protective devices and socially evident in the tendency to avoid going out in the evening hours.

In introducing the Middle Zone, it was suggested that what happens there might be the key to Detroit's future. That suggestion might well be extended to say that what happens in the Middle Zone is the key to the future of urban America. Looking at the Middle Zone in the summer of 1974, that future does not look promising. The forces described here—namely, the outward movement of long term residents, racial transition and its attendant instability, spread of blight, increase of crime, and a decline in the quality of schools and other social services—appear to be dominant. Furthermore, although the processes have been described as if they were independent entities, they comprise an interrelated whole of great complexity. That very complexity tends to point up the scarcity of know-how and means to counteract the processes. Federal, state, and city funds are tied to limited programs that hardly approach the real and complex causes of the problems.

Perhaps one source of optimism is the widespread recognition that the problems exist. Federal (the Department of Housing and Urban Development), state (the Michigan State Housing Development Authority) and city (the Community Development Commission) departments are deeply involved in analyzing the problems. More significantly, the Middle Zone virtually has come alive with a plethora of organizations whose main concern is to attempt to stabilize their community. Thus far these developments largely represent a recognition of the problems rather than a framework for the solution of the problems. For a large part of the Middle Zone, such recognition has come too late. For the remainder, the future remains in doubt.

In assessing that future, the positive elements described in this section cannot be ignored. They include a legacy of solid, attractive, tree-lined residential areas; the vitality of an energetic, confident black community; and the presence of traditional ethnic neighborhoods. If neighborhoods are to be stabilized, and if the Middle Zone is not to become the deteriorated

Inner Zone of the next decade, then the positive elements must be maintained and given support to check the destructive forces of change.

SUBURBAN AREA OF RADIAL DEVELOPMENT

The Suburban Area of Radial Development houses the dominant decisionmaking forces of the Detroit system. A blend of specific leadership activities and characteristic residence types has given this zone a role which in former times, and even today in certain parts of the world, was considered the prerogative of the central city. This blend also has created a lifestyle and outlook that contrasts markedly with those of other zones of the Detroit system.

The Radial Development Zone comprises a series of suburban sectors extending outward from the city of Detroit to the northeast, northwest, east, and south (Figure 2). By far the largest is to the northwest, encompassing much of southern Oakland County, and neatly dissecting the vast, semicircular area of suburban Detroit. Other sectors include a narrow finger of suburban growth along Lake St. Clair toward Mt. Clemens in the northeast, an interrupted corridor extending from West Dearborn to Ypsilanti and Ann Arbor in the west, and a small group of suburbs on the Detroit River to the south.

The spatial development of the zone within the Detroit system can be explained by a simple growth model. First, the nuclei of growth were early suburbs, such as Royal Oak, Birmingham, and Grosse Pointe, that grew along the series of radial arteries extending outward from the city of Detroit. These included a few elite residential suburbs attracted to physical amenities such as Lake St. Clair to the east, Grosse Isle on the Detroit River to the south, and the northeast-southwest belt of lake-filled morainic hills to the northwest. Second, these suburbs were consolidated, extended, and widened during the surge of suburban expansion following World War II that has continued to the present. In the Radial Zone the surge largely reflected the movement of higher income professional and white collar workers attracted by the prestige and amenities of well-established communities. Third, this movement in turn attracted high class shopping centers, professional and

business offices, research centers, and educational institutions. Fourth, continued growth was ensured by the construction of the Detroit area's main expressways. Finally, the zone developed gradually into what it is today —namely, a balanced pattern of upper and middle income residential areas; relatively adequate services and amenities to serve those areas; an excellent expressway network; and the majority of the important service, professional, and leadership activities of the Detroit metropolitan system. The zone has received virtually none of the postwar heavy industrial growth of that system.

During all these growth stages, the particular significance of this Oakland County sector has been reinforced. This sector is in the northwest, Detroit's traditional direction of expansion. It straddles Woodward Avenue, the spine of the Detroit system, as well as the important Grand River artery. The area between these two radial arteries is unique in the Detroit area because no railroad or industrial corridor has preempted and determined its land use and landscape. This has permitted the coalescence of the residential, business, and professional activities of the two arteries. The resulting sector is the largest and most characteristic sector of the Radial Zone.

The high socioeconomic status of the zone is suggested in most indexes of social and economic conditions. Residents of the zone are predominantly white, are wealthier, have more formal education, occupy more expensive and better quality homes, are more mobile, and are more likely to be in executive, professional, and service occupations than the residents in any other part of the Detroit system. If those indexes were mapped, statistics would tend to peak in certain communities, most significantly in Birmingham and Bloomfield Hills in the northwest sector, but also in the Grosse Pointes in the northeast sector, Grosse Isle in the downriver sector, and in West Dearborn and Ann Arbor Township in the western sector. A striking indication of the zone's socioeconomic character is the fact that Oakland County, encompassing the zone's important northwest sector, was the county with the nation's highest average household-effective buying income in 1974.

The overall high socioeconomic status does not mean that the Area of Radial Development is a zone of uniformity. Indeed, a visitor would be struck by the zone's diversity. The flat lake plain terrain of Dearborn or Grosse Pointe contrasts markedly with the rolling, hilly landscape of Bloomfield Hills and Franklin Village. Older deteriorating housing in certain parts of Ferndale and Hazel Park is a striking counterpart to newly built housing in Rochester and Bloomfield Hills. The decidedly urban suburbs of Royal Oak and Ferndale have a quite different character from semirural Avon and Oakland townships. The predominantly Jewish ethnic makeup of suburbs like Oak Park and Southfield differs from the largely Protestant-Catholic composition of the majority of other suburbs. Most noticeably, relatively calm residential communities like Bloomfield Hills, Grosse Pointe, and Grosse Isle stand in direct contrast to bustling, congested commercial centers like Southfield and Troy. In sum, no obvious, tangible uniformity distinguishes this from other zones of the Detroit system. Rather, the key to understanding the Radial Zone is to be found in a certain similarity and/or complementarity of interests, viewpoints, perceptions, and lifestyles.

One important contributor to this similarity is a distinctive group of occupational roles. More so than in any other zone, persons in the Suburban Area of Radial Development are engaged either in administrative, executive, professional, and other leadership occupations or in services catering to those leadership occupations. Moreover, although these pursuits might appear to be diverse, they find a point of identity in their common association with the automobile industry. This association is most direct in the case of those working in administrative and technical offices of General Motors, Ford, and Chrysler. The tie is almost as close in the case of executives and white collar workers in companies involved with industrial design, advertising, public relations, systems analysis, finance, and communications. Finally, the association is found in the case of those engaged in the professions and in a wide variety of other services. The nature of those many occupational pursuits, focusing upon and dependent upon the automobile industry, has led to a professional interaction, a general understanding, and an identity of interests that are distinctive attributes of the Radial Zone.

Another contributor to the zone's identity is a self-contained set of residential, service,

and recreational amenities that are at once distinctive and also enable the zone's residents to be relatively independent of the remainder of the metropolitan system. The zone is well served by shopping centers, from the larger, more urbane Northland, Oakland, and Ann Arbor malls, to the more specialized and sophisticated Grosse Pointe Village, Somerset Mall, and downtown Birmingham. The zone contains excellent public schools, as well as such distinguished private institutions as Cranbrook, Detroit Country Day, and University Liggett. The zone's college population is served by the University of Michigan in Ann Arbor, Michigan State University in East Lansing, and Eastern Michigan University in Ypsilanti, as well as the zone's own Oakland University. Health and professional services are superior to those in other zones of the metropolitan system. The zone is studded with cultural centers like Cranbrook, Meadowbrook, Greenfield Village, Ann Arbor's Rackham Auditorium, and the Grosse Pointe War Memorial. Finally, the zone has a wide variety of amenities—from yacht clubs and golf clubs to theaters and fine restaurants—that more than cater to the zone's recreational needs. Thus, residents seldom have to look elsewhere in the metropolitan system for the general amenities of life. The executive and his white collar employee might commute to other parts of the system five times per week, but they tend to return and spend their nonworking time within their own zone. Events of the Detroit Symphony, the Detroit Institute of Arts, and the Fisher Theater in Detroit might be well and faithfully attended, but preperformance cocktails and after theater snacks normally are consumed in places like West Dearborn, Grosse Pointe, and Bloomfield Hills. When interests and amenities are sought outside the Radial Zone, they are more often found well beyond the Detroit metropolitan area than elsewhere within the metropolitan area.

These amenities of the Radial Zone have helped to promote a general commonality of lifestyle. Many aspects of that lifestyle differ little in different parts of the zone. A similarity of attitudes, concerns, and outlooks are expressed in the zone's many local newspapers. Branches of certain clothing chains crop up in downtown Birmingham, on the "hill" in Grosse Pointe, in Ann Arbor, in Somerset Mall in Troy, but nowhere else in the Detroit region. Certain types of stores—such as ski shops, wine stores, and boutiques—are concentrated in this zone. High schools in Ann Arbor, Brimingham, and Grosse Pointe might be bitter academic and sports rivals, but this rivalry in itself reflects a similarity of interests.

One important aspect of the area's lifestyle is its extension into the recreational areas of northern Michigan. For decades, many residents have had summer homes in communities like Walloon Lake, Harbor Springs, and Mackinac Island. In more recent years, increasing mobility, more leisure time, and modern expressways have brought increasing numbers of the zone's residents to northern Michigan's lake resorts, ski areas, and recreational subdivisions. Although residents look upon this weekend and summer migration as an escape to a different environment, its ultimate effect has been to incorporate that environment into the lifestyle of the Radial Zone. In other words, northern recreation areas have become mere extensions of the zone's living patterns. Many of the zone's residents are more familiar with downtown Traverse City and Petoskey than with downtown Detroit.

The resident's relationships with other zones of the Detroit system are largely transactional. For many the vast area of metropolitan Detroit is perceived as a set of points connected by a series of lines. The points are the familiar places that are part of daily or periodic transactional activities—the G.M. Tech Center, the Fisher Building, Metropolitan Airport, the Detroit Athletic Club, WWJ radio, and the Ford Auditorium. The lines are the expressways, telecommunication lines, and air waves that interconnect those places and tie them to the Radial Zone. The metropolitan area underlying those points and lines tends to be unfamiliar territory. Increasingly it becomes unnecessary to go to other zones, to know what it is like there, or to understand their problems. To a significant degree, the Radial Zone resident is able to abstract himself from those problems and feel that they are outside his own spatial realm.

Emphasizing the self-contained nature of the Radial Zone in no way implies that the zone is static or unaffected by external events. Forces of change engulf this zone as they do other zones of the Detroit system. Many inner portions of the zone display symptoms of the blight that is so pronounced in other parts of the metropolitan area. Outer edges are being transformed rapidly by the actions of specu-

lators and land developers. Traffic congestion plagues certain communities, often more than in other zones. Unprecedented recreational developments in northern Michigan have interrupted the exclusiveness of the zone's weekend living patterns. The threat of school busing influences residential decisions. Drugs, once considered a problem of the distant inner city ghetto, now appear as an integral part of the local high school scene. Residents realize that these external forces are affecting their life patterns, just as they are aware of the economic and social changes—such as federal pressure for improved auto emission standards, competition from foreign automobile imports, and a looming oil crisis—that impinge upon their occupational activities.

To a degree the Radial Zone resident is better able to adjust to these forces of change, and perhaps control them, than the resident of any other zone of the Detroit system. He has at his disposal both the information to know what are possible courses of action, and the financial and political power to take those actions. Traditionally those actions have been of two types. One is the "buffer" type—the use of decisionmaking powers such as political incorporation, pressure on Highway Commissions, and influencing of state legislators to screen out the forces of impending change. The other is the "relinquishment" type. Homeowners in Ferndale and Royal Oak buy homes in Troy and Clawson. An apartment dweller in Southfield moves to a condominium in Rochester. The Jewish Community Center leaves Oak Park to be reestablished in Bloomfield Township. Store owners relinquish their rental options in older shopping centers to rent space in currently fashionable malls. Even residents of prosperous Birmingham are prospective purchasers of property in Avon or Oakland Township. In sum, traditional reactions to forces of change have led to two significant spatial processes. One might be termed the "sifting" process, as certain elements move through the zone, generally in an outward direction. The other is the "shifting" process, as the zone itself extends outward to incorporate a wider area.

A striking yet characteristic aspect of those two spatial processes is the fact that they are so easily incorporated into the framework of the life patterns within the Radial Zone. When residents relinquish one community, they do not thereby give up the lifestyle of that community. Eventually they bring that lifestyle with them. As the locale shifts, the amenities associated with that locale also shift, often with little perceptible break in ongoing life patterns. At present, many residents are moving from Royal Oak, Ferndale and Oak Park as smoothly as they or their parents previously did from Detroit and Highland Park.

In the years to come the boundaries of the Suburban Area of Radial Development will continue to change, in keeping with the processes that have been described here. A more significant question is whether there will be changes in the characteristics utilized to describe the zone. In other words, will the zone's residents continue to control, or adjust to, impinging forces of change and maintain their distinctive lifestyles? To the degree that those forces are tangible, and within the framework of the present American societal structure, the answer would seem to be positive. More than his counterpart in any other zone, the Radial Zone resident has a controlling voice in that structure. It is highly unlikely that a zone that has been introduced by terms like "leadership" and "decisionmaking" would be unable to maintain its distinctive place within and outside of the Detroit system.

SUBURBAN AREA OF INTERSECTORAL DEVELOPMENT

The Suburban Area of Intersectoral Development contains much of the essential manufacturing work force of the Detroit system. A variety of highly skilled tradesmen, blue collar workers, and white collar office workers gives the zone an average income well above that of similar middle income zones in other U.S. metropolitan systems. This relative prosperity, as well as a general similarity in personal and family backgrounds, have contributed to a distinctive set of life patterns and a particular general outlook.

The spatial development of this Intersectoral Zone is connected intimately with the war time and postwar expansion of the automobile industry, an expansion that virtually transferred the industry from its fairly compact concentration in Detroit, Highland Park, Hamtramck, and Dearborn to a series of industrial corridors following the main railroads leading into the city. Those corridors were found in the broad

rural, interstitial areas between the sectors of Radial Development (Figure 2). The establishment of major automobile plants was followed by the swarming of ancillary metal and machinery industries, and the extension of residential subdivisions which caught up with the original factories and eventually engulfed them.

Today, those areas comprise a set of broad suburban wedges extending outward from the Detroit city limits and more or less alternating with the sectors of the Suburban Radial Area of Development. Two wedges dominate. The first is the broad wedge to the north, lying between the Woodward and Gratiot radials. Its postwar development was stimulated by industrial growth along the Mound Road Industrial Corridor and, to a lesser extent, along the Groesbeck Industrial Corridor. The filling in of this wedge explains Macomb County's position as the fastest growing county in the Detroit area during the past two census periods. The second is the equally broad wedge to the southwest, fanning from the Detroit River to encompass much of southern Wayne County. The development of this wedge reflects the auto-industry-dominated Central Wayne Corridor, the steel-chemical-oriented Downriver Corridor, and the "anchoring" effect of the Ford Motor Company complex in Dearborn. A third and narrower wedge stretches westward along the Plymouth Industrial Corridor in the northern part of Wayne County.

The nature of suburban growth within the Intersectoral Zone largely has determined its landscape. With the exception of sites preempted by industry, the zone was open to unfettered, low density sprawl. Generally no older suburbs existed to serve as nuclei for development. Often natural landscape features were obliterated to create monotonous subdivisions. Frequently services and amenities were not provided, so that the extensive shopping plazas serving the area often appear as peripheral afterthoughts rather than integrally planned units. One notable feature of the zone's development was the rapidity and variety of political incorporation. A common form was to take over whole townships, or what was left of whole townships. Thus suburbs like Warren, Sterling Heights, Westland, Taylor, and Southgate have at various periods become the fastest growing cities in the metropolitan area. Overall, however, the political development of the zone has left a haphazard array of incorporated units, some developing into viable and cohesive suburbs, others plagued by poor services, lack of structure, and often premature blight.

Today the visitor to almost any part of the Intersectoral Zone has an image of neverending suburban land. This land has a good deal of variation. Neat, clean, but repetitious bungalow subdivisions give way to new condominium developments. Spacious school buildings surrounded by large playing fields in some suburbs contrast with the smaller inadequate school facilities in others. Gigantic new one story automobile plants with spacious parking lots and impressive landscaping, contrast with the grubby congested streets of tool and die shops that surround them. Large new shopping plazas have a different visual effect than the uncoordinated commercial strip developments on many traffic arteries. Variety, however, does not mean structure. The same visitor will look in vain for "centers," "downtowns," and "main streets" to give him a sense of organization and orientation. He becomes aware that some political pattern exists only when he sees an occasional sign telling him he is now entering the "City of_____".

If this political pattern has little coincidence with the suburbanite's daily activity pattern, it has a profound influence upon his welfare. Political boundaries in the Intersectoral Zone have another meaning. Often they are the means of preserving exclusiveness, of maintaining separation, and of providing buffers against outside encroachment. Most meaningful is a suburb's exclusive claims to the tax base of enterprises within its boundaries. Thus cities like Warren, which houses the General Motors Tech Center and other key automobile plants, are able to maintain among the lowest taxes and some of the finest municipal and school services in the Detroit system. Almost as meaningful is an incorporated unit's ability, by legal or illegal means, to specify the nature of its residents. Most suburbs have thus far been able to exclude low income subsidized federal housing developments, effectively channeling virtually all such housing into only one or two specific suburbs. In the same vein, many suburbs have been able to exclude blacks, a policy that has funneled black suburban migration into those few suburbs, such as Inkster, Ecorse, and River Rouge, that have a long history of black settlement.

The socioeconomic characteristics of the Intersectoral Zone might best be summarized by looking at average family incomes. Although residents are not as affluent as those in the Suburban Area of Radial Development, they are wealthier by far than persons in the Detroit Inner and Middle zones and those in outlying rural zones. Moreover, if comparisons were made with similar middle income suburban zones in other American metropolitan systems, the intersectoral area would rank high. This is explained by the zone's occupational structure.

The Intersectoral Zone houses one of the largest technically skilled work forces in the country. Contrary to popular misconception, the typical member of that work force is not the assembly line worker. Rather, he is the specialist in one of the multitude of complex technical and organizational tasks upon which the American automobile industry depends. Within automobile factories, those specialties include titles like maintenance engineer, press operator, foreman, shipping supervisor, die caster, toolmaker, and quality inspector. Such specialties are repeated in the thousands of private companies—tool and die shops, engineering shops, metal-cutting plants, heat treatment plants—which depend upon the automobile industry and, conversely, upon which the automobile industry ultimately depends. The manufacturing work force is supplemented by workers in shipping companies, freight-handling firms, fuel dealers, lumber specialists, and other firms serving the main manufacturing concerns. This array of specialized production workers is complemented by an equally broad and varied force of office personnel. In sum, the zone provides much of the skilled and experienced technical work force upon which the Detroit, and indeed the American, automobile industry is based.

In many respects the zone's role within the Detroit industrial system corresponds to that played by the Detroit Middle Zone in previous generations. In historical perspective, it is indeed a transplantation of the Middle Zone, as younger families moved out to new subdivisions in keeping with the war time and postwar expansion of industrial activities. The directional bias of this transplantation was decidedly sectoral. Families from Detroit's east side and from Hamtramck moved into the Macomb County wedge; whereas those from Detroit's west side, from East Dearborn, and from River Rouge moved into the western and southwestern wedges. This explains the ethnic makeup of parts of the Intersectoral Zone. Many young families who occupied the zone's new subdivisions were second and third generation offspring of Detroit's older immigrant ethnic communities. Thus parts of Roseville and East Detroit are a youthful extension of Detroit's Gratiot Avenue Italian Colony. The strongly Polish composition of Warren and Sterling Heights reflects families whose parents lived in Hamtramck. The Polish and Hungarian populations of Allen Park, Taylor, and Southgate stem from older concentrations of those nationalities in western and south-western Detroit and River Rouge. If the industrial role analogy is carried further, it might be suggested that the skills and know-how which operate the Chrysler truck assembly plant in Warren, the Ford stamping plant in Woodhaven, and the Great Lakes steel mill in Trenton are a product of experiences gained in the preceding generation in the Dodge Main plant in Hamtramck, the Kelsey-Hayes wheel factory on Livernois, and the iron foundries in Delray, respectively.

The characteristics discussed here—recency of development, sprawl of landscape, relative prosperity, common occupational interests, similar family backgrounds—have had an influence upon the general lifestyles within the zone. Those lifestyles have many facets. They tend to be family oriented, taking pride in homeownership and a personal interest in the local subdivision and the recently incorporated city or village. Activities are largely circumscribed by and dependent upon the personal automobile, as expressed visually by the vast, sprawling parking lots of shopping centers, schools, and commercial facilities. The outdoors is treasured, as typified by an abundance of sporting goods stores, or the hallowed nature of the annual deer season pilgrimage to the north. The zone likely accounts for a considerable proportion of the state sales of power boats, snowmobiles, and motor bikes. The recent boom in house trailer and camper ownership and the increasing desire to purchase lots in the booming northern recreational subdivision developments indicate that those outdoor interests continue unabated. However, those interests have not disassociated the resident from his city background and ethnic heritage, a fact that becomes apparent on a visit to one of the zone's taverns, bars, community halls, bowling alleys, or Friday night fish fries.

In sum, the lifestyle of the Intersectoral Zone incorporates the expansive, consumer-oriented outlook of American suburbia with certain traditional values learned in ethnic communities in the inner city. The blend is not complete, and the style still is being created.

Residents of the Intersectoral Zone have a distinctive set of relationships with, and attitudes toward, other zones in the Detroit system. There is considerable interaction with the Suburban Area of Radial Development, as the residents utilize the amenities of that zone such as shopping, professional services, and restaurants, and as residents of the two zones share certain citywide events such as baseball games, boat shows, conventions, and occasional civic functions. Those shared activities are not carried over into everyday interests and social life, which for the resident are closely identified with his own zone and with persons in that zone. Interaction with the Detroit Inner and Middle zones is of the functional nature described in the introduction to this section. For example, workers from Detroit man the assembly lines of Intersectoral Zone factories. Residents of the zone make visits to parents and grandparents in older city ethnic communities. Otherwise, the attitude of the Intersectoral Zone resident toward the two Detroit zones tends to be clear cut. He is conscious of the problems that exist in those zones, and one of his primary concerns is to keep those problems away from his own life.

In recent years many persons in the Intersectoral Zone have come to feel that their lifestyle is being undermined by a number of unforeseen social changes. Of particular concern is the question of an incorporated unit's control over its own affairs, an important reason for incorporation in the first place. For example, efforts to exclude nonwhites from local communities are increasingly hard to justify at a time when integration is being enforced in other parts of the country. Communities receiving various forms of federal aid find it hard to argue that they should not also provide space for low income public housing projects. Even such a sine quo non as local control over local schools paid for by local taxes is apparently being affected. In the years 1972 and 1973 many of those changes were clearly pointed up by the celebrated school busing issue.

These social forces represent problems from

which many residents believed they had escaped, and often are viewed as threatening a way of life they have struggled hard to attain. Moreover, values now being threatened are values emphasized by a system that has paid lip service to independence and local control. The more dramatic responses to the forces of social change are well publicized, such as the overtly antiblack actions of certain suburban mayors, the flood of "this family won't be bused" signs on house doors and automobile bumpers, as well as numerous confrontations and demonstrations. The insecurity underlying those responses is not always understood, nor is the uncertainty concerning what those social forces will mean in the future.

Even more recently, residents of the Intersectoral Zone have been confronted with a more immediate threat to their accustomed way of life, this time economic. Probably more-so than in other similar suburban zones throughout the country they are affected directly by the likelihood of a continued severe recession. In the past, the relatively high incomes within the zone have mirrored the overall prosperity of the automobile industry. Characteristically, that industry today was more severely affected by the recession of the 1970s than almost any other industry. The Intersectoral Zone, like the Detroit system in general, was faced with a higher than average rate of recession and unemployment. When recessions are long and/or severe, residents of the Intersectoral Zone face an economic crisis that threatens a lifestyle that has been built up during almost three decades. The insecurity brought about by that threat compounds the more long term sense of insecurity brought about by impinging social forces.

It is the degree of this insecurity that differentiates Intersectoral Zone residents from those in the Suburban Area of Radial Development. For in spite of a relatively high economic status, alternatives are limited. Inflation makes it increasingly difficult to maintain an accustomed lifestyle. Recession in the auto industry is a factor beyond their control. They may change jobs, but they do not create jobs or determine where those jobs are going to be. They may move their place of residence, but they are unsure whether their acquired lifestyle will accompany them. Even if a new subdivision today appears isolated from present

forces of social change, there is no assurance that it will remain isolated in the future.

In sum, much of the Suburban Area of Intersectoral Development is affected by processes of social and economic change that had not been foreseen and that still are not fully understood. Although some responses have been defensive and even violent, the majority of residents is more passive, seeing few ways of coping with those forces. The future of the Suburban Area of Intersectoral Development would seem to depend upon how those external forces continue to unfold.

ZONE OF INTERCITY CORRIDOR GROWTH

The Zone of Intercity Corridor Growth expresses the basic urban pattern of southeastern Michigan and is the framework for the ongoing urbanization processes taking place in that region. A close interdependence between the zone's cities and the Detroit metropolis make it an integral part of the Detroit system.

The zone comprises a series of six urban corridors radiating out from Detroit and connecting Detroit with all important cities in its hinterland (Figure 2). In clockwise sequence those corridors are known as the Detroit-Toledo Corridor, the Detroit-Jackson Corridor, the Detroit-Lansing Corridor, the Detroit-Bay City Corridor, the Detroit-Port Huron Corridor, and the Detroit-London (Ontario) Corridor. The Detroit-Bay City Corridor is in the most advanced stages of urbanization, with the Detroit-London Corridor the least advanced.

The development of the corridors has been an important theme in Michigan history. They were the routes of early Indian trails that focused upon Cadillac's Fort Pontchartrain on the Detroit River. They became the sites of military roads during the period of American settlement, and thus the means of settlement of the interior. They dictated the locations of early towns in the area. They have remained the dominant arteries of southern Michigan right up to the present, eventually becoming the framework of the present day expressway system. Today they are the basis of the corridor growth that is the dominant feature of urban land use development.

Similarity in overall historical development does not mean that the zone's various corridors are alike. Each corridor is distinctive. Most significantly, each differs in its degree of urban development, in the functional structure of its cities, and in the nature of its interdependence with metropolitan Detroit.

The dominant corridor by far is the Detroit-Bay City Corridor, interconnecting the cities of Detroit, Pontiac, Flint, Saginaw, and Bay City. The corridor points northwest, the traditional magnet for the Detroit system's growth. Its importance has been reinforced by the functional economic interdependence of its main cities. Largely this reflects the presence of the General Motors Corporation, whose main enterprises are located there (for example, the Pontiac Division in Pontiac, the Chevrolet and Buick divisions in Flint, and the Steering Gear Division in Saginaw). The company not only dominates economic activities but has left its stamp upon the character, appearance, identity, and lifestyles of the cities in the corridor. The corridor continues to be the dominant focus of urban expansion in southeastern Michigan; urban development is virtually complete between Detroit and Bay City.

Second in importance is the Detroit-Jackson Corridor, connecting Detroit, Ypsilanti, Ann Arbor, and Jackson, and extending farther to Battle Creek and Kalamazoo. The corridor is "anchored" by the Ford Motor Company's Dearborn complex, and automobile-related activities are found in other cities. However, the corridor's character is set by other factors. Most important is the presence of several of Michigan's main educational institutions, including Eastern Michigan University in Ypsilanti, The University of Michigan in Ann Arbor, and Western Michigan University in Kalamazoo, as well as distinguished private colleges like Albion College in Albion and Kalamazoo College in Kalamazoo. Those institutions strongly influence the nature and lifestyle of cities in the corridor and promote a high degree of interdependence between those cities and the educational and research institutions of the city of Detroit. Interaction within the Detroit-Jackson Corridor is further enhanced by the presence of the Detroit system's metropolitan airport. Today the chain of urbanization is largely uninterruped between Detroit and Ann Arbor.

The Detroit-Toledo Corridor ranks third in importance. This connects Detroit with an important industrial and commercial center, parallels a strategic link of the Great Lakes waterway, and forms Detroit's main outlet to the population centers, markets, and general economic life of mid-America. However, urban growth in this corridor is not as great as these considerations might warrant. This apparent anomaly would seem to reflect two factors. First, the corridor points away from the northwest, the traditional growth axis of the Detroit system. Second, the intense functional interdependence between its cities, so pronounced in other corridors, is lacking. Thus, despite its important transportational role, the Detroit-Toledo Corridor is less an integral part of the Detroit system, and less a representative segment of that system's society than the corridors to the northwest and west.

The Detroit-Lansing Corridor connects metropolitan Detroit with Brighton, Lansing, and eventually with Grand Rapids. The corridor has not been a dominant focus of urbanization like the two corridors which border it. The main city, Lansing, is relatively distant from Detroit, and intervening towns have not become growth centers. However, this situation is changing rapidly as Detroit sprawls along the Grand River artery; as industrial, educational, and recreational functions spill over from the two adjacent growth arteries; and as distances are reduced by the I-696 expressway. These developments enhance the importance of the one function that sets the character of the corridor —namely, state government. Indeed, this corridor expresses the increasing interdependence between state and metropolis, connecting Lansing—the state capital; Grand Rapids—the state's major nonmetropolitan city; and East Lansing—site of the state's largest undergraduate university; with the Detroit region.

The Detroit-Port Huron Corridor is less developed. It leads to the northeast, away from the Detroit system's major growth axes, and toward Port Huron, one of the zone's smaller urban centers. The recent surge of urban expansion, which already has engulfed the city of Mt. Clemens, will likely continue. However, this reflects more the independent growth of metropolitan Detroit than the functional interdependence among cities of the corridor.

The last corridor connects Detroit with Windsor, Chatham, London, and beyond. The corridor plays a dominant transportational role, connecting the Detroit-Windsor metropolis with southern Ontario and with the eastern United States through the Niagara peninsula. Urban growth has taken place in all of the corridor's cities, but urban coalescence is not as marked as in other corridors. As the "spine" of southwestern Ontario, the Detroit-London Corridor will see increased urban growth in the future. The character of the resulting urban corridor will be less strongly influenced by its interconnections with the Detroit metropolis.

It is likely that intercity corridor growth will continue to set the pattern of ongoing urbanization in Southern Michigan. The processes involved will be expansion of individual cities in the corridors; coalescence, as corridor cities gravitate towards each other; extension of certain corridors; and widening, as corridors encroach over adjacent land. Moreover, incipient urban corridors promise to connect the radial corridors in a circumferential belt—Port Huron-Flint-Lansing-Jackson-Toledo —to create a weblike pattern. As in the past, dominant growth corridors will be those to the northwest and west.

As urbanization progresses, the specialized functional interdependence between cities in individual corridors will intensify, and the resultant character and lifestyle of individual corridors will become increasingly distinctive. It would appear that the essential sectoral patterning of social life in the Detroit system will continue as the system continues to expand.

ZONE OF RURAL CHANGE

The Zone of Rural Change is the part of the Detroit system that is not developed in the sense implied by present-day planners, but its landscape characteristics and activities are determined largely by forces emanating from that system. The zone is more extensive than any other zone, located in between the intercity growth corridors but beyond the contiguous built-up part of metropolitan Detroit (Figure 2). The zone incorporates the northern parts of Oakland and Macomb counties and a smaller portion of western Wayne County in the SMSA as well as a considerable part of

adjacent Monroe, Washtenaw, and St. Clair counties.

There are two physiographic sections. One is the relatively flat glacial lake plain—the Erie-St. Clair Lowland—bordering the northeast-southwest trending waterway between Lakes Huron and Erie and extending roughly twenty-five miles inland from the waterway. This plain traditionally has supported a prosperous mixed agricultural economy of dairying, meat animals, cash crops, and horticultural products. The second part is the hilly, uneven lake-pitted interlobate moraine—the Thumb Upland—bordering the lowland belt to the northwest. This area has been more conducive to recreational developments, although limited patches of dairy farming and fruit growing have been important.

Today those traditional rural activities have become secondary. The main characteristics of different parts of the zone are important in terms of their relationship to ongoing forces of urbanization. These forces include urban sprawl and urban shadow. The first refers to the active land conversion processes taking place at the area's built-up edges. Urban shadow refers to the long stagnation process which appears to condemn a rural area to declining productivity and general sterility. Together they explain the landscape variation in the zone.

One aspect of that landscape variation is the evidence of what appears to be traditional agricultural types, such as dairy farming or field cropping. This evidence generally is illusionary. Closer examination shows that agriculture has declined, both in quality and in intensity. Often operators are too old to manage the farm efficiently, and their children show little interest in farming. More often operating costs—like increased land values, higher taxes, and competition for farm labor— have forced farmers to look for new farms farther away from the urbanization process. Where built-up areas are close, farming is impeded by noise, trespassing, trash, and drainage disruption. All of these factors lead the farmer to invest less time, labor, and capital, particularly in activities that provide a long term financial return.

The second landscape feature is idle land, with vast stretches of neglected grass, weeds, brush, trash, and derelict farm buildings, owned either by speculators or by farmers intending to sell the land at the most profitable time. Because farm abandonment appears to increase at a much faster rate than physical urbanization, the area of derelict land continues to expand. "Idleness" is the most widespread land use in the Zone of Rural Change.

The overall landscape variation is punctuated by spots of more intense activities where landowners temporarily have capitalized upon the recreational needs of nearby suburban residents. For example, horse farms and riding stables are common in many sections, to the degree that Oakland and Washtenaw counties have the highest "horse" densities in Michigan. Elsewhere, cider mills have seen a rejuvenation, offering a range of activities that transcends the simple sale of cider. Trapshooting, golf courses, and other recreational activities are additional amenities offered.

Last, the general appearance of idleness and inactivity in most of the Zone of Rural Change contrasts strikingly with the "sprawl" at the zone's urbanized edges. Here the different actors in the land conversion process—speculator, developer, builder, realtor, utility worker, homeowner, politician, and planner—indulge in the rapid succession of negotiations and decisions ending in development. In such areas the landscape shows the full brunt of change, as land is cleared, utility ditches are dug, streets partitioned, bulldozers utilized, dust created, and the shells of future buildings erected.

The resulting landscape pattern in the Zone of Rural Change is not haphazard. In areas such as the broad intersectoral wedges to the north and southwest, where there has been a relatively even spread of suburban land use into flat and productive agricultural land, there is a distinct sequence of the landscape types described above. Elsewhere the order is not so discernible. The confusing pattern of preexisting land use and the spotty nature of the urban sprawl process have patterned the landscape into something more akin to a mosaic.

Today the zone provides the locale where new processes of change are operating and where new tensions are being created. Many of these processes are physical, associated with urbanization forces which have been discussed. A new subdivision is built at the urban edge. An expressway is extended into a different area. A new automobile plant is built in a nonindustrial village. A sewer line is constructed. Other processes are less obvious. There is a general "sifting" of landowners through the area, largely involving farmers who are forced to give up their farms because of encroaching urbanization but who are not ready to give up farming as a way of life. They sell the original farm and buy another farther away where taxes are lower and urban nuisances are fewer. There is also the steady movement into the zone of suburban residents whose economic activities are tied to the built-up metropolitan area but who wish to escape that area's problems. This escape can involve several jumps in a relatively short time.

Many of the processes operating in the Zone of Rural Change involve movements and migrations, predominantly in an outward direction. The farmer in western Wayne County buys a new farm in Monroe County. The Warren suburbanite who fears school busing of his children buys in a new subdivision in Washington Township. Realtors and developers who have developed the city of Troy, and are developing Avon Township, are now moving their activities to Oakland Township. Ford Motor Company, which first set up a factory in Warren, and later constructed another in the "rural" village of Utica, now builds another in "outlying" Romeo. The sectoral movements so characteristic of other Detroit zones are continued into the Zone of Rural Change.

These processes have produced tensions among the zone's residents. Ironically, the most important source of tension involves conflicting attitudes toward the very factor that created the zone in the first place, namely anticipated growth. Increasing numbers of residents, original landholders and newcomers alike, see growth as a threat to the landscape and lifestyle that attracted them to the area. This tension often leads to resistance. For example, a sewer line which is requisite to rational and planned development in northeast Macomb County is successfully opposed by local residents. Amenities like paved streets bring objections in parts of Oakland Township because they appear to be synonomous with development. A proposed billion dollar shopping center in Bloomfield Township is defeated by residents because it will promote growth and spoil the character of the area. Often the alignments in such confrontations appear to be incompatible. Older farmers side with developers to promote schemes that are opposed by residents who only recently arrived in the area. Plans of local planning commissions are resisted because their very rationality promotes the growth which the residents do not want.

In sum, the Zone of Rural Change has passed out of a previous rural recreational state and is destined for some sort of urban future. When and how that future will be attained is uncertain. Into the foreseeable future, the major part of the zone will remain in its present state of limbo, with a landscape characterized more by waste and idleness than by productive use. Meanwhile local processes are to be observed which are offshoots of the dominant force—urbanization—that has created the zone. The presence of this force emphasizes the integral place of the Zone of Rural Change within the Detroit system.

SUMMARY

In summary, the spatial model portrayed in Figure 2, though highly generalized, provides a convenient and meaningful framework for grouping Detroit society and discussing the different parts of the Detroit system. The zones in the model encompass areas and people with different backgrounds, lifestyles, outlooks, and concerns, and are subjected to quite different external processes. At the time of writing it would appear that the differences between the zones are becoming greater, and their respective societies more divergent. At the same time this increasing social differentiation between the zones does not diminish the essential functional interdependence among them. All continue to be integral parts of the Detroit system.

Forces of Change in the Detroit System

One theme which pervades any discussion of the Detroit system and its regions is change. Indeed, the very essence of the zones discussed above is the forces of change that are engulfing, and to a degree, transforming them. In the remainder of the study those forces are considered more systematically and in greater detail. The consideration is limited to three of the most important forces affecting the Detroit system. These are (1) renewal, which affects all parts of the Detroit system but is most pronounced in the Detroit Inner Zone; (2) racial change, which is most characteristic of the Detroit Middle Zone; and (3) expansion, which emanates from the Suburban Zones and impinges upon the Zone of Rural Change. The final section of this study examines the operation of these three processes in local situations. The present section acts as a bridge to the final section, looking at the three forces of change in the perspective of the total Detroit system.

RENEWAL

Renewal entails the deliberate clearance of existing facilities with the purpose of rebuilding and redeveloping an area into some different and theoretically improved use. Examples include urban renewal, highway construction, school construction, and institutional expansion. Renewal has had a considerable impact upon the Detroit system. This impact reflects a number of factors. First, renewal projects tend to be concentrated in specific areas, where their visual impact tends to be overwhelming. Second, renewal projects have a distinct "rub-off" effect upon adjacent areas. Third, the renewal process affects individuals and families, who must be relocated. Fourth, the renewal process is slow. Years, even decades, pass between the time of announcement and eventual construction. The total effect is that renewal has a detrimental effect upon the appearance, image, and life of the city. Such has been the case for almost two decades in the Detroit inner city, where on the one hand an everexpanding expressway system has virtually chopped up the landscape, and on the other hand an urban renewal system has left many of the remaining parcels in varying states of decay, idleness, and reconstruction. This discussion of renewal begins with federally assisted urban renewal.

Urban Renewal

Although urban renewal includes other elements like neighborhood conservation and code enforcement, the most meaningful and dramatic form is that of complete redevelopment. Within the Detroit area redevelopment is concentrated largely in the Detroit-Highland Park-Hamtramck nucleus, in Pontiac, and in adjacent older suburbs such as East Dearborn, Royal Oak, Ferndale, and Centerline. However, this analysis concentrates on the city of Detroit, where the effects of redevelopment programs have been felt the most.

In aggregate Detroit's urban renewal program encompasses 1,505 acres, which at one

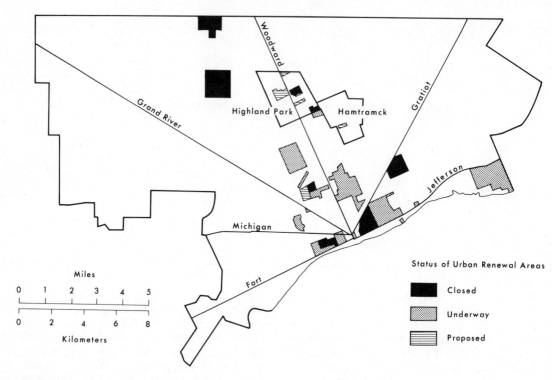

Figure 4.   Urban renewal areas in Detroit, Highland Park, and Hamtramck.

time contained 17,133 housing units and 1,982 businesses. An estimated 7,660 families and 6,730 individuals had to be relocated. With some exceptions, the renewal projects are found within Grand Boulevard, particularly east and west of the central business district and adjacent to the Lodge and Chrysler expressways immediately to the north (Figure 4). Virtually all these areas were residential. They comprised the worst of Detroit's housing stock, although in some areas, such as the University City area, good quality dwellings were included. They also comprised some of the most vital and colorful of Detroit's ethnic and working class communities: "Black Bottom," "Paradise Valley," "Corktown," "Chinatown," and "Bagley" are an important part of Detroit's heritage.

These areas have been and are being renewed for a number of uses, many of which are not residential. Eight renewal projects, comprising 251 acres, are industrial. Three projects, comprising 160 acres, are institutional, notably in The University City and Medical Center area. Five listed projects are commercial, mainly in the central business district. Of the resi-

dential projects, a large proportion are for upper and middle income persons, particularly in the Gratiot, Lafayette, and Elmwood Park areas. Thus far, only a small percentage of the completed renewal areas has been made available for low income housing.

In the summer of 1974 three large parcels comprising 270 acres, and several smaller parcels, lay vacant with no projected use in the near future. The present vacant status of those parcels has been, at one time or another, the status of all renewal lands in Detroit. In effect, vacant land has been a pervasive and accepted part of the Detroit inner city landscape for more than two decades. This land has taken on various hues and physical characteristics, from bare earth and weeds, to green rural-like tranquility, to western sagebrush, and to a recent Detroit specialty, white wooden fences, which give vacant blocks in the heart of the city the appearance of Kentucky horse farms.

As in most American cities, the urban renewal process in Detroit has been long, complicated, and bureaucratic. In any single area the process might be divided into four phases: first, a consideration phase, in which the project is proposed, considered, rumored, announced, and eventually funded; second, a clearing phase, in which property is condemned, residents evicted and relocated, and property demolished; third, a vacant phase, in which land lies idle awaiting purchase and development; and finally, the development phase. Each of these phases has taken its toll in terms of human suffering and landscape deterioration. A detrimental aspect of the renewal process has been the long and uncertain time lag involved during and between each phase. Although some projects have taken at least ten years before the cycle is complete, some have taken twenty years, and some have not yet been completed. The time lag also incorporates changes in national temperament, including some basic changes in the philosophy of urban renewal itself.

One recent change in philosophy might well have an important influence on the future of urban renewal in Detroit. Although the change has been gradual, it clearly divides renewal policies and attitudes into two periods. The first period prevailed throughout much of the program, and was characterized by little real attempt to understand the plight of residents. Projects were discussed and planned with little local participation. Residents felt themselves to be at the mercy of a frightening combination of federal officials, city government, and the institutions that would benefit from development. Redevelopment often took place for private or institutional benefits, or for bureaucratic or financial expediency. The second period, inaugurated in the last few years, is a period of local and resident control, which has been brought about by a complex of factors including federal revenue-sharing stipulations, model neighborhood examples, the growing power of citizens councils, and probably a changing attitude on the part of city officials as to what constitutes "development."

The second period of Detroit's renewal history also has brought forth problems. Many local resident organizations understandably tend to be suspicious of any large scale development projects. As a result, large, worthwhile projects often are rejected or stymied, and actual development, though democratic, has the potential of being piecemeal, unplanned, and destined to bring about early community blight.

Thus, the future quality of urban renewal is open to question in Detroit. But the presence of urban renewal is there. Whatever the nature of eventual development, the process leaves large parts of the city with empty buildings, vacant land, and developments in varying degrees of completion.

Freeway Construction

A second kind of renewal is freeway construction. The Detroit system is well served by one of the most extensive freeway networks in the country. The construction of this network has occurred largely since the passage of the Federal Highway Act of 1956, when the Interstate system was initiated. In the Detroit SMSA alone there were in 1974 almost 200 miles of completed expressways, with approximately sixty-five miles under construction or scheduled for construction. Vast tracts of land formerly used for residential or commercial purposes are now part of the system. Even in the period before 1970 an estimated 20,400 homes in the Detroit metropolitan area had been demolished for expressway construction.

Most completed freeways follow the radial pattern that has been such a dominant feature of the Detroit area's development (Figure 5). The focus is on the central city, as most of the early freeways were designed to bring suburban residents to downtown workplaces. The Ford Freeway, about three miles north of the central business district, is aligned with the river-oriented street pattern of central Detroit, but outside the city it also assumes a radial form. Freeways presently under construction or proposed are designed to improve east-west or north-south connections in outlying or suburban areas. I-275 will traverse most of the north-south length of Wayne County, bypassing Metropolitan Airport and joining I-75 in Monroe County. I-96 will extend directly westward from the Jeffreys Freeway in central Detroit to serve a large western suburban area before being joined by I-275 at Plymouth. Most significantly, the I-696 Freeway paralleling Ten and Eleven Mile Roads is designed to fill the much-needed link among Detroit's northern suburbs. At present, stretches of those routes form broad swaths of bulldozed land sweeping through the suburban landscape. Other stretches are portrayed by rows of standing but vacant buildings from which former residents have been evicted and relocated. These kinds of landscapes have characterized,

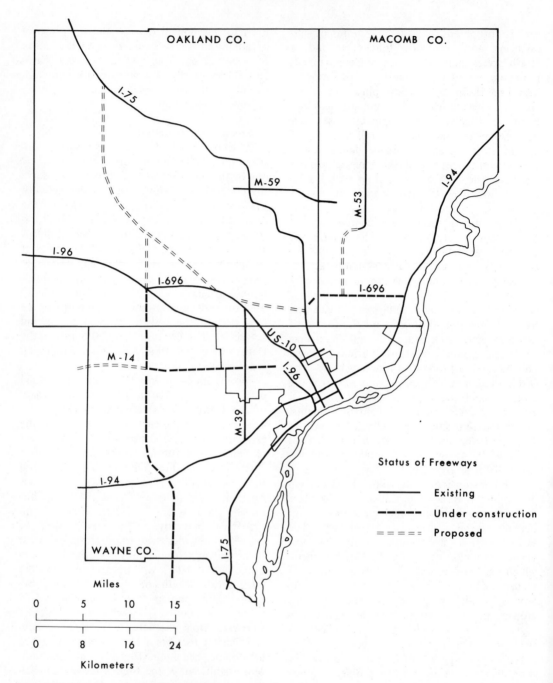

Figure 5. Detroit area freeways, 1974.

at one time or another, all areas where the present expressway system exists. Indeed, they have been an important part of the Detroit metropolitan scene for almost two decades.

Like other forms of renewal, the freeway construction process is lengthy and bureaucratic, with a series of long drawn out phases between initial announcement and final construction. During those phases the personal grief and landscape destruction characteristic of most renewal processes are compounded by the division of neighborhoods, shifting of travel patterns, cutting off of market areas, and increased travel time and congestion. The impact of the process has varied throughout the Detroit area, but it is the Inner Zone that is affected most, because most freeways converge upon the downtown area. In addition to all other adverse effects, many inner city communities have been split up or isolated. For example, the Hubbard-Richard community, a predominantly Mexican-American community west of the central business district, is today practically inaccessible. In suburban areas, lower income areas generally have been affected more than upper income areas. Partly this reflects the attraction in the former of lower property values which reduce right of way costs. Partly, it means that the wealthier have been more articulate, influential, and politically able to divert expressways from personal residential and business areas. In some cases, it means that expressway location has been used by planners as a slum clearance device.

The Detroit area has benefited greatly from the mobility provided by an excellent freeway network. At the same time, the area has paid its price. For almost two decades, the freeway construction process has brought instability and destruction to a considerable part of the metropolitan area.

Institutional Expansion

A third kind of renewal involves the location or expansion of public and private institutions into adjacent residential areas. This includes large scale institutions—such as Wayne State University or the Medical Center—highly visible on the city's landscape. It also includes schools and smaller scale projects that are less apparent but have a great cumulative impact on an area. Often the latter are associated with the changing needs and problems of the city, and include health clinics, drug abuse centers, nursing homes, the Salvation Army, and other religious missions.

The impact of institutional expansion upon the landscape and its residents is like that of other forms of renewal. However, additional factors are often involved. Because land is not always publicly acquired, property speculation can be great where expansion is anticipated. This can mean that residents are faced with unexpected rent increases that they cannot

afford. Moreover, an organized relocation program generally is absent, so that adjustment problems for displacees can be greater than those in federal renewal projects. Finally, many institutions are of the type that are felt to attract "undesirables." A Salvation Army soup kitchen can have an upsetting influence on neighborhood stability, particularly where children are present.

Although impossible to quantify, large tracts of land and large numbers of people are affected by institutional expansion. Examples are present throughout the Detroit area, but the process is most pronounced in the Inner Zone of Detroit. It is in this zone that the greatest number of large expanding institutions are to be found. Moreover, it is here that social agencies and institutions, often excluded from other areas, tend to congregate. Many parts of the Detroit Inner Zone face the prospect of being institutionalized out of existence by those very institutions whose presence is intended to bring about their betterment.

RACIAL CHANGE

The racial change process refers to the change of a residential neighborhood from all white to all black. This process has been rapid in Detroit. Over the past two decades from 7,000 to 9,000 Detroit households changed from white to black each year. Integrated neighborhoods are few. Normally whites accept a few black families in their neighborhoods, but when a critical proportion is reached, a massive exodus of white homeowners follows.

Between 1910 and 1930 Detroit's black population grew rapidly, from 5,700 to 120,000. Even with this increase blacks were a distinct minority in 1930, with 7.6 percent of the city's population. The large scale migration that transformed Detroit into one of the nation's leading black cities is a phenomenon associated with the "boom" years of World War II and the postwar period. Over the past three decades Detroit's black population more than quadrupled, whereas the white population decreased by 56 percent (Table 1). Most incoming blacks have come to the city of Detroit. Of the 757,000 blacks in the Detroit SMSA (18 percent of the SMSA's population), 660,000 are residents of the city of Detroit, and 23,000 of the remainder live in Detroit's enclaves, Hamtramck and

Figure 6. Black population in Detroit, Highland Park, and Hamtramck, 1940-1970. In the oldest ghetto areas the percentage black is decreasing. Source: U.S. Bureau of the Census.

Highland Park. The relatively small number of suburban blacks live in segregated sections of Pontiac and Mt. Clemens or in a limited number of older suburbs such as Inkster, Ecorse, and River Rouge. Most of suburban Detroit is typified by its three largest suburbs—Warren,

Table 1. City of Detroit's Black Population 1910-1970

	Total Population (1000s)	Percent Black	Percent White
1910	466	1.2	98.8
1920	994	4.1	95.9
1930	1569	7.6	92.4
1940	1623	9.2	90.7
1950	1850	16.2	83.6
1960	1670	28.9	70.8
1970	1511	43.7	55.5

Source: U.S. Census of Population

Livonia, and Dearborn—which together in 1970 had a black population of 186 out of a total population of 393,568.

The spatial growth of Detroit's black community can be traced from a near east side nucleus at the turn of the century to the vast, sprawling, but still highly segregated community that it is today (Figure 6). Like many other Detroit immigrants, blacks first settled on the near east side, and by 1910 most of the black community lived in an area south of Gratiot with St. Antoine as its major business thoroughfare. Between 1910 and 1940 extension occurred into adjacent areas to the north and to the east. A narrow corridor extended north past East Grand Boulevard along John R., Brush, Beaubien, St. Antoine, and Hastings streets. The eastern extension was confined to "Black Bottom," an area bounded by Mt. Elliot to the east, Gratiot to the north, and Jefferson to the south. A third area of settlement was a narrow strip on the west side near Lawton between Warren and Tireman.

The doubling of Detroit's black population between 1940 and 1950 brought only a limited spatial expansion of the community, largely an extension of the north-south corridor into Highland Park. At that time a war time and postwar housing shortage prevailed. Families moved in with each other and housing units often were subdivided to accommodate the needs of the growing black population. In the 1940s black Detroit still was a spatially confined "ghetto" in the narrowest sense of the word.

This situation changed dramatically in the 1950s. The suburban building boom literally brought about a spatial "release" of the metropolitan area, which had its repercussions on Detroit's black community. Between 1950 and 1960 no fewer than eighty-three additional census tracts became 50 percent black compared to twenty-four in the previous decade. This involved the extension of all black settlement areas. The most notable trend was the movement into northwest Detroit, in a sector between James Couzens and Grand River (Figure 6).

This dominant northwesterly expansion continued into the 1960s, so that by 1974 the zone of greatest racial transition was located between Greenfield and the Southfield Expressway. On the east side this transition zone is located close to Chalmers Avenue. It is within these areas that the conditions and processes associated with racial change are to be found today. Similar conditions and processes have characterized, at one time or another, all areas of Detroit where racial change has taken place. As has been seen, they have been an essential aspect of the Detroit Middle Zone for more than two decades.

The process of racial change is highly complex. It begins long before transition takes place, as the awareness of impending change creates instability in white neighborhoods. It continues during the period of active transition, when the rapid sequence of events can bring turmoil, neighborhood deterioration, and personal conflicts. It is associated with a myriad of social problems, ranging from confrontation in schools to disruption of city services. It remains long after transition has taken place, because the instability and turmoil of previous periods often leave a legacy of neighborhood depreciation and blight. In recent years efforts have been made by local community groups to

combat the more adverse effects of the transition process. The very existence of those groups is a recognition of the need for neighborhood stabilization and, in most cases, the realization that this stabilization requires a high degree of racial integration. In certain neighborhoods, their efforts have had considerable success. Whether that success is permanent or only temporary is still open to question, and perhaps is the key to the future of the outer parts of the city of Detroit. In areas closer to the city center, the more adverse effects of more than two decades of racial change have left their mark upon the city's landscape.

URBAN EXPANSION

Urban expansion entails the conversion of rural land to urban uses. In a sense the whole Detroit system has undergone expansion at one time or another. Normally, however, the term refers to the rapid suburbanization that has taken place during and since World War II. As has been seen, this suburbanization has led to the creation or expansion of the Suburban Area of Radial Development, the Suburban Area of Intersectoral Development, and the Zone of Intercity Corridor Growth. The rapidity of expansion is indicated in Figure 7, which shows the spread of the Detroit system's built-up area since 1940, and its status in 1970. Though varying in intensity from year to year, the expansion process goes on continually, as is seen in Table 2, which lists the amount of new residential construction in the southeast Michigan region since 1970.

Maps showing the expansion of the built-up area in no way indicate the scope and extent of the urban expansion process. For the process leaves its impact well beyond the edge of the built-up area, as rural areas undergo a slow transition period long before actual urbanization takes place. Although development

Table 2. **Authorized New Dwelling Units in SEMCOG Region, 1970–1974**

1970	1971	1972	1973	1974 (first six months only)
28,486	43,865	39,836	35,762	12,472

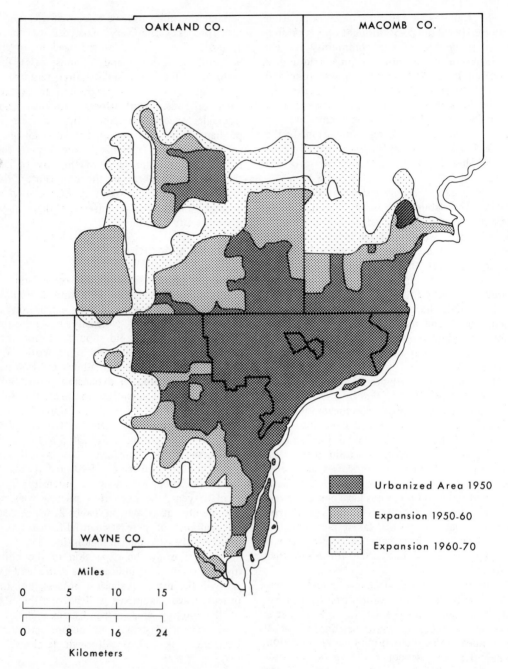

Figure 7. Expansion of the Detroit urbanized area, 1950–1970.

sometimes can take place rapidly, there is normally a period of years, and often decades, between the beginning of agricultural decline and the final urban development. This time lag can be measured in other terms, such as economic recessions and booms, changes in

mortgage rates, changes in zoning ordinances, gasoline crises, and a complex of other factors that not only influence the rate of development, but also whether development will ever take place.

Whatever the factors affecting the nature of

urban expansion, the physical presence of the process is visible throughout the Detroit system. The entire Zone of Rural Change is in one way or another affected by urban expansion processes, and this comprises a major part of southeastern Michigan. As has been the case for almost three decades, the largest area in the Detroit system lies in a state of transition, neither rural nor urban.

SUMMARY

In summary, a large part of the Detroit system today is subject to the impact of one or more of the forces of spatial change that have been described in this chapter. Moreover, an even larger part of the system has been subjected to those forces in the past few decades, and in some places the impact is still visible on the present-day landscape. The total influence of spatial change forces on the Detroit system is summarized by Sinclair in the following quotation from *The Face of Detroit:*

Unfortunately these forces tend to bring with them conditions of instability and uncertainty, which in turn lead to deterioration in areas undergoing change. In outlying parts of the Detroit area, urban sprawl has created large stretches of blighted vacant land, and often has led to unsound and poorly planned developments. Within the city, ghetto expansion has released forces of deterioration well in advance of the "front" of change. Processes associated with highway construction and urban renewal have left a considerable part of the central cities in a state of degenerating limbo. In total, conditions associated with spatial change are responsible for many of the Detroit area's strains.

This section has looked at the forces of change within the broad perspective of the total Detroit system. To describe more intimately how those forces operate, the scale of inquiry now is narrowed to a local level.

Forces of Change at the Local Level: Three Case Studies

The forces of change that are transforming such large parts of the Detroit system also have an impact at the local level. Indeed, all three of the forces described in the previous section have an influence in a wide variety of local situations. This section examines the operation of those forces in a number of selected areas in metropolitan Detroit. Three case studies have been selected. Each stands by itself as an individual entity. At the same time, each can be associated with one of the forces of change discussed in the last section, and identified with one or more of the major zones of the Detroit system analyzed previously. Thus, the Cass Corridor study examines the different forms of renewal taking place in the Detroit Inner Zone. The Northwest Detroit study focuses upon the racial change process, which is such a dominant feature of the Detroit Middle Zone. Finally, the Oakland Township study examines urban expansion at the interface between the Suburban Area of Radial Development and the Zone of Rural Change.

RENEWAL IN THE CASS CORRIDOR

The Cass Corridor is a one-and-a-half square mile inner city neighborhood located between downtown Detroit and Wayne State University, bounded on the east by Woodward Avenue and on the west by the John C. Lodge Expressway (Figure 8). The corridor projects a negative image. To many, the Cass Corridor means prostitution, drug addiction, and skid row. Crime is a serious problem, with homicide,

burglary, and arson relatively commonplace. Housing conditions in the area are among the worst in Detroit. There is an increasing number of abandoned and deteriorated buildings, many occupied by rats. Essential services such as health care and garbage collection are inadequate and appear to be worsening.

There is another side to the story, however. The Cass Corridor is home for about 20,000 people. The majority are poor, with 32.1 percent of families reporting incomes of less than $4,000 in 1969. Many are old, with almost 20 percent of the population sixty-five years of age or over, (compared with 11 percent for the city). Furthermore, many of the people are long time residents and have developed a strong sense of community identity. The area contains a varied ethnic mix. Southern whites are the dominant group, with Third Avenue frequently referred to in the recent past as "The Tennessee Valley" and "Little Kentucky." Cass Avenue is the home of Detroit's small Chinatown, a community displaced by urban renewal from its original location on Michigan Avenue close to downtown. A large black population is housed largely in a public housing project in the southwestern portion of the corridor. Other minorities include American Indians, Indians, Pakistanis, Philipinos, and Koreans, many of whom are students at the Detroit Institute of Technology or employed in the nearby Medical Center.

The character of the Cass Corridor has changed dramatically since the turn of the century, when it was known as "Piety Hill." In 1900 the Cass Corridor consisted of costly,

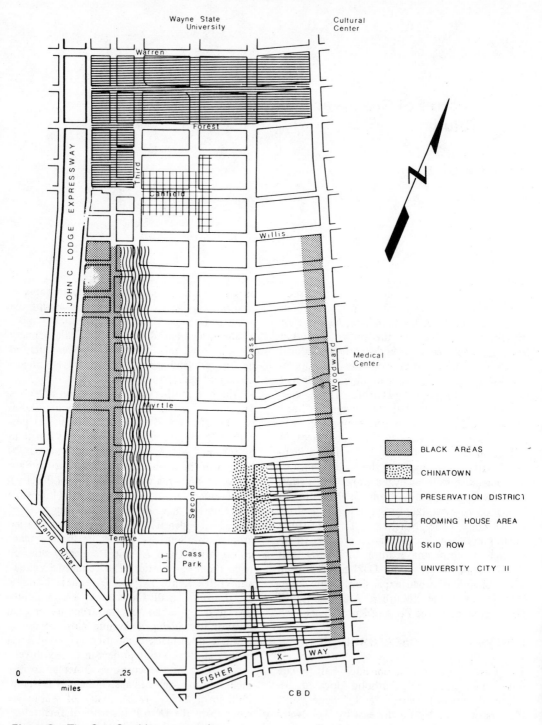

Figure 8. The Cass Corridor community.

durable single family residences housing Detroit's well-to-do. Rapid growth in the automobile industry during the early years of the
twentieth century resulted in major changes
along Woodward Avenue. By the 1920s these
streets, in a three mile strip extending north
from Grand Circus Park, had become the
center of the city's automobile sales. As more
people flocked to Detroit, wealthy families in
the Cass Corridor moved out and were replaced
by middle and lower income people. Old residences were subdivided into apartments and
flats. Many newcomers found accommodation
in the numerous apartment hotels that had
been built in the area. Similar pressures were
placed on the corridor's housing stock during
World War II, when an estimated 200,000
white southerners came to Detroit looking for
work. Increasingly the corridor became an area
of apartments and rooming houses. Thus, up to
the end of World War II, changes throughout
the Cass Corridor were associated with (1) a
changeover from residential use to commercial
use along the major arteries, and (2) the subdivision of residential units and the construction of high density units elsewhere.

In the last two decades a different force has
left its mark on the area. Change has become
associated with renewal, including freeway
construction, institutional expansion, and urban renewal. During the 1950s the John C.
Lodge Expressway was built, cutting a north-
south swath separating the Trumbull community to the west from the Cass Corridor to
the east. Later in the 1960s, the construction of
the Fisher Freeway had a similar dismembering
effect in the southern portions of the corridor.
Other areas have been affected by both direct
and indirect effects associated with institutional expansion. To the north renewal has
been largely synonymous with the growth of
Wayne State University, to the east with the
development of a medical complex, and to the
south with the anticipated extension of the
Detroit Institute of Technology. Moreover,
urban renewal projects in the central city,
particularly those associated with downtown
renewal in the fifties, have caused a spillover
of population into the corridor. Thus, for the
past two decades, and still today, conditions
in the Cass Corridor are affected, and often
determined, by different forms of renewal.
Today, the legacy of those two decades is seen
clearly throughout the corridor.

Renewal Processes in the Cass Corridor

The renewal process in the Cass Corridor takes
on many forms and incorporates a variety
of interacting processes. The most significant
are associated with the expansionist policies
of the educational, medical, and cultural
institutions that abut the corridor on three
sides.

Probably the most striking example of institutional expansion is Wayne State University
which, in its growth from a small city college
to a state university, has acquired large tracts
of community land and property. The university's expansion was slow until the late
1950s, but, in 1959, the Federal Housing Act
made it easier for institutions of higher learning
to expand. Land costs were reduced, the
ability to acquire more land became easier, and
costs were met by city and federal moneys.
A plan for university growth was drawn up that
was to proceed in five phases involving 304
acres. The project was labeled "University
City." The first phase of the project, University
City I, went ahead as scheduled, and by 1968
a forty acre area housing over 3,000 people
had been replaced by a large physical education
complex. In 1966 a law was enacted that prevented any urban renewal project from proceeding without citizen approval and involvement
However, much damage had already been done
through the University City area simply by the
announcement of the 1959 renewal plan.

The second phase of the University City
project involved property in both the Cass
Corridor and the adjacent Trumbull community. Scheduled clearance was interrupted by
a coalition of community organizations, whose
injunction eventually was upheld by the courts.
During the long interval, however, many homeowners had departed, maintenance on houses
and apartment buildings had lapsed, and city
purchases of property had continued. A community plan was drawn up for this area, but
little has been implemented. The present landscape comprises vacant land, demolished houses,
boarded-up houses, and a scattering of residences where residents have remained.

Another phase of the University City project lies south of the university between Woodward and the Lodge Expressway. Much of this
is now owned by the university, but existing
functions remain until university development
catches up. These functions include mixed
university uses and rental apartments and

houses on which few long term improvements are being made. Last, a large area in the northern part of the Cass Corridor is outside the University City project boundaries, but its condition is determined by the possibilities of university expansion. That condition is characterized by uncertainty and property neglect on the one hand, and the speculative ventures of many landowners on the other.

In sum, university expansion has had an adverse impact upon the Cass Corridor. The process has been slow and land acquisition piecemeal. During the long period involved, neighborhoods have deteriorated, houses have been abandoned, and life for remaining residents has become increasingly difficult. A sample quote from *The Community Reporter* indicates some of the difficulties:

> As property value declines so does property taxes, and with that city services. The residents of University City II were finding that they were no longer getting the police protection they once got. Houses are vacated and not boarded up or demolished, much less rehabilitated or replaced. Insurance went up sky-high or was denied altogether. And garbage pick-up and DPW services . . . were unreliable, or almost non-existent.

Wayne State University's expansion has been paralleled by that of other large institutions in and near the corridor. The Detroit Medical Center, comprising 240 acres immediately east of Woodward, is not in the Cass Corridor. However, the "spillover" of its population, which dropped from 85,000 in 1950 to about 20,000 in 1970, has had an indirect impact upon the corridor. Finally, the Detroit Institute of Technology moved into its present location near Cass Park on the southern edge of the area when the S.S. Kresge Company donated its office facility in the mid-1960s. Since that time, there has been some expansion into adjacent streets; the movement of students, many from overseas, into nearby residences; and considerable speculation in anticipation of future growth.

The renewal process has intensified many social problems throughout the Cass Corridor. Detroit's skid row, removed from its previous Michigan Avenue location by a renewal project of the 1950s, has migrated northward into the corridor and now is centered along Third Avenue between Temple and Selden avenues. Changes in occupancy have taken place as buildings in and near renewal areas deteriorated. Often, this meant that former occupants were replaced by alcoholics, drug addicts, prostitutes, and the physically and mentally disabled. Health problems have been compounded. The corridor has one of the highest tuberculosis rates in the country. Arson and crime have increased. All of those social problems have had an adverse affect upon family life and neighborhood stability even in the sounder residential streets.

These social problems have led to another kind of institutional expansion in the Cass Corridor. Social agencies, such as the Salvation Army, Goodwill Industries, Missionary Workers, and Mariner's Inn, and many church missions, have proliferated throughout the area. Though small scale in comparison with the massive public institutions that have been described, their cumulative impact is great. First, they are located throughout the corridor, quite often in what otherwise are residential areas. Second, they expand by taking over adjacent property, forcing residents to move. Third, their presence attracts greater numbers of the socially maladjusted into the area, thus perpetuating the need for their own existence and expansion. *The Community Reporter* reflects the feelings of many residents:

> The Salvation Army does provide many services for needy people. But it is too bad that while they offer those services they are also causing problems within the community. They have admitted that this is not the best place for their programs, but at the same time it is the only place that the "professional do-gooders" and politicians will let them have their building.

As if to justify the fears of many local residents, it was recently announced that the Salvation Army was planning a $3.4 million expansion program, much of it scheduled for the Cass Corridor.

Renewal has led to much speculative activity in the Cass Corridor. For example, university growth has meant an increased demand for student housing. Much of the area between Forest and Canfield is occupied by students. Many realtors and individual entrepreneurs have bought property, fixed it up, and turned out previous residents to accommodate students. Greater profits are realized. First, housing can be subdivided, and rents can be raised when two or more students share a single unit. Second, students—either because of family resources, part time employment, or student financial-aid programs— generally have more financial resources than many community residents, particularly the aged. Similar speculative ventures have occurred in the eastern sections of the Cass Corridor as a result of the growth of the medical complex. In sum, speculation resulting from the renewal process has caused resentment and hardship for many corridor residents.

One unusual form of renewal has had an impact upon a restricted part of the Cass Corridor. West Canfield Avenue between Second and Third avenues, a block of Victorian homes, has been designated a historic preservation district, and work is underway to restore the appearance and charm of what existed almost a century ago. Departments of the city, state, and the federal government have committed funds and facilities for the project. There has been some "rub-off" upon nearby areas as a few buildings on adjacent streets are now being restored in a similar manner. In spite of the limited scope of the whole development and its apparent value to the area, there have been unexpected results. Many local community residents regard the development as a factor that forces up property taxes, attracts middle class professionals into the area, and is a further threat to displace them from their homes.

In sum, the different forms of renewal have conditioned events and the nature of the landscape in the Cass Corridor for a period of twenty years. In some cases, the effects of the renewal processes have been direct—as, for example, where homes are torn down to be replaced by an institutional structure. More often they are indirect. Renewal has been a catalyst stimulating a set of other processes and incorporating a series of elements many of which at first glance have little connection with the renewal process.

The renewal processes operating in the Cass Corridor are perceived in different ways by the many persons who are involved in or affected by those processes. Clearly those perceptions depend upon the outlooks of the individuals involved. Generally, however, those individual viewpoints tend to reflect the divergence of two

conflicting sets of interests—those of the community and those of institutional development. The former are the Cass Corridor residents and a number of community-based organizations that represent them. The latter are the institutional and governmental interests engaged in the renewal process.

Most Cass Corridor residents are involved in day-to-day questions of survival. Residents who have been in the community for a number of years have experienced or witnessed the direct effects of renewal. Many have been turned out of their homes. Others have seen their neighborhoods outlined in abstract "plans" formulated by outside organizations. Although the situation has improved with recent urban renewal legislation, the injustices and insensitivities of the past are not easily forgotten. Actions of the city, the university, and other institutions, no matter how sound, are viewed with suspicion, and as threats to the community.

Through the years, a host of organizations, official and unofficial, have been formed to represent the views of the community. The Citizens Governing Board (CGB), made up of elected representatives from various sections of the corridor, is the link with the Model Neighborhood Agency of which the Cass Corridor is a part. This board must approve federal programs before they can be implemented. The Citizens District Council (CDC), a product of urban renewal legislation, was active in opposing early university plans for expansion, and has developed alternative plans based on community involvement. The Peoples Area Development Corporation (PADCO) was incorporated as an independent, nonprofit development corporation to plan the physical development of the corridor in accordance with the Demonstration Cities Act of 1966. PADCO's role was advisory, to give expression to the needs and aspirations of its citizens. Although a detailed plan and inventory were drawn up, it is questionable whether their plan will be used. The United Community Housing Coalition has been concerned with the education and legal rights of tenants. Among a number of unofficial groups, the People Concerned About Urban Renewal (PCAUR) was at one time effective in countering aspects of the university's expansion plans. The local newspaper, *The Community Reporter*, has played an important role in alerting residents to events that might have an effect on their lives. Finally, the community churches have sponsored a variety of welfare and information programs. In total, these various organizations have met with considerable success. For example, they have caused Wayne State University to change its original plan of low-rise buildings incorporating larger expanses of land to one favoring high-rise development. Probably more important, they have fostered a notable degree of community cohesion. Although the efforts of these various community groups often appear trivial compared to those of the large scale organizations that they oppose, their cumulative efforts have not been in vain.

The institutional and governmental viewpoint is quite different. Those interests view the renewal process as a step toward the revival of the central city. This viewpoint is bolstered by the ongoing developments of the downtown Renaissance Center, and the extension of the Medical and Cultural centers east of Woodward. The New Center and the Burroughs Corporation administrative center complete what is hoped to be one giant institutional and business complex straddling Woodward Avenue from downtown to Grand Boulevard. The institutional attitude toward the plight of Cass Corridor residents has long been one of unconcern. This attitude is slowly changing. Wayne State University is reformulating some long range goals, and shows signs of recognizing community interests.

These divergent interests are brought into focus in the dichotomous outlook concerning the Cass Corridor's future. The resident sees his neighborhood and the corridor in general as a stage manipulated by vested power interests over which he himself has no control. The institutional and renewal interests see their role as revitalizing the central city. Clearly the needs of both groups could be accommodated with the proper attitudes and planning. In the foreseeable future, such accommodation appears most unlikely. Whatever the resolution, however, the effects of renewal processes are clearly outlined on the Cass Corridor landscape. It is appropriate to examine the spatial variation of those effects throughout the study area.

Spatial Variation of Renewal Processes in the Cass Corridor

Renewal processes have had a marked impact upon the corridor's population, which declined from 37,456 in 1950, to 24,113 in 1960, to 19,136 in 1970 (Figure 9). In the 1950–1960 decade some of this loss reflected postwar suburban migration, but much was caused by university expansion and the construction of the John C. Lodge Freeway. The northern part of the corridor showed the greatest losses (68.4 and 49.1 percent respectively) over the decade. The central part of the corridor had the smallest loss. The two northern tracts also had a sharp decline during the 1960–1970 decade, again because of university expansion. During

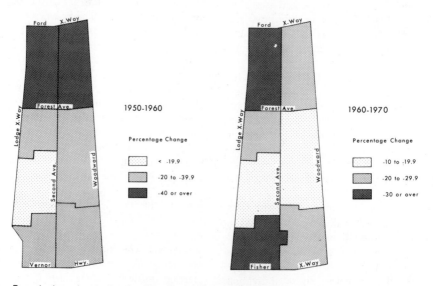

Figure 9. Population change in the Cass Corridor, 1950–1970.

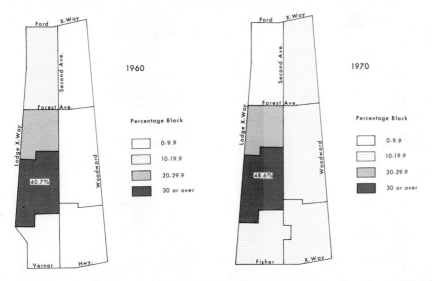

Figure 10. Black population change following urban renewal in the Cass Corridor, 1960-1970.

this decade the construction of the Fisher Freeway caused the population in the two southern tracts to decrease by 32.6 and 24.4 percent respectively. Again, tracts in the middle of the corridor had the smallest population losses. Thus, the pattern of population decline might be considered a contraction on all sides brought about by renewal processes surrounding the corridor.

Renewal has changed the racial composition of the corridor (Figure 10). In 1950 blacks comprised only 2.3 percent of the total population. In no census tract did they exceed 5 percent. Beween 1950 and 1960 the black population increased to 17.8 percent of the total, largely due to the construction of the E.J. Jeffries public housing project in the southwest section of the corridor. The tract that contains this project grew from 1.7 to 40.7 percent black over the decade. Between 1960 and 1970 the black population of the corridor increased to 24.2 percent. Increases in the three tracts bordering Woodward Avenue were related to the demolition of the virtually all-black Detroit Medical Center project area immediately east of Woodward. A decrease in the proportion of blacks in the two northwest tracts of the corridor likely reflects that blacks were affected more directly by the demolition program.

The effects of renewal upon residential stability are indicated in Figure 11, which shows for 1960 and 1970, the number of people who were living in the same housing five years earlier. In 1960 the northern- and southern-most tracts displayed the greatest instability. Turnover in the north reflected the large student population. In the southwest section of the corridor, turnover was associated with skid row transiency and the opening up of the Jeffries housing project. In the southeast, it reflected aged and skid row populations living in rooming houses. The two central tracts were again the most stable. The same basic pattern was manifest in 1970, with increased stability in the tract containing the housing project. Thus, like the pattern of population decline, residential stability patterns show the encroachment on all sides upon the more stable central area.

Land ownership patterns illustrate the effects of institutional expansion as well as the speculative activities associated with anticipated change (Figure 12). Between 1960 and 1973 the most striking change was the decline in the amount of property owned by individuals, and a corresponding increase in that held by educational institutions, realtors and investment brokers, and large corporations. In the northern part of the corridor, particularly north of Forest Avenue, there was an increase in property owned by the university and the city of Detroit. South of the Wayne State renewal area, in a section bounded by Forest, Willis, Third and Cass avenues, realtors and investment corporations are holding large tracts of land. In

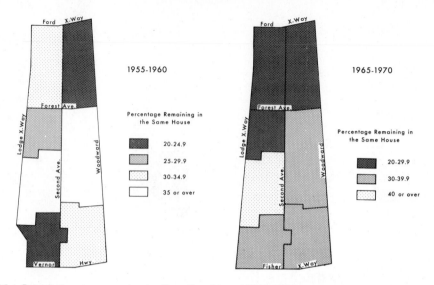

Figure 11. Population turnover in the Cass Corridor, 1955–1960 compared to 1965–1970.

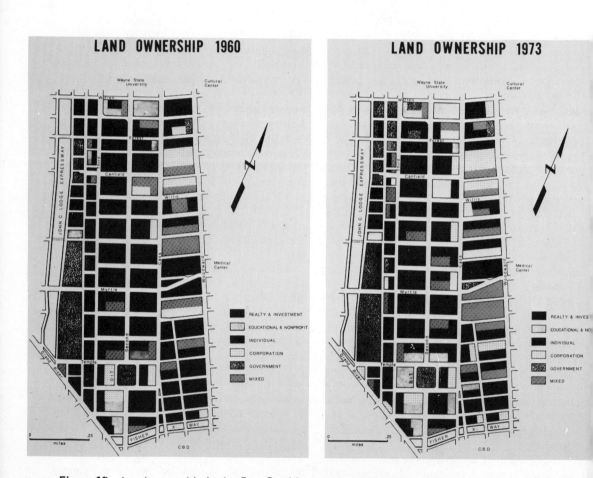

Figure 12. Land ownership in the Cass Corridor community, 1960 and 1973.

the southern part of the corridor, particularly south of Temple, increasing amounts of land are owned by educational institutions and investment companies, reflecting the presence, expansion, and anticipated additional development of the Detroit Institute of Technology. The increase in the amount of property owned by brokers and large corporations between Woodward Avenue and Cass Avenue, particularly between Canfield and Myrtle, was influenced by a proposed development plan incorporating the preservation of Orchestra Hall. In sum, elements associated with institutional expansion have brought about a profound change in the composition and pattern of land ownership in the Cass Corridor. Again, those changes are most pronounced on the outermost edges of the corridor, particularly in the northern and eastern sections, and to a lesser degree to the south.

Certain types of social agencies, such as Salvation Army missions, tend to concentrate in particular areas, but the agencies in general are well distributed throughout the corridor. Thus, unlike that of large institutions, the impact of social agencies upon adjacent residential areas comes from within the corridor, rather than from the edges.

Comparison of housing conditions between 1971 and 1974 indicates that distinct changes have taken place, many of which might be attributed to renewal (Figure 13). As might be expected, conditions in the university renewal area had deteriorated during the period. Likewise, a marked deterioration occurred along Third and Fourth avenues as far north as Canfield. On Third Avenue this represented an extension of skid row conditions, whereas on Fourth this deterioration appears to reflect a physical and psychological isolation from more viable residential areas east of Third. Elsewhere, declining housing conditions are

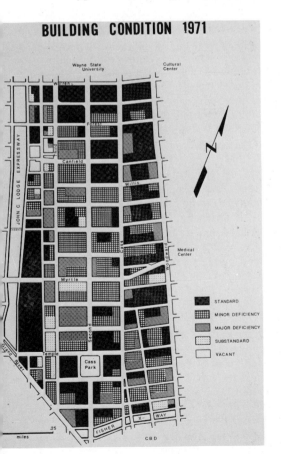 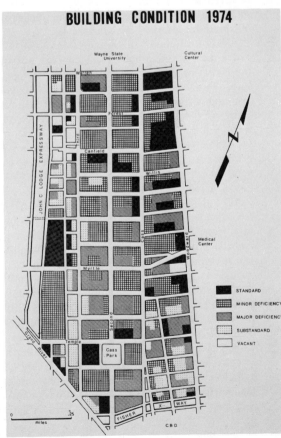

Figure 13. Condition of buildings in the Cass Corridor community, 1971 and 1973.

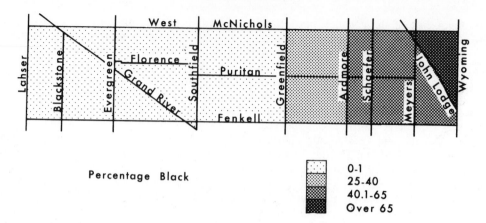

Percentage Black

0-1
25-40
40.1-65
Over 65

Figure 14. Northwest Detroit, black population in 1970. Source: Robert Sinclair, "Ghetto Expansion and the Urban Landscape," *Wiener Geographische Schriften, Festschrift Leopold G. Scheidel,* vol. 2 (1975).

related to stillborn urban renewal projects, the takeover of property by the Detroit Board of Education, and, in the southeast of the corridor, the deterioration of hotel-like quarters inhabited by old and poor individuals.

These different spatial patterns give a clear picture of what is happening within the Cass Corridor. To a large degree that picture is one of deterioration or of instability resulting from speculation about the future. Many of these patterns show the influence of surrounding renewal projects that are shrinking the viable community into a contracting residential core. There is little evidence in those patterns of a "renewal" in the conditions of Cass Corridor residents.

Like many other neighborhoods in the Detroit inner city, the Cass Corridor is subjected to forces of change, many associated with the renewal process. These forces are complex and incorporate a multitude of interrelated elements. They have resulted in hardship and conflict, and have left much of the corridor in a state of physical deterioration. In 1973, there is little indication of a resolution of the conflicts described here, and little overall understanding of the complex interrelationships associated with the forces of change. There is even less indication of a consensus concerning the corridor's future. This frustration and uncertainty allow the elements of conflict and decay to feed upon themselves and become increasingly worse.

RACIAL CHANGE IN
NORTHWEST DETROIT

Northwest Detroit refers to a one mile wide strip extending five miles in an east-west direction between Wyoming and Lahser roads (Figure 14). The greater part of this strip is in the Detroit Middle Zone, but conditions west of the Southfield Freeway are more like those of the Suburban Area of Radial Development. Northwest Detroit currently is undergoing racial change, and the strip exhibits all aspects of that change. The change is associated with the overall northwesterly expansion of Detroit's black population, which has been such a dominant trend during the last two decades.

Traditionally, the northwest Detroit area has had an aura of well-being. Built during the late 1920s and 1930s, the area has been one of solid middle and upper income brick homes on quiet, tree-lined streets. Those streets were crossed at one mile intervals by major arteries, which provided both commercial facilities and excellent access to downtown Detroit and other parts of the city. The area's public and parochial schools had an outstanding reputation, churches were a source of local pride, and city services were excellent. Although the population of 51,113 in 1960 represented a diversity of occupations, incomes, and backgrounds, it was marked by a high degree of residential stability and a common sense of well-being. Among the many neighborhoods in northwest Detroit, two stand out as distinctive. Between Southfield and Evergreen is the prestigious Rosedale Park, inhabited by wealthy professionals, businessmen, and many Detroit civic leaders. In the extreme southwest is the old lower income community of Brightmoor, still dominated by poorly built wooden frame houses, and a cheap, deteriorated commercial strip along Fenkell Avenue.

In the past decade the long-standing residential stability of the area has been affected by a complex of forces associated with racial change. The black proportion of the population increased from less than 1 percent (fifteen persons) in 1960 to 24 percent (12,159 persons) in 1970. In the early 1960s the effects of racial transition were confined to the east and southeast edges of the area, the direction from which black expansion has taken place. By the end of the decade the prospect of racial change had been accepted in all but the westernmost parts of the area, and subsequent development has been conditioned by this fact.

The Process of Racial Change in Northwest Detroit

The steady influx of black population into northwest Detroit since the middle 1960s has been accompanied by white outmigration, so that the term racial succession best describes the process. Because this white suburban movement has involved many families with school age children, the present white population shows a higher than average proportion of older persons, childless couples, and civil servants tied to the city of Detroit by residence requirements. White families still move into some parts of the area, but they have not made up for the numbers who have moved to the suburbs. Thus, there has been an unusual choice of housing for blacks who are able to afford it. Black expansion in the study area initially includes those of middle and upper income, including professionals, businessmen, and white and blue collar workers. However, after this initial black migration, pressures follow from inner city ghetto areas, as poorer blacks, often deprived of former residences by various renewal processes, move into areas already occupied by blacks. Often, wealthier blacks move outward again as additional housing becomes available. Thus, black expansion in the study area involves not only racial transition, but

also a form of succession within the black population.

One of the most important elements associated with the above changes is a series of problems in the area's schools. Partly these problems reflect the overall financial difficulties of the Detroit public school system, but local factors are also involved. First, the dramatic population turnover leads to imbalances in student numbers. Some schools temporarily have declining enrollments due to outward migration. Others are subject to severe overcrowding because incoming black families generally have larger numbers of school age children than the white families they replace. Second, black students, coming from poorer sections of the city, often have more limited educational backgrounds than children brought up in the local area. Finally, public schools have been the scene of violent racial conflicts, gaining national attention during one disturbance in 1969. These factors all have an effect upon the quality of public schools. Parochial schools also have been affected. Traditionally, Roman Catholic schools have played an important educational role in northwest Detroit, and they remain a stabilizing influence in the western sections of the study area (Figure 15). However, many parochial schools have closed, largely for financial reasons, so that persons desiring a parochial educational system have turned elsewhere. Overall, school problems have become one of the most important causes of instability within the study area, and one of the main stimulants to more rapid suburban migration.

A second element is an increase in crime. Crimes reported to the Detroit Police Department increased in the area from 1,324 in 1966, to 3,249 in 1970, to 4,131 in 1972. This increase involves a set of complex and apparently contradictory factors. Although "crime in the streets" is a citywide phenomenon, the greatest concentrations tend to be in slums and more blighted areas of the inner city. To some degree the spread of crime in northwest Detroit reflects (1) the spread of blighted, inner city conditions into parts of the study area, and (2) the instability of the transition process. The impact of increasing crime in the study area is great. Evidence of a violent crime induces thoughts of departure for those financially able to move—whether white in a racially

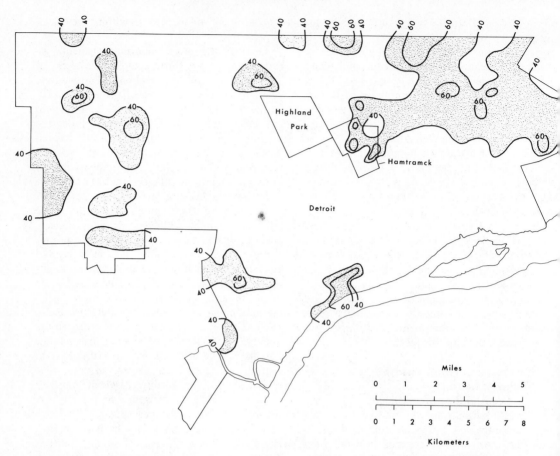

Figure 15. Percentage of elementary school children attending parochial schools in 1970.

changing neighborhood or black in a neighborhood undergoing the spread of blight. Moreover, the fear of crime, and responses to that fear—watchdogs, bricked-over windows, burglar alarms, metal screens, and empty streets—create an appearance of instability and have a further blighting effect upon a neighborhood.

There have been significant changes in northwest Detroit's commercial structure. The one time prosperous "Mile Roads" of the study area have experienced commercial decline, as local residents were attracted to suburban shopping malls, and as the customers replacing them have had less purchasing power. As a result there has been a decline in the quality of merchandise and services; the introduction of different functions, merchandise, and merchandising habits; and an overall advance of neglect and decay. Streets in the eastern part of the study area take on aspects of the inner city ghetto. Many stores are empty or boarded up. Screens,

padlocks, and security guards are part of the local retail scene. Moreover, many of those indexes of commercial decline are found in advance of other aspects of change, in areas otherwise untouched by blight. The psychological impact upon adjacent residential areas is assumed to be considerable.

The rapidly changing situation in the study area incorporates many elements that have no original relationship with the racial change process, but that become an integral part of that process with the passage of time. One such element is associated with the HUD house problem, which has had such detrimental effects in Detroit. The circumstances leading to the presence of such homes have already been described. These circumstances are accentuated in areas of instability, and their evidence is marked within the study area. Many streets in black and mixed neighborhoods are pockmarked with vacant homes, some falling into disrepair, and all presenting an unkempt appearance. The presence of one or more such houses on any street is detrimental to adjacent properties. Potential residents are turned away. Often the result is to hasten the approach of residential blight. Another such element is a general reduction in city services, brought on in the last decade by a consistent decrease in city revenues, with an accompanying decline in civil service morale. The reduction is not so marked in the western part of the study area, largely due to the greater political influence of its residents. In the eastern section, where political influence is not so great and population instability has placed greater demands upon limited services, the effects of the reduction are pronounced. A third and unexpected element is the presence of Dutch Elm disease. A pleasing feature of northwest Detroit is the presence of tall elm trees, which line almost every residential street and blend with brick homes to provide a residential landscape of great beauty. In recent years many of those trees have been afflicted with Dutch Elm disease and have been cut down, leaving many front yards stark and void. The destruction of this element of the cityscape has changed the appearance of some areas, such that it is difficult to distinguish this from other indexes of blight.

In sum, the complex of elements described above has had a blighting effect upon the landscape of the study area. Blight, in promoting residential instability, becomes itself part of the racial transition process, even though many of the contributing elements originally were independent of that process. Blight is not easily eradicated when the racial transition process is complete. Indeed, because the initial expansion of black occupance often is followed by a subsequent movement of poorer blacks, bringing problems of the inner city ghetto, blighted conditions have tended to increase.

Several agents are consciously involved in directing or controlling black expansion in the study area. One is the real estate industry. Certain real estate companies clearly have manipulated the racial transition process for personal gains, which include not only commissions accruing from rapid housing turnover, but also profits made by buying homes at panic rates from departing whites and selling at higher rates to incoming blacks. There have been case examples of the well-known panic-promoting tactics associated with blockbusting. Within the study area at least two lawsuits are underway charging real estate companies with designating "territories" inside which, by agreement, sales to blacks (or whites respectively) are discouraged. The interest of realtors in the transition process is marked by concentrations of short-lived real estate offices along the study area's business streets. Although the more overt practices have become subdued in recent years under the pressures of city ordinances, local community organizations, and press publicity, the real estate element still plays an important role in determining the nature and pattern of black expansion in the study area.

A second and countering agent is the local community councils, which have become the foci of efforts to combat the more deleterious aspects of change in the study area. Activities of these councils include pressuring city government to change zoning laws and improve services, obtaining funds for school improvements, organizing block clubs, and uniting citizen support against real estate blockbusting and the increase in HUD housing. Probably more important, they have fostered much community cohesion. It is no coincidence that most organizations correspond to and take their names from the traditional units of local loyalty in the area, namely the primary and secondary school districts.

As might be expected, the changing situation in northwest Detroit has been the source of conflicts and tensions. The most dramatic type of conflict is racial, beginning with white antipathy toward incoming blacks, and ending with black resentment toward white persons remaining in otherwise black areas. Detroit newspapers have described extreme cases of cross burnings on lawns of incoming black families, as well as harrassment of elderly white couples by black youths. Nevertheless, the most violent confrontations have occurred in the area's schools.

Other types of conflict are less dramatic. They include those divergences in outlooks, perceptions, and responses that tend to be characteristic of changing areas. These conflicts tend to vary throughout the study area. In the rapidly changing central part of the study area, middle and upper middle income blacks, who were early migrants into the area, often resent the later arrival of poorer blacks. Those wealtheir blacks tend to be most conscious of the blight, commercial decline, and deterioration in services that have taken place in much of the study area. Often, their response is to move farther west within the study area.

The white resident of this central area also has a distinct set of attitudes. He is fully aware of the ongoing transition processes and is quite convinced that the area where he lives will be predominantly black within the next few years. Like the middle income blacks of the same area, he is conscious of the blighting processes that are spreading within the area. Moreover, he is able to compare conditions today with those of the somewhat nostalgic past. For the most part, he considers it almost inevitable that he will move out of the area within the next five years. Unlike his black counterpart in the same area, his move is likely to be to a suburb, most likely Farmington, Southfield, or Redford Township.

The wealthier white resident in the western part of the study area has a somewhat different attitude. He also is aware of the changes taking place, and anticipates some racial change within his own neighborhood. However, he tends to believe that the more adverse elements associated with racial change are not inevitable, and that change will not necessarily affect his neighborhood's general stability. Generally, his attitude toward increased integration is more optimistic, and he is less inclined to consider moving from the area. This attitude brings to the fore one other aspect of conflict—namely, the conflict between certain elements of the real estate industry and the organizations attempting to preserve neighborhood stability. It is predominantly in the western part of the study area that this last-named conflict is to be found today.

Though less clear cut than the direct racial confrontations in the eastern part of the study area, these last-named conflicts in the western area have much meaning. They imply an awareness of the blighting elements that have accompanied racial transition, a belief that such elements are not inevitable, a recognition of the need for community efforts to counter those elements, and a realization among many that those efforts must include a considerable amount of integration. At the same time, the very existence of this realization tends to create a "self-fulfilling prophecy" of things to come. Conflicts within the western part of the area are

symptoms of an early stage of the racial transition process, just as the more direct confrontations farther east exemplify a later stage. The outcome of those earlier conflicts might well determine the future of the western parts of the study area.

In summary, racial change in northwest Detroit involves a large number of diverse elements, many of which have no original connection with the racial change process. In time those elements become closely identified with the process and bring about conditions that tend to bring about its continuation. It is appropriate to examine the spatial variation of those conditions throughout the study area.

Spatial Variation of the Racial Change Process in Northwest Detroit

The status of racial transition in northwest Detroit in 1970 is shown in Figure 14. The easternmost square mile has experienced almost complete racial turnover, with all census tracts more than 70 percent black. In the next three square miles the black population comprises more than 50 percent, 25 percent, and 2 percent respectively. In the remaining western areas the percentage is less than one.

The recency of population turnover is illustrated in Figure 16, which expresses the percentage of 1970 residents who were living in the area in 1965. In most of the western part of the area this percentage was between sixty-five and seventy-five, indicating a relatively high degree of stability. Toward the east this percentage declines to forty east of Greenfield and to twenty-five in the two easternmost square miles. This means that population turnover in eastern areas was as much as 75 percent within a five year period. The 1960–1970 population change map indicates aspects of the family structure of new residents (Figure 17). The eastern area shows a considerable population increase, as black families not only filled vacancies created by departing whites, but did so with larger families and consequently greater population densities. With one exception, no significant population change is discerned elsewhere in the study area.

The pattern of active racial turnover in early 1973 is suggested by a map of real estate listings (Figure 18). An east-west profile of numbers of houses for sale resembles a wave, with its crest in the central square mile, be-

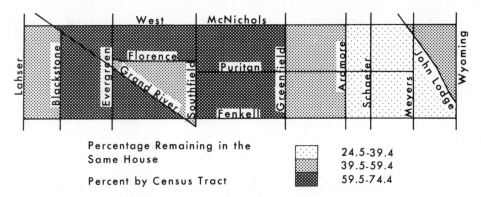

Figure 16. Population turnover in northwest Detroit, 1965–1970.

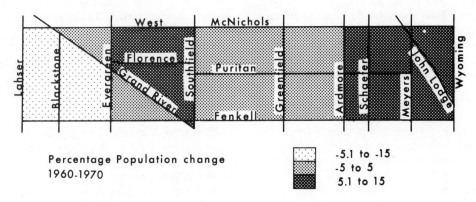

Figure 17. Population change in northwest Detroit, 1960–1970.

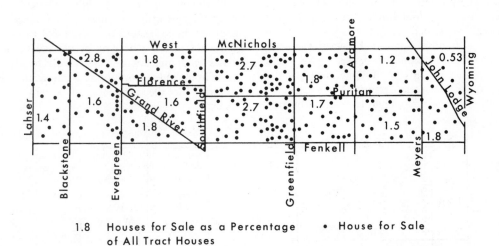

Figure 18. Northwest Detroit, Houses for Sale February 1973. Source: Robert Sinclair, "Ghetto Expansion and the Urban Landscape," *Wiener Geographische Schriften, Festschrift Leopold G. Scheidel,* vol. 2 (1975).

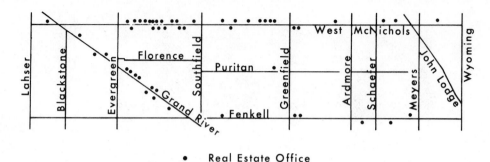

• Real Estate Office

Figure 19. Real estate offices in northwest Detroit, October 1973. Source: Robert Sinclair, "Ghetto Expansion and the Urban Landscape," *Wiener Geographische Schriften, Festschrift Leopold G. Scheidel,* vol. 2 (1975).

tween Greenfield and Southfield. To the west, in front of the wave, the "for sale" density is half as great. To the east, behind the crest of the wave, the "for sale" density is also half as great, but only in the first square mile. It declines to less than 30 percent after the first square mile.

The relationship between the pattern of houses for sale and that of real estate offices is revealing. Reference has been made to the east-west movement of short-lived real estate offices along the commercial arteries of the study area. Figure 19 shows the location of such offices during the summer of 1973. Practically no real estate offices are to be found in the western two miles. Offices in the eastern two miles are relatively few, about three per mile. The greatest concentration, ten and sixteen per mile, is found in the two square miles between Greenfield and Evergreen, closer to the area of active turnover. However, the peak of this concentration is between Greenfield and Evergreen. This is one mile ahead of the area of active racial transition, in an area which remains predominantly white. The pat-

tern of real estate offices would seem to be a portent of other patterns of the future.

Quite a different pattern is shown in the map of housing in FHA mortgage default (Figure 20). In the two easternmost square miles the proportion of such houses is among the highest in the city, ranging from 3.7 to 7 percent. This proportion declines rapidly to the west, and becomes negligible throughout the remainder of the area. This general pattern is expressed more vividly in a map of vacant HUD homes (Figure 21). Virtually all such homes are in the easternmost two square miles. This area already has gone through the racial transition process, and has a relatively stable "for sale" situation. The chain of circumstances that led to mortgage defaults and the presence of vacant HUD homes appears to be initiated well after other change processes have taken place. It might be hypothesized that the rapid turnover of homes in the preceding period led to purchases by families who were unable to afford either home upkeep or mortgage payments. The backwash is the incidence of vacant HUD homes.

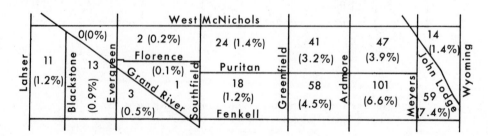

Figure 20. The number (and percentage) of each tract's houses in FHA (HUD) mortgage default, October, 1973, in northwest Detroit.

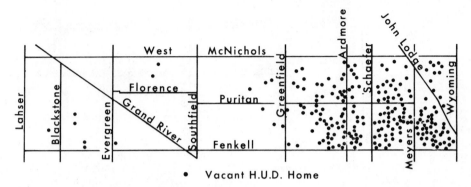

Figure 21. Vacant HUD houses, March 1973. Source: Robert Sinclair, "Ghetto Expansion and the Urban Landscape," *Wiener Geographische Schriften, Festschrift Leopold G. Scheidel*, vol. 2 (1975).

Patterns expressing commercial blight closely parallel those of housing default and vacancy. Figure 22 maps the vacancy status of stores and offices along main commercial arteries in the summer of 1973. The overwhelming concentration in the east is clear, where the percentage of vacancies on some streets is more than 40 percent. The vacancy count declines by more than one-half in the middle section, and with one minor exception becomes even lower in the western sections. Figure 23 maps the incidence of protective devices (iron screens, metal bars, bricked-in windows, etc.) on the windows of commercial structures. Again, the concentration in the east is apparent. The circumstances leading to commercial blight are initiated before and during the time of racial

transition, but become more prevalent after the initial transition has taken place. The commercial condition in the easternmost square mile is akin to that in Detroit's inner city ghetto.

When the different patterns are considered in perspective, a further insight is gained into the complicated process of racial change. Each pattern varies from east to west. The patterns do not coincide, however. If the basic pattern is black-white occupancy change, then racial change in 1973 is concentrated in the middle square mile, between Greenfield and Southfield. Certain patterns, such as that of houses for sale, correspond to this basic pattern. Others, such as those for population, commercial blight, and housing vacancies, are con-

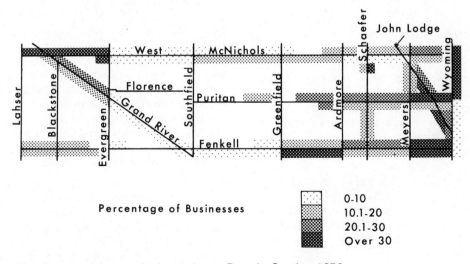

Figure 22. Commercial vacancies in northwest Detroit, October 1973.

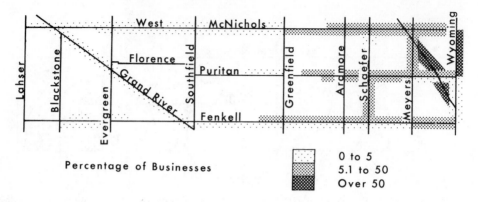

Percentage of Businesses

0 to 5
5.1 to 50
Over 50

Figure 23.   Incidence of storefront protective screens in northwest Detroit, October 1973.

centrated behind (to the east). Others, including
the pattern of real estate offices, show an
intensity well ahead (to the west) of the peak
of racial transition. In sum, the process of
racial change is not confined to the edge of
racial transition. Conditions in large areas
behind this edge reflect that this transition
has taken place in the past. Conditions far in
advance are underlain by the anticipation of
that change.

Like many other areas of the city, our five
mile strip of northwest Detroit in 1973 is a
locale within which the complex forces associated with racial change are to be found. These
forces already have had a profound impact
upon large parts of the area. Whether that impact will be similar in the remainder of the
area, and in other nearby areas, still is to be
determined.

URBAN EXPANSION IN
OAKLAND TOWNSHIP

Oakland Township is a standard thirty-six
square mile survey township in northeastern
Oakland County some thirty miles from downtown Detroit (Figure 24). Long exhibiting the
features associated with the Zone of Rural
Change, the township now appears destined to
undergo the processes associated with direct
urban expansion. That expansion comes from
the south, an apparent continuation of the
process that has engulfed Birmingham, Troy,
Rochester, and Avon Township. Thus the
elements involved are associated with the Zone
of Radial Development.

Traditionally Oakland Township has de-

picted a prosperous rural landscape, on a rolling to hilly upland which is interrupted only in
the southwest by the valley of Paint Creek and
its tributaries. One of the county's earliest
settled townships, it developed rapidly into an
area of prosperous farmers concerned primarily
with dairying and cattle raising. The agricultural scene has been enhanced by the presence
of farming estates, owned by wealthy Detroit
families, farmed by efficient year round managers and used by their owners as summer residences. Several families have turned their land
holdings into game and wildlife preserves. Since
the 1940s affluent nonfarm residents have
appeared on the scene. Their arrival in the
township might be considered part of a slow
ongoing process, which has contributed to,
rather than detracted from, a relatively harmonious symbiosis.

It is this symbiosis that has been disrupted
by forces associated with urban expansion.
Initially these forces were quite subtle. By the
late 1960s the prospect of eventual urbanization had become accepted and the township's
subsequent development was conditioned by
this acceptance. Thus for more than six years
the township has been in the shadow of urban
expansion. It remains in this shadow, but today
development seems so inevitable that the direct
impact stage appears to be approaching.

The Urban Expansion Process in
Oakland Township

Underlying all other aspects of the urban
expansion process in Oakland Township is the
steady influx of wealthy nonfarm persons.
Those migrants are attracted by a beautiful

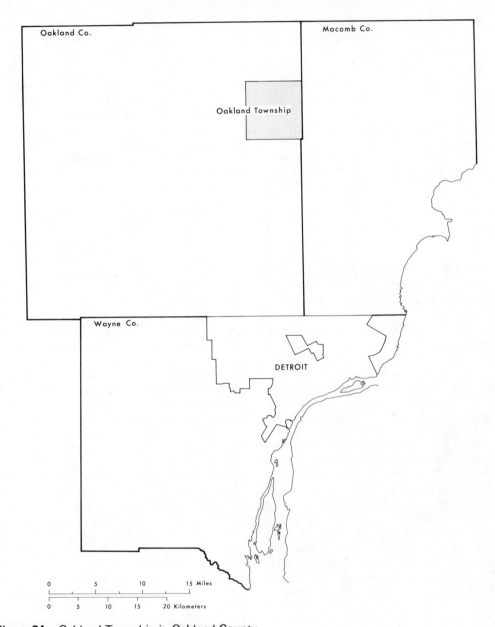

Figure 24. Oakland Township in Oakland County.

landscape, an open rural environment, and the opportunity for exclusive exurbanite living. Some have more specific desires, such as the proximity of reputable private schools, the presence of Oakland University, and even the opportunity to keep horses. For many, prestige is a factor. Automobile executives from the General Motors Tech Center and from Ford and Chrysler Corporations have established homes in the township. Professors and ad-ministrators from Oakland University have been attracted there, as have persons in other professions. There is evidence of an outward "sifting" of families from Detroit's more prestigious communities, such as Birmingham, Bloomfield Hills, and the Grosse Pointes. The high socioeconomic status of Oakland Township's residents is indicated by the fact that 50 percent had incomes between $15,000 and $30,000 in 1970, with more than 12 percent earning more than $30,000. Almost 50 percent had college degrees, and over 20 percent had advanced degrees. In general, it is this category of resident that has accounted for the township's population growth, from about 1,000 in the 1950s, to 5,000 in 1970, to about 10,000 by 1975.

This population influx has been accompanied by basic changes in the township's farming structure. Most farmers in Oakland Township are in their late fifties and early sixties, and many are near retirement. Few of their children have chosen to continue farming, and dependable farm labor has become almost nonexistent. As a result, there has been a gradual decline in the more arduous, intensive, and long term types of farming—quite often a sequence from dairying, to meat animals, to cash crops, and in some places to idle land. Other factors have hastened the process. Farm equipment costs have become exorbitant. Equipment dealers and repairmen have left the local scene. The former agricultural and marketing infrastructure largely has disappeared. Finally, farming operations increasingly have been affected by "nuisances." These include well-known rural-urban problems like frightening livestock, treading on crops, stealing fruit, and throwing garbage; as well as more recent problems, such as the noise and environmental destruction caused by motor bikes in summer and snowmobiles in winter.

One element that has had a great impact upon farmers and nonfarm residents alike is the recent changes in property taxes. In the past few years three factors have combined to bring about what appear to be staggering tax increases. One is the rise accompanying higher land values as the township changed from a rural condition to one of anticipated urbanization. A second is increased millages caused by improved services and planned services (sewer interceptors, increased school populations, etc.). A third is the implementation of recent state regulations that all Michigan private property be assessed at 50 percent of appraised value. Any one of these factors might have been enough to influence decisions of residents and landowners. Occurring together, they have caused farmers to give up farming or move to other agricultural areas, estate owners to reduce or subdivide their property, and land speculators to sell land to developers much earlier than they normally would have.

One event has recently altered the pattern of urban expansion in the township. This is the construction of the Paint Creek sewer interceptor, which is scheduled to serve a district encompassing much of the southwest portion of the township. Normally such a utility is a synonym for suburban growth in the Zone of Rural Change, and the recent spate of real estate activity appears to verify the fact that this part of Oakland Township will be no exception. At the same time, the interceptor has generated great controversy within the township, bringing into focus many of the conflicting attitudes toward growth that are discussed later in this section.

The urban expansion process in Oakland Township is influenced directly and consciously by what might be termed the "development" component. This reflects the actions of decisionmakers who manipulate, convert, develop, and build upon land. The township shows evidence of the well-known complex of landowners, speculators, developers, builders, and managers, serviced by the activities of realtors, bankers, loan companies, insurance companies, lawyers, advertisers, and political pressure groups. At first glance the operations of this complex appear to be at an early stage in Oakland Township, in that the amount of subdivided land is small and scattered. Other factors indicate that the operation is further advanced. Virtually all land within the Paint Creek Sewer Interceptor District is in the hands of speculators or developers. Much land elsewhere in the township belongs to speculators, although often it is rented to local farmers. The development component shows a remarkable degree of external control. The traditional local real estate agent has long since been superseded by companies that have moved their main offices to Birmingham and Bloomfield Hills, and established branch offices in Troy, Rochester, and other suburbs. Development companies in the Paint Creek Sewer Interceptor District also are developing land throughout the Detroit region. Bankers, insurance companies, and law firms which service the developers operate from downtown Detroit or some well-established suburb. The overriding impression is that the development component comprises a well-organized, externally located decisionmaking complex. Today the operations of that complex are at an initial stage. Given the right circumstances, they might well proceed at an unexpectedly rapid pace.

As in any area of change, psychological factors have an influence on events in Oakland Township. One such factor might be termed the Avon Township syndrome. Although many residents of Oakland Township might not fully comprehend the ongoing expansion processes, they can readily observe the consequences of those processes in other suburbs. Often the very mention of such suburbs brings about a psychological reaction. The closest (visibly, physically, and psychologically) of those suburbs is the immediate neighbor to the south, Avon Township, which currently is undergoing the full impact of suburbanization. To many Oakland Township residents "growth" means what is taking place to the south. Whether such growth is viewed favorably (as it is by some) or with distaste (as it is by most), the vision of Avon Township looms large in the actions and decisions made in Oakland Township.

In recent years those actions and decisions have shown a considerable degree of organization. A relatively large proportion of the township's residents are highly educated; are interested in the township's future; and have professional competence in planning, government, and law. Cooperation has taken place among those residents. An outgrowth of this cooperation is the Oakland Township Association, a citizen's group that has actively influenced local government. As a result the township has adopted several unique conservation ordinances (soil and erosion control, wetlands, zoning, purchase of land for recreational purposes, etc.), is formulating a master plan, seeks the advice of county and metropolitan planners, and attempts to involve more residents in important township decisions. The association has become a model for similar citizens organizations throughout the state. The degree to which the Oakland Township Association will be able to control and direct future forces of growth in the township is uncertain. Today, however, the association plays a significant role in the township's development.

Almost inevitably the forces of change in Oakland Township have given rise to tensions and conflicts. Those conflicts are not only connected with the broad forces of urbanization that already have been described; they also include those differences in individual

human perceptions, responses, and opinions that crop up in situations of change. Clearly those differences stem from the particular characteristics and outlooks of individuals. Often, however, they tend to polarize around the divergent attitudes of two general groups of residents. One group comprises the recent immigrants—relatively young, with high incomes, living in wealthy subdivisions in the southern part of the township. The other includes the township's longtime residents—older, with large landholdings (farms or estates), but with relatively low annual incomes. This group lives largely in the middle and northern parts of the township.

The divergence between those two groups is expressed in their general perception of impending urbanization. The more recent subdivision resident is closer to, more experienced with, and has more information about the expansion processes taking place within the township. He tends to be more conscious of the indexes of decline in the rural environment. Most significantly, he observes on a firsthand, day-to-day basis the growth of adjacent Avon Township, and is more able to project the possibility of a similar growth pattern in Oakland Township. The long term resident farther north, though most concerned about increasing taxes and increasing nuisances, appears to be less aware of the deeper implications of the urban expansion process.

The divergence between the two groups can also be observed in their preferences for the township's future development and, more particularly, in the degree to which each group is willing to pay for those preferences. Certain preferences are universal. For example, virtually all Oakland Township residents profess a desire to preserve as much of an open, rural atmosphere as possible. Most residents oppose high density developments. Most prefer to continue traveling outside the township for commercial purposes rather than allowing commercial development within the township. Moreover, most residents show an expression of support for the efforts of the Oakland Township Association. However, opinions differ sharply between the two groups concerning how those preferences should be brought to fruition. The recently arrived subdivision residents favor immediate township purchase of land for future space needs and are willing to pay increased taxes for this purpose. The longtime residents tend to be opposed. Living in the more rural part of the township, the latter do not perceive the loss of open space to be so imminent. Moreover, their larger landholdings would subject them to undue taxation to pay for such purchases. These differences are closely associated with a more general divergence in attitude toward growth. Subdivision residents in the south wish to limit and control residential growth. Longtime residents are more amenable to growth. In sum, it is the newcomers who want fewer newcomers and who, as the longtime residents say, "want to be the very last persons to come into the township."

The resulting conflicts are many and varied. New subdivision residents want to retain the traditional rural "natural beauty" roads, are opposed to new subdivisions, and object to the idea of any industrial or commercial enterprise in the township. Their more northerly counterparts are more interested in sound road maintenance (they are more dependent on it), are not so opposed to new developments, and often see some type of industrial or commercial development as the only solution to soaring property taxes. These differences lead to a somewhat divergent attitude toward

planning. Newcomers are more likely to consult with county planning officials, to promote zoning ordinances, and to support activities of the Oakland Township Association. The longtime residents might show an overt interest, but inherently tend to be suspicious of any ordinance that might threaten their ability to make independent decisions.

In summary, urban expansion in Oakland Township involves a number of diverse and interacting elements. Ironically, many of those elements have no initial connection with the urban expansion process. Almost inevitably they become incorporated into the process and tend to hasten its progress. Certain conditions associated with the urban expansion process are to be observed on the township's landscape. It is appropriate to examine the spatial variation of those conditions.

Spatial Variation of the Urban Expansion Process in Oakland Township

The pattern of immigration into Oakland Township is illustrated by the location of residential subdivisions in the years 1956, 1964, and 1973 (Figure 25). In 1956 plotted land was found only around Cranberry Lake in the north

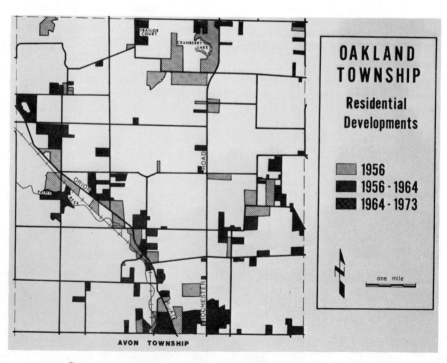

Figure 25. Oakland Township, residential subdivisions, 1956, 1964, 1973.

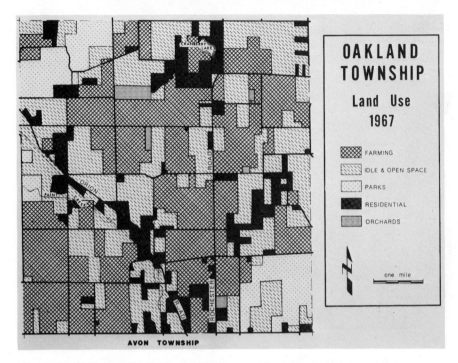

Figure 26. Oakland Township, land use, 1967.

of the township, where the development represented summer weekend cottages, along Orion Road overlooking the scenic Paint Creek Valley, and in a few small patches east of Rochester Road. By 1964 consolidation had taken place around all these nuclei, particularly along the Orion Road artery. Subdivision activity that has taken place since that time has been concentrated along Orion Road and more conspicuously in two sections in the southern part of the township along Orion, Livernois, and Rochester roads. It is in these two last named areas that most subdivision currently is taking place. Today the overall impression in all those residential areas is that of affluent exurbia, from the individual villas nestled in the hills overlooking Paint Creek Valley to the extensive landscaped subdivisions in the southern tiers, to the acreage estates with their horse farms found in other parts of the township. The one exception to this picture of affluence is a set of mobile homes in the far north, the township's concession to a federal regulation requiring some space in every community to be set aside for low income housing.

These residential subdivisions comprise only a small part of the township's total land use, as shown in 1967 and 1973 (Figures 26 and

27). More than five-sixths of Oakland Township is in two categories—farmland and idle open land. The remaining one-sixth is occupied mainly by public parks.

The largest farm acreages are found in a relatively compact area in the center of the township and in a smaller area to the southwest. Farming here, however, is a far cry from the prosperous dairying of the 1950s. Since that period it has changed, first to the raising of cattle and sheep for the local market, and later to the present emphasis on cash crops. These cash crops include hay for the townships 650 recreational horses as well as for ponies in the Detroit's Belle Isle Park, wheat for the mill in nearby Richmond, and corn for sale as feed for farmers farther to the north. By 1973 only one farmer had dairy cattle, while two pastured some beef cattle. The changing nature of farming is also marked by the increase in rented land, which even in 1967 comprised approximately half the farmland. Many farmers have found it more profitable to sell their land and rent it back from the new owners.

Farmland acreage is almost equaled by that of open or idle land. Open land is found throughout the township but is concentrated in the east, along the northern fringe, and in a

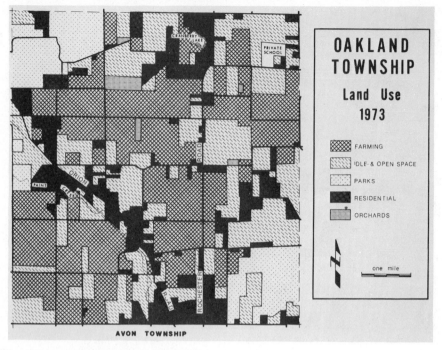

Figure 27. Oakland Township, land use, 1973.

broad belt on both sides of the Paint Creek Valley. Much of this land traditionally has been idle, comprising wetlands, forested land, and the preserves of private landowners who have chosen to keep their land in a relatively natural state. Oakland Township is exceptional in having only a small amount of the neglected, abandoned farmland that is so characteristic of other parts of the Zone of Rural Change. Thus, unlike other parts of that zone, the categories marked "idle and open" continue to have considerable aesthetic appeal. The particular nature of idle land in the township explains why there was no increase in that category between 1967 and 1973.

Perhaps the most revealing spatial pattern is that of land ownership, which can be examined by looking at the ownership categories of large land parcels in 1956, 1967, and 1973 (Figures 28, 29 and 30). In 1956 only a few parcels of land were in the hands of investors. Otherwise land was still owned by families who had been there for fifteen to one hundred years. By 1966 approximately 2,155 acres of land, largely in the center and southwest of the township, had been sold to investors, This corresponded closely with the rented farmland in the

1967 land use map. Between 1967 and 1973 the ownership pattern changed more dramatically, as a further 3,598 acres were sold to investors and 491 acres to developers. By the summer of 1973 few parcels remained in original hands, and the largest remaining parcel, a 750 acre farm, was up for sale.

To a remarkable degree the land ownership pattern explains the pattern of land use. The bulk of the farmland in Oakland Township is not in the hands of farmers, but is owned by investors who lease out their land (often to the original owners) until the time is right for selling (generally to developers). Much of the idle land is also in the hands of investors or developers. In 1973 the most notable ownership trend was the increase in direct purchases by developers and the shortened time span of investor-owned land, a trend prompted by recent tax increases. For example, the aforementioned 750 acre farm was being considered, not by an investor, but directly by a developer.

One of the most significant spatial patterns is that of land values. Although lack of specific information makes the construction of accurate land value maps impossible, local insights enable generalizations to be made. Those gen-

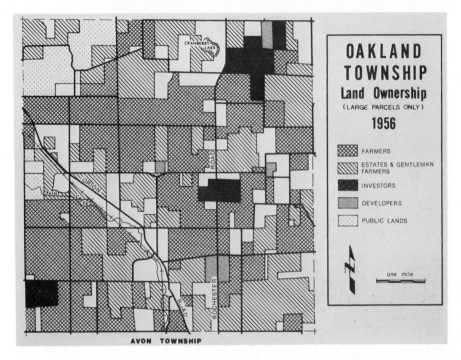

Figure 28. Oakland Township, land ownership, 1956.

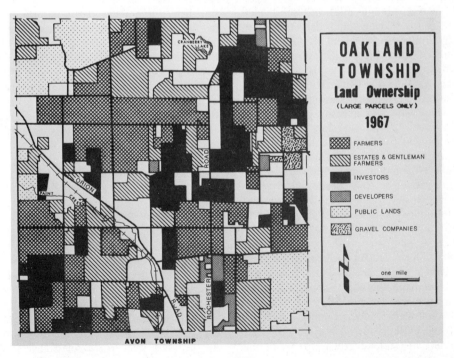

Figure 29. Oakland Township, land ownership, 1967.

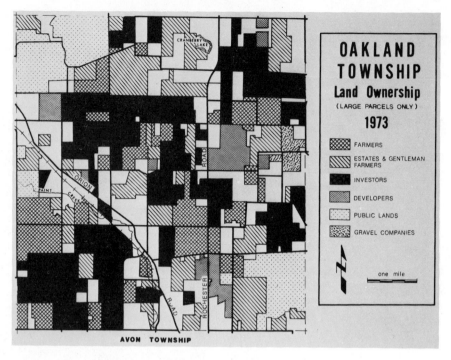

Figure 30. Oakland Township, land ownership, 1973.

eralizations are on two levels—namely, open land (both farmed and idle) and subdivided land. The status of open land is depicted easily. In 1960 farmland in Oakland Township sold for about $600 per acre. In 1967 this land had increased to $2,000 per acre and by 1973 the price was $5,000. Obviously such prices do not reflect the value for farming. The status of subdivided land also is easily portrayed. In 1973 half acre to one acre lots on spacious subdivisions sold for $10,000 and, in spots of particular scenic amenities, for $20,000. Such prices reflect the unique economic status of the township's residents. They also provide a clue to the future development of the township. Either future migrants into the township will continue to be among the wealthiest in the Detroit area, or parts of the township will give way to high density residential developments. Which of those two alternatives will prevail is perhaps the most important question facing Oakland Township.

When considered independently, each of these spatial patterns provides a clue to what is happening in Oakland Township. When the patterns are considered together and in per-

spective, an even clearer picture of the township begins to emerge. It is a picture underlain by the anticipation of change and determined by the uncertainty associated with that change. Like other parts of the Zone of Rural Change, Oakland Township in the mid-1970s had become a stage upon which the complex forces of urban expansion were beginning to impinge. Because of the township's particular socio-economic status, the effects of those forces might well be different than in other parts of the Detroit system. To what degree it will be different cannot now be foreseen.

SUMMARY

The Cass Corridor, the northwest Detroit strip, and Oakland Township are small areas within the Detroit system that in the mid-1970s are affected by different forces of change. Despite the wide disparity among the three areas, and the different forces that are involved, there are elements of similarity in the three cases. Most apparent is the complexity of each situation. At the local level, forces of change involve a myriad of elements. Many of those elements have no initial connection with the basic process involved, but in time they are incorporated into the process and become integral parts of it. Each of the three situations also is characterized by conflict and instability, which extend well beyond the place where the actual change is taking place. Often this conflict remains long after the change has taken place.

The three situations are only slected examples, each unique in itself. At the same time, each is typical in the sense that such complex situations are to be found throughout those parts of the Detroit system where the different forces of change are operating. As has been seen, much of the Detroit metropolitan area is involved. In the mid-1970s these situations pervade and typify every zone of the spatial model described above. In a real sense, they are the very essence of the Detroit system.

Conclusion

A number of basic themes pervade this study. Among them, perhaps the most basic is the theme of diversity. The vast sprawling entity that we call the Detroit system incorporates a rich and varied mosaic of areas, landscapes, and peoples. Clearly this is one of the system's great assets. Diversity has contributed greatly to the remarkable past achievements of the Detroit system. It provides an underlying color and vitality that sometimes is hidden beneath the surface monotony found in much of the area. It is one of the system's sources of promise for the future.

At the same time diversity has its dangers. These occur when diversity leads to differentiation and segregation, a second theme which pervades this study. In its development, the Detroit system has been differentiated into a set of different social areas. Although this differentiation occurs at a number of levels, attention in this study has focused upon the six zones of the spatial model discussed earlier. In many respects the zones constitute different "realms," which are separated by social distance and by different mental and perceptual outlooks. Among those different outlooks, probably the most important is the perception that persons in each zone have of the remainder of the Detroit system. With the passage of time the segregation of these different realms has become more pronounced. This has been accentuated by the spatial expansion of the whole system, which has increased the scope of the different realms.

Persons in one realm can become "locked in" to the activities of their own social world, and come to know and care less and less about other realms. Ignorance of the Detroit zones on the part of the two suburban zones appears to increase as time passes and as the spatial extent of those suburban zones expands. Meanwhile, the lack of knowledge about the outlying zones shown by residents of the Inner Zone continues to increase. In sum, social differentiation, and its accompanying liabilities, tend to become self-perpetuating.

The increasing differentiation of the Detroit system's social realms appears to contradict another theme of this study—namely, the continuing interdependence of different parts of the system. Each zone of our spatial model plays an essential functional role within the total system. That role has its economic aspects. For example, decisionmaking tends to take place in the Suburban Area of Radial Development, whereas much of the skilled technical work force is provided by the Suburban Area of Intersectoral Development. The role played by each zone also has its social aspects. The Inner Zone, for example, has become a haven for publicly supported institutions, and also the receptacle for much that is unwanted or prohibited elsewhere in the system. By contrast, the Zone of Rural Change still provides the breathing space, or the "release force," of the system, giving the feeling that there is still somewhere to go when conditions elsewhere become too unpleasant.

In spite of increasing segregation, the Detroit system still is a functioning entity; it is a system in the most basic sense of the word.

Another dominant theme is that of change. In this study, emphasis has been put upon the broad forces of change that engulf and transform different parts of the system. Such forces are not only disruptive in themselves, they bring instability in advance, and often leave blight in their wake. Virtually every force of change that has been discussed in this study has been responsible for some degree of deterioration, whether in terms of direct destruction, or in terms of "limbo" associated with delay and uncertainty. In aggregate, much of the Detroit system shows the adverse effects of these forces of change.

Even a cursory examination of these forces of change points up another theme of this study—that of complexity. In trying to piece together what is happening in Oakland Township, in northwest Detroit, and in the Cass Corridor, the authors were confronted with such a complex of interrelated elements and events that it was impossible to account for all of them and difficult to put them into perspective. At a larger scale, those complexities become magnified.

When the basic and often contradictory themes woven through this vignette are looked at in perspective, the resulting picture indicates a fundamental dichotomy. On the one hand, all themes bring out elements of strength in the Detroit system. The rich diversity of its landscapes and peoples is one of the system's strongest assets. Even the changes that engulf the system are elements of strength in that change brings about freshness, new outlooks, original adaptations, and the proof of resiliency of areas. These strengths have been present throughout the Detroit system's history and still are evident today.

On the other hand, all of the themes bring out elements of weakness. Diversity can mean the preservation of exclusiveness, and can lead to segregation. Change, no matter how refreshing, also brings about the instability and deterioration that have been amply depicted in these pages. The fundamental dichotomy suggested here is one of the clear impressions to emerge from this study.

Much of the future of the Detroit system depends upon whether the system can capitalize upon the strengths inherent in the themes presented here, or whether it becomes overwhelmed by their weaknesses. If the system can harness the strength, vitality, freshness, and productive capacity of the diverse elements in its makeup, then it has a sound future. However, if the system cannot control and reverse the inherent weaknesses expressed here, its future is less promising. Thus, diversity is a source of strength and should be cherished, but it should not be allowed to lead to the stifling differentiation that often has characterized the past. Forces of change should be welcomed, but they should be prevented from bringing the legacy of instability and deterioration that has been described in this study.

In the immediate future the unfavorable side of the dichotomy appears to have the upper hand. Indeed the weakness inherent in the themes presented in these pages has much to do with the negative image that Detroit presents in the midseventies. As this study is brought to a conclusion, this image is accentuated by a worsening economic climate of the system's industrial base. In the longer term, the prospect might not be so pessimistic. The system includes a population of five million productive people, a rich variety of ethnic and socioeconomic groups, a vigorous black community, a strong industrial structure, and a history of impressive achievements. Today there is some optimism in such diverse examples as the well-publicized Renaissance Center and Fairlane developments, the increased strength of local community councils throughout the metropolitan area, and a new City of Detroit Charter which attempts to remedy past inequities. If these and other developments have some meaning, and if the more favorable side of the dichotomy presented here reasserts itself, the Detroit system would change its present negative image and regain a leadership role which has been characteristic of much of its past.

Bibliography

Atlas and Plat Book of Oakland Township, Michigan, 1956, 1967, and *1973.* Rockford, Ill.: Rockford Map Publishing Co., 1956, 1967, and 1973.

Boyer, Brian D. *Cities Destroyed for Cash: The FHA Scandal at HUD.* Chicago, Ill.: Follett, 1973.

Bunge, William. *Fitzgerald: Geography of a Revolution.* Cambridge, Mass.: Schenkman, 1971.

City of Detroit. *Commercial Land Utilization Study, Volumes I and II.* Detroit, 1974.

City of Detroit, Community Development Commission. Urban Renewal Planning Office. Miscellaneous Statistics.

City of Detroit, Community Renewal Program. *Detroit: The New City.* Detroit, 1966.

University City Urban Renewal Project, 1960.

City of Detroit, Police Department Records..

Deskins, Donald. R., Jr. *Residential Mobility of Negroes in Detroit, 1837–1965.* Ann Arbor, Mich.: University of Michigan, Department of Geography, Michigan Geographical Publication no. 5, 1970.

Detroit Free Press, September 17, 1972, and March 17, 1973.

Detroit Model Neighborhood Agency. *Detroit Model Neighborhood Household Survey— Statistical Tables, Summer of 1972.* Detroit, 1972.

Doxiadis, Constantinos A. *Emergence and Growth of an Urban Region: The Developing Urban Detroit Area.* Vols. I, II and III. Detroit:

Detroit Edison Company, Wayne State University–Doxiadis Associates, 1966.

Hartman, David W. "From 'Piety Hill' to 'Slum Alley'; A Social Analysis of the Schoolcraft Community," Ph.D. Dissertation, Wayne State University, 1975.

Katzman, David M. *Before the Ghetto: Black Detroit in the Nineteenth Century.* Urbana, Ill.: University of Illinois Press, 1973.

Michigan State Housing Development Authority. *Consideration for a Housing Strategy for the City of Detroit.* Report prepared by the American City Corporation for the Michigan State Housing Development Authority. Detroit, 1973.

National Council for Geographic Education. *Metropolitan America: Geographic Perspectives and Teaching Strategies.* The 1972 NCGE Yearbook. Oak Park, Ill., 1972.

Northwest Community Organization (Organization for Citizens Community Councils for Northwest Detroit). Miscellaneous Information.

Oakland Township Association (Oakland Township, Michigan). Miscellaneous Information.

Parkins, Almon E. *The Historical Geography of Detroit.* Lansing, Mich.: Michigan Historical Commission, 1918.

Peoples Area Development Corporation. *A Physical Development Program for PADCO.* Report prepared by William Kessler and Associates, Inc., and Lucas and Edwards, Inc. Detroit, 1973.

Sinclair, Robert. *The Face of Detroit: A*

Spatial Synthesis. Detroit: Wayne State University–National Council for Geographic Education–U.S. Office of Education, 1970.

Sinclair, Robert. "Ghetto Expansion and the Urban Landscape," *Wiener Geographische Schriften, Festschrift Leopold G. Scheidl* vol. 2 (1975).

Smith, William D. *Community Development in the Wayne Area.* Detroit: Center for Urban Studies, Wayne State University, 1970.

Southeast Michigan Council of Governments. Planning and Research Division. Detroit, Michigan. Miscellaneous Statistics and Information.

    1974 Residential Construction in Southeast Michigan. Detroit, 1974.

State of Michigan, Department of State Highways and Transportation. Miscellaneous Statistics.

Sales Management Magazine: 1974 Survey of Buying Power. As quoted in the *Oakland Press,* January 25, 1975.

The *Community Reporter* (Detroit), September 24, 1969, and April 8, 1970.

The Detroit News, March 15, 1973.

Thompson, Bryan. Detroit Area Ethnic Groups, 1971. Map. Wayne State University–Detroit Public Schools TTT Project, 1972.

Transportation and Land Use Study. *A Profile of Southeastern Michigan. Talus Data, 1965.* Detroit, 1968.

United Northwest Detroit Real Estate Association. Multilist of Houses for Sale, February 1973.

U.S. Bureau of the Census. *Census of Population and Housing; 1970 Census Tracts.* Final Report PHC (1)-58 Detroit, Michigan SMSA.

U.S. Bureau of the Census. *Census of Population; 1970. Detailed Characteristics.* Final Report PC (1)-D24 Michigan.

U.S. Bureau of the Census. *Census of Population: 1970. General Economic and Social Characteristics.* Final Report PC (1)-C24 Michigan.

U.S. Bureau of the Census. Miscellaneous publications.

U.S. Department of Housing and Urban Development. Detroit Office Files.

Widick, B.J. *Detroit: City of Race and Class Violence.* Chicago, Ill.: Quadrangle Books, 1972.

Wolf, Eleanor P., and Lebeaux, Charles N. *Change and Renewal in an Urban Community. Five Case Studies of Detroit* New York: Praeger, 1969.

Information for the Cass Corridor, Northwest Detroit, and Oakland Township Case studies was supplemented by field research during the year 1973. Field work included field mapping, structured questionnaires, and informal interviews.

Chapter Six

The Twin Cities of St. Paul and Minneapolis

Images, Identities, and Daily Life

People who have never lived in the Twin Cities depend on visits, friends, and the media for their impressions of the place. Twin Cities residents create their own images, influenced by the same media that inform outsiders. For both groups, the Twin Cities is the Upper Midwest capital, the commercial and transportation gateway to the northwest United States. It is also a sprawling dual-centered metropolis of almost two million persons, enjoying all the advantages that large size permits yet suffering few of the problems that plague older, higher density, single center metropolises with their frequent histories of sharp cultural cleavages. It is a place of surprisingly uniform tastes and a sense that civic problems generally come in manageable proportions.

GEOGRAPHY

The terrain of the Twin Cities region was sculptured by recent glacial activity that left numerous depressions and debris piles that are now lakes and hills. Minneapolis and St. Paul lie on flat areas of sand and gravel washed out from the edges of ice sheets, but they are surrounded by rougher areas left when the glaciers were stationary or retreating rapidly. Local relief in rougher areas averages 200 feet. The glaciers also left swamps, bogs, and sloughs that are ideal breeding places for mosquitos. Despite valiant efforts to control them, mosquitos preclude late evening use of yards and parks for any but the most active or urgent recreations. Unless it is cool or a strong breeze is blowing, mosquitos will drive most people indoors after sundown.

Thanks to the frequent exchange of air, the low population densities, and the small amount of heavy industry in the area, air quality in the Twin Cities is unsurpassed by any United States metropolitan area of over a million people. Temperatures are something else. Over a weather record of 150 years, 108°F in July 1936 was the highest temperature recorded; the lowest reached –41°F in January 1888. In a typical July the temperature stays below 94°F on nine days out of ten and below 85°F on half the days. In a typical January the coldest temperature is above zero on over half the days and stays above –12°F on nine days out of ten. Daily high temperatures normally range from about zero to 38°F in January and from 72 to 94°F in July. The brilliant blue sky on many of the coldest winter days provides an uplift that has no analogue on a steamy July afternoon. Fog is rare. The season of clearer skies but more rain, coming in evening and nighttime showers, runs from early April through September. Winter is drier with only light snow coming from overcast skies. The area has prepared itself for any weather extreme and pays little attention to conditions that would bring many cities to a standstill.

Although the Twin Cities suffer the coldest winters of any major North American metropolis, the bad news is often exaggerated. Many Americans confuse Minneapolis with Minnesota and conclude that the cold winter temperatures in the northern part of the state are typical of the Twin Cities. Actually, when it gets cold in the Twin Cities it usually gets almost as cold in many other cities in the northern United States. Minnesota is a large state, and the distance of places like Bemidji and International Falls, Minnesota, from the Twin Cities is about the same as the distance from Washington, D.C., to Canada, or from New York City to the interior of Maine.

Two kinds of air masses alternate in the Twin Cities. One is cool, clear Canadian air which makes many summer days so perfect and the winter so cold. The other comes from the Pacific Ocean, passing over the Rockies and warming as it descends moving eastward. This air produces warm sunny winter days ideal for outdoor sports. On rare occasions, maritime tropical air from the Gulf of Mexico reaches the Twin Cities at the surface bringing hot humid weather. However, even in the summer Gulf air reaches the area less than 10 percent of the time, even though it predominates in the summer over states as near as Illinois and Missouri. In the Twin Cities, tropical Gulf air frequently overrides the cooler air at the surface and brings evening and nighttime showers.

Even rarer is the occasional summer arrival of air from the Hudson Bay region, holding daytime temperatures in the 60s with accompanying rains, and prompting much discussion and wonder. Summer skies are fair 73 percent of the time, and up to 85 percent of the time during the last three weeks of July. The most common time for thundershowers is around midnight. Summer air in the Twin Cities is usually not tropical air and lacks the moisture content typical over much of the United States. Despite the high latitude (45°), the early summer sun in the Twin Cities is closer to being overhead than it is at the equator. Also, because of the latitude and daylight savings time, the early summer sun sets well after 9:00 P.M., making it possible to read a newspaper out of doors until 9:30 P.M.

Autumn, or Indian Summer, offers fair skies 68 percent of the time, with mild dry days, cool evenings, and only occasional light rain likely at night. This extended period of sunny days has a special beauty for early risers. Twin City lakes are still warm from the summer sun, so when night air cools below its dewpoint gossamer streamers of early morning fog form over the lakes. They rise only a few feet above the water but give added beauty to fiery sunrises over red and orange trees beneath the purple dawn sky. Many residents insist this is the finest season of all.

Early November through December brings the holiday season. The snows begin but fail to last, for the ground is still warm. Around December 10 the snow becomes permanent and most lakes and streams freeze over. This is also the cloudiest season of the year, but the clouds insure the maintenance of the snow cover, enhancing the holiday atmosphere. Visitors during this snow white season are surprised that they can see almost as well outside at night as during the day.

Real winter lasts from New Year's Day to mid-February. Skies clear and the sun shines on the permanent snow cover. Average high temperatures hover around 13°F and winter sports reach full tempo. Ice skaters dot the frozen lakes, skiers dot the low hills, and outside the central cities snowmobilers race across frozen lakes and along roadside trails. The transition to spring starts in mid-February and lasts through March. It is the snowiest part of the year but the snows never last long.

Spring comes suddenly, melting the snow and raising temperatures abruptly to the 70s by May. In early April, following cold front passages, passing showers fall from small thunderclouds forming behind the fronts. These attractive but fast-moving April clouds may bring as many as five brief showers in a single day with sunshine between. Spring—or what passes for it—surprises newcomers to the Twin Cities. Most other major cities lie near major bodies of water which slow down the spring warm-up. In those places lake and sea breezes turn many days that begin warm into cool ones. Twin Cities lakes while often deep are too small and scattered to affect the temperature. They warm quickly in the spring as the Twin Cities warm up.

THE PEOPLE

Complementing a north woods, theater of seasons image is the notion that the Twin Cities are populated by blonde Swedes. Scandinavian-language vaudeville teams that worked out of the Twin Cities at the turn of the century started the image of Minneapolis as New Stockholm. Similarly, Sinclair Lewis's *Main Street*, with its portrayal of Yankee-Scandinavian conflicts, reinforced the idea that Minnesota and the Twin Cities are predominantly Scandinavian.

One does occasionally encounter a Swede or Norwegian in the Twin Cities, but ethnicity is a leitmotiv rather than a dominant chord. Time is one explanation of feeble ethnicity. There are indeed twenty-six pages of Johnsons in the Minneapolis telephone book, but most are second and third generation Americans and many are black. Young persons today may acknowledge their ethnic origins, invoking ethnicity for personal identificational reasons. The importance of Scandinavian foreign stock in the Twin Cities was probably exaggerated to begin with and the exaggeration has increased as the foreign-born groups aged and died. In 1970, the total foreign *stock* (foreign-born plus persons with one or both parents foreign-born) amounted to 17.7 percent of the metropolitan population, but foreign-*born* were only 3.0 percent of the population. Moreover, the foreign stock has never been dominated by any single group. Swedish foreign stock was largest at 3.1 percent of the 1970 population, followed by Germans (2.7 percent), and Norwegians (2.2 percent). No other group except Canadians accounts for 1.0 percent of the Twin Cities population. All Scandinavians lumped together (Swedish, Norwegian, Danish, and Finnish) are but 6.1 percent of the metropolitan population.

This does not imply a complete absence of visible ethnic concentrations, but with few exceptions—such as northeast Minneapolis (Slavic) or the "West Side" of St. Paul (Chicano)—they are well hidden. In 1970 there were about 16,500 people "of Spanish language" in the Twin Cities, of whom no more than 500 were Puerto Rican in origin.

Dispersal also dilutes ethnicity. Census tracts in which more than a fifth of the population consists of foreign stock are rare. Weak ethnic concentrations persist in the Twin Cities but the prosperity of the first and second generations promotes dispersal throughout the metropolitan region. Annual celebrations such as Svenskarnas Dag (Swedish Day), Syttendae Mai (May 17, Norwegian Constitution Day), and St. Patrick's Day (St. Paul only) are well attended, but beyond such well-publicized, highly commercialized events, ethnicity is a sometime thing.

The ethnic homogeneity of the Twin Cities is matched by racial homogeneity. Nonwhites numbered 50,000 in 1970, of whom 32,000 were black. Blacks constituted 1.8 percent of the Twin Cities population; the remaining nonwhites were native Americans (Indians) and Orientals. Almost 10,000 Indians enumerated by the 1970 census form one of the larger metropolitan Indian populations in the nation.

The population of these middle class cities seem well endowed with the attitudes and attributes that bring material success in the American system. The 1969 median family income of $11,680 was well above the $9,590 median for SMSAs over 200,000 population. Only 4.6 percent of Twin Cities families fall below the 1969 poverty level as opposed to 8.5 percent in all metropolitan areas. At the same time, the average income is not raised by the small number of very high incomes; 6.2 percent of the nation's families had 1969 incomes exceeding $25,000, compared with 5.6 percent of all Twin Cities families. Without minimizing the extent of poverty in the Twin Cities, the fact remains that residents are well off economically. The sharp cultural and social gradients that foster tension and conflict in many cities are absent in Minneapolis and St. Paul, producing a metropolis in which social and cultural conflict has rarely attained the proportions it has in other places.

Crime rates are relatively low, the proportion of draftees and enlistees rejected as mentally or physically unsuited for military service has always been low, and education levels and incomes are above national averages. The region's social ethos and general conviction that problems are solvable is evident in the politicians it elects at all levels of government. The progressive image of New Deal Governor Floyd B. Olson, for example, and the violent but successful Teamsters strike of 1934, reflect an abiding grassroots social concern and activism that has often been translated into legislative innovation backed by a willingness to provide concrete backing for education and social legislation. Hubert Humphrey, for example, enjoyed widespread political popularity in the Twin Cities in a political career that began as mayor of Minneapolis. Right down to the local level there is a spirit of openness and honesty in political affairs. The electorate expects open, honest, and efficient government and their expectations are usually fulfilled.

THE "TWIN" CITIES

Failing to distinguish between the two cities is the greatest gap between external image and internal reality. For most nonresidents and for 99 percent of all Minneapolis residents, Minneapolis *is* the Twin Cities (Figure 1). Air travelers are sold tickets to Minneapolis, they board planes going to Minneapolis, and are informed en route of their estimated arrival time in Minneapolis. Should the flight continue beyond Minneapolis, responding to the question, "Are you going to Minneapolis?" with, "No, I'm going to St. Paul" will elicit an ill-concealed sneer from the cabin attendant putting "occupied" signs on through passengers' seats. Dignitaries visiting St. Paul often insult their hosts with an opening comment on "How nice it is to be in Minneapolis (again)." A St. Paul newspaper columnist keeps score on how often St. Paul facilities are mislocated in Minneapolis and vice versa. At last report, the score stood heavily in favor of Minneapolis. The frequency with which St. Paul is incorporated into Minneapolis and the rarity with which

Figure 1. Minneapolis at the Falls of St. Anthony. Grain elevators and ancient milling facilities of General Mills on the far (west) side of the falls and the Pillsbury A Mill on the east side (lower right) commemorate the city's turn of the century livelihood. A sea of parking lots (right center) marks the Gateway renewal area leveled in the 1950s and vigorously rebuilding.

people in Minneapolis think they are in St. Paul dramatizes how people fail to note that St. Paul is a separate city (Figure 2).

Minneapolis and St. Paul are distinct places. They are not identical twins nor are they fraternal, having been founded twenty years and ten miles apart. They started as neighboring rivals but ended up Siamese twins. St. Paul and Minneapolis are inescapably tied by proximity and, like the unhappy Chang and Eng, they sometimes fight. Interurban rivalry no longer generates the silliness and bitterness it produced in the nineteenth century, but it persists. Short-

ly after major league baseball came to the Twin Cities a joke circulated: "Did you hear that they were going to name the team the Minnehaha Twins instead of the Minnesota Twins? ... Minne- for Minneapolis and -haha for St. Paul." Some Minneapolitans assert that they set their watches back fifty years when they go to St. Paul. St. Paul acquired an inferiority complex when Minneapolis became larger. The feeling persists. St. Paulites disguise their jealousy of their neighbor's taller buildings, larger size, and spruce image with smugness and the unmistakable impression that they are

Figure 2. Downtown St. Paul, bounded by railroad facilities and warehouses near the former mouth of Trout Creek (right edge), Interstates 94 and 35-E (top) and the Capitol Approach area (top left), residential areas (far left), and the Mississippi River (foreground). Industrial land uses occupy the flood plain across the river from downtown on St. Paul's "West Side". Although the Mississippi flows from west to east at downtown St. Paul, its path through the Twin Cities area is generally north-south.

cultured and urbane while Minneapolitans are bumptious philistines, but St. Paul is usually the butt of interurban jokes.

Twin Cities residents often describe the difference between St. Paul and Minneapolis in terms of St. Paul being an older, "Eastern" city like Boston, whereas Minneapolis in its business bustle and commercial vitality is more akin to Chicago or Denver. That characterization is accurate, for it acknowledges ethnic, religious, and geographical differences, along with economic ambitions and visual impressions.

St. Paul's earlier start is evident in the larger size of the German and Irish ethnic groups there. It has larger Irish and German foreign stocks than Minneapolis despite its smaller population. Minneapolis remains more Scandinavian than St. Paul; the Norwegian and Swedish groups constitute almost a tenth of the Minneapolis population. Proportions in other ethnic groups are similar in the two cities. Today's stereotypes are residuals of earlier social structures. In 1930, for example, German foreign stock was 13.9 percent of St. Paul's population but only 7.7 percent of the Minneapolis total. Every fifth Minneapolitan was born in Norway or Sweden or had at least one parent who was; every seventh St. Paulite fell into the same category. The Irish were not an especially large group in either city in 1930, but they were twice as important in St. Paul as in Minneapolis.

Past and present ethnic differences have produced relatively little impact on the urban landscape. Even a genuine Scandinavian restaurant is impossible to find. Denmark, Finland, Norway, and Sweden maintain consulates in Minneapolis but they are offices in large buildings and are outwardly indistinguishable from the law offices that surround them. The Scandinavian nations have no representation in St. Paul. In fact, none of them is listed in the St. Paul phone book. When queried about this the Swedish consulate was uncommunicative; the Norwegian consul observed that his offices were not listed in the Madison, Duluth, or Fargo directories, and therefore he could see no good reason why they should be listed in the St. Paul directory. The German consulate is located in Minneapolis but is listed only in the St. Paul telephone directory. There were almost identical numbers of German foreign stock in Minneapolis and St. Paul in 1970, so whereas

location might be a matter of indifference, it is curious that the consulate is not listed in the city in which it is located. But the score is partially evened out by the Mexican consulate, which is located in St. Paul but listed only in the Minneapolis directory. The American Swedish Institute and the Sons of Norway have headquarters in Minneapolis, but the *Volksfest Kultus Haus* is in St. Paul. The St. Paul Irish have no formal organization, but they make a magnificent impression on the urban landscape during the St. Patrick's Day parade.

Relics of these earlier ethnic concentrations are rapidly disappearing, but the religious and moral differences that derive from the earlier and stronger ethnic differences persist. St. Paulites, being more dominantly Southern German, Austrian, and Irish, tend to be Catholics (37 percent). Local wags often remark that it is fitting that the St. Paul Cathedral stands higher and is more imposing than the state capitol building, for that is, or at least was, an accurate reflection of relationships between the powers the edifices memorialize. In St. Paul, flats and houses are still advertised with no location given other than the name of the Catholic parish in which the dwelling is located. Minneapolis is about as Protestant as St. Paul is Catholic. Lutheranism is the dominant faith; Catholics are 20 percent of the population. The headquarters of the Lutheran Brotherhood Insurance Company and the American Lutheran Church bear substantive witness to the strength of the sect in Minneapolis.

Minneapolitans claim that St. Paul is impossible to navigate. Both Minneapolis and St. Paul are laid out in typically midwestern grid patterns except for their central business districts, where streets are parallel and perpendicular to the river. The river churlishly refuses to flow either north-south or east-west; hence both city centers are surrounded by a ring of confusion where the early, river-oriented streets mesh with the cardinal grid. Matters are complicated by the differing topographies of the central areas. Downtown St. Paul is hilly, with a bluff between downtown and the river and another at the western margin of the central area; downtown Minneapolis is flat. The Minneapolis street system is easy to comprehend. A matrix of numbered streets and avenues with cardinal directions appended creates a cartesian space in which finding addresses is simple. St. Paul's street- and house-numbering scheme can scarcely be described as a system. All streets are named with the exception of a few in the CBD. More importantly, there are far fewer than a hundred numbers per block. Many a visitor has set off to walk the "ten blocks" from downtown to an address at 1000 West, only to learn that more than two miles separate the two. St. Paul house numbers were assigned on the basis of water meter installations along early thoroughfares; thus there are usually about three city blocks per hundred numbers. The combination of named streets and irregular numbering creates different conceptions of space and different orientations. Minneapolis residents identify their locations as points and move from one place to another by mentally constructing their own path between origin and destination. People in St. Paul conceive of their locations as areas or neighborhoods because points are too imprecise. They tend to be route-oriented and in asking or giving directions to a destination they will seek or specify the path to be taken rather than the geometric location. St. Paul is a city that must be memorized; its geography cannot be deduced from the street grid.

Ethnic, religious, and geographical differences ultimately result in differences in information flow that perpetuate those differences. Telephone message flows highlight the existence of two separate cities. None of the largest outgoing flows from Twin Cities telephone exchanges crosses the Minneapolis-St. Paul city boundary, nor do any of the second largest outflows. Only at the level of the third largest outflow is the boundary between the two cities breached, and then only for two exchanges. Newspaper circulation patterns also perpetuate separate identities. The *St. Paul Dispatch* and *Pioneer Press* are delivered in St. Paul but not in Minneapolis. The *Minneapolis Star* and *Tribune*, however, penetrate St. Paul, with daily home delivery available in the western half of the city and in many of the suburbs. The Sunday Minneapolis paper is readily available throughout Ramsey County.

Television and radio also affect regional identity. Announcers on the two major stations are careful to say "St. Paul and Minneapolis" as often as they say "Minneapolis and St. Paul." But other things being equal, Minneapolis and its suburbs still get more air time because of

their larger populations. The major station's (WCCO) studios are in downtown Minneapolis and thus the idle chit-chat of disc jockeys and television announcers almost always concerns events there. Because of WCCO's phenomenally large market penetration, this redounds in the favor of Minneapolis.

Differences between the two cities are real and a visitor ignores them at some peril.

WORKING

The 1970 Twin Cities labor force consisted of 760,000 workers. Thus about 42 percent of the total population and about 62 percent of the population over sixteen years of age drew an income from working, males outnumbering females almost two to one. St. Paul has more jobs in manufacturing and transportation than Minneapolis as a result of its earlier start and more important role as a rail transportation center. Correspondingly, St. Paul has fewer jobs in trade, finance, and services. The location of the state capitol and a number of federal offices in St. Paul puts it ahead of Minneapolis in public administration employment. Differences in occupational structure follow from St. Paul's higher manufacturing employment, but the differences are negligible.

The fifteen largest employers engage a fifth of the metropolitan labor force. Some of them loom disproportionately large in making the Twin Cities different from other places. Local government, including public schools (54,000 employees), the University of Minnesota (20,300, one-third of them part time students), federal government (18,500), and the state of Minnesota (15,000) are four of the top five employers in the area. Other important employers include 3M (16,900), Honeywell (13,000), Control Data (10,700), Dayton-Hudson Corporation (10,000), Univac Division of Sperry Rand Corporation (8,800), Northwestern Bell Telephone Company (8,200), Burlington-Northern (6,500), Northwest Airlines (4,700), Northern States Power Company (4,000), General Mills (3,100), and Federal Cartridge (3,000).

Making a living is likely to involve a medium length trip to work because of the Twin Cities low population density and dispersed employment centers. Only 12 percent of the jobs are located in the central business districts; most are located in the remainder of the central cities

and in the first tier of suburbs in Hennepin and
Ramsey Counties. At the same time, the existence of two CBDs acts to reduce distance to
work despite low density by splitting central
employment and thereby putting it closer to
more people.

PLAYING

Although the work ethic is alive and well in the
Twin Cities, all work and no play make a dull
boy. But there is little danger of Twin Cities
residents becoming dullards. They play hard,
whether they do so by watching other people
or whether they are active in sports, pastimes,
and festivals. The region and the local ethos
offer many opportunities for individual and
communal recreation.

Nonresidents are likely to be most familiar
with the organized hoopla of the St. Paul Winter Carnival and the summer Minneapolis Aquatennial; local boosters insure that each receives
some national publicity. The Winter Carnivals
started before World War I and have waxed and
waned in elaborateness since. Minneapolis
chafed for years at the success of the Winter
Carnival and in the 1940s, unable to tolerate
the affront to its dignity any longer, established
the Aquatennial. The Aquatennial Parade occurs downtown, but the rest of the festival is
dispersed throughout the city's network of
lakes and parks.

Smaller festivals and celebrations include St.
Patrick's Day in St. Paul, with a parade and
green beer. Rice Street and Payne Avenue in St.
Paul have sponsored annual festivals for years,
the former with a Swedish accent and the latter
with an Italian flavor. Minnehaha Park in Minneapolis is the traditional location for annual
Norwegian and Swedish celebrations. Recently
the "Snoose Boulevard" festival has recreated
the aura of the turn of the century designation
of Cedar Avenue as Snoose Boulevard, an un-
complimentary recognition of a Scandinavian
preference for chewing snuff. The summer ends
with the Minnesota State Fair, a twelve day
event drawing well over a million persons from
throughout the state.

The Twin Cities offer a normal quota of
spectator sports. Major league baseball, football, hockey, and tennis provide year round
diversion for professional sports buffs. Major
league culture is also much in evidence and remarkably well patronized. The Minnesota Or-

chestra gives three subscription concerts a week
(two in Minneapolis, one in St. Paul) during
its regular season, and the Tyrone Guthrie
Theatre presents eight performances a week
during its season. In addition to the Minnesota
Orchestra and the Guthrie, the St. Paul Chamber Orchestra, and many other orchestras,
chamber groups, choruses, opera companies,
and theatre companies perform throughout the
year.

When Sir Tyrone Guthrie selected Minneapolis as the site for his repertoire theatre, he
established the Twin Cities as a theatrical center
of unusual proportion. About thirty theatres
operate in the Twin Cities, making the area a
major attraction for young actors and actresses.
This abundance of acting talent has attracted
increasing numbers of national advertising
agencies to establish branches in Minneapolis to
use this wealth of talent.

The Twin Cities' physical setting provides
opportunities for participant play in greater
abundance than is the case in most metropolitan regions. Fishing is legal for some species
year round and the region around the Twin
Cities is studded with lakes and rivers that provide adequate to excellent fishing. About a
fourth of the adult populations of Hennepin
and Ramsey counties fish. A common catch
from local lakes includes panfish and northern
pike. The latter can get as large as twenty
pounds or more. Although specimens that size
are increasingly rare within the metropolitan
area, game fishermen hook sizable northerns
often enough to make fishing for them exciting
and worthwhile. Bass fishing at many lakes in
the metropolitan area (including lakes within
the central cities) is excellent; five pound bass
are caught daily and larger ones are not especially newsworthy. The Mississippi and Minnesota rivers yield giant catfish, bass, northern
pike, and walleyed pike (Minnesota's premier
fish).

Boating, whether incidental to fishing or an
end in itself, is also popular. In early 1974,
142,000 boats of all kinds were licensed to residents of Hennepin and Ramsey counties. There
are remarkably few accidents and fistfights
given the number of craft on the water, but increased boating pressure on the metropolitan
area's lakes will eventually lead to zoned use.

Moving through space effortlessly is a delight
that knows no seasonal bounds, and snowmobiles make it possible to do so in the winter, re-

lieving the winter doldrums for the motorboat enthusiast. There were 85,000 snowmobiles licensed to metropolitan residents in 1974, one snowmobile for every twenty-three people. For comparison, there is one boat for every twelve people. Snowmobiles create conflicts. Farmers and property owners adjacent to open areas object to having their property overrun and their tranquility disrupted by the noisy devices, as do cross-country skiers, ice fishermen, and other seekers of outdoor winter quiet. The antagonisms between ice fishermen and snowmobile fans arise because the frozen lakes are the best places to race snowmobiles, most of which will easily go fifty miles per hour, with top speeds for powerful models of seventy or eighty miles per hour.

Twin Cities residents make heavy use of their metropolitan area for outdoor recreation, sometimes creating a nuisance for one another. Voluntary and legislated zoning, rationing, or pricing of lakes, campgrounds, and other facilities when overtaxed will make the region more pleasant for all potential users. For the foreseeable future, high quality fishing, small game hunting, hiking, camping, cross-country and downhill skiing, sailing, and water skiing will continue to be available no more than forty-five minutes drive from the doorstep of any Twin Cities resident.

The Twin Cities area, with about 10 percent of the public ballrooms in the United States, offers an unusual opportunity for young and old. Typically, Friday night's band plays rock and popular music, while on Saturday night and Sunday afternoon it turns to polka and waltz music. The rock crowd tends to be young, but the old-time group is a mixture of ages since many natives and migrants to the area learn to polka and waltz before they are ten years old.

THE GOOD LIFE IN A GOOD PLACE

Unless childhood was a totally dismal experience, a person's hometown remains the best place in the world. Natives hold fond memories of places others abhor. Nevertheless, our collective experience with the Twin Cities and other metropolitan areas encourages the conclusion that the Twin Cities are a better than average place to live. The continental climate serves up winter hardships, summer irritations, and a niggardly spring, but it also produces marked seasonal changes that most residents find bracing. Climate and topography combine to offer nearby recreational opportunities in an abundance and variety few cities can match. A wide range of low density, single family housing alternatives on well-maintained elm-lined streets enables most households to find the housing they want at the location they prefer at reasonable cost. People themselves are well educated and confident. Visitors usually notice an atmosphere of openness and friendliness, a pleasant contrast to the anxieties or desperation of their own cities. Twin Cities residents are bemused by assertions that their amiability is a result of being a decade or so behind Chicago, Los Angeles, and New York. They are cosmopolitan enough to disbelieve that such is the case and self-assured enough to prefer remaining the way they are.

Minnesota was featured as "The State that Works" in a cover story in the August 13, 1973, issue of *Time*. State politics had much to do with the article, yet the essay was a sensible and sensitive portrayal of the state and the metropolitan area. Things *do* work in Minnesota and the Twin Cities and that asset seems to distinguish the metropolitan area from many others. People having business with public officials or private concerns expect their transactions to be accomplished promptly and efficiently, and they usually are. Pettifogging is minimal, whether the business at hand is licensing a canoe or buying a house. Twin Cities residents grouse about the day-to-day irritations of life, but bitterness and despair are rare. The freedom from the hundreds of weekly anxieties and squabbles characteristic of cities in which the average person expects to be gulled every time he or she turns around is perhaps the most refreshing element of Twin Cities life. People feel that life and events are manageable and under control, and they are usually right.

The First Century

The Twin Cities were born in the 1840s, and at least one of the twins was conceived in sin. Civilian settlement was illegal in the St. Paul area before 1837 and before 1851 in Minneapolis because Indian cessions had not yet been obtained. Military authorities at Fort Snelling winked at occasional squatters on the military reservation at the junction of the Minnesota and Mississippi rivers, however, and by the late 1830s several commercial enterprises were established near the fort (Figure 3). A soldier's payday recreation was the same then as now; fifty of the fort's troops spent the night of June 30, 1839, in the guardhouse after visiting Brown's Groggery. Thereupon the fort's martinet commander, Major Plympton, determined to rid the fort of the fleshly attractions purveyed by civilian merchants. After blustering for a year he evicted 150 civilians from the west bank of the river in May 1840. The evictees moved downriver on the east bank to Pig's Eye, the nickname of an earlier refugee publican who had set up shop in a cave. The embryonic village was supplied with a more euphonious name a year later when a log chapel dedicated to St. Paul was erected by Father Lucien Galtier, but St. Paul residents are fond of their disreputable origins.

St. Paul's lusty conception might suggest that the Twin Cities are a happenstance of history, but that is not so. Given the nation's developing economy and the way settlement was spreading, the rise of a great city on the site of St. Paul-Minneapolis was inevitable.

By 1840 American settlement had crossed the Mississippi into what is now Iowa, Missouri, and Kansas, and steam navigation had converted the Ohio-Mississippi-Missouri river network into an efficient transportation system over which goods and people could be shipped quickly and cheaply. The Indian cessions of 1837 opened the St. Croix country at the same time that demand for the region's logs and lumber was growing in the areas to the south that could be reached by river transportation. Entrepreneurs were quick to exploit the "pineries" penetrated by the St. Croix and Rum rivers (Figure 4). Sawmills were established at Marine on the St. Croix (1839), Stillwater (1844), and St. Anthony (1848) and forest products soon became a mainstay of the region's export economy. The territory's extensive timber resources and great agricultural potential guaranteed that Minnesota would prosper, but a more specific set of circumstances guaranteed the emergence of the St. Paul-Minneapolis complex.

St. Paul, with a gradually sloping access through the bluffs to the uplands north of the river bend, became the practical head of navigation on the upper Mississippi, and the Falls of St. Anthony, ten miles upstream, was the largest water power site west of Niagara. River transportation was crucial over the next several decades. St. Paul offered a convenient transfer point before the Mississippi River entered a gorge upstream from Fort Snelling and became impassible at the falls (Figure 5). As a consequence it became the region's first major com-

Figure 3. Fort Snelling, 1844. A significant landmark in the history of Minnesota and the Northwest, the fort was established in 1819 at the Junction of the Minnesota and Mississippi rivers. It effectively extended the authority of the young American nation over the region and paved the way for white settlement. This water color by J.C. Wild shows the Henry H. Sibley house in the foreground and the buildings of the Indian agency behind the post. The painting is in the Minnesota Historical Society collection. Photo courtesy of the Minnesota Historical Society.

mercial center. Meanwhile, sawmilling and flour milling, soon to become the region's dominant industries, got their start largely at St. Anthony Falls where a sixty-five foot drop in the river provided a ready source of power (Figure 6). The ten miles separating the two guaranteed the development of twin cities. A slow riverboat trip might take half a day. Even a trip on the early railroads took forty-five minutes to an hour. The distance separating the cities made consolidation unthinkable given the overland transportation technology of the 1840s and 1850s. Their successful separate development precluded consolidation long before a city ten miles in breadth became thinkable.

In the earliest days the region offered the American and international economies furs and timber. Both were important to the infant Twin Cities. Furs had been a standby of regional production since 1650. Yields were declining by the 1830s, but enough production and trade persisted to provide an early boost for St. Paul, making the city one of the world's major fur centers into the twentieth century. As fashions changed and demand for beaver declined, buffalo hides became more important and the fur frontier shifted into northwestern Minnesota and the Dakota Territory. Traders from the Red River region brought their furs to St. Paul by oxcart in the summer and dogsled in the winter. There they were exchanged for provisions and manufactured goods brought upriver by steamboat. Trade with the Red River country and with surrounding settlements supported St. Paul until the designation of the city as the territorial capital in 1849. St. Paul be-

Figure 4. Minnesota vegetation at the time of European settlement. Hardwood forests surrounded the sites of the Twin Cities and separated the fertile prairie lands southwest from the virgin pine forests in the northeast. The river systems into the pineries delivered logs to sawmills at St. Anthony, Stillwater, and Marine, kicking off a major export industry.

came the state capital in 1858, assuring continuing success.

St. Anthony (the part of Minneapolis east of the Mississippi) started late compared to other sawmilling centers. A mill had been built at St. Anthony Falls in the 1820s to provide Fort Snelling with lumber and squatters settled in the area intermittently. Major Plympton usually evicted them, not, it would appear, because he was sensitive to legal proprieties, but rather because he and a partner had designs on the site. His efforts came to naught, for a sharp operator from the St. Croix, Franklin Steele, managed

to prove a claim on the site and sawmilling and settlement commenced in 1849. Loggers sent timber from the north down the Rum and Mississippi rivers to the mills at St. Anthony.

Nobody familiar with the region had any doubts concerning St. Anthony's ultimate fortunes. The magnificent power site made it clear that a great manufacturing city would develop there. Moreover, Nicollet Island, just above the falls, split the river into two relatively narrow channels and thus provided a bridge site superior to any other in the vicinity. But St. Anthony's growth was retarded for a few more

Figure 5. St. Paul, 1855. When S. Holmes Andrews painted this oil of St. Paul in 1855, the population of the city was less than 5,000. It was a year of unprecedented immigration. Boats brought approximately 30,000 passengers to the Minnesota capital and from there they funneled out to other parts of the territory. Andrews' view of St. Paul shows the Mississippi River in the foreground and the territorial Capitol and First Presbyterian Church in the center and right background. Nothing is known about this artist whose painting is one of the prized items in the Minnesota Historical Society's collections. Photo courtesy of the Minnesota Historical Society.

years because Steele had trouble raising the capital he needed to develop the falls. The area across the river was not opened for settlement until 1851 and conditions remained confused for four years thereafter as squatters and land speculators pressed their conflicitng claims. In 1855 the situation was clarified. All of Hennepin County (which had been organized in 1852), was declared preemption territory: the squatters'claims were recognized. A building boom ensued and on the west side of the river the city of Minneapolis was incorporated in 1856. Steele's Minneapolis Bridge Company opened its suspension bridge over the Mississippi on July 4, 1855, signaling the beginning of the end for St. Anthony. Even though it was detached from Ramsey County and added to Hennepin County in 1856, maintaining a separate corporate existence until 1872, Minneapolis quickly overtook St. Anthony after 1860.

The rivalry of the early centers for political power and population growth is still evident in the locations of state institutions. St. Paul had been designated as capital when the Minnesota Territory was established in 1849, and the state capital remained there despite attempts by land speculators to shift it to St. Peter when statehood was granted in 1858. Stillwater and St. Anthony, naturally envious of St. Paul's good fortune, were mollified when the state penitentiary and the state university were established in 1851. Stillwater, being larger and more influential, got the prison, which appeared to be more lucrative than the university at that time. St. Anthony was designated the site of the university, which did little for St. Anthony in the period before it was incorporated into Minneapolis, but which has been of inestimable importance to Minneapolis and the Twin Cities over the years. St. Peter's

Figure 6. St. Anthony Falls. This painting of the east channel of the Mississippi River in 1857 shows the booming little town of St. Anthony, built close to the falls, as well as the picturesque wildness of the river scenery below the town. On the left is Hennepin Island, with its flour mills and the sluice which carried lumber from sawmills below the rapids for rafting to the lower river. The Winslow House, a well-known early hotel, dominates the hill in the background and in the right foreground stands a wood products factory. The artist painted the town at the high spot in its development, for St. Anthony never recovered from the financial panic which hit only a few months after the picture was painted. In 1872 St. Anthony was combined with Minneapolis, its prosperous rival across the river. Ferdinand Reichardt (1819–1895) was a Danish-born landscape artist who was especially noted for his paintings of Niagara Falls. The original oil is owned by the Minnesota Historical Society. Photo courtesy of the Minnesota Historical Society.

interests were finally acknowledged when an insane asylum was built there in 1866.

Earlier rivalries are also still evident within the Twin Cities themselves. Despite the development of an uninterrupted urban fabric, St. Paul, St. Anthony, and Minneapolis each developed its own residential district for the wealthy. The distances between centers and nineteenth century transportation make St. Paul's separate development understandable, but the early separation of St. Anthony's patrician families from the Minneapolis latecomers is explained by the river obstacle and a single congested bridge across it. After additional perma-

nent bridges were opened in 1873, at Plymouth Avenue upstream from the falls and at 10th Avenue South below the falls, the St. Anthony upper classes began migrating west of the river.

RAPID SETTLEMENT AND URBAN GROWTH, 1860 to 1890

Sawmills, flour mills, banking, railroads, settlement, immigration, agricultural production, and the development of the Twin Cities are so closely intertwined that it is impossible to say which caused which. Growth or change in any one had immediate repercussions for the others.

The repercussions in turn fed more change. Railroads, for example, were chronically short of capital. Yet they had extensive land grants that could be converted to capital if settlers were available to take up the land. Immigrants wanted land, but often had no way of reaching available lands until cheap railroad transportation became available. Once settled and engaged in commercial agriculture, immigrants relied on rail transportation and Twin Cities traders to supply them with manufactured products and imported foodstuffs and on Twin Cities processors to buy their export production. As the Twin Cities prospered from trade, transportation, sawmilling, and flour milling, they took pains to extend the railroads, promote immigration and settlement, and serve as the major market and processing center for the region's agricultural exports. Once such a cycle began, Eastern, European, and Canadian capitalists were eager to provide the investment needed to keep the cycle going. Through a series of such cycles, the entire state was settled between 1860 and 1890 and the population of the Twin Cities increased from 13,000 to 300,000 during the same period.

Railroads were planned during the 1850s but persistent difficulties in obtaining capital prevented actual construction until 1862, when a track was completed between St. Paul and St. Anthony. Five years later the tracks were extended to St. Cloud under the auspices of the St. Paul and Pacific Railroad. Railroad construction continued intermittently throughout the 1870s, and in 1871 a number of important links were completed. The Northern Pacific finished its line between St. Paul and Duluth, providing the Twin Cities with water access to the East. A direct link to Chicago that ran by way of Tomah, Wisconsin, was also finished. Indirect connection with Chicago had existed since 1867. Perhaps most important of all, lines to Breckenridge and Moorhead in the Red River valley were completed in 1871, thus opening the valley to settlement and giving the Twin Cities access to its produce. By 1887 tracks were completed through North Dakota to Great Falls, Montana, and the Twin Cities were first linked with Seattle in 1883.

Railroads from the East Coast had reached Chicago in 1852 and Rock Island in 1854. Thereafter they were increasingly important channels for domestic and overseas immigrants to Minnesota who could travel by train to Rock Island and then by steamer to St. Paul. Foreign immigration accelerated during the 1860s, but the real boom was to come after the Civil War, when direct rail connection to eastern and Great Lakes ports was established. In 1860 native-born persons comprised two-thirds of Minnesota's residents, most of whom had come from the Midwest, New York, Pennsylvania, and New England. By 1880 native-born residents constituted less than one-third of the state's population. Most of the newcomers had come from Scandinavia, Germany, Canada, and Ireland. Recognition of the need for settlers was widespread. The state government established an immigration bureau in 1867. The railroads started their own about the same time. Agents in Europe and in East Coast seaports publicized the state with lyrical descriptions of its fertility and prosperity. More importantly, they arranged ship passage from Europe, met immigrants in ports, housed them while their through passage into the interior was being arranged, and then dispatched them directly to Minnesota's waiting lands.

Until 1870, agricultural settlement was mainly confined to the hardwood forest zone extending from southeastern to north central Minnesota. Settlement of the prairies awaited railroad expansion into the grasslands and solid evidence that prairie land could be successfully cultivated, for it was widely believed that grasslands were less fertile than forest lands.

Demand for wheat helped fuel the drive to settle Minnesota and the Dakotas. Whereas earlier settlers might have spent several years engaged in subsistence agriculture before building up their production to the point that production for sale absorbed most of their efforts, the wheat bonanza of the 1870s brought in bonanza wheat farmers—Yankees using eastern risk capital to develop railroad lands for agriculture. Immigrants followed in the 1880s, steadily expanding the cultivated acreage. Increases in the proportion of cultivated acreage in wheat assumed boom proportions after 1870 for several reasons. Railroads were bringing fresh lands into reach as they marched westward, and wheat offered the kind of immediate return on limited investment that was especially welcome given the frontier's limited capital. Another incentive was the availability of mechanical reapers and threshers that made it possible to harvest acreages that would have been unthinkable two decades earlier. Improved plows and demonstrated success quickly overcame lingering resistance to farming prairies and most of the Minnesota grasslands south of Moorhead were taken up between 1870 and 1880. Finally, and perhaps most important of all, new milling techniques made it possible and desirable to use the hard spring wheats that grew especially well in Minnesota.

Prior to the 1870s wheat was ground between stone wheels, and soft winter wheat was the premium breadstuff because it produced a much better flour than spring wheat. But winter wheat often died during Minnesota's bitter winters. Spring wheat has a hard bran (shell) that shatters during milling. Before 1870 it was virtually impossible to separate the bran from the flour, so there was little demand for hard wheat flour. Purifiers developed in Minnesota and applied on a large scale in Minneapolis transformed the industry by turning spring wheat into the premium breadstuff. It was more nutritious than winter wheat, and after some other milling problems were overcome by replacing millstones with steel and porcelain rollers, spring wheat commanded a higher price than winter wheat.

St. Paul rail men and Minneapolis millers were at the forefront of railroad extension, settlement expansion, and milling innovation. St. Paul's James J. Hill organized the Great Northern Railway out of the old St. Paul and Pacific in 1878. The Northern Pacific line to Duluth provided access to the Great Lakes and thus to eastern and international markets. Although millions of bushels of wheat and millions of barrels of flour moved over the Northern Pacific lines each year, ice at Sault Ste. Marie closed Lake Superior each winter, creating serious shipping congestion during the fall and leaving the Minneapolis millers at the mercy of the hostile Chicago railroads for part of the year. Minneapolis milling interests therefore organized and financed the Soo Line to connect the Twin Cities with Sault Ste. Marie, bypassing both Lake superior and Chicago.

All these developments redounded to the good fortunes of the Twin Cities. Whereas the state's population grew more rapidly than the Twin Cities population up to 1870, between 1870 and 1890 the Twin Cities grew at more than twice the rate of the state. By 1890 almost a fourth of the state's people lived in Minneapolis and St. Paul.

As long as trade and river transportation were dominant, St. Paul retained its premier position. By 1880 the tide had turned; Minneapolis had surpassed St. Paul by 5,500 residents. When Minnesota was but an appendage of the national economy that looked eastward more than it looked west, St. Paul was a gateway to the region and the linchpin between the new territory and the nation's heartland. As settlement expanded to the west and the region became an important producer of goods and foodstuffs, Minneapolis, with its power site and its position between St. Paul and the settlement frontier, was a better location for new enterprise.

St. Anthony Falls was the economic heart of Minneapolis throughout its early history. The Mississippi fell sixty feet in three-fourths of a mile, creating many potential power sites on the river itself. More were soon built by diverting the river into canals that started above the falls and ran parallel to the river a block or two away from it. The water could then be dropped from the canals over mill wheels into tunnels that returned it to the river below the falls. At first the falls were used for sawmilling. By 1869, there were fifteen sawmills at or near the falls that produced over 100 million board feet of lumber annually (Figure 7). After 1870 sawmilling gradually gave way to flour milling in terms of product value, but flour milling increased without diminishing sawmilling. Production increased until 1900. Even though out-

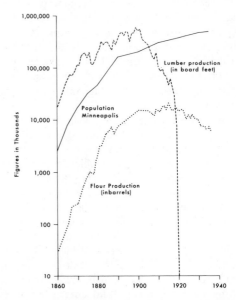

Figure 7. Growth and decline of lumbering and flour milling in Minneapolis, 1860 to 1940. Based on Calvin F. Schmid, *A Social Saga of Two Cities*, Chart 6.

put dropped somewhat thereafter, sawmilling continued to be a mainstay of the Minneapolis economy until 1915, when it declined precipitously, the local timber having been exhausted.

Lumber milling set the stage for flour milling by generating local capital, promoting railroad construction, and stimulating employment and manufacturing. By 1870, at the beginning of the wheat boom, there were thirteen flour mills in Minneapolis that produced more than 250,000 barrels of flour annually. Up to that time they had engaged mostly in custom milling for local use. Larger scale enterprise was hampered by poor rail connections into expanding wheat areas to the west and to eastern markets. But production for export rose rapidly after 1870.

After 1880 the industry began to consolidate. Whereas the twenty mills operating in 1876 were run by seventeen different firms, by 1890 four companies owned almost nine-tenths of the city's milling capacity. C.A. Pillsbury and Company was the largest. The Washburn-Crosby Milling Company (later General Mills) ran a close second.

Thus did Minneapolis become the Mill City, yet ancillary industries provided more jobs than the mills themselves. Thousands worked in companies manufacturing bags, barrels, breakfast foods, livestock feeds, milling machinery, and vegetable oils depending directly on the milling industry. Milling dominated the city's skyline as well as its industrial structure. The mills clustered around the falls and the grain elevators that line the railroad tracks throughout Minneapolis make Mill City a sobriquet that is still appropriate even though milling's heyday ended with World War I.

Meanwhile, back in St. Paul trade, transportation, and diversified industry flourished. River transportation and the fur trade stimulated firms engaged in wholesale and retail trade and others manufacturing the goods that moved in trade. In the prerail era, shoemaking, saddlery, and other leather-fabricating trades were important offshoots of commerce in furs and hides. Although St. Paul did little sawmilling, manufactured wood products firms did flourish. Carriage building, furniture construction, garment making, and hardware manufacturing were other important enterprises in the 1860s. Up to the 1880s, St. Paul retained its lead in wholesale trade, but by 1890 Minneapolis surpassed it. No single industry came to dominate the St. Paul economy the way milling did in Minneapolis. Instead, numerous small firms that depended on St. Paul's role as a transportation and mercantile center provided jobs for St. Paul's residents.

St. Paul's earlier start and firmer financial relationships with the East made it an early banking center, and many of the Twin Cities' banking fortunes started there. Being a government center as well, the city was a favorable environment for ambitious, perceptive financiers like James J. Hill. The eighteen year old Hill had arrived in St. Paul in 1856 with a vague notion of continuing on to the Red River country. The fall wagon train had left, so he took a job as a shipping clerk with a steamboat company. He soon started his own river freight and fuel supply company, which then led him into other commercial ventures. Hill had a prescient grasp of the region's future economic geography and the degree to which the region would depend on railroad transportation. At length the 1873 financial panic provided the opportunity Hill and his backers had been waiting for and by 1878 they had bought the bonds of the bankrupt St. Paul and Pacific. After further financial maneuvers over the succeeding fifteen years, Hill gained sole control of the railroad (redesignated the Great Northern) in 1883 and pushed it through to Seattle a decade later. In 1903 Hill and J.P. Morgan acquired the Northern Pacific and the Chicago, Burlington, and Quincy railroads and proposed to merge the three systems, but were forced to divest themselves of the Northern Pacific and the Burlington by Teddy Roosevelt's trustbusters. Whether a single rail system in the northwestern United States would have been appropriate then is debatable, but the merger of the three railroads in 1972 testifies to Hill's foresight.

The railroads connected both twins to other places equally well and thus conferred no special advantage on either city, yet they were more significant in St. Paul with its earlier emphasis on transportation and related activities. By 1880, the size of St. Paul's railroad operations was evident in the city's labor force composition in the same way that milling and ancillary activities were evident in Minneapolis.

Railroad construction fostered and perpetuated much of the bickering between Minneapolis and St. Paul in the 1860s and 1870s. Left to their own petty devices, the two cities (and perhaps even visionaries like Hill) might well have used rail routes as weapons. Fortunately, local geography left the protagonists few options. Rail lines coming from the East had to follow the broad Mississippi valley. They also had no choice but to leave the valley at St. Paul. The Mississippi flows through a deep gorge between Fort Snelling and St. Anthony Falls. The gorge was too narrow for rails and it dead-ended at the falls in any case. At St. Paul, Trout Creek had carved a gentle gradient between the river and the adjacent uplands, forming an ideal rail path. Once upland, railroads proceeded on to Minneapolis, not only because of the falls and the industry concentrated around them, but also because Nicollet Island and the falls were the best places to bridge the Mississippi. Thus, geology and economics dictated that all the railroads serve both cities regardless of local chauvinists.

The necessity to build trackage, marshaling yards, passenger terminals, warehouses, and car shops in both cities has persistently influenced land use throughout the Twin Cities. Rail yards and tracks govern the location of industry, neighborhood development, and the layout of road networks. The urban problems posed by railroad networks continue. Seven of the railroads serving the Twin Cities a decade ago have now merged into two (Burlington Northern, and the Chicago and Northwestern). The consolidated lines need much less space than they did when there was extensive duplication of facilities. Thus large tracts of railroad land in the Twin Cities are now available for development, some of them at locations adjacent to the central business districts.

CONSOLIDATION, DIVERSIFICATION, AND URBAN GROWTH, 1900–1940

Minnesota's population increase approximated national growth rates after 1900, but the Twin Cities continued to gain more rapidly because of farm-to-city migration. Minneapolis lumber production peaked in 1899, declined between 1900 and 1915, and ceased four years later. The last sawmill closed in 1919. Flour milling continued to increase until 1915 but declined thereafter. After the Panama Canal opened in 1914, Pacific Northwest wheat that had formerly moved through the Twin Cities was shipped east by water. After 1922 revised railroad

tariffs made it cheaper to ship wheat to the East than to ship flour. Successful cultivation of hard winter wheat in Kansas and declining spring wheat production in Minnesota, the Dakotas, and Montana resulting from diversified argiculture combined with higher transportation costs to force Minneapolis millers to shift capacity to Buffalo and Kansas City. Flour milling products constituted over half the value of all commodities manufactured in Minneapolis in 1890. By 1930 they made up less than a fourth. As milling declined in Minneapolis it also dispersed throughout the city. Electric power made it possible to locate mills away from the falls and after 1900 mills and elevators were erected along most of the railroad trackage in Minneapolis.

As flour milling declined in favor of more diversified manufacturing in Minneapolis, St. Paul continued along the diversified lines upon which it had originally embarked. One major outgrowth of St. Paul's location and early trade was the large packing complex at South St. Paul. Meat packing was originally concentrated in St. Paul, but larger facilities were needed to process the output of the more diversified agriculture that was developing in the region. After 1900 Armour and Swift built plants and stockyards in South St. Paul that boosted the town's population from 2,000 in 1890 to 12,000 in 1940. Printing and publishing also developed into major industries during the period. Although most printing firms were small, St. Paul's printing industry was dominated by the West Publishing Company, a firm specializing in law books, and by Brown and Bigelow Co., which prints calendars and other advertising novelties.

On the eve of World War II the Twin Cities were midway in their transition from cities that made their livings by processing the region's agricultural produce to the more cosmopolitan economic centers they were to become in the postwar period when packing, milling, baking, and similar enterprises would decline. But in 1940 the Twin Cities economy was still as much related to the past as it was suggestive of the future.

The urban landscape of Minneapolis and St. Paul, on the other hand, bore slight resemblance to the two nineteenth century towns where it all began. Fifty years of growth at rates exceeding 20 percent per decade had produced a metropolis.

Swedes and Norwegians remained the largest ethnic groups in Minneapolis after 1890. Some Poles and Italians arrived after 1890, the Poles preferring Minneapolis whereas the Italians favored St. Paul. By 1910 Minneapolis had 5,000 Polish-born and 650 Italian-born, whereas St. Paul had 2,000 Italian-born and 2,000 Polish-born. The Polish-born were sometimes ethnic Poles and sometimes Polish Jews. Most of the Polish-born who went to Minneapolis were Poles, but many of the Polish-born who settled in St. Paul were Jewish.

World War I and postwar immigration restrictions combined to stabilize Twin Cities ethnic structure after 1910. In 1930 Scandinavians were dominant throughout the metropolitan region, but less important in St. Paul where the older German and Irish groups were more numerous.

Negroes and Spanish-Americans were recent arrivals in 1940. There were just under 2,000 Americans of Spanish origin in the Twin Cities then and 4,500 Negroes. Negro settlement was an offshoot of the Twin Cities rail business.

Most early Negro settlers were cooks, waiters, and sleeping car porters. Others had been brought north by the meat packers. Mexican-Americans were imported when sugar beets became an important crop in the Red River valley. Rather than make the journey to the Southwest when the harvest was over, many stayed in the Twin Cities and gradually moved into other occupations. American Indians were even less visible in 1940 than they are today. There were but 245 Indians in the Twin Cities then.

By 1940 the transition from an agrarian-based urban economy to a metropolitan manufacturing and service economy was well under way. Both cities' corporate limits were occupied except for a few tracts, and much of the neighborhood churning generated by ethnic migrations and antagonisms was over. Henceforth the Twin Cities' prosperity would depend on a new set of industries and neighborhood turnover would be more dependent on aging and lifestyle changes than on social status.

Inside the Cities

Yankee businessmen founded the Twin Cities as a moneymaking venture, attracting waves of immigrants who wanted a share of the action. The most influential group—Franklin Steele, Caleb Dorr, C.C. and W.D. Washburn, Dorilus Morrison—arrived with the vanguard of lumbermen who had started in New England and worked westward cutting over the Great Lakes forests. They were joined by other Yankee businessmen —Bassett, Pillsbury, Eastman, Welles—who were anxious to harvest the region's forests and fields and supply its residents with goods and services.

PLACES AND PEOPLE IN EARLY DAYS—JOBS FIRST, THEN HOMES

One set of jobs brought money into the area. This basic or export employment, centering on gathering raw materials, on manufacturing, and on shipping goods out of the area, concentrated at the Falls of St. Anthony, at the Nicollet Island river crossing, at the riverboat landing by the mouth of Trout Creek, and later in railroad yards and shops. Additional local service jobs served the needs of residents. These jobs concentrated in downtown centers near the intersections of major streets and horsecar lines.

The local transportation systems (streets, horsecar lines, then streetcar lines) came into contact with regionwide transportation systems (rivers, roads, railroads) in the downtown areas, making the downtowns the principal points of contact between the local economies and the rest of the world. Downtown St. Paul, on the east side of the river, enjoyed better access to

regions east and north of the Twin Cities (Figure 8). The center of St. Paul's downtown grew up west of the riverboat landing and eventually moved inland several blocks, then slowly shifted west to about Seventh and Robert Streets. Downtown Minneapolis, on the west side of the river and west of the milling district, enjoyed unrestricted access to western agricultural areas (Figure 9). Originally three downtown contenders emerged in Minneapolis and St. Anthony—Bridge Square where Washington, Hennepin, and Nicollet avenues met at the western end of the Hennepin Avenue Bridge at Nicollet Island; downtown St. Anthony at the east end of the bridge; and Lower Town on Washington Avenue near the falls . Lower Town was soon crowded out by manufacturers. Downtown St. Anthony, beleaguered by the competition, dropped from the running to become a shopping center for East (of the river) Minneapolis. Meanwhile, the commercial center of downtown Minneapolis migrated southwest toward the high class lake district, settling finally around Seventh and Nicollet.

In each city the export jobs and the downtown lay on the land like a twisted figure eight. Residential areas crowded in on every side, with the rich preempting the most scenic sites. In St. Paul, the small morainic hills directly north of downtown and Dayton's Bluff overlooking the river east of downtown became the fashionable places to live for a while, but then fashion shifted and families abruptly relocated to the bluffs at the east end of Summit Avenue where there was ample room for westward expansion. The

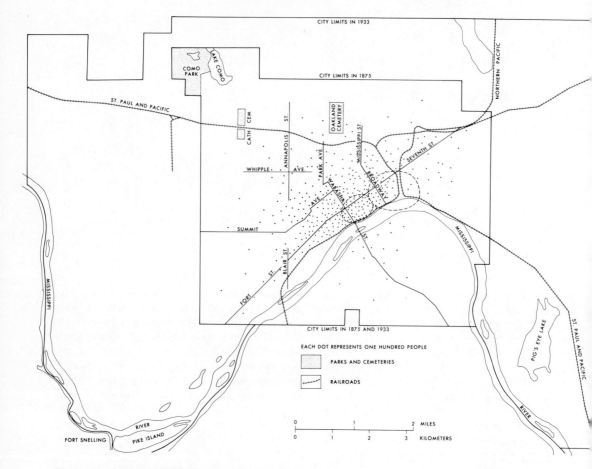

Figure 8. St. Paul in 1875. Rail lines move up Trout Creek to serve areas lying east of the Mississippi River, thereby encouraging population to grow westward from downtown. Based on Calvin F. Schmid, *A Social Saga of Two Cities*, Chart 28.

relatively flat site of early Minneapolis offered little distinctive topography as a preserve for the merchants, millers, and town fathers. Some families, including the Pillsburys, settled between the East Side milling district and the university. Others built houses on Park Avenue, which started at the falls as Cataract Street in early days and ran southward past the Washburn "Fair Oaks" estate. As time passed and the city grew, the southward-bound gold coast swung westward to Lowry Hill and the hills and lakes of Kenwood near Lake of the Isles. A few first families remained in the East Side as the newly rich joined the rush to the southwest lake district.

Before 1900, neighborhood quality generally rose with increasing distance from industry, railroad yards, and the downtown. Congestion,

high densities, and general squalor near the mills gradually gave way to lower densities, higher ground, and cleaner air farther away. At the same time that St. Paul's upper class selected the bluffs west of downtown as the place to live, they assigned to railroad and industrial uses increasing amounts of land east and north of downtown where railroads converged. The same thing happened in Minneapolis. Much East Side land and parcels along the river on the West Side were devoted to railroads and industry as the upper class moved into South and Southwest Minneapolis. The rich, having alternatives, chose to avoid the noise, soot, and odors of transportation, industry, and commerce. In addition they shrewdly avoided the congestion created by a hundred trains and over a thousand railroad cars entering and leaving the

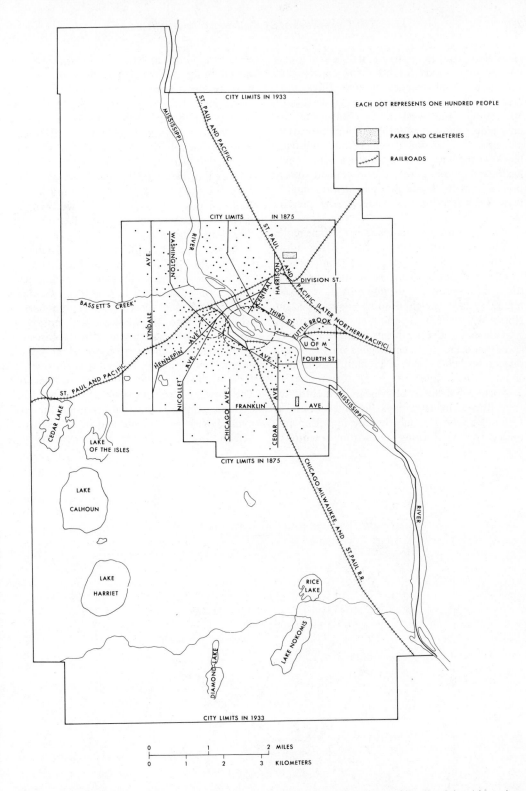

Figure 9. Minneapolis in 1875. Railroads from St. Paul cross the river at Nicollet Island just above St. Anthony Falls, then continue westward hindering easy access between downtown and North Minneapolis. Based on Calvin F. Schmid, *A Social Saga of Two Cities*, Chart 27.

cities daily, blocking streets and isolating certain neighborhoods for hours on end (Figure 10). For several decades in both cities most railroads crossed city streets at grade. South Minneapolis and western St. Paul were the only places enjoying continuous and unrestricted access to their downtowns without railroads blocking the way. So in both cities, early upper income migrations set the dominant directions of growth—Minneapolis southward and St. Paul westward—that continue to the present day.

By the turn of the century, Minneapolis community leaders—Protestant, native-born, and monopolizing finance, civic administration, trade, management, and the professions—lived south and southwest of downtown. A mixed middle class neighborhood developed in North Minneapolis beyond the railroad tracks and Bassett's Creek. Named after a Minneapolis pioneer, the creek begins on the south side of Medicine Lake in Plymouth and flows about fifteen miles to its Mississippi outlet in North Minneapolis above the Plymouth Avenue Bridge. In early days the creek wound a tortuous course through the city in a deep and rugged chasm, blocking travel from downtown

to North Minneapolis except for a few congested bridges. Northeast Minneapolis, carved into residential islands by crisscrossing railroads and strips of industrial land, attracted mainly immigrant Poles, Slovaks, Ukranians, and Italians. A middle class residential neighborhood surrounded the university. Bohemians settled south of the university on the west side of the river, and the main line, yards, and shops of the Chicago, Milwaukee, and St. Paul Railroad running southeast of downtown Minneapolis became the spine of the immigrant Swedish neighborhood.

In St. Paul the elite were well established by 1900 in the Summit Hill neighborhood west of downtown. The city's main middle class neighborhood—settled by Swedes, Germans, Norwegians, and later by large numbers of Irish—developed to the west and northwest. The East Side (east of Rice Street), carved up by railroads and industry, attracted more immigrants from Southern and Eastern Europe, in a fashion analogous to Northeast Minneapolis. The West Side, across the river from downtown, contained mixed industrial activities, the city's main Jewish settlement, and other residential neighborhoods ranging from slums on the flood

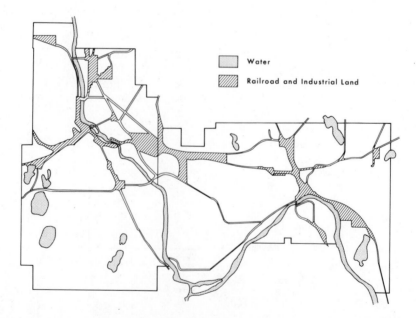

Figure 10. Railroad and industrial corridors carve up Minneapolis and St. Paul into a series of residential islands. The western part of St. Paul and South Minneapolis have been the largest parcels of uncongested land inviting continuous middle class residential development.

plain of the Mississippi to occasional elegant mansions on the high bluffs facing downtown St. Paul.

By the turn of the century the dominant immigrant groups in the Twin Cities were Swedes, Germans, and Norwegians. Poles, Russian Jews, Czechs, Slovaks, Danes, Irish, and Italians remained conspicuous but much less important. Most groups lived in all parts of both cities, but occasional concentrations were high enough to give a predominant ethnic cast to certain parts of both cities. During much of the nineteenth century the Canadian-born represented one of the largest immigrant groups, but they remained inconspicuous except for the few who spoke French.

PEOPLE TODAY

During the 1960s the European foreign stock in the Twin Cities metropolitan area declined 13 percent as death overtook the older age groups. In Minneapolis and St. Paul the decline was even higher. Each city lost about a third of its foreign stock, which dispersed to the suburbs faster than the rest of the population.

Between 1957 and 1971 the city of Minneapolis lost 60 percent of its Jewish population. In contrast with other ethnic groups, large numbers migrated en masse to a couple of suburbs while the Jewish proportion of the area population declined to 2 percent. Near North Minneapolis, which had 38 percent of the area's Jewish population in 1957, lost 94 percent of its Jewish residents during that period. By 1971 more than three out of four Minneapolis area Jews lived in the suburbs, with 48 percent living in St. Louis Park where Jews comprise 20 percent of the population.

The Jewish departure from the Minneapolis Near North left vacant many quality houses which were promptly occupied by black families. Prosperity encouraged the better-off and upwardly mobile black families to move steadily westward and northward away from the North Side ghetto core near 6th Avenue North and Lyndale. As they moved others followed, pushed along by urban renewal projects.

It is uncertain why Minneapolis developed separate black neighborhoods on the North and the South sides, but the Glenwood Avenue North–Fourth Avenue South streetcar line which ran between the two neighborhoods for three generations through downtown Minneap-

olis without a transfer stop may offer a clue. The two ghettos lay separated on the map but remained conveniently linked by a single transit line (Figure 11).

In St. Paul, Mexican and Chicano neighborhoods emerged on the West Side when former Jewish residents abandoned it for better housing across the river on Selby Avenue west of downtown and then for Highland Park southwest of downtown. St. Paul's principal black neighborhood developed at the western edge of downtown at the type of location where black neighborhoods usually develop—the inner precincts of the city's most vigorously expanding middle class residential sector.

There were over 30,000 blacks in the three sprawling ghetto neighborhoods in 1970. Each was small, integrated by ghetto standards elsewhere, and mixed in income, education, age, and occupational characteristics compared to black areas in most other large American cities.

In recent years the black minority—with a sizable number of professionals, civil servants, corporate executives, and foundation personnel—has realized steady acceptance or cooptation into Twin City economic, political, and civic life. Farther down the social ladder, the frequently shrill rhetoric of Indian and Chicano leaders reflects the distance these recent immigrants must travel toward full participation in local affairs.

CHURCHES AND SCHOOLS

Residential neighborhoods grew up around job opportunities. Inside the neighborhoods immigrant groups organized much of their life around churches and schools. The predominant Scandinavian and German origins of the population meant that Twin Cities church members have been overwhelmingly Lutheran or Roman Catholic.

Almost a third of all church members in the area are Lutheran, with the American Lutheran Church, nationally headquartered in Minneapolis, claiming the largest share. The original branches of the Lutheran Church were organized largely around ethnic congregations— Evangelical Lutheran (Norwegian), Augustana Lutheran (Swedish), American Lutheran (German), and United Evangelical Lutheran (Danish). A controversy over public education developed in Twin Cities Lutheran circles during the nineteenth century, but the immigrant press and

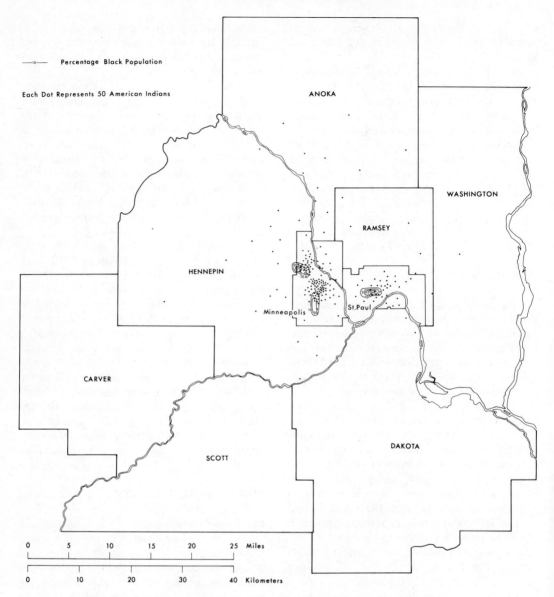

Figure 11.   Black and Indian concentrations in the Twin Cities.

people generally supported the public schools and do so today.

Over 43 percent of church members in 1971 were Roman Catholic. They support an extensive system of territorial parishes serving all parts of the Twin Cities. The United States was considered missionary territory by Rome until 1908. Church authorities in Rome and in the states responded to the threat of Protestantism and the risk of leakage by creating both territorial and personal parishes. Each diocese, including the St. Paul diocese con-taining the Twin Cities, was completely sub-divided by the authority of the local bishop into nonoverlapping areal units called territorial parishes (Figure 12). In addition, national or language-based parishes were formally con-stituted without boundaries as "personal parishes"—e.g., Polish, Slovak, German, Leb-anese—or else resulted from the bishop formally recognizing the ethnic composition of the area served by a territorial parish—e.g., German parishes west of Minneapolis—by designating it a national parish and by assigning to it parish

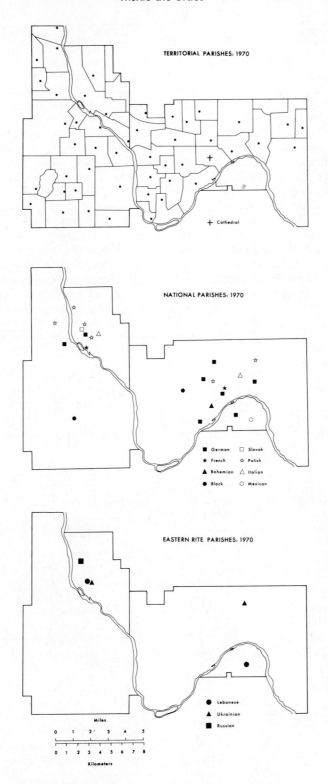

Figure 12. Catholic churches and parishes reveal part of the fabric of immigrant settlement in the Twin Cities. Maps courtesy of Dana Noonan.

priests who were members of the ethnic group and who spoke the language.

Several Catholic and Orthodox parishes of Eastern Rite—e.g., Ukranian, Byzantine, Greek —were also established in Northeast Minneapolis by Eastern Rite Catholic and Orthodox bishops headquartered outside the area. In each type of Catholic parish—territorial, personal, national, or Eastern Rite—an elementary school and occasionally a secondary school was built for the parish children as an alternative to the essentially Protestant-oriented public school system. Besides the Catholic schools, about two dozen additional parochial elementary and secondary schools operate today in the Twin Cities, mainly under Baptist and Lutheran jurisdiction. A few private nondenominational academies operate without institutional support and enroll mainly children from upper income areas.

Patterns of parochial school attendance in the Twin Cities today tell us as much about class structure as about the local geography of religion (Figure 13). The largest and strongest Catholic parochial elementary schools thrive in middle and upper middle class areas having substantial numbers of third and fourth generation Catholic families of Irish, German, and Austrian descent. In the Twin Cities this means the middle and higher income areas of South, Southwest, North, and Northeast Minneapolis, and most of the west half of St. Paul and its eastern edge. Catholic parochial schools have the hardest time surviving in lower income areas, black neighborhoods, and Indian areas, even though a substantial fraction of Indians are Catholic. A significant number of upwardly mobile black families, uncertain about the educational and social environments of the public schools and wanting something distinctive or

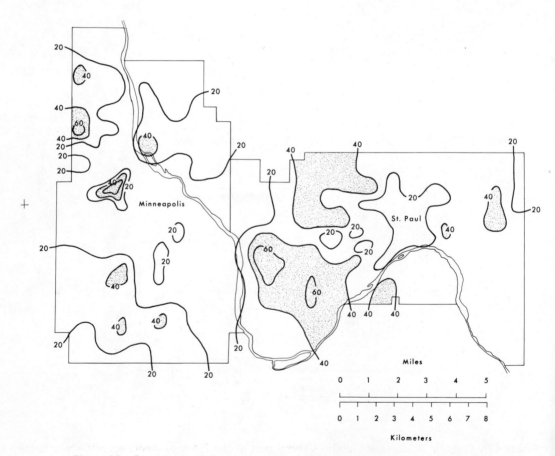

Figure 13. Percentage of elementary school children in nonpublic schools, 1970.

more exclusive for their children, send them to parochial schools. In traditionally Scandinavian middle class South Minneapolis, a number of Lutheran parochial schools enroll fair numbers of students.

Some parents elect to send their children to parochial schools for doctrinal reasons, some prefer the more exclusive atmosphere of an alternative school supervised by a neighborhood parish board of education, and others seek curricular variety. Some Twin Cities parochial schools are more progressive and others are more traditional than the public schools. Race is seldom a reason because public school attendance areas are designed to keep minority enrollments small compared to other cities (Minneapolis, 18 percent in 1973, up from 7 percent in 1963) and because many nonpublic schools enroll a significant number of minority students.

The availability of high quality alternative schools for many families, combined with the relatively high social class and small numbers of minority populations, make it hard to assess the relationships between race, class, schools, and the inclination of families with school age children to move into or out of middle class neighborhoods in either Minneapolis or St. Paul. Parochial schools thrive in such middle class neighborhoods and frequently become—with the church community around them—an important social, political, and neighborhood force attracting new families and retaining the old because of the strong community bonds, long lost in other cities but successfully maintained here.

Moreover, although the parents may hold views different from those of their children, about seven out of ten students surveyed in Minneapolis secondary schools in 1972 said they think it is a good idea for students of different races to go to school together. Some of the highest percentages of students favoring integration were recorded in the city's most integrated schools. Racial attitudes such as these suggest a positive educational picture in other areas as well. Of the public high school students surveyed, a substantial majority liked school, were good students, and were successful after graduation. On national achievement tests in English, Minneapolis eleventh graders scored 49, slightly below the national norm of 52.5. On scores of the American College Testing Program, college-bound

twelfth graders earned a mean score of 20.3 in 1971-1972, doing better than their peers around the nation who averaged 18.8. The city publishes each year the records of continuing high quality of its public school students, a reflection of the willingness of middle class families to live in the city. None of the suburbs publishes its records.

Not to be outdone, St. Paul public schools reported in 1973 that student achievement levels have risen steadily since 1970 after falling each year for the previous five years. The more affluent the family, the better the student seems to do, and the city—always an attractive place for middle class families—evidently is more than holding its own in competition with the suburbs. The 1972 test scores were below 1965, before the decline started, but current results are expected to exceed those of 1965.

Almost half of the 1971 graduates of Minneapolis public high schools were attending college in 1972 and were doing well. Besides the 46 percent in college, 10 percent were enrolled in trade or technical schools, over 37 percent were employed, and 2 percent were in the armed forces.

HOUSING AND NEIGHBORHOODS

From the time of initial settlement until today the growth of the Twin Cities population has been accompanied by a steady expansion in the local housing supply. In fact, the housing inventory has increased even faster, accompanying the sharp decline in average household size in recent generations. Almost all nineteenth century houses were constructed of wood, the cheapest and locally most abundant building material. After the usual series of major fires which swept through nineteenth century midwestern cities, the cities established fire limits, zones around downtown within which only brick and stone buildings were permitted. Their durable construction meant that many of them remain in use today. Fires and the expansion of the downtowns removed most of the housing built before the 1880s.

What little remains of the pre-1890 housing was compactly clustered around the central employment and shopping cores. People and housing huddled within walking distance of downtown. During the economic and population boom of the 1880s the cities became increasingly congested. Reliance on walking, especially during winter, prevented the cities from sprawling outward. Upward expansion was normally impossible because up to the 1880s no one knew how to build economical tall buildings that would support their own weight. Moreover, even if the buildings could be built, a limit of six stories or so existed on the number of flights of stairs a person could climb without collapsing. Thus, one force pulled the cities inward, another kept them low in profile.

Cities like Minneapolis and St. Paul that grew rapidly during the late nineteenth century had only one means of dispersing houses and people, and then only for the privileged classes —the railroad suburbs of the sort found around much larger cities like New York, Boston, Philadelphia, or Chicago. Smaller places like St. Paul and Minneapolis accommodated their pre-1880 growth by cramming the poor and working classes into rather tight quarters with block after block featuring population densities that sometimes reached several hundred people per acre.

Two important inventions of the 1880s removed the constraints preventing the areal expansion of cities and encouraged lower density residential development. One was the construction of steel- and metal-frame buildings, beginning with the Chicago skyscrapers in the mid-1880s, demonstrating how cities could expand upward. Electrification of the horsecar lines and steam-propelled street railways produced the electric streetcar, permitting outward dispersal of the city and giving working class people a chance to live outside the congestion and still move quickly and cheaply to work and shopping.

The new housing during the electric streetcar era was built in neighborhoods served by streetcar lines. Most streetcar lines in Minneapolis were built to serve the South Side, reinforcing growth in that sector of town especially into the southwest lake district (Figure 14). In St. Paul, all the 1884 lines ran west or north of downtown, setting the future course of residential growth. By 1905 the cities' limits had almost reached their present extent. The transit systems of the two cities had merged on Como and on University avenues in St. Paul's Midway district, setting the stage for that area's rise in the 1920s as a major zone of manufacturing and goods handling, close to the railroads of both cities, with plenty

of flat vacant land, easy to reach by streetcar from either city.

The outstanding growth of the Twin Cities during the 1870s and 1880s nurtured extravagant expectations on the part of the streetcar companies' owners and eventually they overbuilt the network to 523 miles. Perhaps taking a cue from railroad magnate James J. Hill who had made a fortune on land grants, the streetcar companies under the management of William King and Thomas Lowry also entered the land business because any land served by the streetcar could be developed for residential use and transfer points between lines were ideal commercial locations. When urban growth fell short of expectations, the surplus land was eventually soaked up by large lots, producing some of the lowest residential densities found among midwestern cities.

St. Paul streetcar lines reached South St. Paul and the stockyards, Stillwater on the St. Croix River, North St. Paul, Wildwood Park, and fashionable White Bear Lake. Minneapolis lines reached out to the towns of Robbinsdale, St. Louis Park, and Hopkins, and to the streetcar suburbs and resort areas on Lake Minnetonka. Trolley lines also connected with interurban lines to Hastings and Anoka. Like streetcar entrepreneurs in other cities, the Twin Cities company built amusement parks at the ends of the out-of-town lines to keep people riding on holidays and weekends. Wildwood Park north of St. Paul and Excelsior Park built in the 1920s on Lake Minnetonka were easily reached from either city and pulled a disproportionate amount of residential construction in these directions.

National and local housing construction rates alternatively waxed and waned with business and immigration cycles. In good times such as the years after 1900 and before World War I incomes rose, immigration increased, and the housing industry boomed. Periods of war and economic recession cut the demand and supply of new housing almost to zero.

The volume of residential construction during each building era, plus the densities permitted by the prevailing urban transportation system, controlled the amounts of land devoted to residents in the Twin Cities in each era (Figure 15). Around the downtowns only traces remain of housing from the walking and horse era (pre-1890). Downtown expansion and

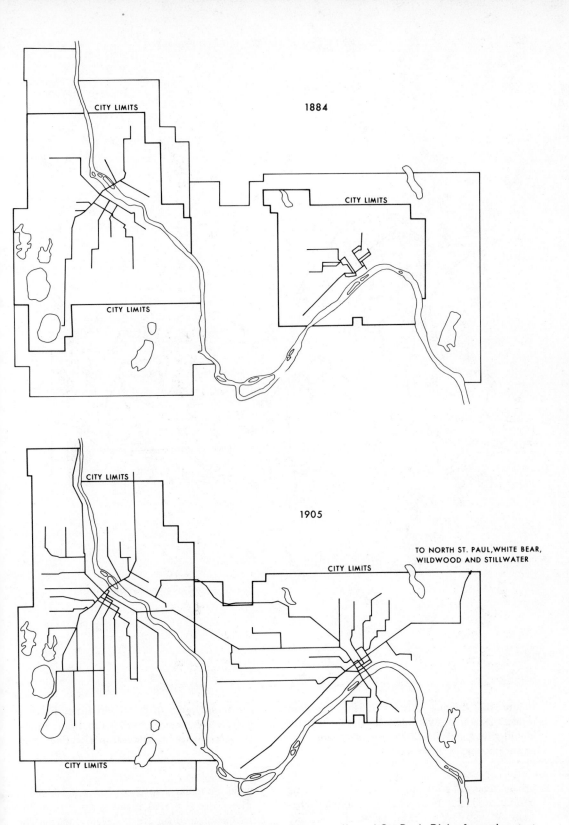

Figure 14. Expansion of the streetcar system in Minneapolis and St. Paul. Right from the start, South Minneapolis and western St. Paul were better served than other parts of the cities. Based on Calvin F. Schmid, *A Social Saga of Two Cities*, Chart 31.

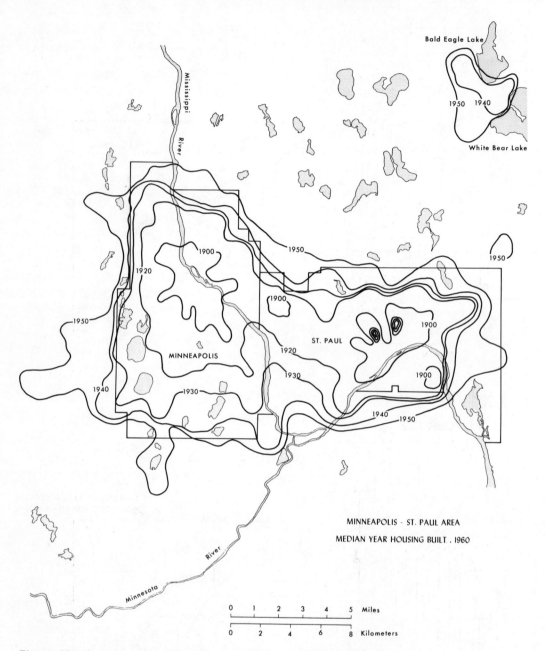

Figure 15. Average year of housing construction in different areas of the Twin Cities in 1960 reflects steady outward growth at ever lower densities. By 1970 most of the area of the map was included in the Twin Cities urbanized area. Patches of urban renewal near downtown St. Paul mean newer housing in those zones.

urban renewal took the rest. The streetcar period produced finger-shaped increments because it was easy to build outward along the lines and harder to expand between them. In the 1920s and 1930s, with cars able to move easily in every direction, a filling-in process yielded a circular-shaped city once again. Then in the postwar period highways out from the cities encouraged suburban development at the built-up margins or leap-frogged beyond.

Architectural styles and consumer tastes of each building era are reflected in each concentric increment. The boundaries between the tree-ring-like increments show up clearly. Troughs in the housing supply profile were sharp and their consequences endure. Every time the nation emerged from a serious depression or war, the cities seemed anxious to adopt new housing styles. In a boom period like the 1920s, duplexes were all the rage. Real estate was bull market, with amateur and professional investors alike thinking they could get rich quick by buying a duplex, renting half to pay for the building, and living in the other half. This scheme worked fine until too many people got into the act and owners found themselves unable to meet mortgage obligations. Yet despite the bankruptcies, the houses remain. Most of the finest duplexes in the Twin Cities represent monuments to the unflappable optimism of the 1920s.

In housing construction, when somebody does something successfully, the normal behavior pattern has been to imitate it repeatedly until a bankruptcy or a depression suggests it is time to stop. Coming out of the Depression, a different group of clients and housebuilders started with fresh styles but the behavior pattern was the same—they built only single family houses. Duplexes and apartment houses led to so many foreclosures during the 1930s that builders stuck to singles in the late 1930s and after 1945. The chronic housing shortage meant that houses could be sold as basements with roofs before they were finished. Builders assumed no one wanted anything but singles. In the mid-1960s, a few venturesome developers began building row houses and apartment houses in Twin City suburbs and discovered a strong market for them. This local experimentation was part of a nationwide trend toward greater balance in the mix of new housing styles and closer attention to household compositions and tastes. Widespread interest in mobile homes is another feature of the current housing scene. There are about 10,000 mobile homes in the Twin Cities area, with about half of them clustered north and northwest of St. Paul in southern Anoka and northern Ramsey Counties.

SHOPPING DISTRICTS AND URBAN TRANSPORTATION ERAS

Every urban transportation era modified the previous pattern of shopping districts and prompted the development of new ones. In the walking and horsecar era almost all commercial activities concentrated in the downtown cores. When streetcar tracks branched out in all directions, outlying commercial districts sprang up. Major centers featuring small department stores, doctor and dentist offices, and a wide variety of other occasional goods and services developed at the intersection of two or more streetcar lines. Other clusters of stores prospered at transit stops by supplying groceries, meat, bakery goods, pharmaceuticals, and other everyday goods and services. Ma and Pa corner stores sold bread and milk to residential areas between streetcar lines.

Farther out, in parts of the cities built up during the era of the recreational automobile, shopping districts grew up on bus and streetcar lines with provision made for car parking and, beyond the lines, at the intersections of major streets and arterials. By 1940, auto-oriented suburban shopping centers were being planned.

During the housing boom that accompanied the post-World War II freeway auto era, car-oriented shopping centers of every size and description appeared at intersections of suburban roads and highways. Shopping center developers transferred from the inner city and the streetcar era the idea of locating stores and shopping centers at traffic intersections and in strips along well-traveled streets, reasoning that if stores at such locations prospered before 1920, analogous locations farther out should work just as well after 1950. But pedestrians could move around transit intersections more easily than cars can negotiate highway intersections—and pedestrians require no parking.

Currently most of the shopping districts along transit lines are steadily going out of business. Neighborhood populations are sparser, poorer, and more mobile than they were fifty years ago. As people move outward they take their business to larger newer shopping centers. Those who remain are usually poorer than those who moved away. Sometimes the newcomers bring different tastes, such as when blacks replaced Jews on Plymouth Avenue in North Minneapolis or on Selby Avenue west of downtown St. Paul. But even the poor often have cars to carry them to larger stores and lower prices in nearby suburban shopping centers.

As retailers, dentists, doctors, and movie houses abandon the old streetcar trunk lines—

Nicollet, Broadway, Central, Lake Street, and
Hennepin in Minneapolis; Seventh Street,
Grand, Selby, University, Snelling, and Rice in
St. Paul—the space is taken over for general
office uses like insurance and real estate or by
specialty goods and services like carpet and re-
upholstery shops, television and electronics
sales and service, pizza shops, second-hand
stores, and the like. In subtle but forceful
ways, new housing added on the edge draws
upper income families outward and erodes the
support base for central city retailers.

Downtown Minneapolis and St. Paul in contrast with other large American cities have been
holding their own in retailing, but the suburban
shopping centers are booming. The leading suburban shopping center developer—Dayton-Hudson Corporation—also operates the leading department store—Dayton's—in each downtown.
The suburban shopping center boom started
in the 1950s and by 1958 the suburbs had 11
percent of the department store trade. By
1967 it had rocketed to 52 percent.

Department store sales in Minneapolis rose
from $130 million in 1958 to $143 million in
1967. Meanwhile suburban Hennepin County
sales went from $23 million to $207 million.
St. Paul did better than Minneapolis during the
same period because of downtown rejuvenation
and slower suburbanization into Ramsey County. While the Minneapolis share of department
store sales dropped from 61 to 28 percent, St.
Paul's share went from 28 to 21 percent.
Looked at another way, Minneapolis department store sales went from $130 million to
$143 million while downtown St. Paul, helped
economically and psychologically by a large
new Dayton's store in 1963, saw sales jump
from $59 million to $107 million.

OPEN SPACE FOR THE TWIN CITIES

The Twin Cities metropolitan area, according to
a study done by the Outdoor Recreation Resources Review Commission in the early 1960s,
had the highest overall opportunities for participation in outdoor recreation of any metropolitan area in the country. There are two
principal reasons. First is the variety of seasons.
The summer is reasonable—not too hot for outdoor activities—and in the winter a continuous
snow cover encourages winter sports. Second,
the Twin Cities has a large amount of open
space available for public use. Within the sub-

urban areas there is a developing system of
regional parks and a large number of lakes
which are public open space (Figure 16). For
weekend recreation beyond one hour's drive
from home there are thousands of lakes and
over ten million acres of public land. Minnesota
is the third largest landowner in the United
States, following only the United State government and the state of Alaska.

Serious concern for open space preservation
came to the Twin Cities area with the New England pioneers who built the region. Most notably, Horace W.S. Cleveland, a gifted and original landscape architect, came to St. Paul from
New England in 1872 bent on the nurturing of
beauty in nature. He presented to the city
council an imaginative plan for parks at Lakes
Como and Phalen—still far distant from the
residential centers of St. Paul. He advocated a
high and commanding hill for state buildings,
a splendid avenue between Minneapolis and St.
Paul, and generous boulevards along the river
flowing through both cities. Cleveland correctly
anticipated a future growth that would make
the cities physically one, scorning "artificial
decorating" for a permanent "heritage of
beauty." St. Paul was slow to respond, but
did acquire Como Park in 1873 over the opposition of shortsighted aldermen who labeled the
park as a playground for the rich who had
carriages to get to it.

Minneapolis was no less lethargic at first,
but when Charles M. Loring, another Maine
native, became president of the newly created Board of Park Commissioners in 1883
he immediately engaged Cleveland as an aide
and adviser and in two years the city purchased
ten major pieces of land for parks. The city acquired the area around Minnehaha Falls and
designed and constructed scenic Minnehaha
Parkway linking the falls and the Minneapolis
lakes. It also acquired wide strips of land
around the city's five largest lakes and dredged
a swamp to create Lake of the Isles (Figure 17).
Many of the city's most expensive houses were
built within a block or two of these lakes,
particularly those to the southwest and along
the Grand Rounds—an elaborate parkway system on the perimeter of three sides of the city.
Most important was an arrangement with St.
Paul whereby lands on both sides of the river
from the university to Fort Snelling were secured for park and parkway use. Loring next
launched a movement for extensive tree plant-

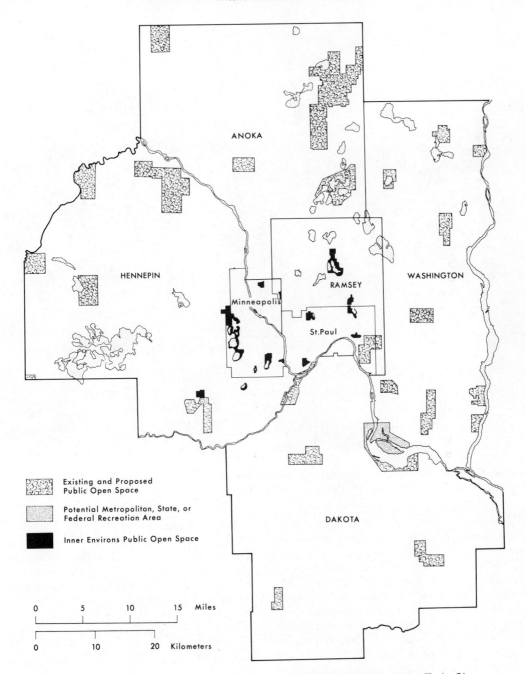

Existing and Proposed
Public Open Space

Potential Metropolitan, State, or
Federal Recreation Area

Inner Environs Public Open Space

ANOKA

HENNEPIN

WASHINGTON

RAMSEY

Minneapolis

St.Paul

DAKOTA

| 0 | 5 | 10 | 15 | Miles |

| 0 | 10 | 20 | Kilometers |

Figure 16. Recreational lakes, rivers, parks, and reserved open space in the Twin City area.

ing to shade the city streets and add beauty to travel ways. Today about the only major Twin Cities water resources remaining to be fully developed as recreational open space are stretches of the Mississippi River. Railroads and industrial uses preempted much of the riverfront in the nineteenth century. Today these uses are obsolete and should be replaced by parkland and housing. The cities, counties, and other public agencies already own much of the land along the river and pressure has begun for the governor to declare the entire stretch of Mississippi in the Twin Cities as a "critical area".

Figure 17. Lake of the Isles, just one of twenty-two lakes and lagoons in "the City of Lakes". Photo courtesy of the Minneapolis Chamber of Commerce.

The Critical Areas Act, passed by the state legislature in 1973, is designed as a permanent method for guiding development within areas of the state which possess important historic, cultural, or esthetic values and where uncontrolled development could result in irreversible damage to important natural resources. Procedurally, a "critical area" is designated by the governor upon the recommendation of the state Environmental Quality Council.

The Minneapolis city charter granted fiscal and operating autonomy to the Board of Park Commissioners. The city is divided into park districts and each district elects a commissioner to a six year term. Three other commissioners are elected at large. The board has its own taxing authority and supervises its own staff independently of the city council. St. Paul parks are managed by a department of the city government.

Besides acquiring and developing new open space, city and county park systems must maintain the health of lakes and trees. Continued urban expansion alters surface water conditions by decreasing the permeability of the ground surface and increasing the rate of runoff. Yet the lakes currently are of higher quality than the runoff. This is a serious water management problem for a region that leans so heavily on its lakes and streams. The runoff water carries increasing loads of pesticides, fertilizers, petroleum, heavy metals, construction debris, glass, salt, sulfur dioxide, and hydrocarbons. Diverting the runoff requires the pumping of Mississippi River water from above the city into the chain of lakes.

While pollution threatens the water, disease threatens many of the region's trees. Over a million stately American elms lining the boulevards and gracing the houses of Minneapolis and St. Paul will die over the next thirty to fifty years of Dutch elm disease carried by beetles who nest in the dead elm branches of live trees. The Minneapolis park board tries to replace 2 to 3 percent of its elms with different species each year as they remove dead, diseased, and damaged trees from public property. Trees on private property receive much less conscientious attention.

St. Paul and suburban areas face the same problem but cannot respond fast enough to slow the spread of the disease. Similar blights threaten red oaks and certain species of maple. The diseases spread fastest through heavy concentrations of a single species, so upper income areas with a rich variety of trees are best protected, while lower income areas with mainly elm trees for shade and decoration will be denuded first and most completely.

Suburban Open Space

Most of the large open space areas in the suburbs are county parks. Few suburban communities have done an adequate job of preserving open space or providing public park space around close-in lakes in the Minneapolis-St. Paul tradition, probably because they are too small to do it. The largest suburban park system is maintained by the Hennepin County Park Reserve District. This system contains 15,000 acres of land—almost all of it in seven large parks. Eighty percent of the land in the Hennepin system is undeveloped; the other 20 percent is utilized for picnicking, camping, nature interpretation centers, and trails. No other metropolitan counties have park systems to compare with the Hennepin system.

There is an extensive and fast-growing private open space system in the suburban areas also. Private golf courses are the most obvious part of this private open space. Private corporations such as Honeywell and 3M have built large corporate parks. There are now many planned unit developments of garden apartments and townhouses which set aside open space owned in common by residents. They also have swimming pools, ponds, garden plots, tennis courts, and picnic areas. The largest planned unit developments contain private open space areas as extensive as many large public parks.

Weekend Open Space

Most open space available for public use lies to the north of the Twin Cities in the forested part of Minnesota. About two-thirds of the forested land is in public ownership. In this forest zone, most recreational use takes place on lakeshores and to a lesser extent in managed public areas such as Itasca State Park, the Boundary Waters Canoe Area, and the Voyageurs National Park area.

Lakeshore cabins accommodate 42 percent of all the person nights spent in weekend recreation accommodations. This is twice as high as the resort percentage (20 percent) and five times as high as the camping percentage (8 percent). The heaviest concentration of lakeshore cabins is in the Brainerd area. This is where the northern pine forests and a lake area are closest to the Twin Cities. The total cabin development in this area forms the third largest built-up area in the state, exceeded only by the Twin Cities and Duluth.

TRANSIT DEVELOPMENT AND POPULATION DENSITIES

The early streetcar company, in a flush of optimism about local growth prospects, built streetcar systems for cities much larger than what eventually appeared, and started the local tradition of low density residential development. After 1920 the private car and the availability of easily developable land on every side of the built-up area promoted suburban development in many directions. Large lakes, bays, an ocean, or a wide river would have confined local growth to fewer places and kept the Twin Cities from becoming the nineteenth lowest density metropolitan area of twenty such areas in the million-plus class in the United States in 1960. Since then, densities have gone even lower.

The lethargic streetcar system never recovered from its post-World War II slump. It completed a conversion to buses in 1954 but catered only to captive ridership, neither promoting its services nor trying to compete with the car. Finally in 1967 a Metropolitan Transit Commission was created by joint agreement of many cities and soon confirmed by the legislature which subjected commission plans to the approval of the Metropolitan Council. The Transit Commission immediately began a long range transit development program starting with the 1970 acquisition of the faltering Twin City Rapid Transit Company and aiming toward an elaborate "family of vehicles" transit system built around proposed fixed guideway high capacity rail transit lines between major centers. Critics of MTC plans argue that the sprawling multi-centered Twin Cities needs no high capacity lines—especially between the centers. Instead, they argue, the area needs a vastly improved and expanded bus system and small vehicles feeding new high density residential developments proposed around the centers (the Metro Council solution), or a personal rapid transit (PRT) system providing stations within walking distance of a majority of residents and non-stop transit service on demand, moving on elevated guideways between any pair of stations. Critics of PRT argue that the perfect PRT system resembles the private car without its cost, pollutants, noise, and intrusions on nonusers. As the argument continues, the Twin Cities retains its title as the metropolitan area that has spent the most money on transit development research without building anything new. But in the long run the thoughtful and vigorous controversy will serve the area well. The one hundred mile Washington, D.C. subway system will cost over $5.5 billion or $55 million per mile. Just the annual interest on such an investment runs between $300 million (in good times) and $600 million (in bad). By way of contrast the 1974 operating revenues of the Metropolitan Transit Commission were $15 million (with a piddling operating deficit of $13 million) on total assets of $41 million and ridership of fifty-four million, and up seven million from 1972. A significant portion of this increase was accounted for by persons over sixty-five and school children who ride free during off-peak hours. The primary source of outside revenue for general operations and debt service for the Transit Commission is an *ad valorum* property tax levied upon the Metropolitan Transit Taxing District.

MTC plans call for continued bus expansion to carry seventy-eight million riders by 1985—or approximately 5 percent of the daily peak hour person trips, up from 3 percent in 1970. The current fleet of over 1,000 buses averages five years of age, compared to fifteen years when public ownership began in 1970. The buses run on 930 miles of routes, up from 521 at time of acquisition.

Besides newer buses and more routes, ridership has been augmented by aggressive advertising campaigns, direct mailings of schedules and "free ride" coupons for new routes: express service between many neighborhoods and downtowns and the university; waiting shelters; better signs and schedule information; electronic control systems; preferential bus access to freeways that meter traffic and ration car access during rush hours; and a reduction in the discriminatory charges on rides between Minneapolis and St. Paul.

While public transit has improved, it still handles a small proportion of daily person trips that are scattered over the region. Approximately 90 percent of these are as drivers or passengers in automobiles, 3 percent by bus, and 7 percent by taxis, motorcycles, and trucks for personal use. Even in the peak hours, when some highways may be congested for forty-five minutes, mass transit is used by only 6 percent of the persons making trips at this time.

Transit's role is more significant as a way of traveling to the downtown where 17 percent of the work force is employed. Transit passengers comprise 19 percent of all trips to the downtown and 22 percent of all rush hour trips (24.1 percent in Minneapolis and 19.2 percent in St. Paul). Even in these high density work areas, however, the auto is the dominant vehicle for transportation with as many people riding as passengers in cars as take the bus and twice as many driving themselves.

As the number of buses, drivers, and longer routes increase, however, the cost of operations grows more rapidly than revenues from the increased number of passengers. The operating subsidies have grown from $1 million in 1971 to $10 million in 1974 and are projected at $33 million by 1976. The consequent cost per ride was 28 cents in 1971, 70 cents in 1974, and is estimated at 85 cents in 1976. The direct public subsidy was less than 1 cent in 1971, 42 cents in 1974, and is estimated at 60 cents in 1976.

HOUSING CHOICE IN THE CITIES AND SUBURBS

Both Minneapolis and St. Paul contain an unusually wide variety of residential areas suiting assorted tastes, needs, and incomes. There is somewhat less variety in the suburbs. Lower income households find little housing there. Most of the area's inexpensive housing lies near the cores of the central cities or huddled in mobile home parks at the edges of the lower income sectors of the urbanized area. Some suburbs explicitly exclude low priced housing. An example is North Oaks at the end of Rice Street in northern Ramsey County, a former country estate owned by James J. Hill. At night barriers close off the entrances to its private streets. Only those who know the combination can push a sequence of buttons to open the gates and enter. Its 5,500 acres resemble a country club more than a residential suburb for 2,500 residents. The streets, lakes, trails, tennis courts, hockey rinks, and other facilities are privately owned and controlled by the homeowners' association to which all must belong. In 1970 the average family income exceeded $31,000, compared to about $13,000 for the average Twin Cities municipality. The average house value was over $51,000 compared to a metropolitan average of $24,000.

The mayor claims that North Oaks residents just want "a reasonable amount of privacy." Anyone who can afford up to $40,000 for a lot can move in. Building plans must be approved by an architectural committee of the homeowner's association. "We're not restrictive," says the mayor. "We just don't want some godawful deal coming in." Apartments and townhouses are prohibited under the zoning ordinances. Only single family houses on large lots are allowed. According to the planning commission chairman, the majority of the North Oaks residents have shown a "preference for perpetuation of the concepts of providing a residential area with large, rustic, residential lots in a private environment." Similar exclusive enclaves include Dellwood, Sunfish Lake, Orono, and recently developed parts of Edina and Minnetonka.

The Metropolitan Council, for its part, argues that North Oaks should provide a balanced housing supply in the community, including multifamily housing. The council worries about the areawide consequences if every suburban community prohibited the construction of low and moderately priced housing. The controversy is essentially political, centering on the desire of upper income persons to create private living spaces to their tastes, insulating themselves from poor persons and metropolitan problems by the use of municipal boundaries, versus the desire of the Metropolitan Council to ensure a choice of neighborhood and housing styles for all citizens—rich or poor. The council has forced many suburbs to make plans for publicly assisted housing as a condition for council approval when the suburbs

apply for funds from various federal park, open space, and sewer programs. The Metro Council is the area review agency that must process and approve all such applications before they go to Washington. The Metro Council recently completed a study of subsidized housing within the seven county Twin Cities metropolitan area. Housing opportunities for lower income persons are increasing slowly throughout the metropolitan area. A total of fifty-four municipalities in the region have some subsidized housing, either planned or existing.

There is a disproportionate concentration of subsidized housing in the two center cities. Minneapolis, for example, has 24 percent of the area's population and 57 percent of the area's subsidized housing. St. Paul has 17 percent of the area's population and 31 percent of the subsidized housing. The suburbs contain about 60 percent of the total population but they include only 12 percent of all federally subsidized housing. Several communities in addition to Minneapolis and St. Paul have slightly higher percentages of subsidized housing than their corresponding percentage of population. Others are approaching their share but most communities have no subsidized housing at all.

Subsidized housing programs are based on a recognition that the gap between the cost of new housing and the ability of low and moderate income people to pay for housing cannot be bridged without governmental financial assistance. Public housing is heavily concentrated in the center cities; 98 percent of all such existing units are located in Minneapolis and St. Paul. There are eighteen HRA's (housing and redevelopment authorities) within the metropolitan area and the number is gradually increasing, but many of those in suburban communities have public housing units only in the proposal stages. Most of the public housing units—70 percent of those in the two central cities; 98 percent of those in suburban and rural areas— have been built or are being planned for the elderly.

In contrast to public housing, other programs aimed primarily at moderate income people operate in Minneapolis and St. Paul. The two center cities contain 81 percent of all such new federally assisted housing. Other programs previously found in the two central cities provide mostly used housing. They include subsidized rental for leasing of housing units, spot acquisitions and subsidized loans for home ownership, and low interest loans or grants for rehabilitation of housing owned by moderate and low income persons. The state in 1973 also developed its own housing program consisting of subsidized loans for new housing and loans and grants for rehabilitation. Both Minneapolis and St. Paul in 1974 also began rehabilitation programs with funds to make loans and grants available for rehabilitation.

When suburbs put walls around their borders and keep out the poor, the aged, and many minorities, they also reduce the bite of the tax collector. In the plushest suburbs a person can build a $100,000 house and have one of the lowest tax bills in the metropolitan area since these suburbs frequently have a substantial commercial and industrial tax base to share the tax load. In 1974 the average tax on a $25,000 house was $401 or 1.60 percent of market value, down from $468 (or 1.87 percent) a year earlier. Yet the taxes on the same house from one jurisdiction to another, making allowance for variation in assessment practices, range from $273 in Inver Grove Heights to $688 in Circle Pines.

Besides disparities in tax treatment, additional disparities exist in expenditure patterns. Such fiscal disparities are a common problem in every American metropolitan area. They disrupt and damage the quality of life. When disparities in tax treatment among jurisdictions reach beyond two to one it means that a resident in the least favored community must tax himself at a rate over twice that assessed on a resident in the most favored community in order to obtain the same level of public services.

Fiscal disparity becomes a serious issue because the fiscal system that cultivates the disparity is inequitable and unfair—persons and families with the same ability to pay are taxed at different rates for the same services just because they live within one set of boundaries with higher value industrial and commercial development instead of another that lacks them. The system that creates fiscal disparities is wasteful because it encourages families and businesses to select locations for individual fiscal advantages (lower tax rates; better services) while ignoring communitywide waste of resources.

In responding to these problems the Minnesota state legislature in 1971 passed three laws—a Fiscal Disparities Act, a substantially changed school aid law, and a municipal state aid law.

The effect of these was to give taxpayers in communities with little or no new tax base from commercial and industrial development a share of the metropolitanwide increment and to provide percentage equalization in municipal and school finance so that places with low returns per mill of tax effort would get more state aid than those with high returns. Thus, each family or business should get the same returns for similar tax effort no matter which community they chose to settle in. To reduce fiscal disparities in the tax base, 40 percent of the tax base attributable to commercial and industrial *growth* in the metropolitan area since 1970 is diverted to a metropolitan equity fund and redistributed to municipalities and school districts based on their population and expenditures. The Fiscal Disparities Act does not interfere directly with the private, suburban preserves of the wealthy, nor does it speed up the production or scattering of low and moderate income housing. What it does is eliminate some of the unfairness that normally accompanies suburbanization.

Population Redistribution

In both central cities the oldest and least desirable neighborhoods today lie within a mile or two of the downtowns. One and two unit wood-frame structures on thirty-five and forty foot lots predominate. The pre–World War I houses made no provision for automobiles, so whatever amenity is provided by the stately elm trees lining the boulevards gets diluted by streets difficult to clean and maintain and clogged by old, well-used cars. Families, especially with children, move when they can to newer houses in better-maintained neighborhoods. Those with the most initiative, information, money, and skill learn how to move to something better, but in leaving they strand a worse-off group. Neighborhood deterioration is mainly a social process with physical consequences. People who move out of a neighborhood are of a higher social class than those left behind, but they usually represent a lower class in the areas they enter. The reverse is often the case in integrated neighborhoods where the black proportion is rising, yet tensions still develop. In south central Minneapolis, at the western edge of Near North Minneapolis, and beyond the western edge of the Summit-University neighborhood in St. Paul, newcomers are often young black business and professional families, with better educations and incomes than the (often elderly) white families from whom they buy their houses. Since blacks are more conspicuous than other immigrant and ethnic groups and are generally thought to be of a lower social class than whites, their entry into a previously all-white area is interpreted as a threat to the status of the neighborhood and to the status of the families living there.

In the long run, then, neighborhood stability becomes a class or status issue rather than a racial question. In order for neighborhoods to remain stable over the long run, property-owning middle class families of mixed ages must continue to want to live in them. This result will come about only when city neighborhoods can offer advantages unavailable in newer suburbs. In Minneapolis and St. Paul, most of the central neighborhoods are undesirable by contemporary Twin Cities standards. They do not attract middle income families committed to house maintenance. As the maintenance-conscious families leave these neighborhoods some homes are turned into rental units and others are sold to lower income families who lack the resources, skills, or interest in maintenance, so that the neighborhoods move even lower in social class and the quality of their day-to-day upkeep.

One of the truly distinctive features of the Twin Cities area is the stable residential areas that surround the aging core in each city. They are found on the outer periphery of Minneapolis at its northwest and northern corners and the northeast and southern corners of St. Paul. The largest and most outstanding, however, lie in two horseshoe-shaped zones opening toward the downtowns—one in South Minneapolis bounded by the West Side chain of lakes, the crosstown Minnehaha Parkway, and the East Side Mississippi River Parkway; and the other in western St. Paul from the North Side lakes west past Lake Como to St. Anthony Park, then south along the river to Highland Park, then back along the river bluffs to Summit Hill. These residential areas may be unmatched among American central cities in their combination of sheer size, beauty, access to magnificent lakes and streams, and the non-threatening mixture of social and racial groups that vie to live in them. Almost all lake and stream frontages are public parks. Fine houses facing the lakes sell in a few days for prices

well over $100,000. House prices away from the water drop sharply block by block to less than $30,000. The neighborhoods remain highly heterogeneous in their income composition, yet all the residents want to live there. Few suburbs can offer so much.

The Metropolitan Setting

The Twin Cities 1960 population distribution was modified by small losses mainly from high density central areas undergoing extensive public and private clearance and rebuilding, and by large gains mainly in the far-flung suburbs north, west, and south of Minneapolis. Middle and upper income newcomers to the area are especially attracted to the suburbs south and west of Minneapolis while an equal number of middle and lower middle income newcomers have settled north and west of Minneapolis. The result has been a slow but steady westward movement of the region's population center.

A generation ago the center of the area's population lay just in Minneapolis between the two downtowns. Today the center of the urbanized area has drifted to just southeast of downtown Minneapolis. In contrast, the center of the St. Louis, Missouri, metropolitan area migrated westward right out of the city, leaving downtown St. Louis increasingly remote from the people it should serve. In the Twin Cities, downtown Minneapolis remains close to the center of the area's population. Some of the area's most desirable residential neighborhoods —once at the edge of the built-up area—increasingly enjoy a position at the very center of the metropolitan area.

Air travelers to the Twin Cities remark on the unexpectedly large and busy Twin Cities International Airport. Upon reaching downtown Minneapolis, where they usually go first (unless they stop along the growing "strip" of hotels west of the airport on I-494), they express surprise that it is not larger, forgetting that another city of almost equal size, with its own vigorous downtown, lies just to the east. Close inspection of daily traffic flows shows that each city draws from its own well-defined commuter suburbs. Each suburb belongs to one city or the other, never to both. As a consequence, the Minneapolis portion of the region might be viewed as two-thirds of the total and St. Paul as one-third.

Recycling the Central Cities

During the past thirty years the doubling in size and population of the Twin Cities created major problems in comprehensive planning, physical development, and governance. The chaotic suburban explosion, made possible by private cars, purchasing power stored up during World War II, and extravagant tastes for large houses on spacious lots, represented an overdue reaction to depression deprivations followed by years of wartime crowding and shortages. Meanwhile, the central cities, which up to World War II had always experienced a modest rate of continuous redevelopment and steady capital investment, entered a temporary phase of net outmigration. Today the pendulum seems to be swinging cityward once again. Instead of abandonment we now see in each city a zone of steady urban redevelopment separated from suburban development by a wide intermediate zone of residential stability.

Both cities are divided into three concentric zones, each with its special redevelopment problems and prospects. At the centers lie the downtowns, surrounded by a zone of transition to residential areas. Second come the aged and usually deteriorating pre–World War I neighborhoods. The outer half of each city forms a zone of stability with attractive well-tended houses inherited from the 1920s, 1930s, and 1940s.

THREE DECADES OF RENEWAL IN MINNEAPOLIS

In 1947 Minneapolis was close to a hundred years old. The "City of Lakes" had reached a population of 500,000 and was ringed by several relatively undeveloped suburbs. The aged parts of the central city foretold of changes to come. The average house was forty years old. Nearly 23,000 families lived in substandard houses and 6,500 were overcrowded, with more than 1.5 persons per room. The city had 700 miles of oiled dirt streets handed down from horse and buggy days. The Washington Avenue skid row, one of the country's largest, was home for 3,000 persons.

The Minnesota state legislature passed the Housing and Redevelopment Act in March 1947, to enable cities to respond to their postwar renewal needs. Later that same year Minneapolis established a Housing and Redevelopment Authority.

By the mid-1950s renewal plans for Gateway Center, the nation's most ambitious downtown redevelopment project when it began, were being completed. The depressing drain of the 1950s when Minneapolis lost 60,000 persons in the productive fifteen to sixty-four age group while gaining 16,000 elderly and 14,000 dependent children, soon gave way to the boom of the 1960s. The Guthrie Theatre was formed, four major league sports arrived, the metropolitan airport was rebuilt and expanded, the metropolitan freeway system was laid out and built, the University of Minnesota grew to over 40,000 students, and economic expansion promised renewed vitality for the second century of Minneapolis.

Gateway Center has now replaced skid row, forming part of a quarter-billion dollar private investment in downtown Minneapolis. For the

first time in fifty years new housing was built
in the heart of the city. The Towers Apartments and Condominiums contain 500 units.
Additional private high-rise apartments and
high-rise public housing for the elderly bring
the total close to 2,000 new units.

The Nicollet Mall provides a pedestrian spine
linking Gateway Center to the heart of the retail district (Figure 18). The tree-lined mall is
reserved for pedestrians and buses only. A
large reflecting pool and sculptered sand garden
at Minoru Yamasaki's Northwestern National
Life building decorate the north end of the
Mall. Completing the downtown redevelopment
is a pedestrian walkway system linking over
twenty downtown blocks by second story sky-

ways over the streets (Figure 19). Most businesses and residents consider the downtown
redevelopment to be an unqualified success.

The core of downtown Minneapolis is divided into a medium density (B4-1) zone and a
high density (B4-2) zone. Surface parking surrounds the core. The reason for high density
core and vacant periphery is economics and
the city zoning code. The zoning code has a
vastly higher parking requirement for developments outside the core. In the medium density zone no parking is required until the
development reaches 400,000 square feet and
in the high density zone no parking until the
800,000 square feet level is reached. Outside
the core, parking must be provided at a rate of

Figure 18. Nicollet Mall in downtown Minneapolis. Photo courtesy of the Minneapolis Chamber
of Commerce.

Figure 19. The climate-controlled Minneapolis skyway system unifies the heart of downtown and separates pedestrian and vehicular movement. Photo courtesy of the Minneapolis Chamber of Commerce.

one space for each 300 square feet of building space over the first 400,000 square feet. Therefore, a 400,000 square foot structure in the high density zone requires no parking, whereas outside that zone parking for 1,320 cars would be required (the Northstar Ramp, downtown's largest, holds 986 cars). Needless to say, this parking requirement acts as a severe constraint to any development outside the core. The only major development to occur outside this core zone has been the Northwestern National Life Insurance building at the north end of the Nicollet Mall at Nicollet and Washington. In order to build the company had to buy from the Housing and Redevelopment Authority a

whole block separate from their building at Hennepin and Second Street North so that they could meet their parking requirement. This lot was then locked into parking and cannot be changed to another use.

This high parking requirement has been both helpful and harmful. On the plus side, it has confined new developments to the core area, facilitating interchange between office and retail functions. The pinnacle of this development is the IDS (Investors Diversified Services) Center at Seventh Street and Nicollet Avenue. The clustering of buildings has resulted in the economic feasibility of employing skyways that are primarily financed and built to connect the intensely used core at the second floor levels (Figure 20). Planners feel the skyway system once installed now tends to cluster development in the core because a skyway link to the rest of the system makes a new development much more financially sound.

Because this parking requirement has worked so well to build a compact retail-office core, it has left many vacant parcels of land around its periphery. Another reason for the vacant lots is that a higher return is to be had from surface parking than from marginal, old-

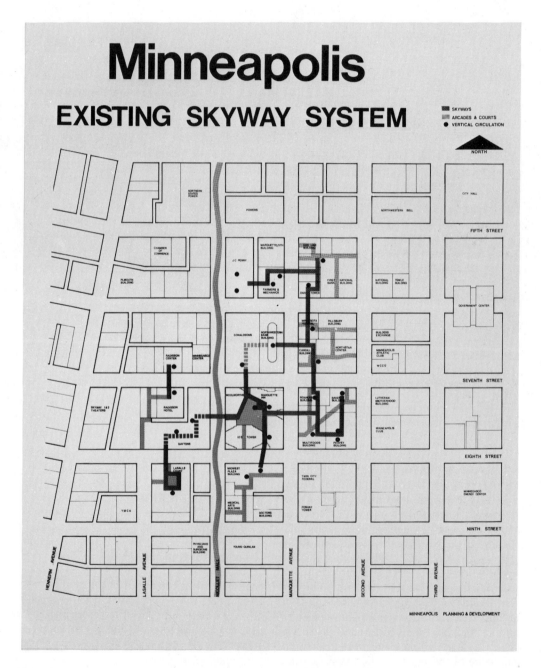

Figure 20. The existing skyway system in downtown Minneapolis. Photo courtesy of the Minneapolis Chamber of Commerce.

er buildings—especially warehouses, loft buildings, obsolete hotels, apartments, and small stores and shops that once served nearby residences. Careful downtown planning has encouraged a compact retail-office center and provided a land bank for expansion of this center. Yet promoting core development has meant hindering progress in the Gateway urban renewal project area. About one-third of the remaining Gateway area land has been designated for office-commercial use. This land seems to be just a few blocks too far away from the core.

Thus the existing downtown pattern is changing. The demand for new private office space over the next few years will require sites that currently lie outside the core or in redeveloped portions of the core. The city of Minneapolis and businessmen's Downtown Council have agreed that all-day parking should be restricted in the core and moved to the periphery of the CBD. Major new office buildings such as the IDS Center were limited in the number of parking spaces they could provide on their site. A revised zoning code will expand the core's B4-1 and B4-2 districts out about one and one-half blocks. The expansion will not only encourage building without provision of parking, but will actually limit the maximum number of spaces that can be built in a particular block. Along with this zoning change, the city will be building municipal parking ramps around the periphery of this CBD to accommodate all-day parking. Commuters will move from ramps to the core on minibuses and through extensions of the skyways.

URBAN RENEWAL AND PUBLIC HOUSING IN ST. PAUL

St. Paul's public renewal programs began with the Federal Urban Renewal Law of 1949. The Housing Authority has since undertaken several federally aided projects. Others began under the Port Authority which is authorized by the legislature to manage and develop river port facilities and its extensive land holdings along the river. The State Capitol Approach Area redevelopment was launched under the State Veteran Service Building Commission. In addition, a large public housing program built over 3,000 units.

Like Minneapolis, the initial emphasis was on redevelopment in which the worst nine-teenth century slum areas were replaced by new and different uses. By now the major blighted areas are gone and emphasis has moved to rehabilitation and conservation—retaining the basic character of communities and neighborhoods but updating the physical plant.

Interest in downtown redevelopment began with a plan by Victor Gruen's firm commissioned in 1958 by a group of St. Paul businessmen. The popular plan failed to materialize when the highway department declined to reroute Interstate 94 to north of the capitol, but the Housing and Redevelopment Authority responded soon with other plans, encouraged by support from the Chamber of Commerce and the Metropolitan Improvement Committee, a group of labor leaders, professionals, and business persons organized to promote citywide renewal and improvement especially for commercial uses. In 1962 the planning board approved the twelve block, forty-three acre Capital Centre renewal project in the heart of downtown. All but a few of the structures had been built before 1920 and most were replaced.

Now that the redevelopment is largely complete, one cluster of blocks is mainly in retail use, commercial and office uses fill another area, and residential areas lie along a zone facing southward toward the river. A skyway system built as part of the public renewal program links more than ten blocks downtown, and plans are underway for a five block tree-lined mall with benches, fountains, and lanes for buses. Sidewalks would be widened to seventeen feet. Financing, like that for the Nicollet Mall, would come from assessments against benefiting merchants and perhaps from federal transit funds.

The new project cost of most past urban renewal activities in St. Paul was financed two-thirds by the federal government and one-third by the city. In Capital Centre, the federal government paid three-fourths of the project costs and St. Paul paid one-fourth plus administrative costs. The city's payments were in cash or credit for noncash grants-in-aid (property improvements such as streets, sewers, lighting, etc. made in the project). The tax receipts from Capital Centre before urban renewal began in 1964 amounted to $710,000 annually. Upon completion, the tax return in the project is estimated to be $2,500,000.

The housing authorities in Minneapolis and in St. Paul have been run vigorously, intelligently, and sensitively, especially in recent years, but a debate continues whether neighborhood rehabilitation efforts will be sufficient to create and maintain stable residential and commercial areas within the low income sections of the cities.

The controversy centers partly on whether the poor should be given a wider choice of dispersed housing opportunities. The South High nonprofit housing project at Cedar Avenue and East 24th Street in Minneapolis is a 212 unit Indian-inspired housing community, the first such project planned and completed by urban Indians anywhere in the country. The residents, almost 40 percent of them Indian, have a governing council of twenty-five who set policy and approve new plans such as a ninety child day care center to be housed in the community center. It is doubtful that an effort to disperse this community would find many supporters.

CAN THE VITALITY BE SUSTAINED?

Like most American cities, Minneapolis and St. Paul came out of World War II with cluttered downtown centers, ragged legacies from the 1920s. Suburbs were booming and downtown abandonment seemed imminent. From today's vantage point we see that reports of the death of the downtowns were greatly exaggerated. Across the country, downtowns were redesigned and rebuilt, some quickly and some only after long delays.

Minneapolis began a steady remodeling of its downtown with the Gateway redevelopment in the early 1950s. The rest of the retail and commercial portion of downtown has been confidently rebuilding ever since. The St. Paul redevelopment effort started later, but once begun with the Capitol Approach, Eastern, and Western redevelopments, spilled into the center of downtown and continues briskly today.

The Twin Cities downtowns are not Atlanta, whose mile-and-a-half business strip along Peachtree Street sports a unified concentration of new office towers, hotels, shopping facilities, landscaped streets, plazas, parks—and a $700 million price tag. Yet certain city-building principles of the 1960s and 1970s remain the same in both places. It all starts with a visionary and somewhat incestuous coalition of business and civic officials who promote bold plans, massive investment of private and public capital, and high standards of coherent urban design

to nurture an image at home and inspire the confidence of investors elsewhere. Meanwhile, the massive expenditure of hundreds of millions of redevelopment dollars is recycled and multiplied within the local economy, helping to produce the vitality investors seek to exploit and triggering additional votes of confidence and further waves of investment. The forecasts become self-fulfilling. The redevelopment business is itself a big business. Stretched out for a long enough time the redevelopment of downtowns can grubstake a sizable chunk of a local economy for an entire generation.

Despite the fanfare and sparkling new images, downtown redevelopments along with debt-financed urban development in general has its critics. "Nicollet Maul" reads the index item for the downtown Minneapolis shopping street in the fourth annual report of the federal Council on Environmental Quality. A typographical error, of course, but capturing well the flavor of the report's comments. The mall was described as "[a] pleasant shopping experience with the feel of the city and the comfort of a suburban mall," but the area around the mall got bad reviews. The report is critical of cities—Minneapolis and Atlanta cited as examples—that are losing or have lost a balance between new high-rise buildings and older, smaller ones, and producing a "bombed out" look in many downtowns. In both Minneapolis and Atlanta, the report continues, the downtown commercial core has developed into a strip little more than a block wide surrounded by acres of parking lots, creating an environment hostile to pedestrians a few steps off Peachtree Street or Nicollet Mall.

Public improvements and urban redevelopment require a continuous stream of private and public investment. In recent years the public portion has come from public borrowing and the day of reckoning is fast approaching when the payments must be made. By 1971 the governments and public service boards in the Twin City area in their various capital improvement programs had raised their bonded indebtedness to over $1.4 billion, excluding bonds issued for public services such as water or airports to be repaid from user fees.

Since bonded indebtedness has risen much faster than either the population or the property tax base, some observers wonder whether the appearances of prosperity reflect genuine prospects for long term vitality. The outstanding local government debt per capita in

Twin City area was $67 in 1950. By 1960 it almost quadrupled to $256. It rocketed to $529 per capita in 1969, then rose 13 percent more in two years to $598 in 1971. Like the extravagant fixed income household that buys and enjoys a new car or house, a sober day of reckoning eventually arrives when the bills must be paid. The Twin Cities experience is not unusual. Since 1960 per capita state and local government expenditures and debt levels have risen much faster than those at the federal level. Moreover, local governments lack convenient sources of revenue to repay their debts. The federal and state personal income tax schedules are structured so that as incomes rise the proportion that is siphoned off as taxes rises even faster—and automatically. Local governments rely heavily on property tax taxes which rise only from new development or by raising assessment levels or mill levies—both politically unpopular.

The fiscal facts raise questions whether the Twin Cities area, or any other major urban region, can continue making a major business of rebuilding itself. Much of the current rebuilding may be just the lengthened shadow of huge debt-financed capital improvements packed into a short span of years.

The Suburbs and Beyond

Surrounding the redeveloping cores and distinctive neighborhoods of the central cities, the ring of suburban development thins outward and merges into the open countryside ten to twenty miles from either the St. Paul or the Minneapolis central business district. Beyond that, for another thirty to eighty miles, branch plants and corporate administrative offices, part time farmers and long distance commuters subtly tie the small towns and countryside into the circulation network of the metropolis—the daily urban system.

THE RESIDENTIAL EXPLOSION—
1946 THROUGH THE 1950S

The legacy from the first fifteen years of postwar development is largely a residential landscape, reflecting capital poured into meeting the most obvious and immediate need—housing. The demand was spurred by four years of soldiers' dreams, the end of war time restrictions, and the need to compensate for the sluggish housing construction during the preceding decade of economic depression (Figure 21). As late as 1955 residential construction accounted for 80 percent of the value of all building permits in the principal developing suburbs of the Twin Cities. Minimal neighborhood commercial services had to be provided and, as an avalanche of youngsters reached school age, classrooms had to be built. Those developments accounted for the scant 20 percent of suburban building permit value which was nonresidential in 1955.

Single family dwellings comprised virtually all of the residential units until the late 1950s (Figure 22). It is well understood that the low mortgage interest rates and loan guarantees provided under federal housing and veterans benefit programs, as well as property tax reductions for owner-occupied homes and income tax deductions on mortgage interest, were major factors explaining the overwhelming preference for single family houses. But there was much reinforcement from other directions. Soldiers had spent a large amount of time dreaming of home; and for those from the Twin Cities and the Upper Midwest home had been an owner-occupied single family house in more than three-fourths of the cases. Furthermore, on PX juke boxes and barracks radios the most popular singers of the time had repeatedly crooned their romantic intentions to settle down at the war's end in some kind of little palace in Dallas or the San Fernando Valley—easily translated to St. Louis Park, Richfield, or Golden Valley.

So early postwar suburbia emerged. Embryonic commercial clusters and explosive expansions of former country school houses appeared at intersections on the skeleton of paved highways beyond the cities' edge. Meanwhile, building on that skeleton, landowners and small developers collectively pushed nearly 2,000 miles of new streets—usually dirt or gravel, sometimes paved—over the pastures and fields and through the woodland and divided the open areas into nearly 200,000 new lots by 1956. At the same time, hundreds of small

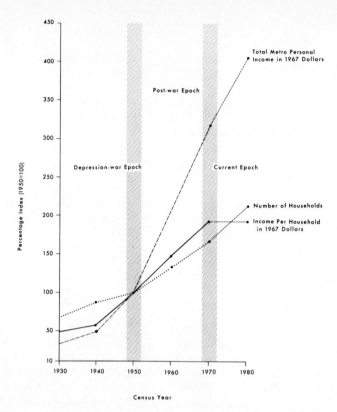

Figure 21. Changing relationships between total personal income, number of households, and income per household in the Twin Cities metropolitan area suggest that a unique post-World War II epoch has ended. Data from U.S. Census.

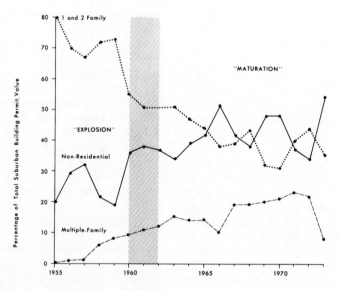

Figure 22. Residential construction in the Twin Cities by type of structure, since World War II. Changing relationships between single family, multiple family, and nonresidential construction in the suburbs suggest distinct periods of residential explosion and maturation of development within the postwar epoch. Data from the Federal Reserve Bank of Minneapolis.

builders erected new houses. Most of the builders had only one, two, or three crews and built perhaps a half dozen to twenty homes in a year. Living space in the average house was less than 1,000 square feet at first, gradually rising to about 1,200 by the mid-1950s. Soon the homes were occupied. Swarms of little children played in the raw streets, on the patches of yet undeveloped but abandoned farmland, around the edges of the ponds and marshes that were never far away. On a quiet summer evening tricycles and toys lay, abandoned for the night, helter-skelter on raw dirt yards. Inside, lights burned late in many homes while young couples taped drywalls, installed cupboards, or painted rooms. Homemade street signs, put up here and there by local residents, substituted for permanent markers which village councils—often still rural-oriented and overwhelmed by new issues —had not yet installed.

Location of New Homes

That was the metropolitan frontier. It advanced relentlessly through those years of residential explosion to enclose one hundred net new square miles of low density subdivision and another eighty-five square miles of medium and high density subdivision by 1956 (Figure 23). Behind the advancing residential frontier, lawns, shrubs, completed houses, and pavement gradually began to soften and order the raw landscape.

The location of new development during this period of residential explosion was constrained by three factors. The most important factor was the existing development pattern and circulation network; others were the organization of the building industry and housing site preferences based on past experience.

At the outset of the postwar boom, virtually all jobs in the metropolitan area were located within the central cities. At the same time most of the land available for expansion of the housing stock lay outside. There was no planned new and different program of development for the transportation and utility system. Hence the pattern of residential expansion had to follow the existing circulation network which joined potential suburban neighborhoods with the central cities. Those facilities were limited. The road grid was as dense as it is anywhere in the midwestern countryside—section line roads and many on the half-section lines. But most were gravel or graded dirt, as they had

been in the 1920s and earlier pioneer times of the automobile. There had been little improvement of rural feeder roads during the Depression and the war years. The web of paved roads in the rural periphery of the Twin Cities was thin. Hence the total network, though dense, was comparatively slow, low capacity, and low quality.

The highest development of paved roads followed five historic spokes of scattered suburban growth. The largest and most important spoke pointed westward from Minneapolis to the hilly, wooded, deeply indented shores of Lake Minnetonka. Another pointed northeastward from St. Paul to the historic attraction of White Bear Lake. A third extended southeast from St. Paul through the long-established railroad-industrial belt along the polluted reach of the Mississippi below the central cities. One more followed flat land southward from Minneapolis through an area of truck farms to the bluffs overlooking the deeply entrenched valley of the Minnesota River. The fifth and least developed followed the rail-industrial zone along the Mississippi above Minneapolis—the route of three of the five major railroads to the northwest.

The spokes along the upper and lower river were the routes of interurban streetcar lines. The Minnetonka and White Bear spokes had been served and reinforced by both suburban rail and interurban trolley lines. A few brittle remnants of the rail era system were still operating at the time the post–World War II boom began—streetcar lines as far west as Hopkins on the old route to Lake Minnetonka, to White Bear Lake, and along the lower river industrial belt beyond the stockyards and packing plants at South St. Paul. Although these lines were still considered important by some, they were ignored by the new suburbanites.

Public sewer or water systems—seldom both in one community—were confined to a handful of small streetcar suburbs—Robbinsdale in the northwest, St. Louis Park and Edina in the west, South St. Paul and North St. Paul on the southeast and northeast. Hence high density development, requiring central sewer and water, was attracted to the periphery of those suburbs or the edges of the central cities. Where houses were built at high density with dependence on individual wells and cesspools, serious problems of sewage accumulation and polluted wells followed within a few years. Notable cases

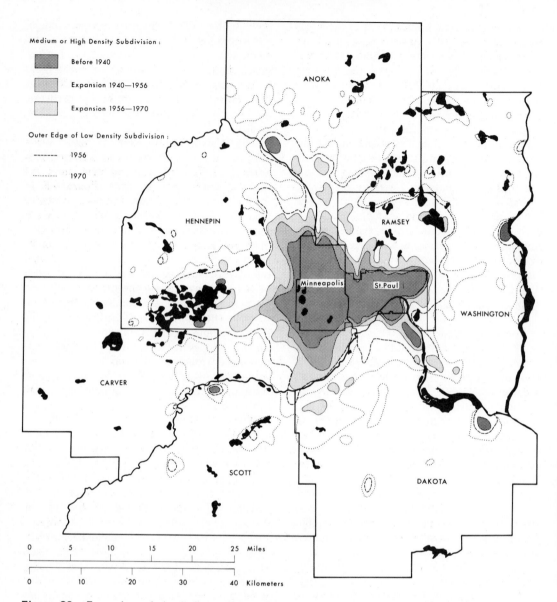

Figure 23. Extension of the built-up Twin City area after World War II. More than 300 square miles of low density subdivision surrounded the prewar medium and high density metropolitan core by 1956. Postwar medium and high density expansion filled in only a fraction of that vast area—forty square miles up to 1956 and another one hundred square miles from 1956 to 1970.

were in Richfield and the eastern part of Bloomington.

The tendency to stick close to existing developments and transportation lines was reinforced by the character of the Twin Cities building industry. Because most housing was built by hundreds of small builders, and there were no really large developers by national

comparison, there were no comprehensively planned new towns such as Park Forest, Illinois, nor anything comparable to the Levittowns, significantly isolated from the main urban mass, beyond the position of the advancing frontier at that time. At the same time, many individual "frontiersmen" and some small builders put up single houses or small clusters on widely scattered, isolated sites in the outer part of the low density zone. That kind of settler has historically consituted about 10 percent of the Twin Cities population and probably also reflects the long-standing decentralization of the building industry and its financing.

Traditional housing site preferences also played an important role in setting the pattern of the postwar residential explosion. In some ways, they influenced the pattern at the broad metropolitan scale. The few large developers of tract housing stayed strictly with the flat glacial outwash plains. There, even in the era of the bulldozer and cheap portable drilling rig, the level surface and sandy soil enabled them to shave a little from the cost of land preparation and utilities. Hence, in the landscape created during that period, as in the older landscapes within Minneapolis, there is a vivid regionalism of more modest and homogeneous housing on the outwash plains and more expensive housing on the rolling morainic uplands.

Perhaps even more interesting is the detail of local differentiation—often from block to block or within blocks—associated with details of the glacial terrain. There are obvious strong preferences for the shores of lakes and ponds, the sides and tops of knobs on the morainic ridges, distinctive groves of birch or conifers or maples or oaks, and creeksides. And in the intricate, disorderly landscape of glacial deposition, these preferences have produced a mixture of housing —and related socioeconomic characteristics whose detail and randomness is at first hard to comprehend for most visitors from most other large American cities. This feature of residential development is probably more pronounced in the early postwar suburbs than it was in the central cities, because even early postwar suburb development was beginning to reflect the new freedom of the automobile era, to be less tied to the flat outwash plains, and to venture more into the hummocky, disordered moraine lands. But the impact of these individual preferences became much more pronounced in the 1960s.

In short, the early postwar residential boom extended and widened the five historic spokes of growth that began in the nineteenth century. High and medium density subdivision expanded mainly north, south, and southwest from Minneapolis on flat, sandy outwash plains, into Brooklyn Center, Crystal, Richfield, east-

ern Bloomington, St. Louis Park, and Hopkins. Development in those areas brought modest housing for middle income families. The principal expansion of medium density subdivision on the rougher glacial moraine land occurred between the spokes, mainly to the southwest of Minneapolis in Edina, with smaller increments west of Minneapolis in Golden Valley and north of the St. Paul Midway in Roseville. Advance of the medium density frontier was slower on the rolling moraine than on the flat outwash plains. The pioneers on the moraine were more likely to be upper middle income and to build larger than average houses on lots ranging in size from one-third to one-half acre. The low density frontier advanced much more rapidly than the medium and high. Though it retained the same spokelike configuration, more of the new growth occurred on moraine land simply because of the greater attenuation toward the big morainic lakes, especially Lake Minnetonka.

Location of New Jobs

Job growth in the suburbs lagged far behind residential growth until the middle or late 1950s. This is reflected in the lag in new building permits for nonresidential purposes. In addition to neighborhood convenience goods and service, many building materials and supply businesses mushroomed in many places, and the vanguard of warehouses and manufacturing firms began to move out from cramped quarters in obsolete multistoried buildings in the central business district of either Minneapolis or St. Paul. The companies shifting at that time were mainly those which had been most affected by the booms in housing and family formation—grocery and appliance distributors, millwork manufacturers and distributors.

The location of initial suburban job growth reflected mainly two factors (Figure 24). For one thing, concentrations of retailing and services followed the old arterials from the city into the former countryside. They represented persistence of the commercial strip idea, nourished in the streetcar era, from the central cities into the suburbs. On the face of it, strip development seemed to have little if any functional value in the new, postwar epoch. The sidewalks of the arterial streets were no longer strung out "depot platforms," where everyone who moved about the city congregated in the process of transferring from vehicle to foot or

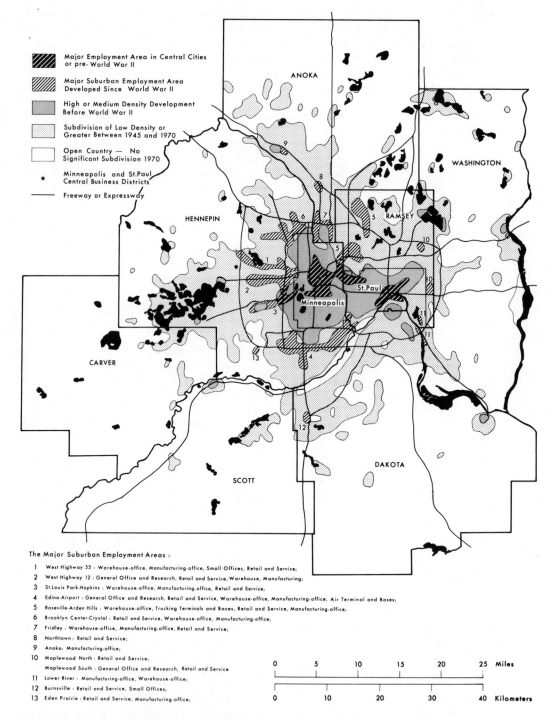

The Major Suburban Employment Areas :

1 West Highway 55 : Warehouse-office, Manufacturing-office, Small Offices, Retail and Service;

2 West Highway 12 : General Office and Research, Retail and Service, Warehouse, Manufacturing;

3 St.Louis Park-Hopkins : Warehouse-office, Manufacturing-office, Retail and Service;

4 Edina-Airport : General Office and Research, Retail and Service, Warehouse-office, Manufacturing-office, Air Terminal and Bases;

5 Roseville-Arden Hills : Warehouse-office, Trucking Terminals and Bases, Retail and Service, Manufacturing-office;

6 Brooklyn Center-Crystal : Retail and Service, Warehouse-office, Manufacturing-office;

7 Fridley : Warehouse-office, Manufacturing-office, Retail and Service;

8 Northtown : Retail and Service;

9 Anoka: Manufacturing-office;

10 Maplewood North : Retail and Service;
   Maplewood South : General Office and Research, Retail and Service

11 Lower River : Manufacturing-office, Warehouse-office;

12 Burnsville : Retail and Service, Small Offices;

13 Eden Prairie : Retail and Service, Manufacturing-office;

Figure 24. Principal suburban employment concentrations developed during the postwar epoch, mostly after 1956, and principal employment concentrations in the central cities.

foot to vehicle. In fact, the suburban arterials generally did not even have sidewalks. On the contrary, the new suburban commercial establishments hugging these streets faced virtually no pedestrian traffic, left too little room for parking, and ignored the popular suburban amenities of landscaping and open space. But perhaps there was less freedom to change the pattern at first than there appeared to be. For any businessman serving a regional clientele faced the question of how his customers would be able to find him. Geographical ignorance was a real problem. The names of a few arterials were well known. They conjured images of landmarks and locations. This was especially true of those which were suburban extensions of well-known Minneapolis and St. Paul commercial strips—Lake Street and Excelsior Boulevard into St. Louis Park and Hopkins, Nicollet and Lyndale avenues southward into Richfield and Bloomington, South Robert Street into West St. Paul, or Central Avenue into Columbia Heights and Fridley, for example.

The principal concentrations of industry were extensions of older rail-industrial strips. The prime example was the extension of the belt along the Milwaukee Railroad adjoining the Lake Street commercial strip from South Minneapolis into St. Louis Park and Hopkins. The origins of the St. Louis Park-Hopkins rail-industry strip go back to the nineteenth century. But it was the scene of rapid and extensive development of new food warehouses and processors and machine industries, mostly transfers from central Minneapolis during the early postwar years. Other agricultural processors and machinery or metal works expanded into the suburban reaches of the North Minneapolis upper river rail-industry strip. And a new generation of "dirty" industries—oil refining and petrochemicals which came mainly with the opening of pipelines from the new Alberta oil fields—extended the lower river rail-industry strip downstream from South St. Paul's packing plants and stockyards.

MATURATION IN THE 1960S AND 1970S

Conditions changed greatly as the years of residential explosion advanced into the late 1950s. The pent-up housing demand from the war and the Depression had been relieved. A vast new market had emerged in the suburbs and it had now become obvious to the leaders of retailing and the service businesses. Also, a vast new real property tax base had accumulated and was continuing to grow and that was obvious to the new generation of elected officials and village administrators who had moved onto the suburban political stage. Meanwhile, the suburbs of the Twin Cities, like those all across the nation, were centers of action as America moved to record high levels of personal income and buying power on which to base the financing of large scale development projects. *The Exploding Metropolis* was replaced by *The Affluent Society* as the popular reading of the time.

New Trends

New trends in suburban development accompanied these changing conditions. There was a shift toward a broader mix of housing types. Apartments, townhouses, and planned unit developments broke the virtual monopoly of the single family dwelling. The apartments and townhouses, as well as a substantial part of the new single family home construction, were located well behind the low density frontier of metropolitan growth. They served to fill in areas closer to the central cities that had been initially developed in scattered tracts at low density. Low density suburban tracts shifted to medium or high density at the rate of about three square miles per year from 1945 through 1956. From 1957 through 1970 the comparable rate was seven square miles per year. The fill-in rate more than doubled. In the latter part of the period, the Twin Cities also saw the emergence of organized innovation in the housing industry, stimulated by higher costs and growing restlessness in the market. So far these innovations have included large, planned communities of factory-assembled homes; cluster development of both single family and multiple units to preserve open space and natural amenities; and the marketing of modular and precut homes.

Meanwhile, suburban job growth began to catch up with population growth. The value of nonresidential building permits in the suburbs leveled out at 40 to 50 percent of the total. That level reflected a succession of new developments—large scale retail shopping malls, industrial parks, office parks, hospitals, high schools, regional community colleges—each a major source of suburban employment. Also, for the first time since early in the century, there was a resurgence of concern about acquiring public open space. There were major acquisitions of parkland when the frontier of development approached the boundaries of the central cities, and again in the latter part of the post–World War II building boom. Both occasions were preceded by periods of rapid residential expansion and relative neglect of public land acquisition. Behind the frontier of urbanization, municipalities bought small remaining parcels and developed them as neighborhood playgrounds. Just ahead of the advancing frontier, county and regional agencies bought tracts of hundreds or thousands of acres for regional parks, nature preservation, public golf courses, and a metropolitan zoo.

At the same time, local governments began to use their vastly increased revenue and bonding capacity to embark on public works programs that had been neglected during the frenetic years of the residential building boom. Street paving, curbing, sewer and water lines, libraries, and civic centers began to transform the suburban landscape and, incidentally, to give institutional substance to the suburban municipal governments. Some of those investments formed an important part of the greatly increased value of nonresidential building permits in the late 1950s and 1960s. While the total annual value of nonresidential building permits in the suburbs grew from typically $60 to $100 million in the mid-1950s to nearly $400 million in the early 1970s, the public share of that total grew from about one-eighth to one-third.

Increasing public control of new development also marked the period of suburban maturation. At the beginning of the postwar boom, fewer than half a dozen suburban communities had any semblance of zoning, subdivision regulations, capital improvement plans, or comprehensive planning commissions. By the early 1960s, of roughly fifty municipalities comprising the area inside the frontier of low density settlement, only three had not yet undertaken at least some of those programs. Meanwhile, to coordinate these local efforts, the state legislature had established the Metropolitan Planning Commission in 1957. The commission was succeeded in the late 1960s by the more powerful Metropolitan Council. Each was the first agency of its kind in the United States. A 1962 survey showed that the

Twin Cities—along with Milwaukee—led the large metropolitan areas of the Midwest in per capita commitment of money and manpower to comprehensive planning. All of those activities reflected the growth of governmental controls over land development and the efforts of both local governments and the larger metropolis to monitor physical change and program public investments. Those commitments grew out of the experiences of both voters generally and community leaders in particular during the chaotic years of explosive residential development.

But figures on governmental efforts tell only part of the story. During the period of maturation, large developers have accounted for an increasing share of total building. Because they have controlled large and diverse tracts of land and large amounts of front-end capital, they have been able to package more comprehensively planned communities. Those efforts have been further encouraged by high land costs and high construction costs. So the integrated design of residential, commercial, and open space over large areas has come from private as well as public initiative.

The end result has been that "planning" has become a symbolic term—perhaps also a buzzword—in suburban development in the 1960s and 1970s—planned communities, planned unit developments, planned residential clusters, planned garden apartments, planned shopping centers, planned educational centers, planned industrial parks, planned mobile home communities, and so on.

The system of freeways and expressways was probably the single most important new ingredient introduced into the suburbs from the late 1950s to the early 1970s. In a general way, those roads greatly increased the overall speed and capacity of transportation. Their effect in the Twin Cities was perhaps even greater than it was in many other metropolitan areas of comparable size. The Twin Cities area built more miles of freeway per capita than any other metropolis in the million or more class because the double downtowns called for two sets of radials rather than one.

But, in addition to its general effects, the freeway system also exerted a crucial influence on the location of all other new investments during this period. The radials reinforced the traditionally easy movement from the central business districts and the Midway district to suburban areas and drastically increased the distance to which activities linked to those districts could penetrate the countryside. The new circumferential routes opened extensive areas of woods and lakeshore in the voids between older radial spokes of growth. The circumferential routes also reduced the travel time between many suburbs by providing more direct routes between them. That was a decentralizing force, and decentralization was further accentuated by the creation of new major nodes in the metropolitan circulation system at the intersections of radial and circumferential freeways.

The freeways interacted with the new standards of affluence and the inertia of established metropolitan and regional markets to guide the location of new jobs and new homes during the period of suburban maturation.

Location of Burgeoning Employment

In 1950 suburban employment numbered about 90,000—roughly 20 percent of the metropolitan total. By 1970 the number of suburban jobs had grown to more than 350,000 and comprised more than 40 percent of the metropolitan total. To be sure, at least one-quarter of these new jobs were in scattered locations.

But much of the suburban employment boom was aggregated in a few major commercial and industrial districts. Several of those locations simply reflected expansion or relocation from the central business districts or the Midway district, across narrow barriers of railroad yards or older development, to nearby freeway interchange areas. Most important in that class are West Highway 55 (Golden Valley, Plymouth), West Highway 12 (Golden Valley, Plymouth, Minnetonka), Roseville-Arden Hills, and Maplewood.

Several of the largest Twin Cities–based corporations led the expansion from the central cities into these new districts. General Mills, Honeywell, and Gamble-Red Owl Stores shifted to the west from Minneapolis. Control Data, Univac, and a complex of trucking firms and suppliers shifted north from the Midway district to Roseville and Arden Hills. And the 3M Corporation built its new headquarters and research center in Maplewood, east of St. Paul. These locational decisions further reinforced the freeway development pattern. Because of the size or monumental nature of the investments and the number of work trips involved, it was essential that the development plans be coordinated with regional transportation plans.

The general pattern of suburban employment growth reflected the century-old pull toward the south and west. Since the frontier of commercial agriculture passed westward across central Minnesota in the 1870s, the locational advantage for distribution firms serving the Upper Midwest region has been on the Minneapolis side of the metropolitan area. Each central city posed a barrier to the other in shipping to the outlying region, and most of the market lies to the west. Regional distributors and services look west and northwest to the Red River valley and the spring wheat region, south and southwest to the northern part of the Corn Belt in southern Minnesota, northern Iowa, eastern South Dakota, and northeast Nebraska.

This directional attraction continued in the era of suburbanization of regional branch offices, warehouses, and related banks, hotels, and restaurants. And it was reinforced by the chance location of the metropolitan airport on the broad outwash plain west of historic Fort Snelling. The result is that the major suburban employment concentrations are largest in the southwest quadrant. From Edina to the airport and extreme southwest corner of St. Paul, subdistricts and strips have coalesced into a new third center of the Twin Cities, comparable to downtown St. Paul in retail sales and office floor space. The new developments in this district have included many shifts or expansions from the central part of Minneapolis, but they have also included many new firms. There are hotels, branch offices, branch plants, retailers, corporate headquarters, and financial institutions—some locally based, some imported—which had not been located in the Twin Cities before.

Altogether, the dozen major suburban concentrations contain about two-thirds of the employment located within the area of post–World War II development—nearly a quarter of a million jobs. They embrace all of the eight major regional shopping malls, with 7.5 million square feet of floor space. They include ten of the eleven major concentrations of suburban offices, with 98 percent of the floor space, or about one-third of the modern office space in the metropolitan area. They also include about three-fifths of the suburban industrial park land, with nearly nine-tenths of the total industrial park land value. In fact, 48 percent of the total suburban industrial park land value is concentrated in the western part of the Edina-airport district—testimony to the pull of the market toward the southwest.

Meanwhile, office and industrial employment that is an integral part of the metropolitan system has grown throughout a zone of metropolitan influence far beyond the suburban belt twenty-five to sixty miles from the downtowns. Home offices of major corporations are dispersed widely through this zone. Most of these are homegrown manufacturing or financial firms, based on accessibility to regional markets, local surplus labor on farms and in small towns, and access to regional resources of management and financing. They tend to be located in or near the principal historic rural trade centers; hence they are also in the main highway and rail corridors. All of them are no farther in time from the Twin Cities airport than Westchester or Fairfield counties are from Kennedy Airport in New York.

Branch plant concentration coincides with the major area of industrial job growth. The pattern is most influenced by accessibility to Twin Cities markets and parent plants, although it is stretched somewhat toward the southwest by the rich farm equipment and supply market of the Corn Belt and northwest by a relatively abundant supply of underemployed farm labor in the marginal dairy country.

With both corporate offices and branch plants in the countryside, and major concentrations of job locations in the suburbs, suburbia and exurbia are integral parts of an extensive, evolving, interacting metropolitan system. Decentralization of employment locations has accompanied suburban maturation and rural assimilation and that decentralization has tended to equalize geographical accessibility to jobs for people who live in all parts of the metropolis. The average home-work trip from most suburban neighborhoods has increased from four to seven miles but is clearly less than the distance from that neighborhood to the nearer of the two central business districts or the Midway.

Location of the New Mix of Homes

To Twin Cities residents, lake shores and wooded hillsides are highly desirable places to live. They combine amenity and prestige in whatever combination one wishes. This view holds within any socioeconomic stratum or from any socioeconomic perspective. The completion of the modern arterial and freeway network in the late 1950s and 1960s opened up vast areas of rolling, lake-studded glacial moraine land which had not been nearly as accessible in earlier years. If the rough terrain and abundance of surface water forced higher land preparation, utility, and construction costs, those barriers fell easily before the unprecedented affluence of the times. The improved highway net and the search for amenity reinforced each other and residential development helped to set the trend away from flatland and railway or streetcar orientation toward moraine land and freeway orientation, and toward larger lots and lower densities for multiple as well as single family dwellings.

There was a new element in the pattern of residential development during this period and it probably has intensified since 1970. On the one hand, there was a record rate of low density expansion, with less contiguity—more leapfrogging—than ever before. At the same time, however, there was also a record rate of medium and high density fill-in of previously low density areas than ever before. The fill-in also showed less contiguity of development than in previous periods. About 70 percent of the new medium density development was adjacent to the contiguous medium and high density metropolitan mass; about 30 percent was not. The record rate of low density expansion and leapfrogging has been noted widely and with alarm. The record rate of fill-in has received much less attention.

The two phenomena probably reflect alternative responses of the housing industry and market to extreme cost increases for capital, land, and construction. Alternative courses of action have been (1) increase density—hence develop close-in locations where central sewer is available—or (2) reduce land costs—hence go farther out than ever before.

The trend is seen by numerous public agencies and organizations as portending a serious problem. The new islands of medium density have received extensions of the sewer network. As a result, sewer trunks crossed intervening areas of remaining low density and those areas now have both land and sewer available. Meanwhile, unsewered developments sprawl in low density islands far beyond the existing or contemplated sewer network. It is feared that those areas will fill in, and their residents will need sewers whose cost will greatly exceed the fiscal capability of the local residents and needlessly strain the resources of the metropolitan sewer board. Hence policies are evolving to inhibit further advances or leaps of the low density frontier and force new development to fill in areas adjacent to the contiguous urban mass or between certain new, medium density islands. The evolving policies favor the medium density approach to the cost squeeze, and discourage the cheap land, low density approach.

Notwithstanding the widespread image of suburbia as a homogeneous or monotonous mass, a vivid and complex regionalism appears to have developed, especially in the period of suburban maturation. The moraine areas—even the outwash plains—have tremendous internal physical diversity. The metropolitan area contains nearly 1,000 "recreational lakes"—so classified by the state Department of Natural Resources. But there are also many more hundreds of small ponds. Because of the detail of small knobs and kettles, the larger lakes have intricate shorelines, with countless bays and islands and varied vistas. The metropolis lies astride the major continental vegetation boundaries between forest and prairie and between broadleaf and coniferous forests. Hence there are rich maple-basswood-white oak forests, birch-aspen groves, ridges and islands of pine, tamarack bogs, and fields in former prairie openings bordering oak woodlands. And there are accompanying differences in bird and animal life.

The distribution of these diverse landscapes has the randomness and kaleidescopic detail with which the glaciers acquired and dumped their burden in the Ice Age. Most Twin Citians are keenly aware of these variations and have preferences among them. Hence the market for residential land and housing has reflected them down to their most minute details. The result is a great diversity and randomness of the residential landscape, with every conceivable combination of socioeconomic and physical features. This phenomenon is unquestionably a great leveler, though it mostly remains to be described and interpreted. If few suburban municipalities are homogeneous physically, few can be homogeneous in family income and related cultural attributes.

The suburban pattern of income differences is accompanied by many other cultural differences (Figure 25). Those also mainly await adequate study and definition. Cultural differences in the suburbs are probably as rich as those among the distinctive old neighborhoods of the central cities. To be sure, there is the concentration of Jewish people which suburbanized from North Minneapolis, or spilled over from the Kenwood district of Minneapolis, to eastern Golden Valley and St. Louis Park. And there is the relatively rapid diffusion and integration of middle income black families into the suburbs.

But most suburban cultural differences will not be found if they are sought in terms of the traditional measures of race, nationality, language, or religion. Yet as one walks and talks in the suburbs, the evidence is abundant that there are vivid and vitally important differences in diet, nutrition, drink, the nature and sources of information, parent-child relationships, family stability, health care, clothing, recreational expenditures. There are geographies of gardening, bowling, golfing, snowmobiling, boat ownership. Insofar as these are related to income, they reflect the intricate pattern of residential land values. But they are also related to values that lead some households to sacrifice for a lakeshore location, others to shun it—or lead to countless other kinds of locational decisions.

Great Variety in the Urbanizing Countryside

Beyond the suburbs, in the urbanizing countryside, the changing residential landscape tells yet another story. The part of this zone twenty-five to sixty miles from the downtowns has the highest percentage growth rates of population in the metropolitan system. The baby boom, housing boom, and schoolroom boom are making their last stand there. The most important factor is the population of local young people with traditional values, to some extent able to shelter those values by staying in their home communities, yet tapping into city-suburban affluence by means of long distance commuting. These people are mostly high school graduates. Hence most of their work trips lead to technical, clerical, or unskilled jobs. Their places of work are not only in the central cities and suburbs but also in the small towns and even in the open country—filling stations, taverns, gravel pits, for example—throughout the metropolitan region. They are mostly in the middle and lower middle income range.

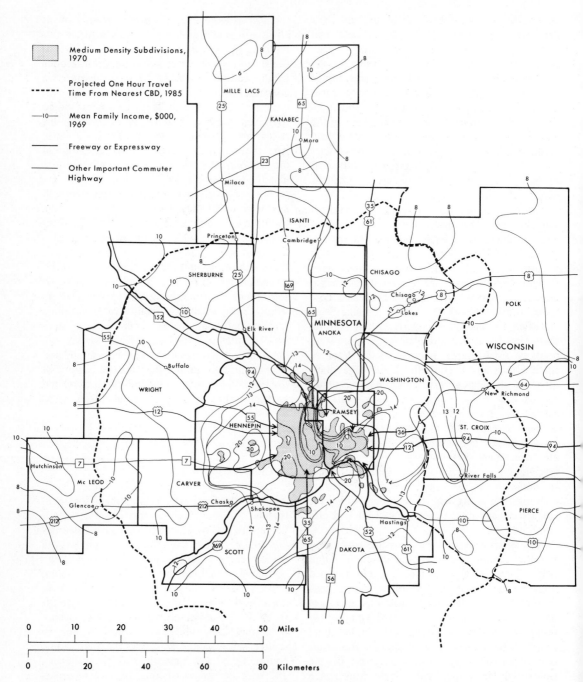

Figure 25. Family income variations in the Twin City area. Geographic variation of mean family income in the counties comprising the Twin City daily urban system.

Also contributing to growth in this zone are emigrants from the central cities and suburbs, making their deepest thrust into the country-side. The emigrants are a heterogeneous lot, with a very wide range of educational and occu-

pational backgrounds, in the middle and upper middle income brackets. They are executives, proprietors, and professionals, to be sure; but the group also includes a wide variety of sales-persons, tradesmen, office clerks, factory workers, and technicians. Some of the proprietors bring their small businesses with them into the countryside. For example one set up his metal fabricating plant in an abandoned creamery near his residential estate; another moved his cabinet shop from the city to a former dairy barn which he rents on a farm near his lake home. In turn, he has remodeled the lake home for comfortable year round occupance.

Finally, there is a growing accumulation of aging and elderly. These people are retired farmers and small town business operators, craftsmen, laborers, and housewives. They are mainly people who are not buying retirement in either an institution or a warmer climate. In most cases their savings are inadequate, though that factor is often reinforced by emotional attachment to the locale. The local retirees are augmented by immigrants who come not only from the Twin Cities but also from other parts of the Midwest, especially Iowa and the industrial cities of Illinois and Indiana. To serve this population there is an expansion of clinic and nursing home facilities comparable to the boom in school classrooms.

New householders in the urbanization zone are creating a rich variety of housing. There is a remodeling boom, with much of the work being done by the residents themselves. Old farmsteads are being remodeled as single family homes. Old houses in the small towns are being remodeled as single family homes or apartment buildings. So are abandoned one or two room schoolhouses in the countryside and old stores at rural crossroads or on the main streets of small hamlets. Mobile homes are situated in farmyards, on small town lots, in courts large and small—usually in the open country or at least beyond the edges of small towns—in subdivisions of one to five acre lots, on lakeshore land, in ten or twenty acre woodlots—perhaps gifts from retiring farmers to their newly married children. Precut houses ranging in size from two to five bedrooms are popular and it is common for the owner and his relatives to provide most of the labor for both the foundation and finishing. Owner-built homes are also common. Their designs are usually conventional, but distinctive features ranging from the ingenious to the outlandish are not uncommon. Finally, there are also conventionally built dwellings ranging from modest to elaborate.

Outbuildings are common. Many are for horses, which are luxury items—though kept by families in a very wide range of incomes. Many outbuildings are for trucks—incidental to the livelihood of so many laborers and tradesmen. But many outbuildings also house a true farming enterprise. For the region has a distinctive kind of suburbanization and intensification of its agriculture. Productivity of farmland ranks among the highest in Minnesota, although the soil quality is only mediocre. Yet the proportion of part time farmers is also among the highest in the state. It is a region of relatively intensive part time farming. It is not uncommon to see a farmer plowing or harvesting by tractor headlight after a day's work at the factory bench, grease rack, or supply room counter.

Population growth areas in the zone of urbanization appear not only on a map of population change but also on the map of family income. For growth is occurring mostly where long distance commuting or branch plants of metropolitan industries are contributing to the basic income. The location of those areas is partly correlated with highway access to city and suburban employment centers. But the pattern is greatly modified by the local patterns of lakeshore and wooded hills and also by accessibility to local employment centers.

There is some concern that exurban settlement will usurp the resource of open land that now surrounds the suburbs and central cities. There is some truth to this. In a way, there is an abundance of open space—about 5,000 square miles without significant development within an hour's driving time of the central business district or the Midway. That is enough to accommodate six to ten centuries of growth even at low outer suburban densities and recent metropolitan population increase rates. On the other hand, if that open space were divided into parcels averaging eight acres, it would last only about a decade at recent growth rates. The latter version of the process is probably nearer reality. Meanwhile, however, there are more than 100,000 acres of public open space within the one hour driving time zone. The newly created Metropolitan Parks and Open Space Board, under the Metropolitan Council, has been given $40 million dollars in bonding power by the Minnesota legislature, and much of the acquisition under that program will be in the exurban zone. Furthermore, key legislative and agency studies have shown that most of the overcrowded state park facilities are in the metropolitan zone of urbanization; hence future state acquisition and protection programs are likely to have a major focus in that area, as well.

Cultural differences also enrich the internal geography of the zone of urbanization. In one sense, the whole zone is a cultural region. For now, at least, it is a unique zone of interaction between city and country. Also, most residents still combine the culture of past rural isolation with the energy of newly increased affluence. Hence, many church congregations are swelling —buildings new structures or enlarging old ones. The zone contains Minnesota's largest concentration of old-time ballrooms, for it has the largest concentration of people who have both the taste for old-time music and the money for live entertainment. The Minnesota Orchestra can attract 2,000 local people to an outdoor symphony in a small town while, not far away, a steam threshing bee in an abandoned farmyard draws 3,000 from the countryside and the suburbs.

Cultural subregions, based on national background and religion, are as vivid in this zone as they are in the older neighborhoods of the central cities, although some are rapidly fading as they are diluted by immigration from the cities and suburbs. Two noteworthy examples are German Catholic concentrations—one centered on the Crow River valley communities of Hanover, Albertville, and St. Michael, along the boundary between Hennepin and Wright Counties; the other around Miesville and New Trier west of Hastings in Dakota County. Among all of the rural areas at similar distance from the central cities, those two were the last to shift their predominant economy out of farming and join the army of rural commuters. Other examples are the Bohemian community, which extends southward from Prior Lake in southern Scott County to New Prague; the French-Canadian community focused on Centerville and Hugo, north of White Bear Lake; and the historic Swedish community centered on the Chisago Lakes area and northern Washington County—scene of the American portions of Moberg's famous novels, *The Immigrants* and *Unto a New Land*.

Racially the urbanization zone is virtually all white. At the time of the 1970 census nonwhites numbered only about 3,000 out of roughly 800,000 total population in the zone. Perhaps it is noteworthy that more than 80 percent of the nonwhite population growth in the

preceding decade occurred in towns with either a branch plant of a major national corporation or a college—both institutions highly sensitive to national and organized social pressures.

JUDGMENT DAY APPROACHES

Reviewing the landscapes that have emerged in the Twin Cities suburbs and beyond since 1945, one can recite the full litany of sins of American suburbia and exurbia. The region is fragmented into scores of autonomous local governments. Its ragged frontier of urbanization, low density, and commuters living sixty miles out are proof of urban sprawl. Many, if not all, of the suburban communities have grown with an imbalance between residential and nonresidential development. Some are almost entirely residential; others heavily commercial or industrial. Hence there are unbalanced community tax bases—some have the advantage of large nonresidential valuations to help the residents pay for municipal services; in others the residents have had to go it alone. The streetcar system was dismantled and the bus system was neglected until very recently. There was neglect of public open space acquisition for many years. There is little public low and moderate income housing outside the central cities. Racial segregation has produced minority ghettoes and virtually all-white neighborhoods.

We now appear to be leaving the era that spawned suburbia and exurbia and entering a new one. The population explosion and the affluent society are, respectively, awash in heavy seas of unprecedented contraception and inflation. The nation is evolving a new perspective on energy consumption in particular and resource consumption in general. That, too, seems certain to affect housing costs, style, and location.

As Twin Citians approach the day of atonement for this age in the life of their metropolis, how will their sins be judged by that Great Urban Model in the Sky?

Priorities and Increasing Management

The post–World War II growth ring of the Twin Cities was built in less than three decades to accommodate a million people. At the minimum, that has been a very large and rapid accomplishment. By comparison, the Minnesota Experimental City—acclaimed as a bold proposal—was to reach a population of one-quarter million in one decade.

Nor was the expansion totally undisciplined. At the beginning of the epoch a large and fast-growing population, with a particular legacy of circumstances from the war-Depression years, was faced with an immediate task and finite resources. In retrospect it is apparent that there were priorities and a crude order of procedure. The community addressed the necessary tasks in the following chronological order: (1) housing and elementary schools; (2) streets, sewers, and highways; (3) commercial and industrial buildings; (4) hospitals, high schools, and churches; and, finally, (5) junior colleges and vocational schools, government and business offices, public open space acquisition and improvement. There were also priorities within each of those broad tasks. For example, single family homes dominated production overwhelmingly during the years when demand was concentrated in young households with a very high birth rate. Then apartment construction escalated when demand shifted heavily toward retirement households and young households with a very low birth rate.

Although the tasks were initiated in chronological order, the effort on each of them has continued once it was begun. Nevertheless, peak years of activity on each task tended to follow soon after its initiation.

Suppose a suitable comprehensive model of urban development and operation had existed in 1945. Suppose further that all of the necessary data had been available and had been collected and entered. And suppose that the consequences of alternative strategies of investment and regulation had been considered and voted upon. In retrospect, again, it is quite plausible that the general priorities and procedures might not have been greatly different from those which actually occurred. One wonders if more "balance" between one family and multiple dwellings would have been acceptable to the people who needed new housing in the late 1940s and 1950s. If the model indicated that more "balance" between housing construction, municipal capital improvements, and nonresidential building would have slowed rectification of the housing shortage and raised prices, would the majority of households have voted for more "balance"? Would abstinence from the automobile, and accompanying pre-Depression residential densities, have been acceptable to a middle income majority in need of housing—given the available data and theory on energy pricing and supplies in 1946 (or twenty years later)?

In short, individual priorities were clear and not hard to justify. They were aggregated into collective priorities through the discipline imposed by the market for labor, materials, land, and money—all in a crude but recognizable way.

Meanwhile, the community has gradually increased the *management* of this expansion process as experience has accumulated. The examples are abundant—metropolitanwide coordination of zoning, hospital planning, solid waste management; metropolitan financing and operation of airports, sewers, and transit; metropolitanwide financing of regional parks; metropolitanwide organizations of county officials, open housing advocacy groups, school officials, and many others. Zoning is becoming increasingly influenced by the timing and location of public capital improvement programs. Performance requirements are increasingly used in connection with zoning to bring aesthetics into the landscape.

The reasons for this increasing management are fundamental. The metropolitan area and its component communities have monitored the changing postwar settlement. They have done it rather poorly, but with gradually growing sophistication. The job has been done by a loose consortium of public agencies, private utilities, scholars and teachers, and citizens organizations. As those groups have monitored and publicized their findings, the general understanding of both the evolving metropolis and its evolving problems has also grown.

The Twin Cities and Minnesota have attracted national attention for their approaches to problems of metropolitan development. It may well be true that the significant accomplishment thus far has not been so much in the anticipation of future problems and preparing for them in advance as it has been in rather quickly grasping current problems and responding to them as an intelligent community.

Nagging Questions
Some questions have been especially stubborn. They were on the public agenda at the beginning of the postwar epoch, they are not yet resolved, and they are likely to persist into the next epoch.

1. On many sides, advocates of local government reorganization argue that the crazy-quilt pattern and multiplicity of local governments in the metropolitan region is irrational and costly. In what ways is that true? Does each different service provided by local government have its own unique optimal service area (threshold and range), unrelated to the vagaries of muncipal and county boundaries? If that is the case, can those services ever be rationalized without establishing special or consolidated districts, separate from the general units of local government—the counties and municipalities? And what then is the appropriate function of the counties and municipalities?

2. Proponents of growth control argue that sprawl is bad because extra costs to the people who do it are borne not by the sprawlers but by the people who live in closer in, higher density areas. Commonly used illustrations are the costs of road improvements and maintenance, school busing, or sewer lines. The questions are: Who is actually subsidized now? By whom? Where? How much? Until those questions are answered it is only frustrating to try to establish equity on the basis of theory. Once the actual situation is well described, it will be much simpler for public officials and their constituents to respond to the ultimate question: Which parts of the system should be subsidized? Where? By whom? Why?

3. It has been observed earlier that evolving policies tend to favor the high density approach to the housing cost squeeze and to discourage the cheap land approach. Yet, important cost-cutting innovations—actual or potential—have been permitted on the low density frontier or beyond, while they have tended to be discouraged or prohibited in the more developed and institutionalized suburbs and central cities. Notable cases are factory-assembled, precut, and owner-built houses. As more sophisticated innovations come in construction, sanitation, or space heating, there will be more need than ever for people and places willing and able to do the testing. What zone will perform the essential experimental and safety valve functions of the relatively unregulated frontier under conditions of controlled growth?

4. Multiple agencies of government have evolved out of the experience of three decades of fast growth. They have responsibility for regulation in the fields of natural resources or environment, health, education, human relations, welfare, and transportation. Their powers are defined and isolated by thousands of pieces of legislation. Yet, their responsibilities within the metropolitan region are interrelated in thousands of ways. For almost any problem that arises, there are existing agencies and powers that can move toward its solution, but such action is almost certain to require coordinated use of multiple powers by multiple agencies. That situation will occur no matter how the agencies are realigned or redefined, for each problem tends to be both complex and unique. The question is: How are these many agencies and laws to be effectively coordinated?

5. Finally, if a new epoch is indeed now breaking upon us, what are going to be the distinctive and important characteristics of that epoch? What will be the resultant major problems of metropolitan operation and the inherent solutions? Which of today's problems in the post–World War II growth rings will—whether they are solved or not—be quietly replaced by new problems of greater urgency in the new epoch?

How, then, will the Twin Citians' postwar development effort be judged? Perhaps it will be on how they met the need to monitor, change, carry on informed discussion, develop understanding, and discipline their response to the problems and issues they perceived. Perhaps Twin Citians in the new epoch will be judged according to their effort to further improve those activities and their ability to respond to tomorrow's problems more quickly and effectively than they did to yesterday's.

David Lanegran and Clarence Shallbetter read an early version of this vignette and offered valuable suggestions for improving it. Their help is gratefully acknowledged.

Bibliography

Blegen, Theodore C. *Minnesota: A History of the State.* Minneapolis: University of Minnesota Press, 1963.

Borchert, John R. *The Twin Cities.* New York: Doubleday and Company, 1959.

——. "The Twin Cities Urbanized Area: Past, Present, Future." *Geographical Review* 51 (1961): 47–70.

Borchert, J.R., and R.B. Adams. *Trade Centers and Trade Areas of the Upper Midwest.* Urban Report no. 3. Minneapolis: Upper Midwest Economic Study, 1963.

Borchert. John R., and Donald P. Yaeger. *Atlas of Minnesota Resources and Settlement.* Minneapolis: University of Minnesota Department of Geography, 1968.

Brown, Ralph H. *Historical Geography of the United States.* New York: Harcourt, Brace and Company, 1948.

Gras, N.S.B. "The Significance of the Twin Cities for Minnesota History." *Minnesota History* 7 (1926): 3–17.

Hart, John Fraser, and Russell B. Adams. "Twin Cities." *Focus* 20, 6 (February 1970): 1–11.

Hartshorne, Richard. "The Twin City District: A Unique Form of Urban Landscape." *Geographical Review* 22 (1932): 431–42.

Henderson, J.M.; A.O. Krueger; R.S. Rodd; and J.S. Adams. *National Growth and Economic Change in the Upper Midwest.* Minneapolis: University of Minnesota Press, 1965.

Lukermann, Fred E. "The Changing Pattern of Flour Mill Location." *The Northwestern Miller,* Vol. 261, nos. 3, 4, 6, 8, 12, 13, 17 (1959).

Robinson, Edward Van Dyke. *Early Economic Conditions and the Development of Agriculture in Minnesota.* University of Minnesota, Studies in the Social Sciences no. 3. Minneapolis: University of Minnesota Press, 1915.

Schmid, Calvin F. *Social Saga of Two Cities.* Minneapolis, 1937.

Schwartz, George M., and George A. Thiel. *Minnesota's Rocks and Waters.* Minneapolis: University of Minnesota Press, 1963.

WPA Writers Project. *Minneapolis: The Story of a City.* Minneapolis, 1940.

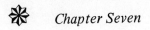 *Chapter Seven*

Seattle

Preface

Two images of Seattle—as "gateway to Alaska" and as the "jet city"—reveal much of the character and history of the place. Seattle was established, grew, and prospered as a regional capital of resource-rich frontier provinces, and as a gateway to Alaska and the Orient. While these functions remain vital to an understanding of the society and economy of Seattle and its hinterland, the "jet city" image reveals a transformation of the city into a more sophisticated industrial and service metropolis, but one somewhat sensitive to the volatility of the dominant Boeing Aircraft Company.

Seattle is a real metropolis and, partly from its isolation, possesses attributes and services of even larger places. Yet, although it is highly interconnected with the rest of the country through flows of goods and migrants, it remains a provincial place, lacking some of the urbane qualities of eastern cities, but lacking their difficult social problems as well.

The city was founded in an area less than favorable for agriculture but in a deep-water setting of hills and lakes and bays permitting easy exploitation of the rich forests. The physical setting is beautiful, transport difficult and constrained, and settlement much influenced by the availability of view or waterfront for houses and level land or waterfront for industry. The endless forests, once cut, provided too much land, encouraging settlement to sprawl over a wide area. Partly because of the variety of terrain the central city retains higher class groups and a strong central business district. It has a distinctive ethnic composition rich in Japanese, Chinese, and native Americans, disproportionately few blacks, and a basic mix of persons of North European origin. Two-thirds of the people live in the suburbs, which are not necessarily affluent or homogeneous. Finally, the superb physical setting, despite the frequent gloom and drizzle, encourages high enthusiasm for boating, hiking, fishing, second homes, and other forms of outdoor recreation.

In the last decade, Seattle has shared with other cities an increasing concern with alternatives to simple growth and newness. This has led to controversies in the Capitol Hill neighborhood, the zoo, Pioneer Square-Skid Road, and the Pike Place Market. Meanwhile, environmental conflicts brew over the Ross Dam project, shoreline disturbance at Nisqually Delta and the Lake Washington bridges, and perhaps over the very nature of the future city.

The Place of Seattle Among Cities

SEATTLE AS A REGIONAL CAPITAL

Seattle is a regional capital with rivals, and perhaps because of them has not attained the preeminence to which many thought it should be destined. Nonetheless, it is a sizable metropolis of about 1.5 million persons with a median family income in 1969 of $11,700, higher than all but five of the large metropolitan areas.

Although seventeenth in size among United States metropolitan areas, it is perhaps fifteenth or sixteenth in functional importance, with high levels of wholesale and retail trade, finance, and transportation services. But while it is the preeminent service center for a large region of the Pacific Northwest and Alaska, its hinterland is sparsely populated and Seattle would never have achieved its present size and importance without its strength in the national and international export of Boeing aircraft. The Alaska-Yukon goldrush, three transcontinental railroads, and World War I shipbuilding propelled Seattle to regional importance, but the relative location and head start of Portland should probably have made the Oregon city the clear-cut regional capital. It remains a strong rival, sharing the highest functions with Seattle over much of the area, shutting out Seattle's influence in Oregon and southern Idaho. Vancouver, B.C., and the international boundary in general also truncate Seattle's "natural" trade area to the north. To a very weak degree as yet, Seattle may be considered a hub of a fairly homogeneous urban network stretching from Vancouver, B.C., to Eugene, Oregon. But unlike Megalopolis the gaps betweeen the cities are long, real, and rural.

Seattle, to the frustration of its boosters, has not quite made the "big leagues" in a variety of popular measures—major league football or baseball, a superior symphony orchestra, and so forth. This is often blamed whether reasonably or not on what Seattle may well be first in, a recreational environment which is supposed to distract residents from spectator activities. But in the words of William Spiedel, a local author: "You can't eat Mount Rainier."

Let us note what is special and not very special about Seattle, and then turn to case studies of some special features or characteristics of Seattle. Some of the forces or conditions that have contributed to the present landscape and economy of Seattle include its isolation from most of the nation and its low density, a marine environment rich in timber and water resources, and its idiosyncratic cultural-economic history.

Seattle's isolation not surprisingly has been both a handicap and an advantage. Certainly its transport position to the mass of the nation's population is poor, undoubtedly discouraging the development of many kinds of industries that need national markets, and making prices higher than in much of the nation— i.e., "slightly higher west of the Rockies." Yet the agricultural, timber, and mineral resources were great enough to induce three transcontinental railroads to terminate in Seattle—Northern Pacific; Great Northern; Chicago, Milwaukee, St. Paul and Pacific—helping to overcome the isolation by encouraging settlement, investment, and trade. Perhaps the isolation also helped attract or bring out the entrepreneurs who despite high transport costs created a variety of industries that successfully compete in national markets. Indeed, peripheral Seattle has traditionally had a high level of industry for a regional capital and this has surely helped maintain its high income levels (Figure 1).

The great distance from the East and even California has at the same time offered some protection to Seattle in its serving local and regional markets. Like Denver, Atlanta, and some other peripheral cities of similar size, Seattle has strong service sectors relative to its size; it is above the national average in retail trade, wholesale trade, finance, communications, and transportation. The latter, to be sure, represents the port or gateway function. A fairly wide variety of regional manufacturing is made possible and easier by this partially captive market of about four million, although its fairly small size restricts the range of goods produced.

Finally, the city's isolation has perhaps resulted in a social structure with substantial tolerance for the unusual, at least in good times.

SEATTLE'S HINTERLAND

The Seattle daily urban system sprawls outward from the center one hundred miles or more. Commuters come from rural areas and small

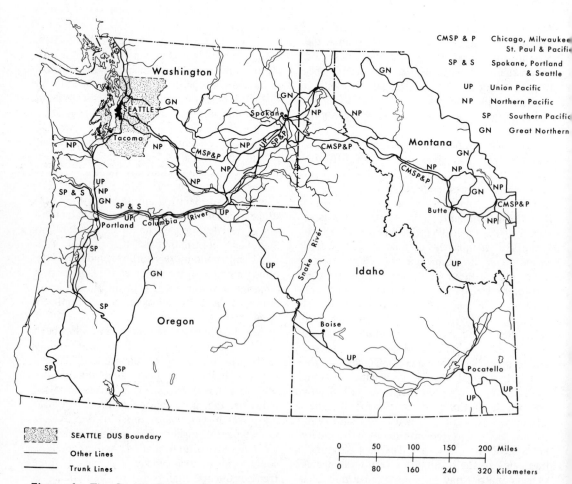

Figure 1. The Pacific Northwest region. Source: Adapted from *Seattle Urban Design Report*, (Seattle: Department of Community Development, 1971).

towns, from near Canada, from the Olympic peninsula, and from east of the Cascade Mountains, using generally high quality Seattle-centered highway and ferry systems. In addition, a high density of second homes and high levels of recreation travel, city newspapers, and especially city television dominate the Puget Sound area. Still, the area is far from homogeneous, there being real divergence in the physical and cultural landscape between the central city, the suburbs, and the semirural hinterland.

Looking beyond the daily urban systems, Seattle's functional economic region is one of the largest in area—including not only Washington and parts of Idaho and Montana, but also Alaska—yet at the same time it is probably one of the smallest in population of the major economic regions. Whereas Seattle may dominate Portland in certain respects, they are fundamentally rivals, and Seattle's influence is superseded by Portland in a fair portion of southern Washington. This simple geographic fact has long irritated Seattle's business community and led to a wide variety of methods to strengthen Seattle's position —for example, by equalizing transport rates for places when in fact it should be cheaper to go to Portland. To the north, the Canadian border and booming Vancouver raise an effective barrier. Seattle's trade area leaps over Canada to embrace Alaska and extends eastward into central Montana. The only change has been a gradual eastward expansion at the expense of Minneapolis, probably a result of a diversion westward of minerals, grains, timber, and livestock that traditionally went east.

In character the Seattle trade area is sparsely populated and dominated by forests and forestry, specialized agriculture, and fishing. Forest production in its hinterland is second only to Portland; wheat production third behind Minneapolis and Kansas City; irrigated production of fruit second only to California. Industry in the hinterland is significant, since forest product manufacturing is widely dispersed. Power-intensive aluminum and related industries are nearly as dispersed, using the relatively cheap and abundant hydroelectric power. Rates are about half the national average, and per capita consumption, largely industrial, about double.

When it comes to scenery, one can note the presence of three national parks within one hundred miles, the most rugged mountains of the nation in both the mainland and Alaska, and waterways and lakes which helped induce the highest levels of small boat ownership in the nation.

SEATTLE AS A FRONTIER COMMUNITY

Seattle is a fairly new city, scarcely more than one hundred years old, and still retains certain qualities of a frontier culture and economy. At least until World War I the economy depended on the exploitation of virgin resources, particularly the forests. The entrepreneurial spirit was vigorous, and continuous economic intrigue determined who got to what resources first with which railway. The proportion of single men was high, partly because of the nature of logging and mining and the need for contract labor to build the railways and work the mines. Seattle was also the end of the line for those who sought success farther on. To this day, Seattle's Skid Road has a large community of forgotten men. The name "Skid Road"—and Seattle's was the first—derives from the fact that logs were skidded down a long hill to Seattle's first lumber mill and that this area was from the beginning the home of a transient population.

Despite effort and money, the city never became staid and traditional. Traditionally it tolerated the new and experimental, different kinds of people and diverse lifestyles. On the other hand, Seattleites lashed out at the Chinese in the 1880s, when they seemed an economic threat, and did little to protest the placement of Japanese-Americans in concentration camps in World War II. By 1970, so far as a socioeconomic profile would indicate, Seattle resembles other large American metropolises, except perhaps in its avoidance thus far of the intensity of social problems of many eastern cities.

The Nature of Its Immigrants

To help exploit its plentiful resources, Seattle attracted a distinctive if not peculiar set of migrants. Besides the original Anglo-Scottish-Irish stock moving on from the Midwest, Seattle became home to unusual concentrations of Germans and, especially, Scandinavians, who began to exercise major cultural and political influence as early as 1900. Sheer distance probably accounts for the small migration of blacks to Seattle. Even today the metropolitan proportion is less than 4 percent, many of whom represent secondary migrants out of Texas and Louisiana by way of California. On the other hand, the Japanese, Chinese, Filipino, and American Indian minority populations are unusually large and significant, totaling about 6 percent of the population. The history of race relations has not been good. Yet by today's standards, the income and occupational situation of minorities relative to the dominant white community is about the best in the country. Intermarriage and housing integration has reached a fairly high level for the Japanese and Chinese communities.

Seattle like California attracted migrants from all over the East during World War II, and indeed has steadily come under the influence of California culture and myths. Also, like California, Seattle was an early center of a "counterculture." Such nonstandardized group behavior has taken many forms in Seattle, however, and reflects its peculiarity in location, environment, and stage of economic maturity. For example, perhaps reflecting its frontier feature, organized religion has always been relatively weak as compared with other parts of the country. Certainly, a smaller proportion of people go to church regularly here than elsewhere. On the other hand, odd religious groups are much in evidence. Seattle is an important center of the tongue-speaking charismatic movement. It is also heavily penetrated by the Mormons and by other sects—such as the Jehovah's Witnesses, the Seventh Day Adventists, and evangelical religious groups.

The peculiarity of Seattleites is also shown a high tolerance of individual rights. Washington, for example, is the only state in the United States where liberal abortion was approved by referendum vote. On the other hand, Seattle, like many other large cities, did not support housing integration—presumably because it was looked upon as a threat to private residential property values.

Some Economic Characteristics

Returning to the economic side, the labor shortage and shipbuilding of World War I led to an early growth of unions. Resistance was as great and violent as elsewhere, culminating in severe labor unrest (especially 1915-1920). Nevertheless, unions became very strong and

for a while fairly radical, at least until the nation's first general strike here in 1919. Even today, Washington is among the most highly unionized states and boasts about the highest wage levels in both industrial and service sectors.

World War I also helped Boeing Aircraft get a start. The early planes depended on the plentiful supplies of spruce for use in their wood frame construction. Following a successful speculation accident Boeing gradually became a competitor to the traditional resource-oriented industries of forest products, food products, and fisheries. Boeing grew to dominance during World War II, and despite a postwar lull and a recent slump Boeing remains a giant employer and generator of exports.

Especially since 1960, however, significant economic diversification has occurred, helping to cushion the volatility of Boeing's sales and employment. Diversification includes the growth of port activities, of service sectors generally, of import-substitution regional manufacuring, and a wide range of export manufacturing.

SEATTLE'S SPECIAL PHYSICAL CONDITION

Seattle is a natural harbor city, but without major river access to the interior. In this respect it is like Boston, Baltimore, Houston, or San Diego. Seattle has succeeded rather well, despite this handicap and a certain degree of isolation. With respect to its port function, Seattle ranks about thirtieth in total tonnage, somewhat below its sixteen to seventeen ranking in overall national importance. Given the inherent superiority of Portland's access to the interior, this is from one perspective a kind of tribute to its competitive spirit; from another, to political manipulations.

Seattle's waterfront is supplemented by many lakes, enhancing the beauty of the landscape at times and places, but also disrupting communication and causing unusual patterns and concentrations of people and transport arteries. Large Lake Washington on the east was for one hundred years a major barrier inland forcing development north and south in an hourglass form. This kind of influence of water bodies is also present in San Francisco but almost no other city approaches the north-south urban distortion now characterizing

Seattle except, even more strikingly, the original city of New York. The urbanized area extends an astounding fifty-two miles north and south (sixty-five miles, if Tacoma is included) and only sixteen miles east and west (and this is very recent). The crossing of Lake Washington by two bridges has led to explosive eastward growth as expected and perhaps threatens the total dominance of the Seattle CBD. Bellevue to the east, with a population of about 100,000, is now the fourth largest city in the state. Such a competitive growth pattern resembles the experience of San Francisco-Oakland or New York-Newark.

Besides the microgeography of lakes as a force to control the outline of the city is the predominantly hilly, irregular topography. Within the city itself, elevation varies from sea level to over 500 feet. As in San Francisco and Los Angeles hillslopes and ridges have been attractive to high value residences, as have the lakeshores, leading to a very irregular pattern of land values (Figure 2). For business purposes the hillsides proved inconvenient and business districts located either in valleys or on hilltops (West Seattle, Queen Anne). The city is located on glacial deposits, so regrading was fairly easy. Some real hills were removed and used to accomplish very large landfills of swampy areas which have proved very valuable for railroad and industrial purposes. Otherwise, very little flat land exists in Seattle.

The physical environment has a profound impact on the morphology of the city, on the economic functions the city performs, and on the behavior of its citizens. The marine climate, and the superb coniferous forests it helps sustain, have regionally and historically been the basis for the development of the region and of Seattle. Even if the forest industries no longer loom large in the city's economy, forest products, grains, fruits, and other primary goods which depend on the abundance of land and moisture still are vital and represent a massive part of regional export income. The influence of the forests is also seen in the predominance of wood construction in housing and perhaps even in endless rows of ugly telephone poles lining the streets.

At another level, the abundance of land and the sheer beauty and richness of the scenic and recreational environment profoundly affect travel and recreational behavior and attract many migrants. At the same time, this

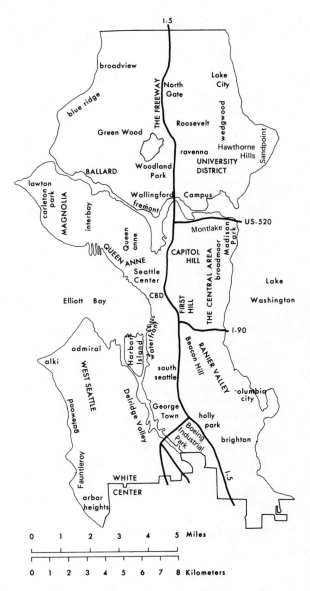

Figure 2.   Neighborhoods in Seattle.

endowment encourages excessive urban sprawl and long distance commuting, leads to adverse impacts on fragile natural environments, and triggers severe conflicts between "economic," "recreational," and "wilderness" uses of land.

Within the city, microgeographic characteristics loom particularly importantly. Subtle differences in view, access to water, and exposure to sun greatly affect land and housing values and greatly distort normal patterns of urban land use.

Seattle's climate is essentially cool, maritime, and drizzly—like western England—from September through June, with a high degree of clouds and drizzle but relatively little hard rain, freezing, or snow; then Mediterranean from July through September, with warm, fairly dry weather and some fog, similar in America only to its neighbors Portland and Vancouver. Winter temperatures resemble cities of the southeast, while those of summer are like northern cities such as Quebec or Winnipeg. The summer is magnificent, but it cannot be denied that the disappearance of the sun for as much as a month—especially in the short hours of December (Seattle, at almost 48° north, is far north of Chicago or New York)—can be depressing. Whether or not climate is really a significant influence, it is true that the suicide rate in Seattle is unusually high, reaching a peak in spring, when the weather, but not necessarily one's prospects, has improved.

Besides the port, Seattle's resource base was essentially the seemingly endless, magnificent forests. In this respect, Seattle is again like its neighbor cities of Portland and Vancouver. However, Seattle itself is no longer as directly dependent on forest product industries as these other cities. Seattle's situation early in the century was not too unlike that of Detroit or Minneapolis about 1850, during the exploitation of the Great Lakes forests. Like San Francisco and Denver, Seattle for a time boomed along with the gold rush in Alaska and the Yukon in 1897.

THE DEMOGRAPHIC PROFILE

Seattle is an intermediate-sized metropolitan area with 531,000 persons within the city limits (ranking twenty-second); 1.2 million in the urbanized area (ranking seventeenth) and 1.4 million in the SMSA (again ranking seventeenth). Thus it is closest in population to such metropolitan areas as Milwaukee, Atlanta, Dallas, Miami, and San Diego, significantly smaller than other regional capitals like Minneapolis-St. Paul, Houston, or St. Louis, but larger than such regional capitals as Denver, Kansas City, Cincinnati, Indianapolis, and New Orleans.

Seattle, with an urbanized area of 413 square miles and a density of only 2,997 persons per square mile, ranks twenty-first of the twenty-five urbanized areas over a million. Population density is thus very low, lower

than any larger metropolitan area except Minneapolis-St. Paul and Dallas, and possibly lower than these, since their incorporated units include much rural land. This does not reflect unbuildable terrain so much as the strong preference for single family homes, traditional wood construction, easy availability of land, and the lack of intense competing agriculture. Reflecting the low density is the high per capita automobile ownership, and 71 percent of the housing stock in single family units, compared to 63 percent nationally. In this respect Seattle most resembles the cities of San Diego or Dallas rather than New York, Boston, or Chicago. Yet despite the high degree of suburbanization and exurbanization and the uneven pace of development at the edge of the built-up areas, the central city of Seattle remains dominant with a strong central business district, perhaps because many wealthier people remain in the city because of its attractive microgeography coupled with a comfortable social environment.

Birth rates have long been below the national average, and despite the attraction of the city for young families, the average age remains at about the national average (like Chicago, Boston, or Los Angeles) and older than such cities as Atlanta, Dallas, or Houston. By 1972, deaths exceeded births in the city of Seattle, and even in the metropolitan area, the rate of natural increase was very low.

Despite a rate of natural increase below the national average, Seattle has experienced rather rapid growth—67 percent in the 1940s, 31 percent in the 1950s, and 43 percent in the urbanized area in the 1960s, exceeding the SMSA growth rate of 29 percent. This growth was sustained by a high level of net inmigration. For 1960-1970 it was 190,000—a rate of 16 percent for the SMSA—far exceeding the natural increase of 12 percent. Among metropolitan areas of Seattle's class or larger, growth during the 1960s was exceeded only by Houston, Dallas, and Washington, D.C., and was about the same as that of San Diego and Denver.

The ethnic composition of Seattle is atypical. With the low proportion of 7 percent blacks in the city and 3 percent in the SMSA Seattle is much like Minneapolis-St. Paul or Denver, and far below the nationwide SMSA average of 13 percent. On the other hand, the 0.8 percent for American Indians is higher than the mean of 0.4 percent. Even more marked is the proportion of Japanese—2 percent locally compared to 0.3 percent nationally—and Chinese—1.2 percent compared to 0.2 percent. Not surprisingly, the pattern is somewhat like that of Vancouver, Portland, San Francisco, and Los Angeles, other major ports of entry for East Asia.

Seattle also has unusually high proportions of people of Scandinavian origin—at least 6 percent compared to a national average of 1 percent—and of Canadian origin—5.2 percent compared to 1.5 percent. The SMSA proportion of foreign stock is much higher than the national average—22 percent compared to 17 percent in 1970—but much below that of Boston or New York. The Scandinavian population either immigrated directly or shifted westward from Minnesota, the Dakotas, and Wisconsin. Minneapolis for example has 10 percent of its population of Scandinavian origin. The Canadian influence reflects Seattle's position near the border. Similarly high are Detroit, Boston, and Portland.

The Jewish population, estimated at 12,000 or 1 percent, is lower than in the majority of metropolitan areas; however, Seattle has one of the larger Sephardic communities.

THE CULTURAL HERITAGE

Culturally, Seattle has about what would be expected for a city of its size and age—occasionally producing outstanding enterprises or personalities, but too small to sustain a high level set of complex activities. The gaps are felt across the board, from opera and symphony to professional sports. More deeply, Seattle shares a common mass culture with California's fads in religion, architecture, clothes, customs, and forms of speech. More subtly, it shares a liberal tradition with Oregon and with its immigrant bases in Minnesota and Wisconsin. Politically these regions and their cities are somewhat alike, having a tradition of progressive or liberal Republicanism, yielding to a slight Democratic dominance since the New Deal.

Finally we may ask what other cities are most like Seattle: Portland and Vancouver in size, economic function and social composition; San Diego in size, industrial composition, and role of the environment; and Denver, Atlanta, and Kansas City in size and as regional wholesale and transportation centers.

The Seattle Economy in Historical Perspective

FROM SAWMILL SETTLEMENT TO REGIONAL METROPOLIS

In 120 years Seattle has been transformed from a rainsoaked sawmill settlement to a major regional metropolis, with a hopeful image of science and scenery. More truthfully, it has become a large, rich, and diverse city, expanding and adding people and characteristics, but never losing those features which brought about its early growth.

Seattle was settled in 1851 by a small band (twelve adults, twelve children) of hard-working individualists. These pioneers had left the Midwest for the Pacific Coast but found Portland, Oregon, at 2,000, entirely too crowded. On arrival at Elliott Bay, it did not take these entrepreneurs long to appreciate their advantageous position on deep water, with easy access to rich timber resources. In the very first year they began to supply timber to booming San Francisco. In 1853, Yesler established the region's first sawmill, providing employment for both white settlers and local Indians and laying the cornerstone for the eventual industrial preeminence of Seattle in the region.

The city was named for Sealth, chief of the local Duwamish Indians, with whom relations were fair, but long term relations between whites and Indians were destructive and hundred year old conflicts, as over territorial fishing rights, remain unresolved today.

Early growth was slow. Seattle was smaller than Olympia, the territorial capital after separation from Oregon, and other settlements,

like Port Townsend on the Olympic Peninsula. In 1860, Seattle was designated the site of the territorial university, not immediately perceived as much of a benefit in a frontier mill town, but eventually to become a significant factor in Seattle's cultural and scientific stature.

Seattle was isolated, and its leading citizens realized the critical importance of acquiring the terminus of one of the railroads into the northwest. The Northern Pacific was first, and was earnestly courted. A decision to send a spur up from the Columbia terminating at Tacoma, rather than crossing the relatively low Snoqualmie Pass just east of Seattle, could well have brought about the eclipse of Seattle. Indeed, long after the Northern Pacific reached Tacoma from Kalama near Portland in 1873, it refused to connect into Seattle, only thirty miles north, since the railroad was after all the leading landowner and developer of Tacoma. Determined Seattle attempted to build its own railways, both north and south. The town grew despite its lack of a rail connection and finally was granted a connection to Tacoma in 1883 when the transcontinental was completed. By 1889, with 37,000 people, it had become the largest town in the newly created state of Washington, despite a disastrous fire that same year.

By 1887 the Northern Pacific completed its main transcontinental line to Tacoma over Stampede Pass, a better connection to Seattle. James J. Hill, with help from Seattle entrepreneurs and Chinese labor, completed the Great Northern to Seattle in 1893. Hill recognized the potential profitability of combining railroading with land and timber ownership and forged an early cooperation with Weyerhauser, who earlier had bought large parts of the forested Northern Pacific land grant and established what became the leading forest product firm of the region to this day.

The depression of the 1890s hit Seattle's basic timber and fish industries hard, but in 1897 the arrival of the steamship *Portland* with gold from Alaska started off a colossal twenty year boom, essentially changing Seattle from a lumber mill town to a commercial, financial, and industrial metropolis. The gold was far from Seattle, but the city's entrepreneurs reaped tremendous advantage as organizers, outfitters, entertainers, and middlemen in the right place at the right time and established a pattern of dominance over Alaska which remains a love-hate relationship. Alaskans resent Seattle's economic dominance, yet benefit from the close economic and social ties. Gold served as the catalyst enabling Seattle to become the dominant commercial and financial center for Washington and to surpass even its older and heretofore larger rival Portland. Many of the thousands of "sourdoughs" pouring through Seattle to Alaska later returned here to settle.

Much wealth continued to be generated through exploitation of the forests, even though the mills and logging might be far from the city, but wealth also came from agriculture and mining. The boom, which raised Seattle's population to 80,000 by 1900 and 237,000 by 1910, also brought two more railroads, the Milwaukee Road (Chicago, Milwaukee, St. Paul, and Pacific) in 1906 and the Union Pacific in 1910, as well as a road over the Cascades. The growth was peopled by immigrants from the Midwest and Europe, particularly Scandinavians, who for a while formed the separate sawmill city of Ballard. Japanese began arriving as laborers in the late 1890s.

In the midst of this boom period was the surprisingly successful Alaska-Yukon Exposition of 1909 which among other benefits provided the University of Washington with a much improved campus.

The euphoria of the period led to the construction of the Chittenden Locks in 1916, a canal connecting Puget Sound to Lake Washington, under the assumption that Lake Washington would become an industrial lake with steel mills and a major navy yard. Fortunately,

the navy yard was established in Bremerton, the steel dream faded, and the impressive locks now serve countless pleasure craft and occasional cargo and navy ships.

As the boom from Alaska-Yukon gold began to fade, Seattle was saved by World War I and the expansion of shipbuilding. The industrial growth of the period together with the labor shortage and perhaps the sheer misery of working conditions promoted the growth of strong unions and radicalism in Seattle and the region after 1900. The militant International Workers of the World had an especially rough history of conflict with company police, the American Legion, and the National Guard as the companies attempted to break the unions. The Russian summer of 1919 was one of intense fear of the Bolsheviks and when the shipyard workers and the Central Labor Council organized the country's first and longest general strike during five days of February 1919 the fears far exceeded any reality of danger. Still, the general strike proved to be a tactical error, and from then on, although Seattle and Washington State became highly unionized, the mood was to shift to one of cooperation rather than confrontation between labor and management.

Radicalism was a real force not only in unions but also in politics off and on from 1900 to 1940, particularly in World War I, and then again in the Depression of the 1930s. Considering the century from 1872 to 1972, it is probably fair to say that Seattle has been relatively more liberal, even radical, and certainly more Democratic in voting behavior than other parts of the West although it never deserved its description (attributed to then Postmaster General James Farley) as the "47 states and the Soviet of Washington." Seattle strongly supported Kennedy in 1960, while the state went Republican, and similarly supported Humphrey, who carried the state in 1968. In the state legislature Seattle normally elects two Democrats for every Republican.

After World War I, Seattle's growth slowed to a trickle. The 1920s were fairly prosperous, as Seattle reverted to dependence on its traditional raw material and service base (Figure 3). The 1930s Depression hit Seattle somewhat harder than the nation as a whole, and Seattle's Hooverville was among the larger and worse examples. It is worth noting that it was in 1936 that Dave Beck and the Team-

Figure 3. Downtown. By the 1930s downtown had moved uptown, where it remains today. The Olympic Hotel on the right is still the focus of Seattle's conventions, tourist buses, and airline terminal connections. The original heart of Seattle can be seen at the bottom of Fourth Avenue in the background.

sters began to emerge from the organizing strike against the Hearst-owned *Seattle Post Intelligencer,* with such tremendous power over labor, and even industry, in the region. But the new union strength was used conservatively, for stability, reflecting Beck's philosophy of negotiating cooperatively from a position of strength.

World War II led to Seattle's second great boom, again based to some extent on shipbuilding but this time preeminently on Boeing aircraft. Boeing had begun in 1916 and supplied planes to the navy in World War I. By persistent experimentation and salesmanship, Boeing survived the postwar slump and obtained a foothold in the small but growing aviation industry. During World War II aircraft employment soared as B-17 Flying Fortress and

B-29 Super Fortress bombers were built. From a 1940 metropolitan population of about 450,000, the 1950 figure reached 700,000. Such dependence on military production brought the expected deep recession at the end of the war. War in Korea again brought renewed prosperity for Boeing, with its B-47 and B-52 bombers, and the city advanced again. However, the marketing of the 707—a 1954 spinoff of the jet tanker for the military—and the subsequent boom in commercial jet aviation, offered a measure of independence on military orders and somewhat greater stability. The metropolitan population reached a million in 1960. Between 1961 and 1968 Boeing employment reached 100,000 as the company came to dominate world jet sales. A variety of other industries prospered as well, including the traditional forest and wood products sectors, recreation-based manufactures and services, and machinery of many kinds. A great expansion of business, service, health, and educational activities took place, both for local consumption and for export. During the 1950 to 1970 period there was a tendency toward concentration of people and economic activities in the greater Seattle metropolitan area, but also a marked decentralization out of the city not only into the suburbs, but into satellite towns and cities. During this boom period Seattle staged a World's Fair in 1962, its second successful exposition, resulting in acquisition of a superior cultural center.

Boeing had overexpanded, however, and was forced in the single year 1969–1970 to cut employment from 100,000 to 38,000 as demand for jet aircraft collapsed. The local and regional depression was severe. Unemployment reached 15 percent, and perhaps 100,000 people left the area, yet the population reached 1.2 million in 1970 in the urbanized area and 1.4 million in the SMSA. The volatility of employment and population makes planning difficult and has severely affected schools, welfare programs, taxes, and the willingness of voters to support improvements. For instance, the vote in favor of rapid transit in 1970 was inversely related to the proportion unemployed.

Since 1970 Boeing has recovered slowly, and other sectors, notably port activities and other manufactures and services, have held up or expanded. By 1973, Seattle had perhaps diversified and grown sufficiently to overcome its excessive dependence on Boeing, and ironically much of this nonaerospace growth has been in the traditional areas of wood, food, transport, and service. Moreover, for the first time in Seattle it is not considered eccentric to raise the question of whether further growth is really desirable.

THE SPECIAL NATURE OF THE SEATTLE ECONOMY

It is common for outsiders to think of the Seattle area as solely dependent upon the Boeing Company. While it remains true that when Boeing's business cools, Seattle shivers, the regional economy has diversified in many directions, providing a broad economic base with Seattle as the hub of a linked complex of urban centers. The cities of Everett and Tacoma, and a number of smaller centers including Bellevue, Bremerton, and Olympia, are closely tied to the central Seattle region.

Seattle's natural environment influenced considerably its industrial development. At the beginning of the city's history settlers began exploiting the natural resources of the region, particularly forests, fisheries, and farmlands. In addition to using these resources for local consumption, the pioneers quickly developed export markets for resource-based products.

The early forest products industry concentrated on the shoreline of Puget Sound. Trees covered the lowlands of western Washington, but their size made it impossible for logs to be moved long distances overland. Logs were put on "skid roads" and drawn by oxen to the shoreline where they were rafted to mills for processing (Figure 4). Most major urban centers on the shore of Puget Sound started as mill towns, catering especially to the San Francisco market created by gold rush demands.

As land was cleared by loggers in the riverbottoms of western Washington, it was often turned over to agricultural purposes. The Duwamish-Green River valley in South Seattle and King County, and the Snohomish-Snoqualmie River valley to the north and east of Seattle are examples of valleys which were settled for agricultural use. In these valley bottoms the soil is quite fertile in comparison to the young soils on the glacial draft on adjacent uplands. Although agricultural activity began in this region with the earliest settlement, the climate, physiography, and topography militated against the development of the region as an agricultural area. An important exception occurred in the 1890s, when the Green and Puyallup River valleys became the national center for hop production for a few years.

The three northern transcontinental railroads gave the Puget Sound region its first direct rail connections to the eastern United States. Demands for forest products increased rapidly, partly because of the general expansion in the nation's economy, and partly because of the depletion in upper Midwest timber supplies. In the period from 1890 to 1920 Washington timber harvests increased sixfold.

The transcontinental railroads' arrival coincided with an important change in the sources of energy used for transportation as well as industrial processing in the forest products in-

Figure 4. (A) Logging, which was the original economic base of Seattle, has been pushed into more remote locations as nearby forests have given way to urban development. Here logs are being tow-rafted from the northern reaches of Puget Sound to ports further south. Much of the lumber produced in recent years has been shipped to Japan.

Figure 4. (B) The loggers' profits are often the naturalists' anathema. The clear-cutting of the area's verdant mountainsides, despite modern methods of reforestation, is regarded by many as ecologically unsound and visually objectionable.

dustry. Steam-powered "donkeys" replaced oxen in hauling logs to yarding areas. Logs were yarded onto railcars for shipment to mills, instead of being rafted up in saltwater. These changes in technology allowed mills to be located away from tidewater.

During this period of rapid growth, Seattle became the railroad center of the region. Not only did Seattle handle most of the eastbound cargo of forest products, but it also served as the distributional center for goods brought to this region from the rest of the nation. Around this basis in trade and transportation, banking and finance developed, making Seattle the center of regional commerce.

Besides the boom in the forest products industry, rapid expansions also occurred in the fishing industry, especially salmon. The catch in Puget Sound increased tenfold from 1875 to 1910, with most of it either salted or canned and shipped East or to Europe. However, overfishing caused sharp declines in the catch after 1913. Subsequent catch levels have continued downward as overfishing has continued and the spawning capabilities of the fish have been endangered by man's disruption of the river systems. Fishing did not generate the level of immigration of the forest products industry, but it was quite influential in attracting Norwegian migrants.

Thus, the early history of this region was colored by periods of rapid expansion associated with the development of resource-based industries serving export markets. Each of these periods of growth has led to expansion in service employment to serve local needs. However, in the long run, capital goods wholesaling and the manufacture of other goods have also been significant and the relative importance of these economic activities has steadily grown as the Seattle regional economy has matured. Meanwhile, production in the formerly dominant lumber, agricultural, and fisheries sectors has been displaced to more remote rural locations.

Today manufacturing industries that serve the forest products, fisheries, agriculture, and food processing industries are important components of the regional economic base. They include producers of heavy motor trucks used for logging, rail cars, boats and ships, marine hardware and machinery, cargo-handling equipment, soft ice cream freezers, cannery and can-making machinery, logging equipment, sawmill machinery, and pulp and paper mill machinery.

The last several decades brought the aerospace, electronics, and metals processing and fabricating industries and specialized garment manufacture.

Like the manufacturing sector, the services sector of the economy has also matured since the turn of the century. The Seattle area now exports a considerable value in services to other regions. Services industries include the insurance industry (SAFECO), education (led by the University of Washington with over 34,000 students), medicine, trade, the port, and governmental activities. The tourist industry throughout the region is also important. Today, about 46 percent of the total value of regional industrial output could be considered basic, or destined for export markets (Figure 5).

The major components of the industrial base of the regional economy are concentrated in several zones. Each zone is dominated by several employers with a few large plants. The remaining elements of the forest products industry are primarily located in Everett and Tacoma; shipbuilding is found in Bremerton and on the Seattle and Tacoma waterfronts; food products processing is located in Seattle, in Tacoma (specialties include Rainier Beer, Crescent Spices, and Nalley Foods), and in Tumwater (Olympia Beer); and the Boeing Company is located primarily in South Seattle, Renton, Everett, Auburn, and Kent. Well-established growth firms exist primarily in the suburban regions, such as Mountlake Terrace (John Fluke Mfg.) and Bellevue (Sundstrand Data Control).

Most of these regional industrial specialties appear to be strongly integrated into national markets and need little from the local economy except labor and local services. They tend to purchase most of their material requirements from other regions and tend to sell most of their output in national and international markets. The notable exceptions to this pattern of backward linkages are the primary resource processing industries, but they have declined greatly in relative importance in the Seattle region.

The pattern of interindustry connections just described is nowhere better illustrated than with the Boeing Company. It started here in part as a speculative venture by William Boeing, the son of a well-to-do Minnesota family associated with the timber industry. During the First World War he decided to enter the airplane manufacturing industry. While Boeing's

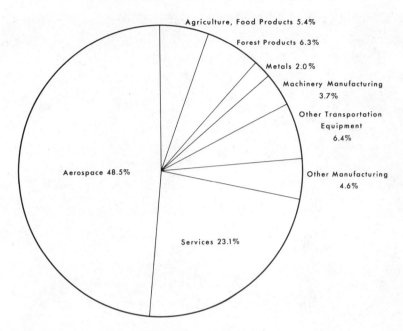

Figure 5. Basic or export workers in the Puget Sound regional economy. The basic workers considered here comprise 46 percent of all workers.

earliest efforts were of marginal success, during the period from 1920–1940 the Boeing Company had a history of brilliant technological developments in aircraft use and construction. Boeing pioneered in the development of airmail service and air passenger service and in the technology of aircraft engines and airframes. Both United Airlines and the Pratt and Whitney Company, now a division of United Aircraft Corporation, were owned at one time by Boeing. Antitrust action and other decisions led to the disposal of all but the airplane manufacturing phase of the company's operations by the early 1940s. During the second World War, Boeing's output expanded dramatically, and in the last twenty-five years the firm has led the development of commercial jet aircraft and has made modest entries into the space market.

Like many capital-goods-producing industries, the aerospace industry suffered from periodic fluctuations in the demand for its product. In recent years these fluctuations have been dramatic at Boeing and have strongly influenced the Seattle region's economy. Boeing buys and sells little in the way of goods regionally, but it is by far the largest employer. Changes in the Boeing employment level have multiplier effects on local services sector em-

ployment and important impacts on the local construction industry. In the period 1963–1968 aerospace employment climbed from 62,000 to 106,000 and then fell by 1971 to only 38,000 (Figure 6).

This massive change in Boeing employment within a decade had a variety of disrupting effects on the Seattle area. During expansion it stimulated vast expansions in housing, business activity, and infrastructure investments, while in the downturn that followed it triggered equally massive social costs in unemployment and welfare, created a stagnant housing and construction industry, and resulted in great burdens for state and local governments. At the bottom of the "Boeing" recession in 1971, the community's dependence on Boeing received scathing treatment. However, as time passed and as Boeing's employment began to increase again, the interest in diversification began to soften. When Boeing expands rapidly, many try to cash in; in times of Boeing-related decline, the company is portrayed as the bad guys. It is no wonder that considerable effort has gone into a program to attract additional industries to this region, although it is widely recognized that growth at any price is undesirable.

Figure 6. "As Boeing goes, so goes the Seattle region." This maxim has certainly been true of the Seattle economy since World War II. Here, in the vast interior of the Boeing 747 assembly plant in Everett, two body sections of a superjet are being joined. The famous Boeing 747 plant at Everett is some thirty miles north of Seattle. In fact, Boeing planes are no longer made in Seattle but in such places as Renton to the south and Everett to the north. The Boeing Space Center is located in the Green River valley far to the south.

Residents of the Seattle region are acutely aware of the high quality of their environment and have mixed emotions about going through another boom caused by a program of industrial diversification. The traditional industrial specialties of the region are relatively pollution free, and there is great concern on the part of government, citizen groups, and industry to assure that new development is equally desirable. Whereas there is disagreement on the geographical distribution that new development ought to take in this region, most feel that it will expand even in the face of a national zero population growth rate. The environment is laden with amenities, and popular fiction argues that, just as hordes have filled up California and Florida, they will move on to other places with desirable environments. Some already decry the "Californication" of the Pacific Northwest, and in truth there is an important migration stream between the Seattle region and California.

While it is too soon to assess accurately the results of the latest efforts to change the composition of Seattle's economy, recent events do not suggest that any new manufacturing activities on the scale of Boeing are likely. The services sector has continued to expand just as it has nationally as people spend more of their income on services. Some major new facilities are envisioned for the region, such as the navy's proposed Trident submarine service base with direct and indirect employment projected at 20,000, and the currently indefinite impacts of the development of North Slope Alaskan oil. However, contemporary forecasts for regional growth are uncertain as to whether the jobs created in these and other basic industrial developments will lead to a labor surplus or shortage. Under any circumstances, it appears that for the next few decades the Seattle region will continue its dependence on industrial activities tied to renewable natural resources found in the Pacific Northwest and Alaska, and an uncertain dependence on the aerospace and related industries.

The Peopling of Seattle

IMMIGRANTS TO A CONTINENT'S EDGE

Unlike the large American cities which were beachheads for arriving hoards of immigrants, were located at important crossroads, were in the path of major urban and industrial developments, or were sunshine salesmen, Seattle has not been an easy place to get to or a place where the living was particularly easy. Practically all Americans who have come to Seattle have made a decision to take great leaps in space to get to a place far away and very different from home. While only seventeenth in population among American metropolitan areas, Seattle is still more than 700 miles from a larger city.

It is this property of being "far out" that has most influenced the nature and variety of Seattle's population. It first attracted an odd lot of frontier-prone adventurers from diverse origins. Today, though unexceptional in size, it is the most important urban focus in the territory west of Minneapolis-St. Paul and north of San Francisco to Alaska. It is the largest regional city—in terms of big money, cultural activity, and educational opportunity —for the entire states of Washington, Idaho, Montana, Alaska, and parts of Oregon. While these areas are thinly populated, they are geographically so diverse that the lumberjack in the Cascade foothills, the Wyoming cowboy, the aspiring musician in Anchorage, the Montana wheat farmer, and the ambitious junior executive in Spokane have all looked to Seattle for metropolitan fulfillment. On the other hand, Seattle has also become home for sizable numbers of Asians, Southern blacks, Scandinavians, and smaller numbers of other ethnic groups. In each case, because of the vast distances separating these groups from their origins, a selective process has been operating. Migrants have generally chosen the city for its challenge and setting rather than its having been chosen for them by family, labor recruitment, and ease of travel. For easterners, getting to Seattle meant coming all the way. With the exception of Alaska it is not on the way to a fresher frontier and, power shortages notwithstanding, it is not on the way to brighter lights.

Once in Seattle, the hardy migrant often found himself far from his family and remote from the influence of American styles and norms. Thus, in what amounts to a rather isolated city—short on history and extralocal traditions, ringed by a diverse environment embracing the sea, islands, mountains, forests and fertile lowlands, and peopled by a disproportionate number of pioneering and individualistic souls —an atmosphere of tolerance developed in which a number of unusual lifestyles has emerged. Only when those who are different raise real or perceived threats to the economic or social well-being of the majority does prejudice and cultural xenophobia rear its head, as it did against the Chinese in the 1880s, the Japanese during World War II, or the blacks and Indians in Seattle today.

Most of the peculiarities of population discussed here apply to the central city of Seattle rather than outlying districts or suburbs elsewhere in the metropolitan region. Proportions and census figures thus relate to the city of Seattle unless otherwise indicated.

THE MAJORITY: IMMIGRANTS FROM BACK EAST

Most of Seattle's population is white, nominally Christian, and at least third generation American. Though original ethnic identity is maintained in Irish, German, French, or Scottish names, such roots are not deemed particularly important. Rather, if for some reason these individualistic souls seek some kind of identity of origin, they are more likely to rally around the state they came from. Like southern California, which has its share of all American immigrants, the Seattle area has its Minnesota Club and Montana Day.

Tavern conversations often are initiated over regional origins. No one really expects anyone over eighteen to have been born in Seattle. Anyone coming from somewhere east of Idaho might be considered an "easterner." Easterners are usually identified as having an accent. New Yorkers are considered almost unintelligible.

Thus, the majority in Seattle are a somewhat rootless lot, imbued with frontier social ethics. Local society cares little for protocol. Mountain climbing is preferred to social climbing. The rich and the famous have listed telephone numbers. Blue jeans pass in most nightspots; never mind the absence of a necktie. Casual relationships blossom in minutes, though the person you just told your life story to may skip town the next day. On the other hand, one might know none of his neighbors and is not supposed to care.

The "natural selection" which has been operating on the population mostly through the mechanism of migration has also occurred in the course of Seattle's economic ups and downs. The depression and widespread unemployment in the early 1970s caused by the Boeing setback is illustrative. Many people left Seattle at the nadir of difficulties for jobs in other parts of the country. Those who stayed, in essence, liked Seattle better than money and scrimped their way through the worst or, in the case of many skilled engineers, formed their own businesses. Thus, Seattle has been left with the more ingenious and the more environmentally oriented.

THE SINGLE AND "SURPLUS" MALE

The remoteness of the Northwest in some senses places it in the category of a separate country. The establishment of settlement by Americans began as a parallel to the English settlement of the United States. Seattle's pilgrims debarked from a small sailing ship in 1851 on a shore as unknown as and more impenetrable than Plymouth in 1620. Although Oregon was already a major settlement by 1851, Seattle's settlers were as isolated from their original homes in the East and Midwest as Plymouth was from England, and were at the edge of a forest with taller trees, amply stocked with Indians and wild beasts.

But at this point the parallel ends. Seattle's settlers were not escaping an atmosphere intolerant of their beliefs. Nor were they interested in agricultural self-sufficiency, despite their remoteness from the American economy as a whole. Rather, they were largely an ambitious lot of young men, with a strong background of pioneer experience, bent on commercial enterprise. They were decidedly "Americanized," as the first census of King County in 1859 showed. It enumerated 302 people, including 301 native white Americans and one Negro. These settlers were hardly a cohesive social unit. Unlike the planned colonial experience, they had stumbled into the Puget Sound country independently, some drawn northward from Oregon's Willamette Valley, others from California's gold rush. Instead of one nucleus of settlement, several had already emerged. Finally, the populace was hardly familial. In the early 1850s single males so dominated the white population of western Washington that there were nine men for every woman. To maintain their claim on acreage men had to live on their land for five years. Their lonely plight was summarized in an 1860 advertisement (cited by Roger Conant) appearing in a local paper:

> Attention Bachelors: Believing that our only chance for a realization of the benefits and early attainment of matrimonial alliances depends upon the arrival in our midst of a number of the fair sex from the Atlantic States, and that, to bring about such an arrival, a united effort and action are called for on our part, we respectfully request a full attendance of all eligible and

sincerely desirous bachelors of this community to assemble on Tuesday evening next ... to devise ways and means to secure this much needed and desireable emigration to our shores.

The notice was signed by ninety-three bachelors.

In response to this situation, Asa Mercer, brother of one of Seattle's first pioneers, began a mail-order bride business. But this hardly solved the problem. The frontier town of Seattle was not aimed toward community so much as enterprise. Its population throughout much of the rest of the nineteenth century continued to be male-dominated as the adventurous and unattached found opportunity as sailors, loggers, and millhands. The Yesler sawmill which produced this situation in the first place emerged as the center of town. And by the

1880s, with the continuing shortage of women, the center of town became a recreational center (Figure 7). Gambling, drinking, prostitution, and burlesque amusement flourished, particularly with the influx of even more men outfitting themselves for the Klondike at the turn of the century.

Today, while the central business district has moved north of Yesler Way, the area south of Yesler still retains some of the characteristics peculiar to men alone (Figure 8). It is Seattle's Skid Road, no longer connoting the transportation of logs as Yesler Way is now a major arterial to the eastern edge of the city, but acting as a service center or miniature central business district for the detached male. In this area, in the shadow of once grand turn of the century buildings now used as warehouses or lofts, are found the cheap hotels which furnish the bare necessities of shelter to the

Figure 7. Toward the end of the nineteenth century, Yesler Way, originally Skid Road, was the major thoroughfare leading east away from the harbor. To the north (left), steep hills impeded development until regrading was accomplished. South of Yesler Way a rowdy red light entertainment district flourished.

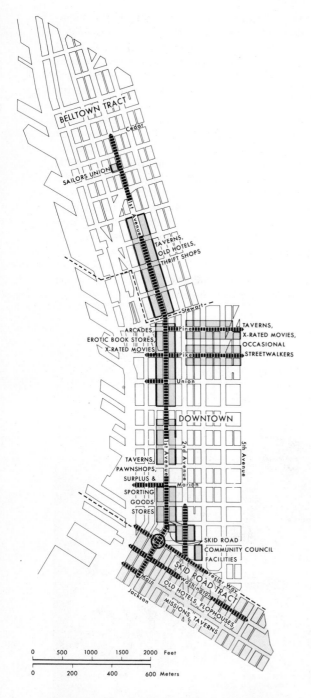

Figure 8. The "ragged edge" of the waterfront is the haunt of Seattle's single and surplus males. Among residents there are about three times as many males as females, mostly single. Tavern density is the highest in the city and other establishments of a furtive nature are also found here.

older men of limited income or the younger man on a binge. Here, too, are the cheap cafes, often using a meal ticket system so that the sober customer can provide himself with the security of nutrition in less sober times. Also here are the missions which administer to the needy, seedy, and down and out, exchanging hot meals or other aid in return for attendance at prayer services. Ironically, this same area caters to another group, which is neither particularly old, detached, or alcoholically prone. Skid Road contains the majority of Seattle's gay bars, perhaps mostly because of the anonymity it offers, but somehow symbolic as reflective of the area's sex ratios.

On First Avenue north of Stewart Street and the CBD is the Belltown area, a string of beer and wine taverns, with virtually all-male patronage. The Skid Road man intermixes with the sailor on shore and the after hours worker. The tavern chain continues on Pike and Pine streets to the east, and these thoroughfares, between busts, are a traditional haunt of Seattle's prostitutes.

An odd kind of symbiosis exists between some of Seattle's arts and crafts merchants and the derelict male. The latter has found a niche in Seattle's center, with its often sweeping views, significant architecture, or potential of a thread of a connection to some extinct moment in history. These qualities may mean little to him, yet his presence helps depress rents, as the big investor is unlikely to locate posh facilities in an area habituated by undesirables. The art merchant's sensitivities may be such that not only is he attracted to the grimy building fallen from grace, but he also may find the derelict colorful and stimulating. Thus, beginning in the late 1960s, art galleries and design shops began opening in refurbished facilities, helped along by low rents, accessibility to downtown, and customers who weren't repulsed by Skid Road. By 1971 whole buildings were being renovated for offices, restaurants, and shops. Rents, of course, began going up, pushing out some of the Skid Road population, along with some of their old hotels and other facilities.

Renovators emphasize the name of the neighborhood as "Pioneer Square" rather than Skid Road. The Skid Road population was squeezed to the north, but rents also got too high for some of the gallery owners who "pioneered" on Skid Road, forcing them out of business. In several instances the Belltown area, toward which the Skid Road population was pushed, was eyed as a potential studio or gallery site.

While Seattle today, like every major American city, has more women than men, there are other remnants besides Skid Road of the surplus detached male days. Seattle has more single men (never married) than single women (never married) and nearly 6 percent of all the population are males living alone, a figure surpassed only by San Francisco among major cities. Seattle still has its famous outfitting shops for the hunter, the climber, the skier, the prospector, the fisherman, the woodsman, and the sailor, and it is the attraction of these traditionally masculine roles which supposedly keeps many in the area.

ETHNIC DIVERSITY

European Influences

A stranger, if given the statistic that 28 percent of the city of Seattle's population is classified as foreign stock—that is foreign born or of foreign or mixed parentage—might expect to find European ethnic districts typical of eastern and midwestern cities. Such areas are generally absent in Seattle for several reasons.

One reason is Seattle's remoteness from eastern ports of European immigration. Those who journeyed overland to the distant Northwest were undoubtedly more independently minded and removed from the old country, needing little of the transitional support which ethnic districts could provide. In some cases, settlement in the Midwest preceded the trip to Seattle. Once in the Northwest they found a rather individualistic society, tolerant of individual differences but to some extent culturally xenophobic. Finally, due to its proximity to the Canadian border and linkage to Alaska via Canada, Canadians make up about one-fifth of Seattle's foreign stock, but Canadian areas even if they existed would be difficult to distinguish from others.

Other European groups such as Irish, Italians, Greeks, and Russians comprise less than 2 percent of the population and with the exception of Greek and Russian churches show few ethnic trademarks on the urban landscape. Germans in Seattle present a different case. Hein-

rich Wilhardt, of German extraction, who later changed his name to Henry Villard, was a key figure in the group who brought the Northern Pacific Railroad to Seattle. Villard disseminated propaganda in Germany encouraging emigration from Germany and settlement on lands owned by the railroad, attracting considerable numbers of Germans to Washington and Seattle. By 1910, German natives comprised nearly 8 percent of the city's population. The Germans, including German Jews, had been very active in commerce and had founded for themselves a large number of fraternal, athletic, and cultural organizations. However, the outbreak of World War I and anti-German sentiment caused a partial exodus of the German population. By 1930, German natives were less than 2 percent of the total population. In 1970, German *stock* comprised approximately the same proportion but there was little tendency toward residential clustering.

Of the various European nationality groups, only Scandinavian settlement developed the ethnic neighborhood pattern. The term Scandinavian here includes only Norwegians and Swedes, Danes being much less numerous and scattered. Together, Norwegian and Swedish foreign stock make up almost 5 percent of Seattle's population. A great deal of the Scandinavian immigration to Seattle occurred in the first decade of the twentieth century following completion of rail connections to the upper Midwest in the 1880s. Minnesota, Wisconsin, Michigan, and the Dakotas were each dotted with Scandinavian agricultural colonies which preserved language and folkways. Seattle's Scandinavians came mainly from these areas, with others arriving directly from Scandinavia via merchant marine vessels. Many of the initial immigrants found employment in fishing and logging, occupations familiar to them. At the turn of the century, the new settlement of Ballard, politically distinct from Seattle at that time, was being developed as a rail head, fishing port, and lumbering focus, simultaneously with the Scandinavian wave of immigration. Despite the passage of time and the rapid assimilation of European peoples which Seattle has afforded, the Ballard area and the adjacent neighborhoods of Phinney and Fremont still retain a concentration of Scandinavians (Figure 9). Some tracts contain up to 30 percent Scandinavian stock. With most of the Scandinavian

SCANDINAVIAN FOREIGN STOCK POPULATION: 1970

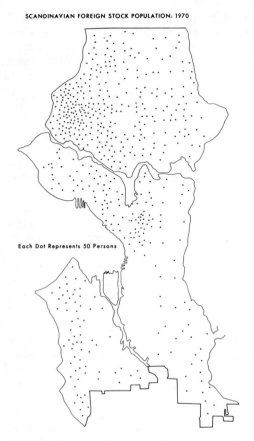

Each Dot Represents 50 Persons

Figure 9. Scandinavian residents are indicated by dots placed in census tracts. Note the concentration in the Ballard area. Norwegian and Swedish immigrants helped settle this section in the 1890s.

restaurants, delicatessens, and bakeries in Seattle, the Ballard landscape also is enhanced by a memorial to Leif Erikson and meeting places for fraternal organizations (Figure 10). But in the Puget Sound region the most Scandinavian-conscious place is undoubtedly Poulsbo, a small fishing town settled by Norwegians which, with one eye on tourism, has painted and decorated all shops in a neo-Norwegian manner.

Easterner Meets Westerner:—The European and Oriental Kaleidoscope

Unlike the European immigrant who had little difficulty fitting into pioneer Seattle, the immigrant from East Asia was notably disadvantaged and segregated. Marked by racial characteristics resembling the American Indian

from whom northwest land had been wrested, satisfied with less remuneration for goods and services than the white pioneer would expect, and, in the case of the Japanese, instant reminders of enemy forces during the Second World War, the Oriental in Seattle has left concentrated imprints in certain parts of the city.

The Chinese were the first to arrive. Chinese contract laborers had been used in California as miners and railroad workers since the gold rush. Under the contract labor system, the men who imported a worker and paid his fare had the right to send him as a member of a labor gang wherever services could be contracted. By the

LEIFR EIRIKSSON

Figure 10. Tribute to the famous Viking sailor Leif Erikson at Ballard. Many of the Norwegians who originally settled in the area came via the Norwegian merchant marine and pioneered in the fishing industry.

1870s the Northwest required cheap labor to mine coal, can salmon, and build the Northern Pacific Railroad. Chinese first imported to California were then drawn northward. In Seattle itself a concentration of Chinese sprang up at the foot of Yesler Way in the 1870s. They were employed in building boardwalks over the swampier parts of downtown, in paving streets, and as domestic servants. Chinese who came independently of labor contracts, or who had completed the tenure of a contract, typically entered the laundry or restaurant businesses. An estimated 300 Chinese lived in Seattle in the early 1880s, with several thousands more located elsewhere in the state of Washington. The completion of the Northern Pacific Railroad in 1883 and the Canadian Pacific Railroad in 1885 unleashed hundreds of unemployed Chinese laborers who headed for Seattle and other coastal cities. By the winter of 1886 this concentration of an unemployed racial minority so disturbed many of the white citizens of Seattle that they formed an anti-Chinese congress to rid Seattle of Chinese. Expulsion of Chinese from small towns all over western Washington had already taken place. After a public riot more than 300 Chinese were assembled and expelled, moving south on steamers or railroad, notably to San Francisco. Those who remained recongregated near Second and Jackson, to the south and east of their original location.

The Chinese Exclusion Act of 1890, which banned immigration from China to the United States after a number of public demonstrations similar to Seattle's, sharply curtailed the growth of the Chinese minority in the city. Not until 1909, when the Alaska-Yukon-Pacific Exposition created a demand for large numbers of common laborers, did the Chinese population begin to grow substantially. At this juncture, in fact, it grew so rapidly that the existing neighborhood could not provide sufficient housing and a second nucleus of Chinese settlement sprang up farther to the south and east, centered around Seventh Avenue and King Street. This district has survived through the decades as the center of the Chinese community. It contains the distinctive buildings of the tongs or clan associations and the rows of angular neon letters proclaiming Chinese restaurants, import shops, and cultural organizations.

Chinatown—or the International District, as it has come to be called due to proximity of Japanese and Filipino institutions—is really only a cultural and commercial center as only several hundred of Seattle's Chinese actually reside there. The residents are generally single older men living in dreary rooms in cheap hotels, something of an Asian surplus male community. Others living in the area are recent immigrants, ignorant of English and working in Chinese-owned establishments. Among this latter group are modern-day counterparts to contract laborers, sometimes paying a debt for being smuggled past immigration officials as well as for passage from East Asia. The census probably undercounts this group (Figure 11).

The rest of the Chinese have generally dispersed east and south. While small numbers of Chinese are found in most parts of the city, Beacon Hill seems to possess the largest concentration. While the term "Chinese" denotes an extraordinary range of subcultures owing to the regional differences within so large a country as China, the origin of Seattle's Chinese is rather homogenous. Some 95 percent of Seattle's 9,200 Chinese have roots in one district of the Canton province of South China. The remaining 5 percent, hailing from various areas of North China, are a rather special group, generally better educated and professional, sometimes called Chinatown's cultural aristocrats.

The history of the Japanese in Seattle is rather different from that of the Chinese. Sizable numbers of Japanese arrived in Seattle only after 1890—the date of the Chinese Exclusion Act. Rather than being predominantly contract laborers, the early urban Japanese included many small businessmen who managed small hotels, grocery stores, and dry cleaning establishments. Contract laborers were used mostly in rural areas on farms, on railroads, and in mines. The original neighborhood of Japanese settlement in Seattle was east of Skid Road, centered around Fifth Avenue between Main and Jackson. This area was immediately north of the second Chinatown established with the Chinese influx that occurred during the Alaska-Yukon-Pacific exposition. This began the era of the International District and in a way foreshadowed today's "Asian student" movement and "Asian power".

During World War I there was increased demand for the services of the Japanese and the Japanese community in Seattle continued to grow. But with Washington's Anti-Alien

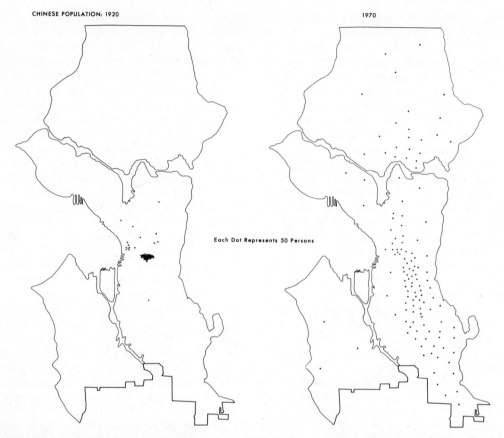

CHINESE POPULATION: 1920   1970

Each Dot Represents 50 Persons

Figure 11. Great changes have taken place in the pattern of Chinese settlement in Seattle between 1920 and 1970. The tightly clustered pattern of 1920 in what is now called the International District has dispersed largely to the southeast. However, the International District is still the commercial and cultural heart of the Chinese community.

Land Law in 1920, making it illegal for foreign-born Japanese to own land, and the Immigration Act of 1924, which practically curtailed all Japanese immigration, growth in the 1920s was severely limited, though already the community had outgrown its original neighborhood and spread eastward along Jackson and Yesler Way.

The Second World War brought grave consequences for the Japanese. All Japanese living on the Pacific Coast west of the Cascades and Sierras were evacuated to interior areas because of the suspicion they aroused. Most of Seattle's Japanese were removed to an isolated area in Idaho and their property in Seattle fell by forced sale into other hands. Often black migrants who had found jobs in the booming war economy found housing in what had been

Japanese neighborhoods. With the closing of the evacuation camps toward the end of the war, many Japanese moved to other parts of the nation rather than return to Seattle. Thus while the census of 1940 reported 6,975 Japanese, only 5,778 were counted in 1950. Since then, during the years of general prosperity, family building, and some new immigration, the community has grown steadily, so that in 1970 there were almost 10,000 Japanese. While a small number continue to reside in the International District, this fraction, like the Chinese there, are generally male, single, and elderly. Major concentrations occur to the east along Yesler Way and to the south on Beacon Hill. In addition, given the growing affluence of the community, Japanese have moved into several suburban areas as well as

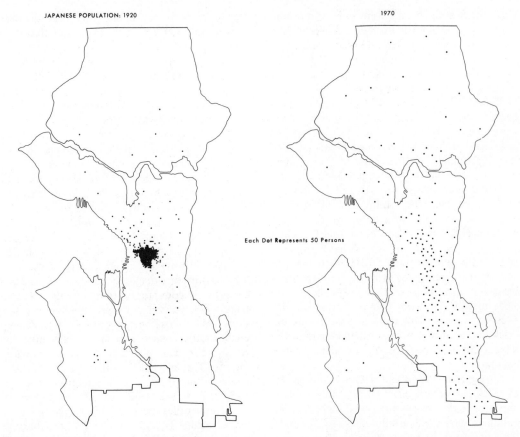

JAPANESE POPULATION: 1920 — 1970 — Each Dot Represents 50 Persons

Figure 12. Like the Chinese, the Japanese have also diffused out of their original neighborhood of settlement. Their movements between 1920 and 1970 were in essentially the same direction. Greater scattering among the Japanese reflects both the forced relocation during World War II and economic assimilation.

practically every neighborhood in Seattle (Figure 12).

Seattle also has a sizable Filipino community, dating back before 1920, although this was the first year that Filipinos were separately counted in the census. First settling in the International District with their fellow Asians, they have also dispersed in much the same directions. In 1970, of the 5,830 Filipinos reported in Seattle, a handful live in the International District where there are a few Filipino restaurants, bars, and organizations, but most have scattered to areas east and south with less concentration than the Chinese and Japanese.

Black Seattle: An Unlikely Feature

Of the forty-eight contiguous states, Washington is the farthest removed from the major southeastern source areas of American blacks. Furthermore, its transportation linkages, before the availability of commercial airlines, were primarily with California to the south and with the upper Midwest to the east, regions which were themselves in possession of very few blacks. Given these geographical constraints, the fact that Seattle should have a sizable black population today attests to the ambitious migration of the black man seeking opportunity.

Ironically, one of the two first settlers in the state of Washington was black—George Bush, who had left Oregon in part because of the law prohibiting blacks in the Willamette Valley. With Michael Simmons he pioneered in the southern end of Puget Sound, near Olympia. But the ensuing pioneer years in Washington and Seattle brought few blacks in Bush's footsteps. In Seattle, blacks were greatly outnumbered by Asians until the Second World War. The 1890 census counted 286 blacks in Seattle, a figure which slowly grew to 3,789 in 1940. During this time, blacks comprised less than 1 percent of the total population.

Before 1890, the small black population of Seattle was living on the northern edge of the town's center. But during the 1890s a clustered settlement of blacks developed in a section of the city atypical of other parts of the country. William Gross, a black who had served in the navy and later owned a Seattle hotel, was given a parcel of land on a hilly part of Madison Street in payment of a debt. At that time, Madison Hill was also a popular area for white citizens; it was attractive, somewhat peripheral, and hardly deteriorating. Gross's settlement in the Madison Hill area attracted other black residents and while white residents in the area initially opposed them, eventually land sales were made. This shift in location of the black community can be ascribed largely to the respect for William Gross in the larger Seattle community.

During the 1920s and 1930s other nuclei of black settlement emerged. An area consisting of mostly single men and deteriorating buildings developed around Jackson Street to the east of the Japanese, while another section around Yesler and 23rd Avenue attracted a more familial population. These three areas described the vertices of a backward letter L and by the late 1930s the spaces inbetween the points were beginning to fill in. They were not the only places in which blacks could live. Since 1920, the first year in which tract statistics were available, at least several hundred blacks were living in other parts of the city. Yet it should be pointed out that in those years before World War II, Seattle had the smallest black population of any major American city (Figure 13).

The wartime influx of blacks attracted by the great number of defense-related jobs in Seattle upset the superficial accommodation by white Seattle of its black population. To some extent blacks were able to move into the housing vacated by the Japanese relocated to Idaho, but this was hardly enough. Wartime housing shortages, intensified by increased white resistance to integrated neighborhoods, caused both doubling up and allocation of the least desirable housing to incoming blacks. And after the war, with continuing boom in defense-related jobs with Boeing, black population in Seattle continued to grow—even as whites were moving to the suburbs. Black population reached 15,666 in 1950, 26,901 in 1960, and 37,868 in 1970. Thus, from only about 1 percent of the city's population in 1940, the black proportion rose to over 7 percent in 1970.

The 1970 census indicates that blacks can be found in virtually all developed areas in King County, including the exclusive suburbs. Generally, however, their proportion in outlying districts is less than 1 percent. More than half the black population continues to live in the Central Area, a wedge of census tracts astride Madison Street and Yesler Way. A good deal of the housing in this area was once Jewish, the Jews having moved in great part to suburbs. Thus a former synagogue has been remodeled to a black community center while a Jewish bakery-delicatessen survives in what is essentially an all-black neighborhood. The eastern edge of the black population concentration reaches the ridge which overlooks Lake Washington. The lakeside of the ridge is expensive lakeview property and is effectively cut off from the cityside by a lack of through streets. At several other places in the periphery of the black residential area similar physical barriers maintain a separation between blacks and affluent whites, and in some places the lakeview alone is enough to keep white families in an area with black neighbors. Thus, in the expansion of black residential areas in Seattle, the nearest places are not always the most likely destination; rather, blacks have generally followed in the paths of other minority groups. Now that the old Jewish areas have largely been relinquished to black ownership there seems to be a trend toward movement southeast to the Beacon Hill area, in the wake of the Japanese.

The origin of the black population currently in Seattle is extremely varied. Much of the migration resulting from kinship and friendship ties stems from Texas and Louisiana. Blacks from these states often migrated westward rather than northward and settled in Los Angeles or San Francisco. A proportion of these then migrated to opportunities northward, and others followed. Another important factor in bringing blacks to Seattle was and continues to be the armed forces. Young black men released from the service have found Se-

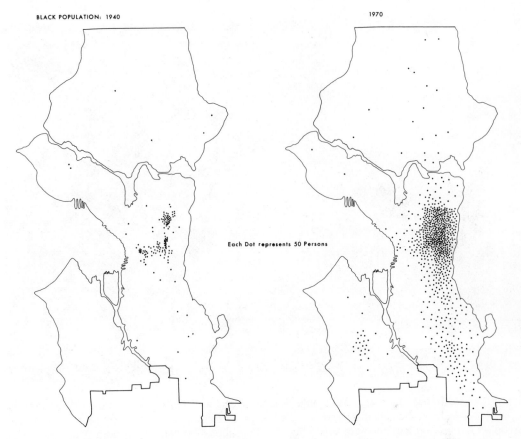

BLACK POPULATION: 1940   1970

Each Dot represents 50 Persons

Figure 13. The 1940 residential distribution of blacks shows the three separate areas of concentration, forming a reversed L, mentioned in the text. The northernmost area is Madison Hill; the 23rd and Yesler area lies to the south, while the westernmost is on the fringe of Skid Road and the International District. A great influx of blacks during and after World War II filled in the areas in between. The 1970 pattern shows the enlarged concentration called the Central Area. In both maps, however, as well as in earlier periods, small numbers of blacks were scattered in different parts of the city.

attle to be a challenging place to work or to continue their education.

While indeed the black population of Seattle faces discrimination, unemployment, and, in many cases, poor housing and neighborhood conditions relative to whites, the overall physical environment in the ghetto is objectively hardly comparable to that found in eastern and midwestern cities. Within Seattle the mean family income for blacks in 1969 was $9,059 compared to $12,871 for whites. The figure for blacks was one of the highest in the nation and the differential one of the smallest. A good deal of the housing in the Central Area consists of well-kept bungalows, particularly

in the valley beyond Madison Hill (Figure 14). Most of the housing is in older single family homes which, though deteriorating and in some spots abandoned, does not at all exhibit the crowding and danger of the tenement slum. The Model Cities program in Seattle, which embraced the Central Area as one of its model neighborhoods, has been rated as one of the best in the country. During its tenure considerable new construction has taken place.

The Return of the Native

Before the first white settlers arrived, most of what is today the Seattle urbanized area was the domain of Duwamish and Suquamish In-

Figure 14. Although there is considerable residential segregation in Seattle, much of the housing in predominantly black neighborhoods consists of well-maintained, smaller single family, owner-occupied homes. Perhaps the lush vegetation makes it look better than it would if the trees were gone.

dians. Their headquarters were in what is now Port Madison on the other side of Puget Sound; several thousand Indians frequented the land around Elliott Bay. "Formal title" to the land was not obtained until 1855 when two million acres of western Washington land were purchased for $150,000 in a treaty which also established reservations for the Indians. This sale is, on the surface, a better deal than Peter Minuet's purchase of Manhattan Island, but the terms of the treaty called for a twenty year installment plan and the exchange of useful articles instead of money. It worked out to about $1.80 worth of trinkets per Indian per year.

The treaty had come about through a meeting between Territorial Governor Stevens and Chief Seattle (Sealth), who presided over the two Indian tribes. Seattle was wise enough to sense that the white man's dominance over the land was inevitable, and in an eloquent speech (quoted by Nard Jones) foretold, "At night when the streets of your cities and villages are silent and you think them deserted, they will throng with the returning hosts that once filled and still love this beautiful land. The White Man will never be alone." While Seattle was speaking of the spiritual, it is in part true in the corporeal.

With the exception of a brief skirmish in 1856, the local Indians more or less left Seattle to the white man. They generally retreated to their reservations or land outside the treaty. Of course, some of Seattle's lonely men took squaws for wives, but the extent of this practice is unknown as separate and extensive enumeration of Indians was not undertaken until 1890.

Census reports reveal that very few Indians lived in Seattle for much of the twentieth century. The Indian population in Seattle was only twenty-two in 1900 and only 222 in 1940.

Seattle old-timers recall picturesque Indian street vendors of baskets and the like. Significant growth occurred in the next thirty years, the population reaching more than 1,700 in 1960 and more than 4,000 in 1970. The figures for 1960 and 1970 area, however, based on self-identification, rather than census takers' opinions. Thus, the earlier figures may reflect an undercount. Despite recent gains, Indians still continue to make up less than 1 percent of the city's population.

The Indians living in Seattle today are by no means a homogeneous group representing the original tribes. Rather, they have been drawn from throughout Seattle's hinterland in the Northwest and Alaska. This area, not long removed from frontier status, has a relatively high proportion of Indians in its population. In western Washington alone there are more than a dozen Indian reservations and on many of these significant economic activity including logging, fishing, and tourism is in progress. Indians represent a small minority, but they are among the least educated. To correct this, special programs in university education and teacher training have been instituted.

Within Seattle, Indians are dispersed more than any other racial minority group, which probably in part reflects the multiplicity of tribes. Light concentrations exist in areas containing public housing projects, reflecting low economic standing. Another concentration occurs in the vicinity of the lower end of the central business district, indicative of that portion of the Indian population on Skid Road. It is estimated that this mostly male group comprises more than 10 percent of the Skid Road inhabitants. Ironically, it was in this same area that Chief Seattle made his prediction. Significantly, a bust of the chief and a totem pole have been erected at the corner of First and Yesler and several blocks to the north is an Indian Community Center (Figure 15).

Mediterranean Migrants: The Case of the Sephardic Jew

Most of the Jewish people in the United States migrated from Germany in the 1840s and from Poland, Russia, and the Ukraine after 1890. A very small proportion of Jews, however, may be traced to Mediterranean areas, vestiges of settlements dating back to the Spanish Inquisition. This latter group is called Sephardic as distinct from the Ashkenazi or Eastern European Jews. Though Seattle has a small community of Ashkenazi relative to other cities, it has a surprisingly large number of Sephardim, numbering over 3,000. Only New York and Los Angeles have more. Moreover, while most American Sephardim are descendants of migrants from England, Holland, and Spanish and Portuguese new world possessions in colonial times, Seattle's group is of much more recent vintage.

The origins of the community can be traced to those chance events which often brought other people to distant Seattle. In 1903, a fisherman named Solomon Calvo who came from Marmara Island in Turkey went ashore in Seattle and was impressed by the city. Upon returning home to Turkey, he persuaded a friend named Jacob Policar to join him in emigration. Calvo began selling fish in the Public Market, while Policar operated a fruit stand. Their success was motivation for acquaintances living on the island of Marmara as well as smaller towns around the Sea of Marmara to follow in their path. In 1904 another Sephardic Jewish immigrant, Nessim Alhadeff, this time from the island of Rhodes, came to Seattle on the basis of information he learned from Greek sailors. Thus, in the ensuing years, both a Rhodes community and a Marmara community of Sephardim developed.

Their native tongue was Ladino, a mixture of Spanish and Hebrew, as opposed to Yiddish, the German-Hebrew dialect spoken by the more numerous Ashkenazi. Their music and foods were influenced by Greeks and Turks, and certain liturgical observances differ sharply from those of the Ashkenazi Jews. Despite the commonality of religion, the early years saw little fraternization between the two groups.

With increasing affluence, the Sephardic Jews moved out of the Central Area where the established Jewish community lived and built their own synagogues in the Seward Park area in the south of Seattle. Although intermarriage between Sephardic Jews and Ashkenazi Jews is not uncommon, the Sephardim have maintained a physical separation and a geographic concentration which has kept much of their unusual culture intact.

THE ADVENTURESOME LIFESTYLE POTPOURRI OF SEATTLE

The West Coast of America—with its diversity of physical environments and climate and with

Figure 15. A bust of Chief Seattle dwells at Pioneer Square, not far from the site where the city's namesake addressed assembled Indians and pioneers prior to treaty arrangements. The totem pole behind the bust, which symbolizes "Indians" to many, was stolen from Alaska. Totem-making tribes were not located in the Puget Sound country. Today, ironically, Indians concentrate in the vicinity of the statue; several taverns frequented by Indians are in the area as well as an Indian Social Center. It is near the railroad station and the docks—both likely foci of Indian migration to the city.

a population which is in large part heir to adventurous pioneers, rugged individualists, and free spirits—has been a likely place in which new lifestyles have spawned or where lifestyles spurned by other places may take hold. Seattle, much like Los Angeles and San Francisco, has its share of youth culture and counterculture.

In his book, *The Dharma Bums,* Jack Kerouac put Seattle on the map of beatnikdom, commenting on the city on his way to the North Cascades where he served as a fire lookout. In the Skagit Valley, just west of these mountains and some sixty miles north of Seattle, there has been a migration of young people attempting alternative lifestyles in rural towns or agricultural settings. As it lies on the freeway which connects southern California to British Columbia, Seattle plays host each summer to footloose and thumb-extended crowds on their way from one scene to another.

Seattle's University District, heavily populated by both students and nonstudents, is an oasis for young people, providing not only youth-oriented goods and services in its commercial area, but connections for transportation, accommodation, and hallucination. The University District became a focus of hippie activities during the 1960s and a bit of the campus came to be called Hippie Hill. Both Capitol Hill and the Fremont area, districts with diverse population having available inexpensive housing, were also centers in which hippies congregated. Today, such areas host the communal lifestyle, in which older homes are rented to groups of unrelated individuals. These districts also are the location of halfway houses for drug addicts, young runaways, and ex-convicts.

Eccentric cults also thrive in Seattle. Some followers of Edgar Cayce, the psychic healer, have made Seattle their center, since Mount Rainier possesses special meaning in some of his readings. "Jesus freaks" abound on the sidewalks of downtown. The Children of God, colonies of proselytizing young Christians, are also very numerous. And the devotees of meditation, organic food, and yoga have all found good karma in Seattle. Here, too, are the Dinky People, a collective accentuating humility, and the Society of Free Space Colonizers who are laying the groundwork for leaving earth.

POCKETS OF WEALTH AND POVERTY

In the Peyton Places, Main Streets, Middletowns, and Metropolises of the United States, social status is clearly stamped on space for all to quickly comprehend. The railroad tracks; a prominent hilltop; a sooty, smelly industrial district; or a fashionable avenue serve to demarcate space in such a way that a resident's class is generally indicated by where he lives.

But in Seattle the individual idiosyncratic nature of the population has conspired with a rugged topography and a sinuous double shoreline to effectively mute the typical symbols and contrasts of income level and prestige found in other cities. Wealth here tends to face away from the city; the homes of the rich are oriented toward choice views across Puget Sound to the Olympic Mountains or across Lake Washington to the Cascade Range. While city skyline views abound along the edges of Lake Union and portions of Capitol Hill, Queen Anne, Beacon Hill, and West Seattle, they are most likely to be from the windows of middle class apartments and homes and older mansions upgraded by young professionals.

There are quite a few vicinities in which may be found the monied classes with 1970 incomes of $25,000 or more. They have not, by any means, simply fled to the suburbs. Most census tracts fronting Lake Washington or Puget Sound, particularly to the north, possess above average family incomes and a disproportionate number of wealthy households. But given the uneven topography, wealth is also occasionally clustered higher on the hillsides. In both cases, transportation arterials, commercial facilities, ridge obstructions, ravines, and what might be called a sense of "residential egalitarianism" have enabled the less prosperous, including working class families, to find residential riches in nearby streets.

Even the few neighborhoods in Seattle which are the local "exclusive" preserves by virtue of their bounded nature and symbolic paraphernalia are juxtaposed with, though protected from, outstanding contrasts. Broadmoor, once the most exclusive community in Seattle complete with ethnically screened residents, is an entry-guarded enclave of substantial eastern style homes surrounded mostly by the University Arboretum and its own golf course. But elsewhere, its high brick wall shields it from a surrounding, substantially black area of varied status. Windermere, with its uniformly wide lawns, rambling newer homes, private park, and distinctive street lamps, occupies land on Lake Washington adjacent to the Sandpoint Naval Air Station. Blue Ridge, on a hillside above Puget Sound, containing varied impressive homes heralded by an equally impressive entrance, also overlooks the railroad tracks.

The locations of lower income families are somewhat more predictable. The southern half of the city, more disturbed by industry and transportation, contains the majority of census tracts in which families below the poverty line live. Areas with the oldest housing—the Central District, lower Capitol Hill, the fringes of downtown, Georgetown (an early industrial nucleus on the Duwamish), and lower Ballard —are the poorest. But as Seattle is a low density newer city and a relatively prosperous one in which many jobs demand high skill levels or education, there are neither the physical nor social conditions to produce the squalor or slum conditions associated with the poorer parts of most American cities.

A few public housing projects have been built in the city but all are small clusters of one or two story structures in widely different locations in the southern half of town. Ironically, one of these projects, High Point, actually crowns the hilltop in West Seattle. Much lower income housing then is relatively inconspicuous, often in smaller older houses and apartments tucked into different parts of the city. The concentrated poverty of Seattle is more visible on Skid Road (discussed earlier in this section), and is produced as much by a culture of alienation as a landscape of economic segregation.

Urban Response to the Natural Environment

THE MAGIC MOUNTAIN— MOUNT RAINIER

"Only the natives can see it," is the standard answer to the perennial question of Seattle visitors who ask "Where is Mount Rainier?" Such an answer reveals much about the climate of western Washington and perhaps even more about the people who reside here. Although Mount Rainier is rarely seen because of the weather, and is much closer to Tacoma— indeed is claimed by Tacoma as *their* mountain —it is truly the magic mountain of Seattle. A major promotional device is to photograph Mount Rainier with a telephoto lens in such a way as to make the unaware viewer think that Mount Rainier rises out of the very navel of another piece of sacred territory, Seattle's central business district (Figure 16).

The importance of the magic mountain is demonstrated locally in many forms. In Seattle, it is "mountain fresh" Rainier Beer; Rainier National Bank; a major social club, the Rainier Club; and until recently a baseball team (now defunct) called the Rainiers. Lately, however, common labels seem more related to aircraft than mountains—for example, the Seattle Pilots (another defunct baseball team) and the Supersonics (professional basketball team)—and one radio station has dubbed Seattle the "Jet City". However, in more realistic terms, a few natives, perhaps mindful of the Emperor's New Clothes, refer to Mount Rainier as Mount Rain-ier. Yet they also continue to treat the mountain in a mystical way as a weather forecasting device, surely superior to the local weather forecasts which must rank among the least reliable in the nation: "If you can see Mount Rainier, it's going to rain; if you can't, it's raining." Regardless, it is a rare day when Mount Rainier is visible all day long (Figure 17). The natives, however, have little difficulty in looking in the right direction for many major streets and landmarks are oriented to the magic mountain—for example, Rainier Avenue and plazas such as at the University of Washington's Rainier Vista.

Such mystical orientation (at least to the outsider), coupled with streets which are highly irregular because of the hilly topography, makes Seattle one of the easiest cities in the United States in which to become disoriented. Of course, bleak days with no visible sun are also a prominent factor in general disorientation. As might be expected, automobile compasses are much in evidence for this reason as well as as a nostalgic reminder to the native that he would rather be sailing than driving.

THE HEAVENLY COVER

Another statement reflecting the climate in Seattle is the common weather forecast of "partly sunny." While this may strike newcomers as odd, it quickly becomes apparent that whereas "partly cloudy" is the standard forecast of sky conditions for other parts of the country, "partly sunny" is fully appropriate for Seattle. The weather bureau reports that some 70 percent of the time about 70 percent of the sky is covered with clouds. As the world-

Figure 16. Mount Rainier as concocted and usually shown for promotional purposes. This shot typically shows downtown Seattle with Mount Rainier dominating the background and is a most interesting type of local photographic fakery. This shot of the downtown area was taken about 1946 from the site of the present Seattle Center.

traveled geographer J.N. Scheepers announced after spending a year in Seattle, "The skies here are no different from places like Cherapunji, India, where more than 400 inches or so of precipitation fall annually."

Heavy precipitation does not accompany such massive cloud cover. Outsiders are amazed to find out, and the natives are quick to tell them, how little precipitation actually occurs in the Seattle area. It averages about thirty-five inches per year, which is about as much as Chicago. The main feature, however, is not how much precipitation falls but how long it takes to fall. It drips, drizzles, and floats suspended most months of the year. And with

such cloud cover, there is little insolation, so evaporation is considerably slower than might be expected. Dampness, mildew, and sweating of windows and the like are common. And inasmuch as it is damp almost continuously, most of the vegetation is very shallow rooted, especially lawn turf. Even a few days of fairly sunny and rainless weather will cause most Pacific Northwest lawns to turn brown and the natives to cry "drought."

The climate in western Washington is much affected by maritime conditions (Figure 18). Consequently, its hottest month is often August rather than July. Hot, however, is clearly too strong a term as contrasted with other

Figure 17. The real Mount Rainier (upper left) as it appears from Seattle is shown here and should be compared with the imaginative work of Figure 16. It is little wonder that the typical visitor, after seeing the typical Chamber of Commerce shot of Mount Rainier, asks "Where is Mount Rainier?" This aerial view is from Lake Washington and it somewhat exaggerates the prominence of Mount Rainier.

areas in the United States. A common statement of outsiders is to the effect that "the coldest winter I ever experienced was summer in Seattle." Air conditioning is unnecessary, although stores and restaurants are increasingly air conditioned. Homes rarely are air conditioned. In fact, furnaces are commonly used a number of days in both July and August.

By contrast, the winters are relatively mild. Some years no snow falls and the temperatures in lowland areas may not dip below freezing. Some characteristically avoid putting antifreeze in their automobiles, only to find that the unusual has happened and the engine block has cracked. When it does snow in Seattle, even a few inches can cripple transportation. Schools close, people abandon their automobiles, and people from the Midwest who ob-

serve such panic first hand commonly curse and blame inexperience on the part of the drivers for the problem. In fact, the many hills in the Seattle area, the lack of snow tire protection, and the common icy conditions of roads in such weather truly do make driving hazardous.

An observer of automobiles in the city would nonetheless be struck by a sizable number of vehicles with the most elaborate equipment for rugged weather. Snow tires with studs are so common as to be a cause of serious road deterioration problems. The basic reason for this is not the periodically severe winter weather in the city, however, but the mania for the Cascade ski slopes an hour or so away to the east. Ski carriers on cartops abound—some even on cars which are owned by nonskiers simply

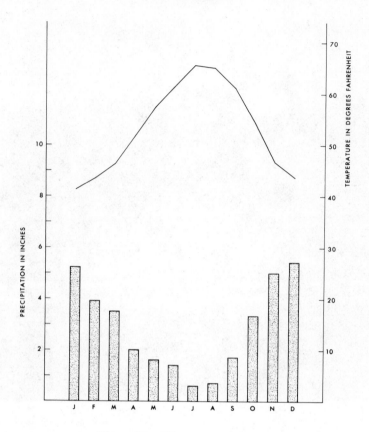

Figure 18. Climatograph of Seattle.

for prestige purposes—and each evening and weekend during winter sees a caravan of vehicles traveling to and from the lighted slopes.

THE OUTDOOR HEDONIST, WASHINGTON STYLE

The climate of Seattle has resulted, paradoxically, in a form of outdoor hedonism. Seattleites have seemingly gone recreation mad like most of the nation, yet the type of recreation sought is specially suited to their climatic conditions. Like millions of other Americans, they seek out ski slopes and go wild over snowmobiles and the like, but they are also avid boaters as a result of the proximity of Puget Sound. There is one registered pleasure boat for every six families. Sailing, cruising, and fishing are major recreational activities.

Yet, because of climatic conditions, some otherwise expected recreational pursuits are very much lacking. The first of these is swimming. Although parks and beaches abound on Puget Sound, these are rarely used by swimmers because of the coolness of water which varies from 55–60° F. Skin divers are a growing exception and many diving clubs exist in the area. Lake Washington, a fresh water lake surrounded by city, is only slightly warmer in summer (65–70°) but much cooler than the sound in winter (42°). The sound beaches are used for sun bathing more than water bathing, or more commonly for picnicking. Another problem of swimming at Puget Sound beaches is the rocky and barnacle-laden shoreland which is also heavily lined with driftwood, much as the result of log rafts used by the timber industry. As would be expected, water skiing is little practiced except by the most spartan types.

The climate also appears to be largely responsible for the general paucity of tennis courts, outdoor swimming pools, and elaborate outdoor barbecue patios. Seattleites commonly have patios Washington-style—covered to keep out the rain. On the other hand, golfing seems to be little affected by the rains, perhaps saying more about golfers than about weather or climate.

REMOVAL OF THE
PRIMEVAL COVER

Few cities started with a more primeval vegetative pattern—great forests of Douglas fir— and few have so completely eradicated it. Unlike most cities wherein man has either heavily used the natural vegetation or added considerably to it with domesticated plants, Seattle has largely removed the original vegetative cover. It has planted many domesticated species in its place, but the overall picture is one of wall-to-wall asphalt and structures rather than one of a verdant forest. Local promoters might quickly and correctly argue that there are still many naturally vegetated areas within Seattle, but this is a scant vestige compared to the original cover of first class forests. In fact, most of the houses hidden by vegetation are outside the Seattle city limits. Thus Seattle in its treatment of its natural vegetation has preferred the artifacts of man to the bounty of nature.

Seattleites had strong commercial motives for removing the natural vegetative cover. The very site on which Seattle stands, somewhat like Butte, Montana, on the site of copper ore, contained a mine of timber. Trees were cut not only to make room for homes but to feed the voracious timber industry. The very center of Seattle became a "skid road" for a timber and lumber mill, one of the first industries in the city. The growth of the city, therefore, literally ate its way into the forest about it and is still doing so.

Whether the natural vegetation would have remained even if it had not been commercially exploitable is doubtful. Because of the persistent but light rainfall and the nature of the coniferous trees themselves, shallow-rooted trees develop. When coupled with the rather violent and not uncommon windstorms of the area, such shallow-rootedness makes any freestanding Douglas fir a potential and dangerous windfall. Thus, it is rare to find tall timber within falling range of dwellings in the Seattle area. Nevertheless, as attempts are made by the more nature conscious clientele of suburbia

to save the trees, such tall timber-laden residential areas abound. During the violent winds, however, newspaper photographs commonly depict certain of these trees that have crashed down on the roofs of nearby homes.

One other aspect of the natural vegetation has also resulted in vast clearing of land. The underbrush in the Pacific Northwest forests is more junglelike than parklike. It is almost impenetrable, being filled with all manner of thorns and berry bushes. The ground area is unusable for outdoor recreation in its purely natural state.

Finally, as is evident on the basis of the climatic features discussed above, sunshine is in short supply and therefore in high demand. The dense natural vegetation keeps the limited available sun from reaching the ground. Moss on the north sides (sometimes all sides) of trees is common and lichenlike substances are quick to accumulate in almost all shaded areas, on concrete steps, brick walls, or shingled roofs. Thus, the typical Seattleite usually opts for as little shade as possible. In fact, the typical "Washington patio" reflects this need. Such patios are not covered simply to keep out the rain, but are characteristically roofed with translucent material to let in all available light.

Despite what has been done to the natural vegetation, it must not be assumed that Seattle is without an abundant domestic vegetation. Flowers abound, as do flowering shrubs. In the early spring and throughout the summer, Seattle is one of the most beautifully flowered cities in North America. Rhododendrons are especially common and startle most visitors because they appear to be a more subtropical type of plant. They are native to the area, however, and thrive because of the cool summers and lack of severely cold winters.

Seattle yards are characteristically landscaped with rock gardens, perhaps a reflection of Japanese influence, and mounds laden with various shrubs. Flowering plums, hawthornes, and various vine plants abound. Roses, although plentiful, are somewhat of a problem because of the dampness, which encourages mildew and various plant diseases. Likewise, the lilac is not in much evidence as compared to warmer areas. Rhododendrons and azaleas are most common. In a few choice spots the strikingly beautiful madrona tree is found and these provide year round greenery. Finally, coniferous plants of all types are common and in some small way provide some nostalgic remembrance of the original vegetative cover.

HIDDEN HOMES

Perhaps also because of a climate that restricts it, visibility is highly valued in the form of view. Houses are commonly advertised as having a peek-a-boo view of Mount Rainier or Lake Washington (usually from a bathroom window) or as having a sweeping vista view of the Cascades, the Olympics, or some other feature. Consequently, a good view is highly prized by Seattleites and they are evidently willing to pay dearly for it. They also place view above almost any other consideration, even a flat lot and a foundation that will not slip away in the next mudslide. Consequently, many houses are perched precariously on steep slopes and a number of them each year are affected by earth slides (Figure 19).

Paradoxically, the houses of many elite forego the views and instead are hidden by vegetation (Figure 20). Most houses in the Highlands, just north of the Seattle city limits, and an exclusive area in Woodway further north, feature wooded and hilly lots rather than view lots. Thus, these people chose housing more in the tradition of the rich and elite of other parts of the nation than the majority of Seattleites. It seems to be characteristic of the upwardly mobile and aspiring middle class in Seattle to give up all other residential comforts for the almighty view. In fairness, however, it must be pointed out that many of the elite have flat lots, wooded surroundings, plus a spectacular view. But for most citizens a choice among these must commonly be made.

THE TERRAIN: BANE OR BOOM?

If you should ask the typical Seattleite about the terrain of Seattle, he would probably tell you how fine and picturesque it is. He would no doubt point out that Seattle has seven hills —perhaps mythical, since no one names the same seven—with great views of the sound and the many lakes. He would insist on how scenic Seattle is as compared with most other cities, and he would be right! Seattle is picturesque. It is visually impressive in the manner of San Francisco. The many hills and the water breaks provide impressive aerial postcard shots. They

also result in a terrain-induced land use pattern with residences on the hills and arterials and business in the valleys. For example, the large Duwamish River alluvial plain to the south encouraged the development of a compact industrial-railroad sector.

Yet upon closer examination it is soon noted that Seattle's site is far from ideal for a large city. In fact, early settlers of Seattle were quick to recognize the imperfections and promptly set out to modify them. Hills were too steep and in the wrong places. Other areas were too low, suffering periodic floods, and even the shores were awkward for shipping. The northern part of the downtown area was too high, the southern part was too low, and the port side of Elliott Bay became too deep too close to shore.

To correct these conditions several massive regradings were undertaken. Streets in one area were raised twenty feet or more. Today a lively tourist curiosity exists in underground tours in the Pioneer Square area. The regrades were representative of the major inadequacies of the Seattle site. The city engineer, R.H. Thompson, undertook one of the most extensive remodeling works of nature on record at that time. Denny Hill was reduced by sluicing 110,000 cubic yards of material by high-powered hydraulic hoses and depositing it around the base of the hill. The Jackson Street area was regraded in 1907, followed by the Dearborn regrade in 1912. Many other hills were also lowered and remodeled in this period. In the process, much of the tideflat area south of downtown was filled in (Figure 21).

The terrain also stood as a type of curse with respect to Lake Union and Lake Washington. These inland bodies of water were unconnected to the sound. Thus, another major modification was undertaken in 1911 by the U.S. Army Corps of Engineers. Locks and a channel to the sound were opened in the late summer of 1916 and, in the process, Salmon Bay was raised slightly and Lake Washington was lowered by twenty-one feet. Today, this lock has allowed the heavier sea water to seep into Lake Union and even threatens Lake Washington with ecological upset (Figure 22).

Lake Washington
Seattleites are fond of pointing out the assets of Lake Washington, a massive 22,138 acre, twenty-seven mile long freshwater body

Figure 19. Hillside homes in the Seattle area. (A) Many homes are precariously perched on steep embankments overlooking Puget Sound. (B) Fabulous views are obtained by some of the wealthy who are fortunate enough to have a fairly level lot on the edge of a steep slope.

(A)

Figure 20. Hidden homes in the Seattle area. In a few areas of Seattle the landscape looks almost unoccupied. Steep slopes, in particular, hide many homes. Because of the steep hillsides, multi-storied residences are much in evidence.

in the very midst of the urban fabric. Its shore-line and scenery attract view-oriented residences, but the lake also interferes with smooth transportation within the urban complex. Moreover, it encourages motorboats with all their pollutants and noise as each shoreline resident plus others beyond try to get their fair share of lake use. In late summer the deafening roar of the hydroplane races is enough to breach the peace of any community other than Seattle (Figure 23).

But the major difficulty with Lake Washington has been its former use as a sewage dumping ground. By the early 1960s ten sewage

Figure 20, continued. Hidden homes in the Seattle area. (B) The third story here is at ground level above.

plants were dumping twenty million gallons of largely untreated sewage into the lake each day. In addition, thousands of septic tanks around the shore were adding their share of pollutants through seepage. The lake had become discolored, most beaches were unsafe for swimming, and algae covered most of the lake shoreline surface.

The cleaning up of Lake Washington is one of the more touted local success stories. In 1961, the Municipality of Metropolitan Seattle (METRO) was established with the explicit purpose of building a modern sewage system which would divert sewage to Puget Sound and replace the septic-tank-laden shorelands. METRO initiated a major sewer system project at a cost

Figure 21. The Denny Regrade as seen in 1929. Such hills as this were sluiced (note sluice on left side of picture) in order to provide a better site for Seattle. Land taken from hills was used to fill low tidewater areas elsewhere.

of some $145 million. Since the lake though large and deep has a rather short flushing time of three years, dramatic results were obtained within a decade. By 1968 phosphorus content in the lake had been reduced from seventy parts per billion to twenty-nine parts per billion. The water was once again fairly clear. Now the problem appears to be underwater plant growth because of the increased sunlight reaching bottom near the shores—plant growth which fouls boat propellers, creating a condition which is visually somewhat analogous to the former conditions of algae.

Lake Union

When Lake Union was first assessed in the nineteenth century it was envisioned as a great inland industrial port. The dream was to con-

nect this body of water to Puget Sound and use it as a protected port, a task not completed until 1916. Consequently, the first industry on the lake was the establishment of Denny's sawmill on the south shore near the downtown area in 1882. By 1906 a great gas plant was established on the north shore. The sawmill is long gone, but the gas plant remained as a shut down, obsolescent, and unsightly landmark. Tentative plans call for converting its peninsula to a lakeside park.

Despite major development of the lake with the opening of the ship canal and the government locks, Lake Union has not met industrial expectations. Instead it has become ringed by a vast assortment of problematic and often conflicting shore use types. Substandard houseboats edge out into the water and create a form

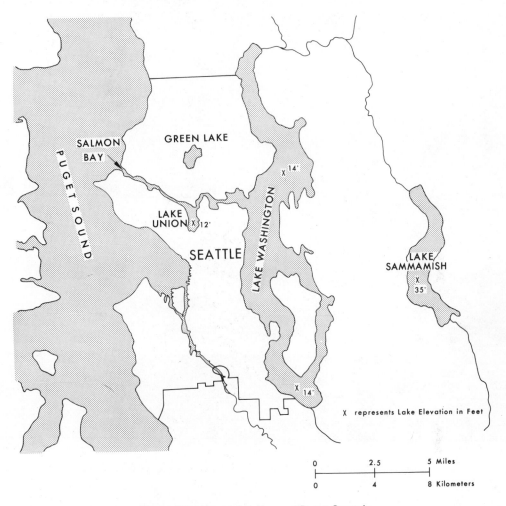

Figure 22. Seattle's lakes and Puget Sound.

of picturesque water-based urban slum. Moored along the shore they are in conflict with other boating use of the lake. Indeed, a five knot speed limit on the lake is policed to keep boat wakes from causing shore disruptions. Apartments invaded the area and block views of residents further back.

Today untidy looking structures crowd the shoreland. Old shabby residences are found next to fashionable apartment buildings and restaurants. Railroad tracks crowd the shorelands in places and obsolescent ships stand foundered in the water, a reminder of better days.

The Port

Another physiographic problem of the early site of Seattle was the harbor. In fact, it was navigational problems which prompted the first settlers to abandon their initial site at Alki Point in West Seattle for what came to be the present shoreland. The portside of downtown Seattle, while adequate for early development, was plagued by water too deep too soon. Pilings could not be extended very far from shore so that even when piers were angled to gain greater length, they simply were inadequate for the big ships of the early twentieth century. Consequently, Harbor Island was developed at the estuary of the Duwamish River. The product of city landfilling and Duwamish River dredging operations, this massive island was developed for private use. As might be expected, the older wharves and piers adjacent to downtown Seattle have become technologically obsolete. Most today are either in disuse

Figure 23. Hydroplane phenomena on Lake Washington in late summer.

or are being used for such things as ferry transport, restaurants, motels, tourist attractions, and general retail operations.

The extremely deep water of Puget Sound at short distances offshore has been beneficial to commerce of late. A foremost example is the massive grain elevator complex on Elliott Bay to the north of the business district. Here the $15 million Pier 86, with forty acres of reclaimed land, receives large grain ships. One of the most automated grain facilities in the world, it can load at a rate of some 3,000 tons per hour and can handle ships up to 1,400 feet long.

In another example one wonders whether nature's endowment of deep water is an asset or a deficit. Much to the concern of some, Puget Sound provides one of the few potential land port possibilities for supertankers.

All Those Ferries

Perhaps the most obvious and dramatic evidence of the physiographic problem of Seattle is shown by its massive bridge and ferry systems. Although water bodies are highly scenic, they are surely more heavily weighted on the deficit side of the economic balance ledger. To the east, Seattle's growth was blocked by Lake Washington, to the north by Lake Union and adjacent water areas, and, most awesome of all, to the west by Puget Sound. The history of Seattle could largely be written from the standpoint of its attempt to "bridge" these great water barriers for spatial spread and development.

Ferries were developed early on both Lakes Washington and Union. Madison Street terminated at ferry slips connected to ferries bound for Kirkland and Laurelhurst. It was not until the early 1940s that Lake Washington was bridged. The famous floating bridge connected Bellevue via Mercer Island to Seattle. On its western end, because of the steep hill, an impressive tunnel was required. Residential development grew rapidly on Mercer Island and in Bellevue. Today Bellevue is the largest suburban expanse outside Seattle and owes most of its growth to improved access to Seattle.

A second floating bridge, the Evergreen, was built across Lake Washington in the early 1960s. This likewise has accelerated growth of settlement on the east side. On the negative side, however, these bridges are bottlenecks, and dangerous ones at that. Many have been killed on the Mercer Island Bridge—sometimes because of malfunctions in the reversible lane. The Evergreen Point Bridge is the most dangerous stretch of road in Washington. It is along these two bridges that traffic congestion is worst.

Today, there is talk of a third and fourth bridge over Lake Washington. The most imminent will carry Interstate 90 parallel to the Mercer Island Bridge. However, inasmuch as the extension of this freeway to Interstate 5 would disrupt much of a low income residential area, it has been bogged down in controversy. From the standpoint of demand there is no question but that greater access to the east is needed, yet it is equally likely that additional roads will encourage even greater traffic across the lake.

The bridging of waters to the north, although less controversial, has been no less difficult or impressive. Major north-south routes all require bridging. Highway 99, locally known as Aurora Avenue, bridges Lake Union waters by the George Washington Bridge. And Interstate 5 bridges the eastern side of Lake Union on an impressive double-decked structure.

To the west, bridging has not as yet been undertaken, except to the south at Tacoma where the famous Narrows Bridge is found (Figure 24). There has been much talk of other bridgings, but to date only ferry services prevail. Consequently, many commute to Seattle from such places as Bremerton on superferries. Today, twenty-one double-ended ferries operate in Puget Sound. Eight ferry routes cross Puget Sound, of which the most important for Seattleites are the Seattle-Winslow, the Seattle-Bremerton, the Edmonds-Kingston, and the Mukilteo-Columbia Beach (Whidbey Island) runs. Each year these ferries carry a total of over 300,000 passengers and 200,000 vehicles —a mere trickle compared to the former San Francisco-Oakland ferry system that carried forty million a year in the 1920s. Such movement, however, given its relatively high costs, is more a reflection of low interaction than high. On the other hand, the relative inaccessibility of the Olympic Peninsula and the many sound islands has helped to preserve amenity-based recreation lands, or at least it has preserved such lands for the wealthy, those who can purchase boats, or those who have leisure time sufficient to justify the purchase of "beach homes" on the island (Figure 25).

Community Enclaves and Topographic Conditions

The lakes and hills which permeate the greater Seattle area encourage frequent intermixtures of different land uses. Fine homes are situated to take advantage of views and special physical amenities almost irrespective of nearby uses. Some elite homes are found next to some of the meanest dwellings. In not a few instances, however, a steep bluff or ravine provides a reasonable buffer zone. Likewise, the hilltops commonly contain housing with the arterials confined to the valleys, a meaningful pattern in terms of cutting down what would otherwise be a series of land use conflicts.

Sharp breaks in relief have also allowed the creation of a number of rather independent suburban communities. Despite their economic reliance on Seattle, these communities remain surprisingly provincial in their appearance and in the outlook of their residents. Such outlying communities as Edmonds, Bothell, Redmond, Renton, and Burien are distinctive communities in their own right. In fact, some of their public and cultural affairs, including art fairs and civic orchestras, occasionally outshine Seattle's. Nonetheless, the residual buildings of the Seattle World's Fair, now the Seattle Center, focus metropolitanwide performances in this center. Community events sponsored by suburbs also use these facilities for their performing arts.

Like most central cities, Seattle continues to lose population, whereas suburban communities multiply and prosper. But Seattle, like most central cities, is trying hard to maintain

Figure 24. The famous Narrows Bridge in Tacoma. Its ill-fated predecessor was blown to pieces by the winds in November 1940. This is one of the few places where the sound has been bridged.

Figure 25. Beach cabins on Puget Sound islands (Camano Island). Note the abundant driftwood on the beach, but the general lack of trees near the cabins. A Cascade Mountain peak, is shown in the background.

its relative importance within the metropolitan complex. The most recent coup was the construction of the massive domed stadium immediately south of the downtown despite careful studies that demonstrate the best site to be outside the central city. Likewise, the Downtown Association is constantly providing promotional assistance for all types of downtown renovation projects ranging from the renewal of Pioneer Square to placing a lid on the freeway in the downtown area in order to create a minipark. Nonetheless, the writing is clearly visible on the urban wall. Most of the growth will go to the suburbs.

Controversy and Conflict in Seattle:
Neighborhood Scale

CAPITOL HILL: THE CHALLENGE OF DIVERSITY

Within a mile of the central business district of most of America's cities are areas whose characteristics have been altered profoundly over the years. Among such areas are those that began as high class residential areas. With passing time and a growing city, the larger homes and more luxurious houses were subdivided into rental rooms and apartments for an immigrant minority. Others became funeral parlors and nursing homes; still others were demolished and replaced by high-rise apartments or commercial structures. Some survived the first phase, only to become the targets of urban redevelopment projects and plans.

The Capitol Hill area in Seattle is something of an exception to this general trend. Though not without important changes nor free of current problems, Capitol Hill still retains an impressive nucleus of well-kept turn of the century mansions. It also has many sterling middle class houses which have been well maintained despite the intrusion of newer residential and commercial structures. Thus, in addition to its older single family houses, it contains modern high-rise apartments and a number of spacious brick apartment houses built during the 1920s. Rather than being solely a residential area, Capitol Hill is also notable for its wide range of shops and small businesses (Figure 26).

Like its structures, the neighborhood also offers a variety of classes and characters. Thus, while so many American cities are stratified

like Seattle by age, class, race, and lifestyle, Capitol Hill not only has the architectural conditions for diversity, it also has the social material. The hill is "home" to the old and the young, the hip and the square, the rich and the poor, the black and the white, the stable and the transient.

Despite its internal diversity, Capitol Hill in some respects is similar throughout. Treating Capitol Hill as a region, the feature of similarity is paradoxically its diversity of structures and people. The core of Capitol Hill, where diversity is most apparent, is Broadway, the major shopping street and the first business district to develop outside downtown. From Pine Street north to Roy Street, Broadway presents an uninterrupted juxtaposition of storefronts. In addition to the contrasts generated by elegant restaurants and drive-ins, by chic boutiques and secondhand shops, the street is also enlivened by churches, nightclubs, theatres, and a community college—a unique mix (Figure 27).

The Edges of Diversity

The western boundary of Capitol Hill is symbolized by alienation. Interstate 5, Seattle's north-south freeway, cuts a broad swath through the city, separating modern apartments on the western slope of Capitol Hill from a light industrial area west of the freeway. Not only is the freeway a barrier to pedestrian and vehicular movement as well as an intense source of noise, but "alienation" is also in a way reflected in the residents. The apartment houses on the western slope of the hill con-

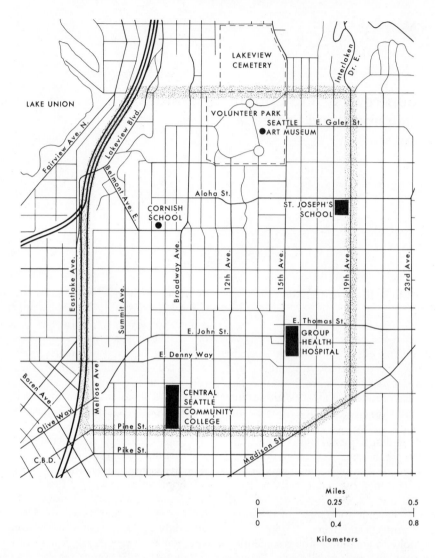

Figure 26. Capitol Hill is an unusually diverse inner city neighborhood perched on a hill east of Lake Union, between downtown and the university. The area was named when Seattle's pioneer promoters envisioned it as a site for the territorial capitol, which went to Olympia instead.

tain many of Seattle's singles and transients. In the census tract including this area there were only 1.44 persons per household compared to 2.94 percent for the metropolitan area as a whole (Figure 28).

Pine Street marks the southern boundary of Capitol Hill. Along this artery a rather solid block of warehouses, small businesses, and automotive services effectively terminates the intermixture of small homes and apartments to the north. That the residential property is

less desirable in this vicinity shows up in the census. The blocks fronting Pine Street are generally the lowest in average rent of any on Capitol Hill, averaging approximately $70 per month as compared to $105 for the hill as a whole.

The eastern boundary, inspiring paranoia, is 19th Avenue. While only a minor arterial, this street is a classic case of racial tension. On the west or Capitol Hill side of 19th the blocks south of Roy Street typically contain 5 to 30

Figure 27. A stroll down Broadway, the commercial heart of Capitol Hill, reveals an unusual mix of businesses including franchised ice cream and drive-in outlets, exclusive furniture stores, taverns catering to different subcultures, and the locksmiths that are indicative of high robbery rates.

percent black residents while across 19th Avenue blacks generally form the majority. Elderly residents worry about muggings, and white mothers living on the west side of 19th Avenue warn their children not to cross the street to the playfield on the other side. The storefronts along the avenue are mostly vacant,

some showing evidence of vandalism. Several houses on the street have been abandoned.

Galer Street forms Capitol Hill's northern boundary which is at the margin of structural diversity. North of Galer Street, single family homes dominate the landscape. There are no high-rise structures and only a few older apart-

Figure 28. In this view to the south, the western edge of Capitol Hill (on left) is terminated by Interstate 5. Downtown is to the rear on the right.

ment houses. Shopping possibilities are minimal. This has come about for a variety of reasons. To the east steep grades prohibit the extension of transit lines. Westward lies Lakeview Cemetery, the last repose of Seattle's founders. Moreover, a steep slope allows only two through streets, fostering a sharp transition of land uses.

The Community of Twenty Thousand Differences

Capitol Hill is home to 20,000 people. Hundreds of others work in the area. Large employers are Central Seattle Community College on Broadway and Group Health Hospital on 15th Avenue. The presence of these facilities, on the hill's two major commercial arteries, has encouraged a development of shops and restaurants beyond that which would be expected on a business street catering to a strictly residential neighborhood.

An unusual assortment of cultural institutions is also found on Capitol Hill. At Harvard Avenue and Roy Street, in a white colonial-style building, dwells Seattle's chapter of the

Daughters of the American Revolution, while across the street the Cornish School, in an unusual baroque stucco edifice, turns out dancers, musicians, and artists. A block away, at Harvard and Broadway, is the Deluxe Tavern, at times a watering spot for Seattle's arty and hip underground. Several blocks to the south, on Pine Street, are found the headquarters of the city's Masons and Oddfellows. Finally, nearly a score of churches dot the neighborhood, from Catholic and Episcopalian to Greek Orthodox and Seventh Day Adventist.

Volunteer Park is the recreational focus of Capitol Hill and is to Seattle as a whole something like what Golden Gate Park is to San Francisco. It houses Seattle's conservatory and the historical collection of Seattle's art museum and features summer band concerts and dramatic performances. In a city where nature "as is" commands so much respect, Volunteer Park is exceptional for its formal layouts of flowers and trees.

The park is also the focus of continuity of wealthy residents in the vicinity. Developed at the turn of the century in commemoration of

Seattle's Spanish-American War volunteers, the park just predated subdivision of the land around it. When building lots were put up for sale in this choice region in 1901, three restrictions designed "to protect the residents of Capitol Hill and to insure the rapid and continued enhancement of values there," were imposed. First, no residence was to cost less than $3,000 (at least $30,000 by today's prices in Seattle). Second, no residence was to be allowed nearer than twenty feet from the sidewalk. Finally, no stores, business blocks, or apartments were permitted on the property. Such restrictions preceded general zoning but applied only to the area north of Roy Street and east of 12th Avenue. The rest of Capitol Hill was allowed to develop more haphazardly. The demarcation line at Roy Street is still clear today. Along Broadway, the shopping district ceases. At 14th Avenue smaller homes and apartments give way to a series of mansions once called "Millionaire's Row." On 19th Avenue, the abandoned houses and storefronts cease at Roy Street where St. Joseph's parish school is built. North of the school one finds tree-lined streets and well-kept middle class homes of the mostly Catholic residents.

We the People

Residents are highly conscious of the diversity of housing, shopping, institutions, and people. In fact it is often a major factor in their being attracted to the area. A business manager in her twenties lives in a modest one bedroom apartment in an older building on Bellevue Avenue. Most of the tenants are elderly or eccentric. She came to Capitol Hill because she thought "it was an outrageous part of town; somewhat integrated but anonymous, and besides my parents were apprehensive about it!" She remains because of its convenience, finding a car unnecessary. A single man in his thirties employed at Group Health Hospital lives outside Capitol Hill but is attracted by the shopping. "There's a lot of the neat, funky old shops, new ones that the hip community has opened up, old ones like the old shoemaker who has gone on his vacation to Greece." Many Group Health employees share his feelings and thus the basically residential area can support a number of unusual small shops and restaurants.

At St. Joseph's Catholic Church at 19th Avenue and Aloha, a middle-aged secretary works part time, living in a middle class single family home in the same vicinity. She feels that Capitol Hill is the most interesting place in Seattle, "because we have all ages, all types, and all colors of people who reside here and work here and have their businesses here ... we have so many older people and we still have many families with young children." Still another person who has assumed a new name lives in a collective of younger people who own and operate a vegetarian restaurant on 15th Avenue. "It's the people on Capitol Hill," he says, "it's like Capitol Hill is the melting pot."

This is not to say that diversity is without its problems. The operator of a tavern on 15th Avenue likes the location, which gives him transient walk-in business, but finds the people abrasive as well as interesting. He lives in a suburban area saying, "I feel fortunate with most of my involvement with the people that I meet in this area but I don't like it for a twenty-four hour a day trip.... When I'm done here, I'm really done." A pharmacist on 19th Avenue for twenty years has belonged to the Capitol Hill Community Council and is now a city councilman. While a Capitol Hill die-hard, he admits that the changing population in his area has caused "negative feelings, and negative approaches and challenges like armed robberies, fire bombings, numerous burglaries, and harassment of all kinds."

A Delicate but Dynamic Balance in Land Use

The diverse conditions that exist on Capitol Hill, whether seen negatively or positively, seem to hinge on an extremely delicate balance of conditions. They were first produced in the 1950s and early 1960s after the original housing stock on the southern part of the hill had aged to the extent that it became more profitable to erect new apartment structures. As the post–World War II baby boom children reached college age, they began occupying cheaper older apartments, built mostly in the 1920s, which for years had been used exclusively by older residents. The construction of Interstate 5 freeway on the western slope of the hill in the early 1960s disrupted that area and enabled rezoning for high-rise as well as three story apartment construction. During subsequent periods of economic boom in Seattle apartment construction began replacing older single family homes following rezoning. In the late 1960s part of the prestige area east of the park was also rezoned for multifamily dwelling construction, though to date none has been built. Rezoning and apartment construction raised appraised land values and congested neighborhoods to an extent intolerable to some homeowners (Figure 29).

It is this process that enabled much of the structural diversity to develop, but the same process continued without limit would lead to diversity's undoing. The Boeing depression of 1969 curtailed the process temporarily. With high vacancy rates, new apartments were not constructed, single homes were not threatened, and apartment owners were less fussy about their tenants. Rents were reduced, helping low income groups find accommodations where it had been difficult previously. Older homes and apartment buildings which had been allowed to

deteriorate during previous years in anticipation of a sale for new apartment construction were once again maintained. Nevertheless, present zoning regulations still make some people uneasy.

The Capitol Hill Community Council is pressing for back-zoning to single family use the areas which are still single family houses. A vice president of the organization explained that "back-zoning reduces the allowed uses of the property to those which characterize the current use of the area." Such a proposal, if adopted, would thus "freeze" the structural differentiation of parts of the hill in its present state.

Should this be successful, however, there are still problems of human interaction. One longtime resident laments the lack of continu-

Figure 29. A new low-rise apartment complex nestles between older single family homes. Where homeowners refuse to move away from such intrusions, a diversity in both structures and residents is allowed to develop.

ity of family homes. "The older people move out," she says, "and they leave very large homes and they are not necessarily purchased by family groups. They're purchased by people for group living experience. . . . In the old days they were always sold to young families who wanted to raise their children and live here for the rest of their lives." A young mother living in an apartment at the southern edge of the hill wants to move. Her reason is "the burglary rate . . . and there's no adequate place for kids."

The diversity of the business community is also threatened. A large new supermarket on Broadway and expansion of Group Health Hospital on 15th Avenue both involved the relocation or extinction of small businesses as well as commercial intrusion into residential areas. A bank and another supermarket have also expanded their parking lots, also razing existing establishments. A community spokesman explains that it has been difficult for the residential community to deal with the business community. In speaking of the supermarket case he deplores the way "they came willy-nilly saying we want this zoning changed, we want to build parking lots across the street that is now residential. In such cases there was immediate uproar from the neighbors." He would like to see more cooperation. A bookstore owner is one person who benefited from the business-residential mix. In starting his used bookstore, he converted an old home partly into a sales area and retained the rest of the space for living.

The Controversy-Diversity Factor

Perhaps diversity is an inevitable generator of controversy. So much of it seems to be common to Capitol Hill. Many elderly people are quite concerned about their personal safety, and it is true that the hill has one of the higher crime rates in the city. When a halfway house for ex-convicts is established within a block of a housing project for the elderly life becomes challenging. But there are some who relish that challenge. A young restaurant owner is one of them. "I'd say it's probably easier to identify with a community of people that think like you do. . . . I wouldn't want to live there. . . ."

THE ZOO

One of the reasons people moved to the suburbs during the 1950s and 1960s was to seek stable neighborhoods in which to live and rear families. Unthinking civic policies and projects made property values and neighborhood stability less secure. Though nearly 50 percent of Seattle's population live in multifamily dwellings, the city thinks of itself as living in single family houses. Part of the city's problem involves a housing stock which is dilapidated and deteriorated. The dispute over future development at Woodland Park is typical of the kind of issue which attracts people to the suburbs.

Woodland Park is the remains of the estate of one of Seattle's early millionaires. The city acquired the park in the early twentieth century and around it has grown a relatively stable urban neighborhood whose quality in part is maintained by proximity to it.

Voters in 1968 approved a bond issue for $4.5 million to redevelop the Woodland Park Zoo. Apparently the definition of "redevelop" was never clear. An architect was hired to produce plans for the zoo. He traveled extensively to view other zoos and came back with a multiphase plan to change the entire character of the zoo and the park which surrounds it. This approach included an "open," natural zoo with animals roaming free within their natural habitat and covering an arterial road which bisected the park.

His plan was excellent but the price tag was more than twice the amount allocated by the voters and it would change the character of the entire park. Opponents said it was the wrong plan for the park. Instead of enhancing a neighborhood park, it created a facility of regional stature. The neighborhood would be walled off from its own playground. On top of it, the zoo which is now free would require a hefty admission charge.

This conflict continues still, highlighting another of the basic policy questions of the region: How does one balance the needs of local communities with the benefits to be gained by the region from major facilities?

PIONEER SQUARE: SKID ROAD REVISITED

This is the heart of old Seattle, and is the heart as well of two contrasting views on what downtown should be. Dormant since the Depression, it began its decline just after World War II. It was the original "skid road," growing up on the only stable spit of land adjacent to the deep waters of Elliott Bay. Rebuilt entirely in brick after the fire of 1889, it served as young Seattle's commercial center for a generation. But by the 1920s downtown growth migrated north, leaving the district to decay for half a century. Few but sailors, longshoremen, and the most unfortunate of transients prowled its streets until the 1960s.

When blue-ribbon committees set to work in 1958 to save the downtown from the suburban shopping center threat, Pioneer Square was already targeted for a major urban renewal project, including the bulldozing of sixteen city blocks of decrepit buildings into a few superblocks. Five major high-rise office towers were proposed, with a four block swath of parking lots. A few old buildings would be saved, but the renewal proposal set out to bulldoze some buildings which were in the process of being restored.

This proposal was a part of the 1963 downtown plan. It called for a ring road to link the central freeway and the Alaskan Viaduct and for razing not only Pioneer Square but also the Pike Place Market, plus the construction of a Waterfront Park, the Westlake Mall, and other urban redevelopment.

The general strategy for downtown was to provide quick access to the center to compete with suburban stores. The central business district would develop as a major office-retail high-rise complex, partly subsidized by urban renewal money. The car was king and would be catered to in an extensive network of parking garages and lots between the growing steel and glass towers. A few small parks would be tucked in odd spaces.

A contrary view rose to political prominence in the latter half of the 1960s. The mayoralty elections of 1969 tipped the balance of power in city government toward environmental values, partly a reaction to the city's freeway projects, designed as extensions of the downtown plan. Besides immersing the freeway plans in a series of controversies, the new attitudes toward downtown focused on Pioneer Square and later on the Public Market as unique urban assets to be restored and preserved rather than bulldozed. One primary value lay in their orientation to people. Smaller scales, an architecture of style, and an orientation to the pedestrian, it was argued, provide a humanistic downtown as opposed to a juggernaut of machines, exhaust, concrete, steel, and glass (Figure 30). Local architects, designers, arts

patrons, and other professionals began to lobby for the Pioneer Square Historical Preservation Ordinance. A few of the old buildings were restored through private efforts and by 1970 a preservation ordinance was passed by a newly elected city council.

Succeeding city ordinances established a forty acre historical district and a commission to govern it. Forbidden to demolish old buildings, property owners have responded with substantial investment (Figure 31). The city has built two cobblestone parks and has planted trees and median planters in an effort to divert through traffic to other streets. Other projects are underway to tie in the old waterfront to the revitalized district.

While responding rapidly to these ministrations, Pioneer Square still faces major problems from the traditional auto-redevelopment vision of downtown. The site of King County Stadium is close by, and efforts are being made to connect the Alaskan Viaduct with I-5 at the southern edge of the historical district.

Both of these plans could spoil future hopes for a people-oriented district. Stadium traffic, parking, and commerce could box Pioneer Square inside parking lots and rows of plastic storefronts. The connection of the viaduct with I-5 will increase auto traffic, noise, odors, and clutter on the entire west and south borders of the district. To forestall this, advocates for the district lobby to double the size of the district to secure its borders right up to the stadium. Meanwhile, increasing numbers of civic activists seriously discuss eliminating the Alaskan Viaduct or diverting it to nonauto uses.

THE PIKE PLACE MARKET: A DEFENSE

William Blake once noted that one could see the universe in a grain of sand. Surely then, Seattle's Pike Place Market must be one of the more legible grains of sand on the shores of urban America, for here, in all its chaos and disheveled splendor, is the very marketplace which has figured so consistently in the history of civilization. Democracy is in part a product of the marketplaces of man—where philosophers discoursed and politicians debated—and here, in Seattle's vital Pike Place Market, democracy colorfully reigns, whether in continuation of philosophers' arguments or in late afternoon bargaining over the price of a summer squash.

Figure 30. When "downtown" moved away from its original hearth, Pioneer Square became a neglected district of warehouses and flophouses, lost souls and soul-saving missions.

Seattle's Pike Place Market is one of the few large and thriving public markets in the country. Almost 200 businesses operate in and around the market. Short of listing each, no adequate description is possible, for one finds gourmet foods and expensive antiques within what is, in effect, a very fine low cost regional shopping center. The market is located between Seattle's central business district and the harbor. Perched since 1907 on the side of a hill above Elliott Bay, it startles the eye with its rambling arcades, ramps, stairways, and passages. Walking through the market, one's nose is outrageously stimulated, one's taste buds tempted to a drool, one's ears ceaselessly barraged with cries of fishhawkers, babies, foreign

Figure 31. The core of restoration in Occidental Avenue. Storefronts have been coordinated to present an unblemished 1890s exterior, though interior prices bespeak the 1970s. With successful redevelopment, rents in the area have also risen, so that many Skid Road facilities have been forced out.

tongues, and singing minstrels—for this market, like all people's markets of the world, is alive (Figure 32).

Integrated and comfortably bizarre, the Pike Place Market has been rhapsodized as a "real place in an unreal time," a place in plastic-wrapped America where real values survive. A place where you can do more than buy fresh locally grown vegetables, local artisan's crafts, Greek figs, old books, kitchen utensils, antique furniture, exotic spices, geoduck clams, and an astounding range of other items. Here is a place where directness can be experienced, where skid row meets suburbia, old meets young, race meets race, buyer meets seller, and stranger can become friend.

Of course, genuine events are created and, in the case of the Pike Place Market, preserved by a public which grows increasingly as disenchanted with packaged urban renewal deals as with packaged food products. There are two stories to tell about Seattle's Pike Place Market. One is about that real place, and the other is about how the people of Seattle acted to keep it from being renewed—surrounded by high-rise apartments, a convention hotel, and a parking garage.

The Pike Place Market was conceived out of necessity, fear, anger, and hope. Prior to 1907, most of the fruit and vegetables grown in the fertile valleys surrounding Seattle were distributed through a commission system. Each

Figure 32. Surrounded by eye-catching displays of artichokes, cantaloupes, casaba melons, and other produce, a market vendor prepares to bag some fresh corn.

farmer consigned his produce to a wholesaler and received his price after the produce was sold. The commission middlemen maintained sheds near the waterfront from which they sold the produce to door-to-door grocery peddlers. By 1906 the cost of produce had become exorbitant, and business seemed suspiciously good for the commission houses, which were soon accused of price fixing, price gouging, and even of dumping fresh produce through trap doors into Elliott Bay. By 1907, door-to-door prices had risen to such an extent that local employers complained they could not keep dependable workmen in the lumber mills because these employees could not afford to feed their families.

In an ambitious move the city government proposed a radical solution to the problem. It proclaimed one Saturday in August 1907 "Mar-

ket Day," when consumers were invited to "meet the producer" and buy food directly from the farmers. Should such a notion catch on, it was asserted, a formal marketplace might be established.

Hence it was that an early consumer protection scheme was largely responsible for the Pike Place Market's inception. But, then as now, middlemen die hard. They canvassed and threatened the farmers, warning them to have nothing to do with this "do-goodism." Perhaps because of threats or because it had been raining for a week, only three farmers arrived with wagonloads of produce at the proclaimed site on Pike Place—itself newly created, terraced out of a bayside cliff. But hoards of customers greeted the three, and each day saw more farmers participating. By the following Saturday, and despite a number of "incidents," seventy farmers backed their wagons against the wooden sidewalks. The market idea was proclaimed a success, and when the market was formally dedicated with bands playing and flags awave, 120 farmers were present.

During the next fifteen years the market thrived, and it was then that the core of what is now called the main market complex was constructed. The multistoried structure housed not only farmers' stalls on its upper level, but a growing assortment of related concessions in lower levels as well. These restaurants, spice shops, and a cornucopia of outlets for other products and services evolved in a unique and intriguing fashion. According to each merchant's individual needs, new market space was designed and added, the result soon being the bizarre labyrinth of complicated ramps and corridors which exists today. During this same period, a number of other market buildings were constructed, sporting names such as the Sanitary Market, the Economy Market, the Corner Market, and the Outlook Market.

Development of the market drew residents into the area and a number of hotels and rooming houses were constructed, some directly over retail businesses in the complex of market buildings. Many seamen and transient workers periodically joined this growing community and a busy cosmopolitan atmosphere prevailed in the market. As the market's fortunes rose, its success and distinctiveness drew international recognition. In the peak years of 1926 and 1932 more than 600 farmers were issued annual marketing permits by the city. The market fared well through the Depression but poorly during World War II. In 1942 citizens of Japanese descent were evacuated from Seattle. Since 70 percent of the market farmers were of Japanese descent, their removal left a serious void. Although many Japanese farmers returned after the war, their overall number never returned to its prewar level.

In a sense, it was realization of the American dream which accounted for the failing fortunes of the Pike Place Market. By the 1960s the number of farmers participating in the market had dropped to fewer than 100. In part this reflected the loss of former farmland to urban use. But the decline also came of the realization of dreams of the founding generation of farmers—to win "a better life" for their sons

and daughters. Meanwhile, large scale farming and changing technologies of refrigeration and transportation completely altered the food-shopping patterns of most urban Americans while they decentralized to the suburbs. Though many Seattle natives nostalgically recall family market day as a weekly part of their childhood, convenience shopping at supermarkets robbed the old market of its former clientele. Until recently, new regular customers seldom made their way to the market, though the area remained a favorite landmark.

With declining fortunes the market began to look shabby and safety code infractions began to nibble at the area's many corners. Code restrictions gradually closed many hotels in the area and the resident population dwindled from fewer than 600 in the mid-1960s to approximately 300 in the early 1970s. The nature of these residents has naturally changed over the years as well; the area is essentially a "high rent skid road," and residents tend to be elderly and poor, but typically self-supporting and proud.

In 1950 came the first major proposal for demolition of the Pike Place Market area. This proposal suggested total demolition and replacement with a 2,000 car parking garage topped by a city park. The plan met with resistance from many residents and, as the city was without funds and legal authority to pursue the matter, the proposal was allowed to die. However, by the early 1960s Seattle's business community was prepared to launch another, stronger redevelopment proposal.

In 1963 the Central Association, a group of downtown businessmen working closely with Seattle City Planning Department, drew up a master plan for the central business district. This was the same plan which was to destory the buildings in Pioneer Square. The proposal for the Pike Place Market area envisioned apartment towers, a major hotel, office buildings, and a 4,000 car parking garage.

Upon receipt of this proposal the city applied for and received an urban renewal planning grant. The resulting plan, completed in 1968, was closely bounded by an independent economic study the city had also commissioned—and which essentially endorsed the plan already proposed by the Central Association. It called for near total demolition and redevelopment of the entire market area. The city adopted the plan in early 1969 and waited for federal approval of urban renewal funds.

Throughout most of the years of renewal planning, the majority of Seattle residents probably never knew much more about the situation than that the poor old market, sadly enough, would have to go. However, by late 1971 that same public passed a toothy initiative which established an historic preservation district around the Pike Place Market. They were guided to this action largely through the efforts of a small citizen group called the Friends of the Market which advocated an understanding and concern for the market unlike that of the city and business interests. The Friends of the Market, formed immediately after the unveiling of the Central Association's plan for the Pike Place district, has been a speckled collection of college professors, lawyers, housewives, and market merchants who declared themselves wholly dedicated "to saving and enhancing the historic Pike Place Market District." The group's main spokesman, quoted in the *Seattle Post-Intelligencer,* December 26, 1965, firmly declared: "Anyone who does not enjoy the market does not like people, does not appreciate life and color and drama.... Those who are indifferent to that which makes it what it is must not be allowed to spoil it for those who do care."

The friends' wide-ranging efforts were generally unsuccessful in changing the nature of the city's renewal plan but did effectively ignite public concern and interest in the market. The issue began to polarize, sides were taken, and the market area was alternately assessed in such terms as:

There was blight there 50 years ago when it was a second class whore district and now it's worse. It's not safe to walk there day or night.

or

The Pike Place Market. It reveals the face of truth. Its roughness reminds me of Seattle's beginnings, its lusty past, the vitality that gave it national notice years ago.

Business interests and their backers are mostly concerned about the area's redevelopment possibilities from a business point of view. They mounted arguments about highest and best economic use, tax base benefits, and so forth. The friends, who claimed to speak "for the people," were more concerned with preserving a unique human ecosystem. Thus the conflict focused on the opposing goals of separate interest groups, although some of the disagreement concerned the actual definition of the market, its meaning, and significances. This difference of understanding was captured by Seattle poet Richard Hugo in "The Pike Place Market":

These market skills go back to deep in Egypt, deep in dynasties of dirt, in minds of cats who hug the market in a storm. Here, it is assumed all things have value. The world will not wear out. Best selling paperbacks with covers bruised by grease: one dime. No bargaining, though produce can be talked down sharply after five.

Who plans to tear this market down? Erect a park? Those militants who hate the old and odd, and dream of homes where lawns are uniformly green . . .
     Let columns rot, progressive mayors deny a city has a private right to be.
     Let the market slide into the sea. . . .

The city's renewal plan was nearing execution in the spring of 1971 when the friends decided to draw up an initiative measure that would create a seven acre Pike Place Market Historical District within which all renovation and construction would be subject to approval by a Market Historical Commission. Double the number of required signatures were collected and the initiative appeared on a general election ballot in the fall of 1971.

As election day approached, the market initiative became the top issue on the ballot. The initiative carried by a substantial margin and was locally hailed as a landmark in the annals of historic preservation in America. Following the election an Historical Commission was duly appointed and city officials redefined the entire project in substantially more preservationist terms. In August 1972, federal funds were finally released for a twenty-two acre area, the seven acre Historical District forming a unique enclave within the larger urban renewal project area.

Thus ends the saga of how Seattle's Pike Place Market was saved from destruction and redevelopment. But living things are, in part, tangible reflections of invisible life processes. The Pike Place Market, like a living human eco-system, must change if it is not to rot away or become a museum. Under conditions of conscious control through the aegis of historical district guidelines which detail allowable changes and permit-granting procedures, plans for a successful maintenance of the market's serendipitous and democratic atmosphere are underway.

Controversy and Conflict in Seattle:
Macro Scale

THE ISSUE OF GROWTH:
LESSER SEATTLE

When Herman Kahn spoke of Pugetopolis in the late 1960s he upset people in the Seattle metropolitan area, but what he said was undeniable. Between Eugene, Oregon, and Vancouver, B.C., and most intensively between Olympia and Bellingham, Washington, a strip city was developing along the Interstate-5 corridor. It was not a continuous urbanscape, of course, but the urban areas kept expanding and, if projections were followed, would eventually lead to one continuous low density urban realm.

Strung like odd-sized beads along the I-5 freeway corridor in the lowland of Puget Sound lies the largest bulk of Washington's population. From Olympia to Tacoma to Seattle to Everett to Bellingham live about 2 million people. Of this number a little over one million live in Seattle-King County (Figure 33). They are an affluent, well-educated population, full of energy and contrary will. Like everyone else in America they are caught in a world where the ground rules are rapidly changing. To their conflicts and decision we shall now direct our attention (Figure 34).

As in many places throughout the country, the issue which is shaping up to be the most important of the decade is growth. Few issues are as emotionally charged. People have made their decisions on it before they even agree what it is. To the business person it is more orders for products and it is greater profits.

To the utilities planner it is the need for more electricity to run the factories to make the products. To the labor leader it is more and more jobs for the union. To the retailer of sporting goods it is more people with money to buy such luxury toys and is coupled with the occasional worry that there may not be enough places for his customers to use their goods. To the environmentalist it is the fear that last year's free-flowing river may be under this year's new dam.

Like many places in the western United States, Seattle is a product of late nineteenth century manifest destiny and reflects the deliberate desires of a mercantile people to build a great and rich city. From the earliest, the settlers who landed at Alki Point in Seattle were aware that Puget Sound was to be a center for East-West trade and that Seattle's Elliott Bay would be the center of the sound. The name they gave to their settlement in the late 1850s was Alki–New York which means "New York–By and By."

Their dream was still strong in the early twentieth century, a time of intense competition between regions of the nation for new capital and population. Growth was the goal and measure. As one pamphlet of the Seattle Chamber of Commerce put it:

> Before many years Alaska will contain as much population as Norway, Sweden, Denmark and Holland combined. Washington, Idaho, Montana and Oregon will eclipse other states of like area, for none equal these

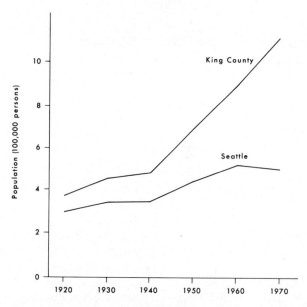

Figure 33. The population and growth of the Seattle area has accelerated since World War II. While the Seattle city population peaked in 1960, King County as a whole has witnessed unabated growth. Population density has declined in King County; this reflects the changing lifestyles of Americans who prefer spacious homes and property and vacate the congested urban areas for distant unincorporated districts. The net result is an evergrowing appetite for land in the country. Growing population and sprawling lifestyles have put pressure on agricultural, recreational, and wilderness lands remote from the city proper.

in the natural advantages of soil, minerals, and climate. Seattle will be the geographical and commercial center of it all!

We think one would be hard put to find such exuberance today when there is a deadlock between the old "cowboy" economy and the new "spaceship" economy.

Easterners coming to Seattle for the first time often wonder at the lack of trees. After all, Seattle is still a frontier town, locked away in the northwest corner of the United States, a town of muddy streets in a forest by an inland sea. Or so runs the popular image, and it is not completely false. Seattle, like most American cities, is still somewhat of a frontier town in the way people use their resources.

In the "cowboy economy" described by economist Kenneth Boulding, the environment and its resources are used as if they were infinite and always available, no matter how fast they are exploited. The cowboy economy was the basis for the development of the towns of

Puget Sound during the nineteenth century. The land and water resources were thought to be so enormous that a forest could be cut or a saltwater marsh filled without disturbing anything but the immediate area.

Nowadays what is emerging in thought and fact is the idea of the "spaceship economy"—using resources over and over. This concept is not a new one. The earth has been recycling its water for millions of years, and people have been recycling their gold and silver for millennia. What is new is that in the Puget Sound region there is now developing a constituency arguing forcefully in all areas for managing growth along lines leading to more of a spaceship economy.

While the issue was developing and even before the battle lines were clearly drawn between proponents of growth and no-growth, the fact that there are limits to growth has been underscored by gas shortages, meat shortages, and the rapidly rising cost of salmon and timber, even in the Pacific Northwest. It came so suddenly

Figure 34. Growth has its limits. As in several other cities, increasing citizen awareness of air pollution and the disruption wrought by freeway construction has led to referenda that have defeated previously envisioned highway projects. Freeway ramps to nowhere are the legacy of attempts to link Interstate 5 with Interstate 90.

that people were still discussing the issue, some even denying it, while gas stations closed at 7:00 P.M. or all weekend.

ROSS DAM, THE ENERGY CRISIS, AND THE ENVIRONMENTALISTS

The Pacific Northwest is well known for its tremendous hydroelectric power resources. Rugged mountains and high precipitation combine to provide an ideal source of power. One dams a valley and allows the mountain torrents to form a lake which then runs through turbines in a power plant to produce electricity. The process is clean; no air or water pollution.

However, not all are happy. The large urban population of Puget Sound has produced a heavy demand for recreation, particularly hiking and camping in the wilderness. Recreational Equipment, Inc., only a few shelves in rented space in the late 1930s, is now a multimillion dollar a year cooperative enterprise selling outdoor equipment all over the nation. Much of it, of course, is used in the Olympic and Cascade mountains surrounding the Puget Sound urban area.

Ninety miles north of Seattle on the Skagit River lies a complex of hydroelectric plants owned by City Light, an electric utility belonging to the people of the city of Seattle. The largest of the installations is Ross Dam. Built in the 1930s, it was designed for further expansion when the power needs of the region demanded it. During the boom times of the 1960s City Light officials concluded that the time had come for development of Ross Dam to its ultimate design size.

Meanwhile, however, hikers, climbers, and other assorted nature lovers had started to expand their sphere of influence. A highway had snaked its way along the Skagit River into the rugged North Cascades and people were discovering the values of wilderness as wilderness. Though they had hoped that the North Cascades National Park established by Congress in 1968 would protect their playground, the national park had been bisected by a narrow strip of national recreation area, which included the Ross Dam area, at the request of City Light officials. Such national recreation areas are more permissive of intense development than national parks, so the goal of raising Ross Dam was still alive.

Conservationists object to the raising of the dam because it would flood several unique valleys containing remnants of the original cedar forest and destroy the habitat for numerous beaver colonies, as well as affecting deer herds and other animals and plants. Industrial interests in Seattle are adamant that the increased power is necessary for continued economic growth. An additional complication is that part of the area to be flooded is in the upper Skagit River valley in British Columbia. Changes in the British Columbian government and increased Canadian nationalism have combined to harden opposition to the Ross Dam expansion north of the border.

At the present time no final decisions have been made, but whatever the outcome, the conflict is the same—how to use a finite resource that is critical for both recreation and economic growth.

THE NISQUALLY DELTA

Flowing down the flanks of Mount Rainier is the Nisqually River, named after the native people of the area. Where the Nisqually enters Puget Sound there is a large delta. It is one of the few large, flat areas suitable for industrial development in southern Puget Sound. It is also one of the few undisturbed river deltas in the region, and it is rich in wildlife.

As in the past, one of the critical factors in determining the growth of the Puget Sound region's cities is American foreign policy with Pacific Rim nations. The Puget Sound region is a logical *entrepot* for trade between the American Midwest and East Asia. The Port authori-

ties, whose jurisdiction includes the Nisqually Delta, perceived that it could be developed into a very large port. Even in the face of consultants' reports which recommended no development on the Nisqually until, perhaps, the 1980s, the port commissioners vigorously pursued their plan to turn the salt marsh into a port. This was in the mid-1960s.

Conservationists objected. The delta was too valuable to waste on a port, they argued. Such facilities should be placed in areas which have already been developed, not natural areas. Besides, existing ports were underutilized. The Nisqually's natural features could be preserved for future generations to enjoy and could allow them the luxury of choice.

The argument has been acrimonious and is not yet entirely over. However, public opinion is swinging toward saving the delta. Purchase of a 1,290 acre tract in the delta by the federal government for use as a wildlife refuge was announced in mid-January 1974, and a governor's task force suggested a "Sound-to-Mountain Park" which includes habitats from the tidal flats to glaciers.

The dispute over the Nisqually Delta has been complicated by the state's Shoreline Management Act. In response to a preservation-oriented shoreline initiative, which was placed on the 1972 ballot by a statewide coalition of conservationists, the legislature developed the less restrictive Shoreline Management Act. Neither proposal carried in the more conservative rural counties of the state. However, the plurality which the legislature's proposal carried in the urbanized Seattle-King County area made it law.

The Shoreline Management Act calls for shoreline plans to be developed by all local jurisdictions under the guidance of the state Department of Ecology. The major questions are where and how development will occur on the region's marine shorelines. Shall superports be allowed and, if so, where? Shall oil be allowed onto the sound to fuel the oil-hungry urban population? How shall the needs of recreation seekers be balanced against the development of aquaculture and fishing? The Nisqually Delta is no longer a resource for the immediate localities to use for their own benefit but a resource of statewide significance whose future will be decided in a broader forum.

TRANSPORTATION AND SEATTLE

Probably the key determinant to urban form is transportation. Seattle is beset by two major conflicts which involve transportation. The most important is the development of the Interstate 90 freeway.

To the east, Seattle is bounded by Lake Washington. At present, two bridges cross the lake to the bedroom suburbs of Bellevue, Kirkland, and other small communities, allowing expansion of urban development east of Lake Washington. Though Seattle proper is still the economic and cultural heart of the metropolitan area, a virtual ring city now encircles the lake.

As part of the National Defense Highway System, Interstate 90 had been planned to cross the lake to Seattle on a third bridge. Downtown interests and other expansionists of the 1950s had supported this project but by the late 1960s serious opposition to a third bridge had surfaced. It is claimed by opponents that the bridge will further destroy the recreational qualities of the lake, upset community structure, and, most importantly, change the form of the entire metropolitan area. As yet undeveloped open space in the foothills of the Cascades would be subdivided and low density residential development based on automobile transportation would be given renewed impetus. Further, it would encourage even more cars to travel to an already clogged downtown.

Proponents of the project claim that the increased access the freeway would provide is vital to the economic health of the commercial core. Without it, the bedroom communities to the east of Seattle will become full-fledged cities in their own right. The issue here is, "What is a city?" The "traditional" postwar view has been that it is a place to work during the day and flee at dusk. Though Seattle still has many fine residential neighborhoods, the population of the city proper declined during the 1960s, while King County's grew.

Though the city administration has not voted opposition to the bridge as a means of encouraging more cars downtown, it has been active in seeking other ways to limit the number of cars going to the urban core. In 1972 the city government requested legislation from the state legislature which would allow it to regulate the price of parking on private lots. Parking lot owners objected to being singled out for regulation and the measure went nowhere. The city is attempting, however, to develop other means for controlling the proliferation of downtown lots.

In the long run, the direction seems clear. Seattle residents have defeated two freeway projects in the past several years and a referendum battle is now brewing over another highway proposal. The "energy crisis" is bringing home to many people the extravagant use of oil and basic changes appear to be emerging.

SEATTLE 2000

In the spring of 1972 the city of Seattle established the Seattle 2000 Commission to help the city administration resolve the sharp differences of opinion about the city's future direction. Seattle 2000 was a series of volunteer citizen task forces on a variety of functional areas such as environment, housing, law and justice, education and communication, and so on. The job of each task force was to develop goals in its subject area for the year 2000. These were to be presented to the mayor and the City Council. After six months of intense discussion among nearly 300 regularly attending members, the commission presented the city government with a fat document of dreams, visions, and much common sense. It was rife with apparent contradictions. For example, the task force on downtown argued that the urban core should maintain itself as the preeminent regional center for employment, shopping, and creation, while the task force on community hoped for balanced neighborhoods where it was possible to live, work, and play.

Yet, through it all there emerged a consistent image of what a city should be. It is a contained, concentrated place built on a human scale. The role of the automobile is to be reduced, the unique characteristics of districts are to be maintained and enhanced, the citizenry is to have an increased role in determining the future of its city. In essence it is the germ of a growth policy for Seattle.

The commission by no means said "zero growth," but it also by no means said "growth is the value and the measure." The local issue was clearly seen not as "no growth" but as "growth: when, where and how?" Concentration of urban development, rather than dispersal, is the issue. Growth was recognized as not only an economic and environmental problem but a psychological necessity and the city was perceived as the crucible of change.

In Seattle and Puget Sound, the limits to growth are being deeply impressed onto the consciousness of the citizenry. There is a realization that some hard choices have to be made about the way in which people want to grow. They want to have their cake and eat it too, to have electricity and the morning paper as well as a hike in the solitude of the wilderness. The ultimate limit to growth is our ability to manage growth. Whether the people who live in the Puget Sound basin will be able to do so remains to be seen, but nobody has even thought about giving up.

Bibliography

Boulding, Kenneth. In M. Jarrett, ed., *Environmental Quality in a Growing Economy*. Baltimore: Johns Hopkins Press, 1966.

Conant, Roger. *Mercer's Belles*. Seattle: University of Washington Press, 1960.

Erickson, Rodney. "The Lead Firm Concept and Regional Economic Growth: An Analysis of Boeing Expansion." Ph.D. dissertation, University of Washington, Seattle, 1973.

Fleming, Douglas K., ed. *Views of Washington State*. Washington, D.C.: Association of American Geographers, 1974.

Jones, Nard. *Seattle*. Garden City, N.Y.: Doubleday, 1972.

Kahn, Herman. *The Year 2000*. New York: Macmillan, 1967.

Kerouac, John. *The Dharma Bums*. New York: Viking Press, 1958.

MacDonald, Alexander. "Seattle Economic Development, 1880–1910." Ph.D. dissertation, University of Washington, Seattle, 1959.

Morgan, Murray. *The Northwest Corner*. New York: Viking Press, 1962.

———. *Skid Road*. New York: Viking Press, 1951.

O'Connor, Harvey. *Revolution in Seattle*. New York: Monthly Review Press, 1964.

Pacific Power and Light Co. *The Pacific Northwest: Economic Growth in a Quality Environment*. Seattle, 1967.

Peterson, Eugene, ed. *Ecology and the Economy*. Vancouver, Wash.: Pacific Northwest River Basin Commission, 1973.

Pohl, Thomas. "Seattle: A Frontier Community." Ph.D. dissertation, University of Washington, Seattle, 1970.

Puget Sound Regional Transportation Study. *Economic Growth in the Puget Sound Area, 1980 Transportation Plan. Reports*. Seattle, 1967.

Schmid, Calvin. "Growth and Distribution of Minority Races in Seattle." Seattle Public Schools, 1964.

Schmid, Calvin, and Schmid, Stanton. "Growth of Cities and Towns, State of Washington." Washington State Planning and Community Affairs Agency. Olympia, 1969.

Seattle, Department of Community Development. Miscellaneous publications, especially:

"Determinant of City Form, 1971"

"Pioneer Square Historical District Bulletin, 1974"

"Pike Place Market Historical District Presentation Plan, 1974"

"The Seattle Central Waterfront, 1972"

Plans developed for various communities: Capitol Hill, South Park, etc.

Seattle 2000 Commission. *Goals for Seattle*. Seattle: City of Seattle, 1973.

Speidel, William. *Sons of the Profits: Seattle Story: 1851–1910*. Seattle: Nettle Creek Publishing Co., 1967.

———. *You Can't Eat Mount Rainier*. Portland, Ore.: Binsford and Mort, 1958.

Stallings, David. "Environmental Cognition and Land Use Controversy: An Environmental

Image Study of Seattle's Pike Place Market."
Ph.D. dissertation, University of Washington,
1975.

Steinbrueck, Victor. *Seattle Cityscape*. Seattle: University of Washington Press, #1, 1962,
#2, 1973.

Wall, B.R. "Log Production in Washington and Oregon." Portland, Ore.: Pacific Northwest
Forest and Range Experiment Station, #42,
1972.

Washington Writer's Project, Washington.
A Guide to the Evergreen State. Portland,
Ore.: Binsford and Mort, 1950.

Index